# GERMAN ENGLISH

## ILLUSTRATED DICTIONARY

FREE AUDIO APP

## Author

**Thomas Booth** worked for 10 years as an English teacher in Poland, Romania, and Russia. He now lives in England, where he works as an editor and English-language materials writer. He has contributed to a number of books in the *English for Everyone* series.

# GERMAN ENGLISH

## ILLUSTRATED DICTIONARY

DK

DK | Penguin Random House

PRODUCED BY
**Author / Editor** Thomas Booth
**Senior Art Editor** Sunita Gahir
**Art Editors** Ali Jayne Scrivens, Samantha Richiardi
**Illustrators** Edward Byrne, Gus Scott
**Project Manager** Sunita Gahir / bigmetalfish design

DK UK
**Senior Editors** Amelia Petersen, Christine Stroyan
**Senior Designers** Clare Shedden, Vicky Read
**Managing Art Editor** Anna Hall
**Managing Editor** Carine Tracanelli
**Jacket Editors** Stephanie Cheng Hui Tan, Juhi Sheth
**Jacket Development Manager** Sophia MTT
**Production Editors** Gillian Reid, Robert Dunn, Jacqueline Street
**Production Controller** Sian Cheung
**Publisher** Andrew Macintyre
**Art Director** Karen Self
**Publishing Director** Jonathan Metcalf

**Translation** Andiamo! Language Services Ltd

DK INDIA
**Desk Editors** Joicy John, Tanya Lohan
**DTP Designers** Anurag Trivedi, Satish Gaur,
Jaypal Chauhan, Bimlesh Tiwary, Rakesh Kumar
**DTP Coordinator** Pushpak Tyagi
**Jacket Designer** Vidushi Chaudhry
**Senior Jackets Coordinator** Priyanka Sharma Saddi
**Managing Editor** Saloni Talwar
**Creative Head** Malavika Talukder

First American Edition, 2023
Published in the United States by DK Publishing
1745 Broadway, 20th Floor, New York, NY 10019


24 25 10 9 8 7 6 5 4 3 2
003–334030–Jun/2023


Published in Great Britain by Dorling Kindersley Limited

A catalog record for this book
is available from the Library of Congress.
ISBN 978-0-7440-8072-8



Printed and bound in China

# Contents

## DAS LEBEN IN DER STADT CITY LIFE



## NAHRUNGSMITTEL UND LEBENSMITTEL FOOD



## DAS LERNEN STUDY

## DIE ARBEIT WORK



## DIE VERKEHRSMITTEL GETTING AROUND



## DER SPORT SPORTS

## DIE FREIZEIT LEISURE



## DIE UMWELT ENVIRONMENT



## DIE NATUR NATURAL WORLD

## DIE INFORMATIONEN REFERENCE

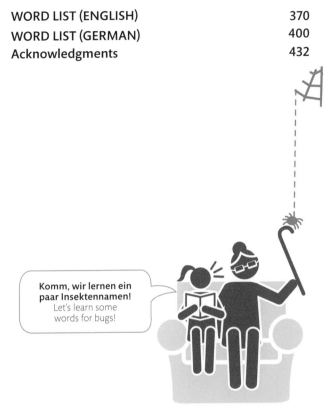

Komm, wir lernen ein paar Insektennamen!
Let's learn some words for bugs!

Ich habe mehr als 10.000 Wörter gelesen!
I have read more than 10,000 words!

# How to use this book

This *German English Illustrated Dictionary* will help you understand and remember more than 10,000 of the most useful words and phrases in German. Each of the 180 units in the dictionary covers a practical or everyday topic (such as health, food, or the natural world), and words are shown in a visual context to cement them in your memory along with their English equivalents. Using the audio app that accompanies the dictionary will help you learn and remember the new vocabulary.

**Unit number** The book is divided into units. The unit number helps you find the unit easily when searching through the contents page.

**Illustrated scenes** Many units include illustrated scenes that make vocabulary easy to understand and remember.

**English words** The English translation is provided for each word.

**Module numbers** Most units are broken down into modules. Every module is identified with a unique number, so you can locate the audio on the app.

**Illustrations** All the entries in the dictionary are illustrated, helping you understand and memorize new vocabulary.

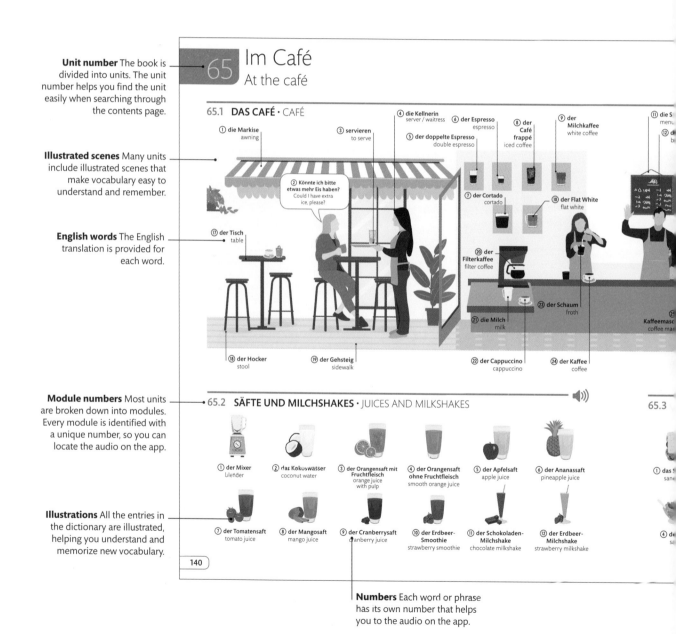

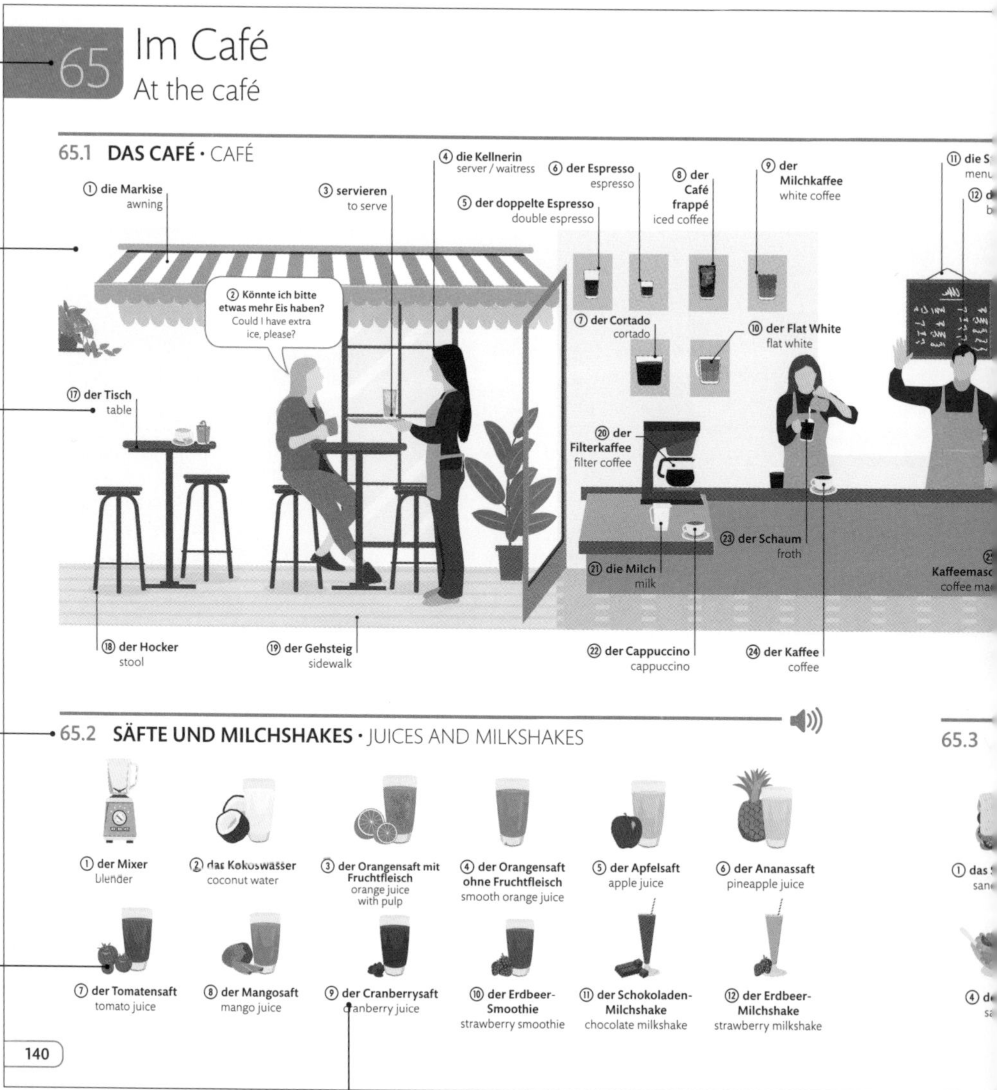


**Numbers** Each word or phrase has its own number that helps you to the audio on the app.

**See also** Each unit has a "see also" box that directs you to other units with useful or related vocabulary.

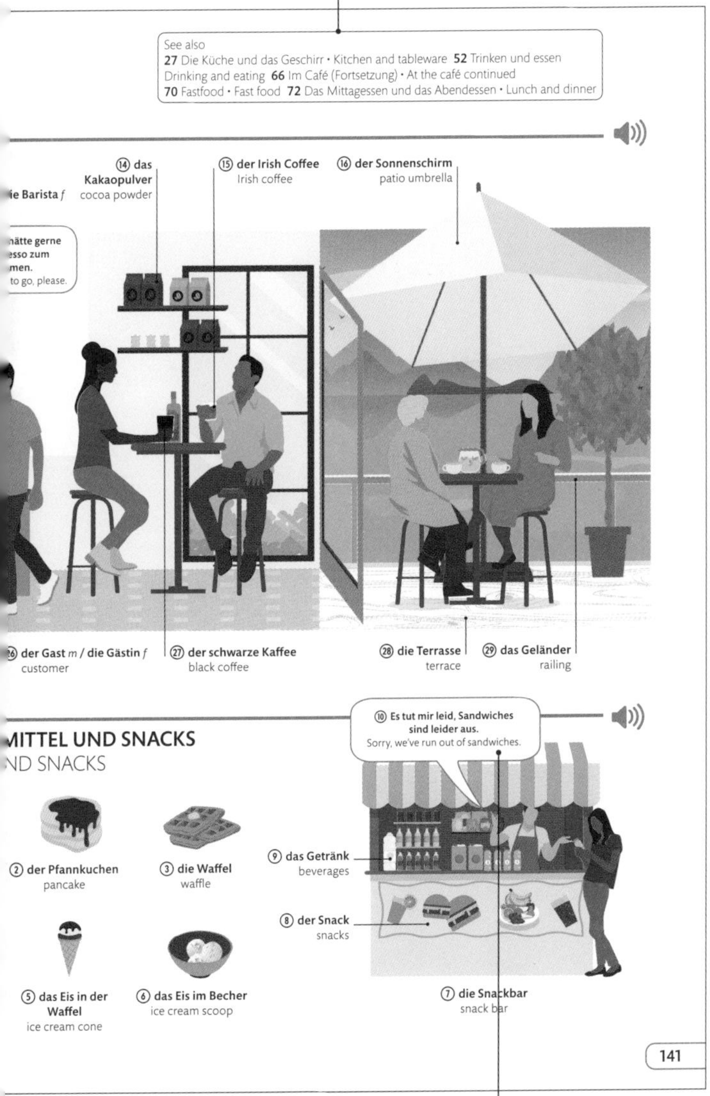


**Speech bubbles** Useful expressions and examples of real-life German appear in speech bubbles throughout the book.

# Gender and articles

All nouns in the dictionary are preceded by the definite article ("the"). In German, nouns are masculine, feminine or neuter. "Der" is used before masculine nouns, "die" is used with feminine and plural nouns, and "das" is used before the neuter. Where "die" is used with a plural, the gender is indicated with *m*, *f* or *n*.

**der Spielzeugladen**
toy shop

**die Schwester**
sister

**das Doppelbett**
double bed

**die Wanderschuhe** *m, pl*
hiking boots

**die Käsesorten** *f, pl*
cheeses

**die Bücher** *n, pl*
books

# Word lists

The German and English word lists at the back of the book contain every entry from the dictionary. All the vocabulary is listed in alphabetical order, and each entry is followed by the unit number or numbers in which it is found, enabling you to look up any word in either German or English. The German words are listed without the articles, so that you can search for words alphabetically. The English word list also provides information about the part of speech (for example noun, verb, or adjective) of each word.

# Audio app

The *German English Illustrated Dictionary* is supported by a free audio app containing every German word and phrase in the book. Listen to the audio and repeat the words and phrases out loud, until you are confident you understand and can pronounce what has been said. The app can be found by searching for "DK Illustrated Dictionary" in the App Store or Google Play.

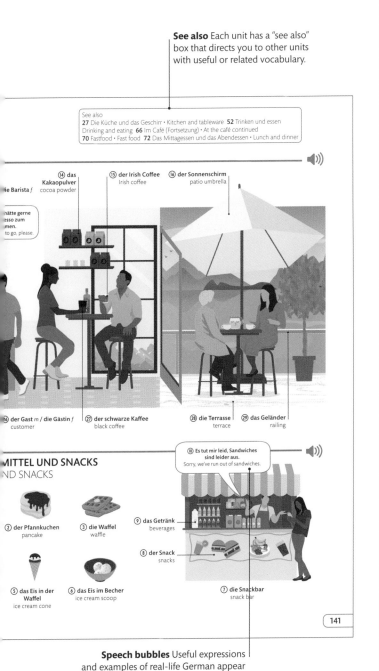

# 01 Körperteile
## Parts of the body

### 1.1 DER MENSCHLICHE KÖRPER · THE HUMAN BODY

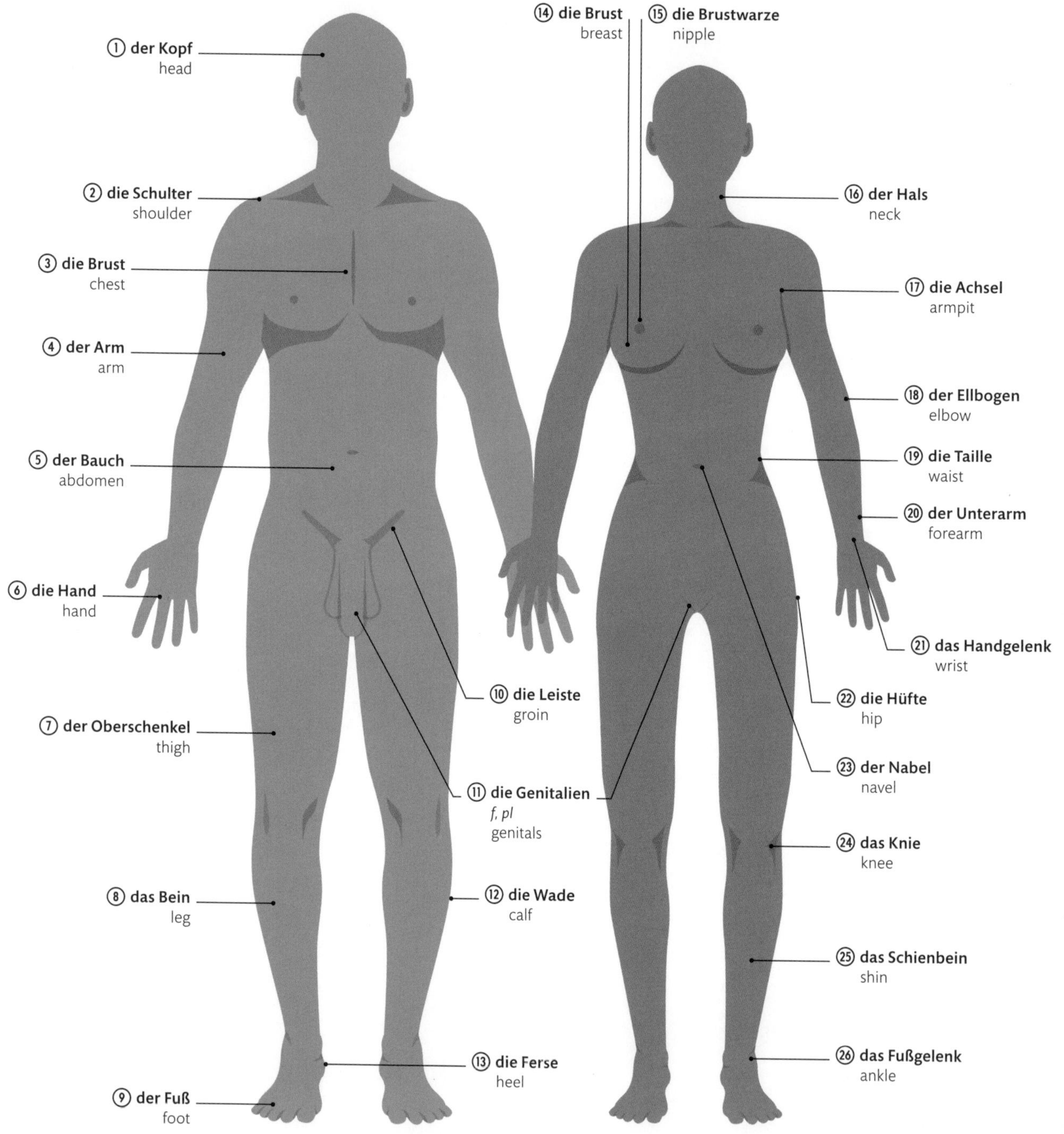

See also
**02** Hände und Füße • Hands and feet **03** Muskeln und Skelett • Muscles and skeleton
**04** Innere Organe • Internal organs **19** Krankheiten und Verletzungen • Illness and injury
**20** Beim Arzt • Visiting the doctor **22** Der Zahnarzt und der Opitker • The dentist and optician

## 1.2 DAS GESICHT • FACE

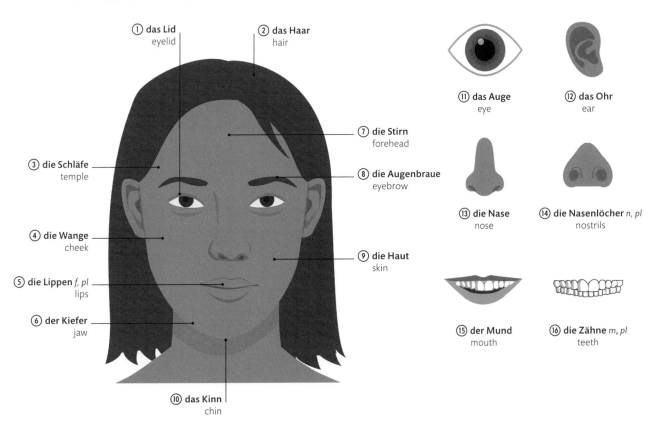

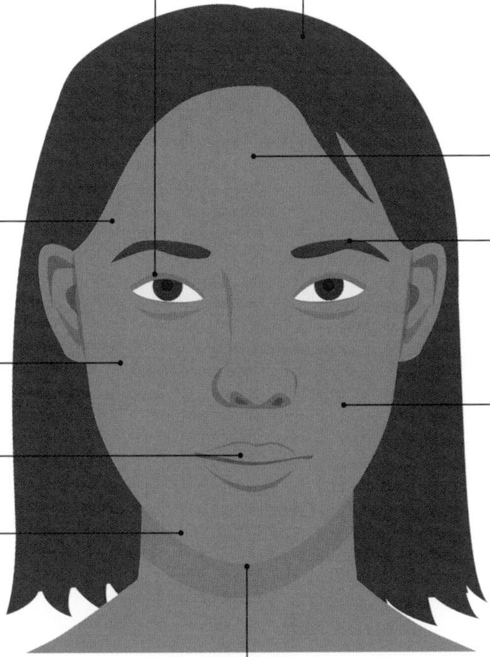


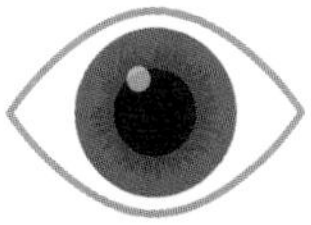

⑪ **das Auge**
eye

⑫ **das Ohr**
ear

⑬ **die Nase**
nose

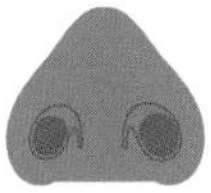

⑭ **die Nasenlöcher** *n, pl*
nostrils

⑮ **der Mund**
mouth

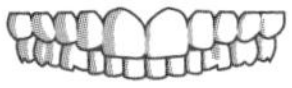

⑯ **die Zähne** *m, pl*
teeth

## 1.3 DIE AUGEN • EYES

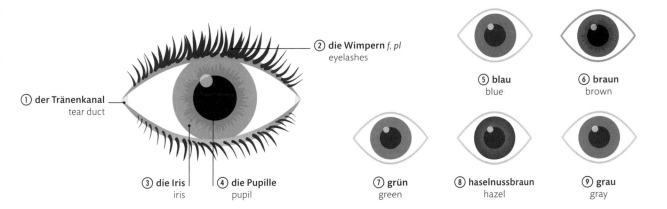

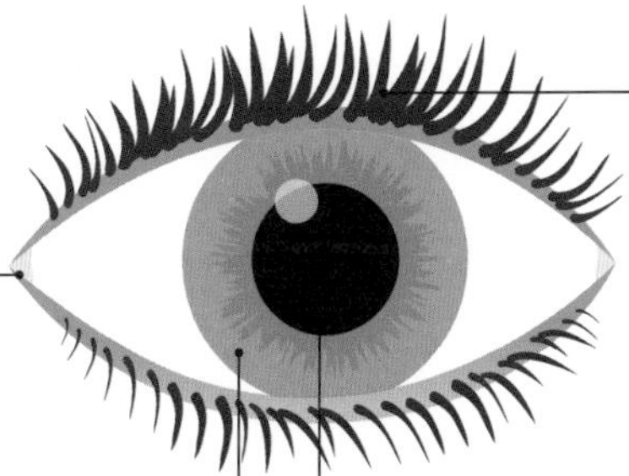


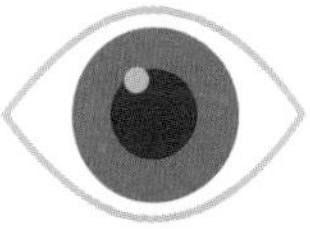

⑤ **blau**
blue

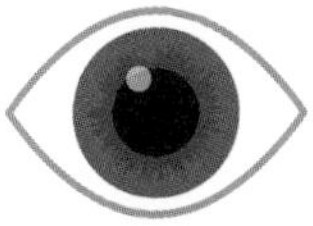

⑥ **braun**
brown

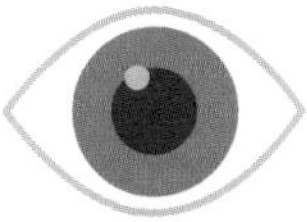

⑦ **grün**
green

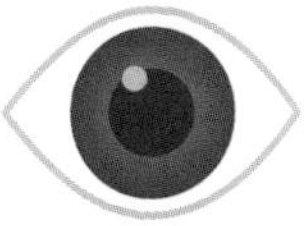

⑧ **haselnussbraun**
hazel

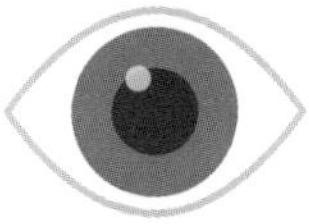

⑨ **grau**
gray

# 02 Hände und Füße

## Hands and feet

## 2.1 DIE HÄNDE · HANDS

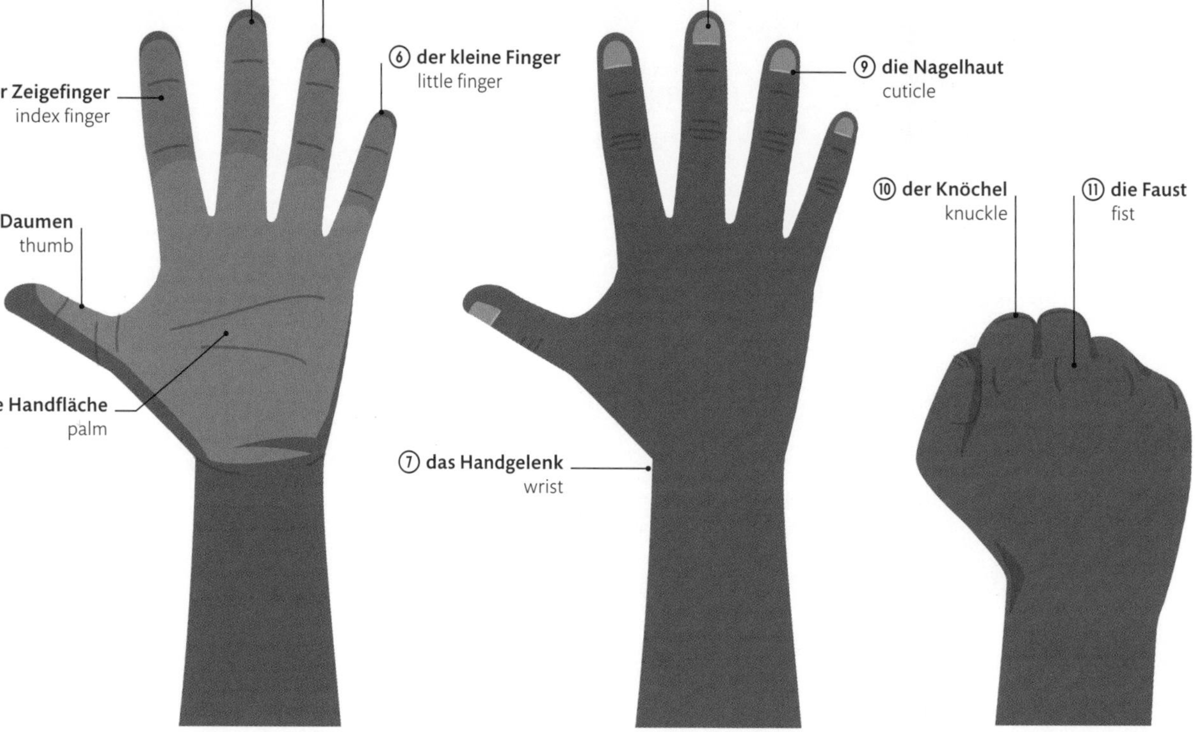


## 2.2 KÖRPERVERBEN · BODY VERBS

① **lächeln**
to smile

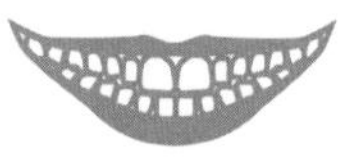
② **grinsen**
to grin

③ **die Stirn runzeln**
to frown

④ **zwinkern**
to wink

⑤ **blinzeln**
to blink

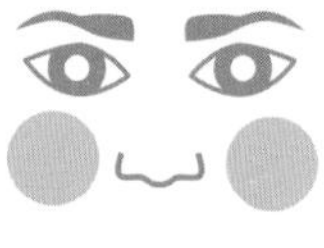
⑥ **rot werden**
to blush

⑦ **gähnen**
to yawn

⑧ **schnarchen**
to snore

⑨ **lecken**
to lick

⑩ **saugen**
to suck

⑪ **atmen**
to breathe

⑫ **den Atem anhalten**
to hold your breath

See also
**01** Körperteile • Parts of the body **03** Muskeln und Skelett • Muscles and skeleton
**19** Krankheiten und Verletzungen • Illness and injury **20** Beim Arzt • Visiting the doctor **21** Das Krankenhaus • The hospital

## 2.3 **DIE FÜSSE** • FEET

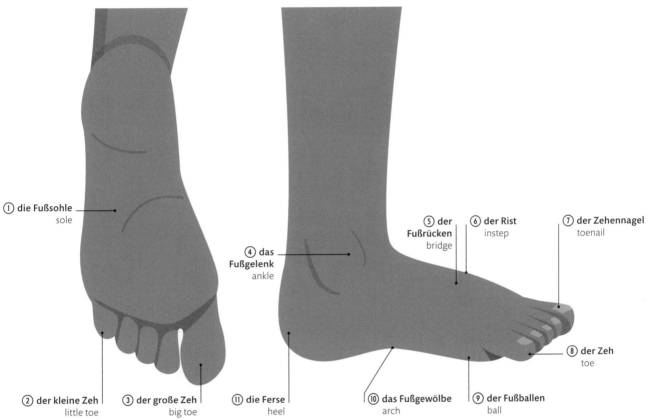

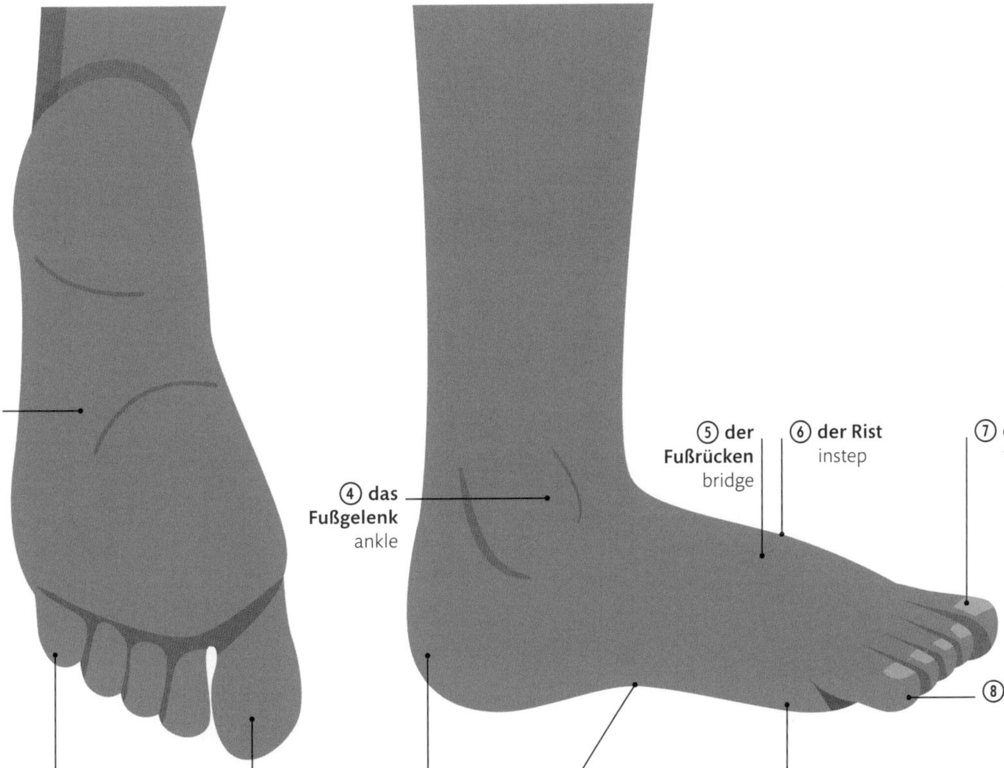

⑬ **lachen**
to laugh

⑭ **weinen**
to cry

⑮ **seufzen**
to sigh

⑯ **winken**
to wave

⑰ **mit den Schultern zucken**
to shrug

⑱ **sich verbeugen**
to bow

⑲ **klatschen**
to clap

⑳ **schwitzen**
to sweat / to perspire

㉑ **zittern**
to shiver

㉒ **niesen**
to sneeze

㉓ **den Kopf schütteln**
to shake your head

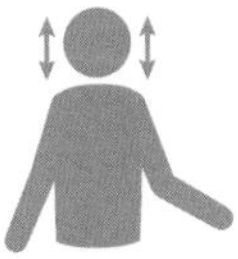
㉔ **nicken**
to nod

# 03 Muskeln und Skelett
## Muscles and skeleton

### 3.1 DIE MUSKELN
MUSCLES

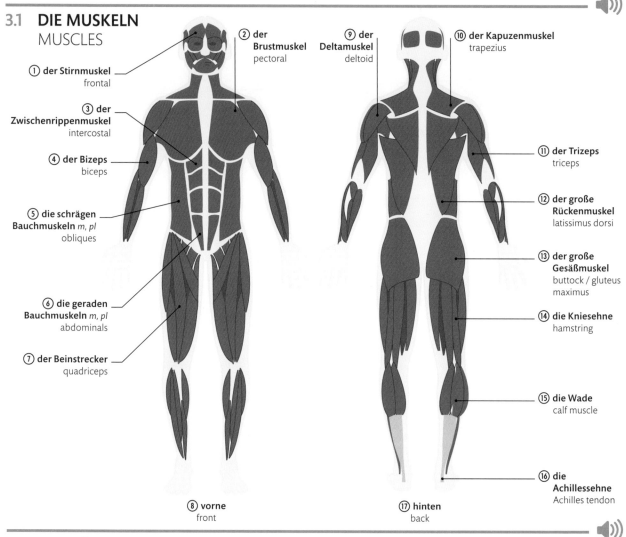

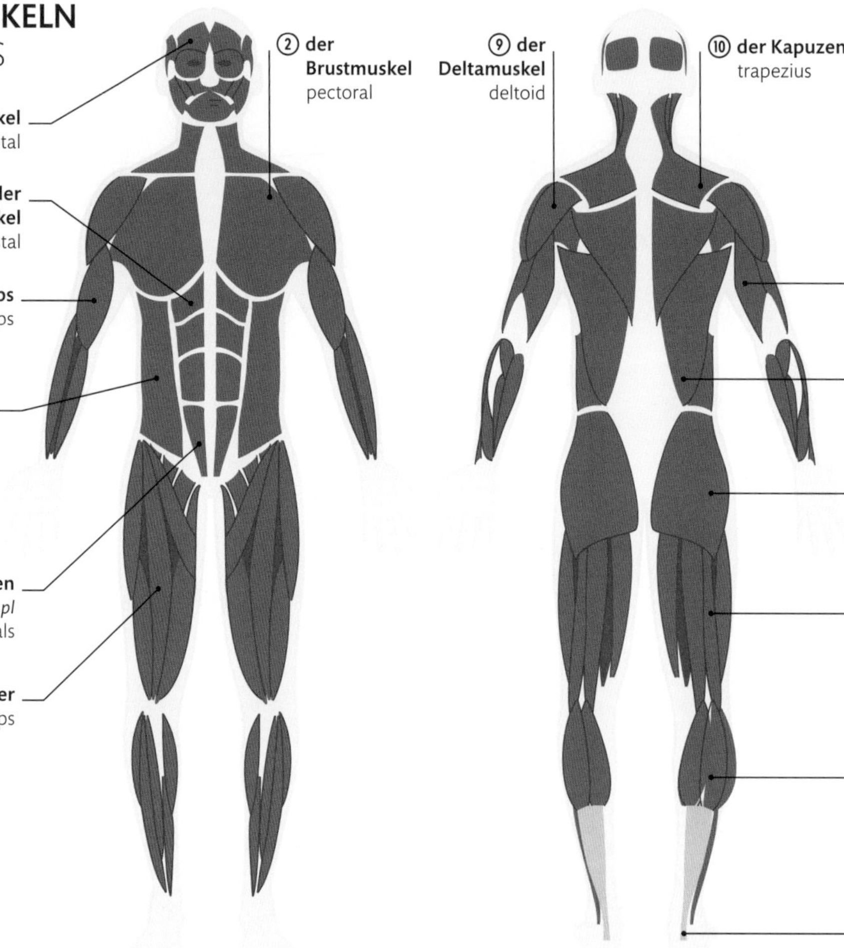

① der Stirnmuskel
frontal
② der Brustmuskel
pectoral
③ der Zwischenrippenmuskel
intercostal
④ der Bizeps
biceps
⑤ die schrägen Bauchmuskeln *m, pl*
obliques
⑥ die geraden Bauchmuskeln *m, pl*
abdominals
⑦ der Beinstrecker
quadriceps
⑧ vorne
front
⑨ der Deltamuskel
deltoid
⑩ der Kapuzenmuskel
trapezius
⑪ der Trizeps
triceps
⑫ der große Rückenmuskel
latissimus dorsi
⑬ der große Gesäßmuskel
buttock / gluteus maximus
⑭ die Kniesehne
hamstring
⑮ die Wade
calf muscle
⑯ die Achillessehne
Achilles tendon
⑰ hinten
back

### 3.2 DIE ZÄHNE · TEETH

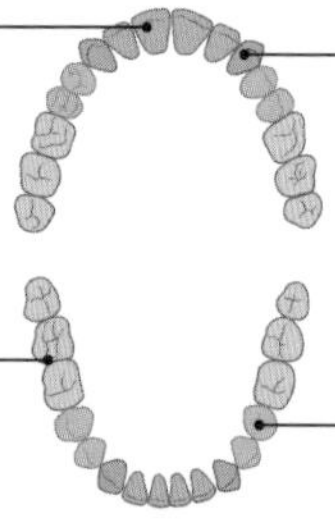

① die Schneidezähne *m, pl*
incisors
② die Eckzähne *m, pl*
canines
③ die Backenzähne *m, pl*
molars
④ die vorderen Backenzähne *m, pl*
bicuspids

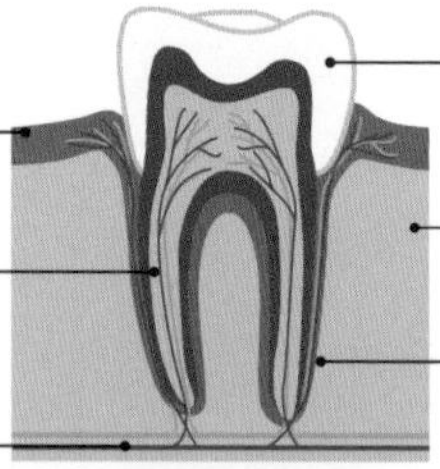

⑤ das Zahnfleisch
gum
⑥ das Zahnmark
pulp
⑦ der Nerv
nerve
⑧ der Zahnschmelz
enamel
⑨ der Knochen
bone
⑩ die Wurzel
root
⑪ der Zahn
tooth

See also
**01** Körperteile • Parts of the body **02** Hände und Füße • Hands and feet
**04** Innere Organe • Internal organs **19** Krankheiten und Verletzungen • Illness and injury **20** Beim Arzt • Visiting the doctor **21** Das Krankenhaus • The hospital

## 3.3 DAS SKELETT • SKELETON

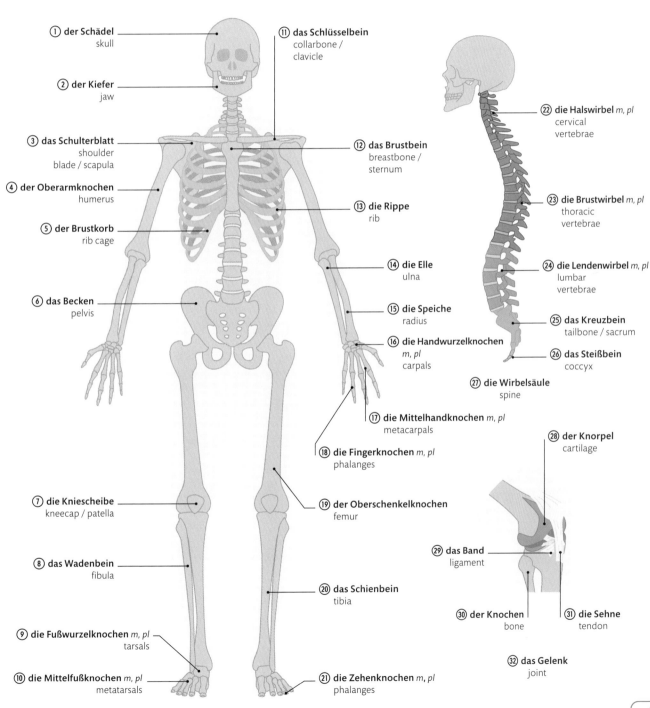

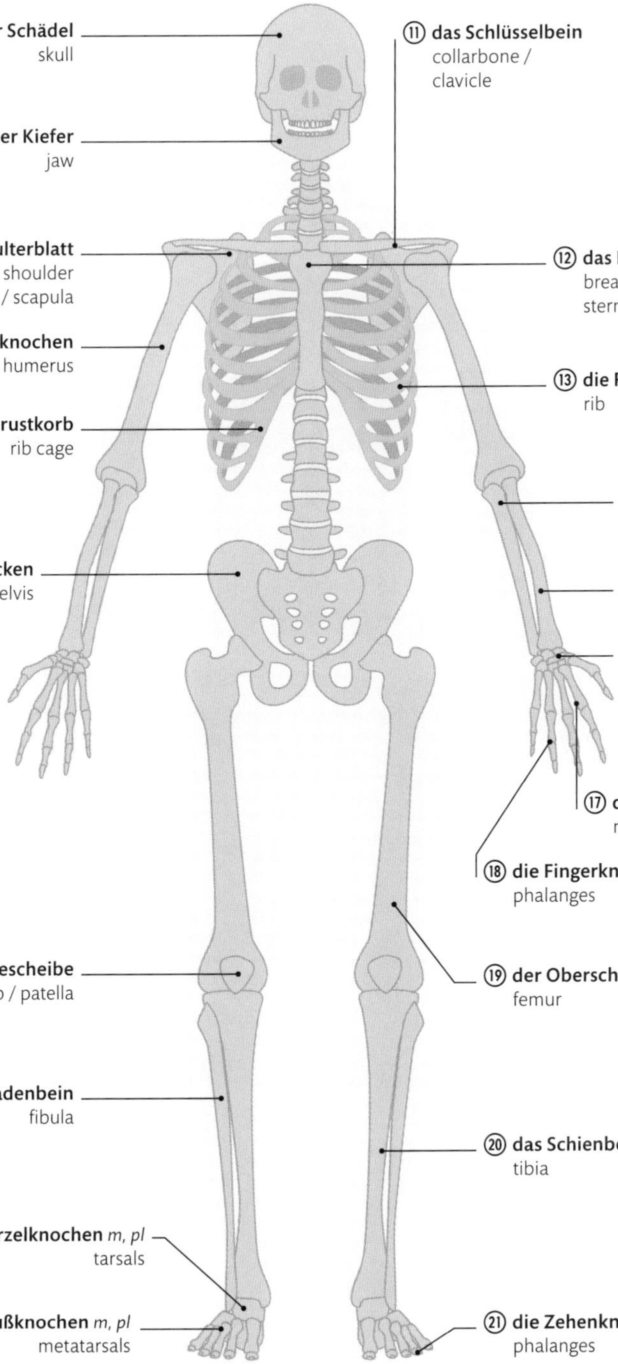


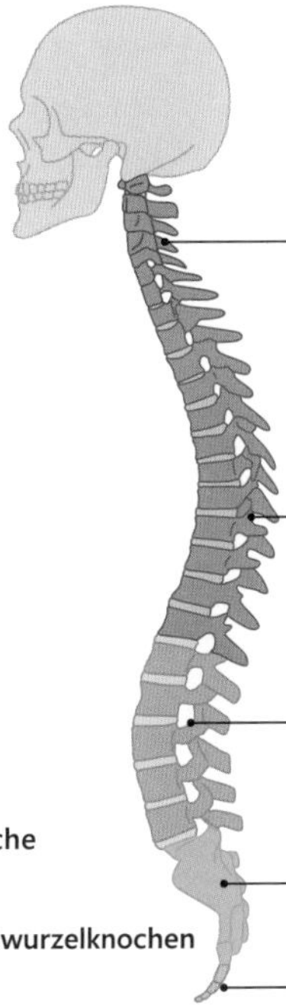


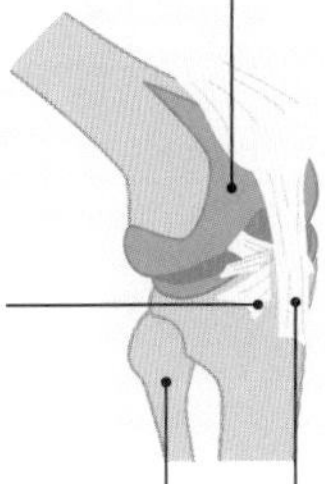

# 04 Innere Organe
## Internal organs

## 4.1 INNERE ORGANE · INTERNAL ORGANS

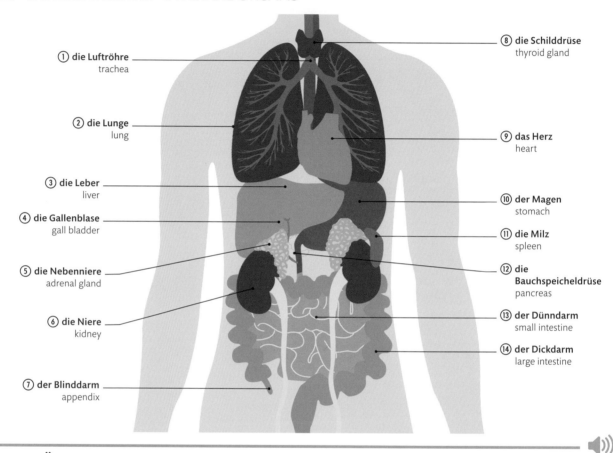

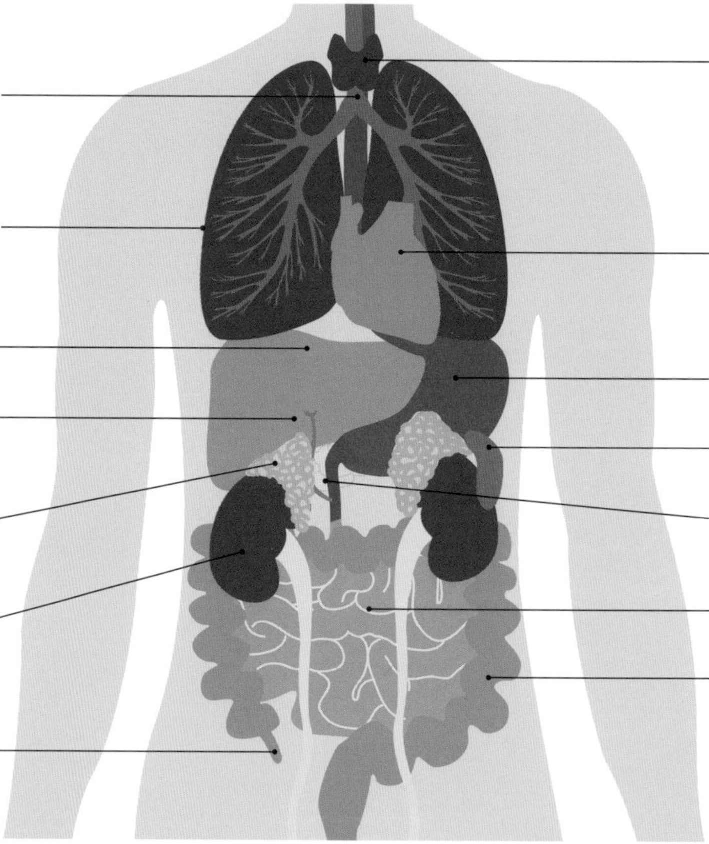


## 4.2 KÖRPERSYSTEME · BODY SYSTEMS

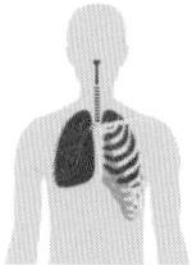
① **die Atemwege** *m, pl*
respiratory

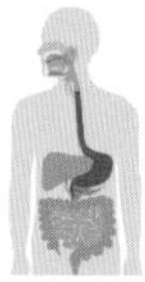
② **der Verdauungstrakt**
digestive

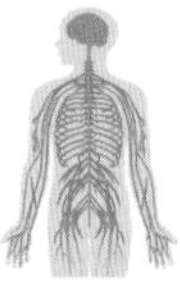
③ **das Nervensystem**
nervous

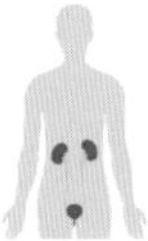
④ **der Harntrakt**
urinary

⑤ **das endokrine System**
endocrine

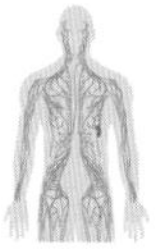
⑥ **das Lymphsystem**
lymphatic

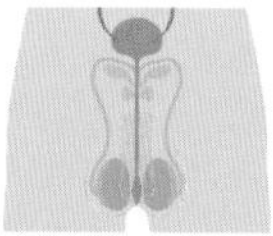
⑦ **das Fortpflanzungssystem**
reproductive

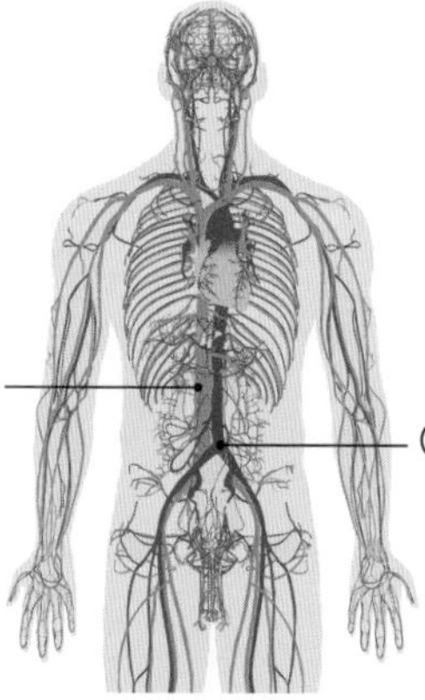

⑧ **der Blutkreislauf**
cardiovascular

See also
**01** Körperteile • Parts of the body **03** Muskeln und Skelett • Muscles and skeleton
**19** Krankheiten und Verletzungen • Illness and injury **20** Beim Arzt • Visiting the doctor
**21** Das Krankenhaus • The hospital

## 4.3 DER KOPF • HEAD

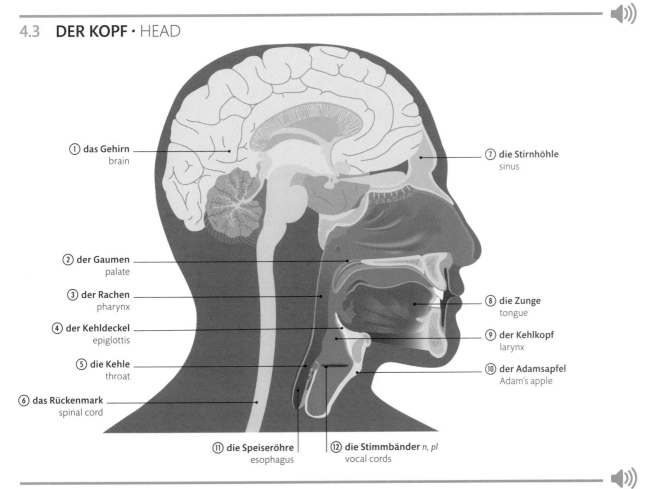

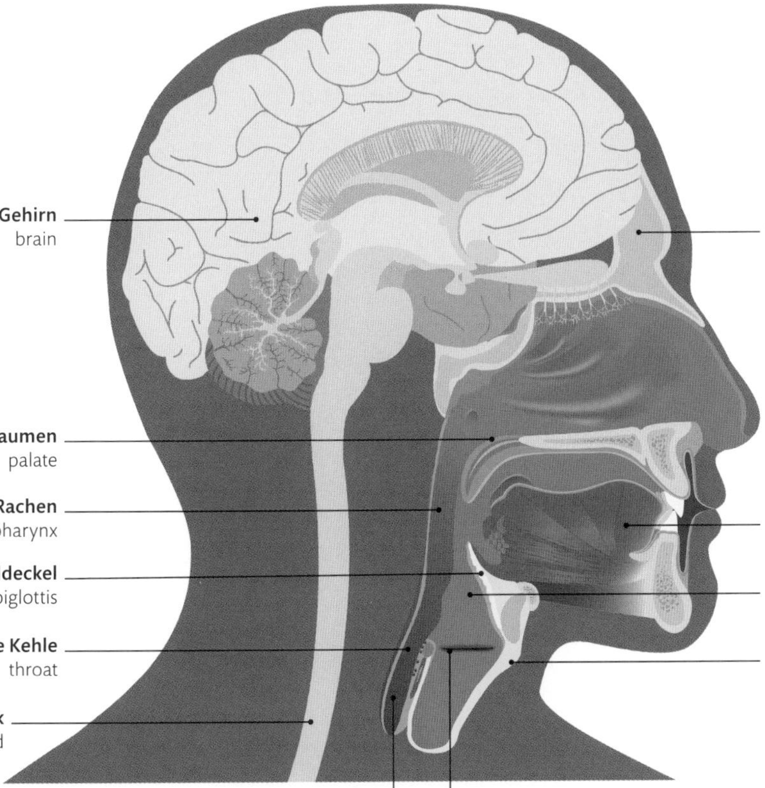


## 4.4 DIE FORTPFLANZUNGSORGANE • REPRODUCTIVE ORGANS

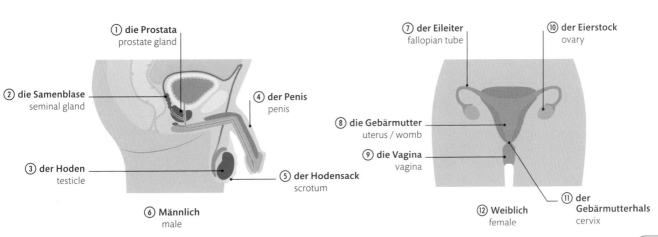

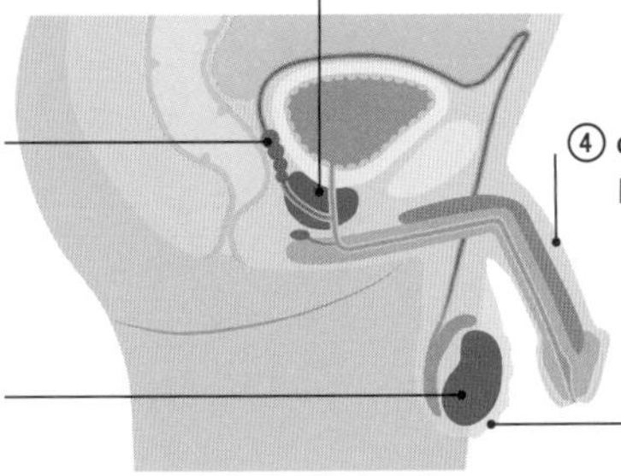


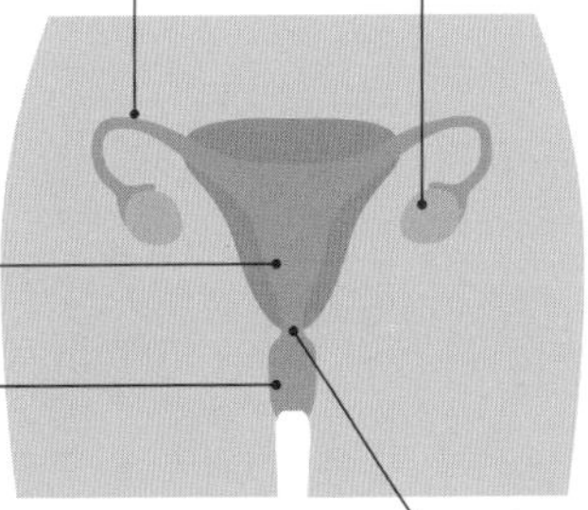

# 05 Die Familie
## Family

### 5.1 **CARLOS FAMILIE** · CARLOS'S FAMILY

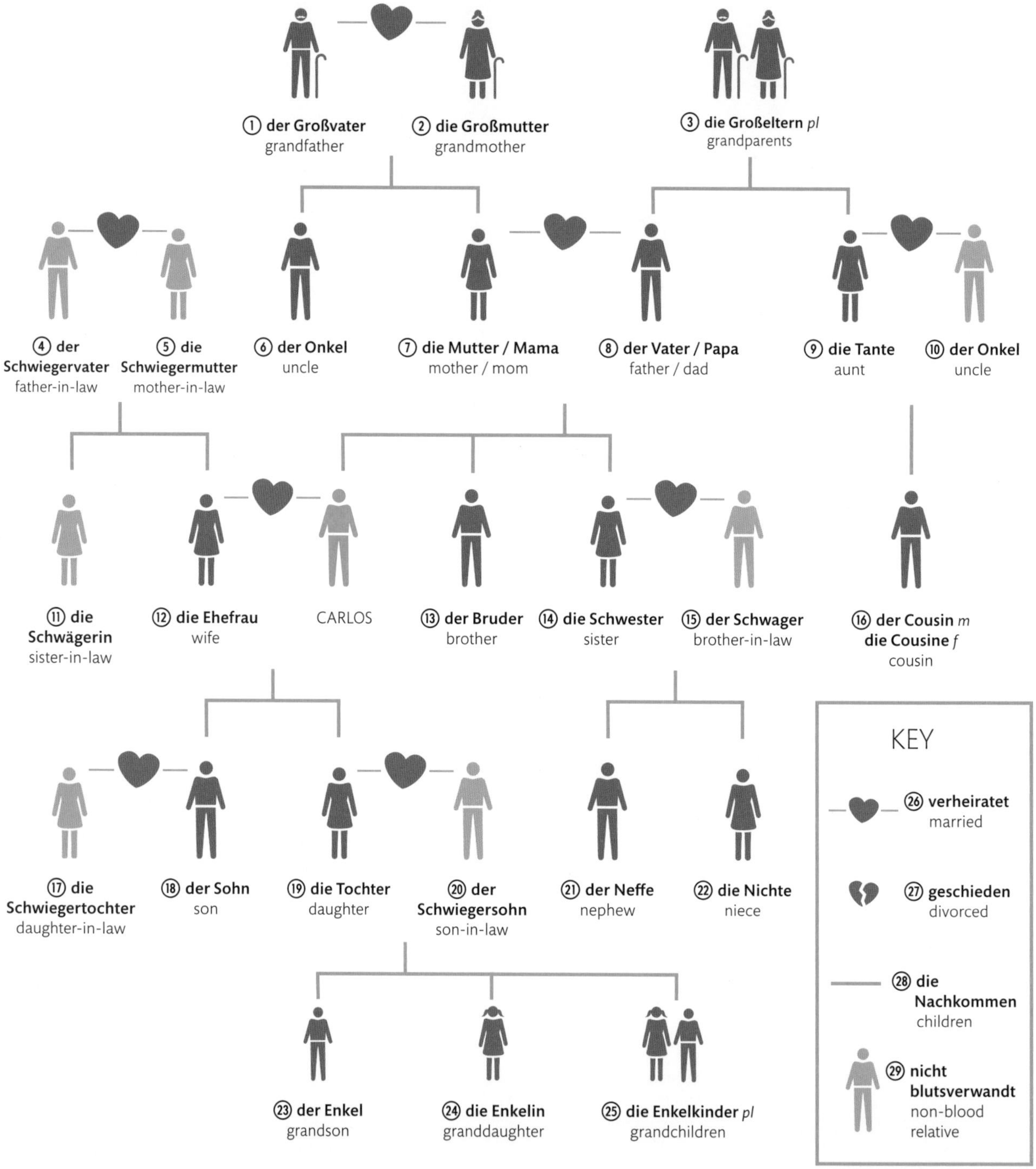

① der Großvater
grandfather
② die Großmutter
grandmother
③ die Großeltern *pl*
grandparents
④ der Schwiegervater
father-in-law
⑤ die Schwiegermutter
mother-in-law
⑥ der Onkel
uncle
⑦ die Mutter / Mama
mother / mom
⑧ der Vater / Papa
father / dad
⑨ die Tante
aunt
⑩ der Onkel
uncle
⑪ die Schwägerin
sister-in-law
⑫ die Ehefrau
wife
CARLOS
⑬ der Bruder
brother
⑭ die Schwester
sister
⑮ der Schwager
brother-in-law
⑯ der Cousin *m* die Cousine *f*
cousin
⑰ die Schwiegertochter
daughter-in-law
⑱ der Sohn
son
⑲ die Tochter
daughter
⑳ der Schwiegersohn
son-in-law
㉑ der Neffe
nephew
㉒ die Nichte
niece
㉓ der Enkel
grandson
㉔ die Enkelin
granddaughter
㉕ die Enkelkinder *pl*
grandchildren
KEY
㉖ verheiratet
married
㉗ geschieden
divorced
㉘ die Nachkommen
children
㉙ nicht blutsverwandt
non-blood relative

See also
**07** Lebensereignisse • Life events
**08** Schwangerschaft und Kindheit • Pregnancy and childhood

## 5.2 SARAHS FAMILIE
SARAH'S FAMILY

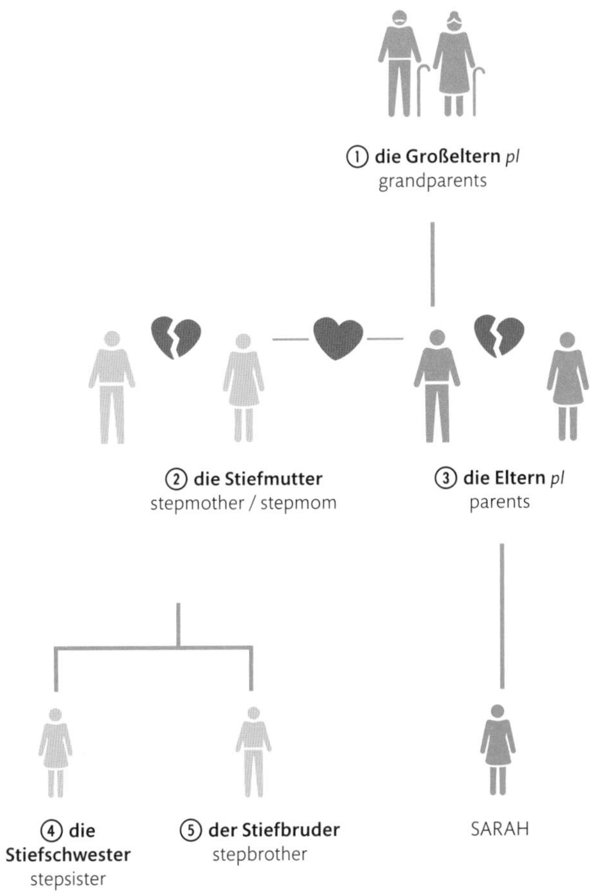


## 5.3 BEZIEHUNGEN • RELATIONSHIPS

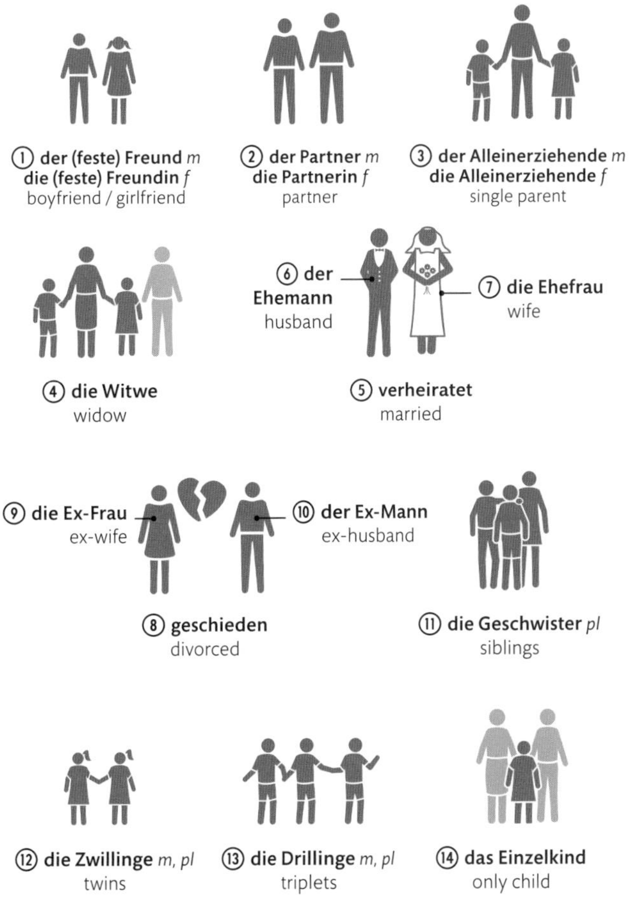


## 5.4 AUFWACHSEN • GROWING UP

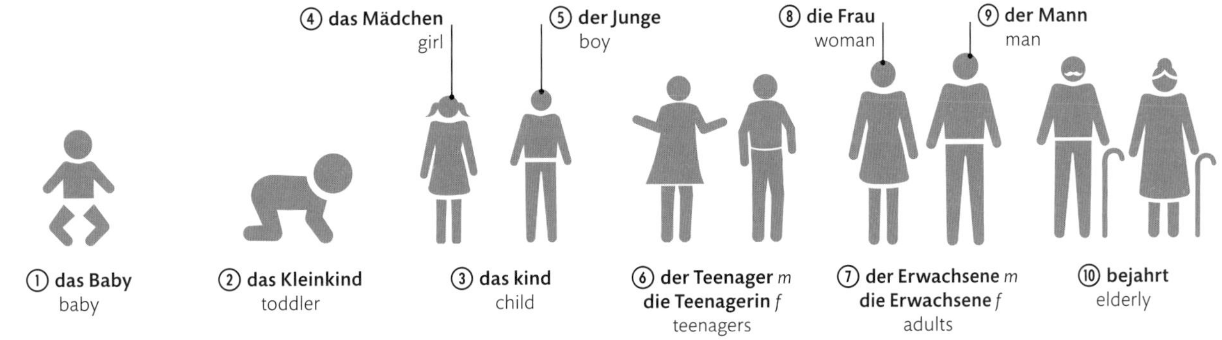

# 06 Gefühle und Stimmung
## Feelings and moods

### 6.1 GEFÜHLE UND STIMMUNG · FEELINGS AND MOODS

① **zufrieden**
pleased

② **fröhlich**
cheerful

③ **glücklich**
happy

④ **erfreut**
delighted

⑤ **verzückt**
ecstatic

Ha Ha!
⑥ **amüsiert**
amused

⑦ **dankbar**
grateful

⑧ **glücklich**
lucky

⑨ **interessiert**
interested

?
⑩ **neugierig**
curious

??
⑪ **fasziniert**
intrigued

⑫ **erstaunt**
amazed

⑬ **überrascht**
surprised

⑭ **stolz**
proud

⑮ **aufgeregt**
excited

⑯ **begeistert**
thrilled

⑰ **ruhig**
calm

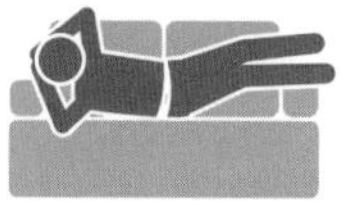
⑱ **entspannt**
relaxed

⑳ **Danke. Das Essen war hervorragend.**
Thank you. I really enjoyed the meal.
⑲ **wertschätzend**
appreciative

㉑ **selbstbewusst**
confident

㉒ **hoffnungsvoll**
hopeful

㉓ **mitfühlend**
sympathetic

㉔ **genervt**
annoyed

㉕ **eifersüchtig**
jealous

㉖ **peinlich berührt**
embarrassed

See also
**10** Eigenschaften • Personality traits **24** Gesunder Körper, gesunder Geist • Healthy body, healthy mind **93** Nützliche Fähigkeiten für den Arbeitsplatz • Workplace skills

(28) **Ich habe schon wieder nicht bestanden. Ich bin sehr enttäuscht.**
I failed the exam again. I'm very disappointed.

(27) **enttäuscht**
disappointed

(29) **besorgt**
worried

(30) **ängstlich**
anxious

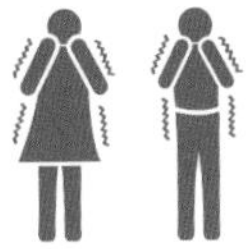

(31) **nervös**
nervous

(32) **erschrocken**
frightened

(33) **verängstigt**
scared

(34) **in Schrecken versetzt**
terrified

(35) **traurig**
sad

(36) **unglücklich**
unhappy

(37) **den Tränen nah**
tearful

(38) **elend**
miserable

(39) **depressiv**
depressed

(40) **einsam**
lonely

(41) **verärgert**
irritated

(42) **frustriert**
frustrated

(43) **sauer**
angry / mad

(44) **wütend**
furious

(45) **angeekelt**
disgusted

(46) **lustlos**
unenthusiastic

(47) **müde**
tired

(48) **erschöpft**
exhausted

(49) **verwirrt**
confused

(50) **gelangweilt**
bored

(51) **abgelenkt**
distracted

(52) **ernst**
serious

(53) **gleichgültig**
indifferent

(54) **gestresst**
stressed

(55) **schuldbewusst**
guilty

(56) **unbeeindruckt**
unimpressed

(57) **aufgelöst**
upset

(58) **schockiert**
shocked

# 07 Lebensereignisse
## Life events

### 7.1 BEZIEHUNGEN • RELATIONSHIPS

① **der Nachbar** *m*
**die Nachbarin** *f*
neighbor

② **der Freund** *m*
**die Freundin** *f*
friend

③ **der Bekannte** *m*
**die Bekannte** *f*
acquaintance

④ **der Kollege** *m*
**die Kollegin** *f*
colleague

⑤ **der Brieffreund** *m*
**die Brieffreundin** *f*
pen pal

⑥ **das Paar**
couple

⑦ **der beste Freund** *m*
**die beste Freundin** *f*
best friend

⑧ **der Partner** *m*
**die Partnerin** *f*
partner

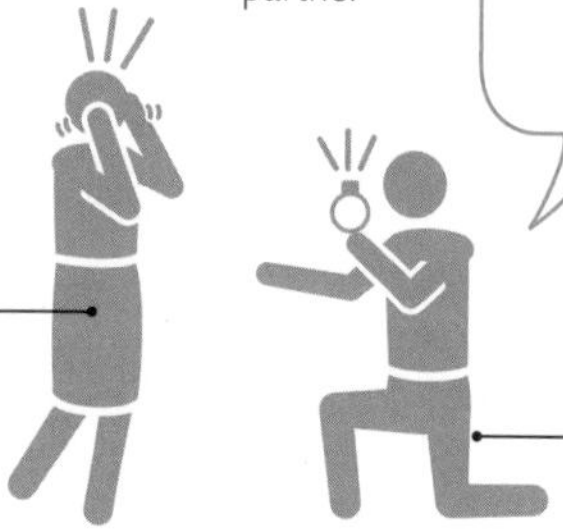
⑨ **Willst du mich heiraten?**
Will you marry me?

⑩ **die Verlobte**
fiancée

⑪ **der Verlobte**
fiancé

⑫ **die Verlobten** *pl*
engaged couple

⑬ **die Braut**
bride

⑭ **der Bräutigam**
groom

⑮ **das Ehepaar** *pl*
married couple

### 7.2 LEBENSEREIGNISSE • LIFE EVENTS

① **geboren werden**
to be born

② **die Geburtsurkunde**
birth certificate

③ **in den Kindergarten gehen**
to go to preschool

④ **eingeschult werden**
to start school

⑤ **Freunde finden**
to make friends

⑥ **einen Preis gewinnen**
to win a prize

⑦ **einen Abschluss machen**
to graduate

⑧ **auswandern**
to emigrate

⑨ **einen Job annehmen**
to get a job

⑩ **sich verlieben**
to fall in love

⑪ **heiraten**
to get married

See also
**05** Die Familie • Family **08** Schwangerschaft und Kindheit • Pregnancy and childhood **19** Krankheiten und Verletzungen • Illness and injury **73** An der Schule • At school **80** An der Universität • At college **92** Bewerbungen • Applying for a job **131** Reise und Unterkunft • Travel and accommodation

## 7.3 FESTE UND FEIERLICHKEITEN • FESTIVALS AND CELEBRATIONS

① **der Geburtstag**
birthday

② **das Geschenk**
present

③ **die Geburtstagskarte**
birthday card

④ **Weihnachten** *n*
Christmas

⑤ **Silvester** *n*
New Year

⑥ **Fasching** *m*
carnival

⑦ **Erntedank** *m*
Thanksgiving

⑧ **Ostern** *n*
Easter

⑨ **Halloween** *n*
Halloween

⑩ **Kwanzaa** *n*
Kwanzaa

⑪ **das Passahfest**
Passover

⑫ **Diwali** *n*
Diwali

⑬ **der Tag der Toten**
Day of the Dead

⑭ **das Fest des Fastenbrechens**
Eid al-Fitr

⑮ **das Holi-Fest**
Holi

⑯ **Chanukka** *n*
Hanukkah

⑰ **Vaisakhi** *n*
Baisakhi / Vaisakhi

⑫ **die Hochzeit**
wedding

⑬ **die Hochzeitsreise**
honeymoon

⑭ **der Jahrestag**
anniversary

⑮ **ein Kind bekommen**
to have a baby

⑰ **das Weihwasser**
holy water

⑯ **die Taufe**
christening / baptism

⑱ **der Bar Mitzwa die Bat Mitzwa**
bar mitzvah / bat mitzvah

⑲ **den Hadsch machen**
to go on Hajj

⑳ **in Rente gehen**
to retire

㉑ **sich scheiden lassen**
divorce

㉒ **ein Testament aufsetzen**
to write a will

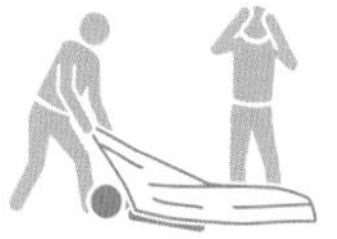
㉓ **sterben**
to die

㉔ **die Beerdigung**
funeral

# 08 Schwangerschaft und Kindheit
Pregnancy and childhood

## 8.1 SCHWANGERSCHAFT UND GEBURT · PREGNANCY AND CHILDBIRTH

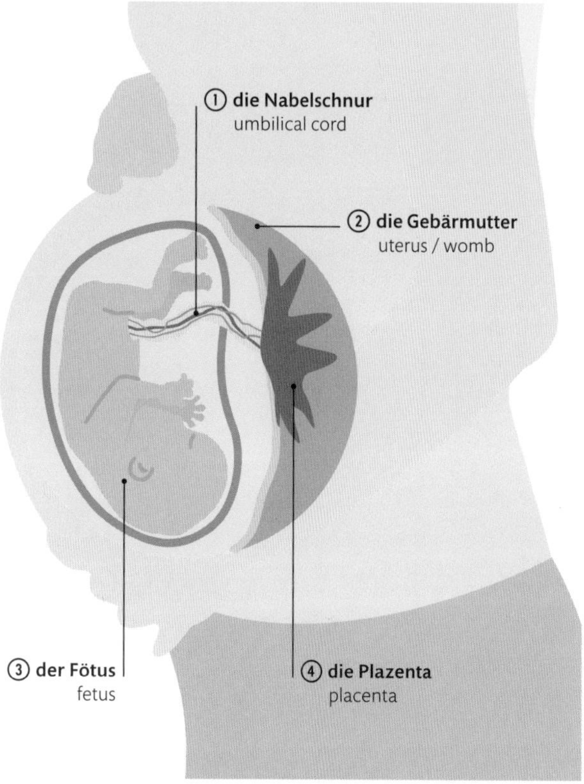


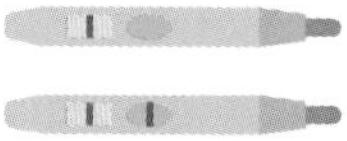

⑤ der Schwangerschaftstest
pregnancy test

⑥ schwanger
pregnant

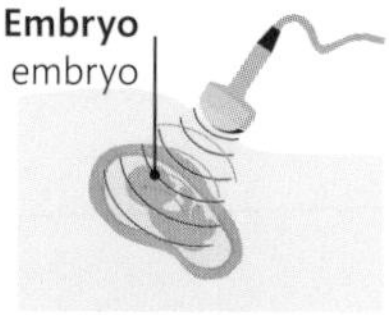


⑦ der Ultraschall
ultrasound

⑨ der Geburtstermin
due date

⑩ der Geburtshelfer *m*
die Hebamme *f*
midwife

⑪ der Entbindungsarzt *m*
die Entbindungsärztin *f*
obstetrician

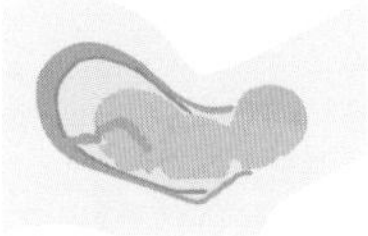

⑫ die Geburt
birth

⑬ das Neugeborene
newborn baby

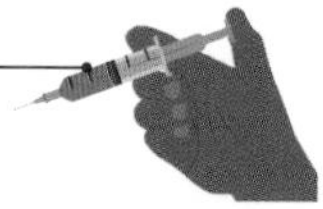

⑭ die Impfung
vaccination

⑮ der Brutkasten
incubator

## 8.2 SPIELE UND SPIELZEUGE · TOYS AND GAMES

① die Puppe
doll

② das Puppenhaus
dollhouse

③ das Stofftier
plush toy

④ das Brettspiel
board game

⑤ die Bauklötze *m, pl*
building blocks / building bricks

⑥ der Ball
ball

⑦ der Kreisel
top

⑧ das Jo-Jo
yo-yo

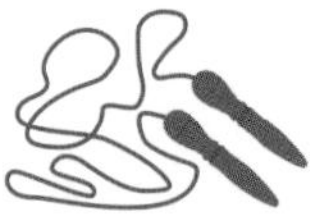

⑨ das Springseil
jump rope

⑩ das Trampolin
trampoline

⑪ das Puzzle
jigsaw puzzle

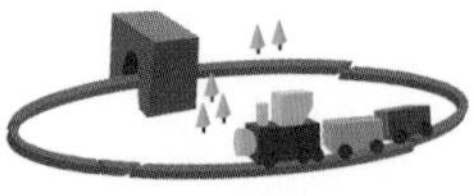

⑫ die Spielzeugeisenbahn
train set

See also
**05** Die Familie • Family **13** Kleidung • Clothes **20** Beim Arzt • Visiting the doctor
**21** Das Krankenhaus • The hospital **30** Das Schlafzimmerr • Bedroom

## 8.3 DIE KINDHEIT • CHILDHOOD

① **der Buggy**
stroller

② **der Kinderwagen**
baby carriage

③ **der Hochstuhl**
high chair

④ **der Schnuller**
pacifier

⑤ **die Rassel**
rattle

⑥ **das Babyfon**
baby monitor

⑦ **das Treppengitter**
stair gate

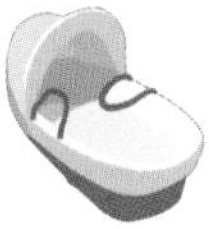
⑧ **das Babykörbchen**
Moses basket

⑨ **die Babybadewanne**
baby bath

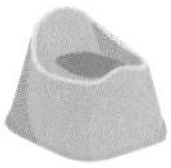
⑩ **das Töpfchen**
potty

⑪ **das Feuchttuch**
wet wipe

⑫ **das Kleinkind**
toddler

⑬ **die Wundschutzcreme**
diaper rash cream

⑭ **die Windel**
diaper

⑮ **die Windeltasche**
diaper bag

⑯ **der Laufstall**
playpen

⑱ **der Sauger**
nipple

⑰ **das Fläschchen**
bottle

⑲ **die Milchnahrung**
baby formula

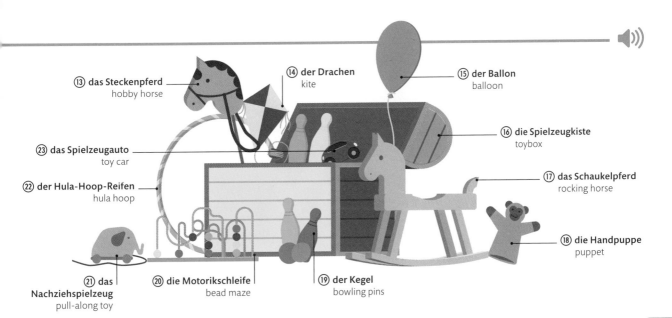

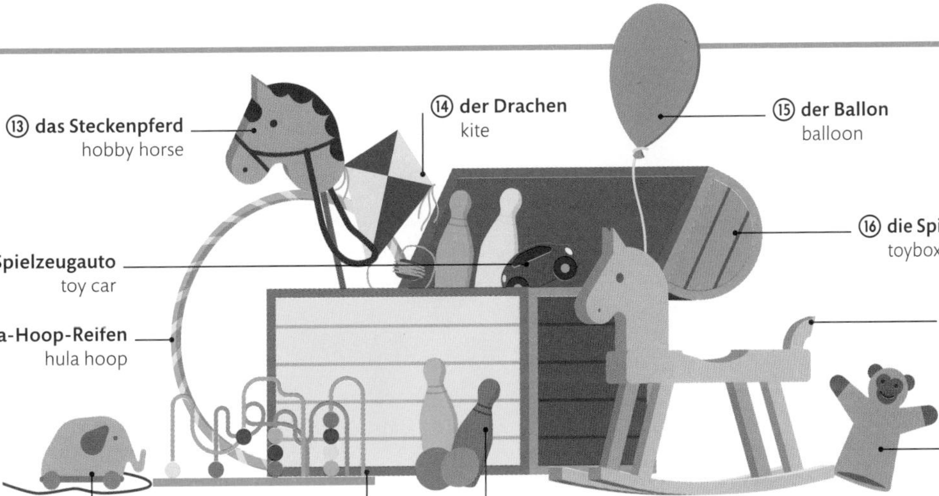
⑬ **das Steckenpferd**
hobby horse

⑭ **der Drachen**
kite

⑮ **der Ballon**
balloon

⑯ **die Spielzeugkiste**
toybox

㉓ **das Spielzeugauto**
toy car

⑰ **das Schaukelpferd**
rocking horse

㉒ **der Hula-Hoop-Reifen**
hula hoop

⑱ **die Handpuppe**
puppet

㉑ **das Nachziehspielzeug**
pull-along toy

⑳ **die Motorikschleife**
bead maze

⑲ **der Kegel**
bowling pins

# 09 Die Alltagsroutine

## Daily routines

### 9.1 VORMITTAG UND NACHMITTAG · MORNING AND AFTERNOON

① **der Wecker klingelt**
alarm goes off

② **aufwachen**
to wake up

③ **aufstehen**
to get up

④ **sich duschen**
to take (or have) a shower

⑤ **sich baden**
to take (or have) a bath

⑥ **sich schminken**
to put on makeup

⑦ **sich rasieren**
to shave

⑧ **sich die Haare waschen**
to wash your hair

⑨ **sich die Haare föhnen**
to dry your hair

⑩ **ein Hemd bügeln**
to iron a shirt

⑪ **sich anziehen**
to get dressed

⑫ **sich die Zähne putzen**
to brush your teeth

⑬ **sich das Gesicht waschen**
to wash your face

⑭ **sich die Haare bürsten**
to brush your hair

⑮ **das Bett machen**
to make the bed

⑯ **frühstücken**
to have (or eat) breakfast

⑰ **das Mittagessen einpacken**
to pack your lunch

⑱ **das Haus verlassen**
to leave the house

⑲ **zur Arbeit gehen**
to go to work

⑳ **in die Schule gehen**
to go to school

㉑ **fahren**
to drive

㉒ **mit dem Bus fahren**
to catch the bus

㉓ **mit dem Zug fahren**
to catch the train

㉔ **die Zeitung lesen**
to read a newspaper

㉕ **ankommen**
to arrive

㉖ **früh ankommen**
to arrive early

㉗ **pünktlich ankommen**
to arrive on time

㉘ **zu Mittag essen**
to have (or eat) lunch

㉙ **die E-Mails checken**
to check your emails

㉚ **eine Pause machen**
to take a break

㉜ Es tut mir leid, dass ich schon wieder zu spät gekommen bin.
I'm sorry I'm late again.

㉛ **zu spät kommen**
to arrive late / to be late

See also
**11** Fähigkeiten und Handlungen • Abilities and actions **29** Kochen • Cooking
**81** Auf der Arbeit • At work **82** Im Büro • In the office **171** Die Zeit • Time
**178** Geläufige Verben • Common phrasal verbs

## 9.2 DER ABEND • EVENING

① **die Arbeit beenden**
to finish work

④ Am schönsten ist es zu Hause!
There's no place like home!

② **die Arbeit verlassen**
to leave work

③ **Überstunden machen**
to work overtime

⑤ **nach Hause kommen**
to arrive home

⑥ **das Abendessen kochen**
to cook dinner

⑦ **zu Abend essen**
to have (or eat) dinner

⑧ **den Tisch abräumen**
to clear the table

⑨ **abspülen**
to do the dishes

⑩ **Radio hören**
to listen to the radio

⑪ **fernsehen**
to watch TV

⑫ **Tee oder Kaffee trinken**
to drink tea or coffee

⑬ **den Müll hinausbringen**
to take out the trash

⑭ **die Kinder ins Bett bringen**
to put the children to bed

⑮ **ins Bett gehen**
to go to bed

⑯ **den Wecker stellen**
to set the alarm

⑰ **einschlafen**
to go to sleep

## 9.3 ANDERE AKTIVITÄTEN OTHER ACTIVITIES

① **Hausaufgaben machen**
to do homework

② **Gassi gehen**
to walk the dog

③ **den Hund / die Katze füttern**
to feed the dog / cat

④ **Lebensmittel einkaufen**
to buy groceries

⑤ **sich mit Freunden treffen**
to go out with friends

⑥ **in ein Café gehen**
to go to a café

⑦ **Freunde anrufen die Familie anrufen**
to call a friend / to call your family

⑧ **den Rasen mähen**
to mow the lawn

⑨ **Sport machen**
to exercise

⑩ **mit den Kindern spielen**
to play with your kids

⑪ **Rechnungen bezahlen**
to pay the bills

⑫ **ein Nickerchen machen**
to take a nap

⑬ **das Auto putzen**
to clean the car

⑭ **ein Instrument spielen**
to play a musical instrument

⑮ **sich mit Freunden unterhalten**
to chat with friends

⑯ **online chatten**
to chat online

⑰ **die Blumen gießen**
to water the plants

⑱ **ein Paket verschicken**
to send a package

# 10 Eigenschaften

Personality traits

## 10.1 PERSONEN BESCHREIBEN · DESCRIBING PERSONALITIES

① **nett**
friendly

② **unfreundlich**
unfriendly

③ **gesprächig**
talkative

④ **enthusiastisch**
enthusiastic

⑤ **ernst**
serious

⑥ **bestimmt**
assertive

⑦ **kritisch**
critical

⑧ **fürsorglich**
caring

⑨ **empfindlich**
sensitive

⑩ **unsensibel**
insensitive

⑪ **vernünftig**
reasonable

⑫ **unvernünftig**
unreasonable

⑬ **freundlich**
kind

⑭ **unfreundlich**
unkind

⑮ **geheimniskrämerisch**
secretive

⑯ **erwachsen**
mature

⑰ **kindisch**
immature

⑱ **vorsichtig**
cautious

⑲ **großzügig**
generous

⑳ **mutig**
brave

㉑ **witzig**
funny

㉒ **gemein**
mean

㉓ **geduldig**
patient

㉔ **ungeduldig**
impatient

㉕ **faul**
lazy

㉖ **optimistisch**
optimistic

㉗ **aufgeschlossen / extrovertiert**
outgoing

㉘ **leidenschaftlich**
passionate

㉙ **höflich**
polite

㉚ **unhöflich**
rude

㉛ **schüchtern**
shy

㉜ **intelligent**
intelligent

㉝ **nervös**
nervous

㉞ **selbstbewusst**
confident

㉟ **albern**
silly

㊱ **selbstsüchtig**
selfish

See also
**05** Die Familie • Family **06** Gefühle und Stimmung • Feelings and moods **11** Fähigkeiten und Handlungen • Abilities and actions **93** Nützliche Fähigkeiten für den Arbeitsplatz • Workplace skills

(38) **Die Arbeit kann warten.**
My work can wait until later.

(37) **entspannt**
laid-back

(39) **ehrgeizig**
ambitious

(40) **spontan**
spontaneous

(41) **romantisch**
romantic

(42) **ruhig**
calm

(43) **exzentrisch**
eccentric

(44) **ehrlich**
honest

(45) **unehrlich**
dishonest

(46) **hilfsbereit**
supportive

(47) **impulsiv**
impulsive

(48) **zuverlässig**
reliable

(49) **unzuverlässig**
unreliable

(50) **talentiert**
talented

(51) **arrogant**
arrogant

(52) **rücksichtsvoll**
considerate

(53) **abenteuerlustig**
adventurous

(54) **nahbar**
approachable

(55) **unnahbar**
unapproachable

(56) **entscheidungsfreudig**
decisive

(57) **akkurat**
meticulous

(58) **ungeschickt**
clumsy

(59) **gedankenlos**
thoughtless

# 11 Fähigkeiten und Handlungen
## Abilities and actions

### 11.1 FÄHIGKEITEN UND HANDLUNGEN BESCHREIBEN
DESCRIBING ABILITIES AND ACTIONS

① **sehen**
to see

② **schmecken**
to taste

③ **riechen**
to smell

④ **kriechen**
to crawl

⑩ **Tanzen macht mir Spaß!**
I love to dance.

⑪ **Mir auch!**
Me too!

⑨ **tanzen**
to dance

⑤ **schlagen**
to hit

⑥ **spielen**
to play

⑦ **treten**
to kick

⑧ **werfen**
to throw

⑫ **fangen**
to catch

⑬ **laufen**
to run

⑭ **hüpfen**
to hop

⑮ **springen**
to jump

⑯ **schleichen**
to creep

⑰ **schütteln**
to shake

⑱ **arbeiten**
to work

⑲ **blasen**
to blow

⑳ **(einen Schneemann) bauen**
to make (a snowman)

㉑ **buchstabieren**
to spell

㉒ **(die Hausaufgaben) machen**
to do (homework)

㉓ **abschreiben**
to copy

㉔ **bauen**
to build

㉕ **graben**
to dig

㉖ **reparieren**
to repair

㉗ **richten**
to fix

㉘ **sich hinsetzen**
to sit down

㉙ **aufstehen**
to stand up

㉚ **verstehen**
to understand

㉛ **hinfallen**
to fall

㉜ **heben**
to lift

㉝ **addieren**
to add

㉞ **subtrahieren**
to subtract

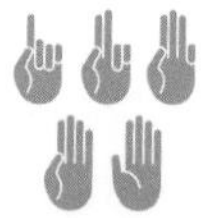
㉟ **zählen**
to count

See also
**09** Die Alltagsroutine • Daily routines **93** Nützliche Fähigkeiten für den Arbeitsplatz • Workplace skills **178** Geläufige Verben • Common phrasal verbs

㊱ **zuhören**
to listen

㊲ **reden**
to talk

㊳ **sprechen**
to speak

㊴ **schreien**
to shout

㊵ **singen**
to sing

㊶ **schauspielern**
to act

㊷ **flüstern**
to whisper

㊸ **denken**
to think

㊹ **entscheiden**
to decide

㊺ **sich erinnern**
to remember

㊻ **vergessen**
to forget

㊼ **helfen**
to help

㊽ **auf etwas deuten**
to point

㊾ **packen**
to pack

㊿ **auspacken**
to unpack

(51) **fliegen**
to fly

(52) **fahren**
to ride

(53) **klettern**
to climb

(54) **lecken**
to lick

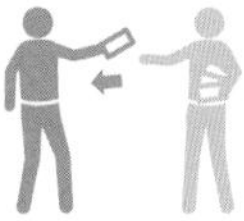
(55) **nehmen**
to take

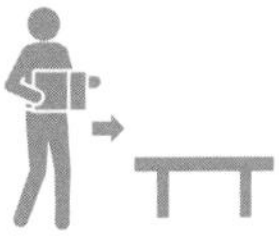
(56) **bringen**
to bring

(57) **mitnehmen**
to pick up

(58) **eintreten**
to enter

(59) **verlassen**
to exit

(60) **gewinnen**
to win

(61) **heben**
to raise

(62) **tragen**
to carry

(63) **jonglieren**
to juggle

(64) **festhalten**
to hold

(65) **umziehen**
to move

(66) **schieben**
to push

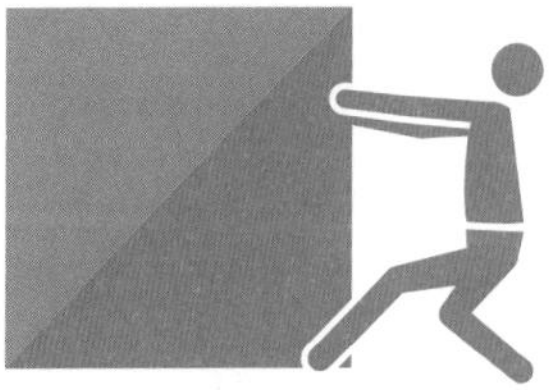
(67) **ziehen**
to pull

# 12 Aussehen und Haar
## Appearance and hair

### 12.1 ALLGEMEINES AUSSEHEN
GENERAL APPEARANCE

① **mittelgroß** medium height
② **groß** tall
③ **klein** short

④ **schön** beautiful

⑤ **gutaussehend** handsome

⑥ **jung** young

⑦ **mittleren Alters** middle-aged

⑧ **alt** old

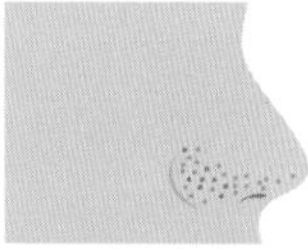

⑨ **die Poren** *f, pl* pores

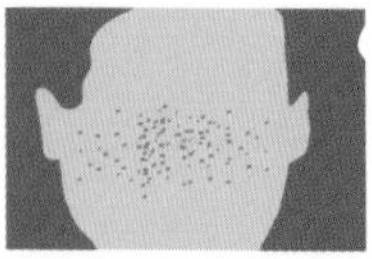

⑩ **die Sommersprossen** *f, pl* freckles

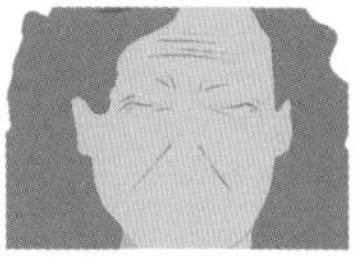

⑪ **die Falten** *f, pl* wrinkles

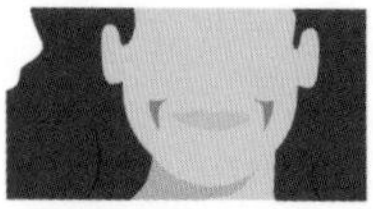

⑫ **die Grübchen** *f, pl* dimples

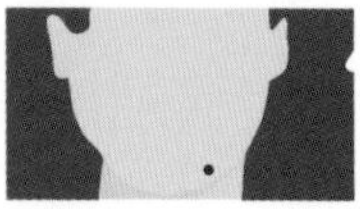

⑬ **das Muttermal** mole

### 12.2 DAS HAAR · HAIR

① **das Haar stylen** to style your hair

② **die Haare waschen** to wash your hair

③ **die Haare schneiden lassen** to have (or get) your hair cut

④ **die Haare hochbinden** to tie your hair back

⑤ **die Haare wachsen lassen** to grow your hair

⑥ **sich rasieren** to shave

⑦ **langes Haar** long hair

⑧ **kurzes Haar** short hair

⑨ **schulterlanges Haar** shoulder-length hair

⑩ **der Seitenscheitel** side part

⑪ **der Mittelscheitel** center part

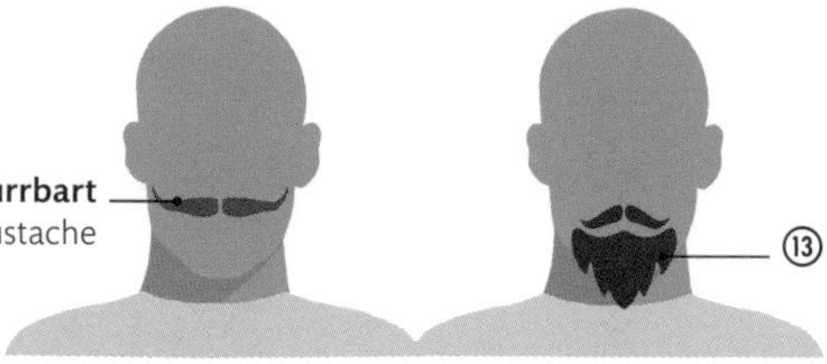

⑫ **der Schnurrbart** mustache
⑬ **der Kinnbart** goatee

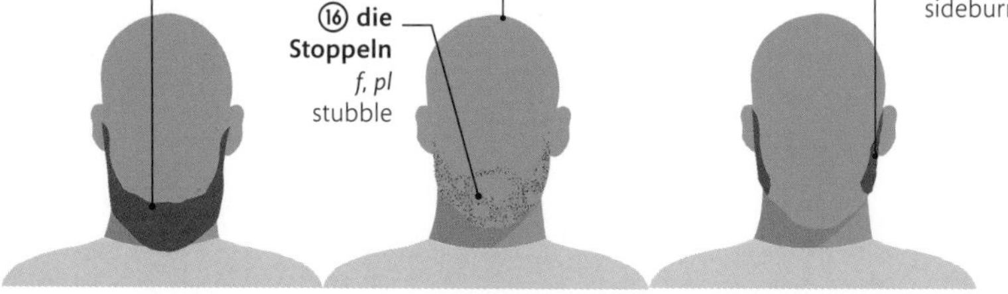

⑭ **der Bart** beard
⑮ **die Glatze** shaved head
⑯ **die Stoppeln** *f, pl* stubble
⑰ **die Kotelette** sideburns

⑱ **die Gesichtsbehaarung** facial hair

See also
**13-15** Kleidung • Clothes **16** Accessoires • Accessories
**17** Schuhe • Shoes **18** Beauty • Beauty

**19 der Bürstenschnitt**
crew cut

**20 glatzköpfig**
bald

**21 das glatte Haar**
straight hair

**22 das wellige Haar**
wavy hair

**23 das lockige Haar**
curly hair

**24 das gekräuselte Haar**
frizzy hair

**25 der Pferdeschwanz**
ponytail

**26 der Flechtzopf**
braid

**27 die Rattenschwänze**
pigtails

**28 der Bob**
bob

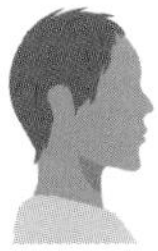

**29 sehr kurzes Haar**
crop

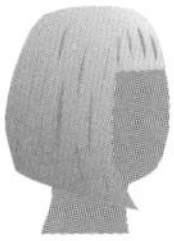

**30 die Perücke**
wig

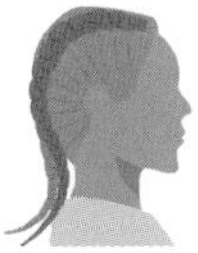

**31 der Französische Zopf**
French braid

**32 der Dutt**
bun

**33 die Strähnchen**
*n, pl*
highlights

**34 der Afro**
Afro

**35 die Rastazöpfe**
*m, pl*
braids

**36 die Cornrows**
*f, pl*
cornrows

**37 das normale Haar**
normal hair

**38 das fettige Haar**
greasy hair

**39 das trockene Haar**
dry hair

**40 die Schuppen**
*f, pl*
dandruff

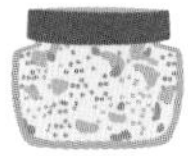

**41 das Haargel**
hair gel

**42 das Haarspray**
hair spray

**43 das schwarze Haar**
black hair

**44 das braune Haar**
brown hair

**45 das blonde Haar**
blond / blonde hair

**46 das rote Haar**
red hair

**47 das kastanienbraune Haar**
auburn hair

**48 das graue Haar**
gray hair

**49 das Glätteisen**
straightening iron

**50 der Lockenstab**
curling iron

**51 die Haarbürste**
hairbrush

**52 der Kamm**
comb

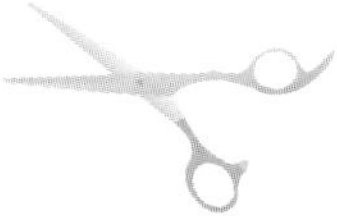

**53 die Haarschere**
hair scissors

**54 der Haarföhn**
hair dryer

# 13 Kleidung
## Clothes

### 13.1 KLEIDUNG BESCHREIBEN • DESCRIBING CLOTHES

① **das Leder**
leather

② **die Baumwolle**
cotton

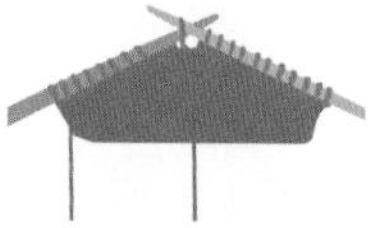
③ **aus Wolle**
woolen

④ **die Seide**
silk

⑤ **die Synthetikfaser**
synthetic

⑥ **der Jeansstoff**
denim

⑦ **einfarbig**
plain

⑧ **gestreift**
striped

⑨ **kariert**
checkered

⑩ **gepunktet**
polka dot

⑪ **das Paisleymuster**
paisley

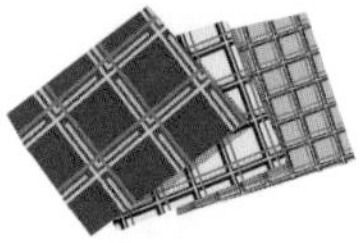
⑫ **das Schottenkaro**
plaid

⑬ **locker**
loose / baggy

⑭ **figurbetont**
fitted

⑮ **eng**
tight

⑯ **faltig**
crumpled

⑰ **kurz**
cropped

⑱ **klassisch**
vintage

### 13.2 ARBEITSBEKLEIDUNG UND UNIFORMEN • WORK CLOTHES AND UNIFORMS

③ **die Kochuniform**
chef's uniform

④ **die Schürze**
apron

⑤ **der Laborkittel**
lab coat

⑥ **die Feuerwehruniform**
firefighter's uniform

⑦ **der Overall**
coveralls

See also
12 Aussehen und haar • Appearance and hair 14-15 Kleidung (Fortsetzung) Clothes continued 16 Accessoires • Accessories 17 Schuhe • Shoes

## 13.3 BABYKLEIDUNG UND KINDERKLEIDUNG • KIDS' AND BABIES' CLOTHES

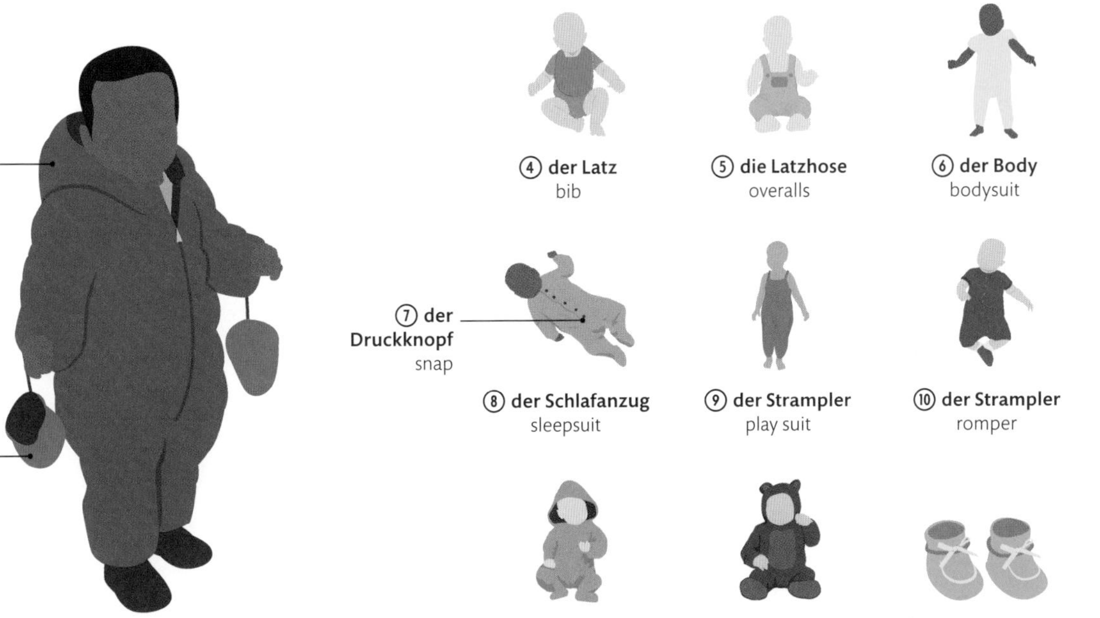

① **die Kapuze**
hood

② **die Fäustlinge** *m, pl*
mittens

③ **der Schneeanzug**
snowsuit

④ **der Latz**
bib

⑤ **die Latzhose**
overalls

⑥ **der Body**
bodysuit

⑦ **der Druckknopf**
snap

⑧ **der Schlafanzug**
sleepsuit

⑨ **der Strampler**
play suit

⑩ **der Strampler**
romper

⑪ **der Strampler**
onesie

⑫ **das Kostüm**
costume

⑬ **die Babystiefel** *m, pl*
booties

⑧ **die Militäruniform**
military uniform

⑨ **die OP-Kleidung**
scrubs

⑩ **die Cargohose**
cargo pants

⑪ **die Warnweste**
high-visibility jacket

⑫ **der Überwurf**
tabard

⑬ **die Schuluniform**
school uniform

⑭ **das Schulhemd**
school shirt

⑮ **die Schulkrawatte**
school tie

# Kleidung (Fortsetzung)
Clothes continued

## 14.1 FREIZEITKLEIDUNG · CASUAL CLOTHES

① **Ich trage meine Freizeitkleidung lieber als meine Arbeitskleidung.**
I prefer this casual outfit to my formal work clothes.

⑦ **Nach der Arbeit trage ich gerne Jeans und ein T-Shirt.**
After work, I like to change into jeans and a T-shirt.

② **die Bluse**
blouse

③ **der Pullover**
sweater

④ **der Rock**
skirt

⑤ **die Falte**
pleat

⑥ **der Saum**
hem

⑧ **das T-Shirt**
T-shirt

⑨ **die Streifen** *m, pl*
stripes

⑩ **die Jeans**
jeans

⑪ **das Sweatshirt**
sweatshirt

⑫ **die Short**
shorts

⑬ **die Bermudashort**
bermuda shorts

⑭ **die Strickjacke**
cardigan

⑮ **das Trägerhemd**
tank top

⑯ **das Kleid**
dress

⑰ **die Leggings**
leggings

⑱ **das kurzärmelige Hemd**
short-sleeved shirt

⑲ **das Polohemd**
polo shirt

⑳ **der Sonnenhut**
sun hat

㉑ **der V-Ausschnitt**
V-neck

㉒ **der Rundhals**
round neck

See also
**12** Aussehen und haar • Appearance and hair **15** Kleidung (Fortsetzung) Clothes continued **16** Accessoires • Accessories **17** Schuhe • Shoes

## 14.2 **SCHLAFBEKLEIDUNG** • NIGHTWEAR

① **das Leibchen**
camisole

② **die Pantoffeln** *m, pl*
slippers

③ **die Schlafmaske**
eye mask

④ **der Schlafanzug**
pajamas

⑤ **das Nachthemd**
nightgown / nightie

⑥ **der Bademantel**
bathrobe

## 14.3 **UNTERWÄSCHE** • UNDERWEAR

① **die Unterhose**
panties

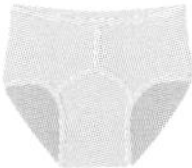
② **der Slip**
briefs

③ **die Boxershorts** *f, pl*
boxer shorts

④ **die Socken** *f, pl*
socks

⑤ **der BH**
bra

⑥ **das Unterkleid**
slip

⑦ **das Unterhemd**
undershirt

⑧ **die Strumpfhose**
pantyhose

⑨ **die Strümpfe** *m, pl*
stockings

⑩ **das Mieder**
corset

⑪ **das Strumpfband**
garter

⑫ **der Strumpfhalter**
garter belt

## 14.4 **KLEIDUNGSVERBEN** • VERBS FOR CLOTHES

① **tragen**
to wear

② **anprobieren**
to fit

③ **anziehen**
to put on

④ **ausziehen**
to take off

⑤ **binden**
to fasten

⑥ **lockern**
to unfasten

⑦ **(jemandem) stehen**
to suit (someone)

⑧ **sich umziehen**
to change / to get changed

⑨ **aufhängen**
to hang up

⑩ **zusammenlegen**
to fold

⑪ **aufkrempeln**
to turn up

⑫ **etwas anprobieren**
to try something on

# 15 Kleidung (Fortsetzung)

## Clothes continued

### 15.1 FORMELLE KLEIDUNG · FORMAL WEAR

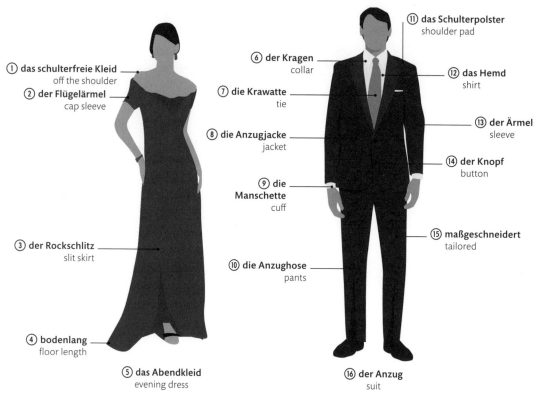

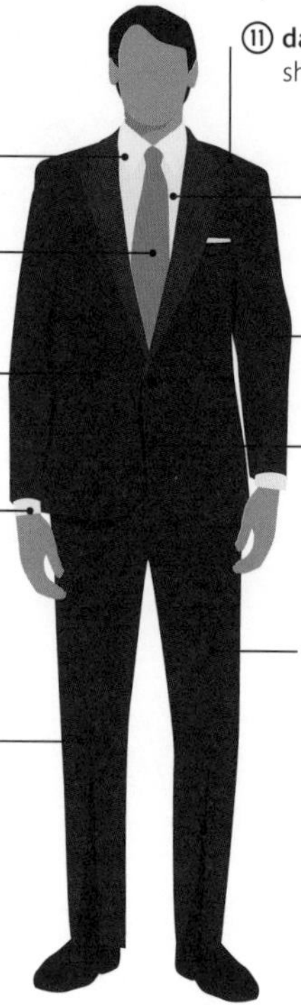

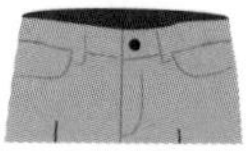

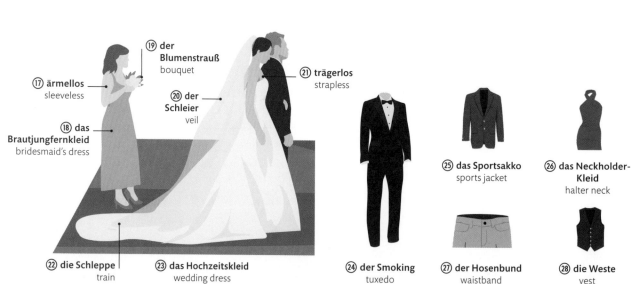

See also
**12** Aussehen und haar • Appearance and hair
**16** Accessoires • Accessories **17** Schuhe • Shoes

## 15.2 JACKEN • COATS

① **die Regenjacke**
raincoat

③ **der Anorak**
anorak

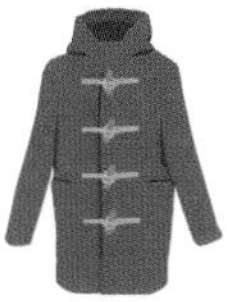

④ **der Dufflecoat**
duffle coat

⑤ **der Poncho**
poncho

⑥ **die Jeansjacke**
denim jacket

⑦ **die Steppjacke**
quilted jacket

⑧ **die Bomberjacke**
bomber jacket

⑨ **der Umhang**
cloak

⑩ **der Trenchcoat**
trench coat

## 15.3 SPORTKLEIDUNG • SPORTSWEAR

① **der Trainingsanzug**
tracksuit

② **der Sport-BH**
sports bra

③ **die Jogginghose**
sweatpants

④ **der Gymnastikanzug**
leotard

⑤ **das Trikot**
soccer jersey

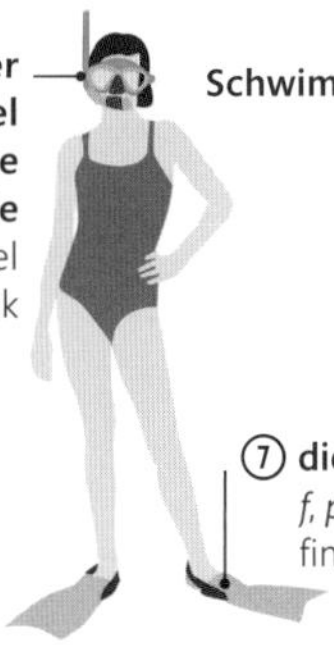


⑧ **der Badeanzug**
swimsuit

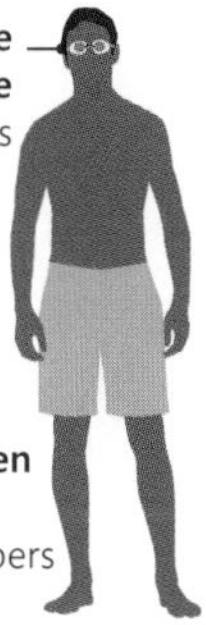


⑩ **die Badehose**
swim trunks

## 15.4 TRADITIONELLE KLEIDUNG TRADITIONAL CLOTHES

① **die Agbada**
agbada

② **das Flamenco-Kleid**
flamenco dress

③ **die Lederhose**
lederhosen

④ **der Kimono**
kimono

⑤ **der Thawb**
thawb

⑥ **der Sari**
sari

⑦ **der Kilt**
kilt

⑧ **der Sarong**
sarong

⑨ **die Folklorebluse**
folk blouse

# 16 Accessoires
Accessories

## 16.1 **MODEACCESSOIRES** · FASHION ACCESSORIES

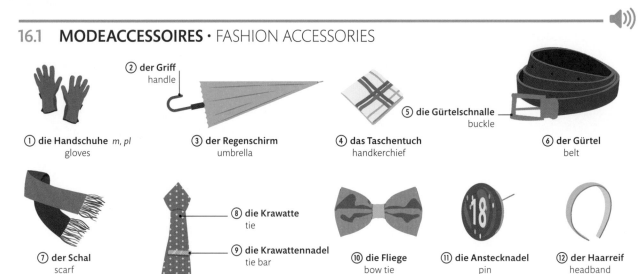

① **die Handschuhe** *m, pl*
gloves

② **der Griff**
handle

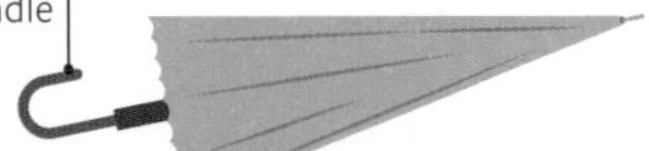

③ **der Regenschirm**
umbrella

④ **das Taschentuch**
handkerchief

⑤ **die Gürtelschnalle**
buckle

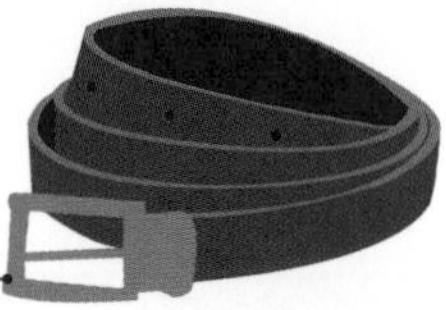

⑥ **der Gürtel**
belt

⑦ **der Schal**
scarf

⑧ **die Krawatte**
tie

⑨ **die Krawattennadel**
tie bar

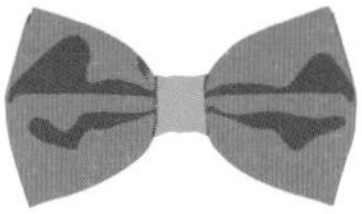

⑩ **die Fliege**
bow tie

⑪ **die Anstecknadel**
pin

⑫ **der Haarreif**
headband

## 16.2 **SCHMUCK** · JEWELRY

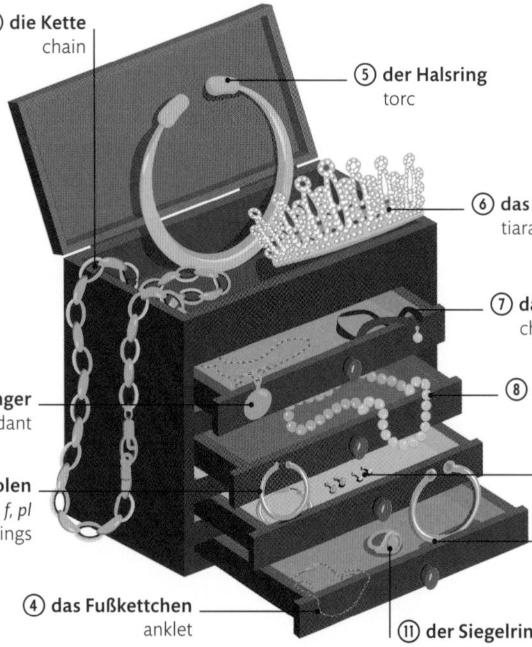

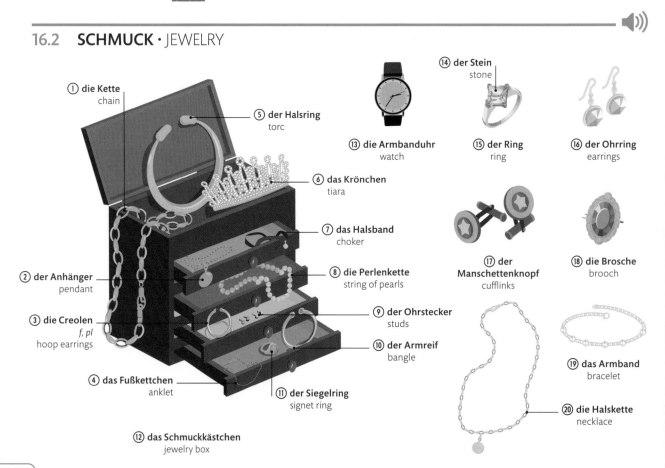

① **die Kette**
chain

② **der Anhänger**
pendant

③ **die Creolen**
*f, pl*
hoop earrings

④ **das Fußkettchen**
anklet

⑤ **der Halsring**
torc

⑥ **das Krönchen**
tiara

⑦ **das Halsband**
choker

⑧ **die Perlenkette**
string of pearls

⑨ **der Ohrstecker**
studs

⑩ **der Armreif**
bangle

⑪ **der Siegelring**
signet ring

⑫ **das Schmuckkästchen**
jewelry box

⑬ **die Armbanduhr**
watch

⑭ **der Stein**
stone

⑮ **der Ring**
ring

⑯ **der Ohrring**
earrings

⑰ **der Manschettenknopf**
cufflinks

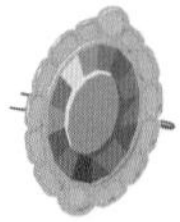

⑱ **die Brosche**
brooch

⑲ **das Armband**
bracelet

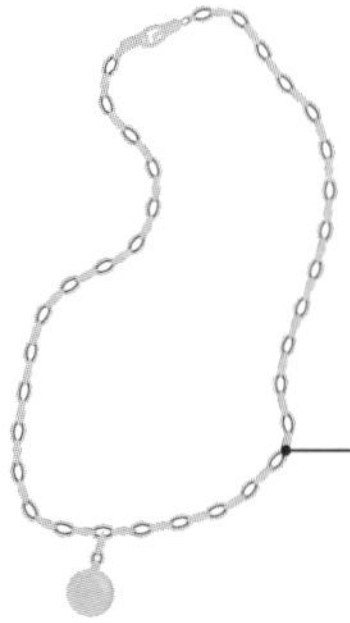

⑳ **die Halskette**
necklace

See also
**12** Aussehen und haar • Appearance and hair
**13-15** Kleidung • Clothes **17** Schuhe • Shoes

## 16.3 KOPFBEDECKUNGEN • HEADWEAR

① **die Schiebermütze**
flat cap

② **die Baseballkappe**
baseball cap

③ **die Bommelmütze**
pom pom beanie

④ **der Hidschab**
hijab

⑤ **die Jarmulke**
yarmulke

⑥ **der Turban**
turban

⑦ **das Barett**
beret

⑧ **der Fedora**
fedora

⑨ **die Sherlock-Holmes-Mütze**
deerstalker

⑩ **der Fes**
fez

⑪ **der Cowboy-Hut**
cowboy hat

⑫ **der Sombrero**
sombrero

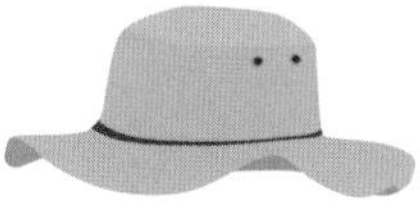

⑬ **der Sonnenhut**
sun hat

⑭ **die Ballonmütze**
newsboy cap

⑮ **der Panamahut**
panama

⑯ **der Strohhut**
boater

⑰ **die Mütze**
beanie

⑱ **der Glockenhut**
cloche

## 16.4 TASCHEN • BAGS

① **die Aktentasche**
briefcase

② **der Rucksack**
backpack

③ **der Geldbeutel**
wallet

④ **die Reisetasche**
duffel

⑤ **die Handtasche**
purse

⑥ **der Koffer**
suitcase

⑦ **der Griff**
handle

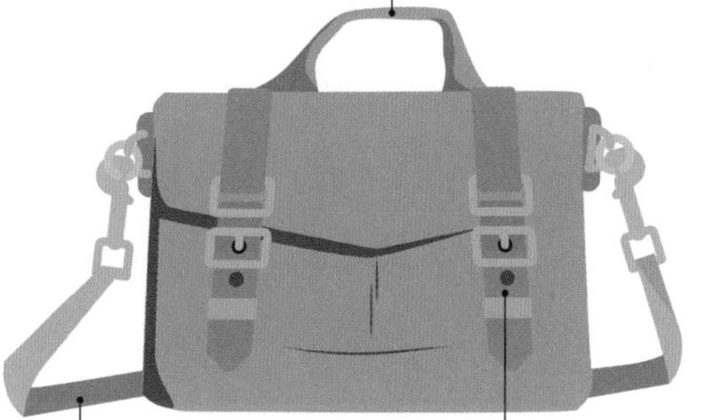

⑧ **der Schulterriemen**
shoulder strap

⑨ **die Schließe**
fastening

⑩ **die Umhängetasche**
shoulder bag

# 17 Schuhe
## Shoes

### 17.1 **SCHUHE UND ZUBEHÖR** · SHOES AND ACCESSORIES

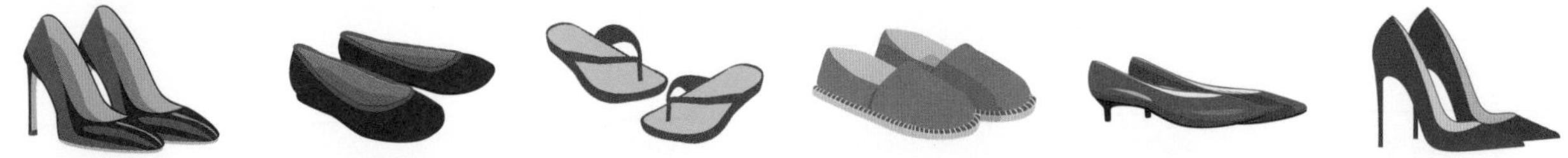

① **die Stöckelschuhe** *m, pl*
high-heeled shoes

② **die flachen Schuhe** *m, pl*
flats

③ **die Flipflops** *m, pl*
flip-flops

④ **die Espandrillen** *f, pl*
espadrilles

⑤ **die Kitten-Heel-Schuhe** *m, pl*
kitten heels

⑥ **die Stilettos** *m, pl*
stilettos

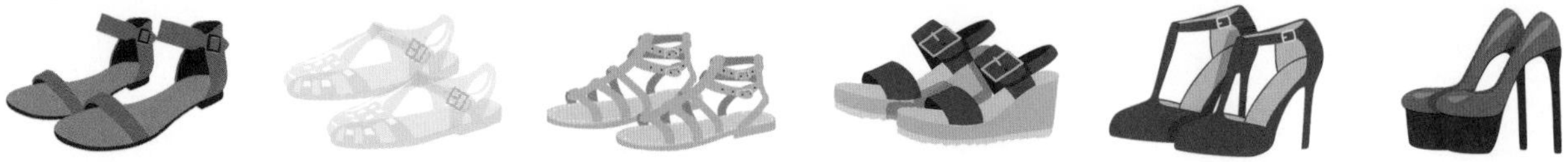

⑦ **die Sandalen** *f, pl*
sandals

⑧ **die Gummisandalen** *f, pl*
jelly sandals

⑨ **die Römersandalen** *f, pl*
gladiator sandals

⑩ **die Keilabsatz-Sandalen** *f, pl*
wedge sandals

⑪ **die T-Strap-Pumps** *m, pl*
T-strap heels

⑫ **die Plateauschuhe** *m, pl*
platforms

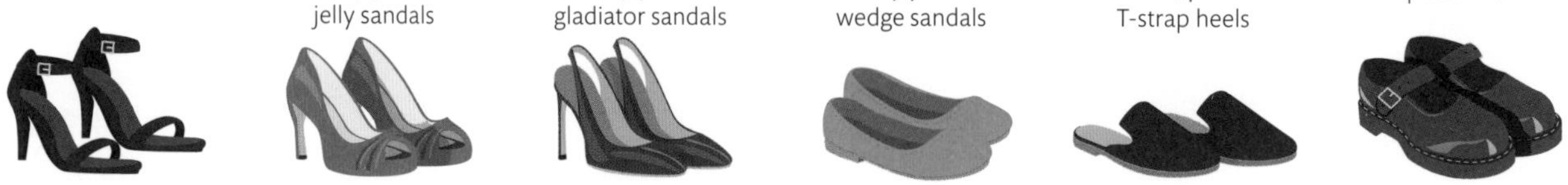

⑬ **die Schuhe mit Fesselriemen** *m, pl*
ankle strap heels

⑭ **die Peep-Toes** *m, pl*
peep toes

⑮ **die Schuhe mit Fersenriemen** *m, pl*
slingback heels

⑯ **die Ballerinas** *m, pl*
ballet flats

⑰ **die Pantoffeln** *m, pl*
mules

⑱ **die Spangenschuhe** *m, pl*
Mary Janes

### 17.2 **STIEFEL** · BOOTS

① **die Arbeitsschuhe** *m, pl*
work boots

② **die Chelsea-Boots** *m, pl*
Chelsea boots

③ **die Wanderschuhe** *m, pl*
hiking boots

④ **die Stiefeletten** *f, pl*
ankle boots

⑤ **der oberschenkellange Stiefel**
thigh-high boot

⑦ **die Desert-Boots** *m, pl*
chukka boots

⑫ **die Schnürstiefel** *m, pl*
lace-up boots

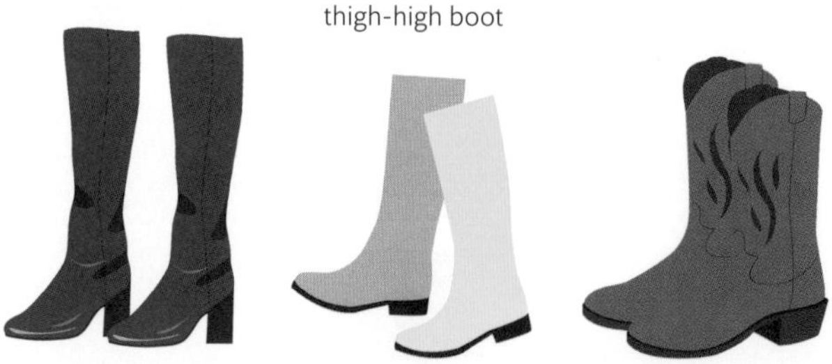

⑬ **die kniehohen Stiefel** *m, pl*
knee-high boots

⑭ **die Regenstiefel** *m, pl*
rain boots

⑮ **die Cowboy-Stiefel** *m, pl*
cowboy boots

See also
12 Aussehen und haar • Appearance and hair 13-15 Kleidung • Clothes
16 Accessoires • Accessories 40 Gartengeräte • Garden tools

⑲ **die Oxford-Schuhe**
Oxfords

⑳ **die Derbys**
Derby shoes

㉑ **die Slipper**
slip-ons

㉒ **die Mokassins**
moccasins

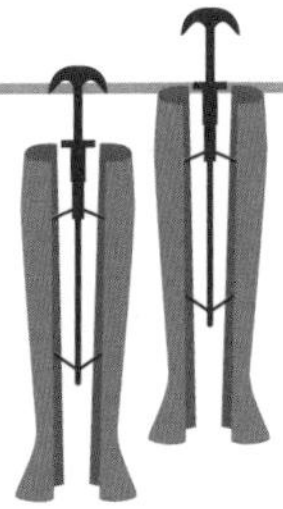
㉓ **der Schaftformer**
boot shapers

㉔ **der Schuhspanner**
shoe trees

㉕ **die Clogs**
*m, pl*
clogs

㉖ **die Schnallenschuhe**
*m, pl*
buckled shoes

㉗ **die Schlappen**
*m, pl*
slides

㉘ **die Schlappen**
*m, pl*
slippers

㉙ **die Schnürsenkel**
*m, pl*
shoelaces

㉚ **die Einlagen**
*f, pl*
insoles

㉛ **die Slipper**
*m, pl*
loafers

㉜ **die Bootsschuhe**
*m, pl*
boat shoes

㉝ **die Kinderschuhe**
*m, pl*
kids' shoes

㉞ **die Herrenhalbschuhe** *m, pl*
brogues

㉟ **die Schuhcreme**
shoe polish

㊱ **die Schuhbürste**
shoe brush

## 17.3 SPORTSCHUHE • SPORTS SHOES

① **die Laufschuhe (mit Spikes)** *m, pl*
running spikes

② **die Stollenschuhe**
*m, pl*
baseball cleats

③ **die Laufschuhe**
*m, pl*
running shoes

④ **die Knöchelturnschuhe**
*m, pl*
high-tops

⑤ **die Golfschuhe**
*m, pl*
golf shoes

⑦ **die Zunge**
tongue

⑥ **der Turnschuh**
sneaker

⑧ **der Radschuh**
cycling shoe

⑨ **der Skischuh**
ski boot

⑩ **die Wasserschuhe**
*m, pl*
water shoes

⑪ **die Reitstiefel**
*m, pl*
riding boots

⑫ **die Tabi-Schuhe**
*m, pl*
tabi boots

⑬ **die Stollenschuhe**
*m, pl*
soccer cleats

# 18 Beauty
## Beauty

### 18.1 MAKE-UP · MAKEUP

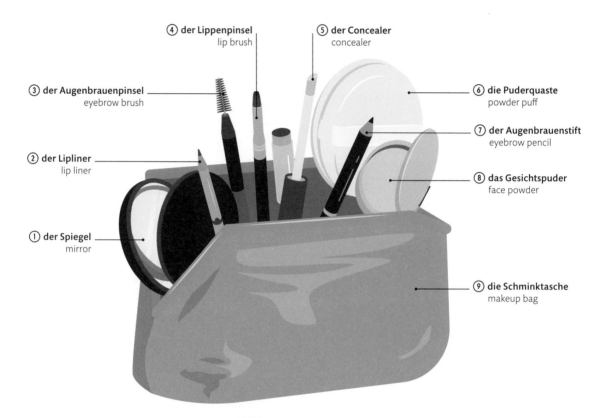

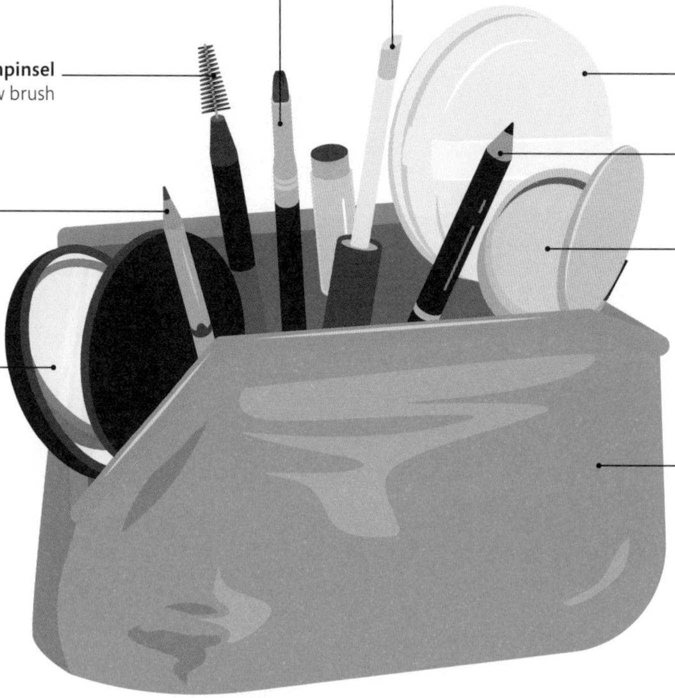

⑩ **das Rouge**
blush

⑪ **der Eyeliner**
eyeliner

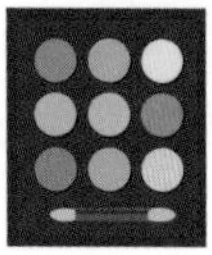

⑫ **der Lidschatten**
eyeshadow

⑬ **die Foundation**
foundation

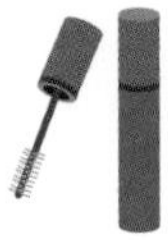

⑭ **die Wimperntusche**
mascara

⑮ **der Lippenstift**
lipstick

### 18.2 HAUTTYPEN · SKIN TYPE

① **normal**
normal

② **trocken**
dry

③ **fettig**
oily

④ **empfindlich**
sensitive

⑤ **der Mischtyp**
combination

See also
**12** Aussehen und haar • Appearance and hair **13-15** Kleidung • Clothes
**16** Accessoires • Accessories **17** Schuhe • Shoes **31** Das Badezimmer • Bathroom

## 18.3 **MANIKÜRE** • MANICURE

① **die Nagelschere**
nail scissors

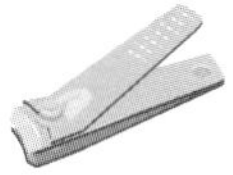

② **der Nagelknipser**
nail clippers

③ **der Nagellack**
nail polish

④ **der Nagellackentferner**
nail polish remover

⑤ **die Nagelfeile**
nail file

⑥ **die Handcreme**
hand cream

## 18.4 **TOILETTENARTIKEL UND SCHÖNHEITSKUREN**
## TOILETRIES AND BEAUTY TREATMENTS

① **die Feuchtigkeitscreme**
moisturizer

② **das Gesichtswasser**
toner

③ **der Gesichtsreiniger**
face wash

④ **der Gesichtsreiniger**
cleanser

⑤ **das Parfüm**
perfume

⑥ **das Aftershave**
aftershave

⑦ **der Lippenbalsam**
lip balm

⑧ **das Schaumbad**
bubble bath

⑨ **der Wattebausch**
cotton balls

⑩ **das Haarfärbemittel**
hair dye

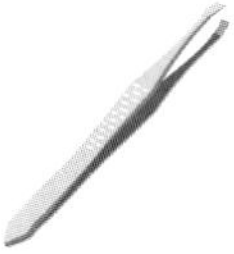

⑪ **die Pinzette**
tweezers

⑫ **das Wachs**
wax

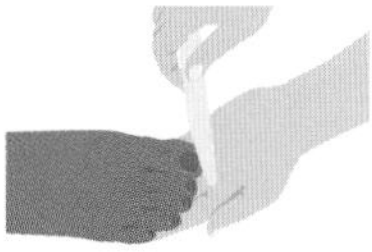

⑬ **die Pediküre**
pedicure

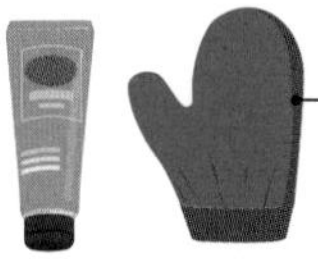

⑮ **der Applikationshandschuh**
tanning mitt

⑭ **der Selbstbräuner**
self tanner

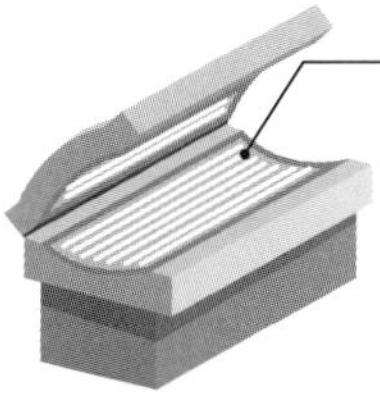

⑰ **die UV-Röhre**
UV tubes

⑯ **die Sonnenbank**
tanning bed

⑱ **die Schutzbrille**
tanning goggles

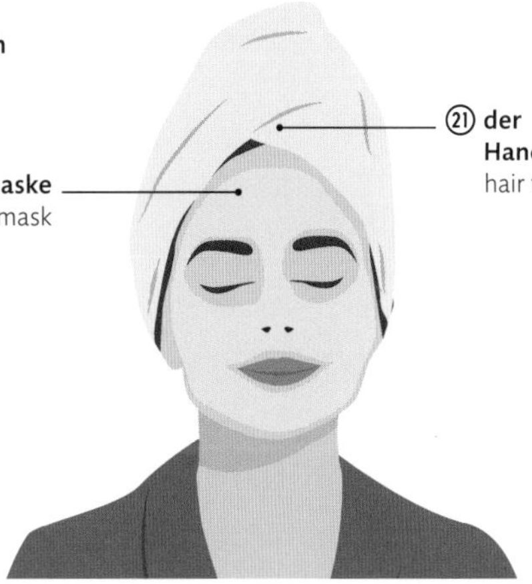

㉑ **der Handtuchturban**
hair towel wrap

⑳ **die Gesichtsmaske**
face mask

⑲ **die Gesichtsbehandlung**
facial

# 19 Krankheiten und Verletzungen

## Illness and injury

### 19.1 KRANKHEITEN • ILLNESS

① **die Grippe**
flu

② **die Erkältung**
cold

③ **der Husten**
cough

④ **die laufende Nase**
runny nose

⑤ **das Virus**
virus

⑥ **das Fieber**
fever

⑦ **der Schüttelfrost**
chills

⑧ **die Halsschmerzen** *m, pl*
sore throat

⑨ **die Mandelentzündung**
tonsillitis

⑩ **die Kopfschmerzen** *m, pl*
headache

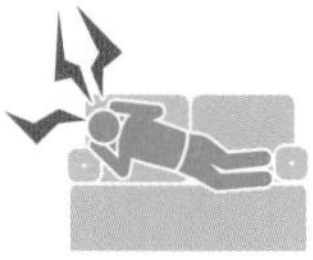
⑪ **die Migräne**
migraine

⑫ **der Schwindel**
dizzy

⑬ **die Lebensmittelvergiftung**
food poisoning

⑭ **die Vergiftung**
poisoning

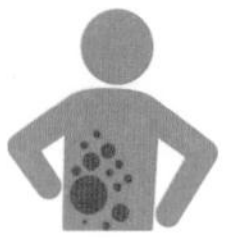
⑮ **der Ausschlag**
rash

⑯ **die Windpocken**
chickenpox

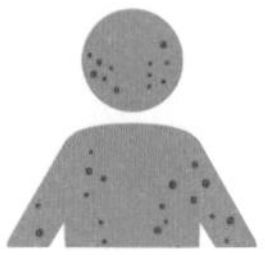
⑰ **die Masern**
measles

⑱ **der Mumps**
mumps

⑲ **das Ekzem**
eczema

⑳ **das Asthma**
asthma

㉑ **die Allergie**
allergy

㉒ **der Heuschnupfen**
hay fever

㉓ **die Infektion**
infection

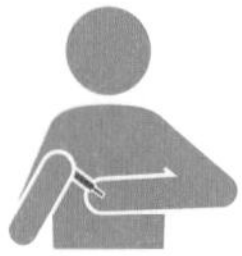
㉔ **der Diabetes**
diabetes

㉕ **der Stress**
stress

㉖ **das Nasenbluten**
nosebleed

㉗ **die Übelkeit**
nausea

㉘ **die Blinddarmentzündung**
appendicitis

㉙ **der Bluthochdruck**
high blood pressure

㉚ **die Symptome** *n, pl*
symptoms

㉛ **der Krampf**
cramp

㉜ **die Rückenschmerzen** *m, pl*
backache

㉝ **der Schmerz**
pain

㉞ **die Bauchschmerzen** *m, pl*
stomachache

㉟ **die Schlaflosigkeit**
insomnia

㊱ **der Durchfall**
diarrhea

See also
**01** Körperteile • Parts of the body **03** Muskeln und Skelett • Muscles and skeleton
**04** Innere Organe • Internal organs **20** Beim Arzt • Visiting the doctor
**21** Das Krankenhaus • The hospital

## 19.2 **VERLETZUNGEN** • INJURY

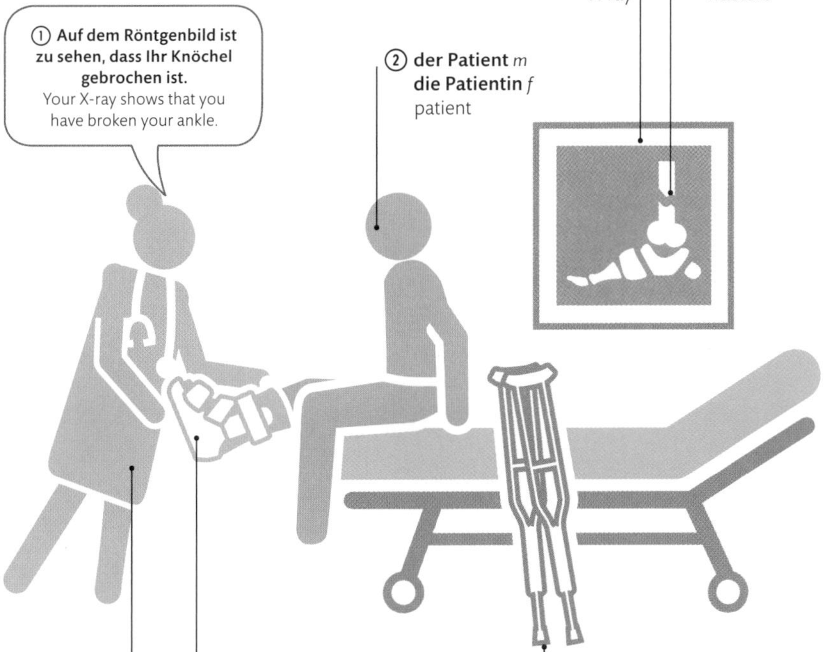
① **Auf dem Röntgenbild ist zu sehen, dass Ihr Knöchel gebrochen ist.**
Your X-ray shows that you have broken your ankle.

② **der Patient** *m* **die Patientin** *f*
patient

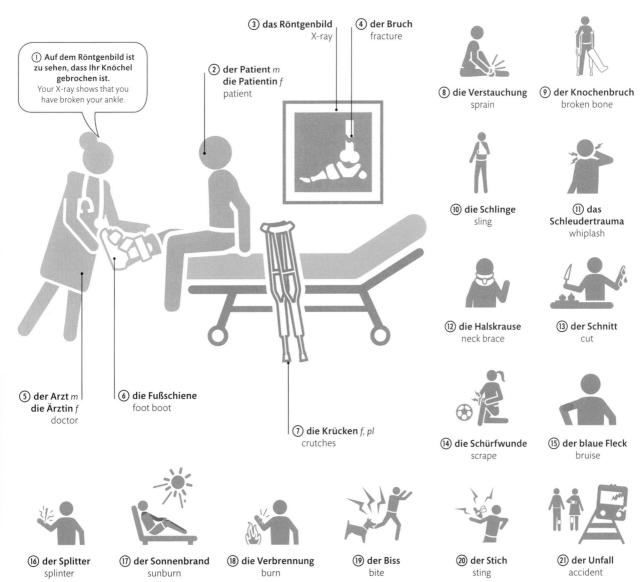

③ **das Röntgenbild**
X-ray

④ **der Bruch**
fracture

⑤ **der Arzt** *m* **die Ärztin** *f*
doctor

⑥ **die Fußschiene**
foot boot

⑦ **die Krücken** *f, pl*
crutches

⑧ **die Verstauchung**
sprain

⑨ **der Knochenbruch**
broken bone

⑩ **die Schlinge**
sling

⑪ **das Schleudertrauma**
whiplash

⑫ **die Halskrause**
neck brace

⑬ **der Schnitt**
cut

⑭ **die Schürfwunde**
scrape

⑮ **der blaue Fleck**
bruise

⑯ **der Splitter**
splinter

⑰ **der Sonnenbrand**
sunburn

⑱ **die Verbrennung**
burn

⑲ **der Biss**
bite

⑳ **der Stich**
sting

㉑ **der Unfall**
accident

㉒ **die Wunde**
wound

㉓ **die Blutung**
hemorrhage

㉔ **die Blase**
blister

㉕ **die Gehirnerschütterung**
concussion

㉖ **die Kopfverletzung**
head injury

㉗ **der elektrische Schlag**
electric shock

# 20 Beim Arzt

## Visiting the doctor

### 20.1 DIE BEHANDLUNG · TREATMENT

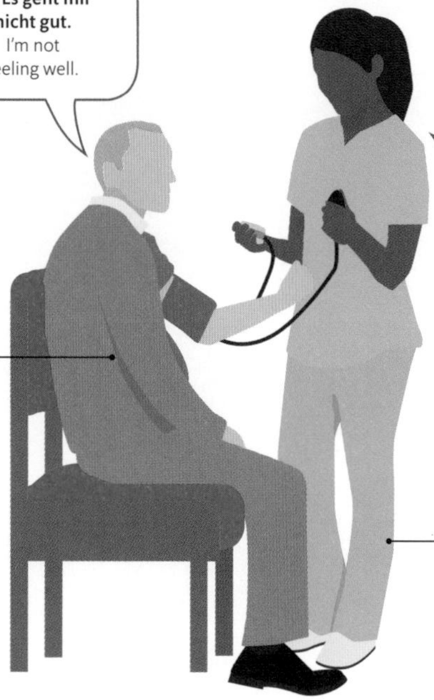

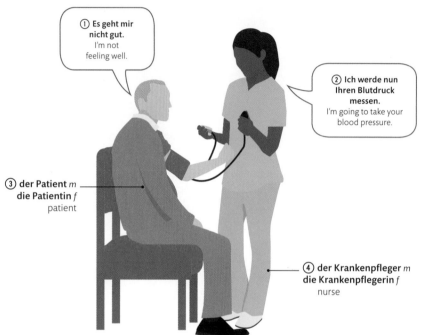

① **Es geht mir nicht gut.**
I'm not feeling well.

② **Ich werde nun Ihren Blutdruck messen.**
I'm going to take your blood pressure.

③ **der Patient** *m*
**die Patientin** *f*
patient

④ **der Krankenpfleger** *m*
**die Krankenpflegerin** *f*
nurse

⑤ **der Blutdruck**
blood pressure

⑥ **der Arzt** *m*
**die Ärztin** *f*
doctor

⑦ **die Arztpraxis**
doctor's office

⑧ **das Wartezimmer**
waiting room

⑨ **der Termin**
appointment

⑩ **die Untersuchung**
medical examination

⑪ **die Impfung**
inoculation / vaccination

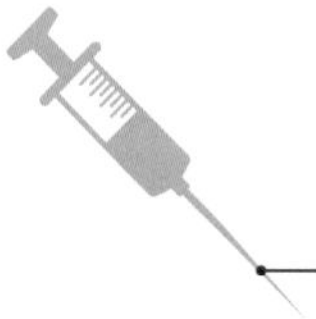

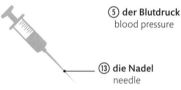

⑬ **die Nadel**
needle

⑫ **die Spritze**
syringe

⑭ **die Blutuntersuchung**
blood test

⑮ **die Untersuchungsergebnisse** *n, pl*
test results

⑯ **das Rezept**
prescription

⑰ **die Medizin**
medicine / medication

⑱ **die Tablette**
pills / tablets

⑲ **die Waage**
scale

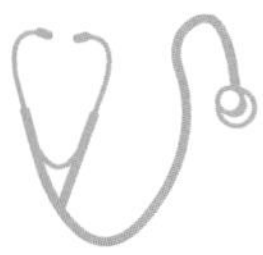

⑳ **das Stethoskop**
stethoscope

㉑ **der Inhalator**
inhaler

㉒ **das Nasenspray**
nasal spray

㉓ **der Mundschutz**
face mask

㉔ **die Schlinge**
sling

㉕ **der Verband**
dressing

㉖ **der Mull**
gauze

㉗ **das Heftpflaster**
tape

㉘ **das Thermometer**
thermometer

㉙ **das Ohrthermometer**
ear thermometer

See also
**01** Körperteile • Parts of the body **02** Hände und Füße • Hands and feet
**03** Muskeln und Skelett • Muscles and skeleton **04** Innere Organe • Internal organs
**19** Krankheiten und Verletzungen • Illness and injury **21** Das Krankenhaus • The hospital

## 20.2 **DER ERSTE-HILFE-KASTEN** • FIRST-AID KIT

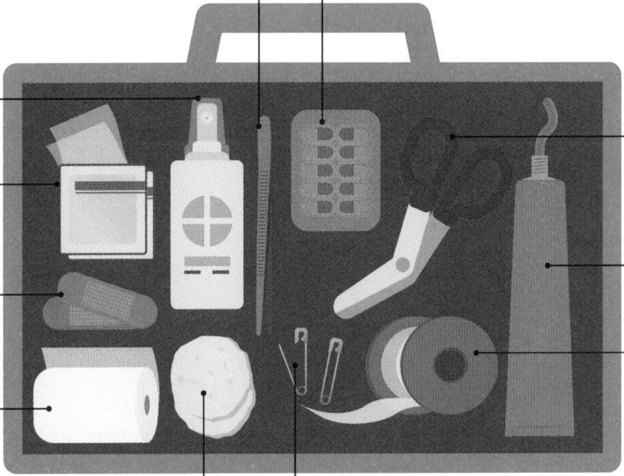

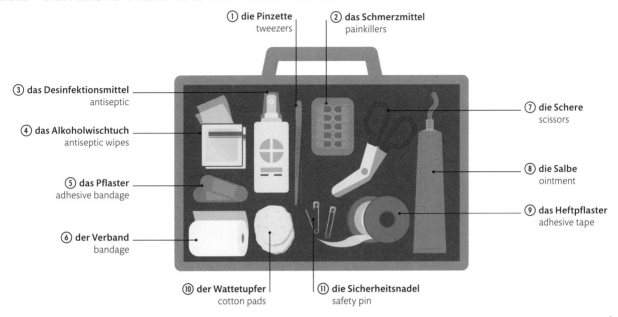

① **die Pinzette** tweezers
② **das Schmerzmittel** painkillers
③ **das Desinfektionsmittel** antiseptic
④ **das Alkoholwischtuch** antiseptic wipes
⑤ **das Pflaster** adhesive bandage
⑥ **der Verband** bandage
⑦ **die Schere** scissors
⑧ **die Salbe** ointment
⑨ **das Heftpflaster** adhesive tape
⑩ **der Wattetupfer** cotton pads
⑪ **die Sicherheitsnadel** safety pin

## 20.3 **KRANKHEITSVERBEN** • VERBS TO DESCRIBE ILLNESS

① **sich übergeben** to vomit
② **niesen** to sneeze
③ **husten** to cough
④ **schmerzen** to hurt / to ache
⑤ **bluten** to bleed
⑥ **in Ohnmacht fallen** to faint

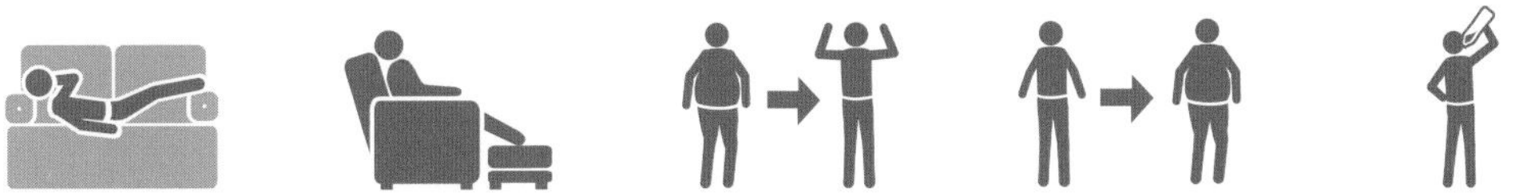

⑦ **sich hinlegen** to lie down
⑧ **sich ausruhen** to rest
⑨ **abnehmen** to lose weight
⑩ **zunehmen** to gain weight
⑪ **Wasser trinken** to drink water

⑫ **Sport machen** to exercise
⑬ **heilen** to heal
⑭ **sich erholen** to recover
⑮ **sich besser fühlen** to feel better

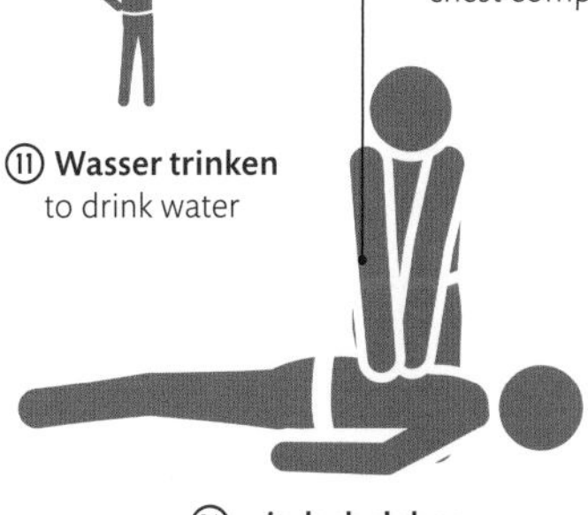

⑯ **wiederbeleben** to resuscitate
⑰ **die Herzdruckmassage** chest compressions

# 21 Das Krankenhaus
## The hospital

### 21.1 IM KRANKENHAUS · AT THE HOSPITAL

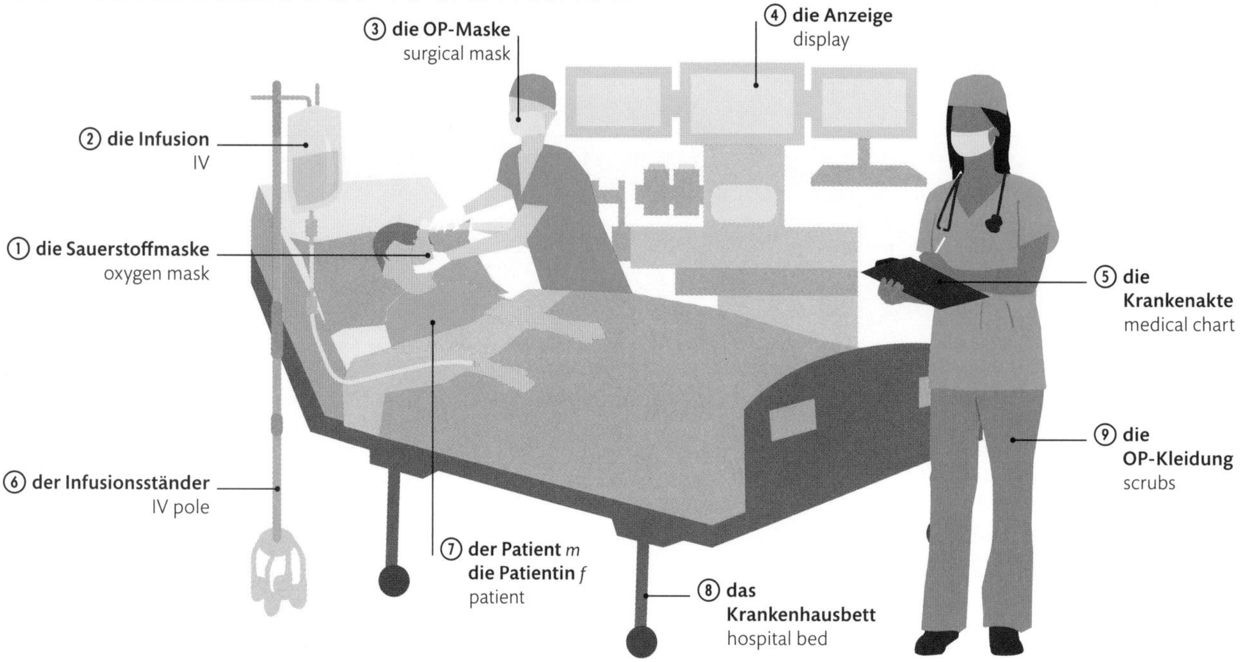

⑩ **das Krankenhaus**
hospital

⑪ **der Krankenwagen**
ambulance

⑫ **der Rettungssanitäter** *m*
**die Rettungssanitäterin** *f*
paramedic

⑬ **die Trage**
stretcher

⑭ **der Chirurg** *m*
**die Chirurgin** *f*
surgeon

⑮ **der Arzt** *m*
**die Ärztin** *f*
doctor

⑯ **der Krankenpfleger** *m*
**die Krankenpflegerin** *f*
nurse

⑰ **die Stationshilfskraft**
orderly

⑱ **der Rollstuhl**
wheelchair

⑲ **die Aufnahme**
scan

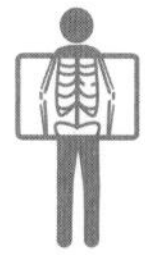

⑳ **das Röntgen**
X-ray

㉑ **die Blutuntersuchung**
blood test

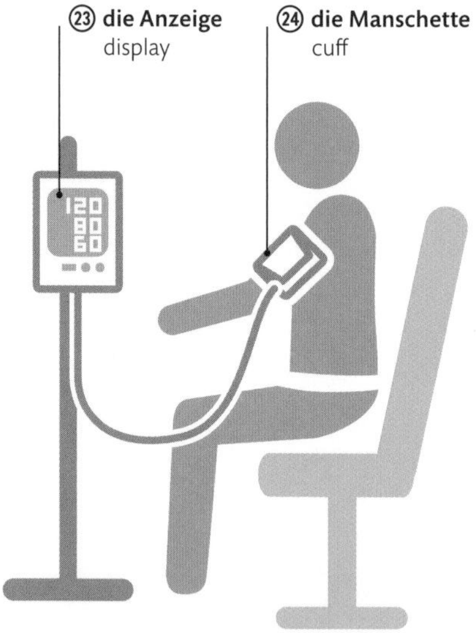


㉒ **das Blutdruckmessgerät**
blood pressure monitor

See also
**01** Körperteile • Parts of the body **03** Muskeln und Skelett • Muscles and skeleton
**04** Innere Organe • Internal organs **19** Krankheiten und Verletzungen • Illness and injury **20** Beim Arzt • Visiting the doctor

25 **das Skalpell**
scalpel

26 **die Naht**
stitches

27 **der Schönheitseingriff**
plastic surgery

28 **die Behandlung**
treatment

29 **die Operation**
operation

30 **der OP-Tisch**
operating table

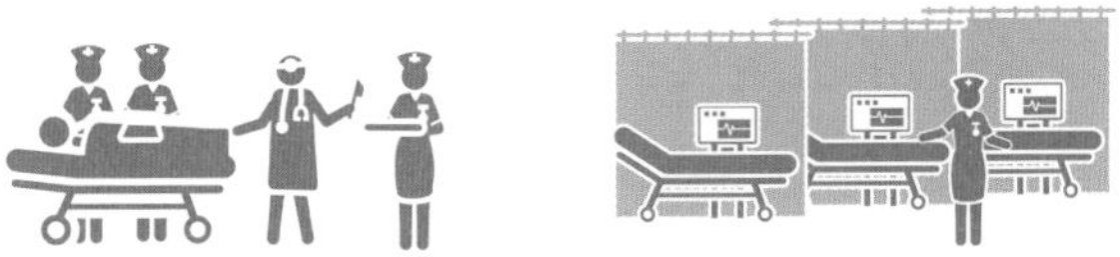

31 **der OP-Saal**
operating room

32 **die Notaufnahme**
emergency room

33 **die Intensivstation**
intensive care unit

34 **der Aufwachraum**
recovery room

35 **das Einzelzimmer**
private room

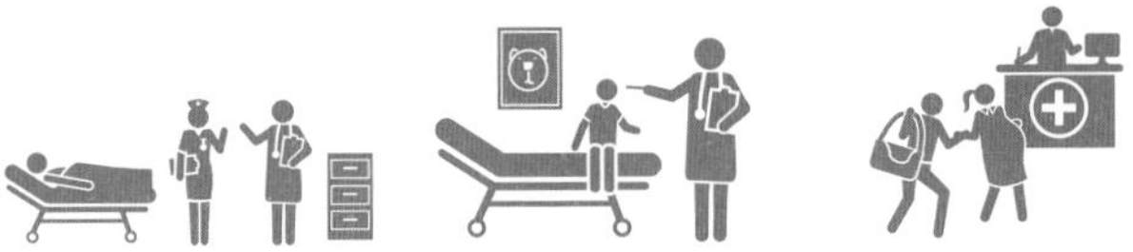

36 **die Station**
ward

37 **die Kinderstation**
children's ward

38 **die Entbindungsstation**
maternity ward

39 **einweisen**
to admit

40 **entlassen**
to discharge

41 **ambulant**
outpatient

## 21.2 ABTEILUNGEN • DEPARTMENTS

1 **HNO (Hals, Nase, Ohren)**
ENT (ear, nose, and throat)

2 **die Kardiologie**
cardiology

3 **die Orthopädie**
orthopedics

4 **die Neurologie**
neurology

5 **die Radiologie**
radiology

6 **die Pathologie**
pathology

7 **die Pädiatrie**
pediatrics

8 **die Dermatologie**
dermatology

9 **die Gynäkologie**
gynecology

10 **die Chirurgie**
surgery

11 **die Physiotherapie**
physical therapy

12 **die Urologie**
urology

13 **die Geburtshilfe**
maternity

14 **die Psychiatrie**
psychiatry

15 **die Augenheilkunde**
ophthalmology

16 **die Endokrinologie**
endocrinology

17 **die Onkologie**
oncology

18 **die Gastroenterologie**
gastroenterology

# 22 Der Zahnarzt und der Optiker
The dentist and optician

## 22.1 BEIM ZAHNARZT · DENTIST'S OFFICE

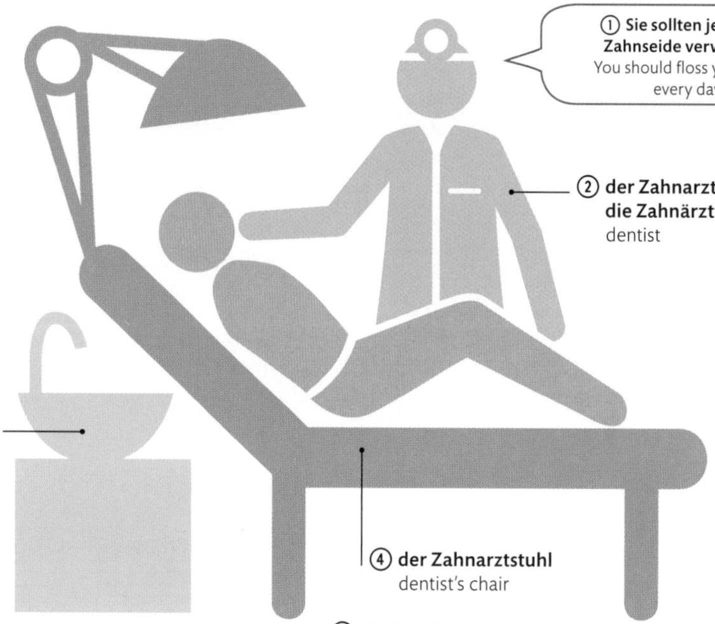

① **Sie sollten jeden Tag Zahnseide verwenden.**
You should floss your teeth every day.

② **der Zahnarzt** *m*
**die Zahnärztin** *f*
dentist

③ **das Waschbecken**
basin

④ **der Zahnarztstuhl**
dentist's chair

⑤ **die Routineuntersuchung**
check-up

⑥ **der Zahnschmerz**
toothache

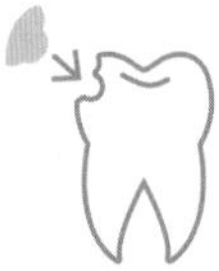

⑦ **die Füllung**
filling

⑧ **der Zahnbelag**
plaque

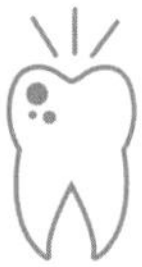

⑨ **der Karies**
decay

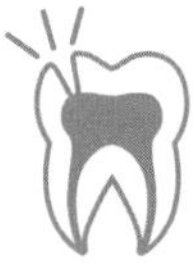

⑩ **das Loch**
cavity

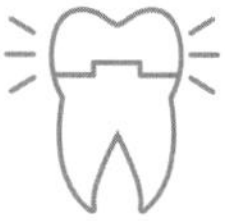

⑪ **die Krone**
crown

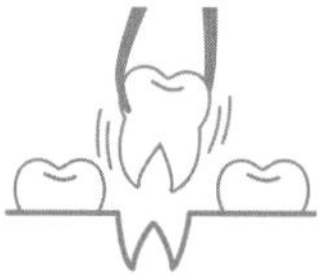

⑫ **einen Zahn ziehen**
extraction

⑬ **die Milchzähne** *m, pl*
baby teeth

⑭ **die Zahnspange**
braces

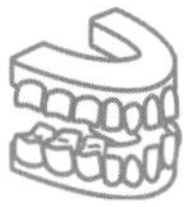

⑮ **das künstliche Gebiss**
dentures / false teeth

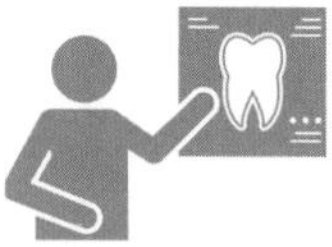

⑯ **die Zahnröntgenaufnahme**
dental X-ray

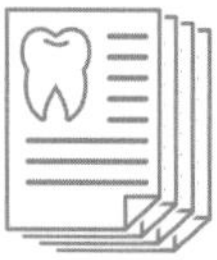

⑰ **die zahnärztliche Krankengeschichte**
dental history

⑱ **der Bohrer**
drill

⑲ **der Spiegel**
dental mirror

⑳ **die Sonde**
probe

㉑ **die Zahnzwischenraumbürste**
interdental brush

㉒ **das Bleichen**
whitening

㉓ **der Zahnpfleger** *m*
**die Zahnpflegerin** *f*
dental hygienist

㉔ **die Zahnseide**
dental floss

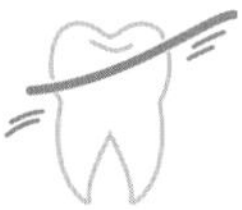

㉕ **Zahnseide benutzen**
to floss

㉖ **die Zähne putzen**
to brush

㉗ **ausspülen**
to rinse

See also
01 Körperteile • Parts of the body 03 Muskeln und Skelett • Muscles and skeleton
20 Beim Arzt • Visiting the doctor 21 Das Krankenhaus • The hospital
31 Das Badezimmer • Bathroom

## 22.2 BEIM OPTIKER • OPTICIAN

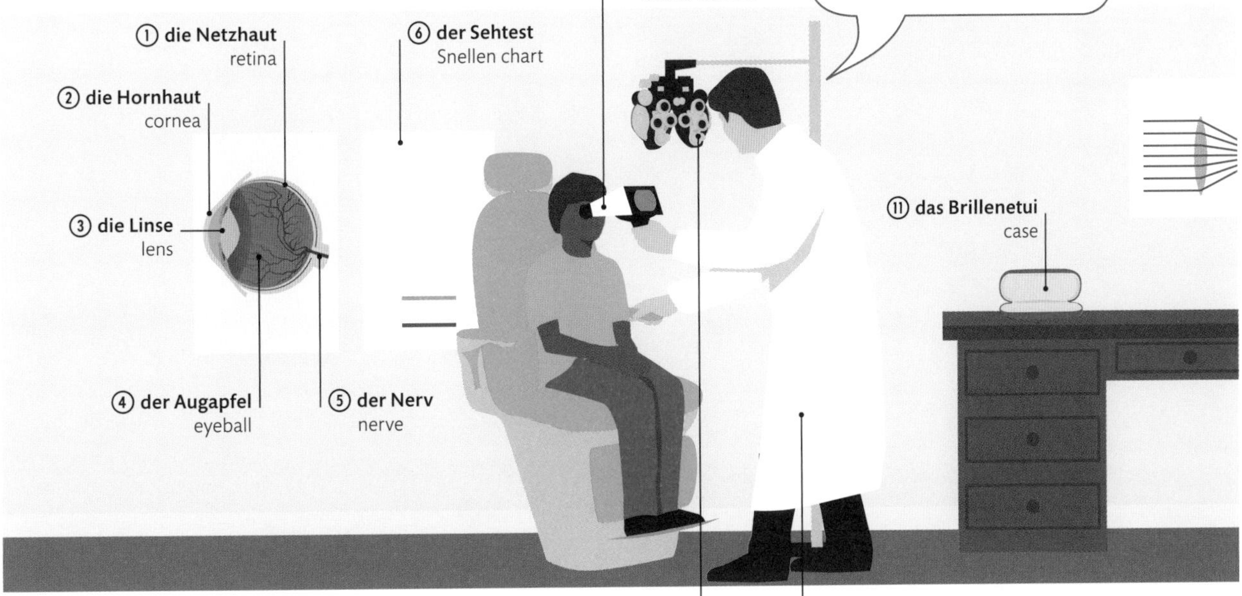


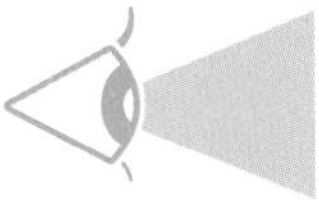
⑫ **die Sehkraft**
vision

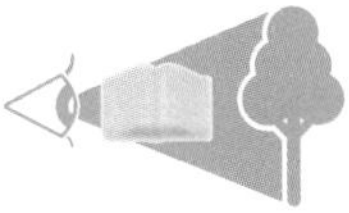
⑬ **weitsichtig**
farsighted

⑭ **kurzsichtig**
nearsighted

⑮ **die Träne**
tear

⑯ **der graue Star**
cataract

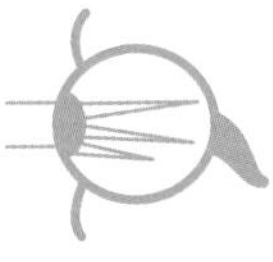
⑰ **die Hornhautverkrümmung**
astigmatism

⑱ **die Lesebrille**
reading glasses

⑲ **die Gleitsichtbrille**
bifocal

⑳ **das Monokel**
monocle

㉑ **das Opernglas**
opera glasses

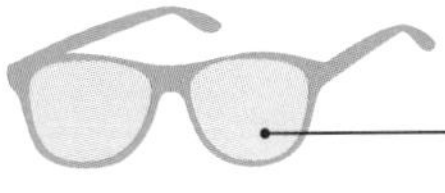
㉒ **die Brille**
glasses

㉓ **das Brillenglas**
lens

㉔ **die Sonnenbrille**
sunglasses

㉕ **das Brillenputztuch**
lens cleaning cloth

㉖ **die Kontaktlinse**
contact lenses

㉗ **die Kontaktlinsenflüssigkeit**
contact lens solution

㉘ **die Kontaktlinsendose**
lens case

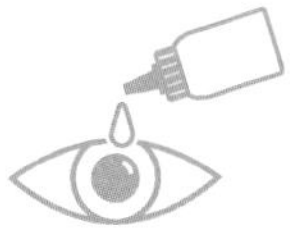
㉙ **die Augentropfen** *m, pl*
eye drops

# 23 Die Ernährung
Diet and nutrition

## 23.1 EIN GESUNDER LEBENSSTIL • HEALTHY LIVING

① **das Eiweiß**
protein

② **die Kohlenhydrate** *n, pl*
carbohydrates

③ **die Ballaststoffe** *m, pl*
fiber

④ **das Milchprodukt**
dairy

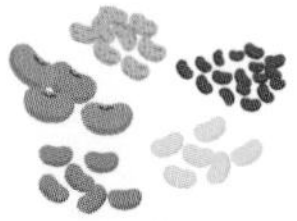
⑤ **die Hülsenfrüchte** *f, pl*
legumes

⑥ **der Zucker**
sugar

⑦ **das Salz**
salt

⑧ **die gesättigten Fettsäuren** *f, pl*
saturated fat

⑨ **die ungesättigten Fettsäuren** *f, pl*
unsaturated fat

⑩ **die Kalorien** *f, pl*
calories / energy

⑪ **die Vitamine** *n, pl*
vitamins

⑫ **die Mineralstoffe** *m, pl*
minerals

⑬ **das Kalzium**
calcium

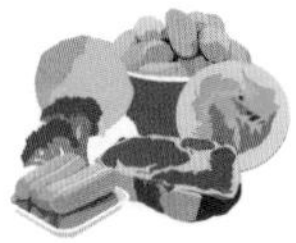
⑭ **das Eisen**
iron

⑮ **das Cholesterin**
cholesterol

⑯ **der Detox**
detox

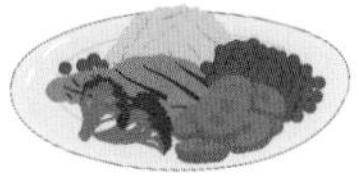
⑰ **die ausgewogene Ernährung**
balanced diet

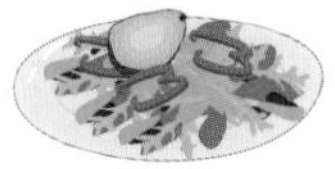
⑱ **die kalorienbewusste Ernährung**
calorie-controlled diet

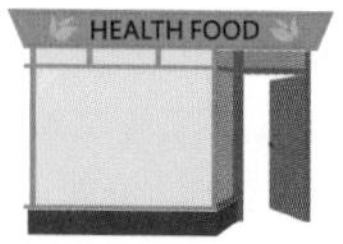

⑲ **der Bioladen**
health food store

⑳ **die Bioabteilung**
organic food section

㉑ **die lokalen Erzeugnisse** *n, pl*
local produce

㉒ **Ich kaufe gerne Bioobst und -gemüse.**
I like to buy organic fruit and vegetables.

㉓ **der Wochenmarkt**
farmers' market

See also
**03** Muskeln und Skelett • Muscles and skeleton **19** Krankheiten und Verletzungen • Illness and injury
**24** Gesunder Körper, gesunder Geist • Healthy body, healthy mind **29** Kochen • Cooking
**48** Der Supermarkt • The supermarket **52-72** Nahrungsmittel und Lebensmittel • Food

**㉔ das industriell verarbeitete Lebensmittel**
processed food

**㉕ die Superfoods**
superfoods

**㉖ Bio-**
organic

**㉗ das Nahrungsergänzungsmittel**
supplement

**㉘ die Zusatzstoffe** *m, pl*
additives

**㉙ ohne Milchprodukte** *n, pl*
dairy-free

**㉚ vegetarisch**
vegetarian

**㉛ vegan**
vegan

**㉜ pescetarisch**
pescatarian

**㉝ glutenfrei**
gluten-free

**㉞ abnehmen**
to lose weight

**㉟ die Fertignahrung**
convenience food

**㊱ energiereich**
high-calorie

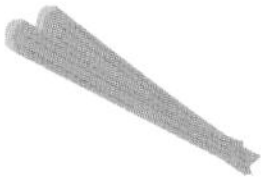

**㊲ kalorienarm**
low-calorie

**㊳ sich bei etwas einschränken**
to cut down on

**㊴ auf etwas verzichten**
to give up

**㊵ eine Diät machen**
to go on a diet

**㊶ zu viel essen**
to overeat

## 23.2 LEBENSMITTELALLERGIEN
FOOD ALLERGIES

**① die Nussallergie**
nut allergy

**② die Erdnussallergie**
peanut allergy

**③ die Meeresfrüchteallergie**
seafood allergy

**④ die Laktoseintoleranz**
lactose intolerant

**⑤ die Glutenunverträglichkeit**
gluten intolerant

**⑥ die Milchallergie**
dairy allergy

**⑦ die Weizenallergie**
wheat allergy

**⑧ die Eiallergie**
egg allergy

**⑨ die Sesamallergie**
sesame allergy

**⑩ die Sojaallergie**
soy allergy

**⑪ die Sellerieallergie**
celery allergy

**⑫ die Sulfitallergie**
sulfite allergy

**⑬ allergisch**
allergic

**⑭ die Senfallergie**
mustard allergy

**⑮ intolerant**
intolerant

# 24 Gesunder Körper, gesunder Geist
## Healthy body, healthy mind

### 24.1 **YOGA** · YOGA

① **die Yogahose**
yoga pants

② **die Yogamatte**
mat

③ **der Kopfstand**
headstand

④ **der Yogakurs**
yoga class

⑤ **Tief ein- und wieder ausatmen.**
Take a deep breath in, and then breathe out.

⑥ **das Kind**
child's pose

⑦ **die Kobra**
cobra pose

⑧ **der Krieger**
warrior pose

⑨ **der Drehsitz**
seated twist

⑩ **das Dreieck**
triangle pose

⑪ **die sitzende Vorbeuge**
seated forward fold

⑫ **die Totenhaltung**
corpse pose

⑬ **die Krähe**
crow pose

⑭ **der Stuhl**
chair pose

⑮ **die Berghaltung**
mountain pose

⑯ **die Brücke**
bridge pose

⑰ **die Bretthaltung**
plank pose

⑱ **der Bogen**
bow pose

⑲ **die Taube**
pigeon pose

⑳ **der Baum**
tree pose

㉑ **der herabschauende Hund**
downward dog

㉒ **die geschlossene Winkelhaltung im Sitz mit Fußsohlen aneinander**
bound ankle pose

㉓ **das Kamel**
camel pose

㉔ **das Rad**
wheel pose

㉕ **der Halbmond**
half moon pose

㉖ **der Delfin**
dolphin pose

See also
**03** Muskeln und Skelett • Muscles and skeleton **04** Innere Organe • Internal organs
**19** Krankheiten und Verletzungen • Illness and injury **20** Beim Arzt • Visiting the doctor
**21** Das Krankenhaus • The hospital **23** Die Ernährung • Diet and nutrition **29** Kochen • Cooking

## 24.2 **BEHANDLUNGEN UND THERAPIEN** • TREATMENTS AND THERAPY

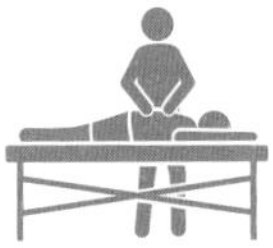
① **die Massage**
massage

② **das Shiatsu**
shiatsu

③ **die Chiropraktik**
chiropractic

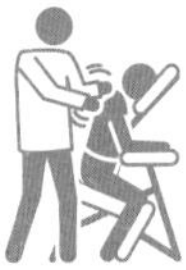
④ **die Osteopathie**
osteopathy

⑤ **die Reflexzonenmassage**
reflexology

⑥ **die Meditation**
meditation

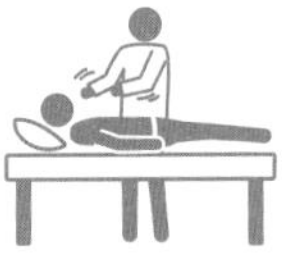
⑦ **das Reiki**
reiki

⑧ **die Akupunktur**
acupuncture

⑨ **das Ayurveda**
ayurveda

⑩ **die Hypnosetherapie**
hypnotherapy

⑪ **die Hydrotherapie**
hydrotherapy

⑫ **die Aromatherapie**
aromatherapy

⑬ **die Kräuterheilkunde**
herbalism

⑭ **die ätherischen Öle** *n, pl*
essential oils

⑮ **die Homöopathie**
homeopathy

⑯ **die Akupressur**
acupressure

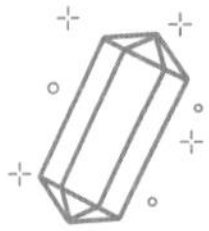
⑰ **die Heilsteinbehandlung**
crystal healing

⑱ **die natürliche Behandlung**
naturopathy

⑲ **das Fengshui**
feng shui

⑳ **die Dichtungstherapie**
poetry therapy

㉑ **die Gestaltungstherapie**
art therapy

㉒ **die Tiertherapie**
pet therapy

㉓ **die Naturtherapie**
nature therapy

㉔ **die Musiktherapie**
music therapy

㉕ **die Entspannung**
relaxation

㉖ **die Achtsamkeit**
mindfulness

㉗ **der Berater** *m*
**die Beraterin** *f*
counselor

㉘ **die Psychotherapie**
psychotherapy

㉚ Heute wollen wir uns über Stress bei der Arbeit unterhalten.
Today, we're talking about stress at work.
㉙ **die Gruppentherapie**
group therapy

# 25 Ein Ort zum Leben
A place to live

## 25.1 HÄUSER · HOUSES

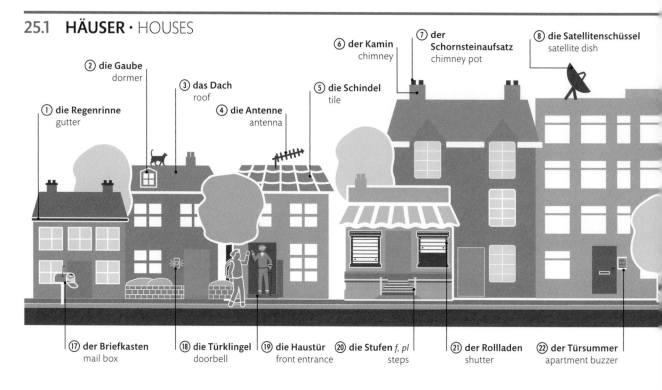

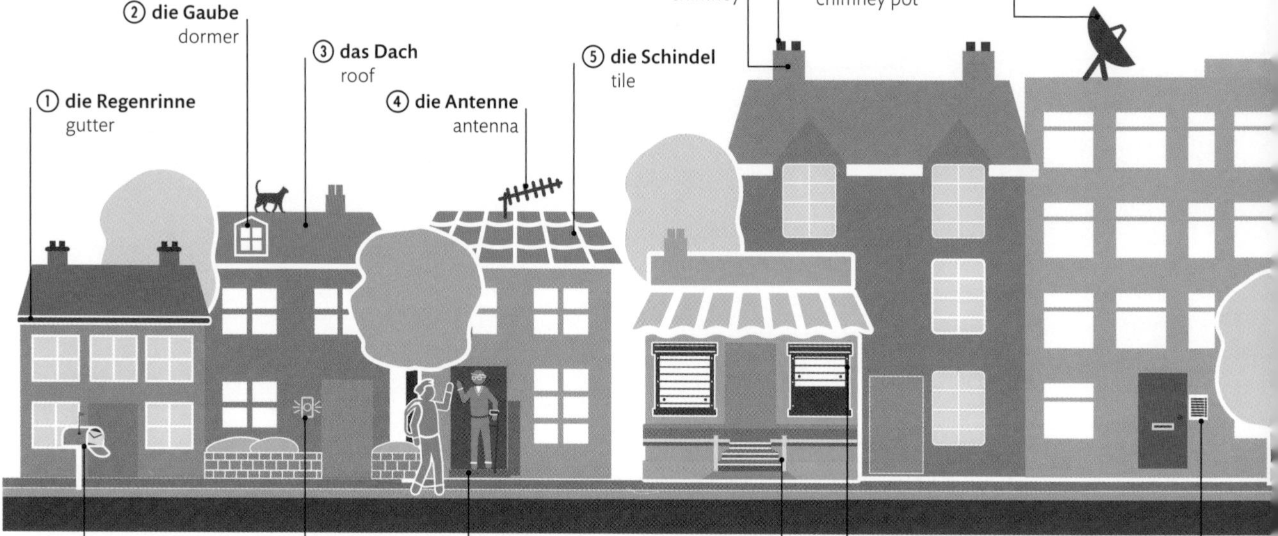


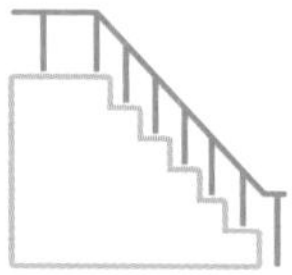
㉚ **die Treppe**
staircase / stairs

㉛ **unten**
downstairs

㉜ **oben**
upstairs

㉝ **der Keller**
basement

㉞ **das Erdgeschoss**
first floor

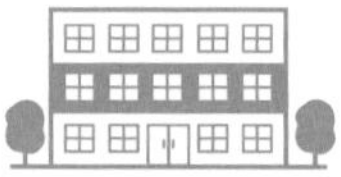
㉟ **der erste Stock**
second floor

㊶ **die Wohnung**
apartment

㊱ **die Terrasse**
patio / terrace

㊲ **die Terrassentür**
patio doors / French doors

㊳ **der Balkon**
balcony

㊴ **der Hof**
courtyard

㊵ **die Gegensprechanlage**
intercom

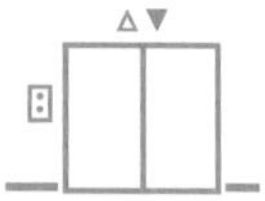
㊷ **der Aufzug**
elevator

㊸ **das Planschbecken**
wading pool

㊹ **der Whirlpool**
jacuzzi

㊺ **die Hütte**
shed

㊻ **die Tonne**
dumpster

See also
**32** Haus und Heim • House and home **34** Hausarbeit • Household chores
**37** Wohnraumverschönerung • Renovating **42-43** In der Stadt • In town
**44** Gebäude und Architektur • Buildings and architecture

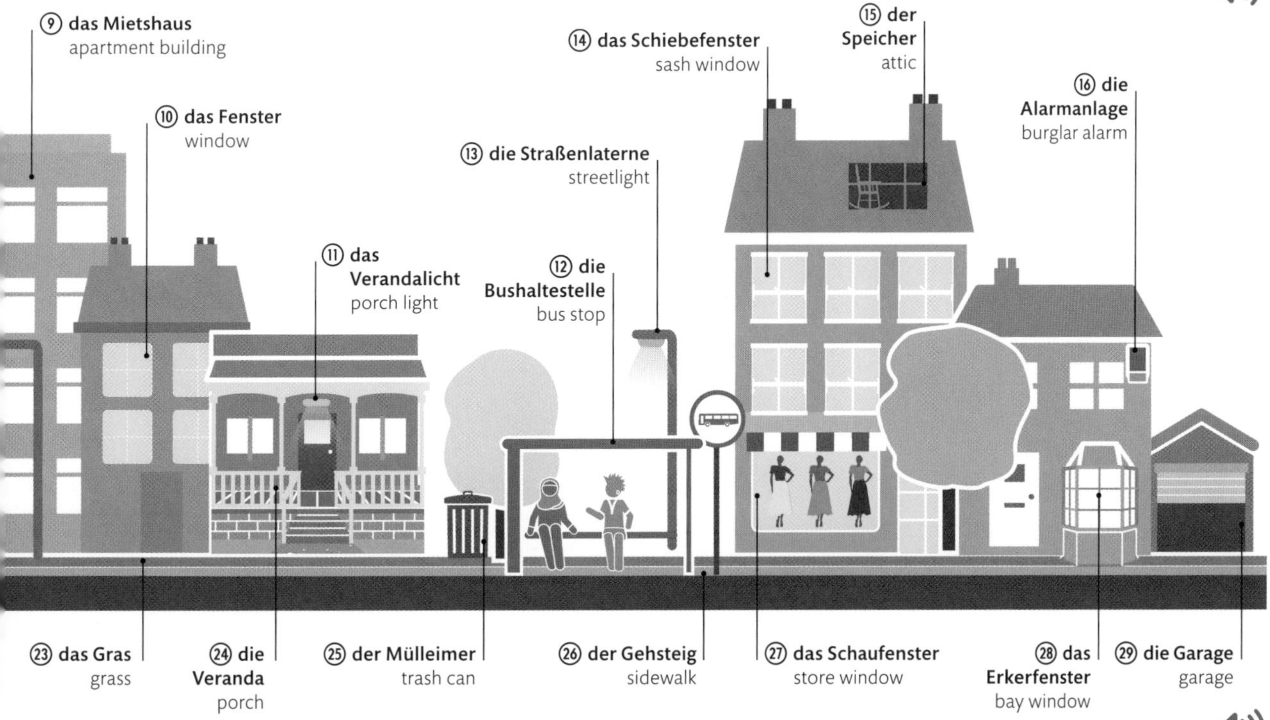


## 25.2 DER GANG • HALLWAY

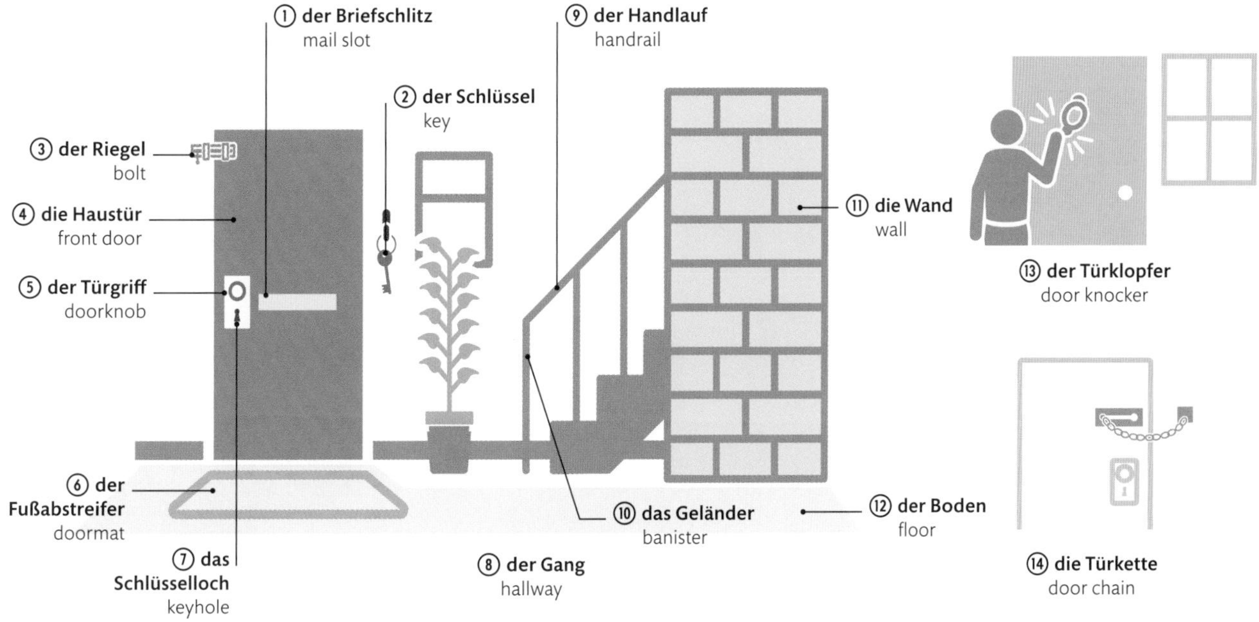

# 26 Das Wohnzimmer und das Esszimmer

## Living room and dining room

### 26.1 DAS WOHNZIMMER · LIVING ROOM

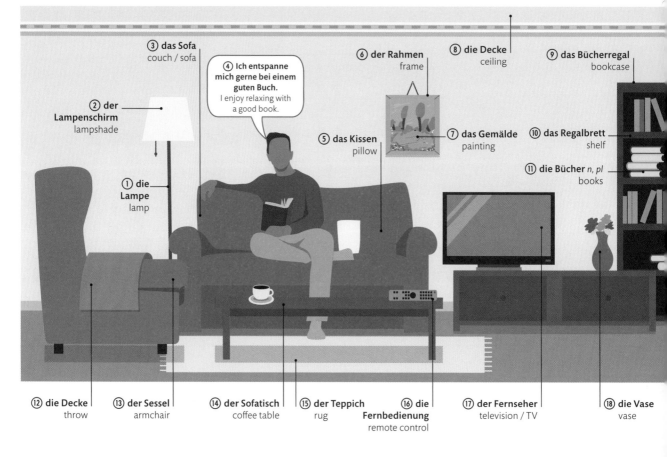

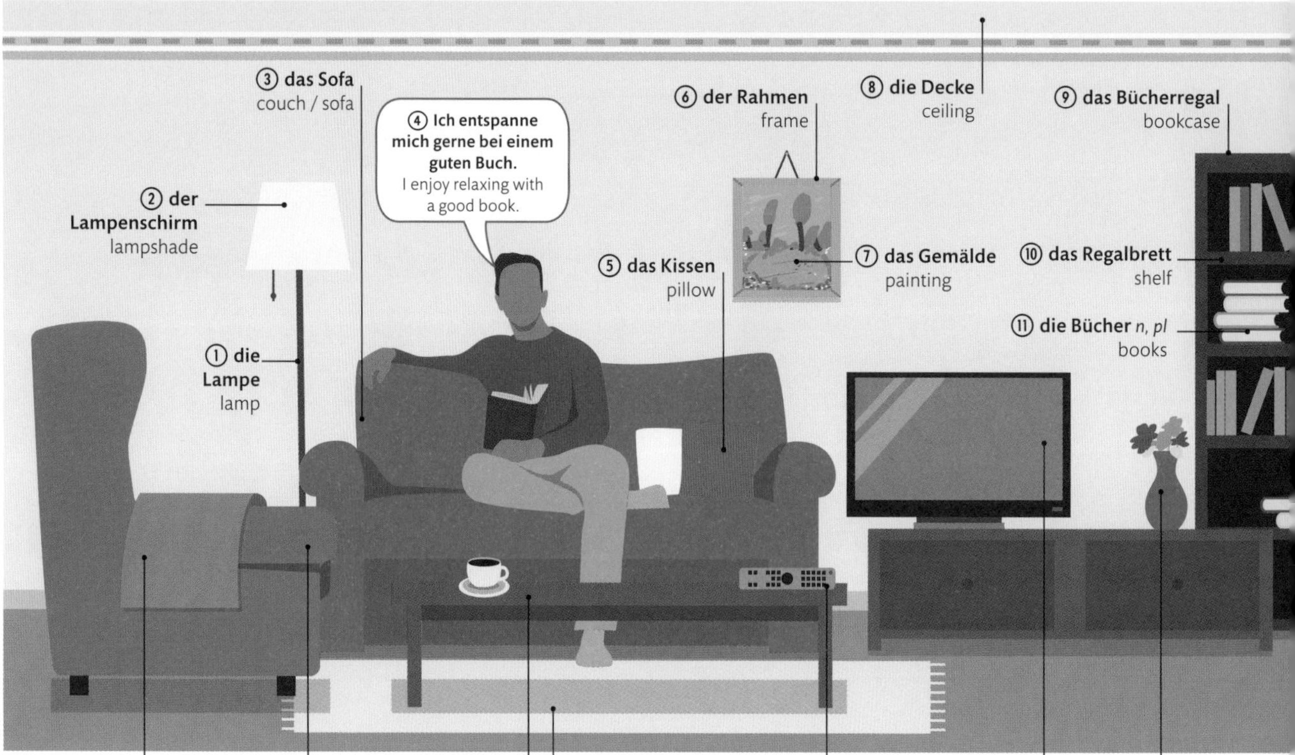

⑲ **der Kamin**
fireplace

⑳ **der Kaminsims**
mantlepiece

㉑ **die Jalousie**
Venetian blinds

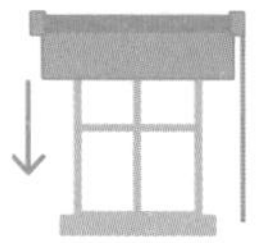

㉒ **der Rollladen**
roller shade

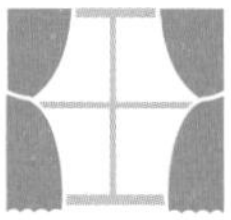

㉓ **die Tüllgardine**
curtains

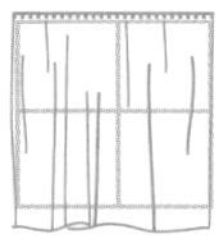

㉔ **der Netzvorhang**
sheer curtain

㉕ **das Ausziehsofa**
sofa bed

㉖ **der Schaukelstuhl**
rocking chair

㉗ **der Schemel**
foot stool

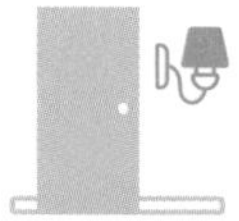

㉘ **die Wandleuchte**
sconce

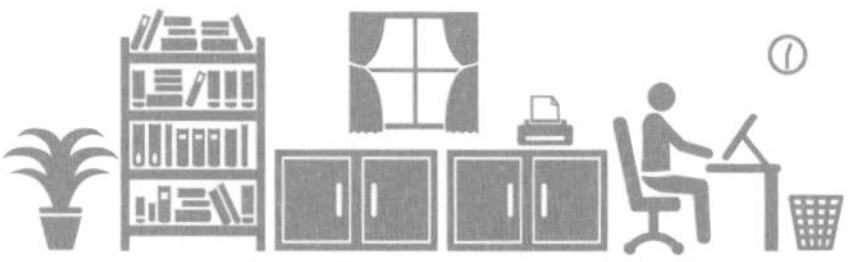

㉙ **das Arbeitszimmer**
home office

See also
**25** Ein Ort zum Leben • A place to live **27** Die Küche und das Geschirr • Kitchen and tableware **34** Hausarbeit • Household chores **71** Das Frühstück • Breakfast **72** Das Mittagessen und das Abendessen • Lunch and dinner **136** Unterhaltung zu Hause • Home entertainment

## 26.2 DAS ESSZIMMER • DINING ROOM

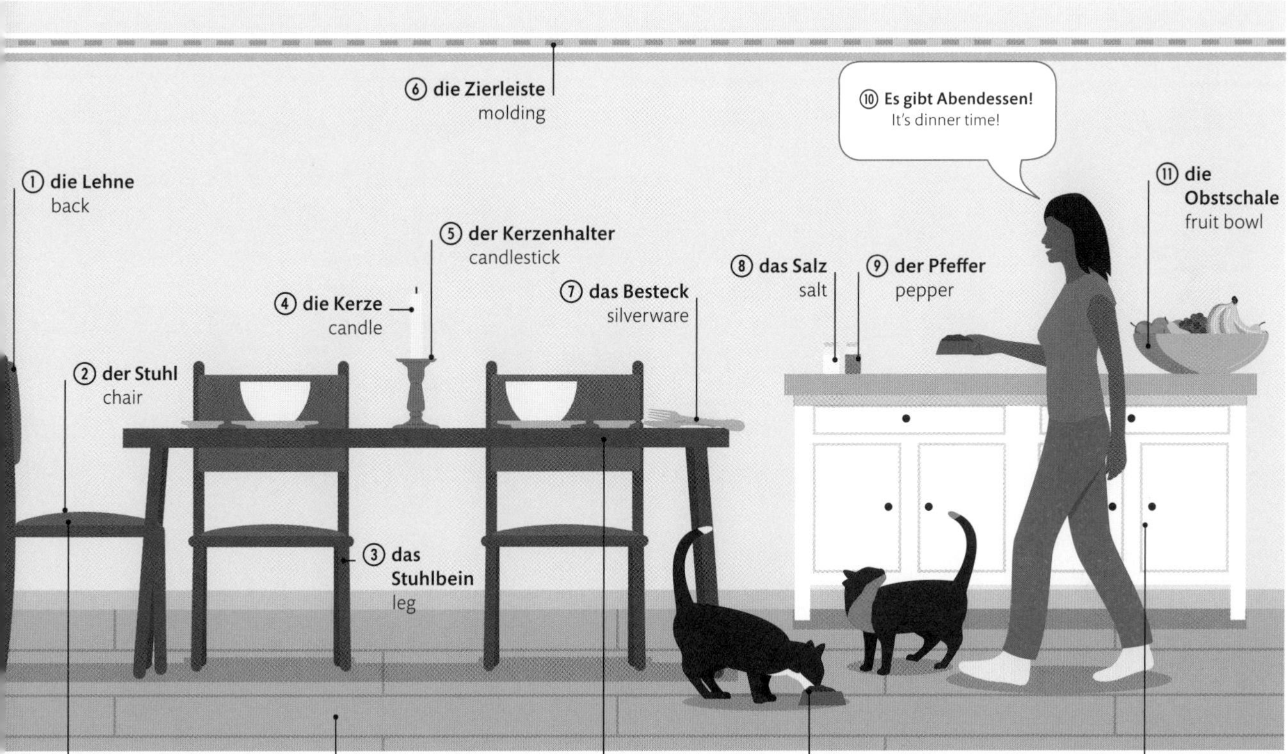


**⑫ die Sitzfläche**
seat

**⑬ die Holzdiele**
floorboards

**⑭ der Tisch**
table

**⑮ der Napf**
food bowl

**⑯ die Anrichte**
sideboard

**⑰ den Tisch decken**
to set the table

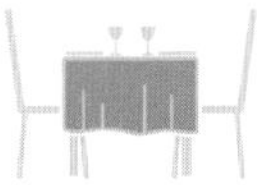

**⑱ die Tischdecke**
tablecloth

**⑲ das Tischset**
place mat

**⑳ das Frühstück**
breakfast

**㉑ das Mittagessen**
lunch

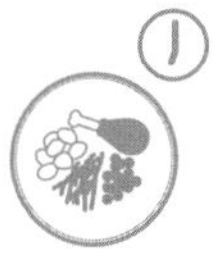

**㉒ das Abendessen**
dinner

**㉓ der Gastgeber** *m*
**die Gastgeberin** *f*
host / hostess

**㉔ hungrig**
hungry

**㉕ satt**
full

**㉖ die Portion**
portion

**㉗ die Dinnerparty**
dinner party

# 27 Die Küche und das Geschirr

Kitchen and tableware

## 27.1 KÜCHENGERÄTE · KITCHEN APPLIANCES

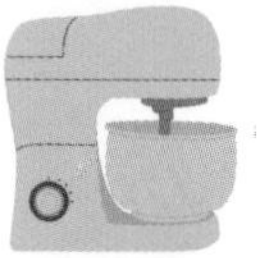

① **das Rührgerät**
mixer

② **der Toaster**
toaster

③ **der Mixer**
blender

④ **die Spülmaschine**
dishwasher

⑤ **der Wasserkocher**
electric kettle

⑥ **der Reiskocher**
rice cooker

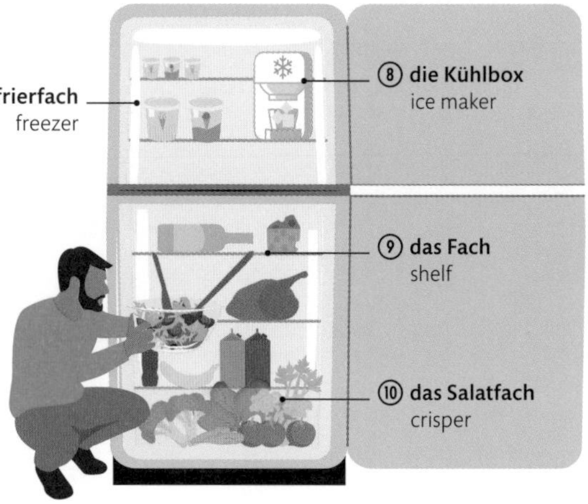

⑦ **das Gefrierfach**
freezer

⑧ **die Kühlbox**
ice maker

⑨ **das Fach**
shelf

⑩ **das Salatfach**
crisper

⑪ **der Kühlschrank**
fridge / refrigerator

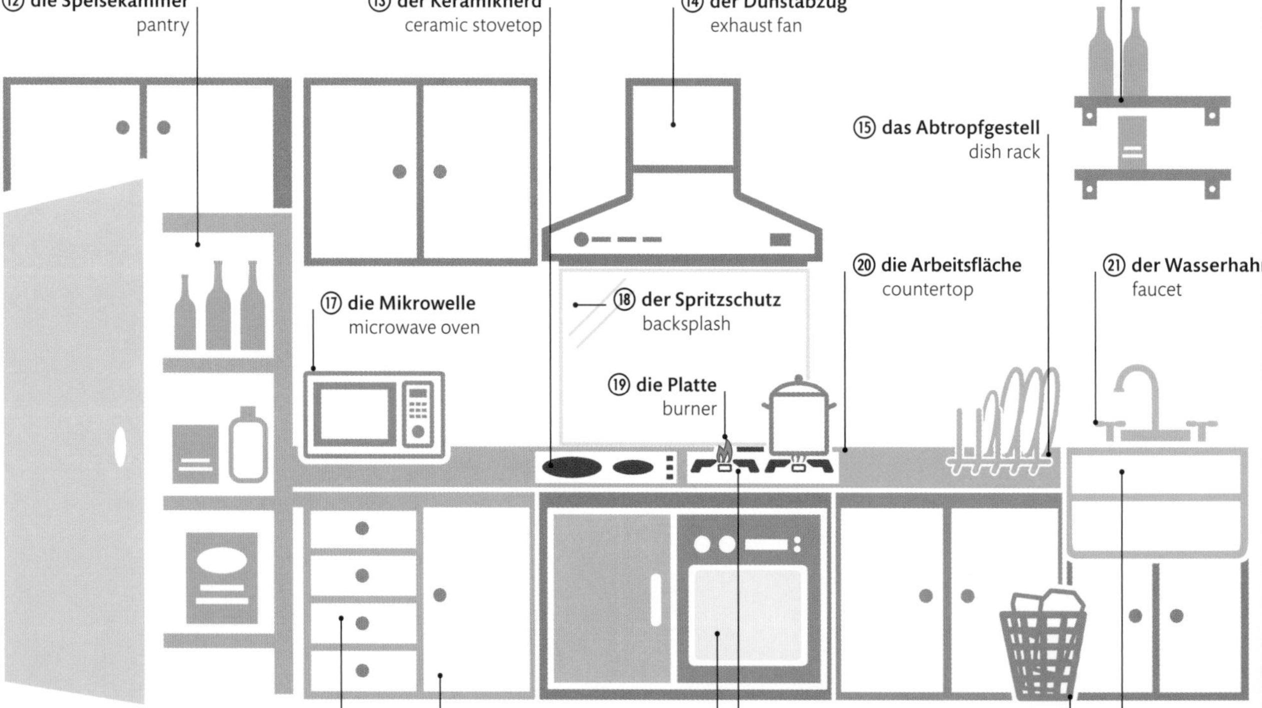

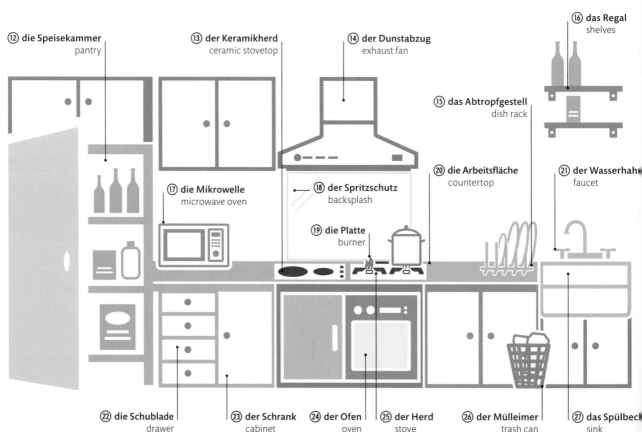

⑫ **die Speisekammer**
pantry

⑬ **der Keramikherd**
ceramic stovetop

⑭ **der Dunstabzug**
exhaust fan

⑮ **das Abtropfgestell**
dish rack

⑯ **das Regal**
shelves

⑰ **die Mikrowelle**
microwave oven

⑱ **der Spritzschutz**
backsplash

⑲ **die Platte**
burner

⑳ **die Arbeitsfläche**
countertop

㉑ **der Wasserhah**
faucet

㉒ **die Schublade**
drawer

㉓ **der Schrank**
cabinet

㉔ **der Ofen**
oven

㉕ **der Herd**
stove

㉖ **der Mülleimer**
trash can

㉗ **das Spülbec**
sink

See also
**28** Küchenutensilien • Kitchenware **29** Kochen • Cooking **59** Kräuter und Gewürze • Herbs and spices **60** In der Vorratskammer • In the pantry **71** Das Frühstück • Breakfast **72** Das Mittagessen und das Abendessen • Lunch and dinner

## 27.2 DAS GESCHIRR • TABLEWARE

① **die Gabel**
fork

② **das Messer**
knife

③ **der Esslöffel**
tablespoon

④ **der Teelöffel**
teaspoon

⑤ **der Suppenlöffel**
soup spoon

⑥ **der Servierlöffel**
serving spoon

⑦ **das Besteck**
silverware

⑧ **das Buttermesser**
butter knife

⑨ **die Essstäbchen** *n, pl*
chopsticks

⑩ **die Kelle**
ladle

⑪ **der Essteller**
dinner plate

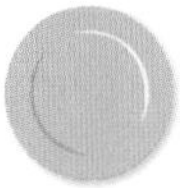
⑫ **der Beilagenteller**
side plate

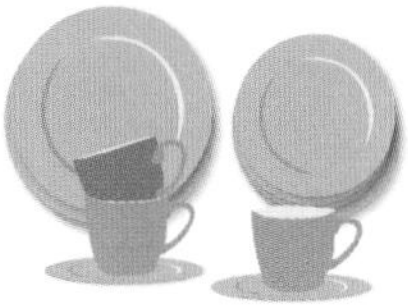
⑬ **das Geschirr**
dinnerware

⑭ **die Kaffeetasse**
coffee cup

⑮ **die Teetasse**
teacup

⑯ **die Tasse**
mug

⑰ **der Espressokocher**
espresso maker

⑱ **die Teekanne**
teapot

⑲ **das Gedeck**
place setting

⑳ **die Serviette**
napkin

㉑ **der Serviettenring**
napkin ring

㉒ **die Schüssel**
bowl

㉓ **die Suppenschüssel**
soup bowl

㉔ **die Reisschüssel**
rice bowl

㉕ **der Eierbecher**
egg cup

㉖ **das Sushi-Set**
sushi set

㉗ **der Messbecher**
measuring cup

㉘ **das Becherglas**
tumbler

㉙ **das Weinglas**
wineglass

㉚ **das Pint-Glas**
pint glass

㉛ **die Stielgläser** *n, pl*
stemware

㉜ **die Gläser** *n, pl*
glasses / glassware

㉝ **das Einmachglas**
jar

㉞ **der Becher**
sippy cup

㉟ **der Sake-Becher**
sake cup

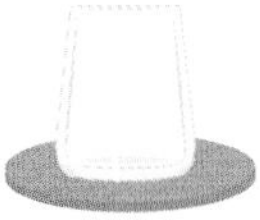
㊱ **der Untersetzer**
coaster

# Küchenutensilien
Kitchenware

## 28.1 DIE KÜCHENAUSSTATTUNG · KITCHEN EQUIPMENT

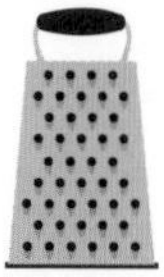
① **die Reibe** grater

② **der Schäler** peeler

③ **der Schneebesen** whisk

④ **das Küchenmesser** kitchen knife

⑤ **das Brotmesser** bread knife

⑥ **die Küchenschere** kitchen scissors

⑦ **das Hackbeil** cleaver
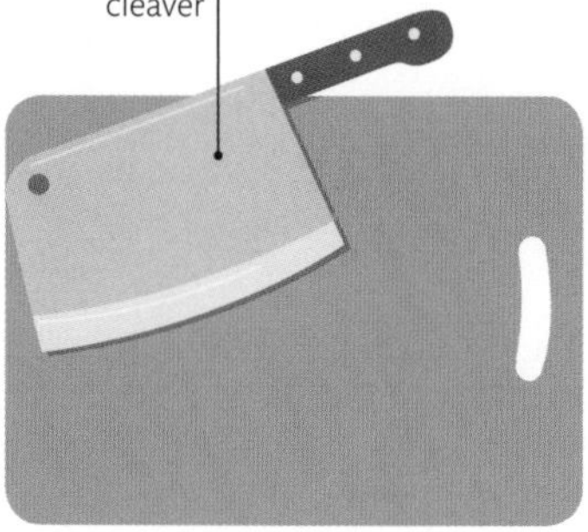
⑫ **das Schneidbrett** cutting board

⑧ **der Messerschleifer** knife sharpener

⑨ **der Fleischklopfer** meat tenderizer

⑩ **der Spieß** skewer

⑪ **der Dosenöffner** can opener

⑬ **der Flaschenöffner** bottle opener

⑭ **der Korkenzieher** corkscrew

⑮ **der Holzlöffel** wooden spoon

⑯ **der Schaumlöffel** slotted spoon

⑰ **der Pfannenwender** spatula

⑱ **der Apfelentkerner** apple corer

⑲ **der Stampfer** masher

⑳ **die Knoblauchpresse** garlic press

㉑ **die Bratengabel** carving fork

㉒ **der Eislöffel** scoop

㉓ **der Griff** handle
㉔ **der Deckel** lid
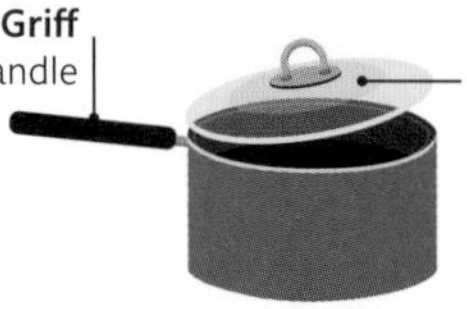
㉕ **der Stieltopf** saucepan

㉖ **die Pfanne** frying pan

㉗ **die Grillpfanne** grill pan

㉘ **der Wok** wok

㉙ **der Durchschlag** colander

㉚ **der Bratenwender** flipper

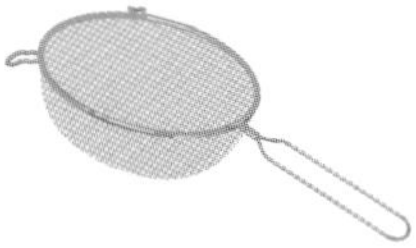
㉛ **das Sieb** sieve

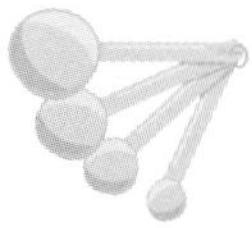
㉜ **die Messlöffel** *m, pl* measuring spoons

㉝ **der Mörser** mortar
㉞ **der Stößel** pestle

㉟ **Mörser und Stößel** *m* mortar and pestle

See also
**27** Die Küche und das Geschirr • Kitchen and tableware **29** Kochen • Cooking
**59** Kräuter und Gewürze • Herbs and spices **60** In der Vorratskammer • In the pantry
**71** Das Frühstück • Breakfast **72** Das Mittagessen und das Abendessen • Lunch and dinner

㊱ **die Tajine**
tagine

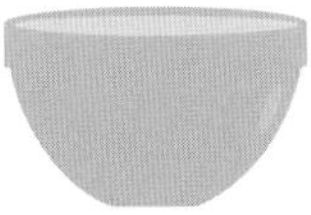

㊲ **die Rührschüssel**
mixing bowl

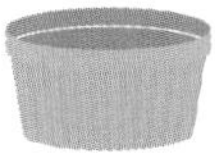

㊳ **die Souffléform**
soufflé dish

㊴ **das Auflaufförmchen**
ramekin

㊵ **die Kasserole**
casserole dish

㊶ **der Frittierkorb**
frying basket

㊷ **die Butterschale**
butter dish

㊸ **der Wecker**
timer

㊹ **die Eieruhr**
egg timer

㊺ **die Zitronenpresse**
lemon squeezer

㊻ **die French Press**
coffee press / cafetière

㊼ **das Bratenthermometer**
meat thermometer

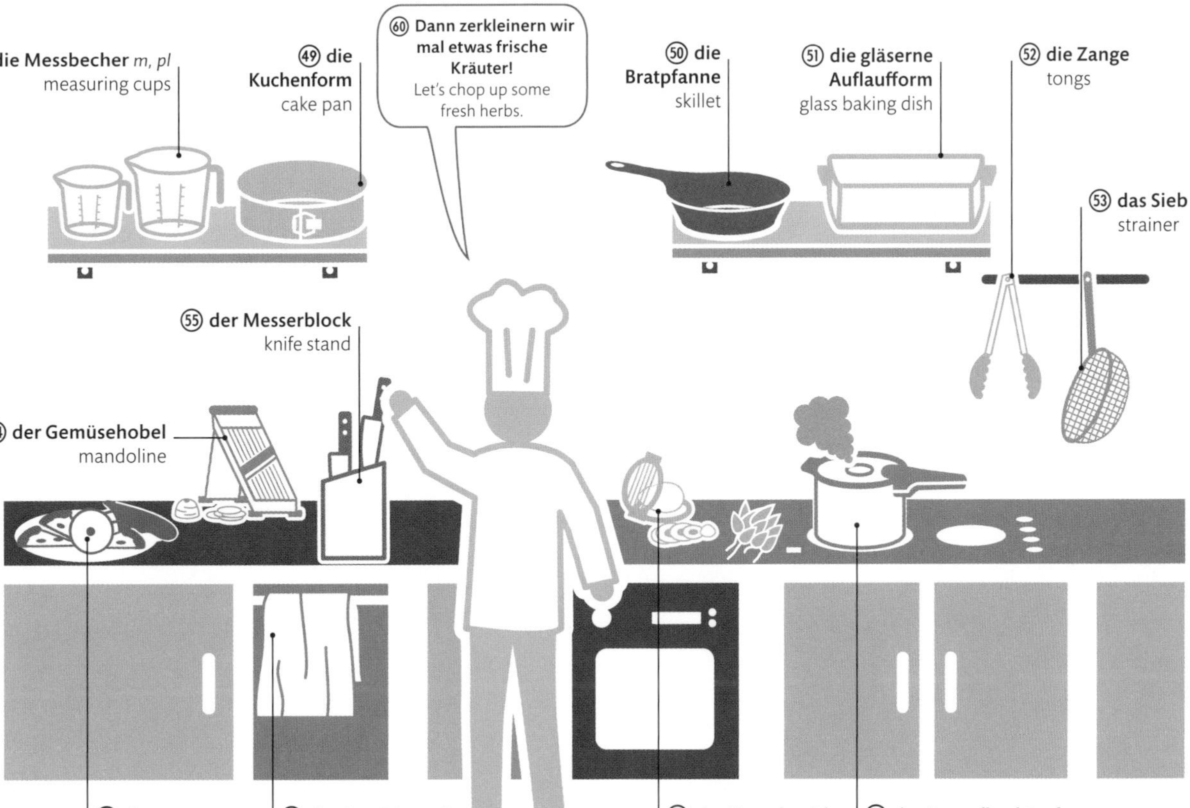

# 29 Kochen
Cooking

## 29.1 KOCHVERBEN · COOKING VERBS

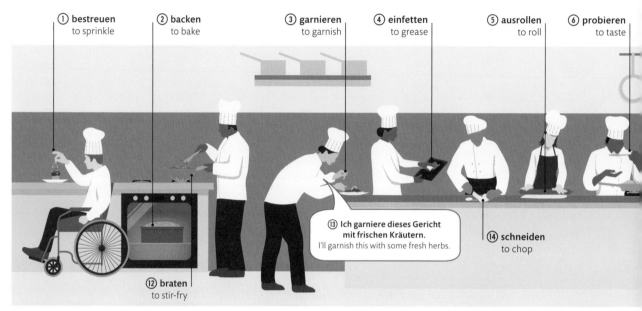

① **bestreuen** to sprinkle
② **backen** to bake
③ **garnieren** to garnish
④ **einfetten** to grease
⑤ **ausrollen** to roll
⑥ **probieren** to taste

⑬ Ich garniere dieses Gericht mit frischen Kräutern.
I'll garnish this with some fresh herbs.
⑭ schneiden
to chop
⑫ braten
to stir-fry

⑳ **grillen** to broil

㉑ **rösten** to roast

㉒ **braten** to fry

㉓ **pochieren** to poach

㉔ **köcheln** to simmer

㉕ **kochen** to boil

㉖ **einfrieren** to freeze

㉗ **hinzugeben** to add

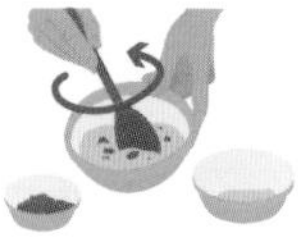
㉘ **mischen** to mix

㉙ **umrühren** to stir

㉚ **verrühren** to whisk

㉛ **zerstampfen** to mash

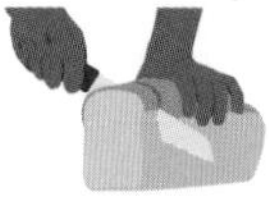
㉜ **in Scheiben schneiden** to slice

㉝ **eine Prise** a pinch

㉞ **ein Schuss** a dash

㉟ **eine Handvoll** a handful

㊱ **zerhacken** to mince

㊲ **schälen** to peel

㊳ **schneiden** to cut

㊴ **reiben** to grate

㊵ **gießen** to pour

See also
**27** Die Küche und das Geschirr • Kitchen and tableware **28** Küchenutensilien • Kitchenware **59** Kräuter und Gewürze • Herbs and spices **60** In der Vorratskammer • In the pantry **62-63** Die Bäckerei • The bakery **71** Das Frühstück • Breakfast **72** Das Mittagessen und das Abendessen • Lunch and dinner

⑦ **dünsten**
to steam

⑧ **Kannst du mir bitte eine Karotte in Würfel schneiden?**
Can you dice a carrot for me, please?

⑨ **Eier schlagen**
to beat eggs

⑩ **Mir sind die Zwiebeln angebrannt. Sie sind ruiniert!**
I've burned the onions. They are ruined!

⑪ **in der Mikrowelle erwärmen**
to microwave

⑮ **Butter schmelzen**
to melt butter

⑯ **zerlegen**
to carve

⑰ **würfeln**
to dice

⑱ **anbrennen**
to burn

⑲ **anschwitzen**
to sauté

## 29.2 **BACKEN** • BAKING

① **die Schürze**
apron

② **der Ofenhandschuh**
oven mitt

③ **die Kuchenform**
cake pan

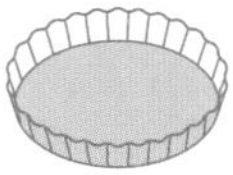
④ **die Pastetenform**
flan pan

⑤ **die Pie-Form**
pie pan

⑥ **der Backpinsel**
pastry brush

⑦ **das Nudelholz**
rolling pin

⑧ **das Backblech**
baking pan

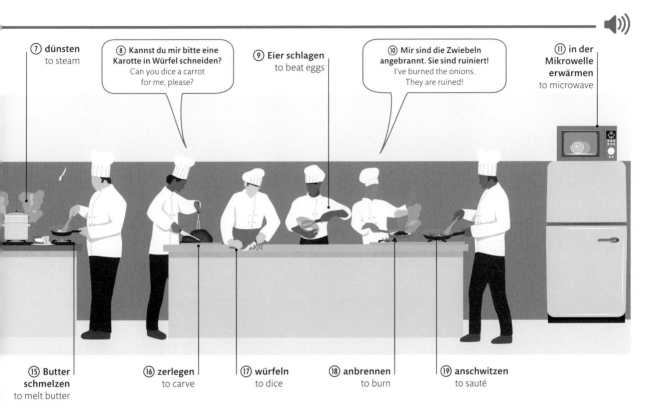

⑨ **die Muffinform**
muffin tin

⑩ **das Kuchengitter**
cooling rack

⑪ **die Glasur**
icing

⑫ **der Spritzbeutel**
piping bag

⑬ **die Waage**
scale

⑭ **der Messbecher**
measuring cup

⑮ **dekorieren**
to decorate

# 30 Das Schlafzimmer
Bedroom

## 30.1 DAS SCHLAFZIMMER · BEDROOM

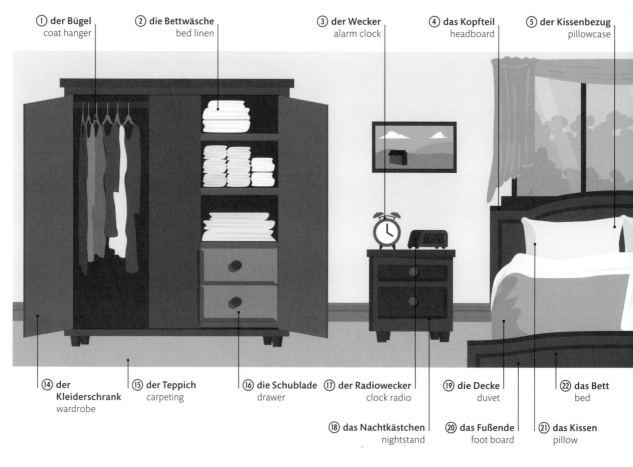

(27) **das Einzelbett**
twin bed

(28) **das Doppelbett**
double bed

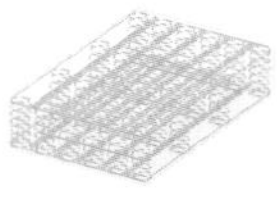

(29) **die Boxspring-Matratze**
box spring

(30) **der Polsterhocker**
Ottoman

(31) **die Wäschetruhe**
linen chest

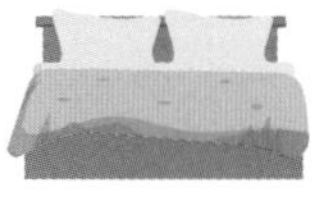

(32) **der Überwurf**
throw

(33) **die Steppdecke**
quilt

(34) **die Decke**
blanket

(35) **die Heizdecke**
electric blanket

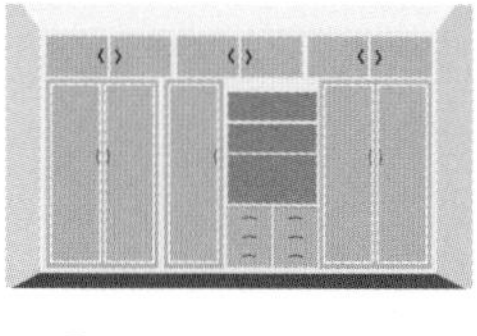

(36) **der Einbauschrank**
closet

(37) **die Wärmflasche**
hot-water bottle

See also
**08** Schwangerschaft und Kindheit • Pregnancy and childhood **13-15** Kleidung • Clothes
**25** Ein Ort zum Leben • A place to live **32** Haus und Heim • House and home

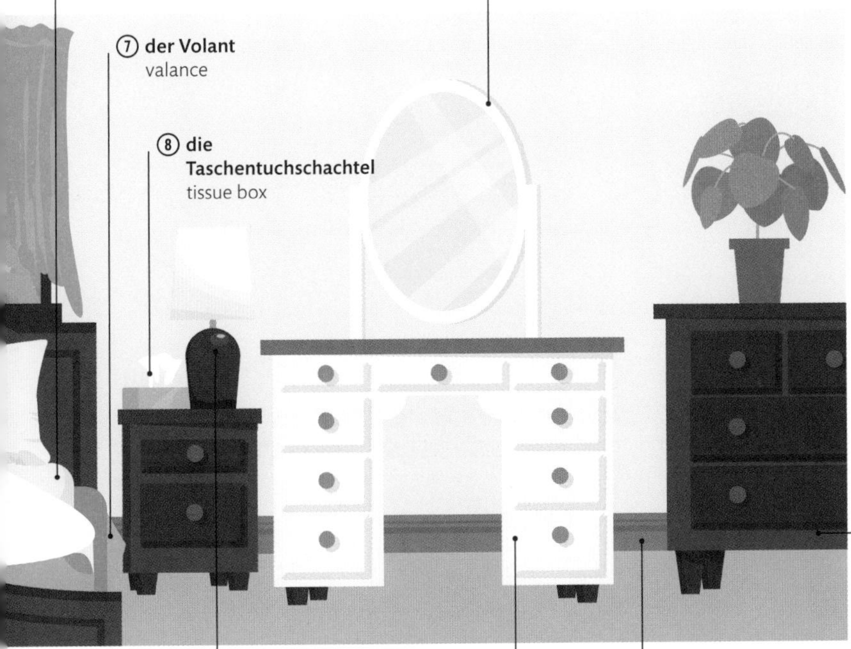

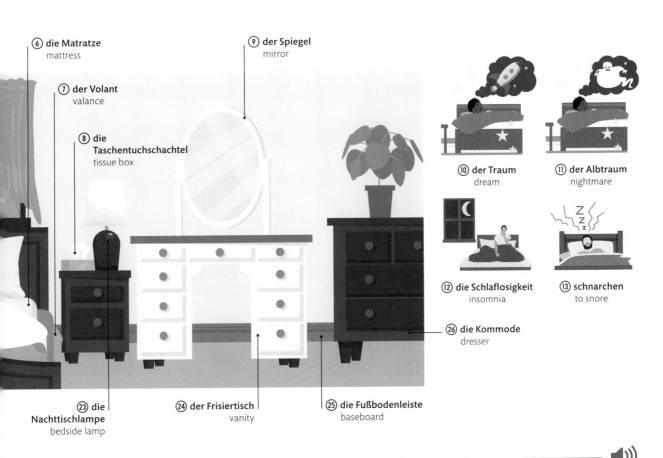

⑥ **die Matratze**
mattress

⑦ **der Volant**
valance

⑧ **die Taschentuchschachtel**
tissue box

⑨ **der Spiegel**
mirror

㉓ **die Nachttischlampe**
bedside lamp

㉔ **der Frisiertisch**
vanity

㉕ **die Fußbodenleiste**
baseboard

㉖ **die Kommode**
dresser

⑩ **der Traum**
dream

⑪ **der Albtraum**
nightmare

⑫ **die Schlaflosigkeit**
insomnia

⑬ **schnarchen**
to snore

## 30.2 DAS KINDERZIMMER • NURSERY

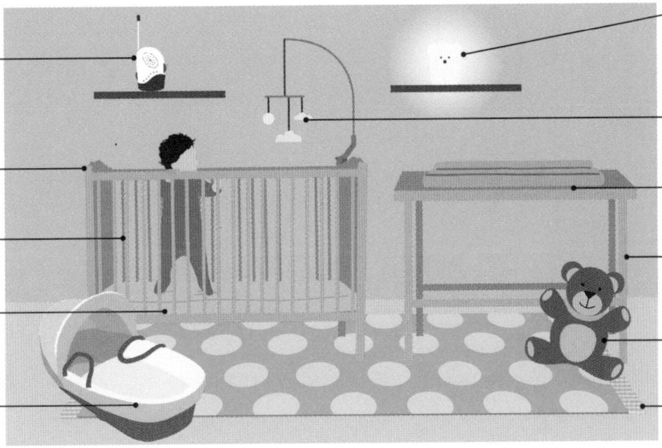

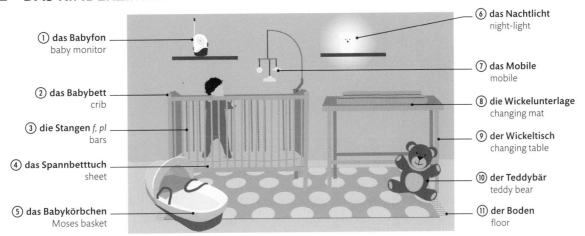

① **das Babyfon**
baby monitor

② **das Babybett**
crib

③ **die Stangen** *f, pl*
bars

④ **das Spannbetttuch**
sheet

⑤ **das Babykörbchen**
Moses basket

⑥ **das Nachtlicht**
night-light

⑦ **das Mobile**
mobile

⑧ **die Wickelunterlage**
changing mat

⑨ **der Wickeltisch**
changing table

⑩ **der Teddybär**
teddy bear

⑪ **der Boden**
floor

# 31 Das Badezimmer
Bathroom

## 31.1 IM BADEZIMMER · IN THE BATHROOM

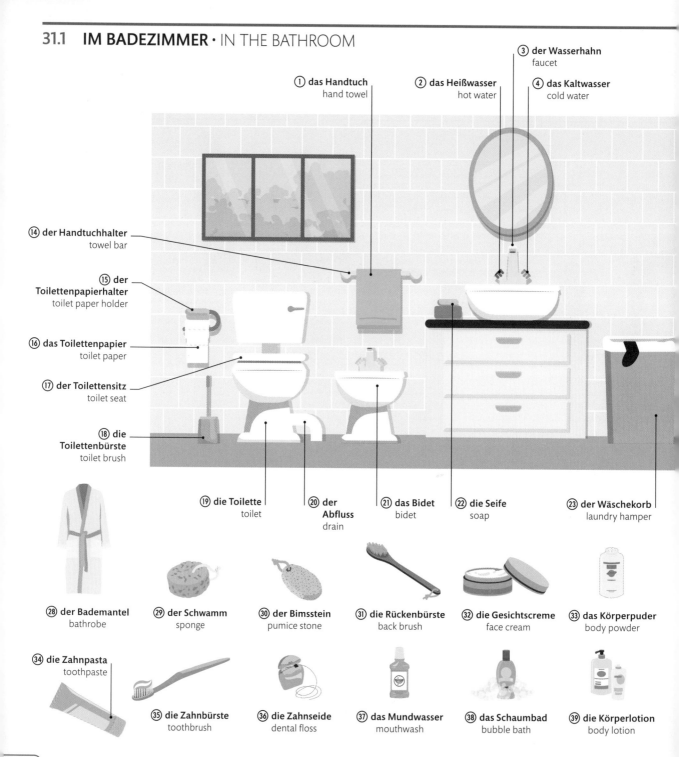

① **das Handtuch** hand towel
② **das Heißwasser** hot water
③ **der Wasserhahn** faucet
④ **das Kaltwasser** cold water
⑭ **der Handtuchhalter** towel bar
⑮ **der Toilettenpapierhalter** toilet paper holder
⑯ **das Toilettenpapier** toilet paper
⑰ **der Toilettensitz** toilet seat
⑱ **die Toilettenbürste** toilet brush
⑲ **die Toilette** toilet
⑳ **der Abfluss** drain
㉑ **das Bidet** bidet
㉒ **die Seife** soap
㉓ **der Wäschekorb** laundry hamper

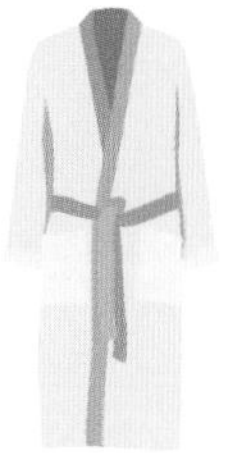

㉘ **der Bademantel** bathrobe

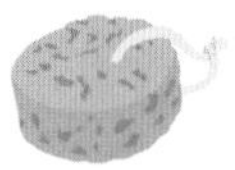

㉙ **der Schwamm** sponge

㉚ **der Bimsstein** pumice stone

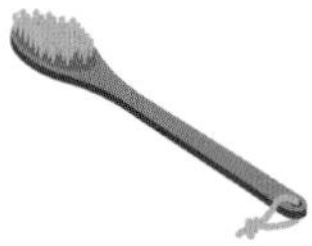

㉛ **die Rückenbürste** back brush

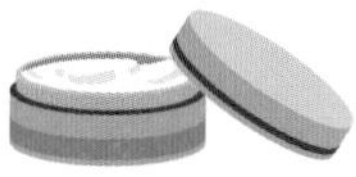

㉜ **die Gesichtscreme** face cream

㉝ **das Körperpuder** body powder

㉞ **die Zahnpasta** toothpaste

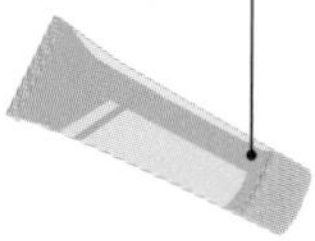

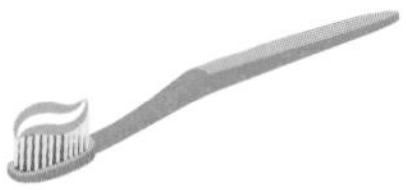

㉟ **die Zahnbürste** toothbrush

㊱ **die Zahnseide** dental floss

㊲ **das Mundwasser** mouthwash

㊳ **das Schaumbad** bubble bath

㊴ **die Körperlotion** body lotion

See also
**18** Beauty • Beauty **25** Ein Ort zum Leben • A place to live **32** Haus und Heim • House and home
**33** Elektrizität und Sanitärtechnik • Electrics and plumbing

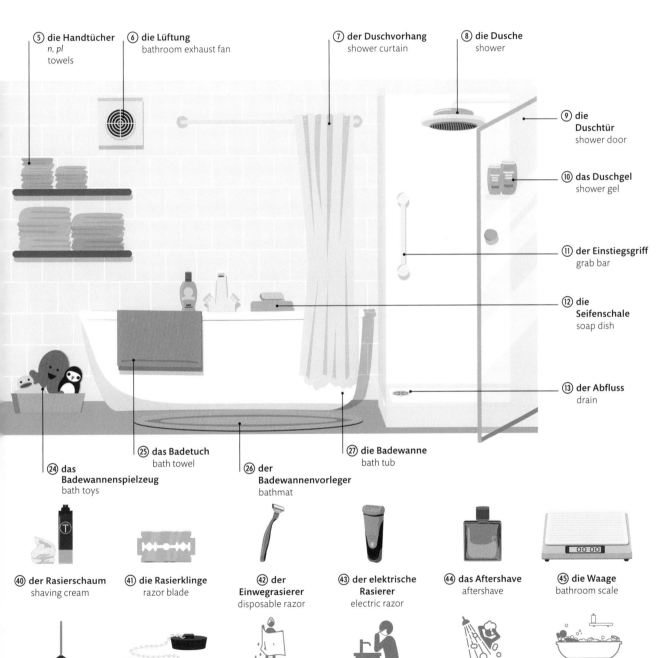

⑤ **die Handtücher** *n, pl* towels

⑥ **die Lüftung** bathroom exhaust fan

⑦ **der Duschvorhang** shower curtain

⑧ **die Dusche** shower

⑨ **die Duschtür** shower door

⑩ **das Duschgel** shower gel

⑪ **der Einstiegsgriff** grab bar

⑫ **die Seifenschale** soap dish

⑬ **der Abfluss** drain

㉔ **das Badewannenspielzeug** bath toys

㉕ **das Badetuch** bath towel

㉖ **der Badewannenvorleger** bathmat

㉗ **die Badewanne** bath tub

㊵ **der Rasierschaum** shaving cream

㊶ **die Rasierklinge** razor blade

㊷ **der Einwegrasierer** disposable razor

㊸ **der elektrische Rasierer** electric razor

㊹ **das Aftershave** aftershave

㊺ **die Waage** bathroom scale

㊻ **die Gummiglocke** plunger

㊼ **der Stöpsel** plug

㊽ **sich abtrocknen** to dry yourself

㊾ **sich rasieren** to shave

㊿ **duschen** to take (or have) a shower

51 **baden** to take (or have) a bath

# Haus und Heim
## House and home

### 32.1 HAUSARTEN • TYPES OF HOUSES

① **das Einfamilienhaus**
detached house

② **die Doppelhaushälfte**
duplex

③ **das Reihenhaus**
row house

④ **das Stadthaus**
town house

⑤ **das Cottage**
cottage

⑥ **die Villa**
villa

⑦ **der Bungalow**
ranch house

⑧ **das Anwesen**
mansion

⑨ **der Wohnwagen**
mobile home

⑩ **die Blockhütte**
cabin

⑪ **das Baumhaus**
tree house

⑫ **die Berghütte**
chalet

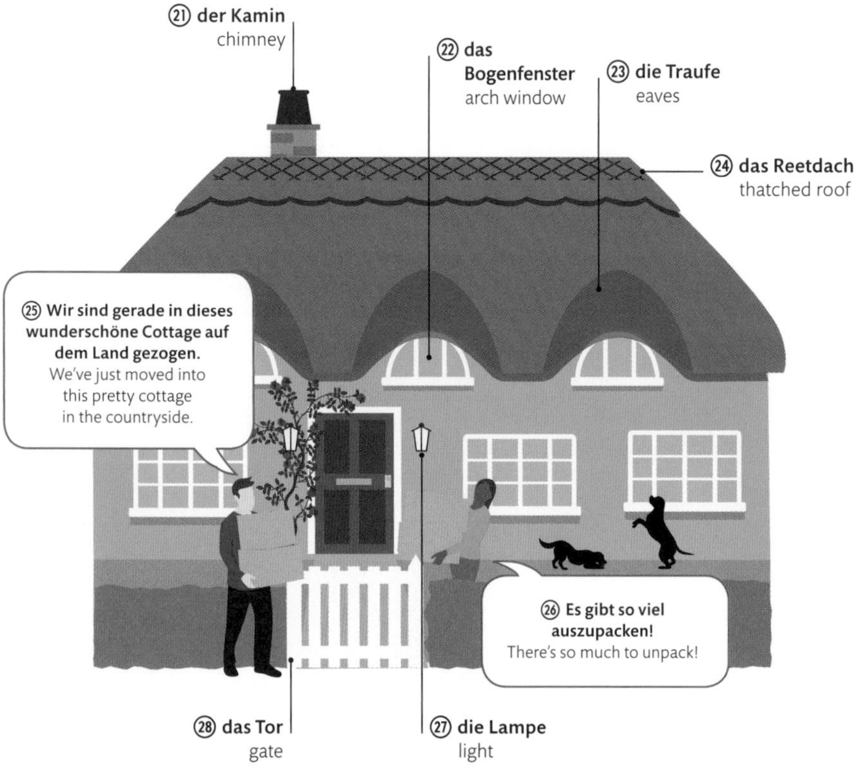
㉑ der Kamin
chimney
㉒ das Bogenfenster
arch window
㉓ die Traufe
eaves
㉔ das Reetdach
thatched roof
㉕ Wir sind gerade in dieses wunderschöne Cottage auf dem Land gezogen.
We've just moved into this pretty cottage in the countryside.
㉖ Es gibt so viel auszupacken!
There's so much to unpack!
㉘ das Tor
gate
㉗ die Lampe
light

㉙ **das Cottage mit Reetdach**
thatched cottage

⑬ **die Jurte**
yurt

⑭ **die Hütte**
hut

⑮ **der Wigwam**
wigwam

⑯ **das Iglu**
igloo

⑰ **das Tipi**
teepee

⑱ **das Hausboot**
houseboat

⑲ **das Fertighaus**
prefab house

⑳ **das Pfahlhaus**
stilt house

See also
**25** Ein Ort zum Leben • A place to live **33** Elektrizität und Sanitärtechnik • Electrics and plumbing **35** Heimwerken • Home improvements **37** Wohnraumverschönerung • Renovating **42-43** In der Stadt • In town **44** Gebäude und Architektur • Buildings and architecture

## 32.2 EIN HAUS KAUFEN ODER MIETEN • BUYING AND RENTING A HOUSE

① **der Makler** *m*
**die Maklerin** *f*
realtor

② **die Immobilie**
real estate

③ **ein Haus besichtigen**
to view a house

④ **möbliert**
furnished

⑤ **unmöbliert**
unfurnished

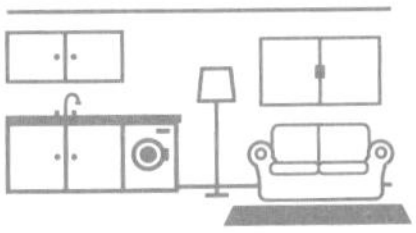

⑥ **der offene Wohnbereich**
open-plan

⑦ **der Parkplatz**
parking space

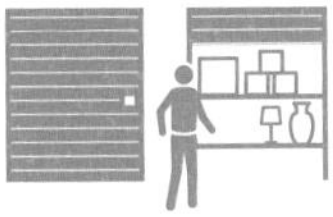

⑧ **der Lagerraum**
storage

⑨ **sparen**
to save up

⑩ **kaufen**
to buy

⑪ **besitzen**
to own

⑫ **die Kartons** *m, pl*
boxes

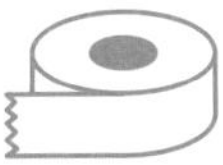

⑬ **das Klebeband**
tape

⑭ **die Schlüssel** *m, pl*
keys

⑮ **packen**
to pack

⑯ **das Umzugsauto**
moving truck

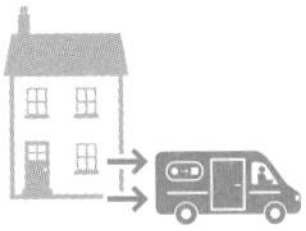

⑰ **ausziehen**
to move out

⑱ **einziehen**
to move in

⑲ **auspacken**
to unpack

⑳ **vermieten**
to rent out

㉑ **mieten**
to rent

㉒ **der Mietvertrag**
lease

㉓ **der Mieter** *m*
**die Mieterin** *f*
tenant

㉔ **der Vermieter** *m*
**die Vermieterin** *f*
landlord

㉕ **die Kaution**
deposit

㉖ **den Mietvertrag kündigen**
to give notice

㉗ **der Kredit**
mortgage

㉘ **die Rechnungen** *f, pl*
bills

㉙ **der Untermieter** *m*
**die Untermieterin** *f*
roomer

㉚ **der Mitbewohner** *m*
**die Mitbewohnerin** *f*
roommate

㉛ **das Wohngebiet**
residential area

# 33 Elektrizität und Sanitärtechnik
## Electrics and plumbing

### 33.1 DIE ELEKTRIZITÄT · ELECTRICITY

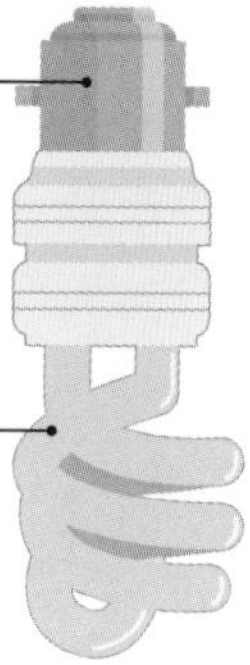

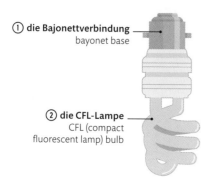

① **die Bajonettverbindung**
bayonet base

② **die CFL-Lampe**
CFL (compact fluorescent lamp) bulb

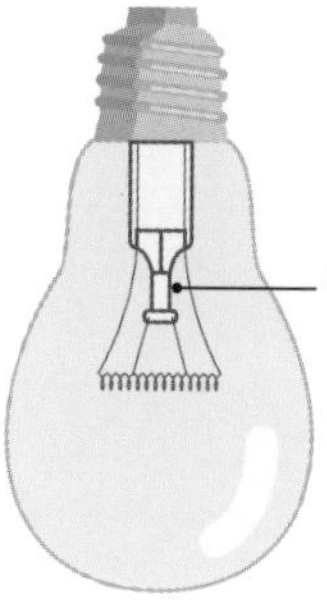

③ **die Glühbirne**
incandescent bulb

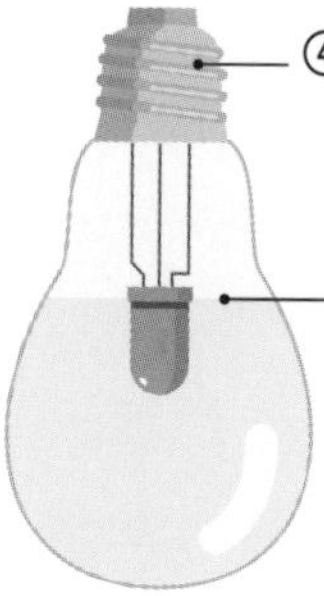

④ **die Schraubverbindung**
screw base

⑤ **die LED-Lampe**
LED (light emitting diode) bulb

⑥ **das Leuchtmittel**
light bulbs

⑦ **die Steckdose**
socket

⑧ **der Lichtschalter**
light switch

⑨ **der Gleichstrom**
direct current

⑩ **der Wechselstrom**
alternating current

⑪ **der Generator**
generator

⑫ **die Gasheizung**
gas space heater

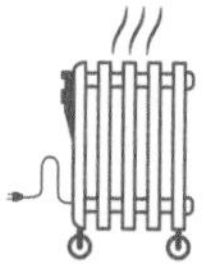

⑬ **die Ölheizung**
oil-filled radiator

⑭ **das Heizgebläse**
fan space heater

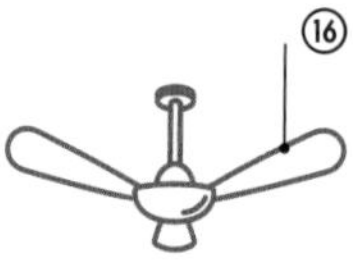

⑮ **der Deckenventilator**
ceiling fan

⑯ **der Ventilatorflügel**
blade

⑰ **der Ventilator**
fan

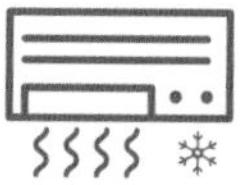

⑱ **die Klimaanlage**
air conditioning

⑲ **der Strom**
power

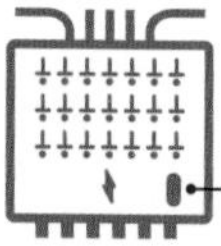

⑳ **der Sicherungskasten**
fuse box

㉑ **der Schutzschalter**
breaker

㉒ **das Ampere**
amp

㉓ **die Phase**
live

㉔ **der Nullleiter**
neutral

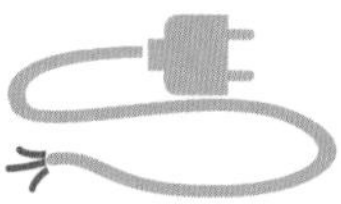

㉕ **die Drähte** *m, pl*
wires

㉖ **die Erdung**
ground

㉗ **die Spannung**
voltage

㉘ **der Stecker**
plug

㉙ **der Kontakt**
pin

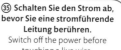

㉟ **Schalten Sie den Strom ab, bevor Sie eine stromführende Leitung berühren.**
Switch off the power before touching a live wire.

㉚ **der Stromzähler**
electricity meter

㉛ **der Transformator**
transformer

㉜ **der Stromausfall**
power outage

㉝ **der Netzstrom**
utility power

㉞ **die Verdrahtung**
wiring

See also
**31** Das Badezimmer • Bathroom **35** Heimwerken • Home improvements **36** Werkzeuge • Tools
**37** Wohnraumverschönerung • Renovating **87** Der Bau • Construction

## 33.2 SANITÄRTECHNIK • PLUMBING

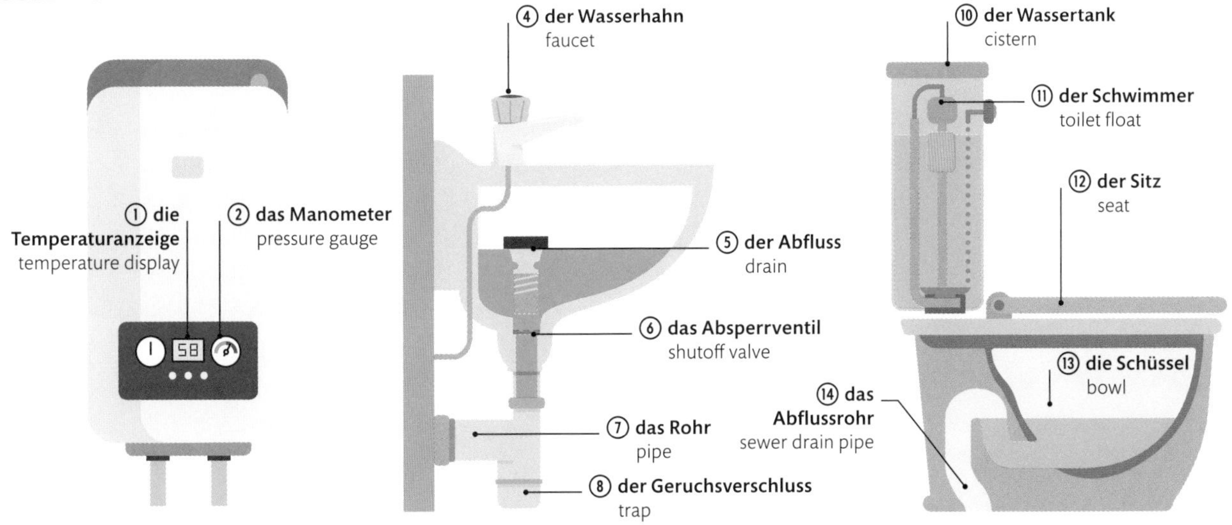


③ **der Boiler**
on-demand boiler

⑨ **das Waschbecken**
sink

⑮ **die Toilette**
toilet

⑯ **der Heizkörper**
radiator

⑰ **der Wasserhahn**
faucet

⑱ **plötzlich undicht werden**
to spring a leak

⑲ **einen Klempner rufen** *m* **/ eine Klempnerin rufen** *f*
to call a plumber

⑳ **reparieren**
to repair

㉑ **installieren**
to install

## 33.3 ABFALL • WASTE

① **der Abfalleimer**
trash can

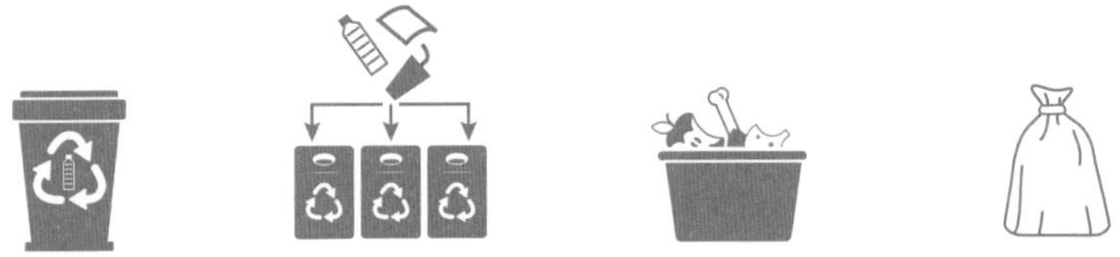

② **die Recycling-Tonne**
recycling bin

③ **der Recyclinghof**
sorting unit

④ **der Kompost**
food compost bin

⑤ **der Müllbeutel**
trash bag

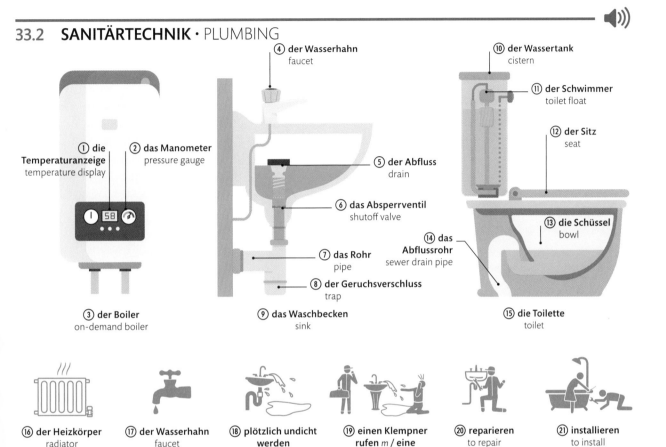

⑥ **der Biomüll**
biodegradable waste

⑦ **der Sondermüll**
hazardous waste

⑧ **der Elektroschrott**
electrical waste

⑨ **der Bauschutt**
construction waste

# 34 Hausarbeit

## Household chores

### 34.1 AUFGABEN IM HAUSHALT · HOUSEHOLD TASKS

① **das Bett beziehen**
to change the sheets

② **das Bett machen**
to make the bed

③ **das Haustier füttern**
to feed the pets

④ **die Blumen gießen**
to water the plants

⑤ **das Auto putzen**
to wash the car

⑥ **den Boden kehren**
to sweep the floor

⑦ **den Boden schrubben**
to scrub the floor

⑧ **den Ofen putzen**
to clean the oven

⑨ **die Fenster putzen**
to clean the windows

⑩ **das Gefrierfach abtauen**
to defrost the freezer

⑪ **den Teppich saugen**
to vacuum the carpet

⑫ **abstauben**
to dust

⑬ **das Bad putzen**
to clean the bathroom

⑭ **aufräumen**
to clean up

⑮ **Lebensmittel einkaufen**
to buy groceries

⑯ **die Wäsche machen**
to do the laundry

⑰ **die Wäsche aufhängen**
to hang clothes

⑱ **die Kleidung bügeln**
to do the ironing

⑳ Normalerweise erledige ich die Hausarbeit abends.
I usually do the housework in the evening.

⑲ **den Boden wischen**
to mop the floor

㉑ **die Wäsche zusammenlegen**
to fold clothes

㉒ **den Tisch decken**
to set the table

㉓ **den Tisch abräumen**
to clear the table

㉔ **die Spülmaschine einräumen**
to load the dishwasher

㉕ **die Spülmaschine ausräumen**
to unload the dishwasher

㉖ **die Oberflächen abwischen**
to wipe the surfaces

㉗ **das Geschirr spülen**
to do the dishes

㉘ **das Geschirr abtrocknen**
to dry the dishes

㉙ **den Müll hinausbringen**
to take out the trash

See also
**09** Die Alltagsroutine • Daily routines **25** Ein Ort zum Leben • A place to live **33** Elektrizität und Sanitärtechnik • Electrics and plumbing **35** Heimwerken • Home improvements
**37** Wohnraumverschönerung • Renovating **39** Gartenarbeit • Practical gardening

## 34.2 **WÄSCHE UND PUTZEN** • LAUNDRY AND CLEANING

① **der Scheuerschwamm**
scouring pad

② **der Schwamm**
sponge

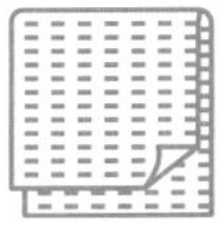

③ **das Tuch**
cloth

④ **das Staubtuch**
duster

⑤ **der Staubwedel**
feather duster

⑥ **der Abzieher**
squeegee

⑦ **der Eimer**
bucket

⑧ **der Mopp**
mop

⑨ **die Scheuerbürste**
scrubbing brush

⑩ **die Kehrschaufel**
dustpan

⑪ **der Kehrbesen**
brush

⑫ **der Besen**
broom

⑬ **der Recyclingmüll**
recycling bin

⑭ **der Müllbeutel**
trash bag

⑮ **das Putzmittel**
polish

⑯ **der Oberflächenreiniger**
surface cleaner

⑰ **der WC-Reiniger**
toilet cleaner

⑱ **der WC-Stein**
automatic toilet cleaner

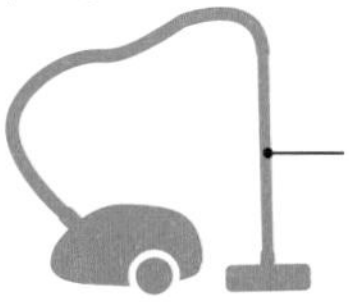

⑳ **das Saugrohr**
suction hose

⑲ **der Staubsauger**
vacuum cleaner

㉑ **die Gummihandschuhe** *m, pl*
rubber gloves

㉒ **der klare Essig**
white vinegar

㉓ **die schmutzige Wäsche**
dirty clothes

㉔ **der Wäschekorb**
laundry hamper

㉕ **die Waschmaschine**
washing machine

㉖ **der Trockner**
tumble dryer

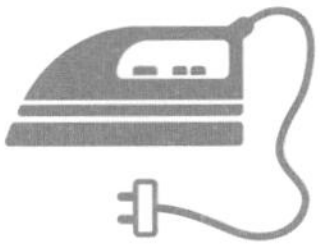

㉗ **das Bügeleisen**
iron

㉘ **das Bügelbrett**
ironing board

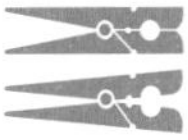

㉙ **die Wäscheklammer**
clothes pin

㉚ **die Wäscheleine**
clothesline

㉛ **das Waschmittel**
laundry detergent

㉜ **der Weichspüler**
fabric softener

㉝ **die Spülmaschine**
dishwasher

㉞ **das Geschirrspültab**
dishwasher tablets

㉟ **das Geschirrspülmittel**
dishwashing liquid

㊱ **die Bleiche**
bleach

# Heimwerken
## Home improvements

### 35.1 **WERKZEUG UND HEIMWERKERZUBEHÖR** · TOOLS AND DIY EQUIPMENT

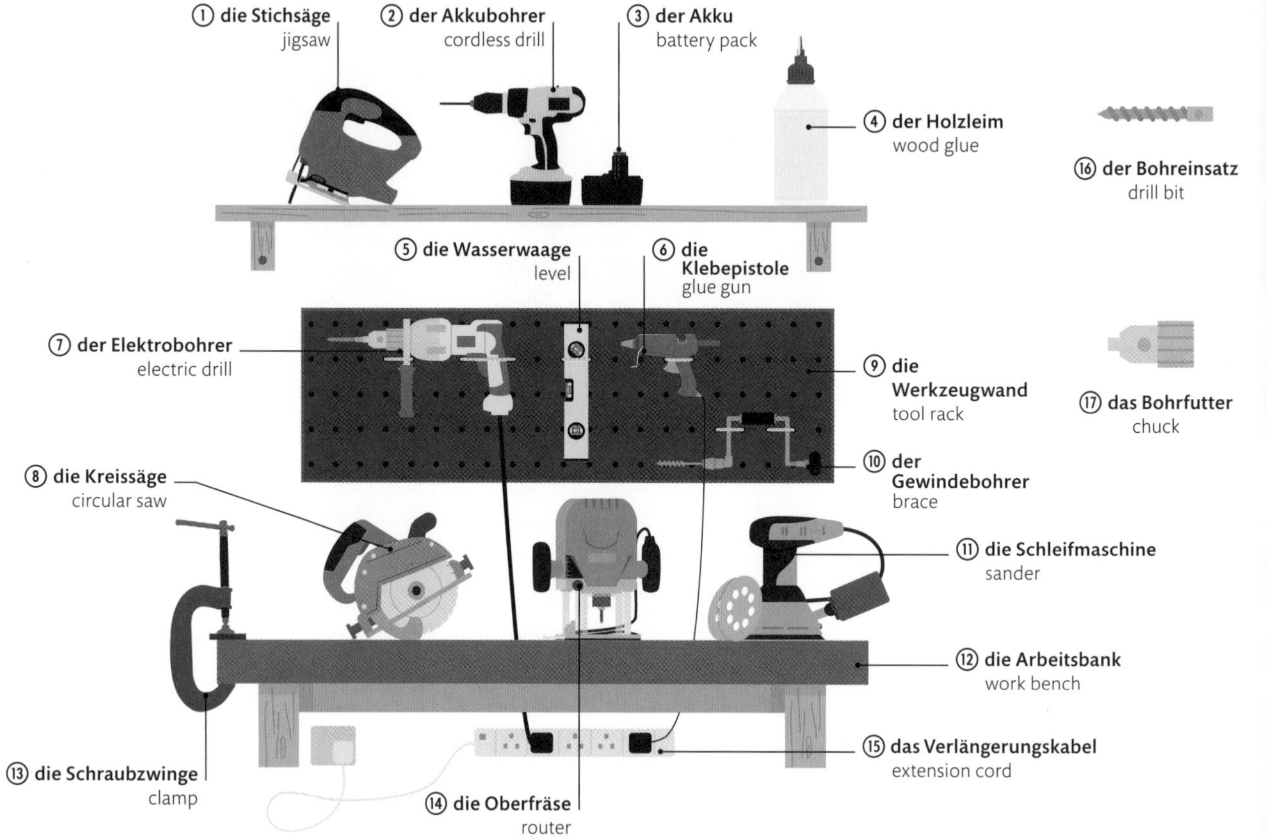


### 35.2 **HEIMWERKERVERBEN** · DIY VERBS

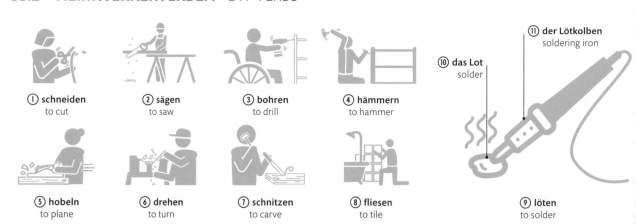

① **schneiden**
to cut

② **sägen**
to saw

③ **bohren**
to drill

④ **hämmern**
to hammer

⑤ **hobeln**
to plane

⑥ **drehen**
to turn

⑦ **schnitzen**
to carve

⑧ **fliesen**
to tile

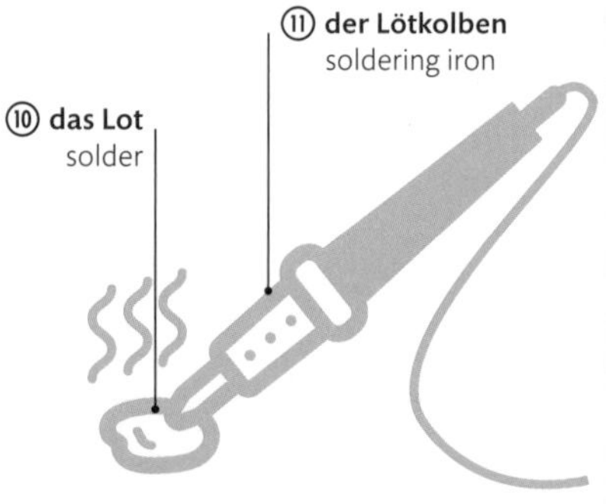

⑨ **löten**
to solder

See also
**33** Elektrizität und Sanitärtechnik • Electrics and plumbing **36** Werkzeuge • Tools **37** Wohnraumverschönerung • Renovating **87** Der Bau • Construction

## 35.3 WERKSTOFFE • MATERIALS

① **das Holz**
wood

② **das Hartholz**
hardwood

③ **das Weichholz**
softwood

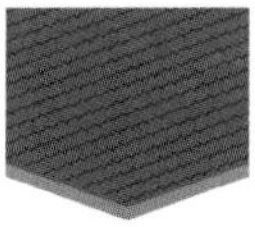
④ **die Hartfaserplatte**
hardboard

⑤ **die Spanplatte**
particle board

⑥ **das Sperrholz**
plywood

⑦ **die MDF-Platte**
MDF

⑧ **die Fliese**
tiles

⑨ **der Beton**
concrete

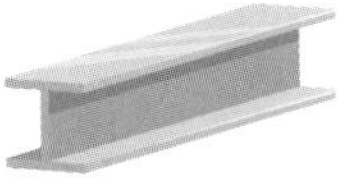
⑩ **das Metall**
metal

⑪ **der Draht**
wire

⑫ **die Steinplatte**
flagstone

⑬ **das Isoliermaterial**
insulation

⑭ **der Sand**
sand

⑮ **der Kies**
gravel

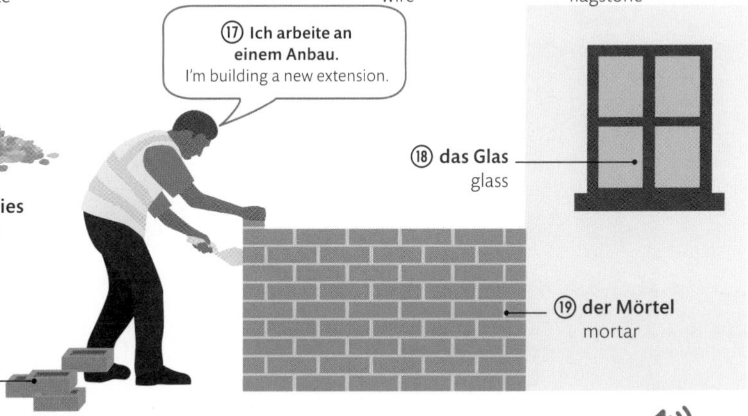
⑰ **Ich arbeite an einem Anbau.**
I'm building a new extension.

⑯ **die Ziegel** *m, pl*
bricks

⑱ **das Glas**
glass

⑲ **der Mörtel**
mortar

⑫ **einen Teppich verlegen**
to install a carpet

⑬ **den Abfluss (des Waschbeckens) frei machen**
to unclog the sink

⑭ **das Haus neu verkabeln**
to rewire the house

⑮ **mauern**
to lay bricks

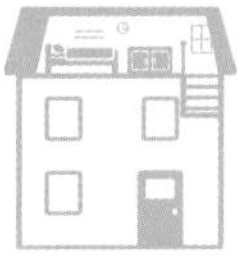
⑯ **das Dachgeschoss umbauen**
to convert the attic

⑰ **einen Vorhang nähen**
to make curtains

⑱ **ein Regal aufhängen**
to put up shelves

⑲ **eine Glühbirne wechseln**
to change a light bulb

⑳ **den Abfluss (der Toilette) frei machen**
to unclog the toilet

㉑ **eine Wand einreißen**
to knock down a wall

㉒ **eine Wand streichen**
to paint a wall

㉓ **einen Zaun reparieren**
to fix a fence

# 36 Werkzeuge
## Tools

### 36.1 DER WERKZEUGKASTEN · TOOLBOX

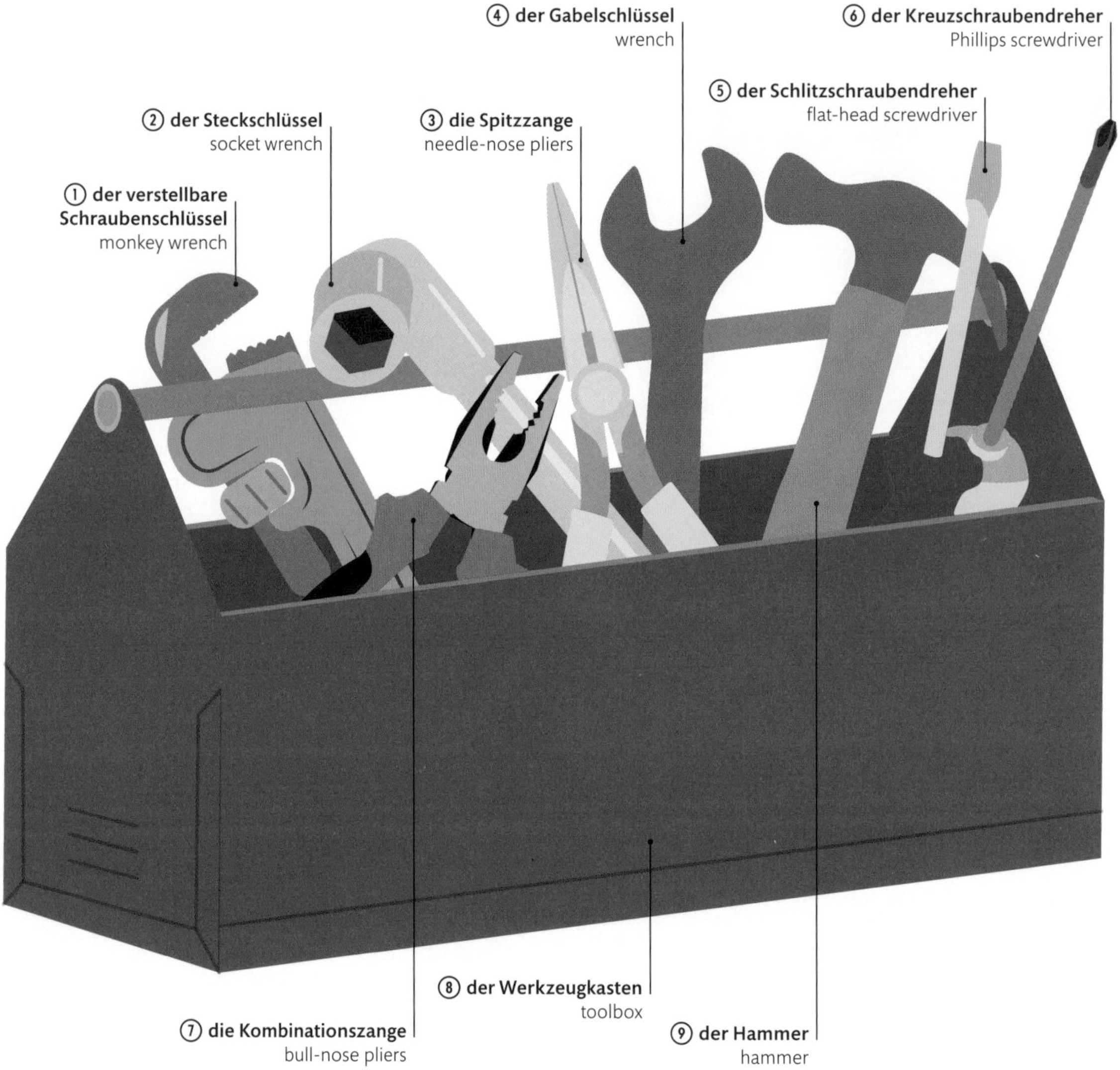


### 36.2 BOHREINSÄTZE · DRILL BITS

① **der Metallbohrer** metal bit

② **der Steinbohrer** masonry bit

③ **der Holzbohrer** carpentry bit

④ **der Flachfräsbohrer** flat wood bit

⑤ **der Torxeinsatz** security bit

⑥ **die Reibahle** reamer

See also
**33** Elektrizität und Sanitärtechnik • Electrics and plumbing **35** Heimwerken • Home improvements **37** Wohnraumverschönerung • Renovating **87** Der Bau • Construction

## 36.3 WERKZEUGE • TOOLS

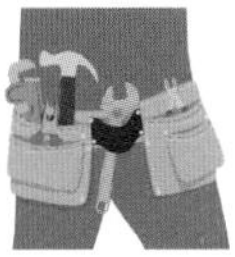
① **der Werkzeuggürtel**
tool belt

② **der Nagel**
nail

③ **die Schraube**
screw

④ **die Schraube**
bolt

⑤ **die Unterlegscheibe**
washer

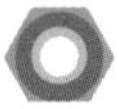
⑥ **die Mutter**
nut

⑦ **der Inbusschlüssel**
Allen wrenches

⑧ **das Maßband**
tape measure

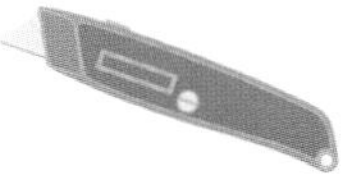
⑨ **das Teppichmesser**
utility knife

⑩ **die Bügelsäge**
hacksaw

⑪ **der Fuchsschwanz**
tenon saw

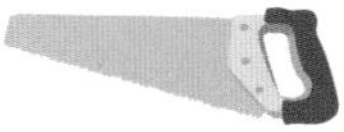
⑫ **die Handsäge**
handsaw

⑬ **der Hobel**
plane

⑭ **der Handbohrer**
hand drill

⑮ **der Schraubenschlüssel**
wrench

⑯ **der Meißel**
chisel

⑰ **die Feile**
file

⑱ **der Wetzstein**
sharpening stone

⑲ **die Leiter**
ladder

㉑ **die Abisolierzange**
wire strippers

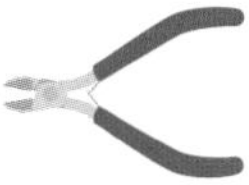
㉒ **der Seitenschneider**
wire cutters

㉓ **das Isolierband**
insulating tape

㉔ **der Rohrschneider**
pipe cutter

㉕ **die Gummiglocke**
plunger

㉖ **der Gummihammer**
mallet

㉗ **die Axt**
ax

㉘ **die Stahlwolle**
steel wool

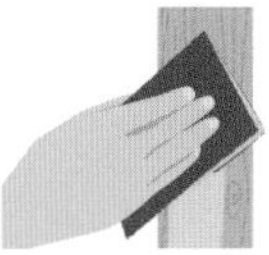
㉙ **das Schleifpapier**
sandpaper

㉚ **die Schutzbrille**
safety goggles

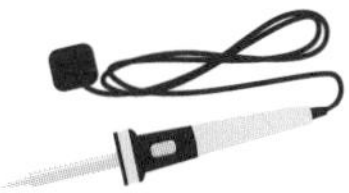
㉛ **der Lötkolben**
soldering iron

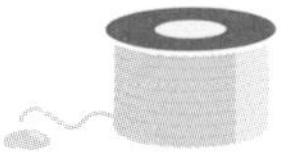
㉜ **das Lot**
solder

㉞ **die Wasserwaage**
level

# 37 Wohnraumverschönerung
## Renovating

### 37.1 RENOVIERUNG · HOUSEHOLD RENOVATION

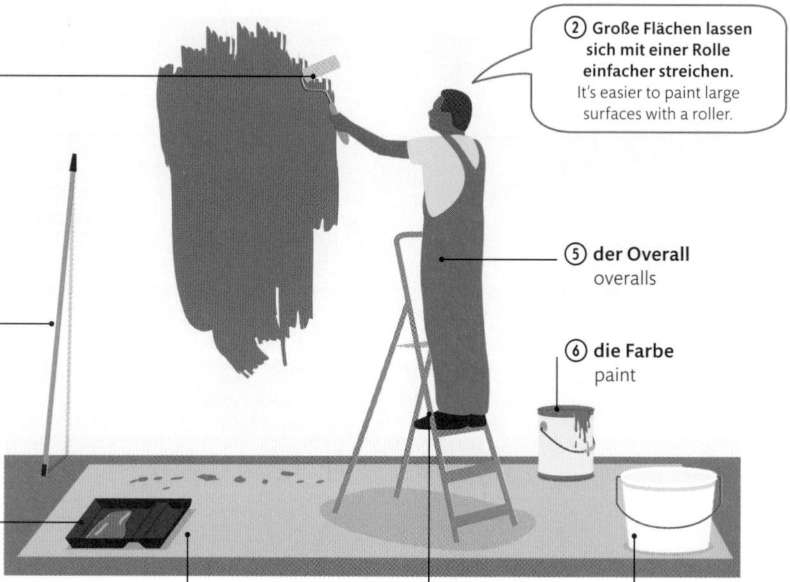

② Große Flächen lassen sich mit einer Rolle einfacher streichen.
It's easier to paint large surfaces with a roller.

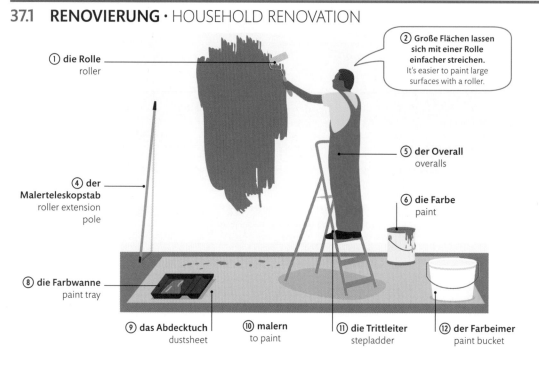

① **die Rolle**
roller

④ **der Malerteleskopstab**
roller extension pole

⑤ **der Overall**
overalls

⑥ **die Farbe**
paint

⑧ **die Farbwanne**
paint tray

⑨ **das Abdecktuch**
dustsheet

⑩ **malern**
to paint

⑪ **die Trittleiter**
stepladder

⑫ **der Farbeimer**
paint bucket

③ **der Pinsel**
paintbrush

⑦ **der Schwamm**
sponge

⑬ **der Malerkrepp**
masking tape

⑭ **das Teppichmesser**
utility knife

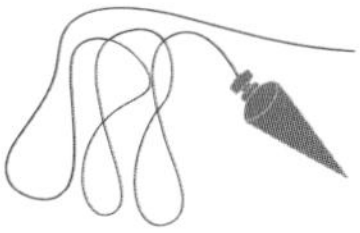

⑮ **das Lot**
plumb line

⑯ **das Schleifpapier**
sandpaper

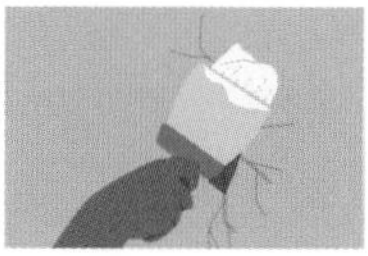

⑰ **die Füllmasse**
spackle

⑱ **der Terpentinersatz**
mineral spirits

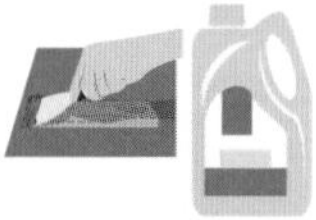

⑲ **das Abbeizmittel**
paint stripper

⑳ **der Putz**
plaster

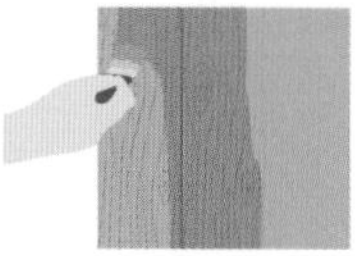

㉑ **die Grundierung**
sealer

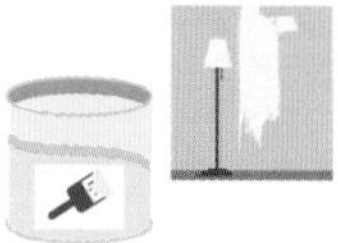

㉒ **der Voranstrich**
primer

㉓ **die Dispersionsfarbe**
paint

㉔ **die matte Farbe**
matte

㉕ **die glänzende Farbe**
gloss

㉖ **die Schablone**
stencil

㉗ **das Lösungsmittel**
solvent

㉘ **die Dichtmasse**
sealant / caulk

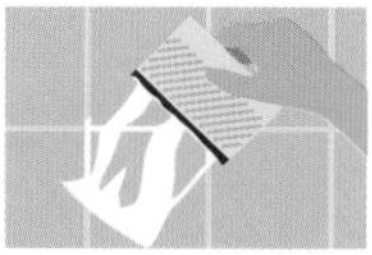

㉙ **der Fugenmörtel**
grout

㉚ **das Holzschutzmittel**
wood preserver

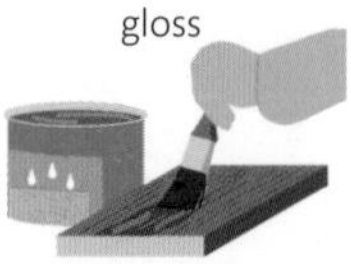

㉛ **der Lack**
varnish

See also
**32** Haus und Heim • House and home **33** Elektrizität und Sanitärtechnik • Electrics and plumbing **34** Hausarbeit • Household chores **35** Heimwerken • Home improvements

32 **die Schere**
scissors

33 **das Schrankpapier**
lining paper

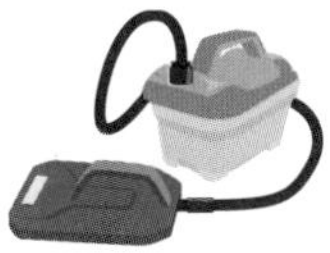

34 **der Tapetenlöser**
wallpaper stripper

35 **der Spachtel**
scraper

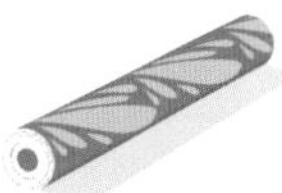

36 **die Tapetenrolle**
wallpaper roll

37 **die Tapetenbordüre**
wallpaper border

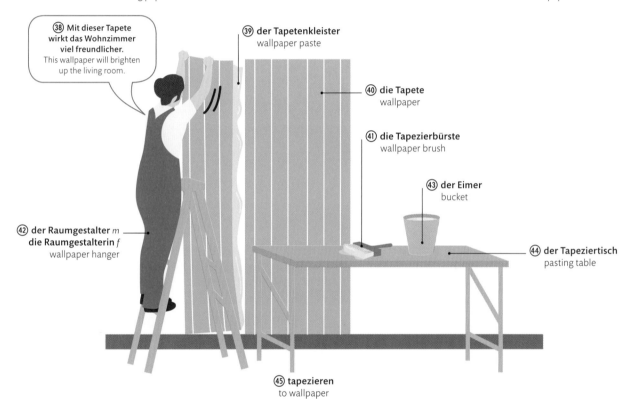

38 **Mit dieser Tapete wirkt das Wohnzimmer viel freundlicher.**
This wallpaper will brighten up the living room.

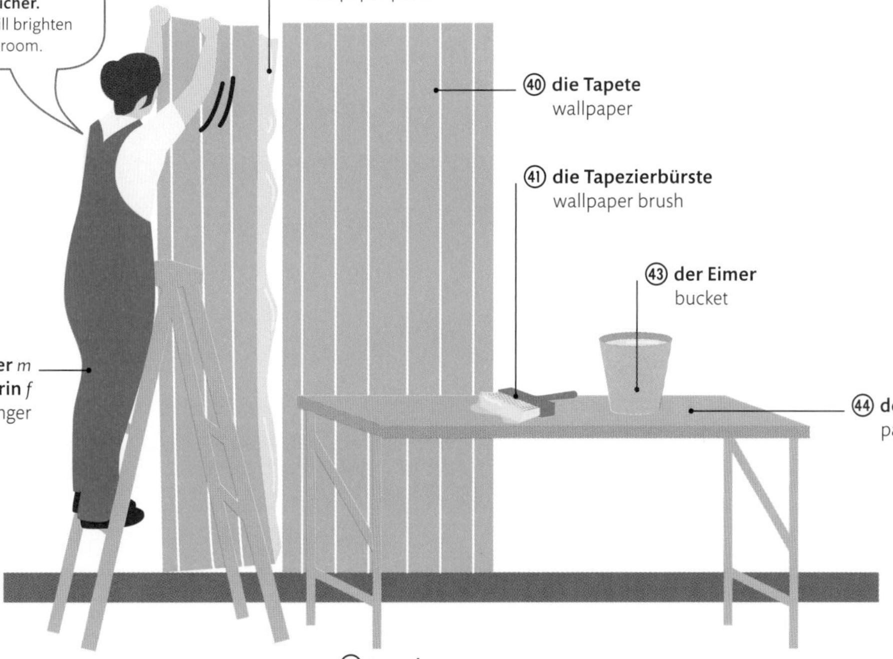

39 **der Tapetenkleister**
wallpaper paste

40 **die Tapete**
wallpaper

41 **die Tapezierbürste**
wallpaper brush

42 **der Raumgestalter** *m*
**die Raumgestalterin** *f*
wallpaper hanger

43 **der Eimer**
bucket

44 **der Tapeziertisch**
pasting table

45 **tapezieren**
to wallpaper

## 37.2 GESTALTUNGSVERBEN • VERBS FOR RENOVATION

1 **entfernen**
to strip

2 **verspachteln**
to spackle

3 **schleifen**
to sand

4 **verputzen**
to plaster

5 **aufhängen**
to hang

6 **fliesen**
to tile

# 38 Gartenpflanzen und Zimmerpflanzen
## Garden plants and houseplants

### 38.1 BLUMEN UND PFLANZEN IM GARTEN · GARDEN PLANTS AND FLOWERS

① **der Löwenzahn**
dandelion

② **die Nachtkerze**
evening primrose

③ **die Distel**
thistle

④ **die Tulpe**
tulip

⑤ **das Maiglöckchen**
lily of the valley

⑥ **die Nelke**
carnation

⑧ **das Gänseblümchen**
daisy

⑨ **die Butterblume**
buttercup

⑩ **der Mohn**
poppy

⑪ **das Stiefmütterchen**
pansy

⑫ **die Geranie**
geranium

⑬ **der Fingerhut**
foxglove

⑮ **die Lupine**
lupin

⑯ **die Rose**
rose

⑰ **die Sonnenblume**
sunflower

⑱ **die Orchidee**
orchid

⑲ **die Begonie**
begonia

⑳ **die Lilie**
lily

㉒ **das Veilchen**
violet

㉓ **der Krokus**
crocus

㉔ **die Narzisse**
daffodil

㉕ **der Flieder**
lilac

㉖ **die Gardenie**
gardenia

㉗ **der Lavendel**
lavender

㉙ **die Ringelblume**
marigold

㉚ **die Azalee**
azalea

㉛ **die Chrysantheme**
chrysanthemum

㉜ **der Rhododendron**
rhododendron

㉝ **der Hibiskus**
rose of Sharon / hibiscus

㉟ **das Geißblatt**
honeysuckle

㊱ **die Iris**
iris

㊲ **der Lotus**
lotus

㊳ **die Glyzine**
wisteria

㊴ **das Kapkörbchen**
African daisy

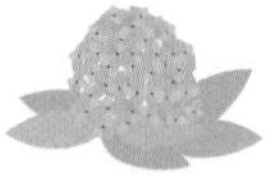
㊵ **die Hortensie**
hydrangea

See also
**39** Gartenarbeit • Practical gardening **40** Gartengeräte • Garden tools
**41** Gartenelemente Garden features **167-169** Pflanzen und Bäume • Plants and trees

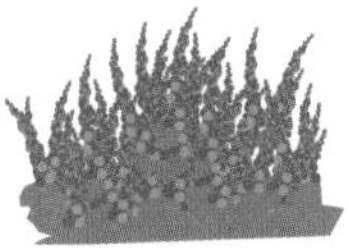
⑦ **das Heidekraut**
heather

⑭ **die Kamelie**
camellia

㉑ **das Pampasgras**
pampas grass

㉘ **die Protea**
protea

㉞ **der Rosmarin**
rosemary

㊶ **der Lorbeerbaum**
bay tree

## 38.2 ZIMMERPFLANZEN • HOUSEPLANTS

① **das Einblatt**
peace lily

② **der Bogenhanf**
snake plant

③ **die Grünlilie**
spider plant

④ **die Palmlilie**
yucca

⑤ **der Drachenbaum**
dragon tree

⑥ **der Bonsai**
bonsai tree

⑦ **das Köstliche Fensterblatt**
Swiss cheese plant

⑧ **die Sukkulenten** *f, pl*
succulents

⑨ **der Chinesische Geldbaum**
Chinese money plant

⑩ **der Gummibaum**
rubber plant

⑪ **das Schildblatt**
umbrella plant

⑫ **die Punktblume**
polka dot plant

⑬ **die Efeutute**
marble queen

⑭ **die Efeutute**
jade pothos

## 38.3 DER BLÜTENAUFBAU • FLOWER ANATOMY

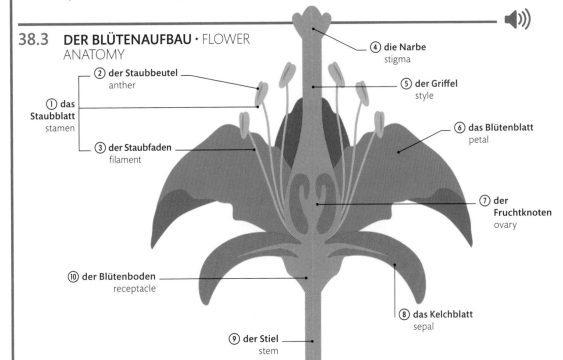

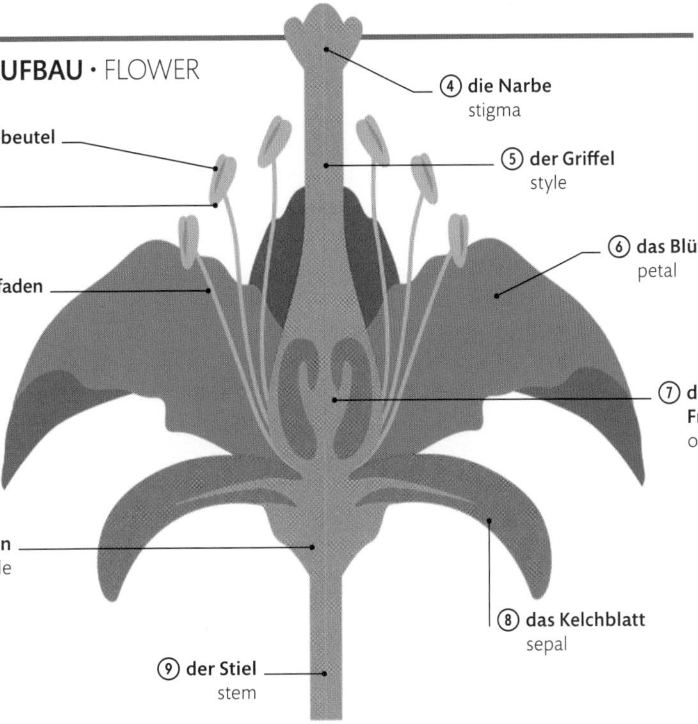

# 39 Gartenarbeit
## Practical gardening

### 39.1 VERBEN FÜR DIE GARTENARBEIT · GARDENING VERBS

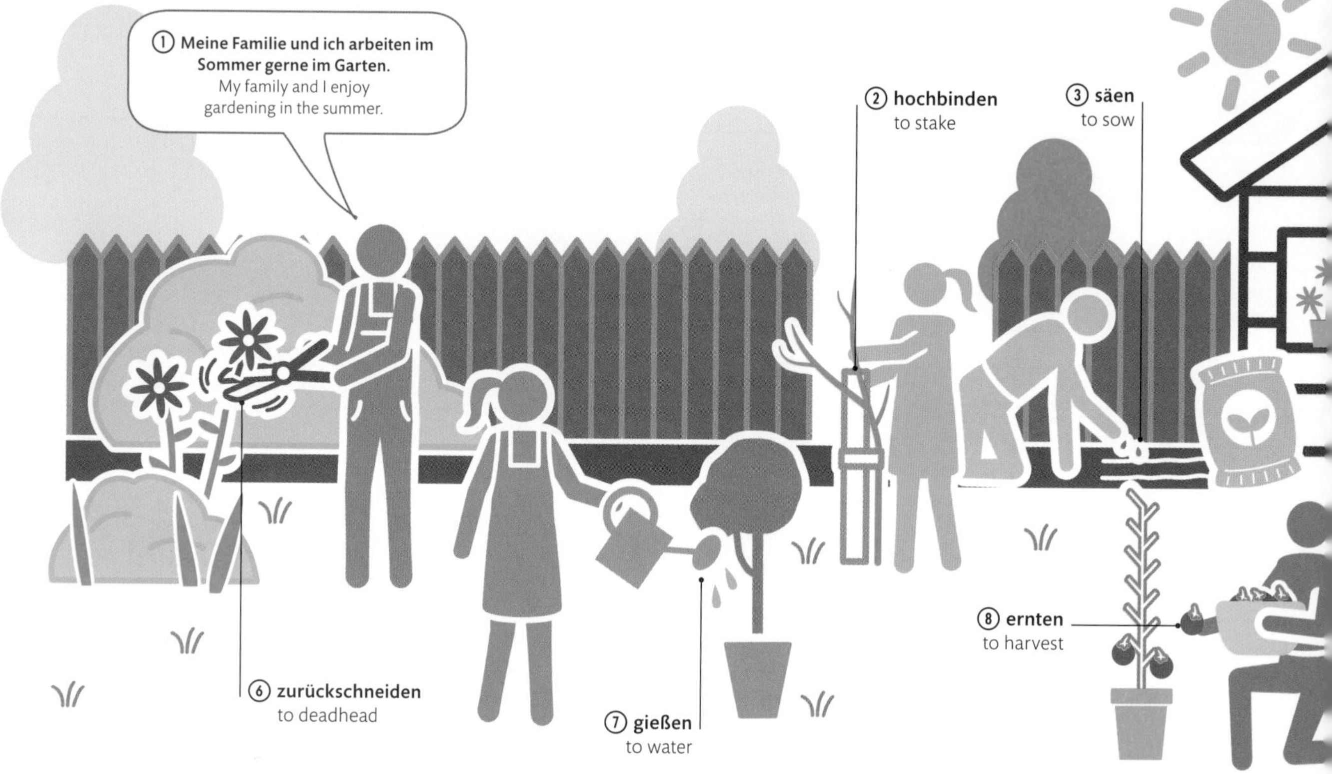

⑮ **den Rasen mähen**
to mow the lawn

⑯ **Gras verlegen**
to lay sod

⑰ **rechen**
to rake (soil)

⑱ **zusammenrechen**
to rake (leaves)

⑲ **belüften**
to aerate

⑳ **das Frühbeet**
cold frame

㉔ **aufpfropfen**
to graft

㉕ **vermehren**
to propagate

㉖ **anpflanzen**
to plant

㉗ **mulchen**
to mulch

㉘ **das Unkraut jäten**
to do the weeding

㉙ **umsetzen**
to transplant

㉞ **kultivieren**
to cultivate

㉟ **zuschneiden**
to trim

㊱ **stutzen**
to prune

㊲ **fällen**
to chop

㊳ **sieben**
to sieve

㊴ **den Garten gestalten**
to landscape

See also
**38** Gartenpflanzen und Zimmerpflanzen • Garden plants and houseplants **40** Gartengeräte Garden tools **41** Gartenelemente • Garden features **167-69** Pflanzen und Bäume • Plants and trees

④ **der Gartenschuppen**
potting shed

⑤ **graben**
to dig

⑨ **umtopfen**
to pot

⑩ **das Knochenmehl**
bone meal

⑪ **der Ableger**
plant cutting

⑫ **das Gewächshaus**
greenhouse

⑬ **der Schuppen**
shed

⑭ **die Entwässerung**
drainage

㉑ **oberflächlich düngen**
to top dress

㉒ **pflegen**
to tend

㉓ **am Spalier aufziehen**
to train

㉚ **einsprühen**
to spray

㉛ **der Flüssigdünger**
plant food

㉜ **Bio-**
organic

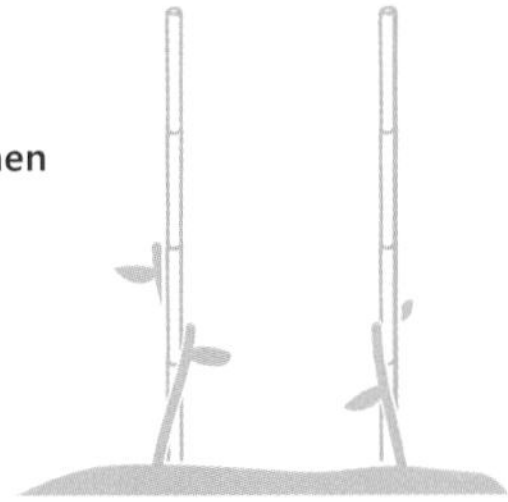

㉝ **die Rankhilfe**
training / support cane

㊵ **der Dünger**
fertilizer

㊶ **düngen**
to fertilize

㊷ **der Unkrautvernichter**
weedkiller

## 39.2 BODENARTEN
TYPES OF SOIL

② **die Humusschicht**
topsoil

① **der Boden**
soil

③ **der Unterboden**
subsoil

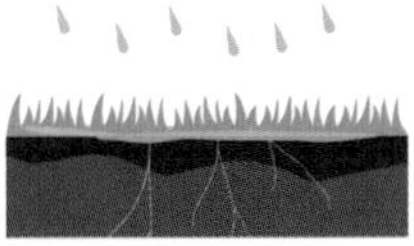

④ **die Versickerung**
leaching

⑤ **die Oberfläche**
surface

⑥ **der Lehm**
loam

⑦ **der Torf**
peat

⑧ **der Kalk**
chalk

⑨ **der Sand**
sand

⑩ **der Schluff**
silt

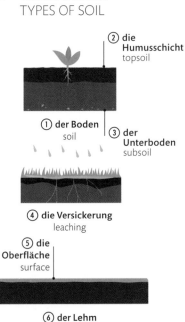

⑪ **der Ton**
clay

# 40 Gartengeräte
## Garden tools

### 40.1 **GARTENGERÄTE** · GARDENING EQUIPMENT

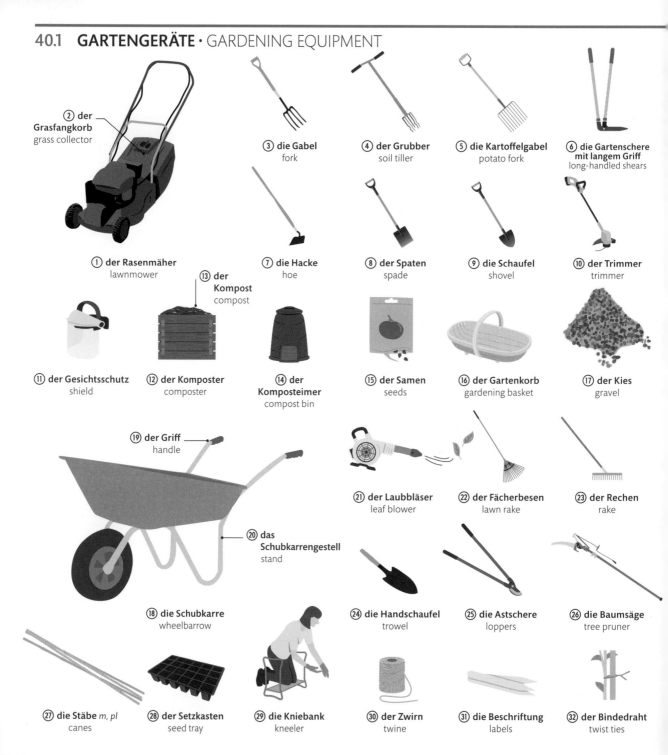

② **der Grasfangkorb**
grass collector

① **der Rasenmäher**
lawnmower

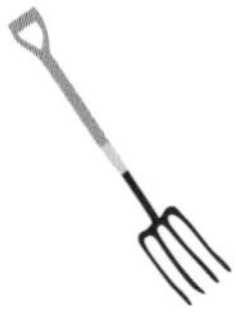

③ **die Gabel**
fork

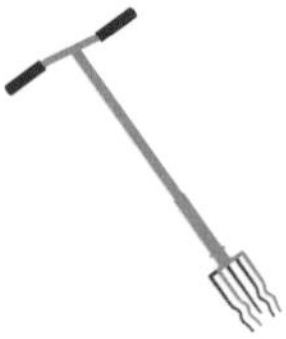

④ **der Grubber**
soil tiller

⑤ **die Kartoffelgabel**
potato fork

⑥ **die Gartenschere mit langem Griff**
long-handled shears

⑦ **die Hacke**
hoe

⑧ **der Spaten**
spade

⑨ **die Schaufel**
shovel

⑩ **der Trimmer**
trimmer

⑪ **der Gesichtsschutz**
shield

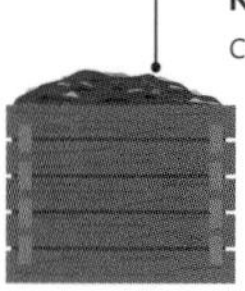

⑬ **der Kompost**
compost

⑫ **der Komposter**
composter

⑭ **der Komposteimer**
compost bin

⑮ **der Samen**
seeds

⑯ **der Gartenkorb**
gardening basket

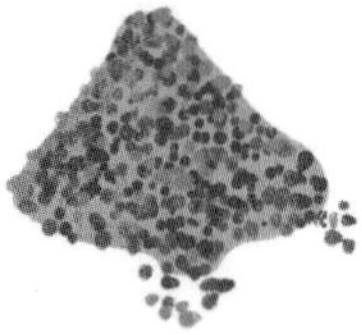

⑰ **der Kies**
gravel

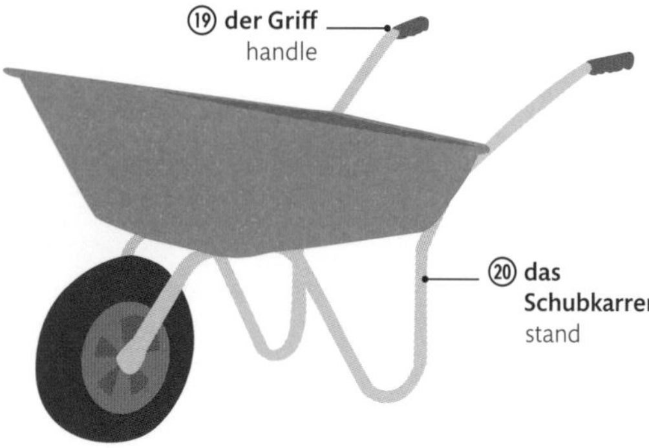

⑲ **der Griff**
handle

⑳ **das Schubkarrengestell**
stand

⑱ **die Schubkarre**
wheelbarrow

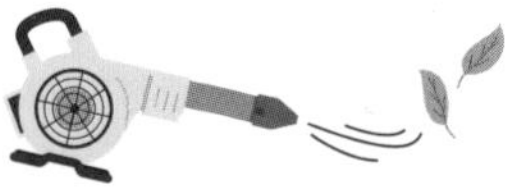

㉑ **der Laubbläser**
leaf blower

㉒ **der Fächerbesen**
lawn rake

㉓ **der Rechen**
rake

㉔ **die Handschaufel**
trowel

㉕ **die Astschere**
loppers

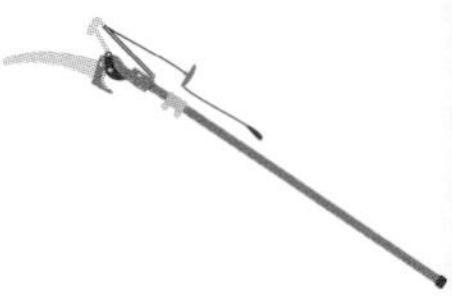

㉖ **die Baumsäge**
tree pruner

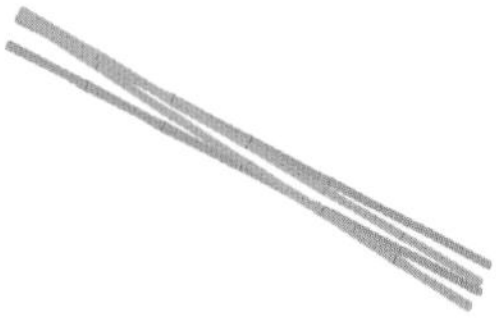

㉗ **die Stäbe** *m, pl*
canes

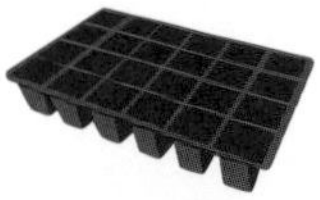

㉘ **der Setzkasten**
seed tray

㉙ **die Kniebank**
kneeler

㉚ **der Zwirn**
twine

㉛ **die Beschriftung**
labels

㉜ **der Bindedraht**
twist ties

See also
**38** Gartenpflanzen und Zimmerpflanzen • Garden plants and houseplants **39** Gartenarbeit • Practical gardening **41** Gartenelemente • Garden features **167-169** Pflanzen und Bäume • Plants and trees

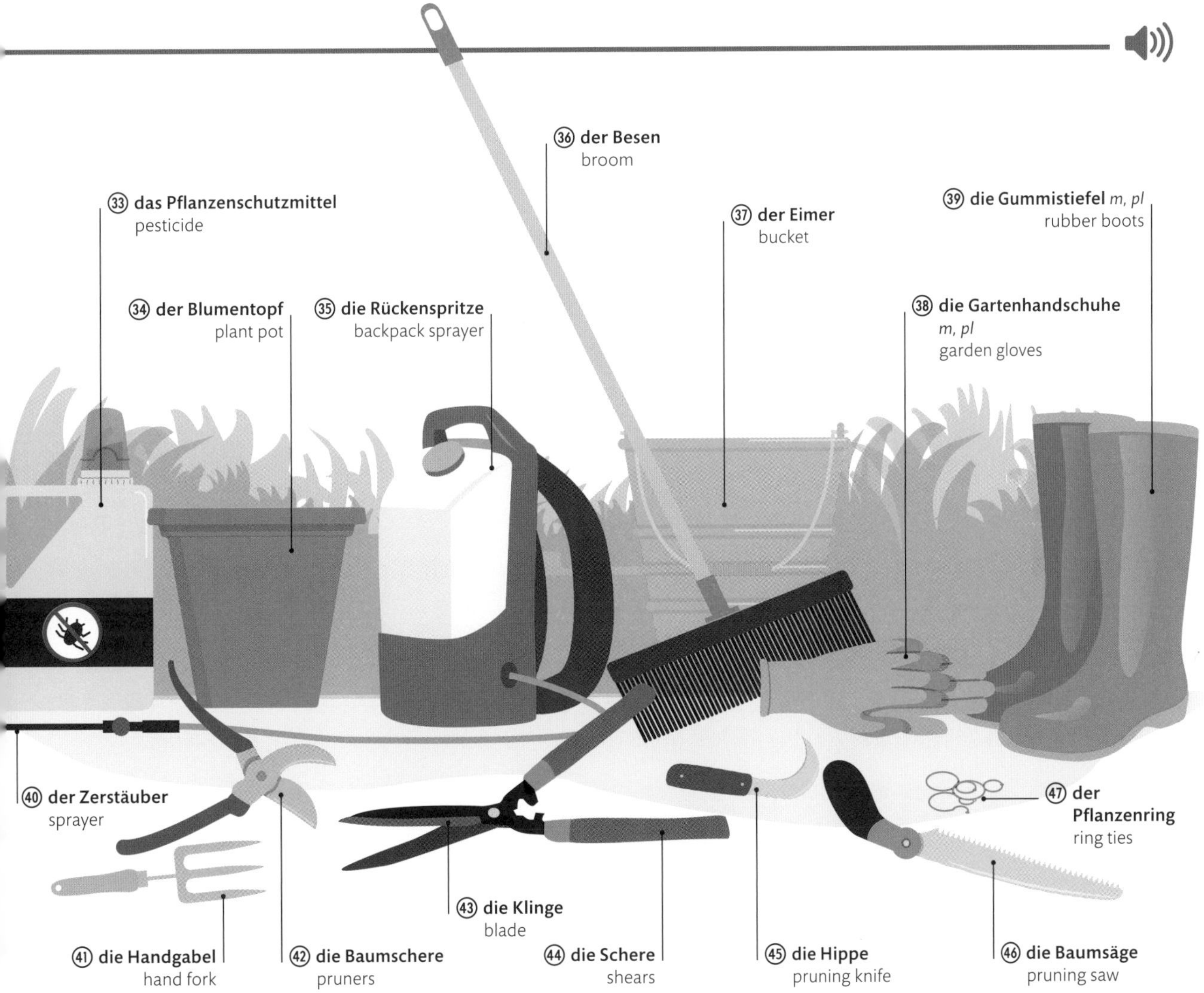


## 40.2 GIESSEN • WATERING

1 **die Gießkanne**
watering can

2 **der Sprühkopf**
spray nozzle

3 **der Rasensprenger**
sprinkler

4 **die Schlauchtrommel**
hose reel

5 **die Düse**
nozzle

6 **der Gartenschlauch**
garden hose

# 41 Gartenelemente
## Garden features

### 41.1 GARTENTYPEN UND GARTENELEMENTE · GARDEN TYPES AND FEATURES

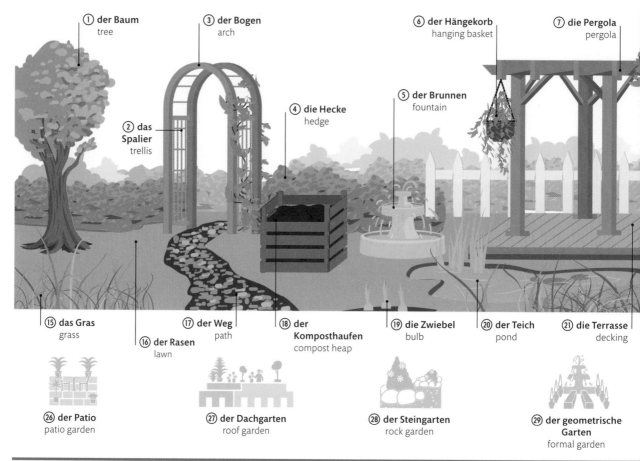

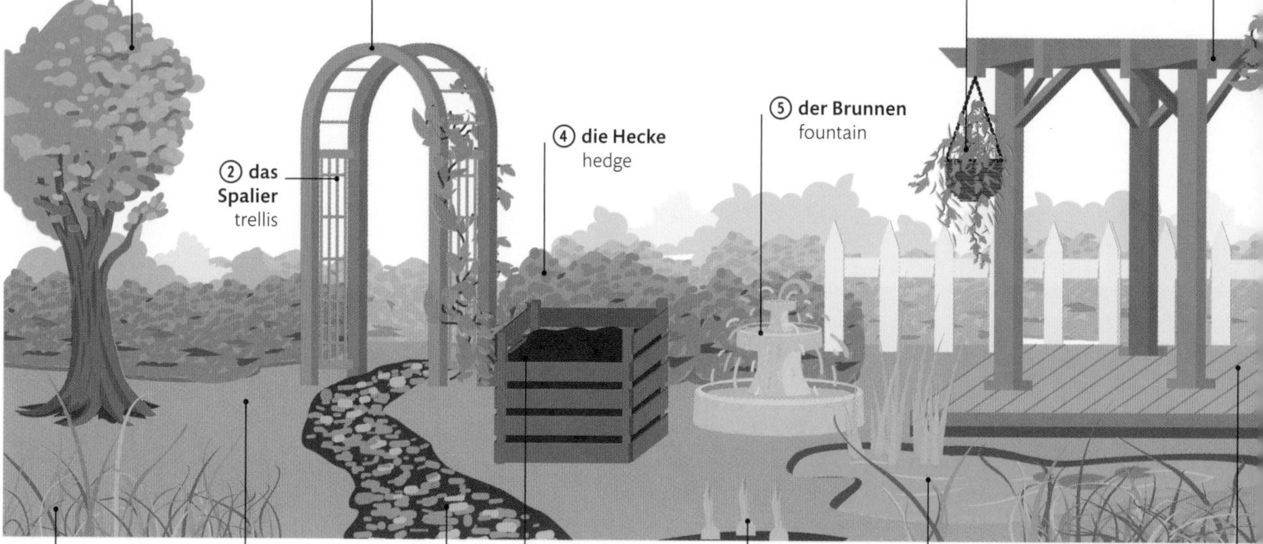

㉖ **der Patio**
patio garden

㉗ **der Dachgarten**
roof garden

㉘ **der Steingarten**
rock garden

㉙ **der geometrische Garten**
formal garden

### 41.2 PFLANZENARTEN · TYPES OF PLANTS

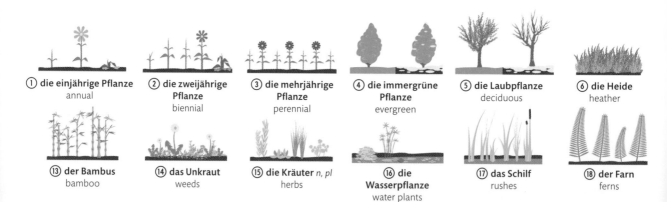

① **die einjährige Pflanze**
annual

② **die zweijährige Pflanze**
biennial

③ **die mehrjährige Pflanze**
perennial

④ **die immergrüne Pflanze**
evergreen

⑤ **die Laubpflanze**
deciduous

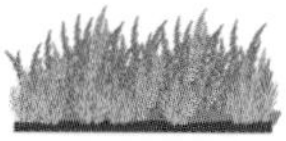

⑥ **die Heide**
heather

⑬ **der Bambus**
bamboo

⑭ **das Unkraut**
weeds

⑮ **die Kräuter** *n, pl*
herbs

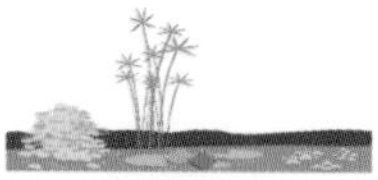

⑯ **die Wasserpflanze**
water plants

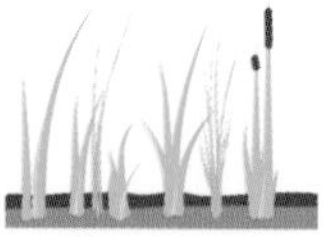

⑰ **das Schilf**
rushes

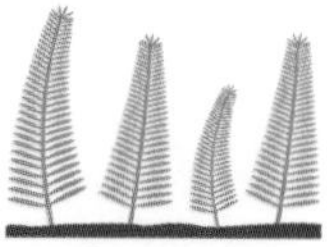

⑱ **der Farn**
ferns

See also
**38** Gartenpflanzen und Zimmerpflanzen • Garden plants and houseplants **39** Gartenarbeit • Practical gardening **40** Gartengeräte • Garden tools **167-169** Pflanzen und Bäume • Plants and trees

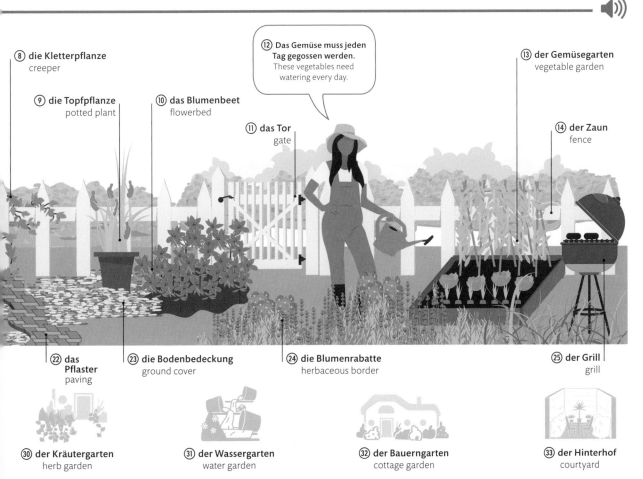

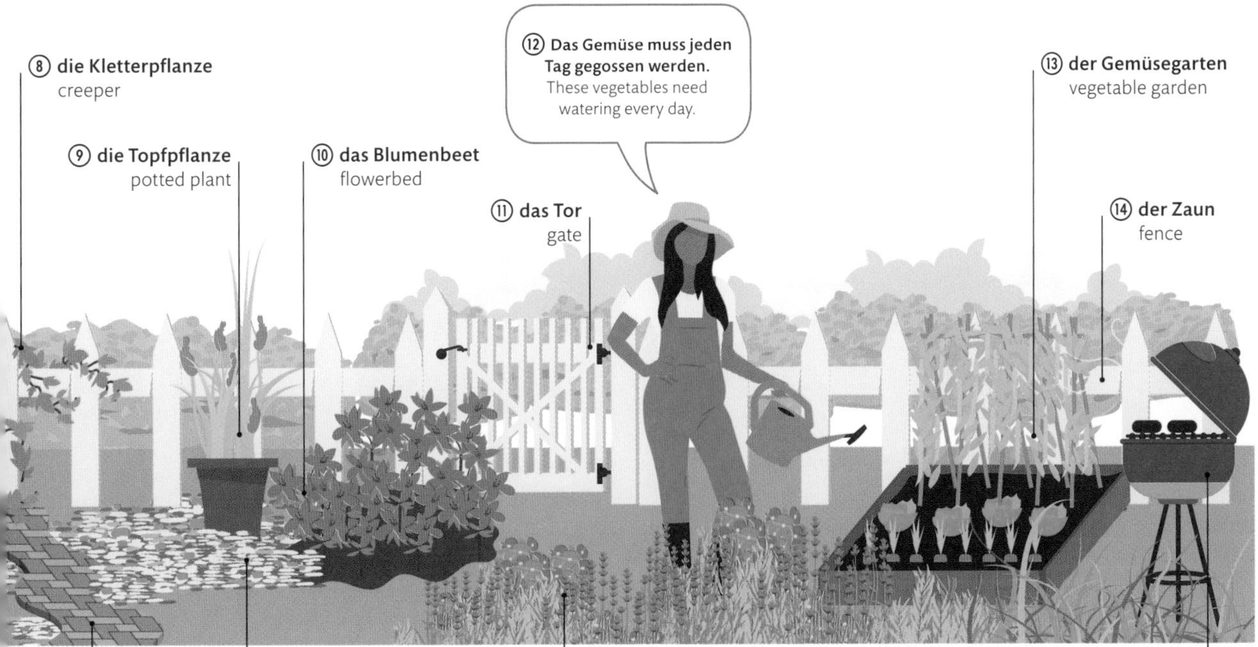

㉚ **der Kräutergarten**
herb garden

㉛ **der Wassergarten**
water garden

㉜ **der Bauerngarten**
cottage garden

㉝ **der Hinterhof**
courtyard

⑦ **die Palme**
palms

⑧ **der Nadelbaum**
conifers

⑨ **der Formschnitt**
topiary

⑩ **die Kletterpflanze**
climber

⑪ **die Zierpflanze**
ornamental plants

⑫ **die Schattenpflanze**
shade plants

⑲ **die Gebirgspflanze**
alpine plants

⑳ **die Sukkulente**
succulents

㉑ **der Kaktus**
cacti

㉒ **das Gebüsch**
shrubs

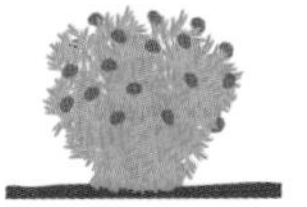

㉓ **der Blütenstrauch**
flowering shrub

㉔ **die Gräser** *n, pl*
grasses

# 42 In der Stadt
## In town

### 42.1 GEBÄUDE UND ANDERE MERKMALE
BUILDINGS AND OTHER FEATURES

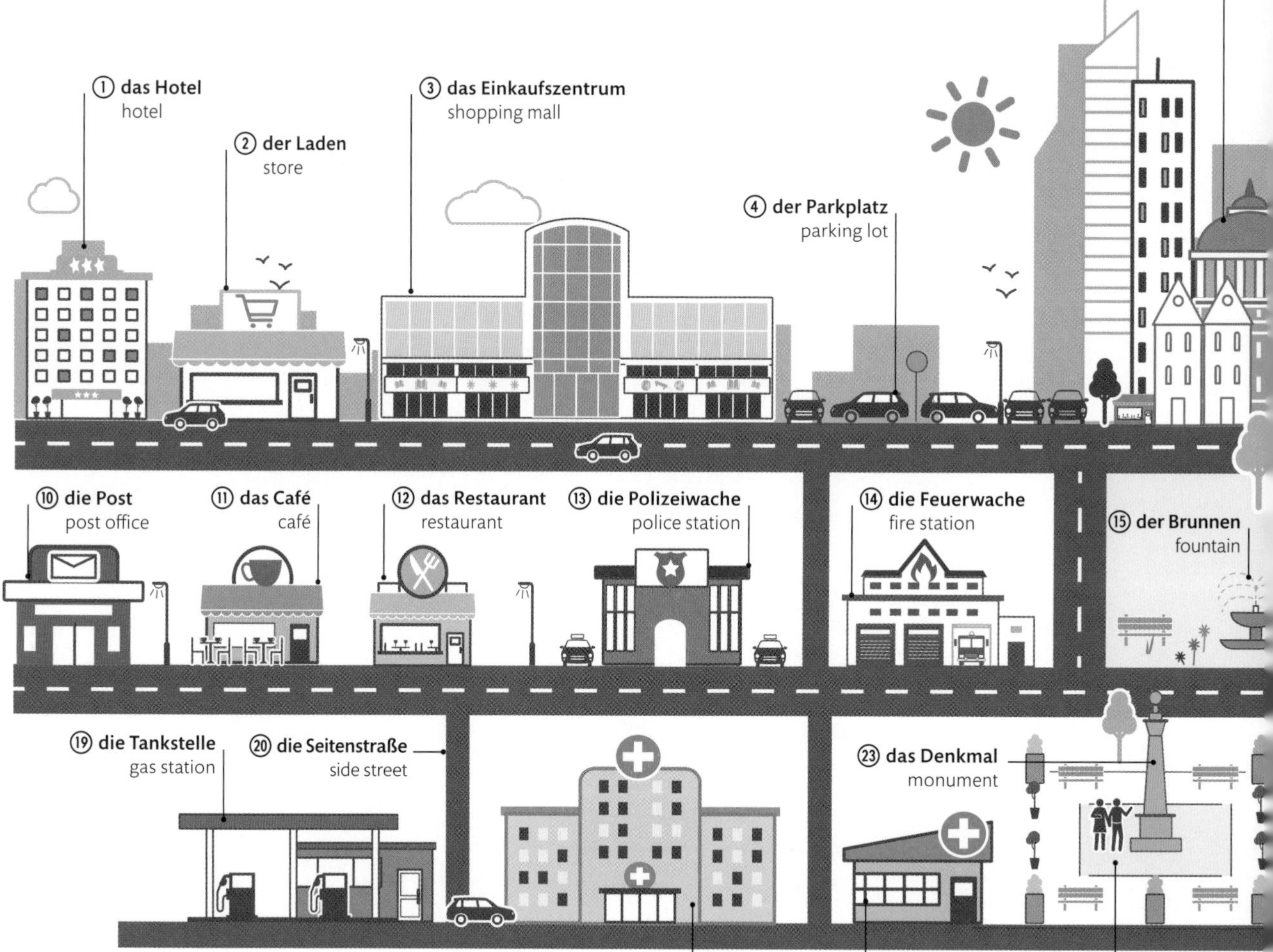

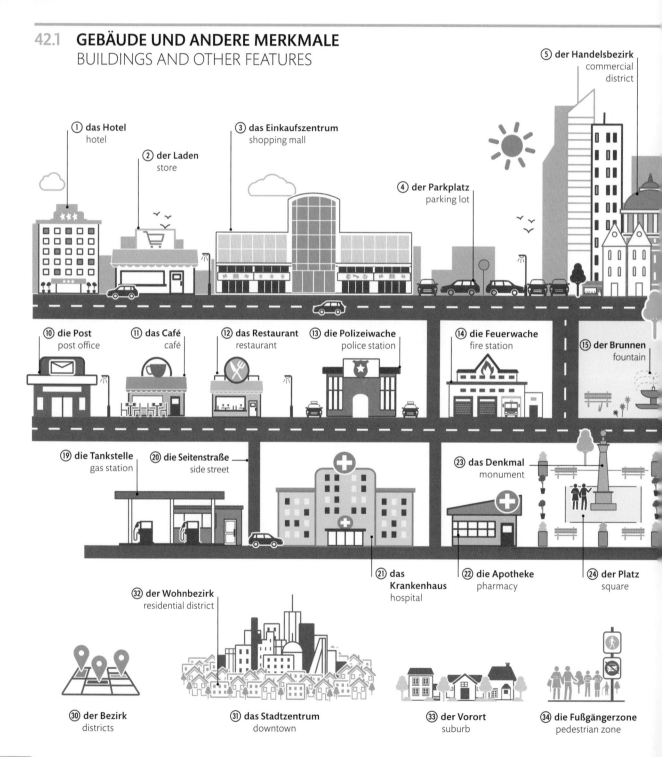

- ① **das Hotel** – hotel
- ② **der Laden** – store
- ③ **das Einkaufszentrum** – shopping mall
- ④ **der Parkplatz** – parking lot
- ⑤ **der Handelsbezirk** – commercial district
- ⑩ **die Post** – post office
- ⑪ **das Café** – café
- ⑫ **das Restaurant** – restaurant
- ⑬ **die Polizeiwache** – police station
- ⑭ **die Feuerwache** – fire station
- ⑮ **der Brunnen** – fountain
- ⑲ **die Tankstelle** – gas station
- ⑳ **die Seitenstraße** – side street
- ㉑ **das Krankenhaus** – hospital
- ㉒ **die Apotheke** – pharmacy
- ㉓ **das Denkmal** – monument
- ㉔ **der Platz** – square

㉚ **der Bezirk**
districts

㉜ **der Wohnbezirk**
residential district

㉛ **das Stadtzentrum**
downtown

㉝ **der Vorort**
suburb

㉞ **die Fußgängerzone**
pedestrian zone

See also
**25** Ein Ort zum Leben • A place to live **43** In der Stadt (Forsetzung) • In town continued **44** Gebäude und Architektur • Buildings and architecture **46** Einkaufen • Shopping **47** Im Einkaufszentrum • The shopping mall **102** Züge • Trains **104** Am Flughafen • At the airport **106** Der Hafen • The port

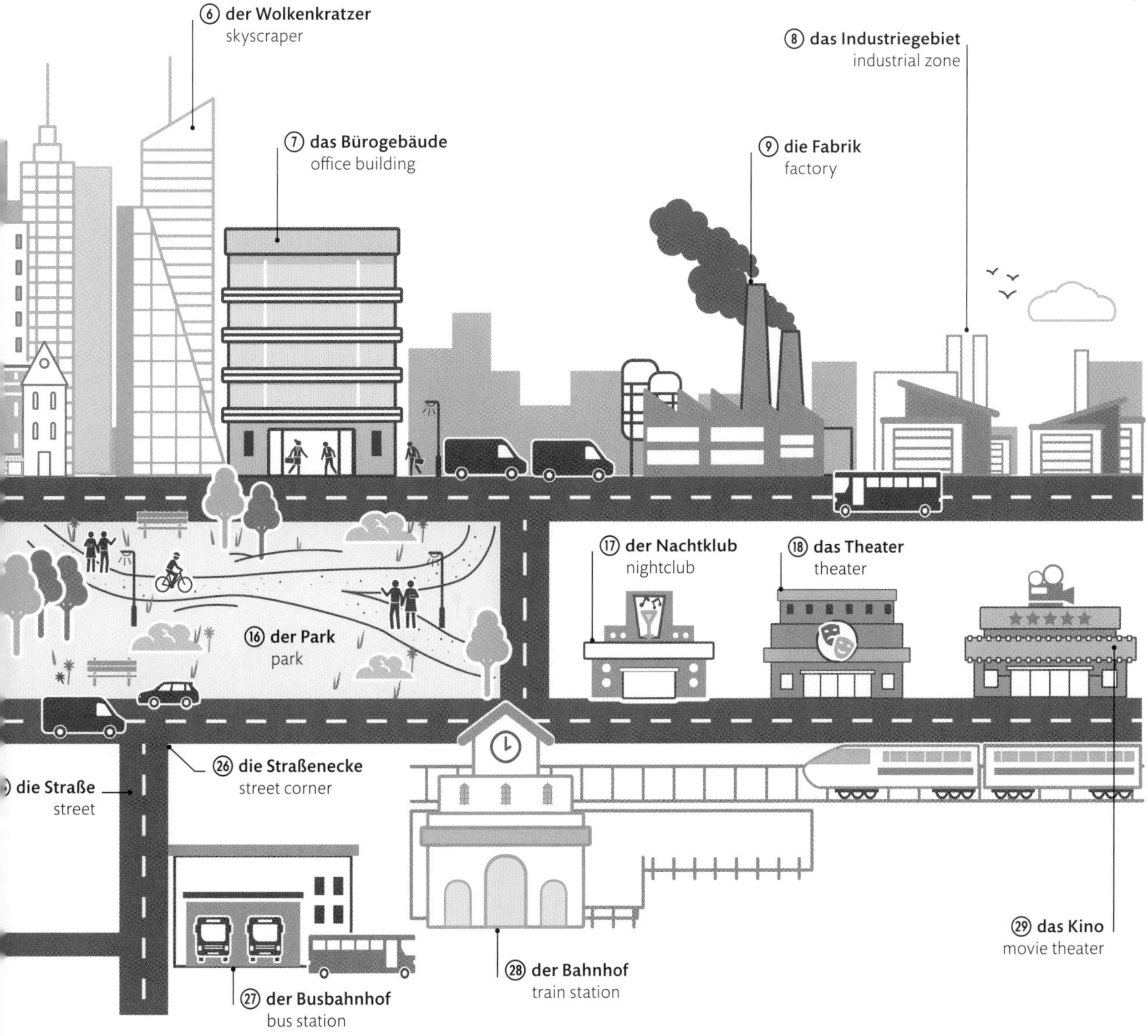

㉟ **die Gasse**
alley

㊱ **der Berufsverkehr**
rush hour

㊲ **die Einbahnstraße**
one-way system

㊳ **die Touristeninformation**
tourist office

# In der Stadt (Fortsetzung)
In town continued

## 43.1 GEBÄUDE UND ANDERE MERKMALE • BUILDINGS AND OTHER FEATURES

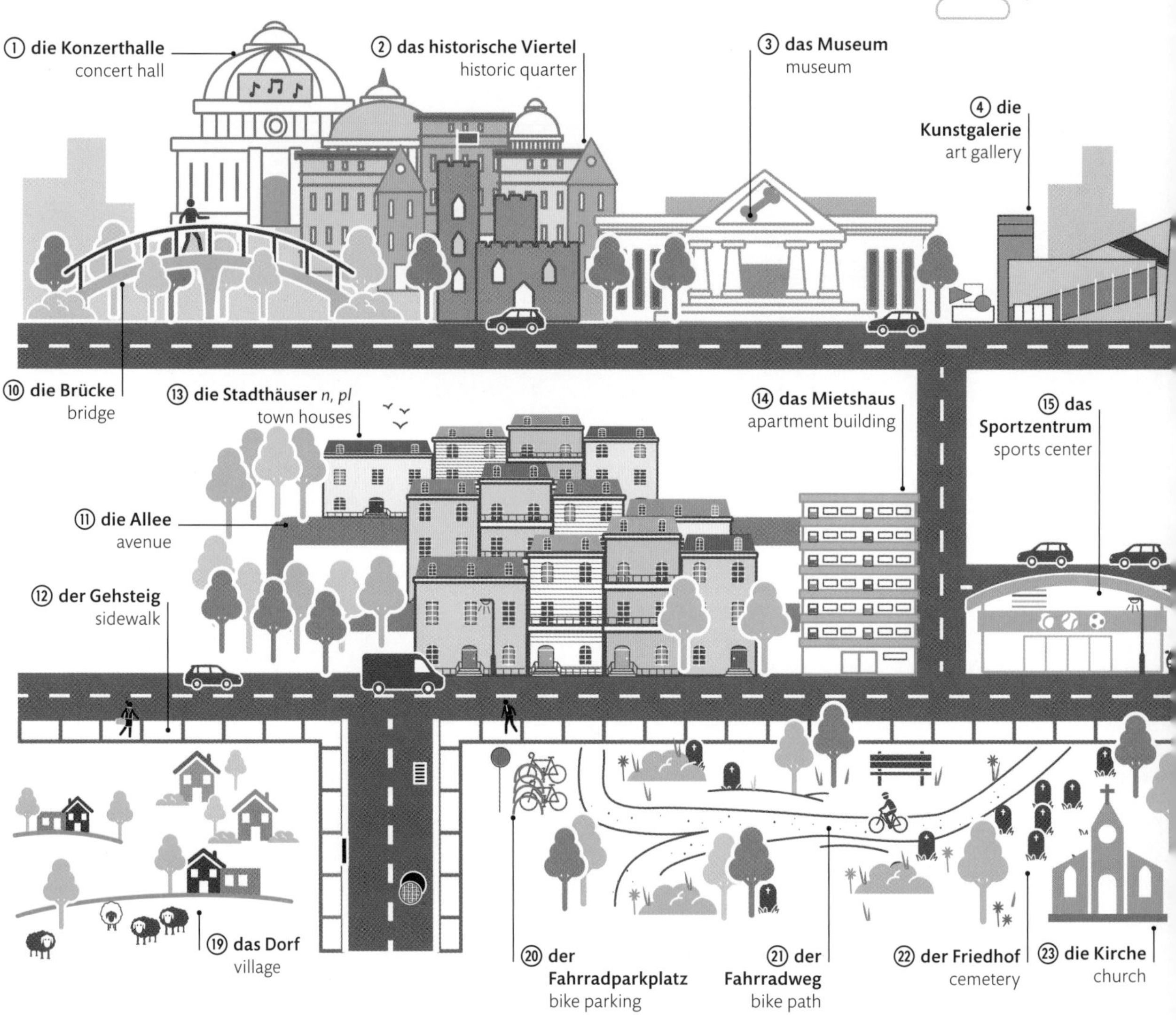

㉚ das Einsteigloch
manhole

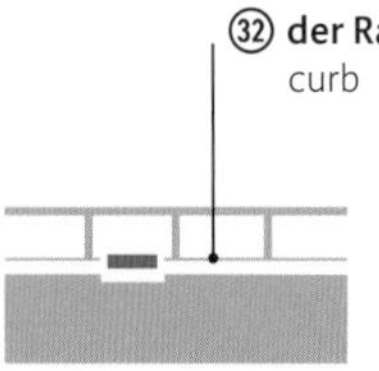


㉛ die Rinne
gutter

㉝ der Abfluss
drain

㉞ das Straßenschild
street sign

㉟ der Poller
bollards

See also
**25** Ein Ort zum Leben • A place to live **44** Gebäude und Architektur • Buildings and architecture
**46** Einkaufen • Shopping **47** Im Einkaufszentrum • The shopping mall **102** Züge • Trains
**104** Am Flughafen • At the airport **106** Der Hafen • The port

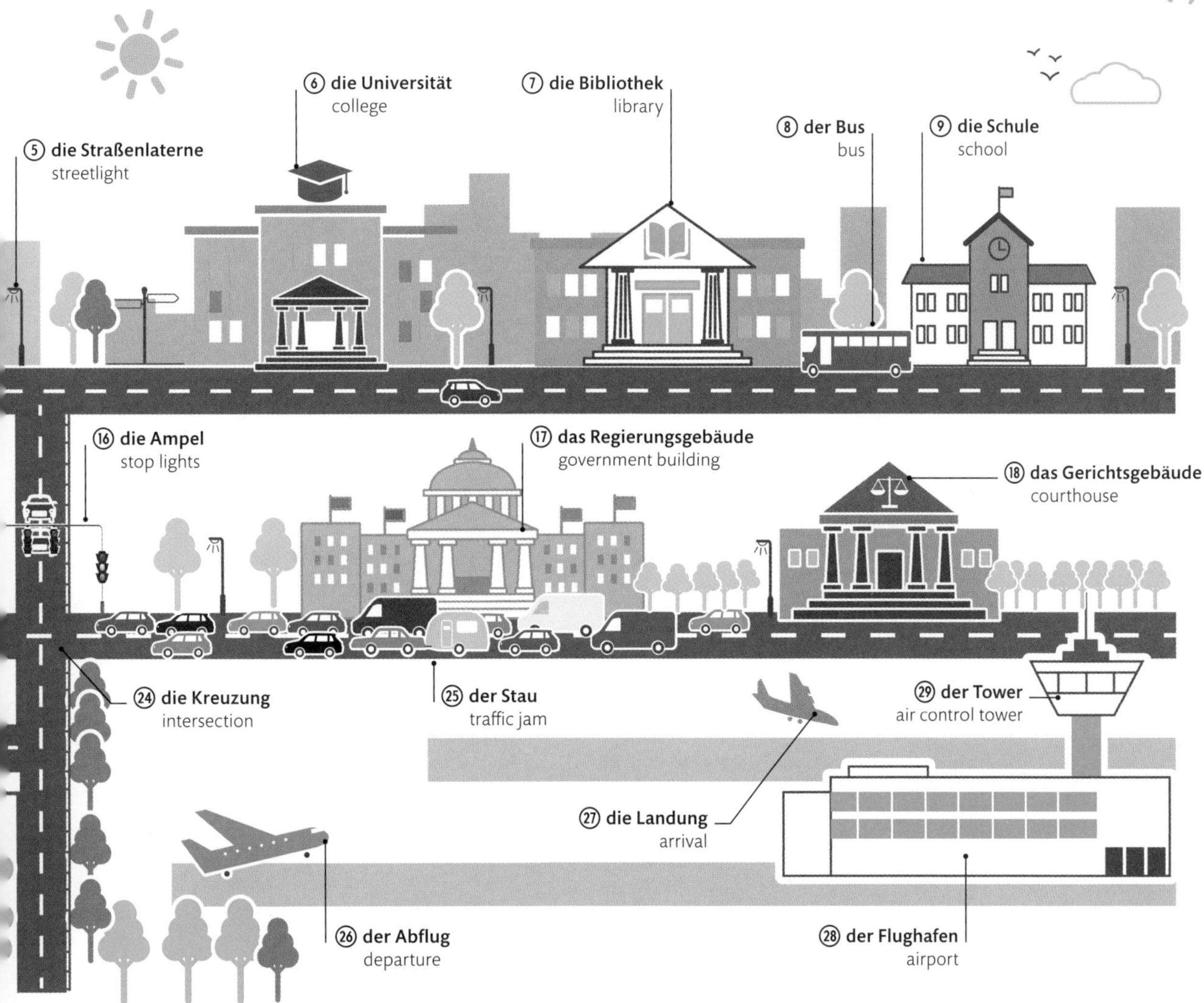


## 43.2 DER SPIELPLATZ • PLAYGROUND

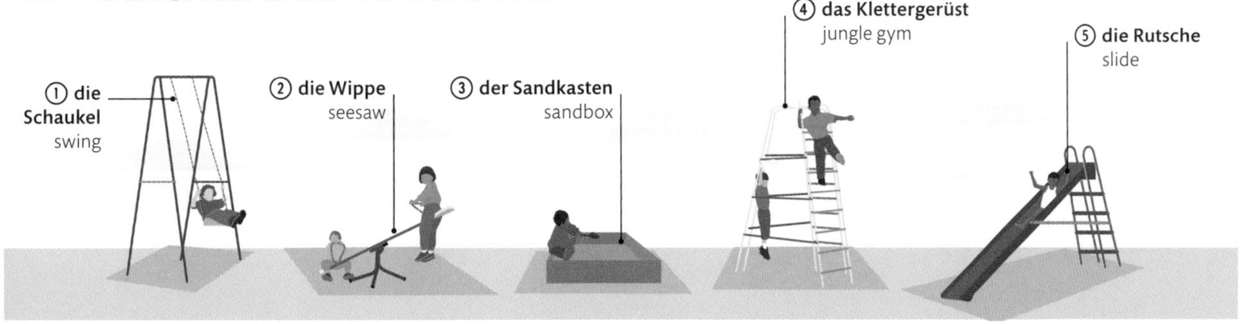

# 44 Gebäude und Architektur
## Buildings and architecture

### 44.1 GEBÄUDETYPEN · TYPES OF BUILDINGS

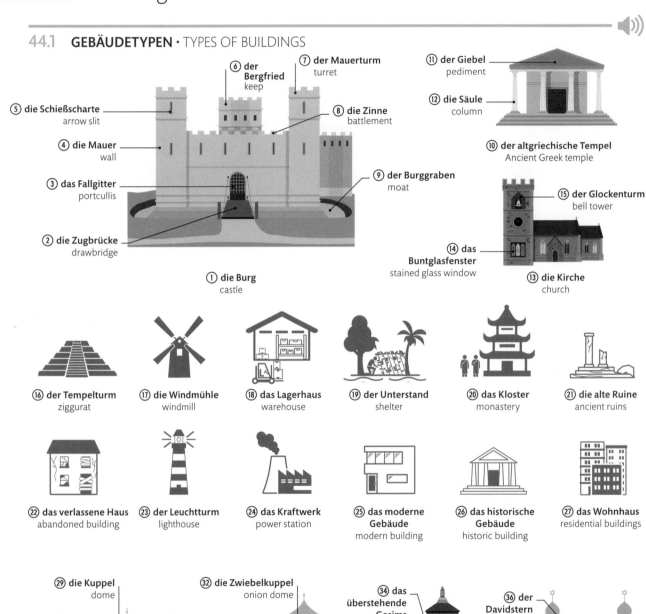

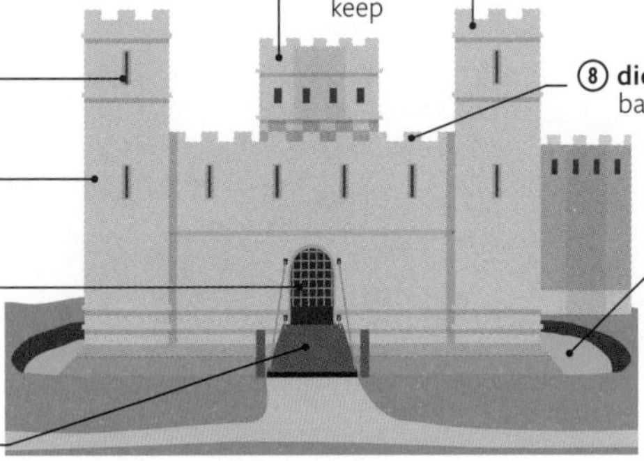


① **die Burg**
castle

⑩ **der altgriechische Tempel**
Ancient Greek temple

⑬ **die Kirche**
church

⑯ **der Tempelturm**
ziggurat

⑰ **die Windmühle**
windmill

⑱ **das Lagerhaus**
warehouse

⑲ **der Unterstand**
shelter

⑳ **das Kloster**
monastery

㉑ **die alte Ruine**
ancient ruins

㉒ **das verlassene Haus**
abandoned building

㉓ **der Leuchtturm**
lighthouse

㉔ **das Kraftwerk**
power station

㉕ **das moderne Gebäude**
modern building

㉖ **das historische Gebäude**
historic building

㉗ **das Wohnhaus**
residential buildings

㉘ **die Moschee**
mosque

㉛ **die orthodoxe Kirche**
Orthodox church

㉝ **der Tempel**
temple

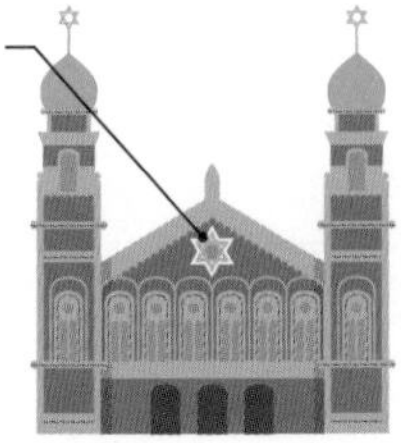


㉟ **die Synagoge**
synagogue

See also
**25** Ein Ort zum Leben • A place to live **32** Haus und Heim • House and home **42-43** In der Stadt • In town **132** Sightseeing • Sightseeing

## 44.2 BERÜHMTE GEBÄUDE UND DENKMÄLER • FAMOUS BUILDINGS AND MONUMENTS

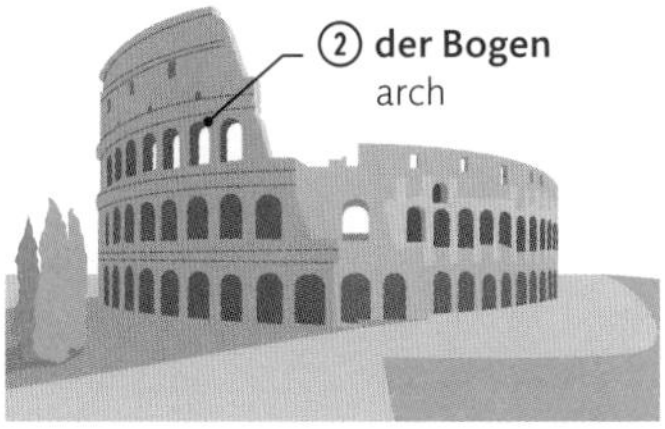


① **das Kolosseum**
the Colosseum

③ **die Pyramiden von Giseh**
the Pyramids of Giza

④ **die Große Moschee von Djenné**
the Great Mosque of Djenné

⑦ **das Weiße Haus**
the White House

⑧ **das Taj Mahal**
the Taj Mahal

⑨ **die Verbotene Stadt**
the Forbidden City

⑩ **die Basilius-Kathedrale**
St. Basil's cathedral

⑪ **das Opernhaus von Sydney**
Sydney Opera House

⑫ **die Burg von Himeji**
Himeji Castle

⑬ **der Big Ben**
Big Ben

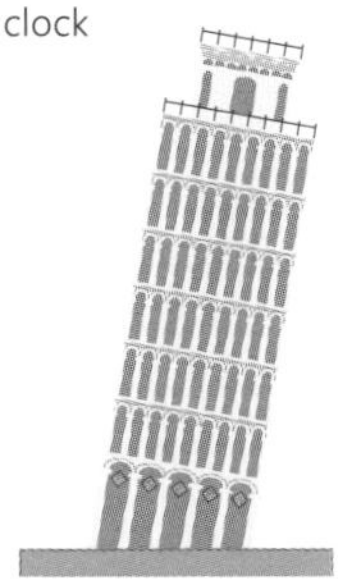

⑮ **der Schiefe Turm von Pisa**
the Leaning Tower of Pisa

⑯ **der Eiffelturm**
the Eiffel Tower

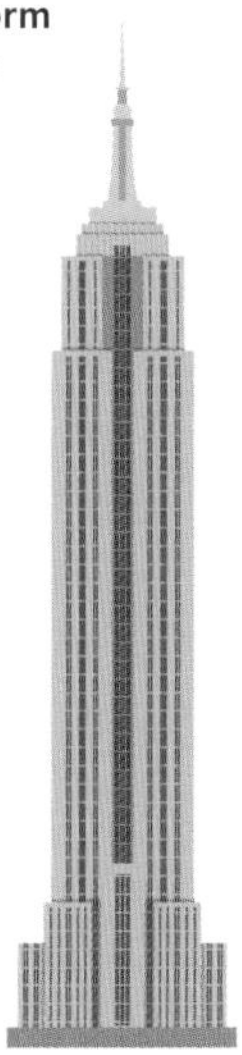

⑱ **das Empire State Building**
the Empire State Building

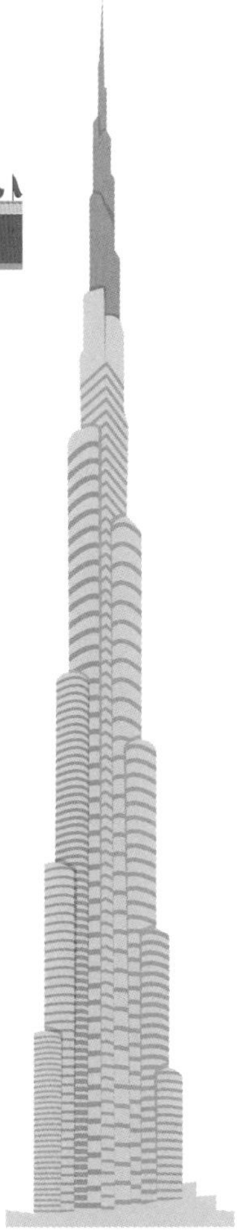

⑲ **der Burj Khalifa**
Burj Khalifa

# 45 Bank und Post
## The bank and post office

### 45.1 DIE BANK · BANK

① **der Filialleiter** *m* **die Filialleiterin** *f*
branch manager

② **der Bankmitarbeiter** *m* **die Bankmitarbeiterin** *f*
cashier

③ **Ich möchte gerne $400 auf mein Sparkonto einzahlen.**
I'd like to deposit $400 into my savings account.

④ **einzahlen**
to deposit

⑤ **der Schalter**
counter

⑥ **der Kunde** *m* **die Kundin** *f*
customer

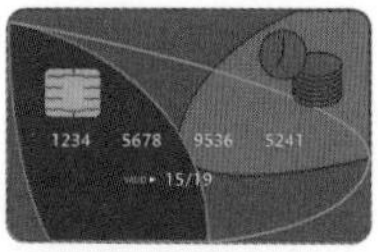


⑦ **die Kreditkarte**
credit card

⑧ **die Debitkarte**
debit card

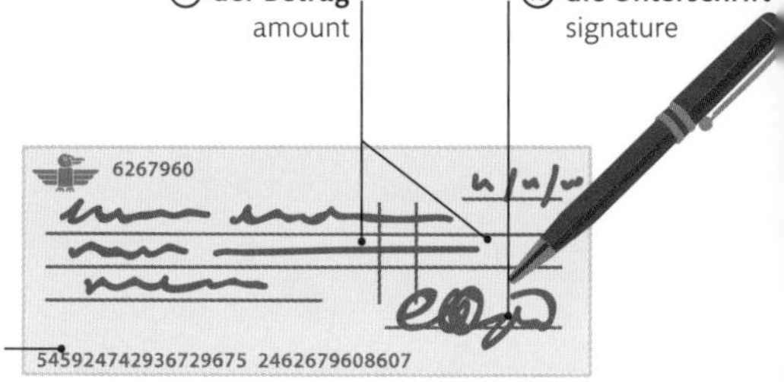


⑨ **der Betrag**
amount

⑩ **die Unterschrift**
signature

⑪ **die Kontonummer**
account number

⑫ **der Scheck**
check

⑬ **das Sparkonto**
savings account

⑭ **die Ersparnisse** *n, pl*
savings

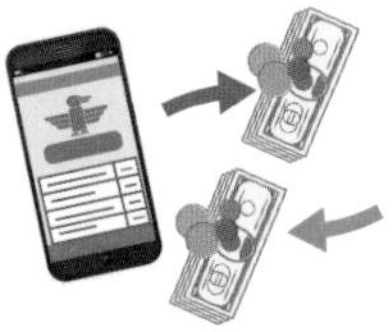

⑮ **das Girokonto**
checking account

⑯ **die Lastschrift**
direct debit

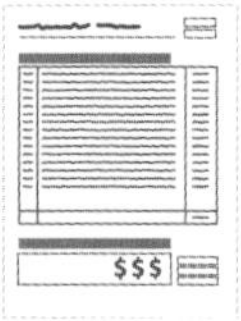


⑰ **der Kontoauszug**
bank statement

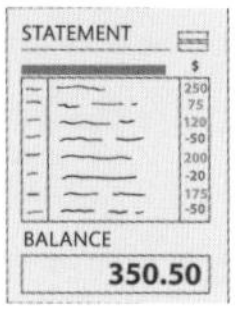


⑱ **schwarze Zahlen schreiben**
in the black / in credit

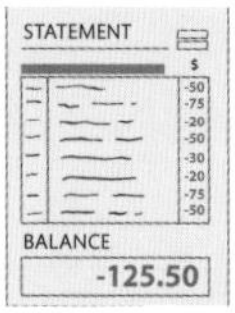


⑲ **rote Zahlen schreiben / Schulden haben**
in the red / in debt

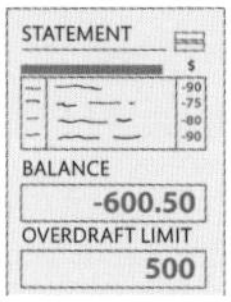


⑳ **der Dispo**
overdraft

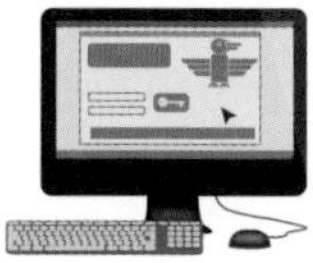

㉑ **das Online-Banking**
online banking

㉒ **der Zinssatz**
interest rate

㉓ **das Darlehen**
bank loan

㉔ **der Immobilienkredit**
mortgage

㉕ **Geld abheben**
to withdraw money

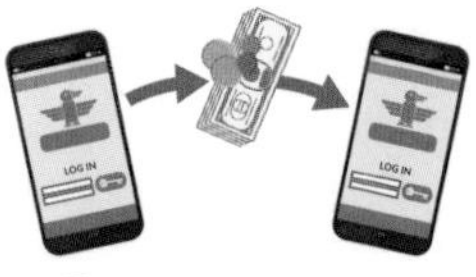


㉖ **Geld überweisen**
to transfer money

See also
**94** Geld und Finanzen • Money and finance
**131** Reise und Unterkunft • Travel and accommodation

## 45.2 DAS GELD • MONEY

① **die Währung**
currency

② **die Münze**
coins

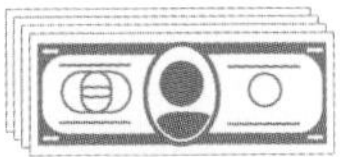

③ **der Geldschein**
bills

④ **die PIN**
PIN

⑤ **das Kartenlesegerät**
card machine

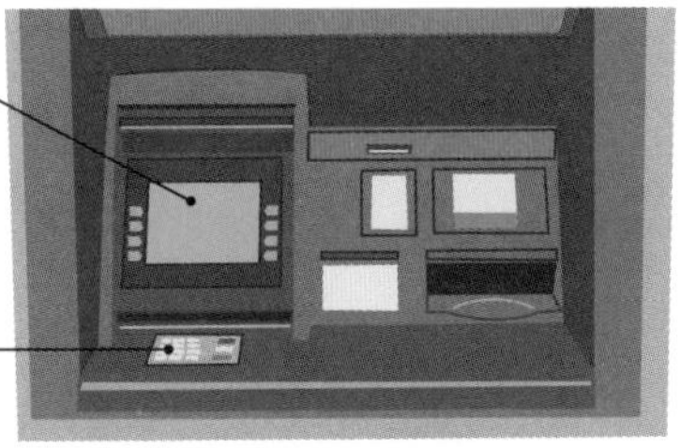

⑥ **der Bildschirm**
screen

⑦ **die Tastatur**
keypad

⑧ **der Geldautomat**
cash machine / ATM

⑨ **der Wechselkurs**
exchange rate

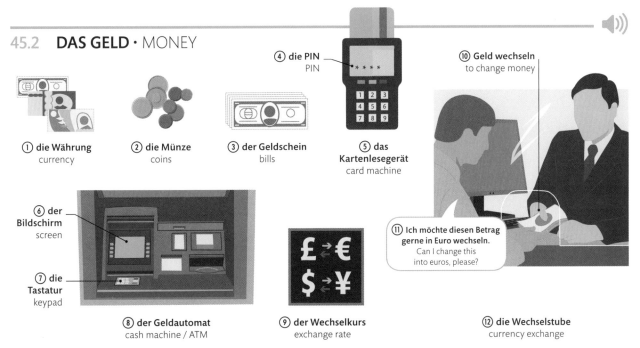

⑩ **Geld wechseln**
to change money

⑪ **Ich möchte diesen Betrag gerne in Euro wechseln.**
Can I change this into euros, please?

⑫ **die Wechselstube**
currency exchange

## 45.3 DIE POST • POST OFFICE

① **der Postmitarbeiter** *m*
**die Postmitarbeiterin** *f*
postal worker

② **die Waage**
scale

③ **der Brief**
letter

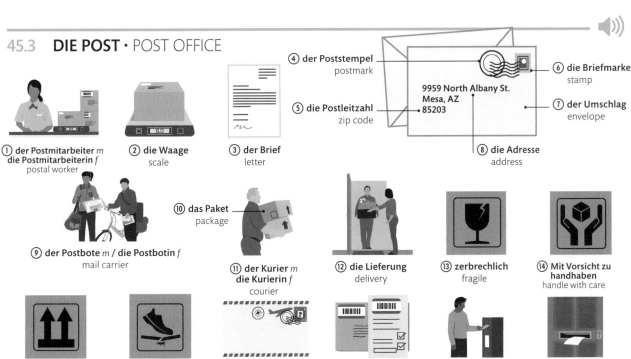

④ **der Poststempel**
postmark

⑤ **die Postleitzahl**
zip code

⑥ **die Briefmarke**
stamp

⑦ **der Umschlag**
envelope

⑧ **die Adresse**
address

⑨ **der Postbote** *m* **/ die Postbotin** *f*
mail carrier

⑩ **das Paket**
package

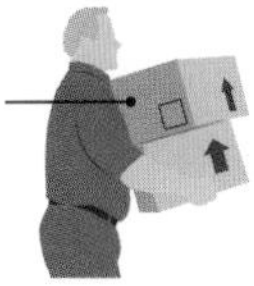

⑪ **der Kurier** *m*
**die Kurierin** *f*
courier

⑫ **die Lieferung**
delivery

⑬ **zerbrechlich**
fragile

⑭ **Mit Vorsicht zu handhaben**
handle with care

⑮ **diese Seite nach oben**
this way up

⑯ **nicht biegen**
do not bend

⑰ **die Luftpost**
airmail

⑱ **das Einschreiben**
registered mail

⑲ **der Briefkasten**
mailbox

⑳ **der Briefschlitz**
mail slot

# 46 Einkaufen
## Shopping

### 46.1 IN DER FUSSGÄNGERZONE · ON THE HIGH STREET

① **Diese Sachen haben wir im Ausverkauf bekommen!**
We bought these at the sale.

② **der Gebrauchtwarenladen**
thrift shop

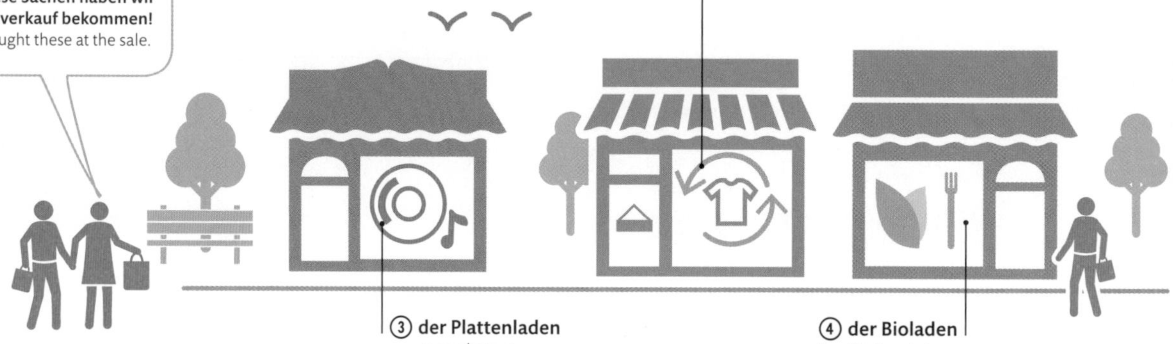

③ **der Plattenladen**
record store

④ **der Bioladen**
health food store

⑤ **der Geschenkladen**
gift shop

⑥ **die Boutique**
boutique

⑦ **der Juwelier**
jeweler

⑧ **der Künstlerbedarf**
art store

⑨ **der Antiquitätenladen**
antiques store

⑩ **der Spielzeugladen**
toy store

⑪ **der Optiker**
optician

⑫ **der Baumarkt**
hardware shop

⑬ **die Schlosserei**
key cutting shop

⑭ **das Elektronikgeschäft**
electronics shop

⑮ **der Heimtierhandel**
pet store

⑯ **das Reisebüro**
travel agent

⑰ **der Wochenmarkt**
street market

⑱ **der Fischladen**
fishmonger

⑲ **die Metzgerei**
butcher

⑳ **die Bäckerei**
bakery

㉑ **das Lebensmittelgeschäft**
grocery shop

㉒ **das Feinkostgeschäft**
delicatessen

㉓ **die Konditorei**
bakery

㉔ **das Café**
café / coffee shop

㉕ **der Spirituosenladen**
liquor shop

㉖ **der Zeitungskiosk**
newsstand / kiosk

㉗ **der Buchladen**
bookshop

㉘ **der Schuhladen**
shoe store

See also
**42-43** In der Stadt • In town **47** Das Einkaufszentrum The shopping mall **48** Der Supermarkt • The supermarket

㉙ **das Gartencenter**
garden center

㉚ **der Florist** *m*
**die Floristin** *f*
florist

㉛ **der Schneider** *m*
**die Schneiderin** *f*
tailor

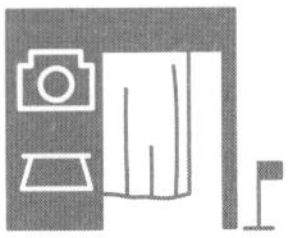

㉜ **der Fotoautomat**
photo booth

㉝ **die Wäscherei**
Laundromat

㉞ **die Reinigung**
dry cleaner's

㉟ **die Einkaufstour**
shopping spree

㊱ **der Schaufensterbummel**
window shopping

㊲ **Ich habe vergessen, Milch auf die Einkaufsliste zu schreiben.**
I forgot to put milk on my shopping list.

㊳ **die Einkaufsliste**
shopping list

## 46.2 EINKAUFSVERBEN • SHOPPING VERBS

① **aussuchen**
to choose

② **verkaufen**
to sell

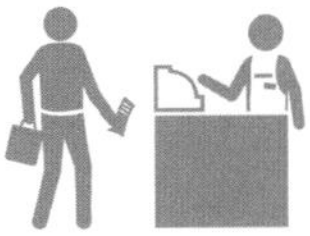

③ **kaufen**
to buy

④ **haben wollen**
to want

⑤ **passen**
to fit

⑥ **bezahlen**
to pay

⑦ **anprobieren**
to try on

⑧ **verhandeln**
to haggle

⑨ **sich beschweren**
to complain

⑩ **umtauschen**
to exchange

⑪ **erstatten**
to refund

⑫ **zurückgeben**
to return

## 46.3 ONLINE-BESTELLUNGEN • ORDERING ONLINE

① **in den Einkaufswagen legen**
to add to the cart

② **der Wunschliste hinzufügen**
to add to wishlist

③ **zur Kasse gehen**
to proceed to checkout

④ **bestellen**
to order

⑤ **die Bestellung verfolgen**
to track your order

# 47 Das Einkaufszentrum
## The shopping mall

### 47.1 DAS EINKAUFSZENTRUM · SHOPPING MALL

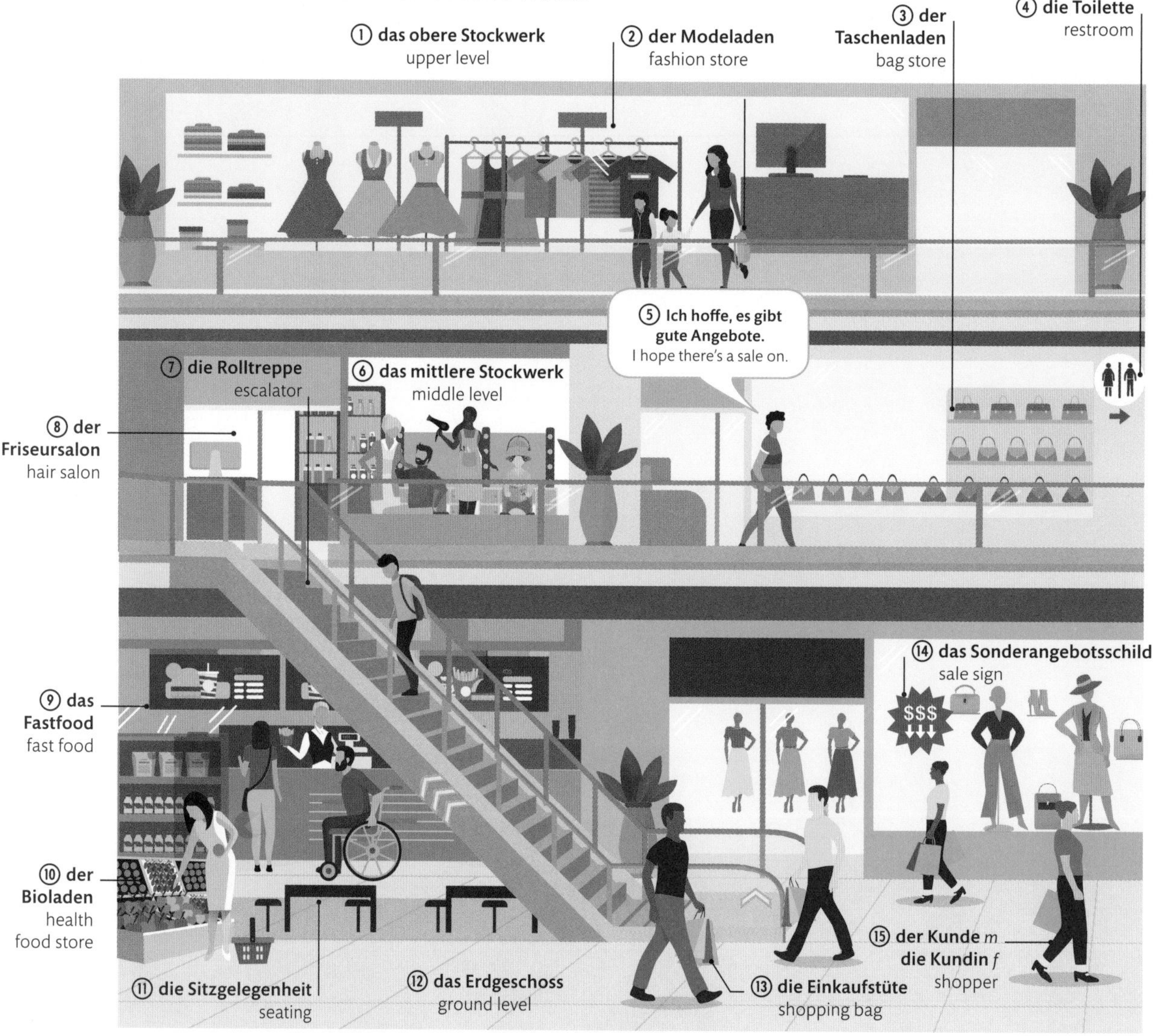

See also
**13-15** Kleidung • Clothes **16** Accessoires • Accessories **17** Schuhe • Shoes
**18** Beauty • Beauty **42-43** In der Stadt • In town **46** Einkaufen • Shopping

㉔ **die Umkleide**
changing rooms

㉕ **die Damenmode**
womenswear

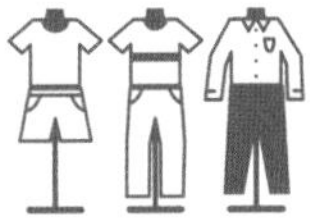
㉖ **die Herrenmode**
menswear

㉗ **der Wickelraum**
baby changing facilities

㉘ **die Kinderabteilung**
children's department

㉙ **das Markenprodukt**
designer labels

㉚ **das Sonderangebot**
sale

㉛ **die Unterwäsche**
lingerie

㉜ **die Einrichtungsgegenstände** *m, pl*
home furnishings

㉝ **das Preisschild**
price tag

㉞ **die Beleuchtung**
lighting

㉟ **die Elektrogeräte** *n, pl*
electrical appliances

㊱ **die Treuekarte**
loyalty card

㊲ **der Handwerkerbedarf**
DIY (do it yourself)

㊳ **die Beauty-Abteilung**
beauty

㊴ **der Kundenservice**
customer service

㊵ **die Parfümerie-Abteilung**
cosmetics

㊶ **der Gastronomiebereich**
food court

## 47.2 AM BLUMENSTAND • FLOWER STALL

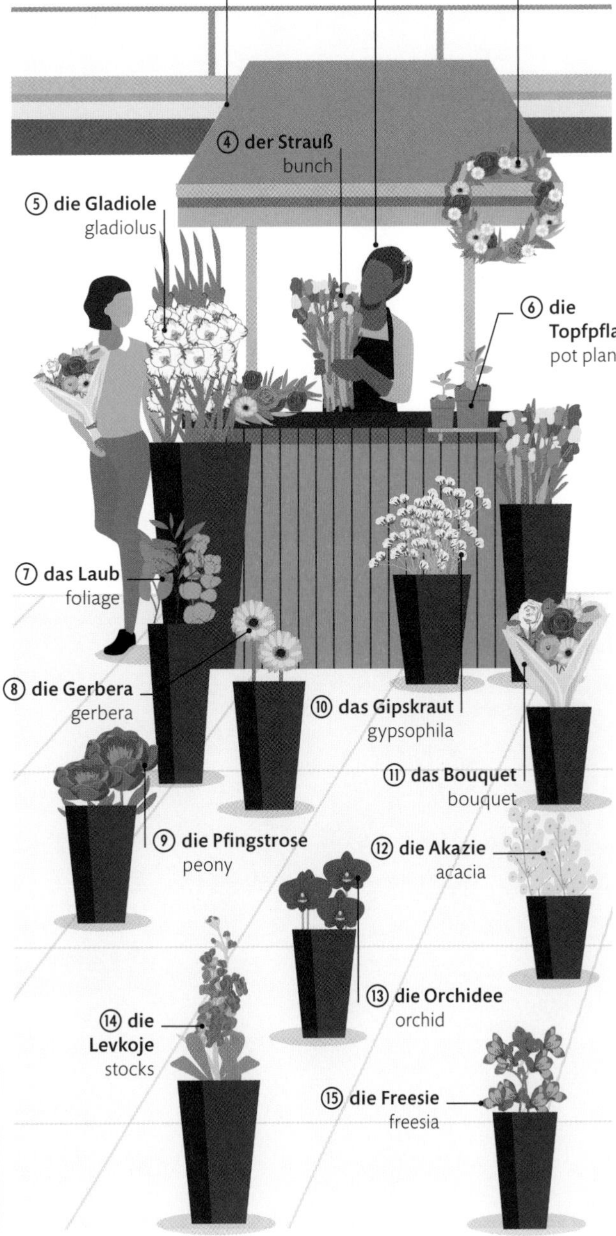

# 48 Der Supermarkt
## The supermarket

### 48.1 DER SUPERMARKT · SUPERMARKET

① **geöffnet**
open

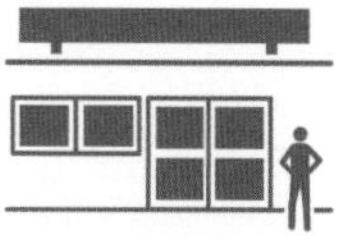
② **geschlossen**
closed

③ **der Kunde** *m*
**die Kundin** *f*
customer

④ **der Beleg**
receipt

⑤ **das Sonderangebot**
special offer

⑥ **das Schnäppchen**
bargain

⑦ **die große Auswahl**
wide range

⑧ **die Schlange**
line

⑨ **das Kartenlesegerät**
card machine

⑩ **das Online-Shopping**
online shopping

⑪ **der Lieferant** *m*
**die Lieferantin** *f*
delivery man

⑫ **die Lieferung nach Hause**
home delivery

### 48.2 AN DER KASSE · CHECKOUT

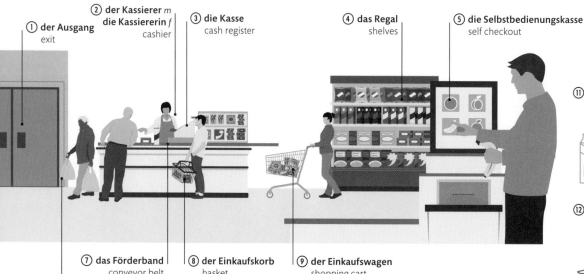

① **der Ausgang**
exit

② **der Kassierer** *m*
**die Kassiererin** *f*
cashier

③ **die Kasse**
cash register

④ **das Regal**
shelves

⑤ **die Selbstbedienungskasse**
self checkout

⑪ **der Barcode**
barcode

⑫ **der Scanner**
scanner

⑦ **das Förderband**
conveyor belt

⑧ **der Einkaufskorb**
basket

⑨ **der Einkaufswagen**
shopping cart

⑥ **die Einkaufstüte**
shopping bag

⑩ **die Kasse**
checkout

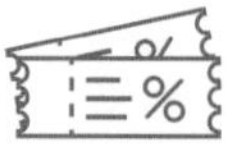
⑬ **der Gutschein**
coupon

See also
**46** Einkaufen • Shopping **53** Fleisch • Meat **54** Fisch und Meeresfrüchte • Fish and seafood **55-56** Gemüse • Vegetables **57** Obst • Fruit **58** Obst und Nüsse • Fruit and nuts **59** Kräuter und Gewürze • Herbs and spices **60** In der Vorratskammer • In the pantry **61** Milchprodukte • Dairy produce **62-63** Die Bäckerei • The bakery

## 48.3 **SUPERMARKTABTEILUNGEN** • AISLES / SECTIONS

① **das Gebäck**
bakery

② **die Milchprodukte** *n, pl*
dairy

③ **das Müsli**
breakfast cereals

④ **die Konserven** *f, pl*
canned food

⑤ **die Süßigkeiten** *f, pl*
candy

⑥ **das Gemüse**
vegetables

⑦ **das Obst**
fruit

⑧ **Fleisch und Geflügel** *n, n*
meat and poultry

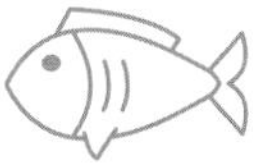

⑨ **der Fisch**
fish

⑩ **die Feinkostabteilung**
deli

⑪ **das Gefriergut**
frozen food

⑫ **die Fertiggerichte** *n, pl*
convenience food

⑬ **die Getränke** *n, pl*
drinks

⑭ **die Haushaltsprodukte** *n, pl*
household products

⑮ **die Hygieneartikel** *m, pl*
toiletries

⑯ **die Babyartikel** *m, pl*
baby products

⑰ **die Elektronik**
electrical goods

⑱ **die Tiernahrung**
pet food

## 48.4 **DER KIOSK** • NEWSSTAND / KIOSK

① **die Zeitung**
newspaper

② **die Zeitschrift**
magazine

③ **der Comic**
comic

④ **die Postkarte**
postcard

⑤ **die Karte**
tourist map

⑥ **die Briefmarke**
stamps

⑦ **die Fahrkarte**
travel card

⑧ **die SIM-Karte**
sim card

⑨ **der Riegel**
snack bar

⑩ **die Chips** *m, pl*
chips

⑪ **das Wasser**
water

# 49 Die Apotheke
## The pharmacy

### 49.1 DIE APOTHEKE • PHARMACY

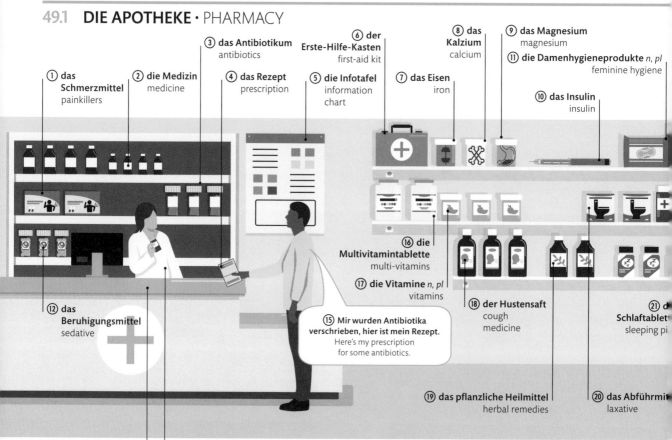

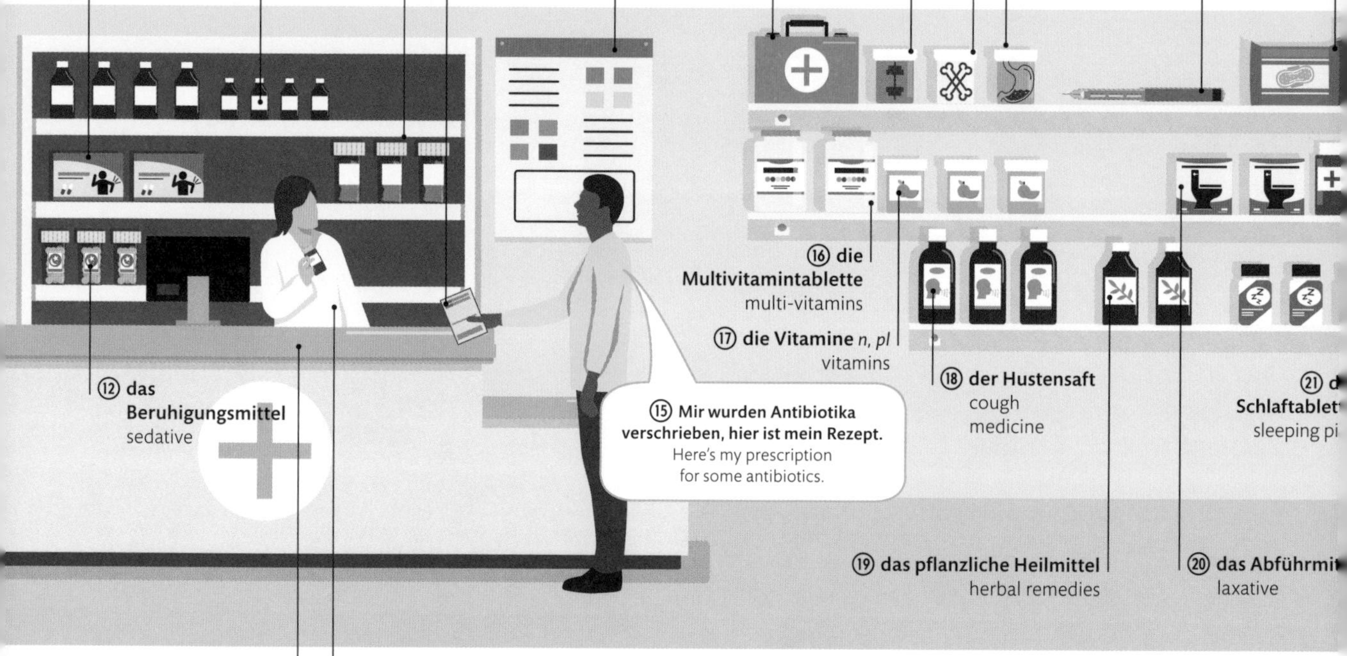

1 das Schmerzmittel
painkillers
2 die Medizin
medicine
3 das Antibiotikum
antibiotics
4 das Rezept
prescription
5 die Infotafel
information chart
6 der Erste-Hilfe-Kasten
first-aid kit
7 das Eisen
iron
8 das Kalzium
calcium
9 das Magnesium
magnesium
10 das Insulin
insulin
11 die Damenhygieneprodukte n, pl
feminine hygiene
12 das Beruhigungsmittel
sedative
13 die Ausgabe
dispensary
14 der Apotheker m
die Apothekerin f
pharmacist
15 Mir wurden Antibiotika verschrieben, hier ist mein Rezept.
Here's my prescription for some antibiotics.
16 die Multivitamintablette
multi-vitamins
17 die Vitamine n, pl
vitamins
18 der Hustensaft
cough medicine
19 das pflanzliche Heilmittel
herbal remedies
20 das Abführmi
laxative
21 d
Schlaftablet
sleeping pi

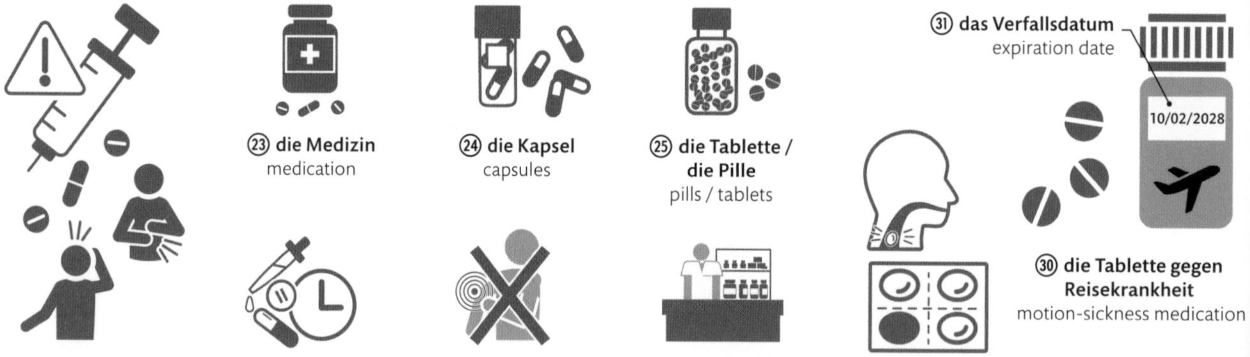

22 die Nebenwirkungen f, pl
side effects
23 die Medizin
medication
24 die Kapsel
capsules
25 die Tablette / die Pille
pills / tablets
26 die Dosierung
dosage
27 entzündungshemmend
anti-inflammatory
28 das nicht verschreibungspflichtige Arzneimittel
over-the-counter drugs
29 das Halsbonbon
throat lozenge
30 die Tablette gegen Reisekrankheit
motion-sickness medication
31 das Verfallsdatum
expiration date
10/02/2028

See also
**19** Krankheiten und Verletzungen • Illness and injury **20** Beim Arzt • Visiting the doctor **21** Das Krankenhaus • The hospital **46** Einkaufen • Shopping

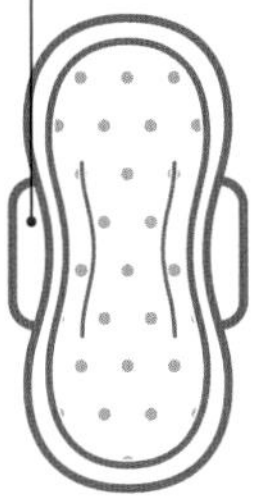
㉝ **der Flügel**
wings

㉜ **die Binde**
sanitary pad

㉞ **der Tampon**
tampon

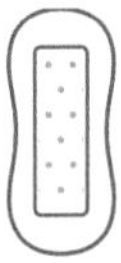
㉟ **die Slipeinlage**
panty liner

㊱ **die Inkontinenzeinlage**
incontinence pads

㊲ **das Zäpfchen**
suppository

㊳ **das Deodorant**
deodorant

㊴ **die Hautpflege**
skin care

㊵ **die Sonnencreme**
sunscreen

㊶ **die Sonnencreme**
sunblock

㊷ **der Verband**
bandage

㊸ **das Heftpflaster**
adhesive bandage

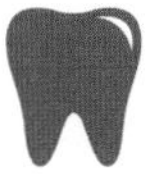
㊹ **die Zahnpflege**
dental care

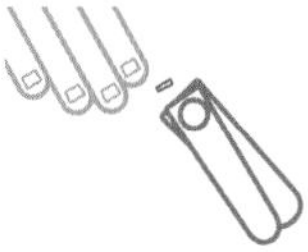
㊺ **die Nagelzange**
nail clippers

㊻ **das Feuchttuch**
wet wipes

㊼ **das Taschentuch**
tissue

㊽ **die Einlage**
insoles

㊾ **die Lesebrille**
reading glasses

㊿ **das Insektenmittel**
insect repellent

(51) **die Kontaktlinse**
contact lens

(52) **die Kontaktlinsenflüssigkeit**
lens solution

(53) **die Spritze**
syringe

(54) **der Inhalator**
inhaler

(55) **die Tropfen** *m, pl*
drops

(56) **das Nahrungsergänzungsmittel**
supplement

(57) **löslich**
soluble

(58) **die Salbe**
ointment

(64) **der Messlöffel**
measuring spoon

(63) **der Sirup**
syrup

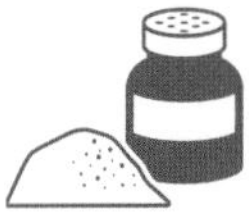
(59) **das Pulver**
powder

(60) **das Spray**
spray

(61) **das Gel**
gel

(62) **die Creme**
cream

# 50 Die Rettungsdienste
## Emergency services

### 50.1 DIE NOTAUFNAHME · ACCIDENT AND EMERGENCY

② Bring mir den Defibrillator!
Bring me the defibrillator!

① **der Rettungssanitäter** *m*
**die Rettungssanitäterin** *f*
paramedic

③ **der Scheinwerfer**
headlights

④ **das Blaulicht**
emergency vehicle beacon

⑤ **der Erste-Hilfe-Kasten**
first-aid bag

⑥ **der Rettungswagen**
ambulance

⑦ **die Battenburg-Markierung**
Battenburg markings

⑧ **die Luftnotrettung**
air ambulance

⑨ **die Krankenwagentrage**
ambulance stretcher

⑩ **die Tragbahre**
pole stretcher

⑪ **die Notaufnahme**
emergency department

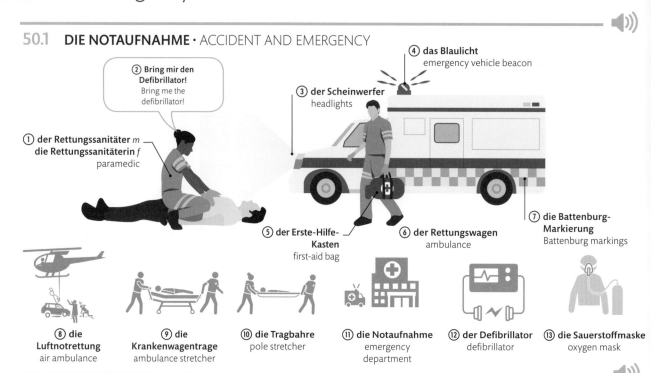

⑫ **der Defibrillator**
defibrillator

⑬ **die Sauerstoffmaske**
oxygen mask

### 50.2 DIE FEUERWEHR · FIRE BRIGADE

① **der Rauchmelder**
smoke alarm

② **der Feueralarm**
fire alarm

③ **der Notausgang**
fire escape

④ **die Feuerwache**
fire station

⑤ **der Druckluftzylinder**
compressed-air cylinder

⑥ **der Feuerlöscher**
fire extinguisher

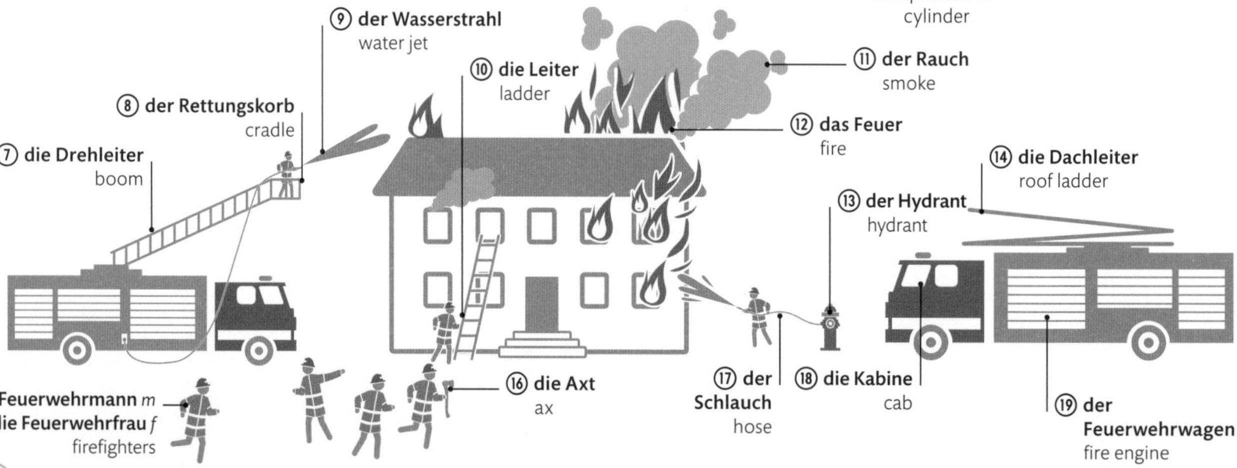

⑦ **die Drehleiter**
boom

⑧ **der Rettungskorb**
cradle

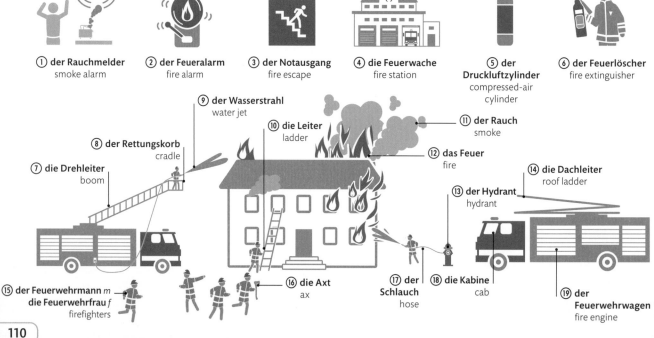

⑨ **der Wasserstrahl**
water jet

⑩ **die Leiter**
ladder

⑪ **der Rauch**
smoke

⑫ **das Feuer**
fire

⑬ **der Hydrant**
hydrant

⑭ **die Dachleiter**
roof ladder

⑮ **der Feuerwehrmann** *m*
**die Feuerwehrfrau** *f*
firefighters

⑯ **die Axt**
ax

⑰ **der Schlauch**
hose

⑱ **die Kabine**
cab

⑲ **der Feuerwehrwagen**
fire engine

See also
**19** Krankheiten und Verletzungen • Illness and injury
**21** Das Krankenhaus • The hospital **85** Recht • Law

## 50.3 DIE POLIZEI • POLICE

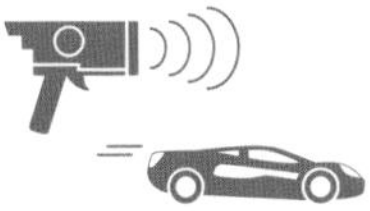

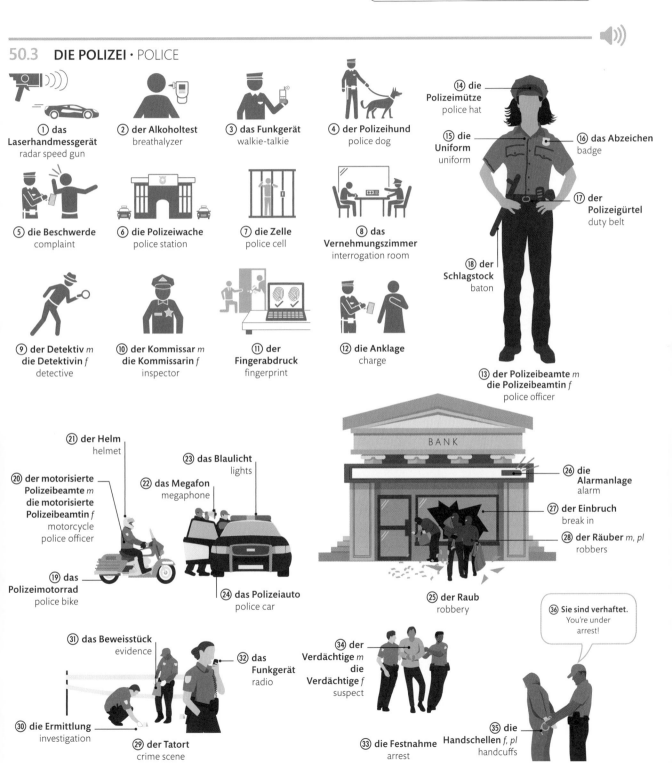

① **das Laserhandmessgerät**
radar speed gun

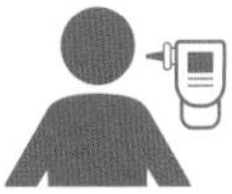

② **der Alkoholtest**
breathalyzer

③ **das Funkgerät**
walkie-talkie

④ **der Polizeihund**
police dog

⑤ **die Beschwerde**
complaint

⑥ **die Polizeiwache**
police station

⑦ **die Zelle**
police cell

⑧ **das Vernehmungszimmer**
interrogation room

⑨ **der Detektiv** *m*
**die Detektivin** *f*
detective

⑩ **der Kommissar** *m*
**die Kommissarin** *f*
inspector

⑪ **der Fingerabdruck**
fingerprint

⑫ **die Anklage**
charge

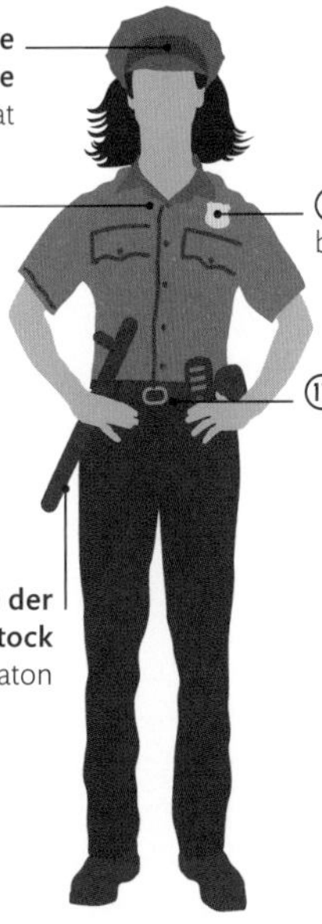

⑭ **die Polizeimütze**
police hat

⑮ **die Uniform**
uniform

⑯ **das Abzeichen**
badge

⑰ **der Polizeigürtel**
duty belt

⑱ **der Schlagstock**
baton

⑬ **der Polizeibeamte** *m*
**die Polizeibeamtin** *f*
police officer

㉑ **der Helm**
helmet

⑳ **der motorisierte Polizeibeamte** *m*
**die motorisierte Polizeibeamtin** *f*
motorcycle police officer

⑲ **das Polizeimotorrad**
police bike

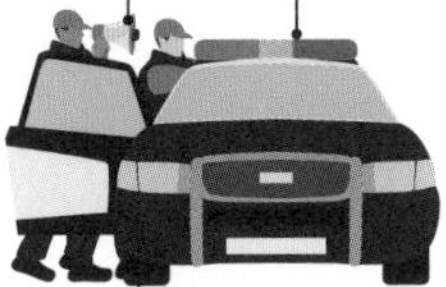

㉓ **das Blaulicht**
lights

㉒ **das Megafon**
megaphone

㉔ **das Polizeiauto**
police car

㉖ **die Alarmanlage**
alarm

㉗ **der Einbruch**
break in

㉘ **der Räuber** *m, pl*
robbers

㉕ **der Raub**
robbery

㉛ **das Beweisstück**
evidence

㉜ **das Funkgerät**
radio

㉚ **die Ermittlung**
investigation

㉙ **der Tatort**
crime scene

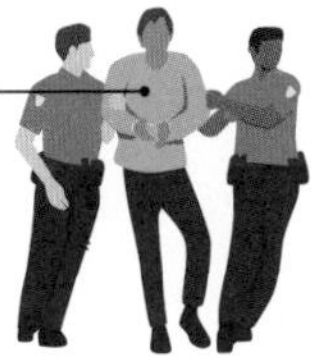

㉞ **der Verdächtige** *m*
**die Verdächtige** *f*
suspect

㉝ **die Festnahme**
arrest

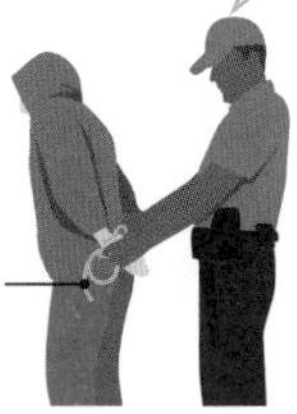

㊱ **Sie sind verhaftet.**
You're under arrest!

㉟ **die Handschellen** *f, pl*
handcuffs

# 51 Energie und Stromversorgung
## Energy and power supply

### 51.1 ATOMENERGIE UND FOSSILE BRENNSTOFFE · NUCLEAR ENERGY AND FOSSIL FUELS

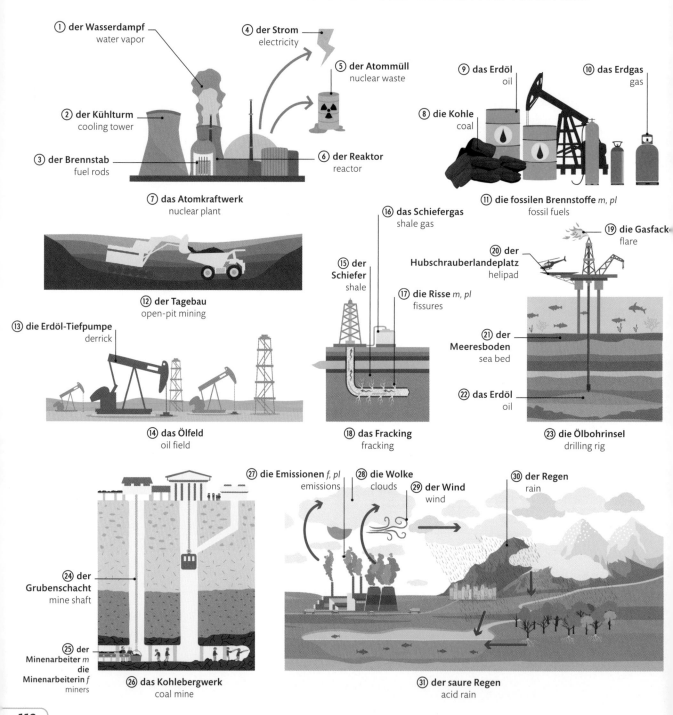

① **der Wasserdampf** water vapor
② **der Kühlturm** cooling tower
③ **der Brennstab** fuel rods
④ **der Strom** electricity
⑤ **der Atommüll** nuclear waste
⑥ **der Reaktor** reactor

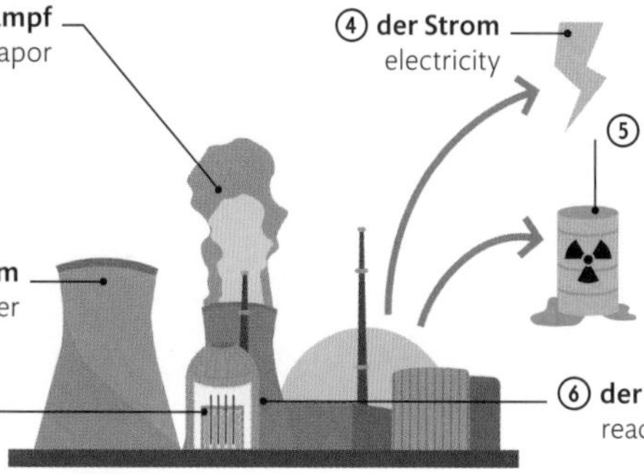

⑦ **das Atomkraftwerk** nuclear plant

⑧ **die Kohle** coal
⑨ **das Erdöl** oil
⑩ **das Erdgas** gas

⑪ **die fossilen Brennstoffe** *m, pl* fossil fuels

⑫ **der Tagebau** open-pit mining

⑬ **die Erdöl-Tiefpumpe** derrick

⑭ **das Ölfeld** oil field

⑮ **der Schiefer** shale
⑯ **das Schiefergas** shale gas
⑰ **die Risse** *m, pl* fissures

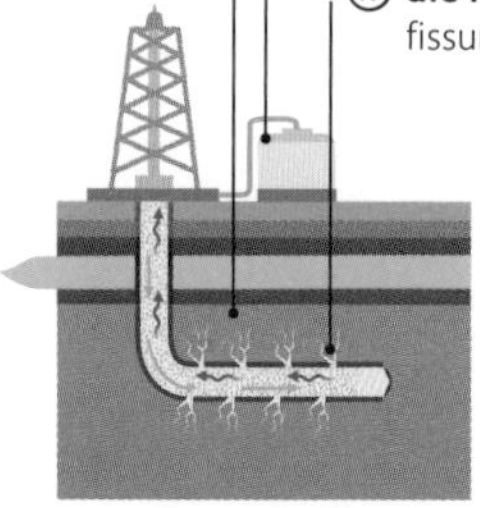

⑱ **das Fracking** fracking

⑲ **die Gasfack[el]** flare
⑳ **der Hubschrauberlandeplatz** helipad
㉑ **der Meeresboden** sea bed
㉒ **das Erdöl** oil

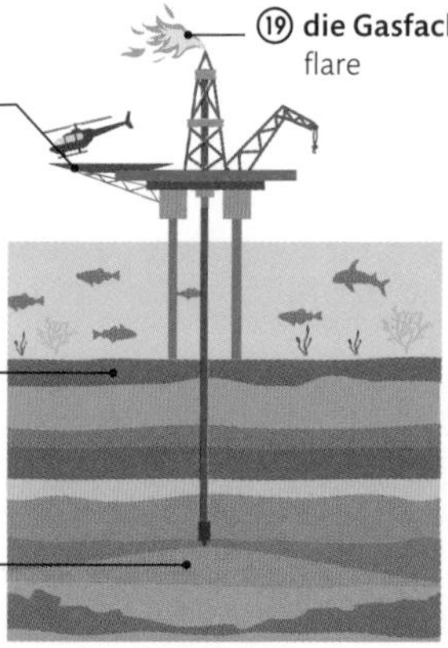

㉓ **die Ölbohrinsel** drilling rig

㉔ **der Grubenschacht** mine shaft
㉕ **der Minenarbeiter** *m* **die Minenarbeiterin** *f* miners

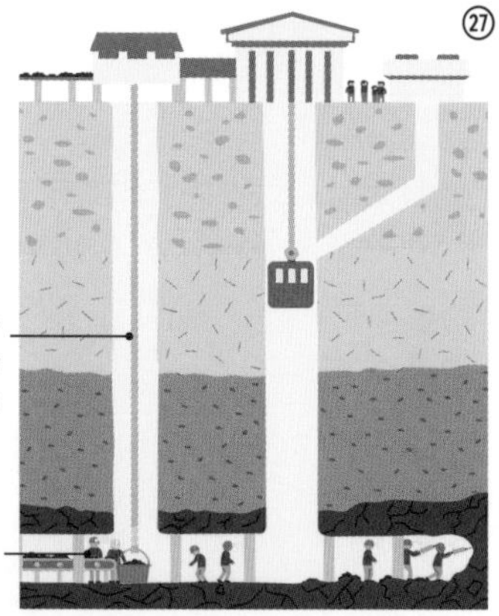

㉖ **das Kohlebergwerk** coal mine

㉗ **die Emissionen** *f, pl* emissions
㉘ **die Wolke** clouds
㉙ **der Wind** wind
㉚ **der Regen** rain

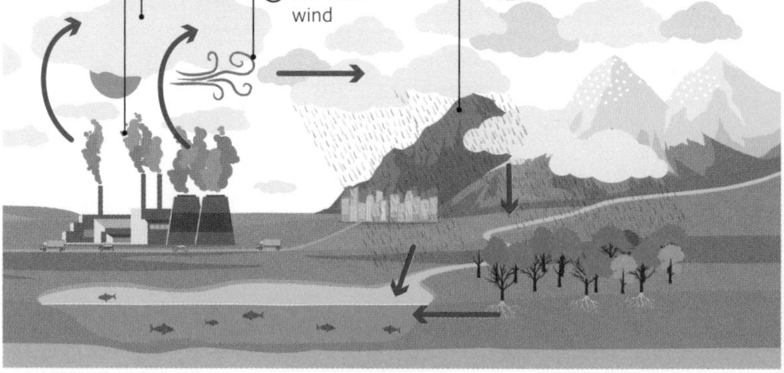

㉛ **der saure Regen** acid rain

See also
**33** Elektrizität und Sanitärtechnik • Electrics and plumbing **42-43** In der Stadt • In town
**145** Der Planet Erde • Planet Earth **155** Klima und Umwelt • Climate and the environment

## 51.2 ERNEUERBARE ENERGIEN • RENEWABLE ENERGY

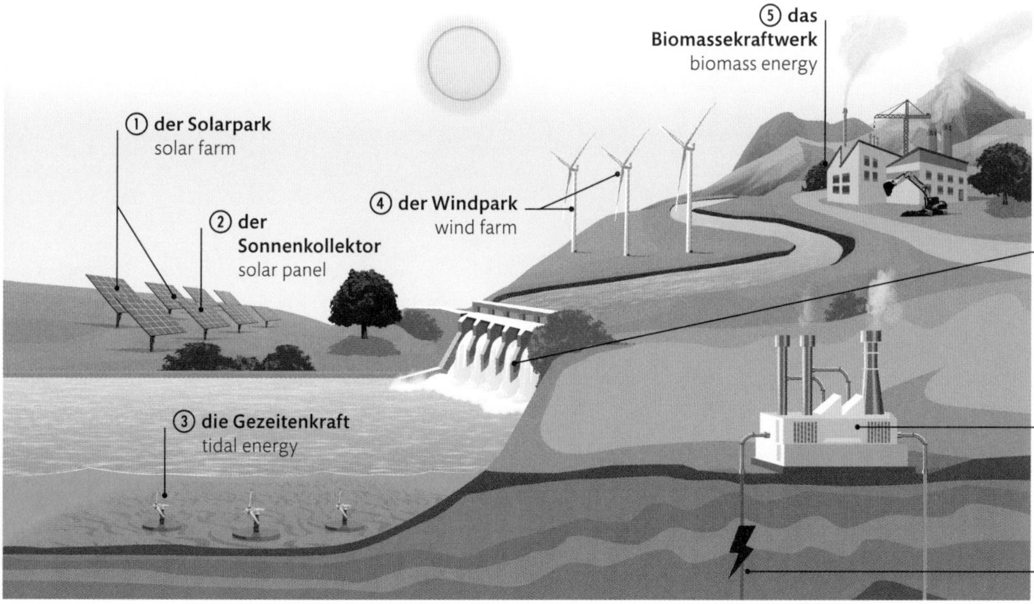


⑨ **die grüne Energie** green energy

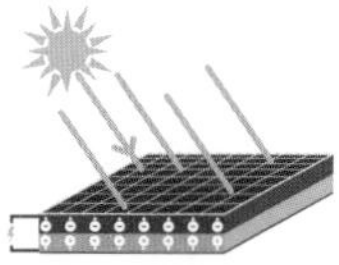

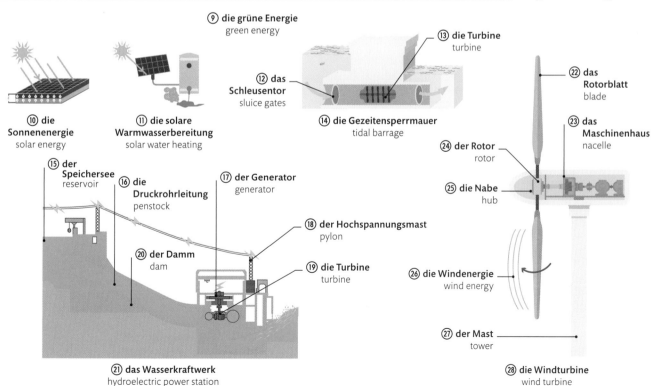

⑩ **die Sonnenenergie** solar energy

⑪ **die solare Warmwasserbereitung** solar water heating

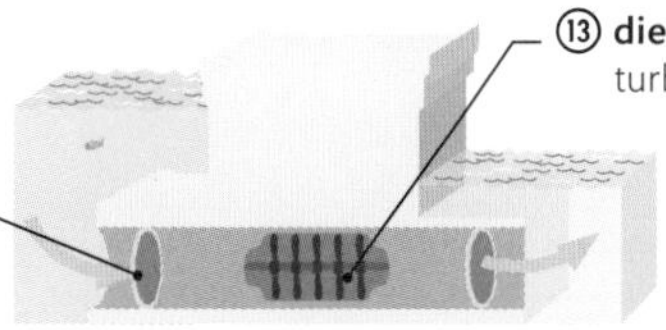


⑭ **die Gezeitensperrmauer** tidal barrage

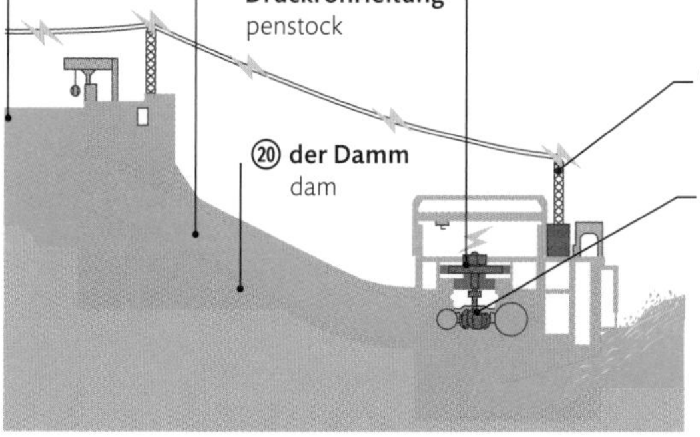


㉑ **das Wasserkraftwerk** hydroelectric power station

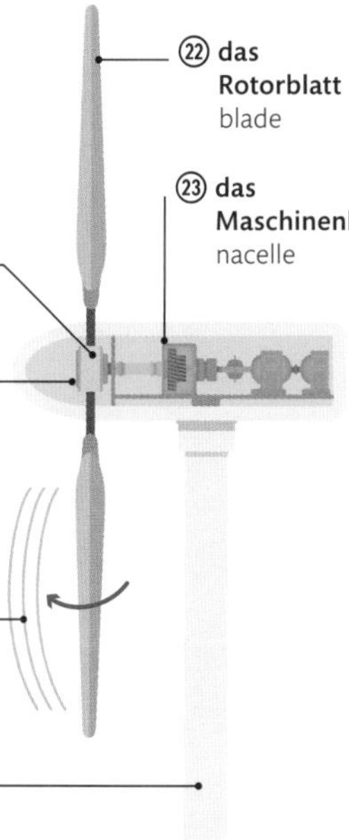


㉘ **die Windturbine** wind turbine

# 52 Trinken und essen
## Drinking and eating

### 52.1 GETRÄNKE · DRINKS

① **der Kaffee**
coffee

② **der Tee**
tea

③ **der Kakao**
hot chocolate

④ **der Kräutertee**
herbal tea

⑤ **der Eistee**
iced tea

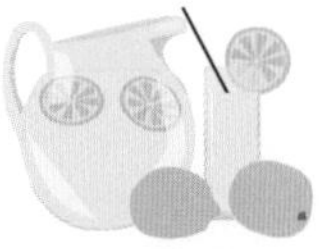
⑥ **die Limonade**
lemonade

⑦ **der Saft**
juice

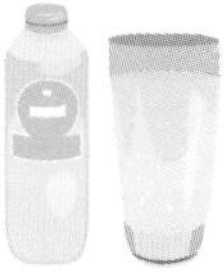
⑧ **das Mineralwasser**
mineral water

⑨ **das Leitungswasser**
tap water

⑩ **der Smoothie**
smoothie

⑪ **die Orangeade**
orangeade

⑫ **die Cola**
cola

⑬ **der Milchshake**
milkshake

⑭ **der Energydrink**
sports drink / energy drink

⑮ **der Rotwein**
red wine

⑯ **der Weißwein**
white wine

⑰ **der Rosé**
rosé wine

⑱ **das Bier**
beer

### 52.2 BEHÄLTER · CONTAINERS

① **die Flasche**
bottle

② **das Glas**
glass

③ **der Karton**
carton

④ **das Einmachglas**
jar

⑤ **die Tüte**
bag

⑥ **die Packung**
package

⑦ **die Box**
box

⑧ **die Dose**
can

⑨ **die Thermoskanne**
thermal flask

⑩ **die Schüssel**
bowl

⑪ **die luftdichte Box**
airtight container

⑫ **das Einmachglas**
Mason jar

See also
**27** Die Küche und das Geschirr • Kitchen and tableware **28** Küchenutensilien
Kitchenware **29** Kochen • Cooking **52-72** Nahrungsmittel und Lebensmittel • Food

## 52.3 **ADJEKTIVE** • ADJECTIVES

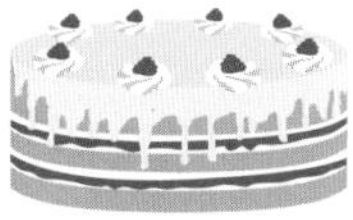
① **süß**
sweet

② **herzhaft**
savory

③ **sauer**
sour

④ **salzig**
salty

⑤ **bitter**
bitter

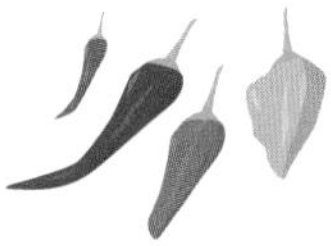
⑥ **scharf**
spicy / hot

⑦ **frisch**
fresh

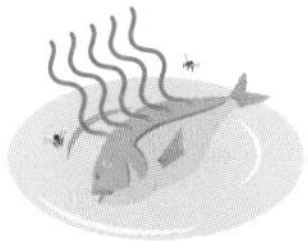
⑧ **verdorben**
bad

⑨ **stark**
strong

⑩ **gekühlt**
iced / chilled

⑪ **sprudelnd**
carbonated / sparkling

⑫ **still**
non-carbonated / still

⑬ **schwer**
rich

⑭ **saftig**
juicy

⑮ **knackig**
crunchy

⑯ **hervorragend**
delicious

⑰ **eklig**
disgusting

⑱ **lecker**
tasty

## 52.4 **VERBEN FÜR DAS TRINKEN UND ESSEN**
DRINKING AND EATING VERBS

① **essen**
to eat

② **kauen**
to chew

③ **probieren**
to taste

④ **Prost!**
Cheers
⑤ **zu Abend essen**
to dine

⑥ **knabbern**
to nibble

⑦ **abbeißen**
to bite

⑧ **schlucken**
to swallow

⑨ **nippen**
to sip

⑩ **trinken**
to drink

⑪ **herunterstürzen**
to gulp

# 53 Fleisch
## Meat

### 53.1 DER METZGER · THE BUTCHER

① **Bio-**
organic

② **freilaufend**
free-range

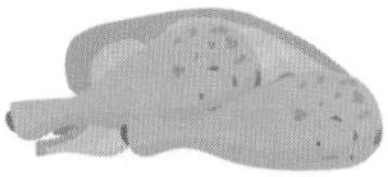
③ **das weiße Fleisch**
white meat

④ **das rote Fleisch**
red meat

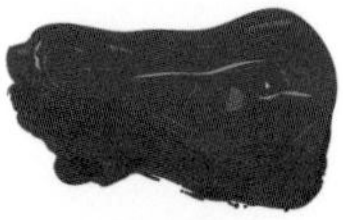
⑤ **das magere Fleisch**
lean meat

⑥ **das Hackfleisch**
ground meat

See also
**29** Kochen • Cooking **52** Trinken und essen • Drinking and eating **54** Fisch und Meeresfrüchte • Fish and seafood **69** Im Restaurant • At the restaurant **72** Das Mittagessen und das Abendessen • Lunch and dinner **165** Bauernhoftiere • Farm animals

## 53.2 **FLEISCHSORTEN** • TYPES OF MEAT

① **das Lamm** lamb
② **das Schwein** pork
③ **das Rind** beef
④ **das Kalb** veal
⑤ **der Hirsch** venison
⑥ **die Ziege** goat

⑦ **das Kaninchen** rabbit
⑧ **das Wildschwein** wild boar
⑨ **das gekochte Fleisch** cooked meat
⑩ **das rohe Fleisch** raw meat
⑪ **das gepökelte Fleisch** cured meat
⑫ **das geräucherte Fleisch** smoked meat

## 53.3 **GEFLÜGEL** • POULTRY

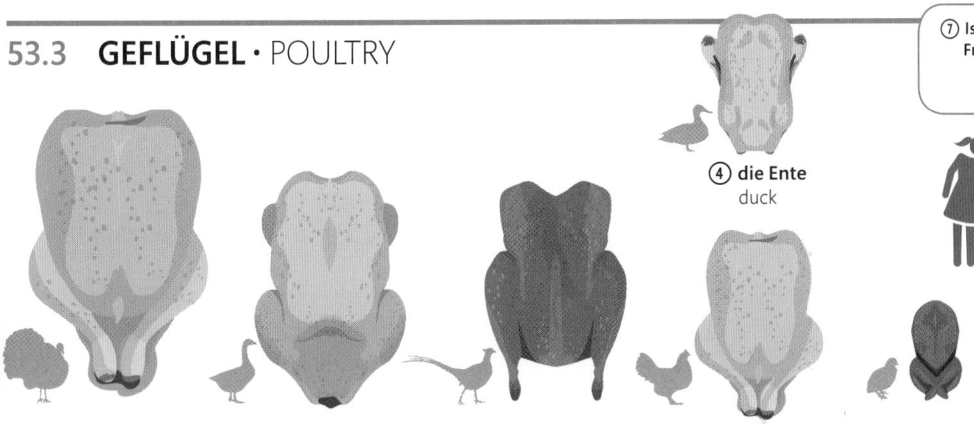

① **der Truthahn** turkey
② **die Gans** goose
③ **der Fasan** pheasant
④ **die Ente** duck
⑤ **das Huhn** chicken
⑥ **die Wachtel** quail

⑦ **Ist das ein Huhn aus Freilandhaltung?**
Is this chicken free-range?

⑧ **Ja, es stammt von einem Bauern aus der Umgebung.**
Yes, it's locally sourced.

## 53.4 **FLEISCHTEILE** • CUTS OF MEAT

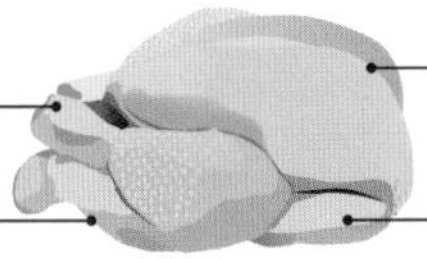

① **der Schlegel** leg
② **die Keule** thigh
③ **die Brust** breast
④ **der Flügel** wing

⑤ **die Rippe** rib
⑥ **das Filet** filet
⑦ **die Fleischstücke** *n, pl* cuts

⑧ **die Keule** cut
⑨ **der Schnitt** slice
⑩ **das Herz** heart
⑪ **die Zunge** tongue
⑫ **die Niere** kidney
⑬ **die Innereien** *f, pl* offal

# 54 Fisch und Meeresfrüchte
## Fish and seafood

### 54.1 **FISCH** · FISH

① **das Lachsfilet**
salmon fillet

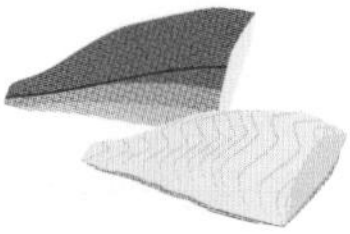
② **der Schellfisch**
haddock tail

③ **der Rochenflügel**
skate wing

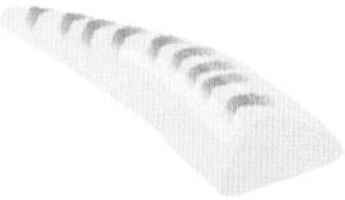
④ **das Kabeljaufilet**
cod fillet

⑤ **die Sardine**
sardines

⑥ **die Rotbarbe**
red mullet

⑧ **die Makrele**
mackerel

⑨ **die Scholle**
sole

⑩ **die Seebrasse**
sea bream

⑪ **der Seeteufel**
monkfish

⑫ **der Seebarsch**
sea bass

⑬ **der Katzenwels**
catfish

㉔ Ich hätte gerne vier Forellenfilets.
Can I have four trout fillets, please?

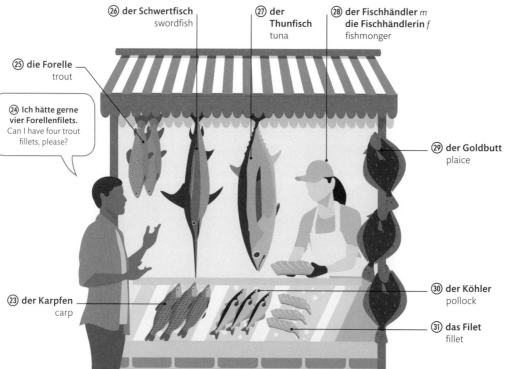

㉖ **der Schwertfisch**
swordfish

㉗ **der Thunfisch**
tuna

㉘ **der Fischhändler** *m*
**die Fischhändlerin** *f*
fishmonger

㉕ **die Forelle**
trout

㉙ **der Goldbutt**
plaice

㉓ **der Karpfen**
carp

㉚ **der Köhler**
pollock

㉛ **das Filet**
fillet

㉜ **der Fischkasten**
fish box

⑮ **die Regenbogenforelle**
rainbow trout

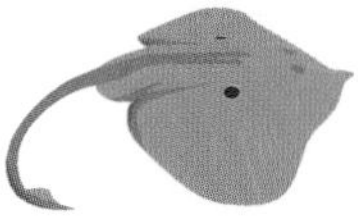
⑰ **der Rochen**
skate

⑲ **der Hering**
herring

㉑ **der Schlankwels**
basa

See also
**29** Kochen • Cooking **52** Trinken und essen • Drinking and eating **55-56** Gemüse Vegetables **69** Im Restaurant • At the restaurant **72** Das Mittagessen und das Abendessen • Lunch and dinner **166** Leben im Ozean • Ocean life

⑦ **der Weißling**
whiting

⑭ **der Heilbutt**
halibut

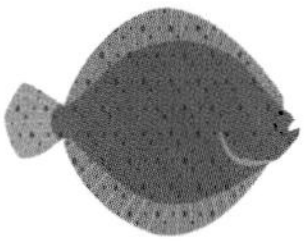
⑯ **der Steinbutt**
turbot

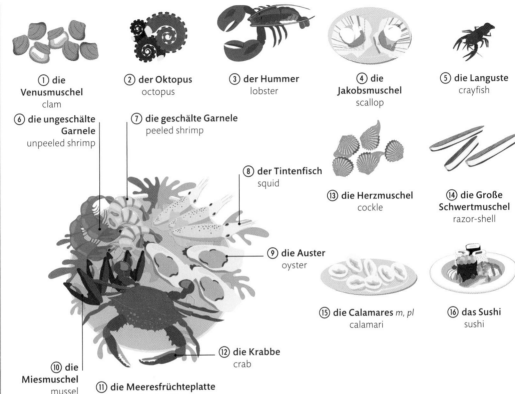

⑱ **der Aal**
eel

⑳ **der Barsch**
perch

㉒ **der Zander**
pike perch

## 54.2 **MEERESFRÜCHTE** • SEAFOOD

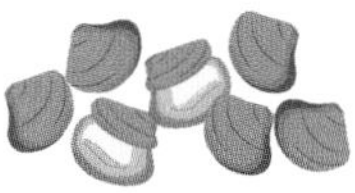
① **die Venusmuschel**
clam

② **der Oktopus**
octopus

③ **der Hummer**
lobster

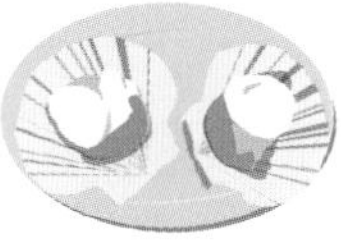
④ **die Jakobsmuschel**
scallop

⑤ **die Languste**
crayfish

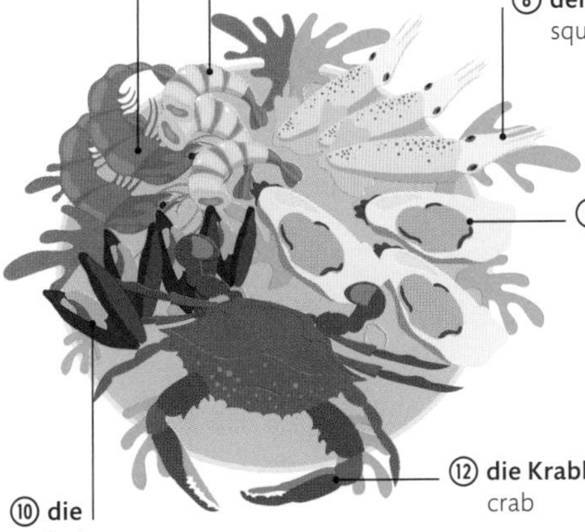


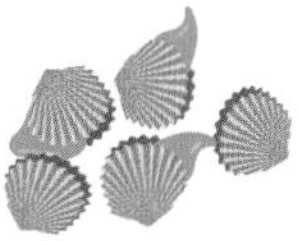
⑬ **die Herzmuschel**
cockle

⑭ **die Große Schwertmuschel**
razor-shell

⑮ **die Calamares** *m, pl*
calamari

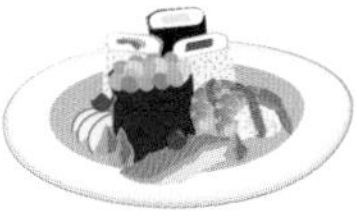
⑯ **das Sushi**
sushi

## 54.3 **ZUBEREITUNG** • PREPARATION

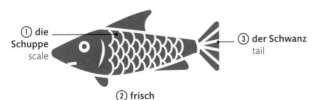

② **frisch**
fresh

④ **gefroren**
frozen

⑤ **geräuchert**
smoked

⑥ **gesalzen**
salted

⑦ **entschuppt**
descaled

⑧ **ausgenommen**
cleaned

⑨ **entgrätet**
boned

⑩ **die Lende**
loin

# 55 Gemüse
Vegetables

## 55.1 GEMÜSE · VEGETABLES

① **die Saubohne**
fava beans

② **die Stangenbohne**
runner beans

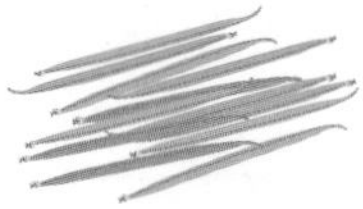

③ **die Grüne Bohne**
green beans

④ **die getrocknete Bohne**
dried beans

⑤ **der Sellerie**
celery

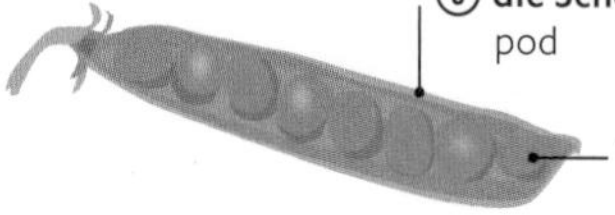

⑧ **die Schote**
pod

⑨ **die Erbse**
pea

⑦ **die Speiseerbse**
garden peas

⑩ **die Zuckererbse**
snow peas

⑪ **die Okra**
okra

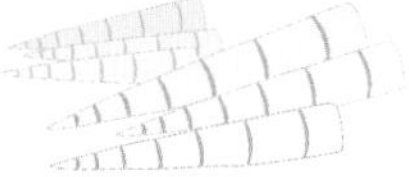

⑫ **der Bambus**
bamboo

⑬ **die Bohnensprosse**
bean sprouts

⑮ **der Chicorée**
chicory

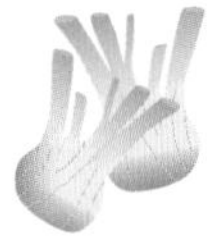

⑯ **der Fenchel**
fennel

⑰ **das Palmherz**
palm hearts

⑱ **der Jungmais**
baby corn

⑲ **der Kolben**
kernel

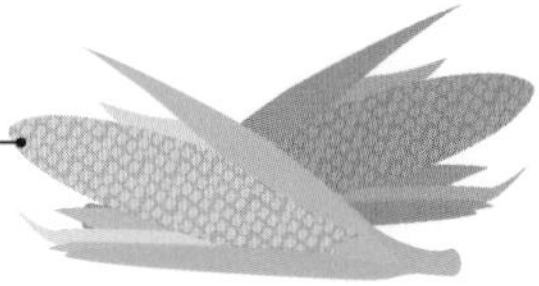

⑳ **der Mais**
corn

㉓ **die Endivie**
endive

㉔ **der Löwenzahn**
dandelion

㉕ **der Mangold**
Swiss chard

㉖ **der Grünkohl**
kale

㉗ **der Sauerampfer**
sorrel

㉘ **der Spinat**
spinach

㉛ **der Pak Choi**
bok choi

㉜ **der Kohlrabi**
kohlrabi

㉝ **der Rosenkohl**
Brussels sprouts

㉞ **der Frühkohl**
spring greens

㊲ **das Röschen**
floret

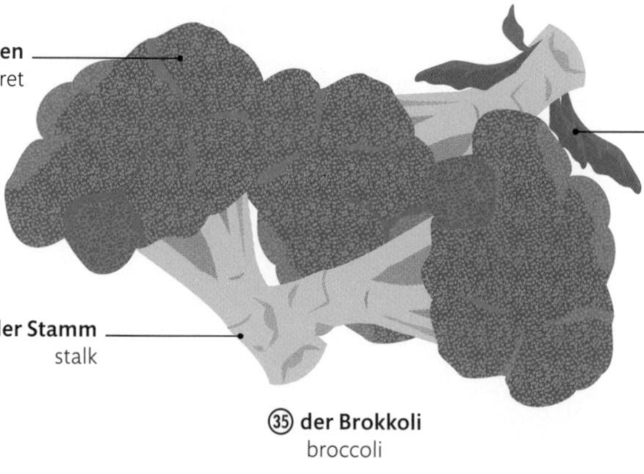

㊳ **das Blatt**
leaf

㊱ **der Stamm**
stalk

㉟ **der Brokkoli**
broccoli

See also
**29** Kochen • Cooking **52** Trinken und essen • Drinking and eating **56** Gemüse (Fortsetzung) • Vegetables continued **57** Obst • Fruit **58** Obst und Nüsse • Fruit and nuts **59** Kräuter und Gewürze • Herbs and spices **69** Im Restaurant • At the restaurant **72** Das Mittagessen und das Abendessen • Lunch and dinner

⑥ **der Baumkohl**
collards

⑭ **der Wirsing**
savoy cabbage

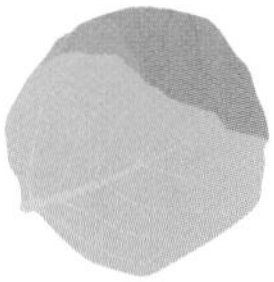

㉑ **der Weißkohl**
cabbage

㉒ **der Rotkohl**
red cabbage

㉙ **der Palmkohl**
cavolo nero

㉚ **die Rote-Bete-Blätter** *n, pl*
beet greens

㊵ **das Pestizid**
pesticides

㊴ **das Biogemüse**
organic vegetables

## 55.2 SALATGEMÜSE • SALAD VEGETABLES

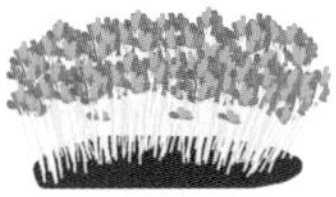

① **die Kresse**
cress

② **der Rucola**
arugula

③ **der Eisbergsalat**
iceberg lettuce

④ **der Römersalat**
romaine lettuce

⑤ **das Romanasalatherz**
little gem

⑥ **die Frühlingszwiebel**
spring onion

⑦ **die Cocktailtomate**
cherry tomatoes

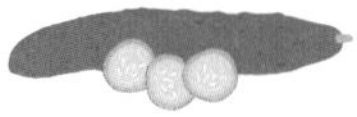

⑧ **die Salatgurke**
cucumber

⑨ **der Friséesalat**
frisée

⑩ **die Brunnenkresse**
watercress

⑪ **der Radicchio**
radicchio

⑫ **der Kopfsalat**
lettuce

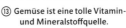

⑬ **Gemüse ist eine tolle Vitamin- und Mineralstoffquelle.**
Vegetables are a great source of vitamins and minerals.

⑭ **der Salat**
salad

# 56 Gemüse (Fortsetzung)

Vegetables continued

## 56.1 IM LEBENSMITTELGESCHÄFT · AT THE GROCERY STORE

① **die Steckrübe** turnip

② **das Radieschen** radish

③ **die Pastinake** parsnip

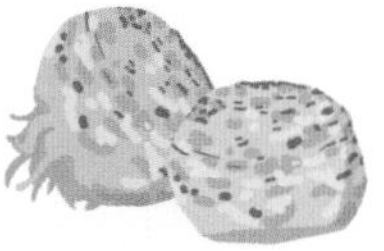
④ **der Knollensellerie** celeriac

⑤ **der Maniok** cassava

⑥ **die Kartoffel** potato

⑦ **die Wasserkastanie** water chestnut

⑧ **die Yamswurzel** yam

⑨ **die Rote Bete** beet

⑩ **die Kohlrübe** rutabagas

⑪ **der Topinambur** Jerusalem artichoke

⑫ **die Tarowurzel** taro root

⑬ **der Meerrettich** horseradish

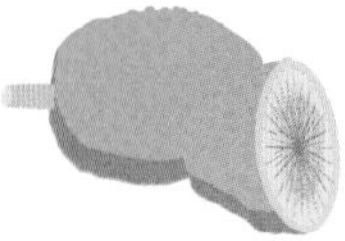
⑭ **die Brotfrucht** breadfruit

⑮ **die Schalotte** shallot

⑯ **die Chilischote** chili

⑰ **die Eiertomate** plum tomato

⑱ **die Spargelspitze** asparagus tip

⑲ **das Artischockenherz** artichoke heart

⑳ **der Austernpilz** oyster mushroom

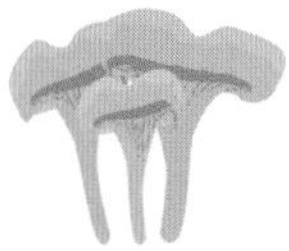
㉑ **der Pfifferling** chanterelle

㉒ **der Shiitake** shiitake mushroom

㉓ **der Trüffel** truffle

㉔ **der Enoki** enoki mushroom

㉕ **die Zucchini** marrow

㉖ **der Moschuskürbis** butternut squash

㉗ **der Eichelkürbis** acorn squash

㉘ **der Kürbis** pumpkin

㉙ **der Riesenkürbis** buttercup squash

㉚ **die Bischofsmütze** patty pan

㉛ **frisch** fresh

㉜ **gefroren** frozen

㉝ **konserviert** canned

㉞ **roh** raw

㉟ **gekocht** cooked

㊱ **scharf** hot / spicy

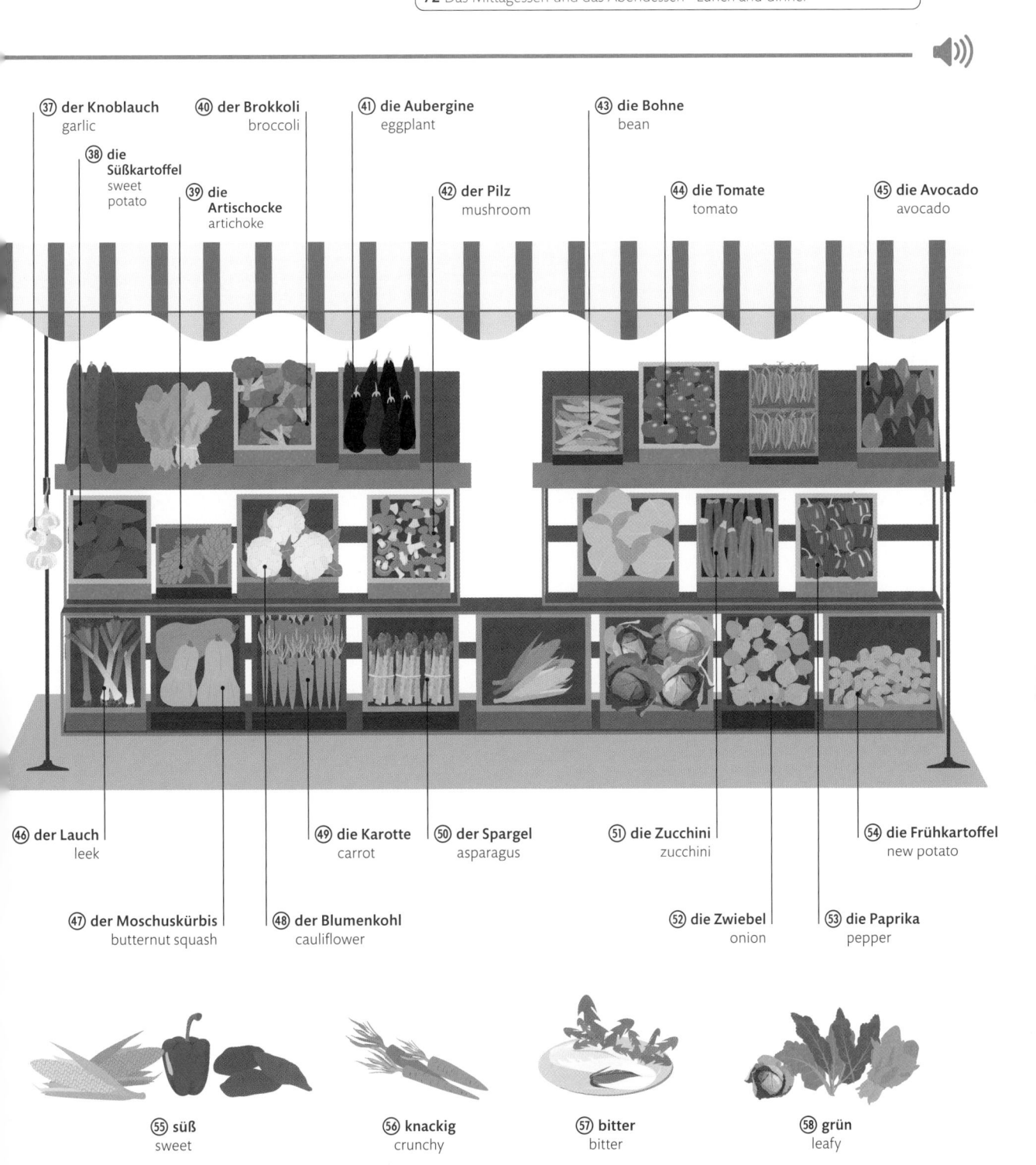

See also
**29** Kochen • Cooking **52** Trinken und essen • Drinking and eating **57** Obst
Fruit **58** Obst und Nüsse • Fruit and nuts **69** Im Restaurant • At the restaurant
**72** Das Mittagessen und das Abendessen • Lunch and dinner

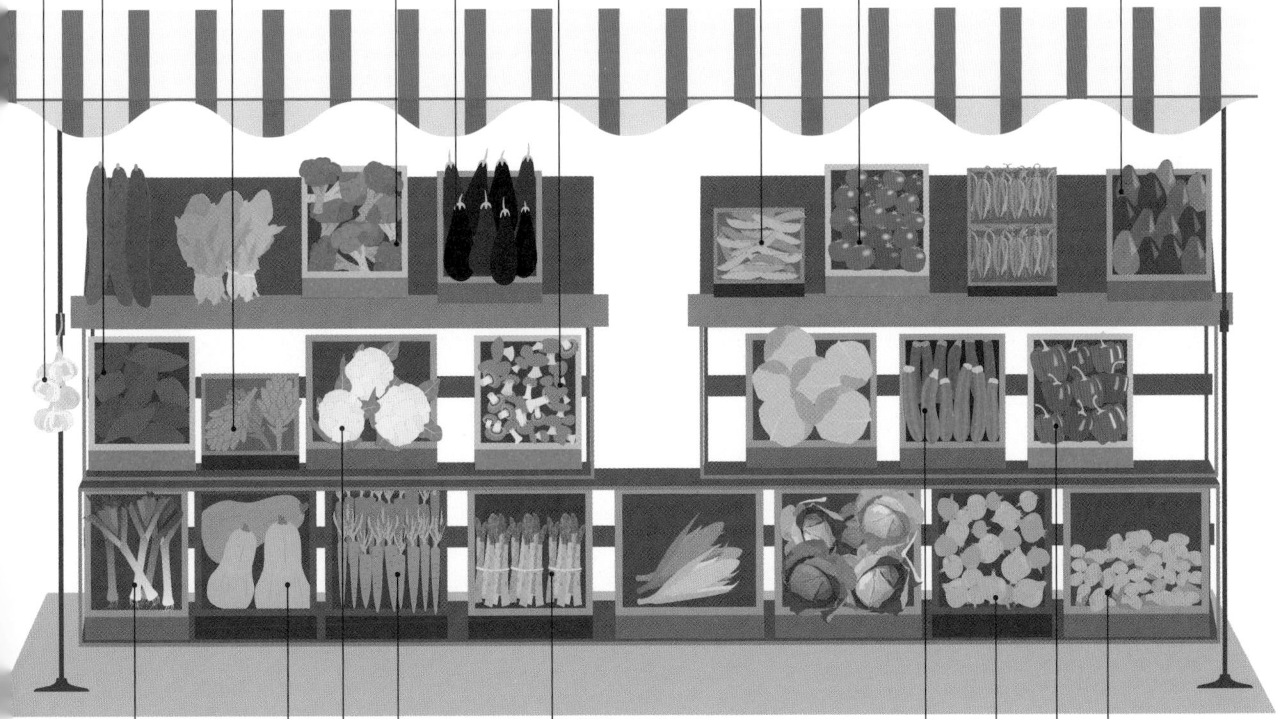

55 **süß**
sweet

56 **knackig**
crunchy

57 **bitter**
bitter

58 **grün**
leafy

# 57 Obst

## Fruit

### 57.1 ZITRUSFRÜCHTE · CITRUS FRUIT

① **die Orange** orange
② **die Blutorange** blood orange
③ **die Tangelo** ugli fruit
④ **die Pampelmuse** pomelo
⑤ **die Grapefruit** grapefruit
⑥ **das Segment** segment

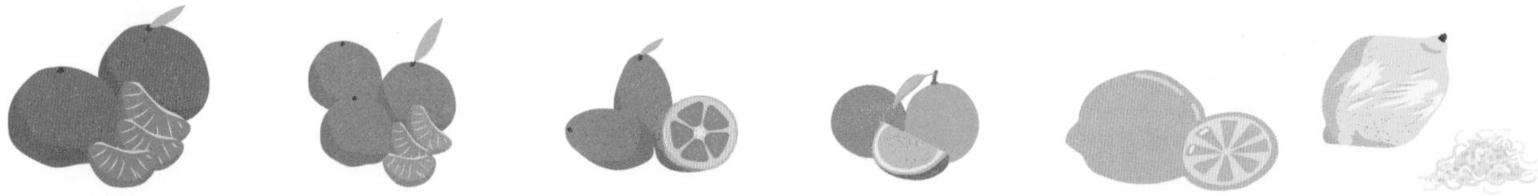

⑦ **die Klementine** clementine
⑧ **die Satsuma** mandarin orange
⑨ **die Kumquat** kumquat
⑩ **die Limette** lime
⑪ **die Zitrone** lemon
⑫ **die Zitronenschale** zest

### 57.2 OBST BESCHREIBEN · DESCRIBING FRUIT

① **die Kokosnussschale** coconut shell
② **hart** hard
③ **weich** soft
④ **kernlos** seedless

⑤ Diese Birnen sind reif und können geerntet werden.
These pears are ripe and ready to pick.

⑥ **ernten** to pick

⑦ **der Frühling** spring
⑧ **der Sommer** summer
⑪ **süß** sweet
⑫ **sauer** sour
⑬ **reif** ripe
⑭ **verdorben** rotten

⑨ **der Herbst** fall
⑩ **die Saisonfrucht** seasonal fruit
⑮ **knackig** crisp
⑯ **das Kerngehäuse** core
⑰ **die Ballaststoffe** *m, pl* fiber
⑱ **das Fruchtfleisch** pulp

See also
**29** Kochen • Cooking **52** Trinken und essen • Drinking and eating **55-56** Gemüse • Vegetables
**58** Obst und Nüsse • Fruit and nuts **65-66** Im Café • At the café **69** Im Restaurant • At the restaurant
**71** Das Frühstück • Breakfast **72** Das Mittagessen und das Abendessen • Lunch and dinner

## 57.3 BEEREN UND STEINFRÜCHTE • BERRIES AND STONE FRUIT

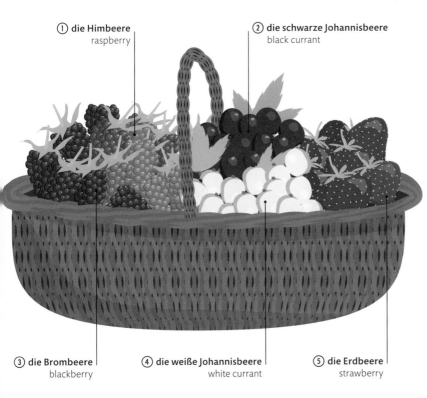

① **die Himbeere**
raspberry

② **die schwarze Johannisbeere**
black currant

③ **die Brombeere**
blackberry

④ **die weiße Johannisbeere**
white currant

⑤ **die Erdbeere**
strawberry

⑥ **der Obstkorb**
basket of fruit

⑦ **die Cranberry**
cranberry

⑧ **die Blaubeere**
blueberry

⑨ **die Loganbeere**
loganberry

⑩ **die Andenkirsche**
cape gooseberry

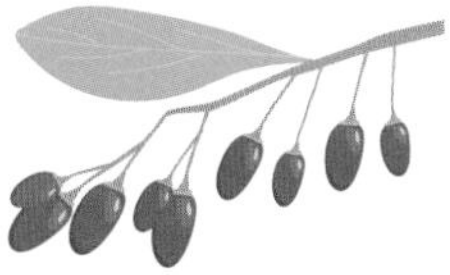

⑪ **die Goji-Beere**
goji berry

⑫ **die Stachelbeere**
gooseberry

⑬ **die rote Johannisbeere**
red currant

⑭ **die Heidelbeere**
bilberry

⑮ **die Holunderbeere**
elderberry

⑯ **die Weintraube**
grapes

⑰ **die Maulbeere**
mulberry

⑱ **der Pfirsich**
peach

⑲ **die Nektarine**
nectarine

⑳ **die Aprikose**
apricot

㉑ **die Mango**
mango

㉒ **die Pflaume**
plum

㉓ **die Kirsche**
cherry

㉔ **die Dattel**
date

㉕ **die Lychee**
lychee

# 58 Obst und Nüsse

Fruit and nuts

## 58.1 MELONEN · MELONS

① **die Wassermelone**
watermelon

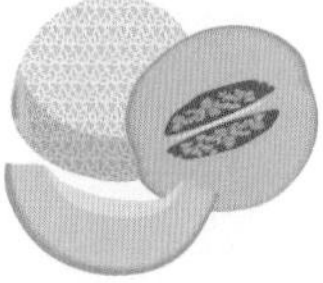

② **die Kantalupe**
cantaloupe

③ **die Honigmelone**
honeydew melon

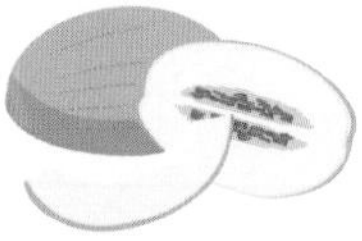

④ **die Gelbe Kanarische**
Canary melon

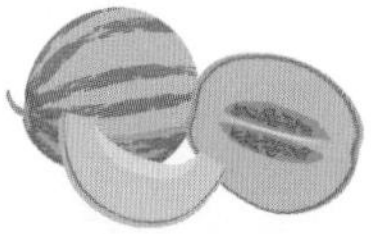

⑤ **die Charentais-Melone**
charentais

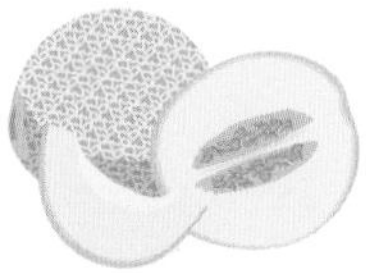

⑥ **die Galiamelone**
galia

## 58.2 WEITERES OBST · OTHER FRUIT

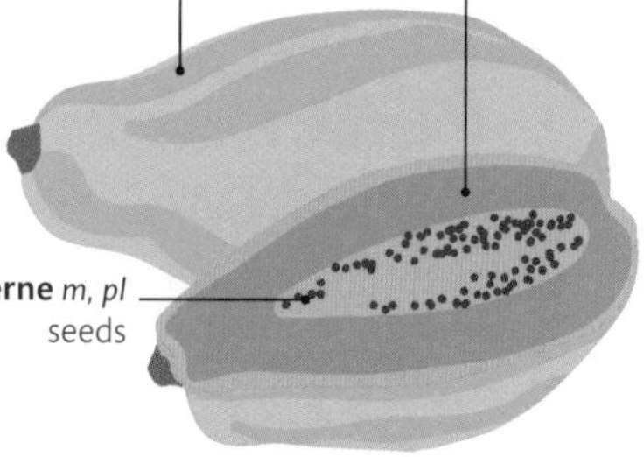


① **die Papaya**
papaya

⑤ **die Quitte**
quince

⑥ **die Passionsfrucht**
passion fruit

⑦ **die Guave**
guava

⑧ **die Sternfrucht**
starfruit

⑨ **die Kakifrucht**
persimmon

⑩ **die Ananas-Guave**
feijoa

⑪ **die Ananas**
pineapple

⑫ **die Kaktusfeige**
prickly pear

⑬ **die Baumtomate**
tamarillo

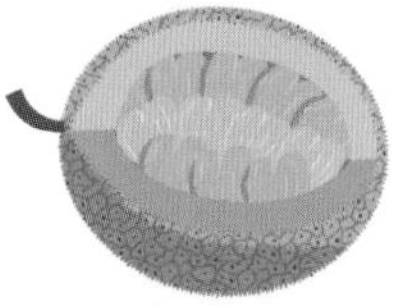

⑭ **die Jackfrucht**
jackfruit

⑮ **die Mangostinfrucht**
mangosteen

⑯ **der Granatapfel**
pomegranate

⑰ **die Banane**
banana

⑱ **die Kiwi**
kiwi

⑲ **der Apfel**
apple

⑳ **der Holzapfel**
crab apples

㉑ **die Birne**
pear

㉒ **der Rhabarber**
rhubarb

See also
**29** Kochen • Cooking **52** Trinken und essen • Drinking and eating **55-56** Gemüse Vegetables **57** Obst • Fruit **65-66** Im Café • At the café **69** Im Restaurant • At the restaurant **71** Das Frühstück • Breakfast **72** Das Mittagessen und das Abendessen • Lunch and dinner

## 58.3 **NÜSSE UND TROCKENFRÜCHTE** • NUTS AND DRIED FRUIT

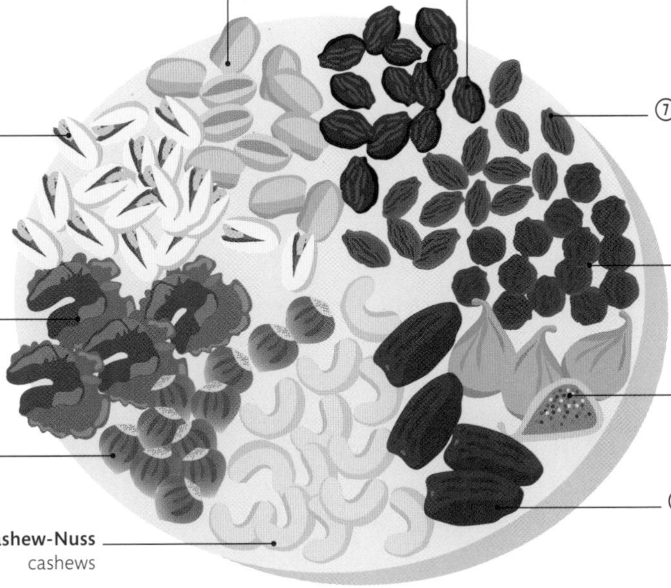

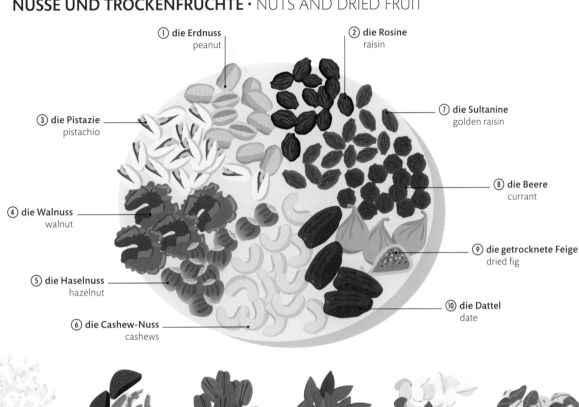

① **die Erdnuss**
peanut

② **die Rosine**
raisin

③ **die Pistazie**
pistachio

④ **die Walnuss**
walnut

⑤ **die Haselnuss**
hazelnut

⑥ **die Cashew-Nuss**
cashews

⑦ **die Sultanine**
golden raisin

⑧ **die Beere**
currant

⑨ **die getrocknete Feige**
dried fig

⑩ **die Dattel**
date

⑪ **der Pinienkern**
pine nuts

⑫ **die Paranuss**
brazil nuts

⑬ **die Pekannuss**
pecans

⑭ **die Mandel**
almonds

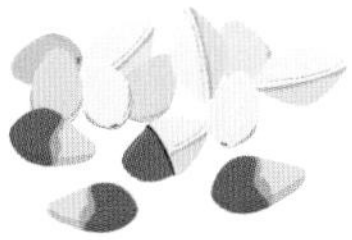

⑮ **die Ginkgonuss**
ginkgo nuts

⑯ **die Kolanuss**
kola nuts

⑰ **die Kastanie**
chestnuts

⑱ **die Macadamianuss**
macadamias

⑲ **die getrocknete Aprikose**
dried apricots

⑳ **die Dörrpflaume**
prunes

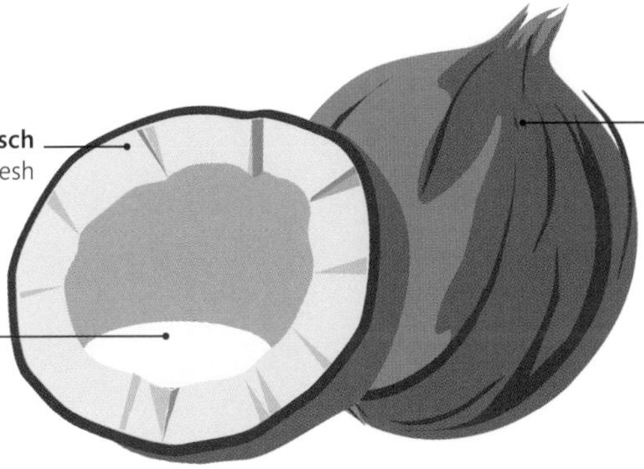

㉓ **das Fruchtfleisch**
flesh

㉒ **das Kokoswasser**
coconut water

㉔ **die Schale**
shell

㉑ **die Kokosnuss**
coconut

# 59 Kräuter und Gewürze
## Herbs and spices

### 59.1 **GEWÜRZE** · SPICES

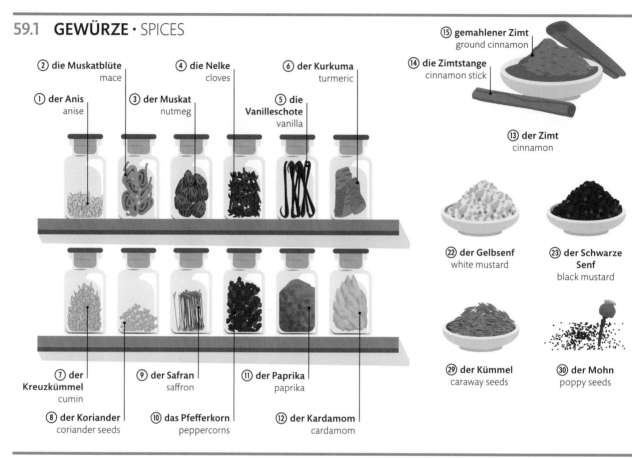

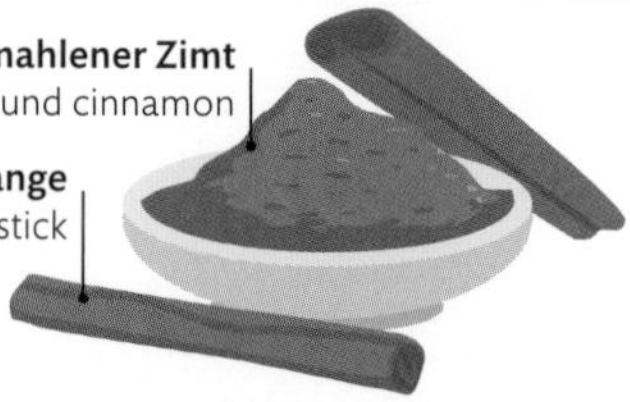


⑬ **der Zimt**
cinnamon

㉒ **der Gelbsenf**
white mustard

㉓ **der Schwarze Senf**
black mustard

㉙ **der Kümmel**
caraway seeds

㉚ **der Mohn**
poppy seeds

### 59.2 **KRÄUTER** · HERBS

① **der Fenchel**
fennel

② **der Lorbeer**
bay leaf

③ **die Petersilie**
parsley

④ **der Schnittlauch**
chives

⑤ **die Minze**
mint

⑥ **der Koriander**
cilantro

⑬ **der Thymian**
thyme

⑭ **der Salbei**
sage

⑮ **der Estragon**
tarragon

⑯ **der Majoran**
marjoram

⑰ **das Basilikum**
basil

⑱ **der Oregano**
oregano

See also
**29** Kochen • Cooking **52** Trinken und essen • Drinking and eating **53** Fleisch
Meat **55-56** Gemüse • Vegetables **60** In der Vorratskammer • In the pantry

⑯ **der Sternanis**
star anise

⑰ **der Sumach**
sumac

⑱ **das Fünfgewürz**
five spice

⑲ **die Ras el-Hanout**
ras el hanout

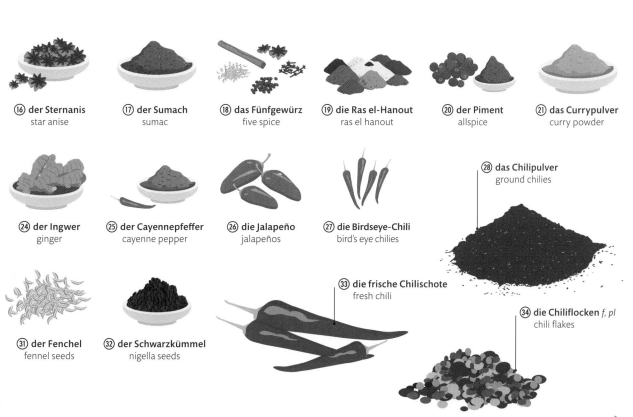

⑳ **der Piment**
allspice

㉑ **das Currypulver**
curry powder

㉔ **der Ingwer**
ginger

㉕ **der Cayennepfeffer**
cayenne pepper

㉖ **die Jalapeño**
jalapeños

㉗ **die Birdseye-Chili**
bird's eye chilies

㉘ **das Chilipulver**
ground chilies

㉛ **der Fenchel**
fennel seeds

㉜ **der Schwarzkümmel**
nigella seeds

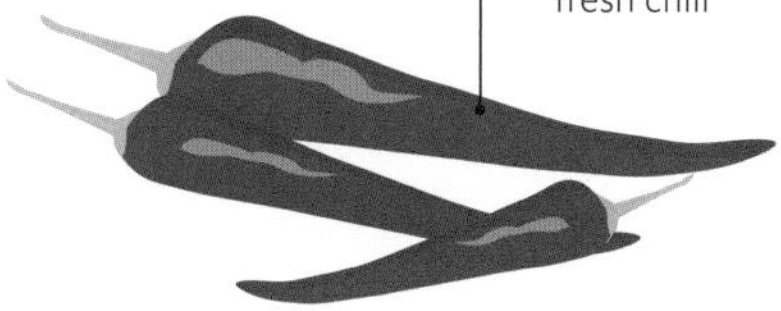
㉝ **die frische Chilischote**
fresh chili

㉞ **die Chiliflocken** *f, pl*
chili flakes

⑦ **der Ysop**
hyssop

⑧ **der Dill**
dill

⑨ **der Rosmarin**
rosemary

⑩ **der Kerbel**
chervil

⑪ **das Maggikraut**
lovage

⑫ **der Sauerampfer**
sorrel

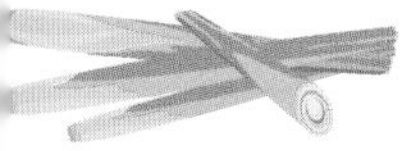
⑲ **das Zitronengras**
lemongrass

⑳ **die Zitronenmelisse**
lemon balm

㉑ **das Gurkenkraut**
borage

㉒ **der Bockshornklee**
fenugreek leaves

㉓ **das Kräutersträußchen**
bouquet garni

# 60 In der Vorratskammer
## In the pantry

### 60.1 **ÖLE** · BOTTLED OILS

① **das Öl** oil

② **das Palmöl** palm oil

③ **das Sonnenblumenöl** sunflower oil

④ **das Rapsöl** canola / rapeseed oil

⑤ **das Maisöl** corn oil

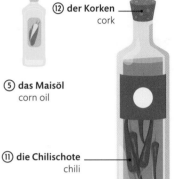

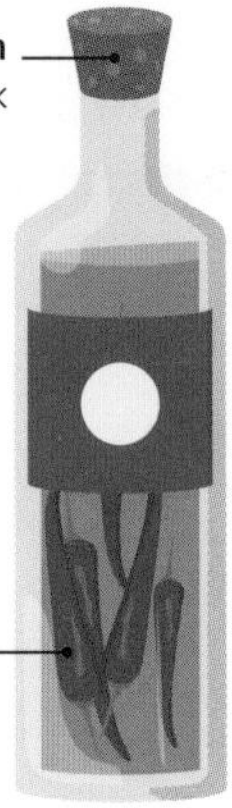


⑩ **das aromatisierte Öl** flavored oil

⑥ **das Sojaöl** soybean oil

⑦ **das Erdnussöl** peanut oil

⑧ **das Haselnussöl** hazelnut oil

⑨ **das Kokosnussöl** coconut oil

⑬ **das Sesamöl** sesame oil

⑭ **das Mandelöl** almond oil

⑮ **das Walnussöl** walnut oil

⑯ **das Traubenkernöl** grapeseed oil

⑰ **das Olivenöl** olive oil

### 60.2 **SÜSSER AUFSTRICH** · SWEET SPREADS

① **das Zitronenmus** lemon curd

② **die Himbeermarmelade** raspberry jam

③ **die Erdbeermarmelade** strawberry jam

⑤ **der kristallisierte Honig** crystalized honey

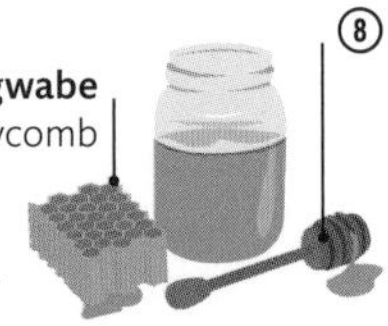


⑥ **der Honig** honey

⑨ **die Zitrusmarmelade** marmalade

⑩ **der Ahornsirup** maple syrup

⑪ **die Erdnussbutter** peanut butter

⑫ **der Schokoaufstrich** chocolate spread

⑬ **das eingemachte Obst** preserving jar

See also
**27** Die Küche und das Geschirr • Kitchen and tableware **29** Kochen • Cooking **52** Trinken und essen • Drinking and eating **53** Fleisch • Meat **55-56** Gemüse • Vegetables **65-66** Im Café • At the café **69** Im Restaurant • At the restaurant

## 60.3 WÜRZSAUCEN • SAUCES AND CONDIMENTS

## 60.4 SAUERKONSERVEN • PICKLES

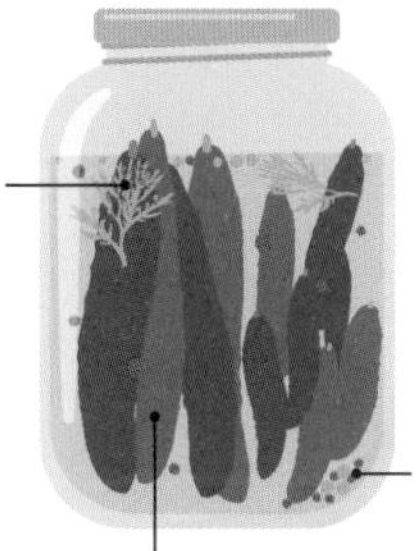

# 61 Milchprodukte
## Dairy produce

### 61.1 DER KÄSE · CHEESE

① **der Hartkäse**
hard cheese

② **der Schnittkäse**
semi-hard cheese

③ **der halbfeste Käse**
semi-soft cheese

④ **der Schmelzkäse**
soft cheese

⑤ **der Schafskäse**
sheep's milk cheese

⑥ **der Ziegenkäse**
goat's cheese

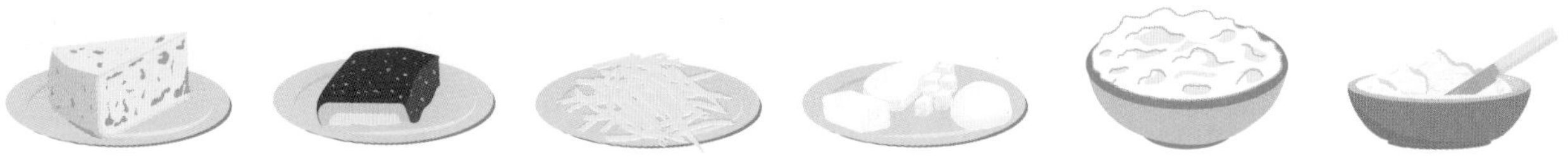

⑦ **der Blauschimmelkäse**
blue cheese

⑧ **die Rinde**
rind

⑨ **der geriebene Käse**
grated cheese

⑩ **der frische Käse**
fresh cheese

⑪ **der Hüttenkäse**
cottage cheese

⑫ **der Frischkäse**
cream cheese

### 61.2 EIER · EGGS

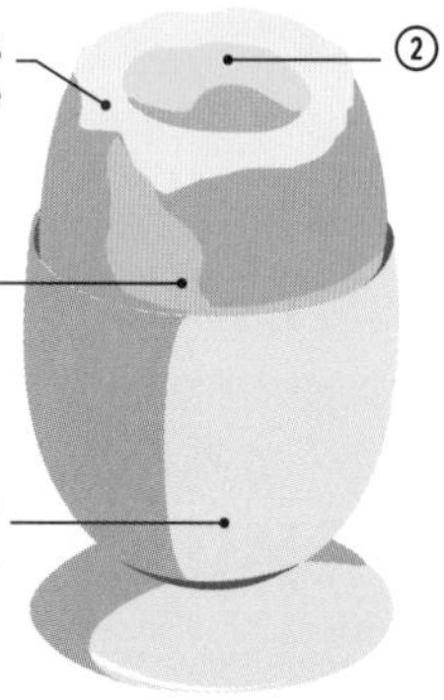

① **das Eiweiß**
egg white

② **das Eigelb**
yolk

③ **die Eierschale**
shell

④ **der Eierbecher**
egg cup

⑤ **das gekochte Ei**
boiled egg

⑥ **das Spiegelei**
fried egg

⑦ **das Rührei**
scrambled eggs

⑧ **das pochierte Ei**
poached egg

⑨ **das Omelett**
omelet

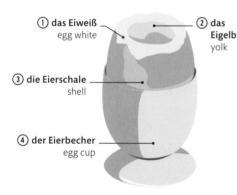

⑩ **das Gänseei**
goose egg

⑪ **das Entenei**
duck egg

⑫ **das Hühnerei**
chicken egg

⑬ **das Wachtelei**
quail egg

### 61.3 MILCH · MILK

① **pasteurisiert**
pasteurized

② **die Rohmilch**
unpasteurized

③ **laktosefrei**
lactose free

④ **homogenisiert**
homogenized

⑤ **fettfrei**
fat free

⑥ **das Milchpulver**
powdered milk

See also
**29** Kochen • Cooking **52** Trinken und essen • Drinking and eating **65-66** Im Café At the café **69** Im Restaurant • At the restaurant **71** Das Frühstück • Breakfast

## 61.4 MILCHPRODUKTE • MILK PRODUCTS

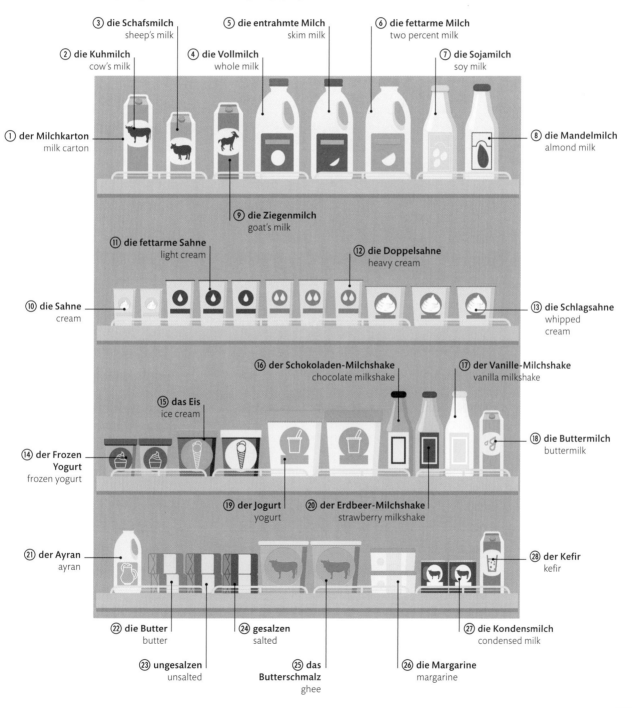

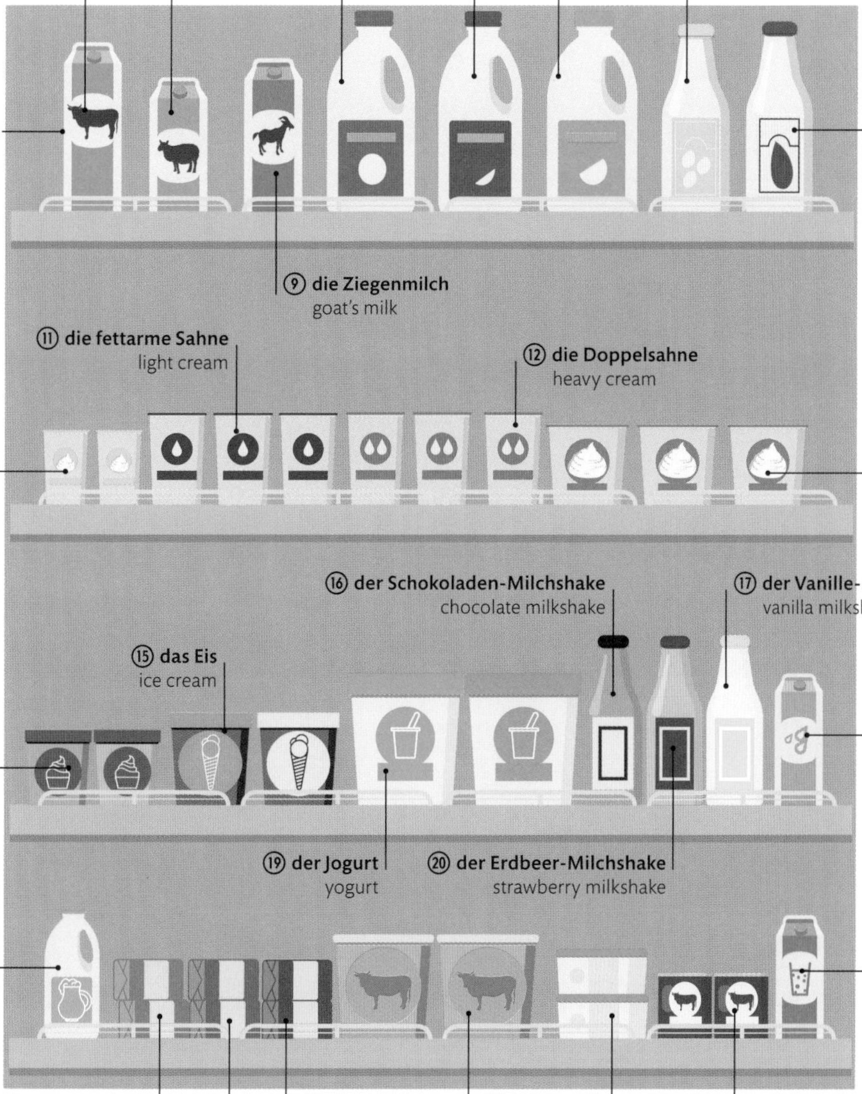

# 62 Die Bäckerei
## The bakery

## 62.1 **BROT UND MEHL** · BREADS AND FLOURS

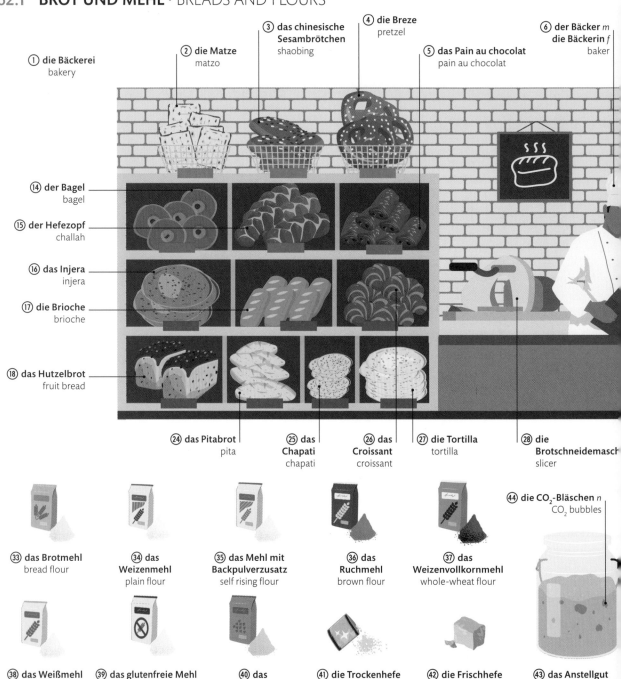

① **die Bäckerei**
bakery

② **die Matze**
matzo

③ **das chinesische Sesambrötchen**
shaobing

④ **die Breze**
pretzel

⑤ **das Pain au chocolat**
pain au chocolat

⑥ **der Bäcker** *m*
**die Bäckerin** *f*
baker

⑭ **der Bagel**
bagel

⑮ **der Hefezopf**
challah

⑯ **das Injera**
injera

⑰ **die Brioche**
brioche

⑱ **das Hutzelbrot**
fruit bread

㉔ **das Pitabrot**
pita

㉕ **das Chapati**
chapati

㉖ **das Croissant**
croissant

㉗ **die Tortilla**
tortilla

㉘ **die Brotschneidemasch**
slicer

㉝ **das Brotmehl**
bread flour

㉞ **das Weizenmehl**
plain flour

㉟ **das Mehl mit Backpulverzusatz**
self rising flour

㊱ **das Ruchmehl**
brown flour

㊲ **das Weizenvollkornmehl**
whole-wheat flour

㊳ **das Weißmehl**
white flour

㊴ **das glutenfreie Mehl**
gluten-free flour

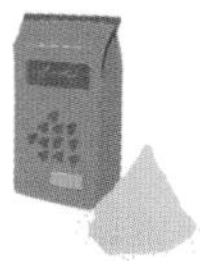

㊵ **das Buchweizenmehl**
buckwheat flour

㊶ **die Trockenhefe**
dried yeast

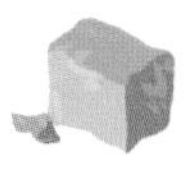

㊷ **die Frischhefe**
fresh yeast

㊹ **die $CO_2$-Bläschen** *n*
$CO_2$ bubbles

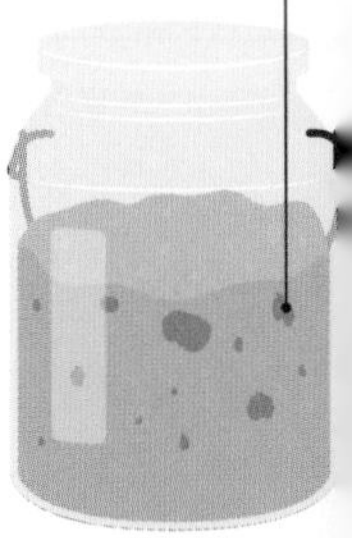

㊸ **das Anstellgut**
sourdough starter

See also
**29** Kochen • Cooking **52** Trinken und essen • Drinking and eating
**63** Die Bäckerei (Fortsetzung) • The bakery continued **65-66** Im Café • At the café **69** Im Restaurant • At the restaurant **71** Das Frühstück • Breakfast

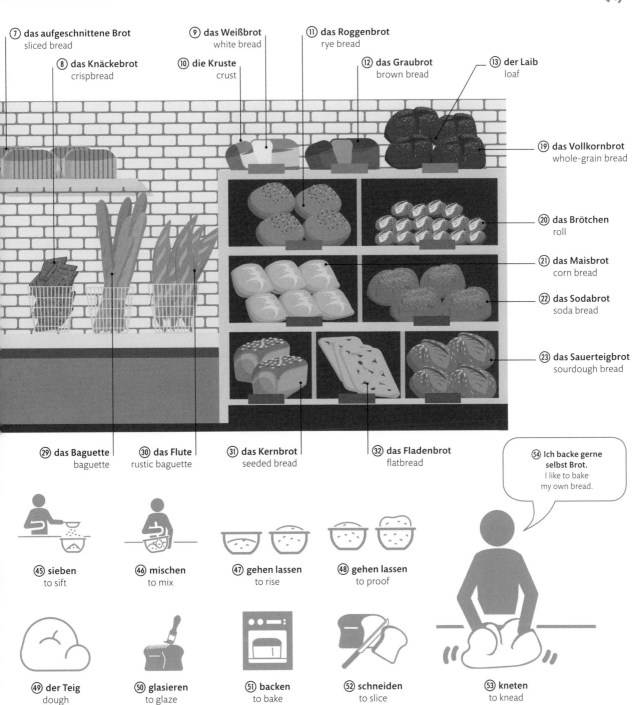

⑦ **das aufgeschnittene Brot**
sliced bread

⑧ **das Knäckebrot**
crispbread

⑨ **das Weißbrot**
white bread

⑩ **die Kruste**
crust

⑪ **das Roggenbrot**
rye bread

⑫ **das Graubrot**
brown bread

⑬ **der Laib**
loaf

⑲ **das Vollkornbrot**
whole-grain bread

⑳ **das Brötchen**
roll

㉑ **das Maisbrot**
corn bread

㉒ **das Sodabrot**
soda bread

㉓ **das Sauerteigbrot**
sourdough bread

㉙ **das Baguette**
baguette

㉚ **das Flute**
rustic baguette

㉛ **das Kernbrot**
seeded bread

㉜ **das Fladenbrot**
flatbread

㊺ **sieben**
to sift

㊻ **mischen**
to mix

㊼ **gehen lassen**
to rise

㊽ **gehen lassen**
to proof

㊾ **Ich backe gerne selbst Brot.**
I like to bake my own bread.

㊾ **der Teig**
dough

㊿ **glasieren**
to glaze

51 **backen**
to bake

52 **schneiden**
to slice

53 **kneten**
to knead

# Die Bäckerei (Fortsetzung)
The bakery continued

## 63.1 KUCHEN UND NACHSPEISEN · CAKES AND DESSERTS

① **der Brandteig**
choux pastry

② **der Blätterteig**
puff pastry

③ **der Filoteig**
phyllo

⑬ **die Konditorcreme**
crème pâtissière

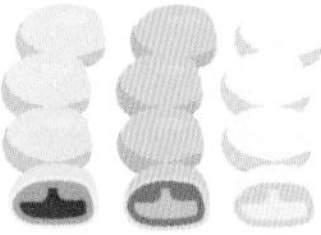
⑭ **das Mochi**
mochi

⑮ **der Donut**
donut

⑯ **der Berliner**
jelly donut

⑰ **der Schokodonut**
chocolate donut

⑱ **der Muffin**
muffin

⑲ **die Baklava**
baklava

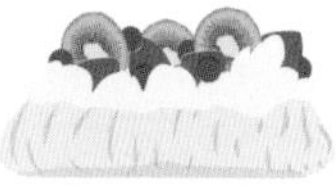
⑳ **die Pavlova**
pavlova

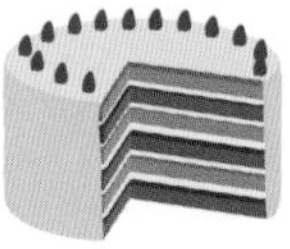
㉑ **der Schichtkuchen**
layer cake

㉒ **der Rührkuchen**
sponge cake

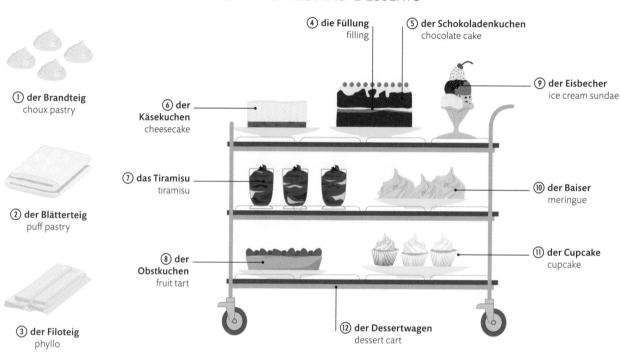

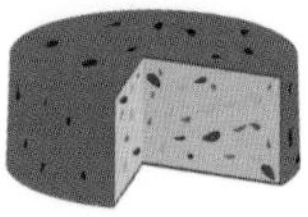
㉓ **das Früchtebrot**
fruitcake

㉔ **die Torte**
gateau

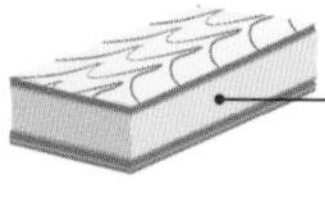
㉖ **der Vanillepudding**
custard

㉕ **die Cremeschnitte**
Napolean

㉗ **das Eclair**
éclair

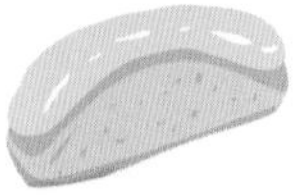
㉘ **das Iced Bun**
iced bun

㉙ **das Plundergebäck**
pastry

㉚ **der Milchreis**
rice pudding

See also
**29** Kochen • Cooking **52** Trinken und essen • Drinking and eating **67** Süßigkeiten • Candy **71** Das Frühstück • Breakfast

## 63.2 KEKSE • COOKIES AND BISCUITS

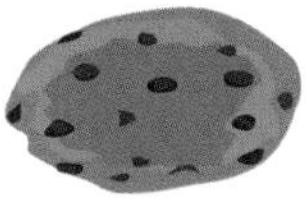

① **der Schokoladen-Cookie**
chocolate chip cookie

② **der Florentiner**
Florentine

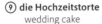

③ **das Mürbegebäck**
shortbread

④ **die Makrone**
macaron

⑤ **der Lebkuchenmann**
gingerbread man

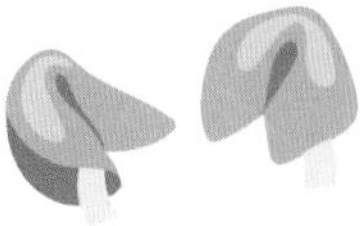

⑥ **der Glückskeks**
fortune cookies

## 63.3 KUCHEN ZU FEIERLICHEN ANLÄSSEN • CELEBRATION CAKES

⑨ **die Hochzeitstorte**
wedding cake

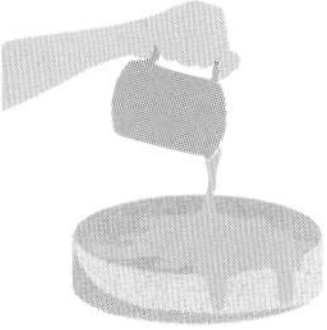

⑩ **glasieren**
to glaze

⑪ **backen**
to bake

⑫ **dekorieren**
to decorate

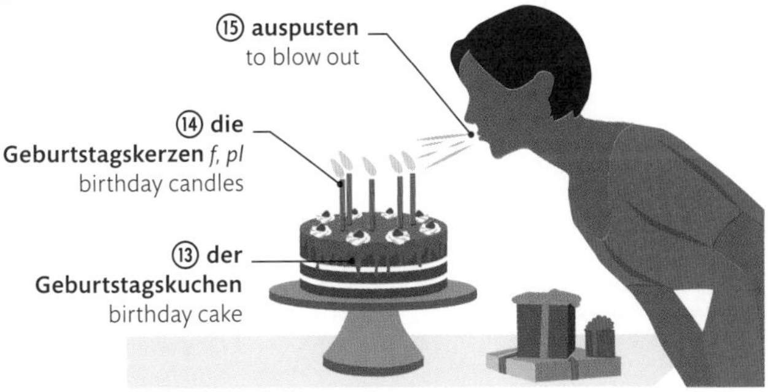

# Im Feinkostladen
## The delicatessen

## 64.1 **DAS FEINKOSTGESCHÄFT** · DELICATESSEN

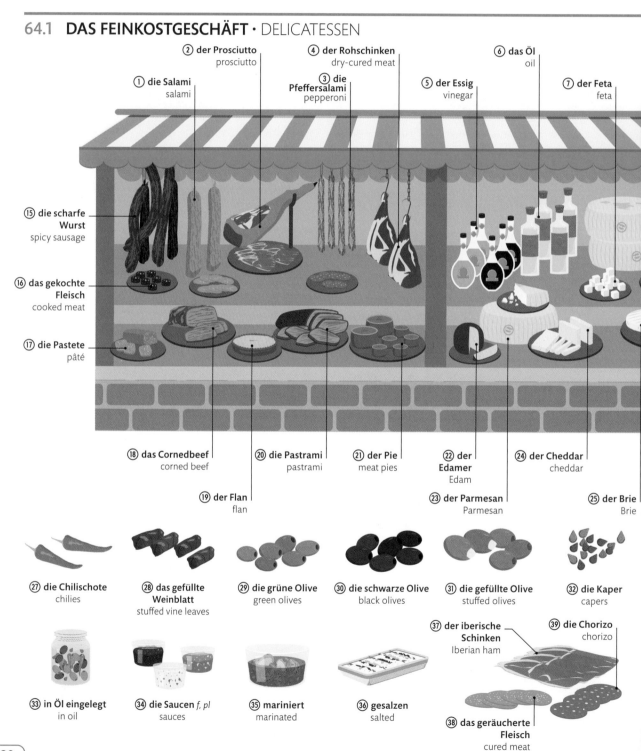

㉗ **die Chilischote**
chilies

㉘ **das gefüllte Weinblatt**
stuffed vine leaves

㉙ **die grüne Olive**
green olives

㉚ **die schwarze Olive**
black olives

㉛ **die gefüllte Olive**
stuffed olives

㉜ **die Kaper**
capers

㉝ **in Öl eingelegt**
in oil

㉞ **die Saucen** *f, pl*
sauces

㉟ **mariniert**
marinated

㊱ **gesalzen**
salted

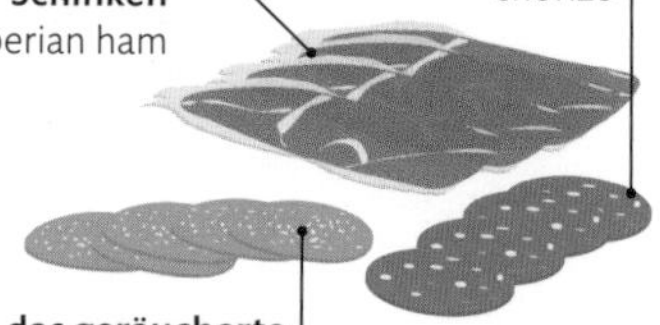

See also
**29** Kochen • Cooking **52** Trinken und essen • Drinking and eating **53** Fleisch • Meat **60** In der Vorratskammer • In the pantry **61** Milchprodukte • Dairy produce **65-66** Im Café • At the café **69** Im Restaurant At the restaurant **71** Das Frühstück • Breakfast **72** Die Mittagessen und das Abendessen • Lunch and dinner

⑧ **die Rinde**
rind

⑨ **Probieren Sie diese verschiedenen Käsesorten!**
Try these different types of cheese!

⑩ **der Paneer**
paneer

⑪ **der Halloumi**
halloumi

⑫ **der Mozzarella**
mozzarella

⑬ **der Manchego**
manchego

⑭ **die Käsesorten**
*f, pl*
cheeses

㉖ **der Camembert**
Camembert

㊵ **der Räucherlachs**
smoked salmon

㊶ **die geräucherte Makrele**
smoked mackerel

㊷ **der geräucherte Schellfisch**
smoked haddock

㊸ **der Räucherfisch**
smoked fish

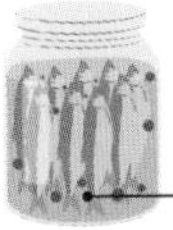

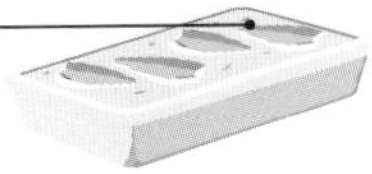

㊻ **die Sardine**
sardines

㊺ **die Anchovi**
anchovies

㊹ **in Lake eingelegt**
in brine

㊼ **der marinierte Fisch**
marinated fish

## 64.2 PASTA UND NUDELN
### PASTA AND NOODLES

① **die Lasagne**
lasagne

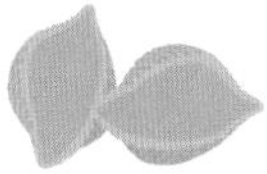

② **die Muschelnudel**
conchiglie / shells

③ **die Fusilli**
fusilli

④ **die Makkaroni**
macaroni

⑤ **die Gnocchi**
gnocchi

⑥ **die Penne**
penne

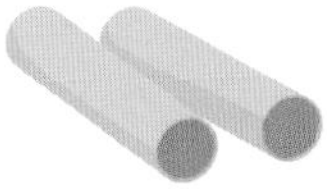

⑦ **die Cannelloni**
cannelloni

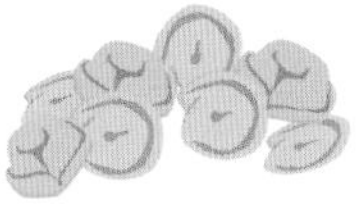

⑧ **die Tortellini**
tortellini

⑨ **die Nudeln**
noodles

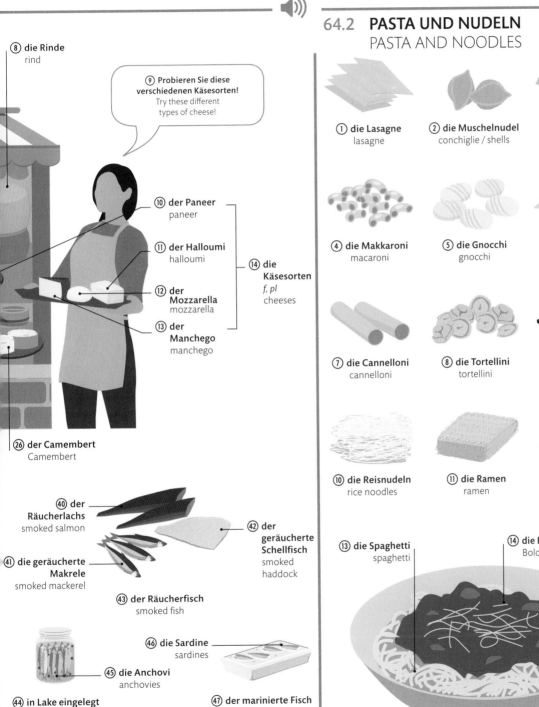

⑩ **die Reisnudeln**
rice noodles

⑪ **die Ramen**
ramen

⑫ **die Udon**
udon

⑬ **die Spaghetti**
spaghetti

⑭ **die Bolognesesauce**
Bolognese sauce

# 65 Im Café
## At the café

### 65.1 DAS CAFÉ • CAFÉ

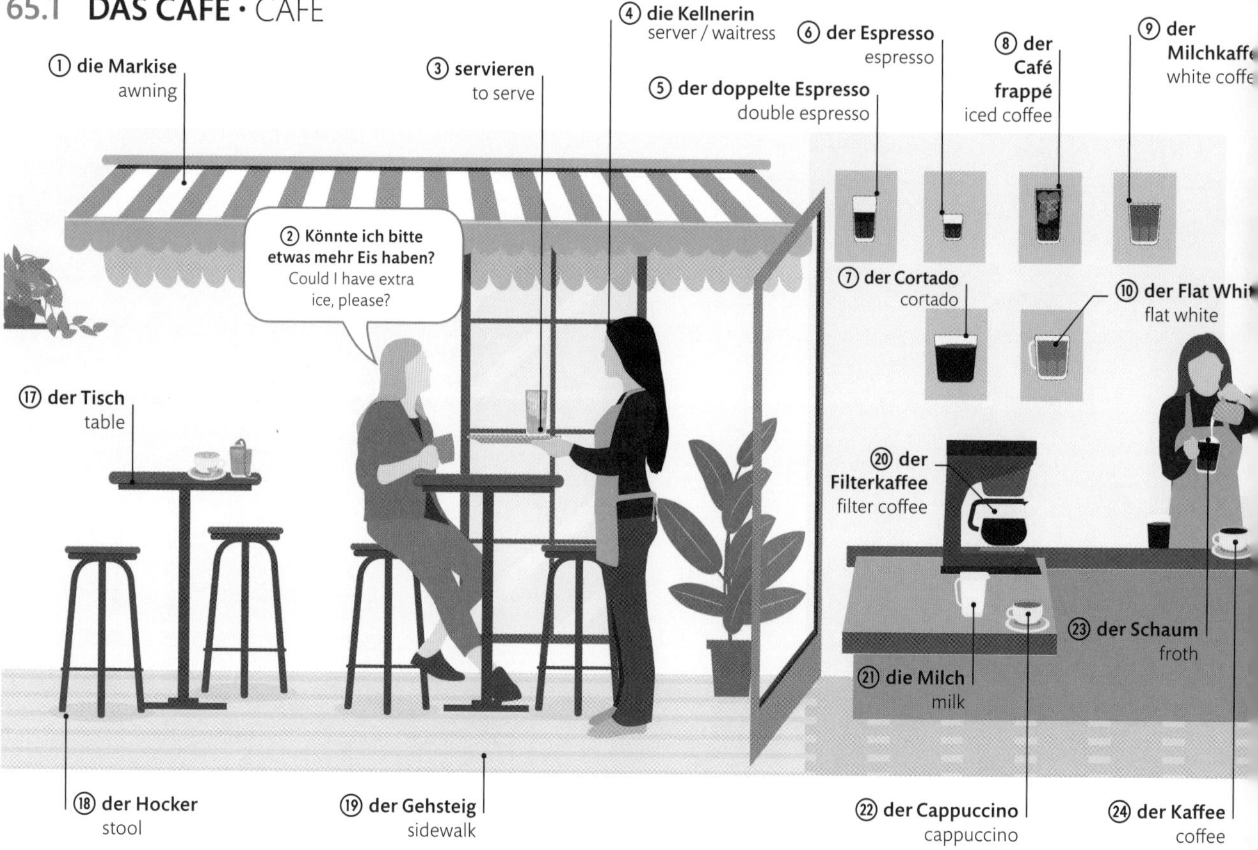

(1) die Markise
awning
(2) Könnte ich bitte etwas mehr Eis haben?
Could I have extra ice, please?
(3) servieren
to serve
(4) die Kellnerin
server / waitress
(5) der doppelte Espresso
double espresso
(6) der Espresso
espresso
(7) der Cortado
cortado
(8) der Café frappé
iced coffee
(9) der Milchkaffe
white coffe
(10) der Flat Whi
flat white
(17) der Tisch
table
(18) der Hocker
stool
(19) der Gehsteig
sidewalk
(20) der Filterkaffee
filter coffee
(21) die Milch
milk
(22) der Cappuccino
cappuccino
(23) der Schaum
froth
(24) der Kaffee
coffee

### 65.2 SÄFTE UND MILCHSHAKES • JUICES AND MILKSHAKES

(1) der Mixer
blender
(2) das Kokoswasser
coconut water
(3) der Orangensaft mit Fruchtfleisch
orange juice with pulp
(4) der Orangensaft ohne Fruchtfleisch
smooth orange juice
(5) der Apfelsaft
apple juice
(6) der Ananassaft
pineapple juice
(7) der Tomatensaft
tomato juice
(8) der Mangosaft
mango juice
(9) der Cranberrysaft
cranberry juice
(10) der Erdbeer-Smoothie
strawberry smoothie
(11) der Schokoladen-Milchshake
chocolate milkshake
(12) der Erdbeer-Milchshake
strawberry milkshake

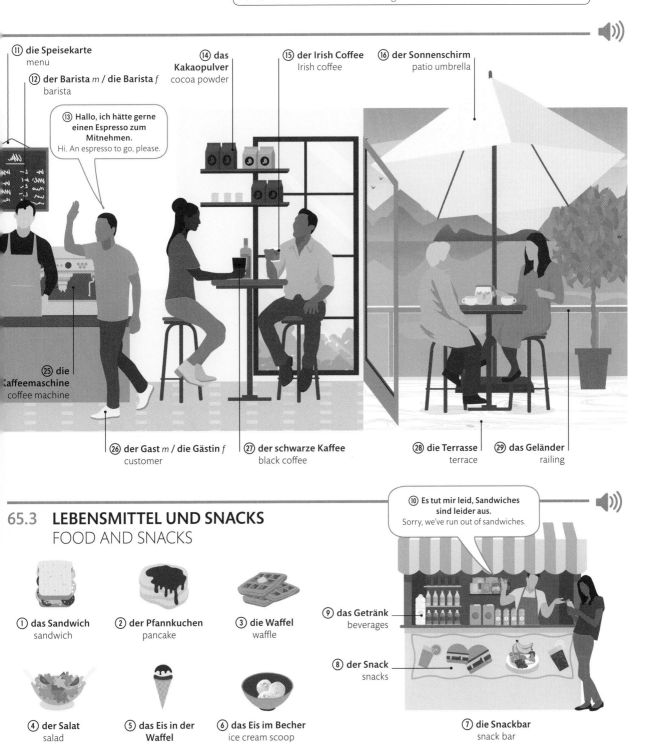

See also
**27** Die Küche und das Geschirr • Kitchen and tableware **52** Trinken und essen Drinking and eating **66** Im Café (Fortsetzung) • At the café continued
**70** Fastfood • Fast food **72** Das Mittagessen und das Abendessen • Lunch and dinner

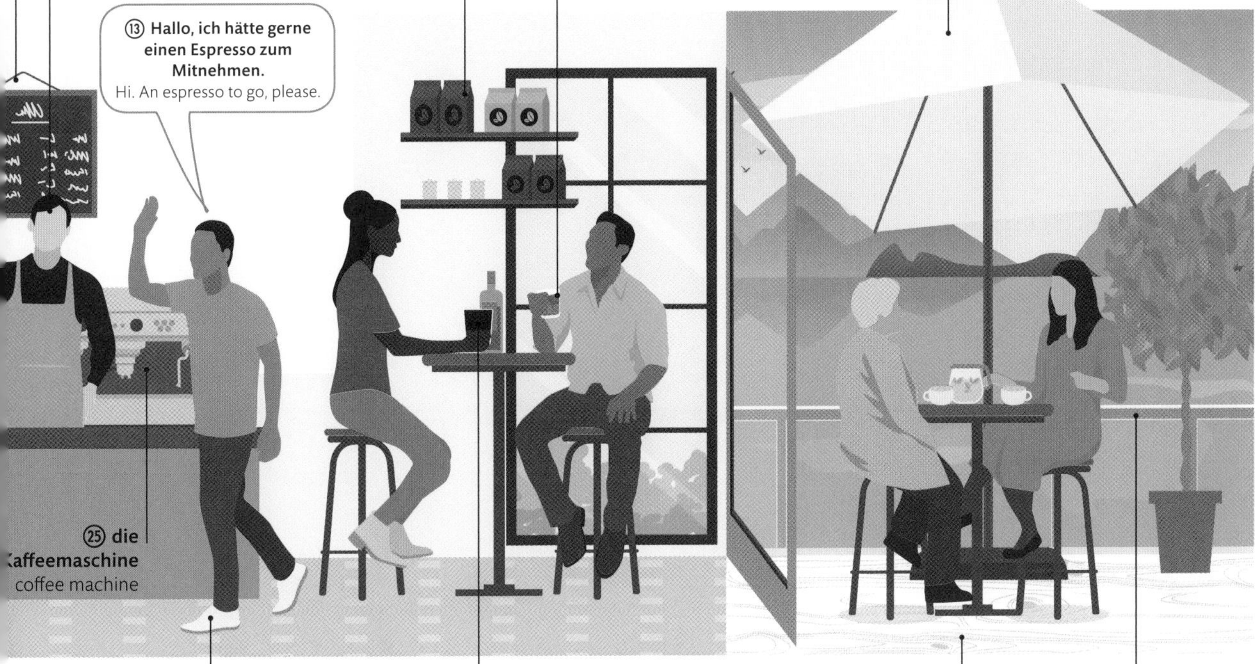


## 65.3 LEBENSMITTEL UND SNACKS
FOOD AND SNACKS

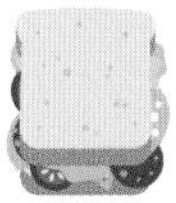
① **das Sandwich**
sandwich

② **der Pfannkuchen**
pancake

③ **die Waffel**
waffle

④ **der Salat**
salad

⑤ **das Eis in der Waffel**
ice cream cone

⑥ **das Eis im Becher**
ice cream scoop

⑦ **die Snackbar**
snack bar

# Im Café (Fortsetzung)
## At the café continued

See also
**27** Die Küche und das Geschirr • Kitchen and tableware **52** Trinken und essen• Drinking and eating **72** Das Mittagessen und das Abendessen Lunch and dinner

### 66.1 **TEE** • TEA

# 67 Süßigkeiten
## Candy

See also
**48** Der Supermarkt • The supermarket
**62-63** Die Bäckerei • The bakery

### 67.1 IM SÜSSIGKEITENLADEN • CANDY STORE

(5) **das Gummibärchen**
soft candy

(11) **die Bonbons** *n, pl*
hard candy

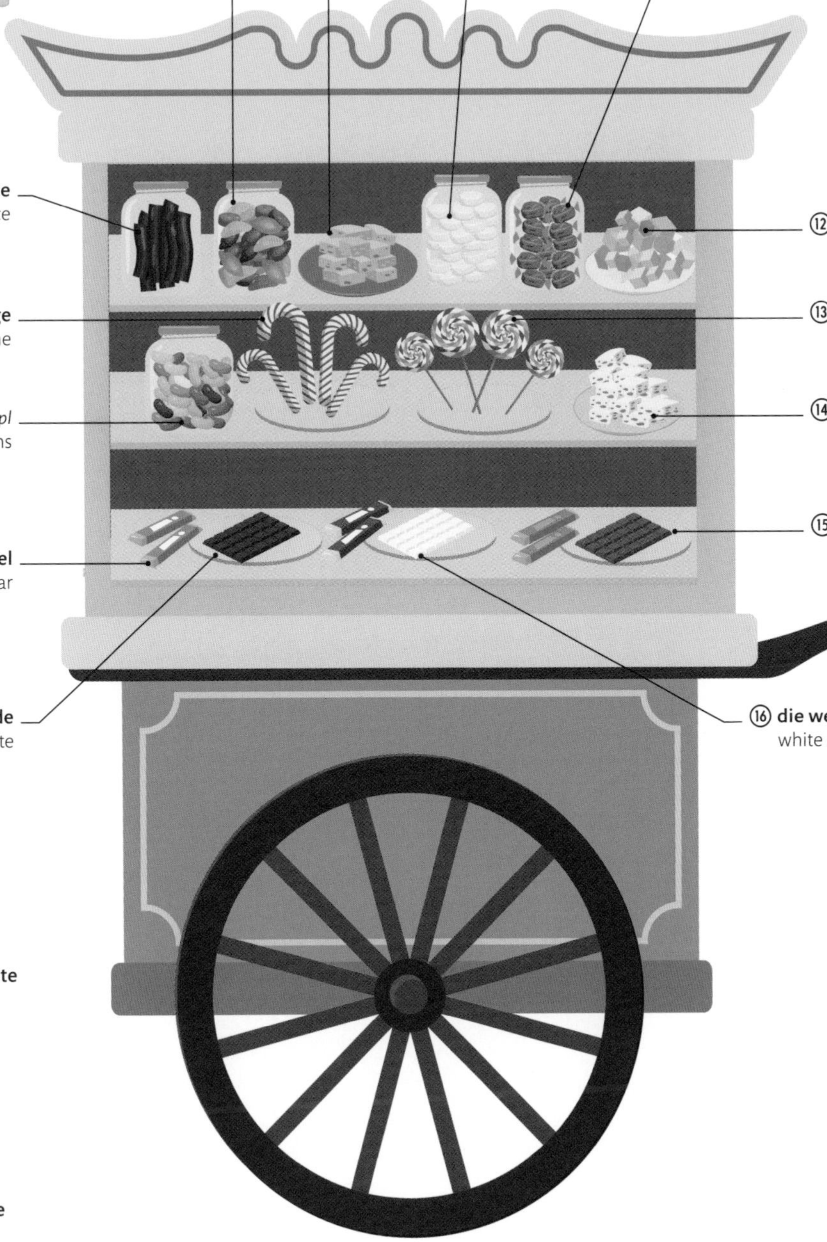

(1) **der Fruchtgummi**
fruit gummies

(2) **das Halva**
halva

(3) **das Minzbonbon**
mint

(4) **das Sahnebonbon**
toffee

(6) **die Lakritze**
licorice

(7) **die Zuckerstange**
candy cane

(8) **die Geleebonbons** *n, pl*
jelly beans

(9) **die Schokoladentafel**
chocolate bar

(10) **die Zartbitterschokolade**
dark chocolate

(12) **das Lokum**
Turkish delight

(13) **der Lutscher**
lollipop

(14) **das Nugat**
nougat

(15) **die Milchschokolade**
milk chocolate

(16) **die weiße Schokolade**
white chocolate

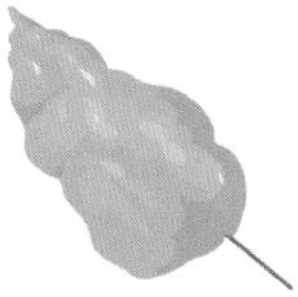

(17) **die Zuckerwatte**
cotton candy

(18) **selbst gemischte Süßigkeiten** *f, pl*
penny candy

(19) **der Marshmallow**
marshmallow

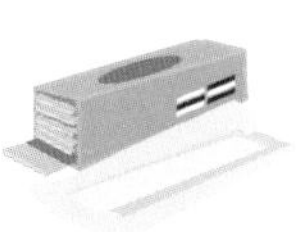

(20) **der Kaugummi**
chewing gum

# 68 In der Bar
## At the bar

### 68.1 DIE BAR · BAR

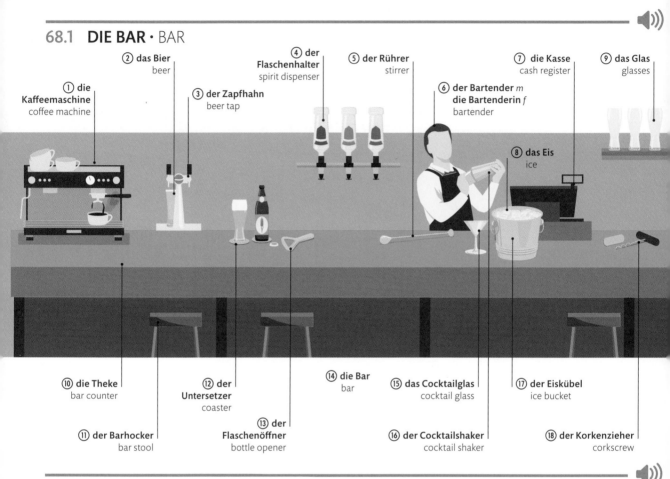

① die Kaffeemaschine
coffee machine

② das Bier
beer

③ der Zapfhahn
beer tap

④ der Flaschenhalter
spirit dispenser

⑤ der Rührer
stirrer

⑥ der Bartender *m*
die Bartenderin *f*
bartender

⑦ die Kasse
cash register

⑧ das Eis
ice

⑨ das Glas
glasses

⑩ die Theke
bar counter

⑪ der Barhocker
bar stool

⑫ der Untersetzer
coaster

⑬ der Flaschenöffner
bottle opener

⑭ die Bar
bar

⑮ das Cocktailglas
cocktail glass

⑯ der Cocktailshaker
cocktail shaker

⑰ der Eiskübel
ice bucket

⑱ der Korkenzieher
corkscrew

### 68.2 BIER UND WEIN · BEER AND WINE

① das Lagerbier
lager

② das Pilsner
Pilsner

③ das Weizenbier
wheat beer

④ das India Pale Ale
Indian pale ale (IPA)

⑤ das Ale
ale

⑥ das Starkbier
stout

⑦ das alkoholfreie Bier
alcohol-free beer

⑧ der Rotwein
red wine

⑨ der Weißwein
white wine

⑩ der Rosé
rosé

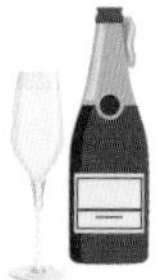

⑪ der Sekt
sparkling wine

⑫ der Champagner
Champagne

See also
**52** Tricken und essen • Drinking and eating **69** Im Restaurant • At the restaurant
**72** Das Mittagessen und das Abendessen • Lunch and dinner

## 68.3 GETRÄNKE • DRINKS

① **das Mineralwasser**
mineral water

② **der Cidre**
cider

③ **der Rum**
rum

④ **Rum und Cola** *m*
rum and cola

⑤ **der Wodka**
vodka

⑥ **der Wodka Orange**
vodka and orange

⑦ **der Gin Tonic**
gin and tonic

⑧ **der Martini**
Martini

⑨ **der Cocktail**
cocktail

⑩ **der alkoholfreie Cocktail**
mocktail

⑪ **der Sherry**
sherry

⑫ **der Portwein**
port

⑬ **der Whisky**
whiskey

⑭ **der Whisky mit Wasser**
Scotch and water

⑮ **der Branntwein**
brandy

⑯ **der Likör**
liqueur

⑰ **mit Eis**
with ice

⑱ **ohne Eis**
without ice

⑳ **doppelt**
double

⑲ **einfach**
single

㉑ **ein Shot**
shot

㉒ **das Maß**
measure

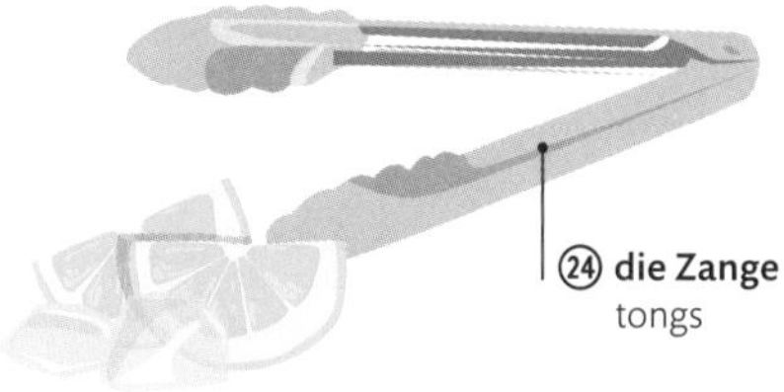

㉔ **die Zange**
tongs

㉓ **Eis und Zitrone** *n / f*
ice and lemon

## 68.4 BARSNACKS • BAR SNACKS

① **die Chips** *m, pl*
chips

② **die Nüsse** *f, pl*
nuts

③ **die Mandeln** *f, pl*
almonds

④ **die Cashew-Nuss** *f, pl*
cashews

⑤ **die Erdnüsse** *f, pl*
peanuts

⑥ **die Oliven** *f, pl*
olives

# 69 Im Restaurant
## At the restaurant

### 69.1 DAS RESTAURANT · RESTAURANT

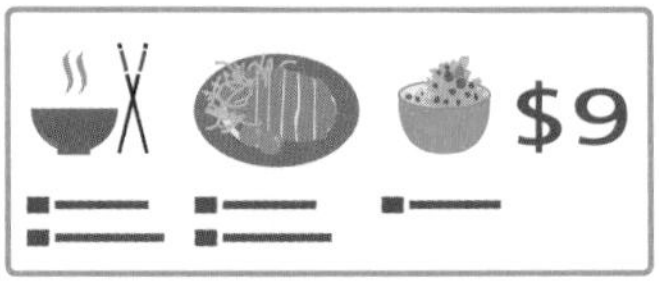

**⑱ das Menü**
fixed menu

**⑲ der Brunch**
brunch

**⑳ die Mittagskarte**
lunch menu

**㉑ das À-la-Carte-Menü**
à la carte menu

**㉒ die Tageskarte**
specials

**㉓ das Kindermenü**
kids meal

**㉔ das Buffet**
buffet

**㉕ das Dreigängemenü**
three-course meal

**㉖ die Suppe**
soup

**㉗ die Vorspeise**
appetizer

**㉘ die Hauptspeise**
entrée

**㉙ die Beilage**
side / side order

**㉚ die Käseplatte**
cheese platter

**㉛ das Dessert**
dessert

**㉜ das Getränk**
beverage

**㉝ der Kaffee**
coffee

**㉞ der Digestif**
digestif

See also
**27** Die Küche und das Geschirr • Kitchen and tableware **52** Trinken und essen • Drinking and eating **53** Fleisch • Meat **54** Fisch und Meeresfrüchte • Fish and seafood **55-56** Gemüse • Vegetables **72** Das Mittagessen und das Abendessen • Lunch and dinner

⑤ **der Preis**
price

⑥ **das Tablett**
tray

⑧ **die Küche**
kitchen

⑨ **der Koch** *m*
**die Köchin** *f*
chef

⑩ **der Assistenzkoch** *m*
**die Assistenzköchin** *f*
commis chef

⑦ **Ich wünsche guten Appetit!**
Enjoy your meal!

⑮ **die Abendkarte**
dinner menu

⑯ **der Kellner**
server / waiter

⑰ **der Dessertwagen**
dessert cart

㉟ **der Sommelier** *m*
**die Sommelière** *f*
sommelier

㊱ **essen gehen**
to eat out

㊲ **einen Tisch reservieren**
to make a reservation

㊳ **absagen**
to cancel

㊴ **bestellen**
to order

㊵ **die Rechnung**
check

㊶ **getrennt zahlen**
to pay separately

㊷ **die Rechnung aufteilen**
to split the check

㊸ **der Bedienungszuschlag**
service charge

㊹ **Bedienung enthalten**
service included

㊺ **Bedienung nicht enthalten**
service not included

㊻ **das Trinkgeld**
tip

㊼ **der Beleg**
receipt

㊽ **das Bistro**
bistro

# 70 Fastfood
## Fast food

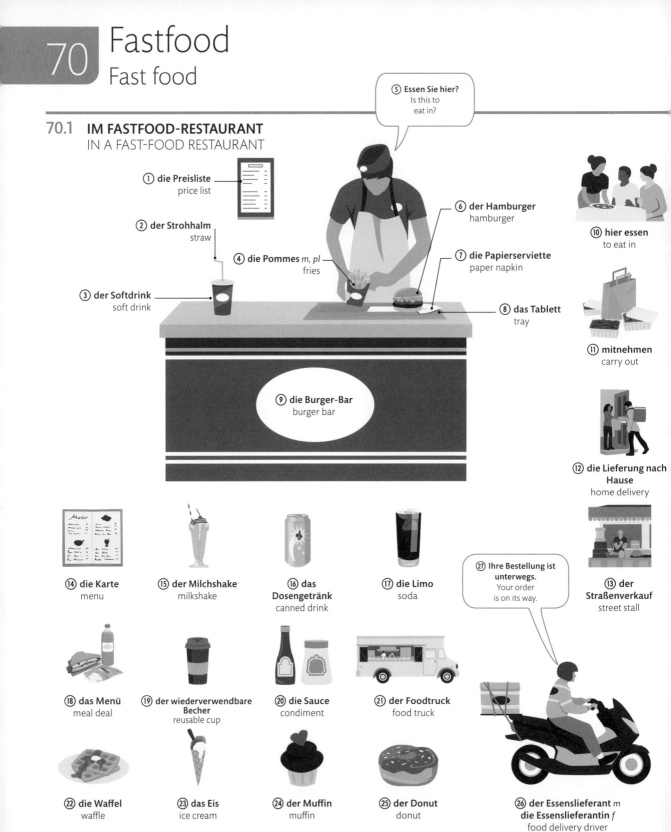

### 70.1 IM FASTFOOD-RESTAURANT
IN A FAST-FOOD RESTAURANT

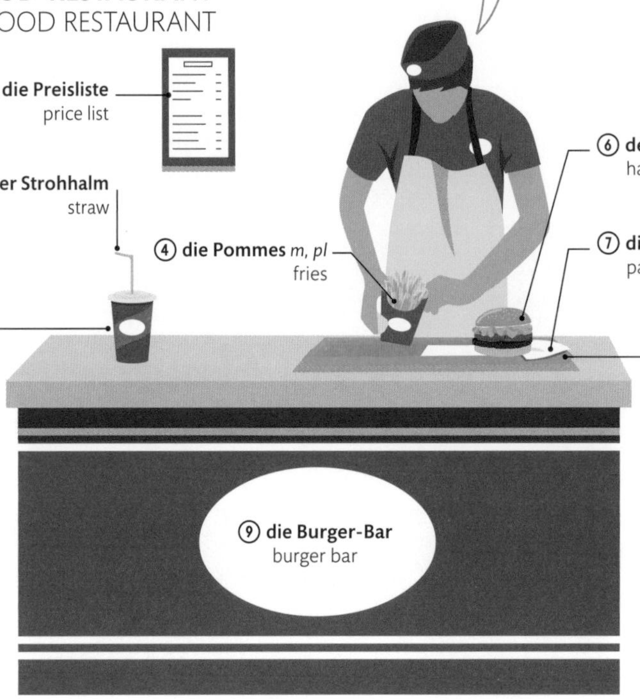

① **die Preisliste** price list

② **der Strohhalm** straw

③ **der Softdrink** soft drink

④ **die Pommes** *m, pl* fries

⑤ **Essen Sie hier?** Is this to eat in?

⑥ **der Hamburger** hamburger

⑦ **die Papierserviette** paper napkin

⑧ **das Tablett** tray

⑨ **die Burger-Bar** burger bar

⑩ **hier essen** to eat in

⑪ **mitnehmen** carry out

⑫ **die Lieferung nach Hause** home delivery

⑬ **der Straßenverkauf** street stall

⑭ **die Karte** menu

⑮ **der Milchshake** milkshake

⑯ **das Dosengetränk** canned drink

⑰ **die Limo** soda

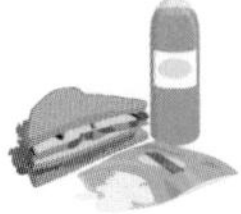

⑱ **das Menü** meal deal

⑲ **der wiederverwendbare Becher** reusable cup

⑳ **die Sauce** condiment

㉑ **der Foodtruck** food truck

㉒ **die Waffel** waffle

㉓ **das Eis** ice cream

㉔ **der Muffin** muffin

㉕ **der Donut** donut

㉗ **Ihre Bestellung ist unterwegs.** Your order is on its way.

㉖ **der Essenslieferant** *m* **die Essenslieferantin** *f* food delivery driver

See also
**52** Trinken und essen • Drinking and eating **60** In der Vorratskammer • In the pantry **65** Im Café • At the café **67** Süßigkeiten • Candy

**㉙ der Cheeseburger**
cheeseburger

**㉚ der Hähnchenburger**
chicken sandwich

**㉘ der vegetarische Burger**
veggie burger

**㉛ der Burger**
burger

**㉜ die Chicken Nuggets** *n, pl*
chicken nuggets

**㉝ das frittierte Hähnchen**
fried chicken

**㉞ der Kartoffelpuffer**
hash browns

**㉟ Fish and Chips** *pl*
fish and chips

**㊳ der Senf**
mustard

**㊲ der Ketchup**
ketchup

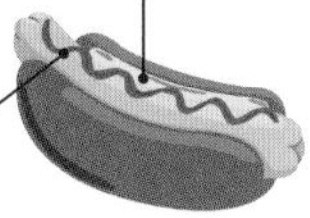

**㊱ der Hotdog**
hot dog

**㊴ der Spieß**
kebab

**㊵ die Rippe**
ribs

**㊶ die Nudeln** *f, pl*
noodles

**㊷ die Klöße** *m, pl*
dumplings

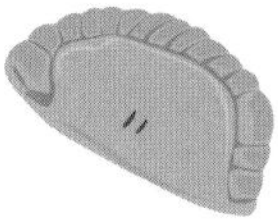

**㊸ die Empanada**
empanada

**㊺ die Füllung**
filling

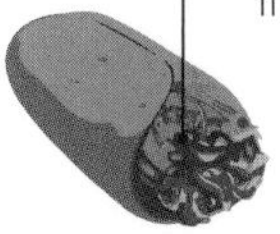

**㊹ der Wrap**
wrap

**㊻ die Crêpe**
crêpe

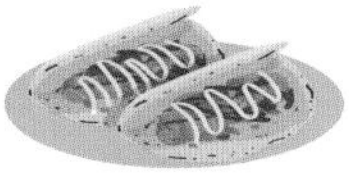

**㊼ der Taco**
taco

**㊽ die Falafel**
falafel

**㊾ die Nachos** *m, pl*
nachos

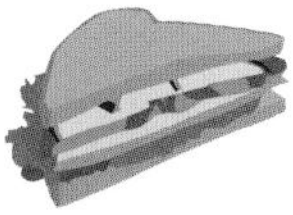

**㊿ das Sandwich**
sandwich

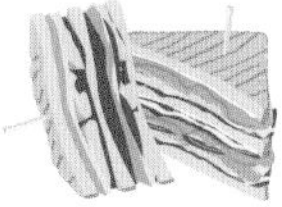

**51 das Club-Sandwich**
club sandwich

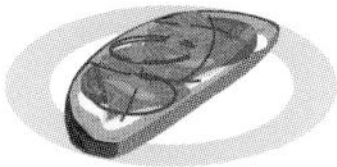

**52 das belegte Brot**
open sandwich

**53 der Pizzaofen**
pizza oven

**54 die Pizza**
pizza

**55 der Belag**
topping

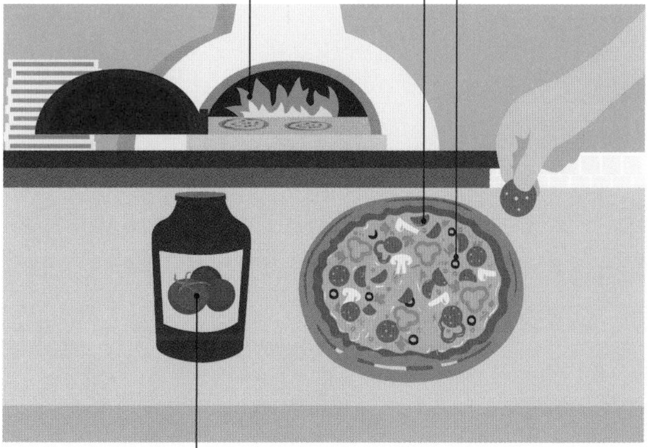

**56 die Tomatensauce**
tomato sauce

**57 die Pizzeria**
pizzeria

# 71 Das Frühstück
## Breakfast

### 71.1 DAS FRÜHSTÜCKSBUFFET · BREAKFAST BUFFET

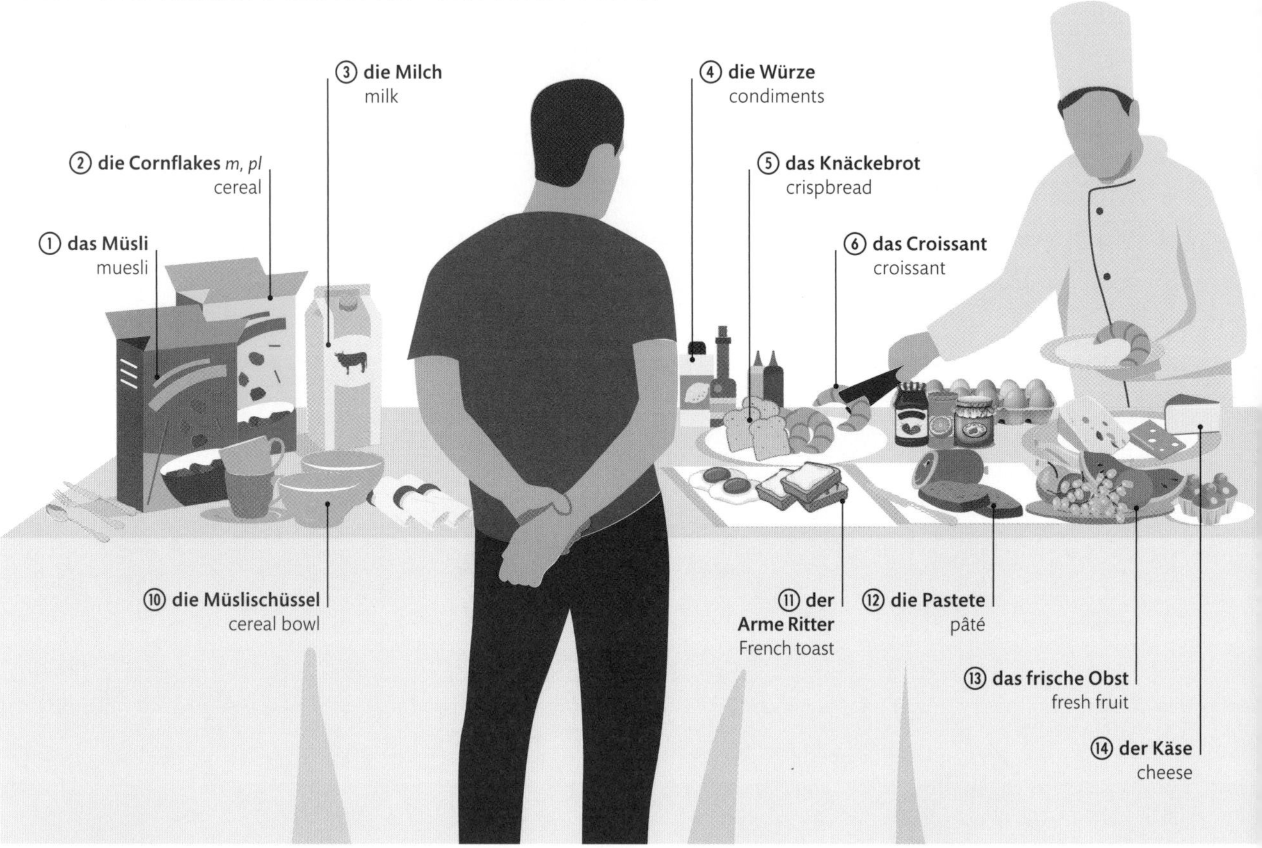

**⑰ der Schinken**
ham

**⑱ das getoastete Sandwich**
toasted sandwich

**⑲ das Omelett**
omelet

**⑳ der Avocadotoast**
avocado toast

**㉑ der Bagel**
bagel

**㉒ die Zimtschnecke**
cinnamon rolls

**㉕ die Marmelade**
jam

**㉖ die Zitrusmarmelade**
marmalade

**㉗ der Honig**
honey

**㉘ der Tee**
tea

**㉙ der Kaffee**
coffee

**㉚ der Fruchtsaft**
fruit juice

See also
29 Kochen • Cooking 52 Trinken und essen • Drinking and eating 53 Fleisch • Meat
57 Obst • Fruit 58 Obst und Nüsse • Fruit and nuts 61 Milchprodukte • Dairy produce
64 Im Feinkostladen • The delicatessen 65-66 Im Café • At the café

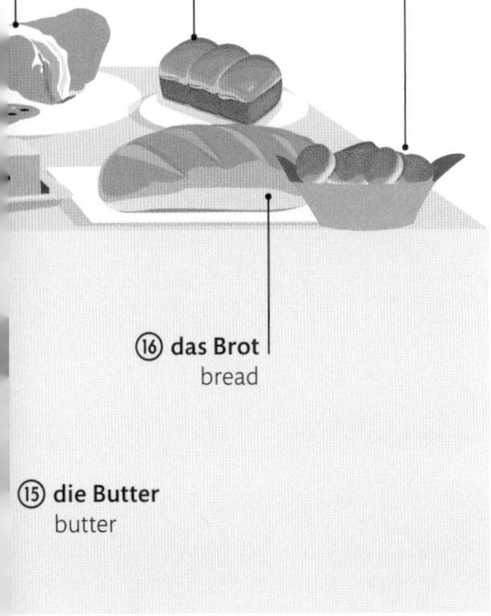

㉓ **die Waffel**
waffles

㉔ **die Sahne**
cream

㉛ **die Trockenfrüchte** *f, pl*
dried fruit

㉜ **der Fruchtjoghurt**
fruit yogurt

## 71.2 DAS WARME FRÜHSTÜCK · COOKED BREAKFAST

① **das Würstchen**
sausage

② **die Frikadellen** *f, pl*
sausage patties

③ **der Bacon**
bacon

④ **der Bückling**
kippers

⑤ **der Räucherlachs**
smoked salmon

⑥ **die geräucherte Makrele**
smoked mackerel

⑦ **die Blutwurst**
black pudding

⑧ **die Niere**
kidneys

⑨ **das Rührei**
scrambled eggs

⑩ **das pochierte Ei**
poached egg

⑪ **das gekochte Ei**
boiled egg

⑫ **das Eiweiß**
egg white

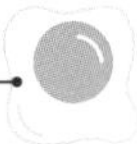
⑬ **das Eigelb**
yolk

⑭ **das Spiegelei**
fried egg

⑮ **der Toast**
toast

⑯ **die gebratenen Pilze** *m, pl*
fried mushrooms

⑰ **der Kartoffelpuffer**
hash browns

⑱ **die gegrillte Tomate**
grilled tomato

⑲ **die Dosentomaten** *f, pl*
canned tomato

⑳ **die Baked Beans** *f, pl*
baked beans

㉑ **das Frühstücksbrötchen**
breakfast roll

㉒ **der Frühstücksburrito**
breakfast burrito

㉓ **das Kartoffelplätzchen**
potato cakes

㉔ **der Pfannkuchen**
pancakes

㉕ **der Haferbrei**
oatmeal

# 72 Das Mittagessen und das Abendessen
Lunch and dinner

## 72.1 MAHLZEITEN UND GERICHTE · MEALS AND DISHES

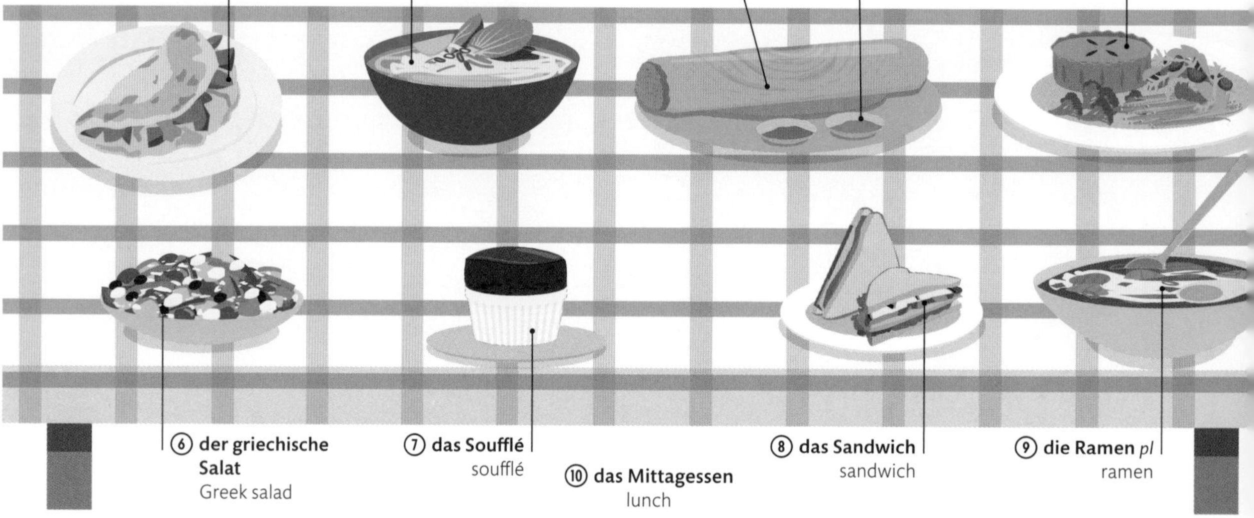

① **das Omelett** omelet
② **die Nudelsuppe** noodle soup
③ **der Dosa** dosa
④ **das Chutney** chutney
⑤ **der Pie** meat pie
⑥ **der griechische Salat** Greek salad
⑦ **das Soufflé** soufflé
⑧ **das Sandwich** sandwich
⑨ **die Ramen** *pl* ramen
⑩ **das Mittagessen** lunch

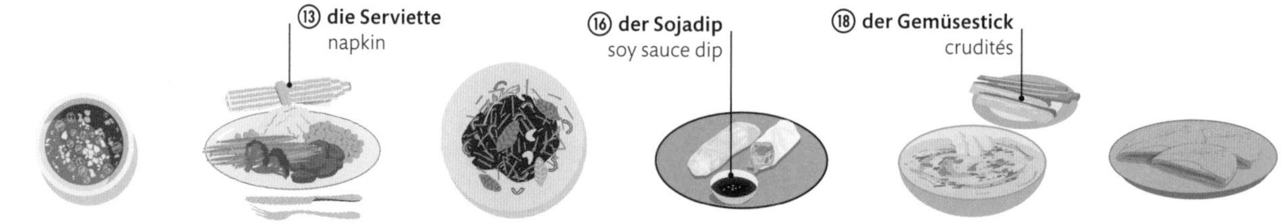

⑪ **die Suppe** soup
⑫ **das gekochte Gemüse** cooked vegetables
⑬ **die Serviette** napkin
⑭ **das Pfannengemüse** stir-fry
⑮ **die Sommerrolle** summer roll
⑯ **der Sojadip** soy sauce dip
⑰ **der Hummus** hummus
⑱ **der Gemüsestick** crudités
⑲ **das Pitabrot** pita bread

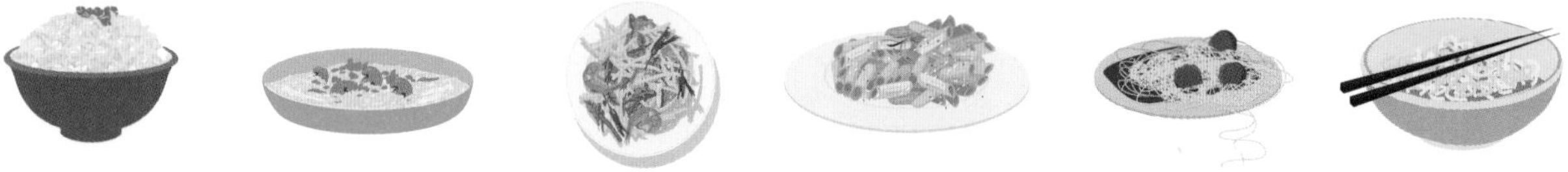

⑳ **der Reis** rice
㉑ **der Risotto** risotto
㉒ **die Paella** paella
㉓ **die Pasta** pasta
㉔ **der Fleischkloß** meatballs
㉕ **die Nudeln** *f, pl* noodles

㉖ **die Beilage** side dishes
㉗ **die Frühlingsrolle** spring roll
㉘ **der Salat** chopped salad
㉙ **das Dressing** dressing
㉚ **das eingemachte Gemüse** pickles
㉛ **die Würze** condiments

See also
**27** Die Küche und das Geschirr • Kitchen and tableware **29** Kochen • Cooking **52** Trinken und essen • Drinking and eating **53** Fleisch • Meat **55-56** Gemüse • Vegetables **65-66** Im Café • At the café **69** Im Restaurant • At the restaurant

42 **das Abendessen**
dinner

## 72.2 ZUBEREITUNG • FOOD PREPARATION

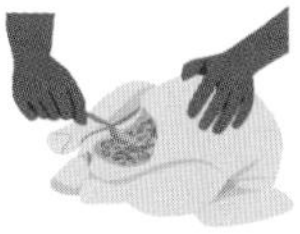
1 **gefüllt**
stuffed

2 **gegrillt**
grilled

3 **mariniert**
marinated

4 **in Sauce**
in sauce

5 **pochiert**
poached

6 **gekocht**
boiled

7 **gebacken**
baked

8 **in der Pfanne gebraten**
stir-fried

9 **gebraten**
fried

10 **frittiert**
deep-fried

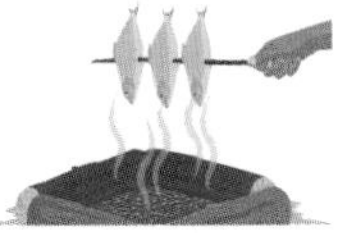
11 **geräuchert**
smoked

12 **gedünstet**
steamed

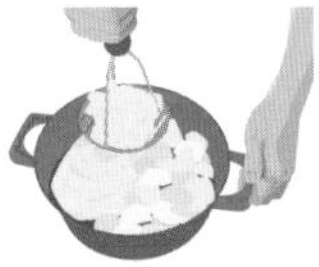
13 **gestampft**
mashed

14 **mit Dressing versehen**
dressed

15 **gepökelt**
cured

16 **eingelegt**
pickled

17 **koscher**
kosher

18 **halal**
halal

# 73 In der Schule
## At school

### 73.1 SCHULE UND LERNEN · SCHOOL AND STUDY

① **die Schule**
school

② **das Klassenzimmer**
classroom

③ **die Klasse**
class

④ **der Lehrer** *m*
**die Lehrerin** *f*
teacher

⑤ **das Whiteboard**
whiteboard

⑥ **der Schüler** *m*
**die Schülerin** *f*
pupil

⑦ **der Schreibtisch**
desk

⑧ **die Schüler** *pl*
school students

⑨ **die Schultasche**
school bag

⑩ **das Schulbuch**
literature

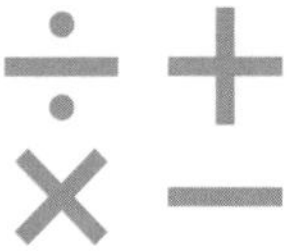
⑪ **Mathematik** *f*
math

⑫ **Geografie** *f*
geography

⑬ **Geschichte** *f*
history

⑭ **Naturwissenschaften** *f, pl*
science

⑮ **Chemie** *f*
chemistry

⑯ **Physik** *f*
physics

⑰ **Biologie** *f*
biology

⑱ **Englisch** *n*
English

⑲ **Fremdsprachen** *f, pl*
languages

⑳ **Handwerk** *n*
design and technology

㉑ **Informatik** *f*
information technology

㉒ **Kunst** *f*
art

㉓ **Musik** *f*
music

㉔ **Schauspiel** *n*
drama

㉕ **Sport** *m*
physical education

㉖ **der Rektor** *m*
**die Rektorin** *f*
principal

㉗ **die Hausaufgaben** *f, pl*
homework

㉘ **die Unterrichtsstunde**
lesson

㉙ **die Prüfung**
exam

㉚ **der Aufsatz**
essay

㉛ **die Note**
grade

㉜ **das Lexikon**
encyclopedia

㉝ **das Wörterbuch**
dictionary

㉞ **der Atlas**
atlas

㉟ **der Test**
test

See also
**74** Mathematik • Mathematics **75** Physik • Physics **76** Chemie • Chemistry **77** Biologie • Biology **79** Geschichte • History **80** An der Universität • At college **83** Computer und Technologie • Computers and technology

## 73.2 SCHULVERBEN • SCHOOL VERBS

① **lesen**
to read

② **schreiben**
to write

③ **fragen**
to question

④ **eine Prüfung machen**
to take a test

⑤ **lernen**
to learn

⑥ **zeichnen**
to draw

⑦ **antworten**
to answer

⑧ **buchstabieren**
to spell

⑨ **wiederholen**
to review

⑩ **eine Prüfung wiederholen**
to retake

⑪ **sich Notizen machen**
to take notes

⑫ **etwas besprechen**
to discuss

⑬ **nicht bestehen**
to fail

⑭ **bestehen**
to pass

⑮ **Ich habe meine Prüfung bestanden!**
I've passed my test.

## 73.3 MATERIALIEN • EQUIPMENT

① **der Bleistift**
pencil

② **der Spitzer**
pencil sharpener

③ **der Stift**
pen

④ **die Feder**
nib

⑤ **der Radiergummi**
eraser

⑥ **der Buntstift**
colored pencils

⑦ **die Federmappe**
pencil case

⑧ **das Lineal**
ruler

⑨ **das Zeichendreieck**
triangle

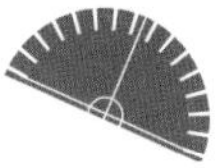
⑩ **der Winkelmesser**
protractor

⑪ **der Taschenrechner**
calculator

⑫ **der Zirkel**
compass

⑬ **das Schulbuch**
textbook

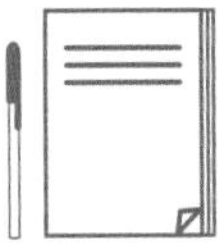
⑭ **das Heft**
notebook / exercise book

⑮ **der Projektor**
digital projector

⑯ **der Textmarker**
highlighter

⑰ **die Büroklammer**
paper clip

⑱ **der Hefter**
stapler

# 74 Mathematik
## Mathematics

### 74.1 FORMEN · SHAPES

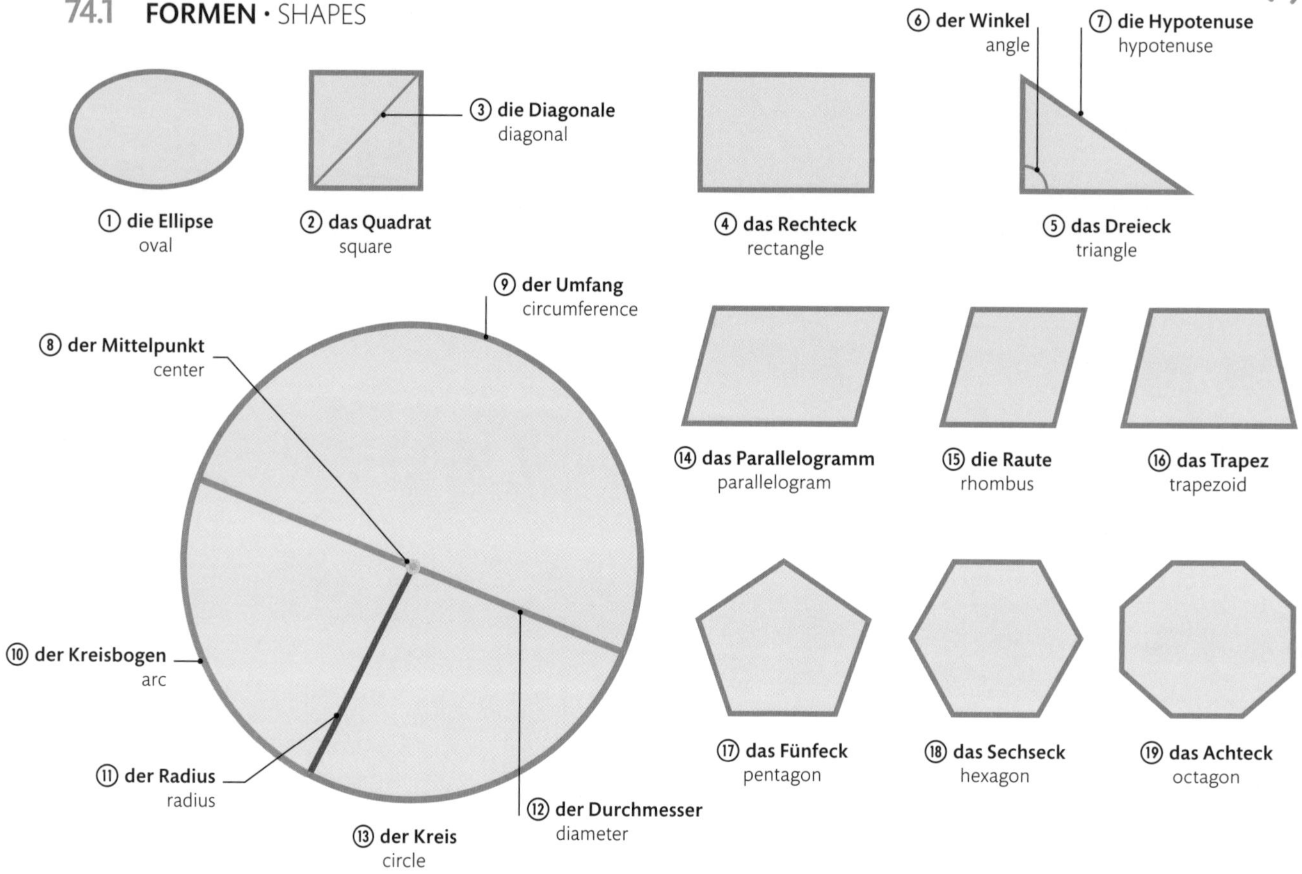

① die Ellipse
oval
② das Quadrat
square
③ die Diagonale
diagonal
④ das Rechteck
rectangle
⑤ das Dreieck
triangle
⑥ der Winkel
angle
⑦ die Hypotenuse
hypotenuse
⑧ der Mittelpunkt
center
⑨ der Umfang
circumference
⑩ der Kreisbogen
arc
⑪ der Radius
radius
⑫ der Durchmesser
diameter
⑬ der Kreis
circle
⑭ das Parallelogramm
parallelogram
⑮ die Raute
rhombus
⑯ das Trapez
trapezoid
⑰ das Fünfeck
pentagon
⑱ das Sechseck
hexagon
⑲ das Achteck
octagon

### 74.2 KÖRPER · SOLIDS

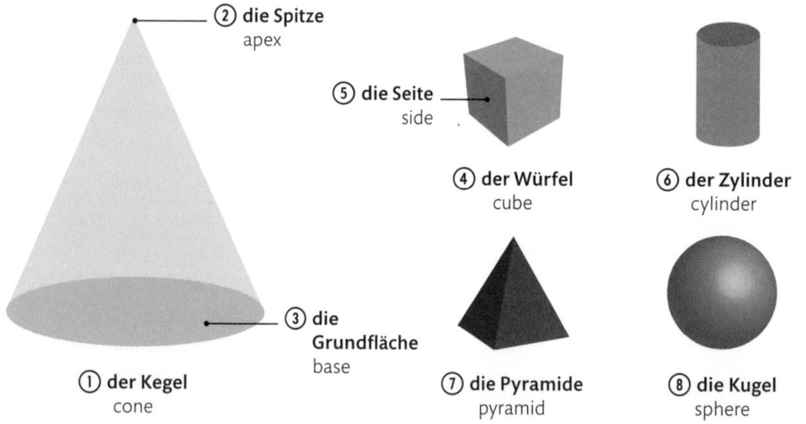

① der Kegel
cone
② die Spitze
apex
③ die Grundfläche
base
④ der Würfel
cube
⑤ die Seite
side
⑥ der Zylinder
cylinder
⑦ die Pyramide
pyramid
⑧ die Kugel
sphere

### 74.3 LINIEN · LINES

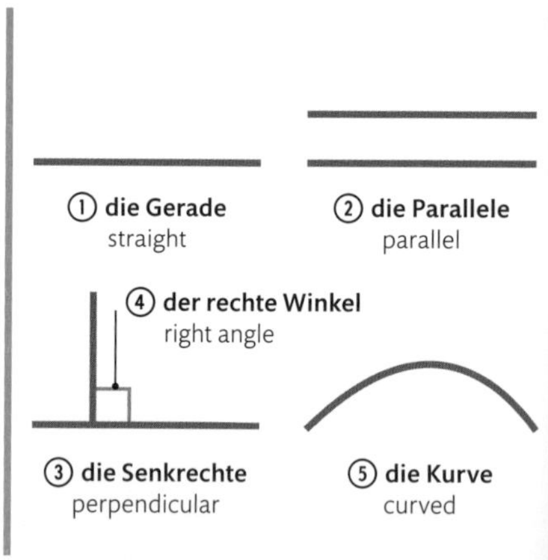

① die Gerade
straight
② die Parallele
parallel
③ die Senkrechte
perpendicular
④ der rechte Winkel
right angle
⑤ die Kurve
curved

See also
**73** In der Schule • At school **94** Geld und Finanzen • Money and finance
**173** Zahlen • Numbers **174** Gewichte und Maße • Weights and measures

## 74.4 MESSUNGEN • MEASUREMENTS

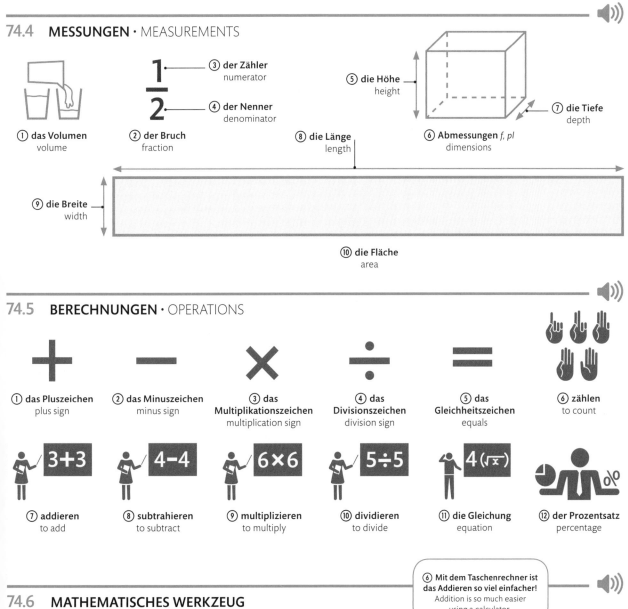

① **das Volumen**
volume

② **der Bruch**
fraction

③ **der Zähler**
numerator

④ **der Nenner**
denominator

⑤ **die Höhe**
height

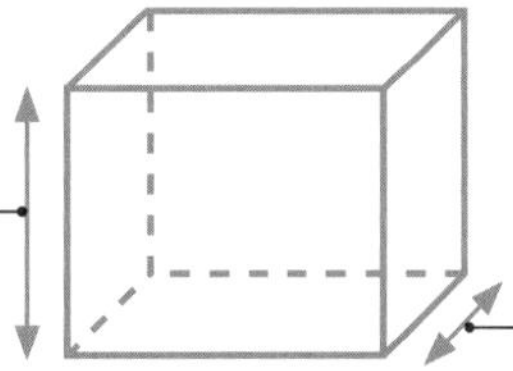

⑥ **Abmessungen** *f, pl*
dimensions

⑦ **die Tiefe**
depth

⑧ **die Länge**
length

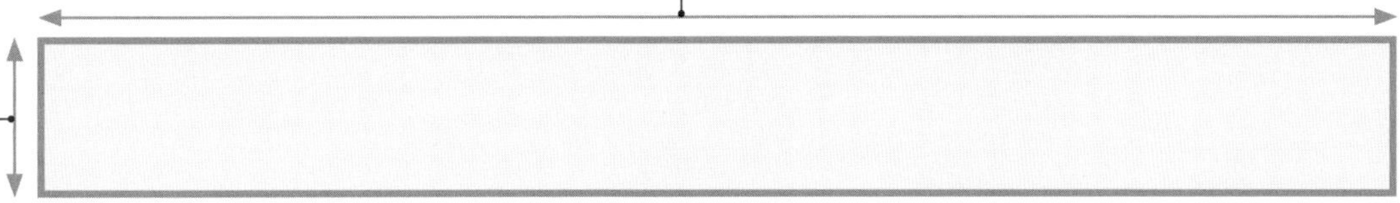

⑨ **die Breite**
width

⑩ **die Fläche**
area

## 74.5 BERECHNUNGEN • OPERATIONS

① **das Pluszeichen**
plus sign

② **das Minuszeichen**
minus sign

③ **das Multiplikationszeichen**
multiplication sign

④ **das Divisionszeichen**
division sign

⑤ **das Gleichheitszeichen**
equals

⑥ **zählen**
to count

⑦ **addieren**
to add

⑧ **subtrahieren**
to subtract

⑨ **multiplizieren**
to multiply

⑩ **dividieren**
to divide

⑪ **die Gleichung**
equation

⑫ **der Prozentsatz**
percentage

## 74.6 MATHEMATISCHES WERKZEUG
MATHEMATICAL EQUIPMENT

① **das Zeichendreieck**
triangle

② **der Winkelmesser**
protractor

③ **das Lineal**
ruler

④ **der Zirkel**
compass

⑥ **Mit dem Taschenrechner ist das Addieren so viel einfacher!**
Addition is so much easier using a calculator.

⑤ **der Taschenrechner**
calculator

# 75 Physik
Physics

## 75.1 PHYSIK · PHYSICS

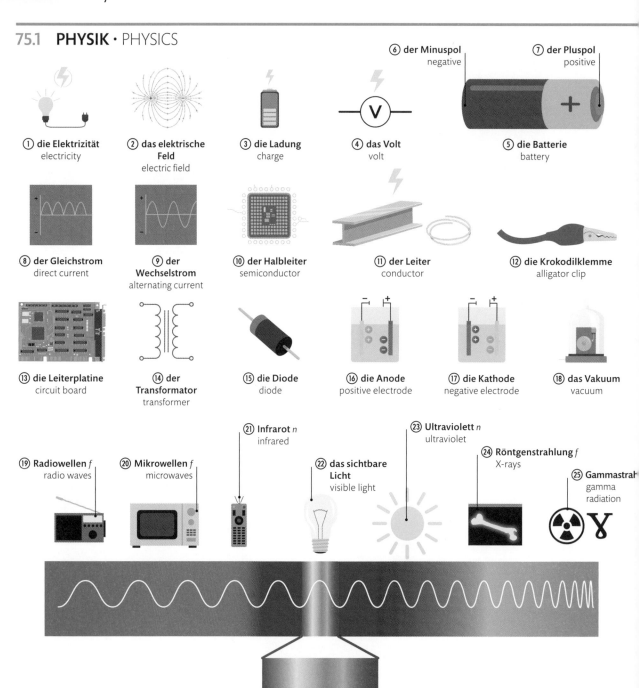

(1) **die Elektrizität**
electricity

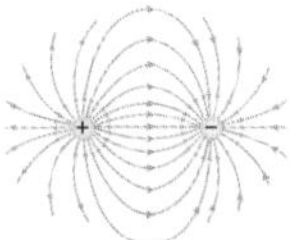



(2) **das elektrische Feld**
electric field

(3) **die Ladung**
charge

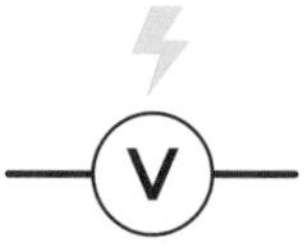



(4) **das Volt**
volt

(6) **der Minuspol**
negative

(7) **der Pluspol**
positive

(5) **die Batterie**
battery

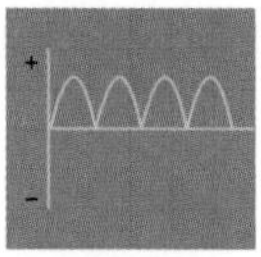



(8) **der Gleichstrom**
direct current

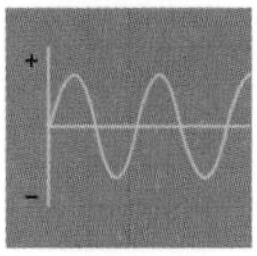



(9) **der Wechselstrom**
alternating current

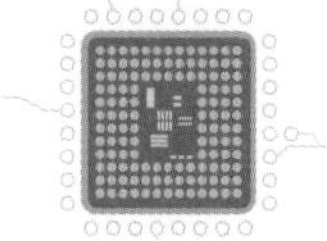

(10) **der Halbleiter**
semiconductor

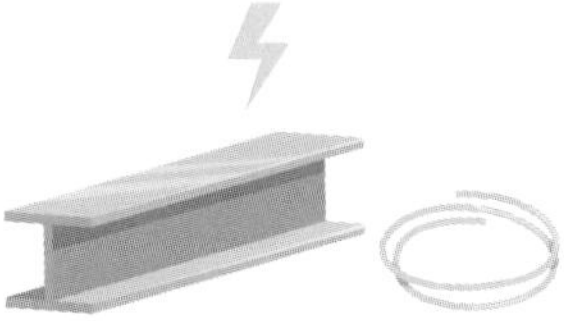

(11) **der Leiter**
conductor

(12) **die Krokodilklemme**
alligator clip

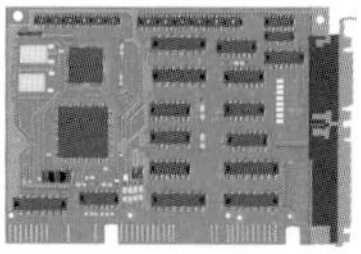

(13) **die Leiterplatine**
circuit board

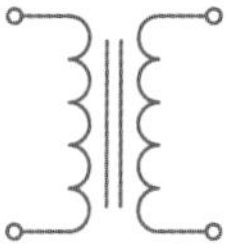

(14) **der Transformator**
transformer

(15) **die Diode**
diode

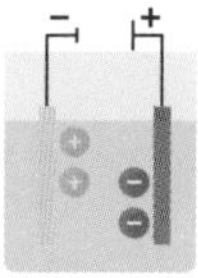



(16) **die Anode**
positive electrode

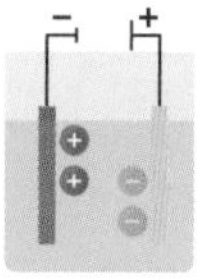



(17) **die Kathode**
negative electrode

(18) **das Vakuum**
vacuum

(19) **Radiowellen** *f*
radio waves

(20) **Mikrowellen** *f*
microwaves

(21) **Infrarot** *n*
infrared

(22) **das sichtbare Licht**
visible light

(23) **Ultraviolett** *n*
ultraviolet

(24) **Röntgenstrahlung** *f*
X-rays

(25) **Gammastrah**
gamma radiation

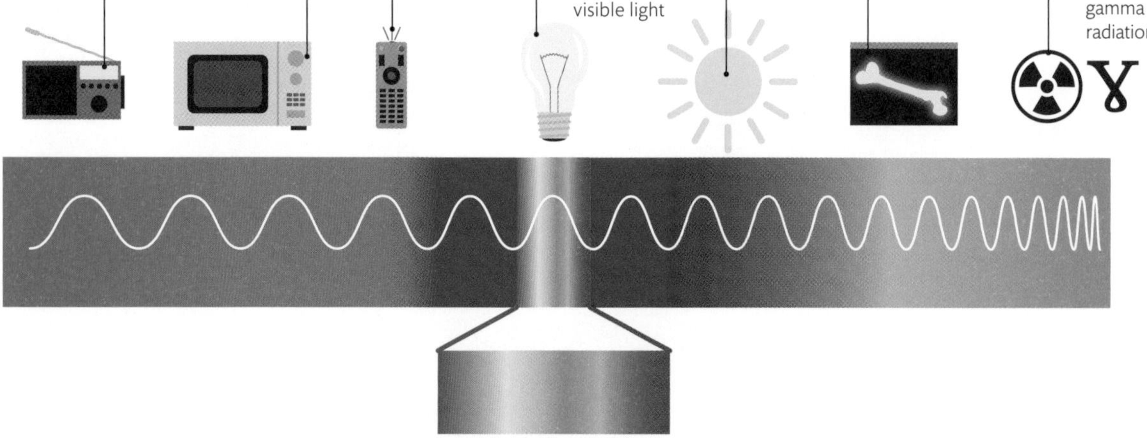



(26) **das elektromagnetische Spektrum**
electromagnetic spectrum

See also
**73** In der Schule • At school **74** Mathematik • Mathematics **76** Chemie • Chemistry
**77** Biologie • Biology **78** Das Periodensystem • The periodic table

⑰ **der Nordpol**
north pole

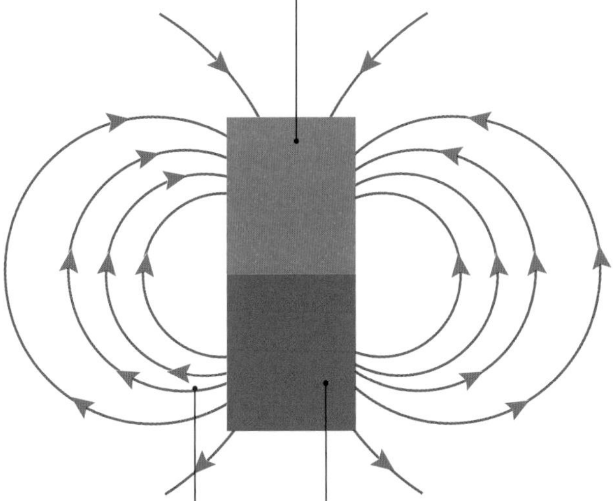

㉘ **das Magnetfeld**
magnetic field

㉙ **der Südpol**
south pole

㉚ **der Magnet**
magnet

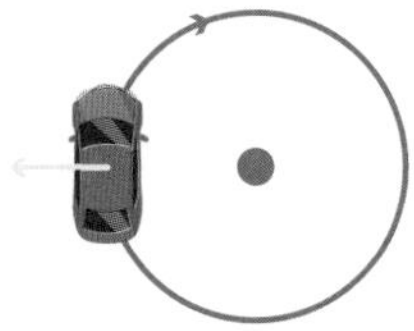

㉛ **die Zentrifugalkraft**
centrifugal force

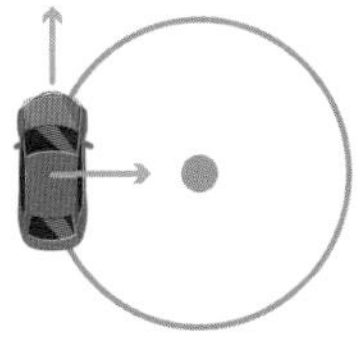

㉜ **die Zentripetalkraft**
centripetal force

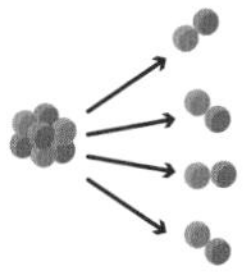

㉝ **die Spaltung**
fission

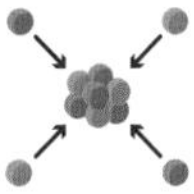

㉞ **die Fusion**
fusion

㉟ **die Radioaktivität**
radioactivity

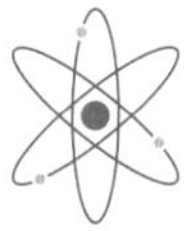

㊱ **das Teilchen**
particle

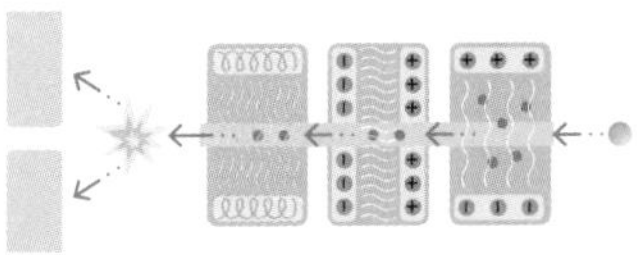

㊲ **der Teilchenbeschleuniger**
particle accelerator

## 75.2 **OPTIK** • OPTICS

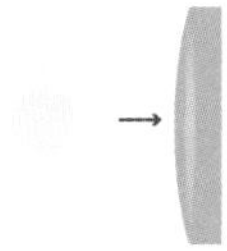

① **die Linse**
lens

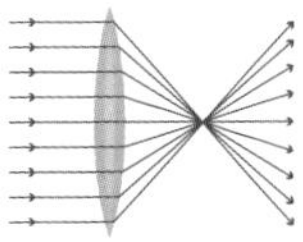

② **die konvexe Linse**
convex lens

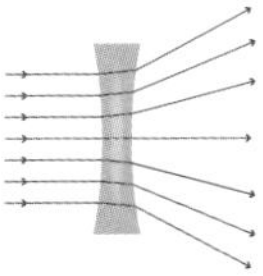

③ **die konkave Linse**
concave lens

④ **der Laser**
laser

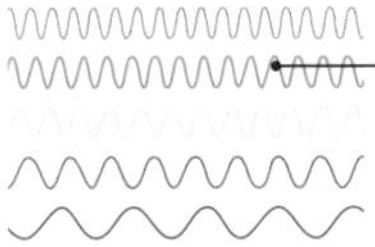

⑤ **die Welle**
wave

⑥ **die Wellenlänge**
wavelength

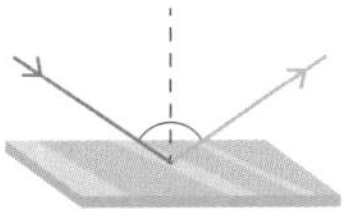

⑦ **die Reflexion**
reflection

⑧ **die Brechung**
refraction

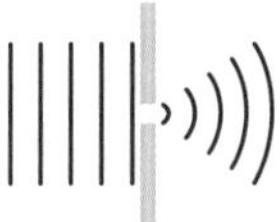

⑨ **die Beugung**
diffraction

⑩ **das Prisma**
prism

⑫ **Ich untersuche die Streuung des Lichts.**
I'm studying the dispersion of light.

⑪ **die Streuung**
dispersion

# 76 Chemie
## Chemistry

### 76.1 IM LABOR · IN THE LABORATORY

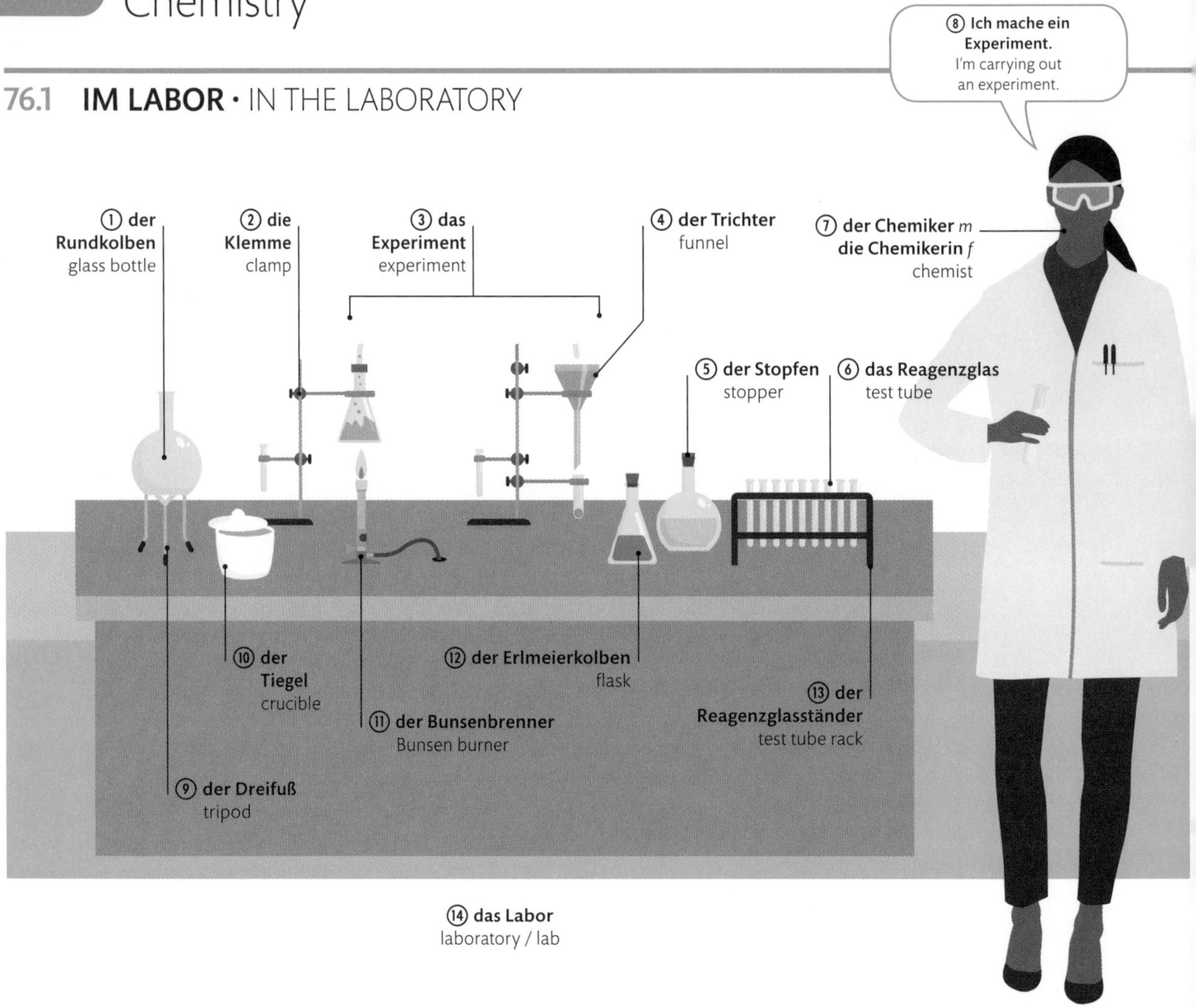

⑧ Ich mache ein Experiment.
I'm carrying out an experiment.
① der Rundkolben
glass bottle
② die Klemme
clamp
③ das Experiment
experiment
④ der Trichter
funnel
⑦ der Chemiker m
die Chemikerin f
chemist
⑤ der Stopfen
stopper
⑥ das Reagenzglas
test tube
⑩ der Tiegel
crucible
⑫ der Erlmeierkolben
flask
⑬ der Reagenzglasständer
test tube rack
⑪ der Bunsenbrenner
Bunsen burner
⑨ der Dreifuß
tripod
⑭ das Labor
laboratory / lab

0.00


⑮ **die Waage**
scale

10:23.00


⑯ **der Zeitmesser**
timer

⑰ **das Thermometer**
thermometer

⑱ **die Zange**
tongs

⑲ **der Spatel**
spatula

⑳ **der Stößel**
pestle

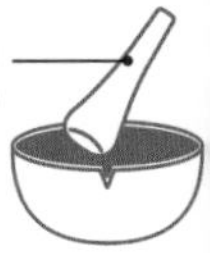

㉑ **der Mörser**
mortar

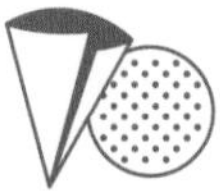

㉒ **das Filterpapier**
filter paper

㉓ **die Pipette**
dropper

㉔ **die Pipette**
pipette

㉕ **der Becher**
beaker

㉖ **der Glasstab**
glass rod

㉗ **die Schutzbrille**
safety goggles

See also
**73** In der Schule • At school **74** Mathematik • Mathematics **75** Physik • Physics
**77** Biologie • Biology **78** Das Periodensystem • The periodic table

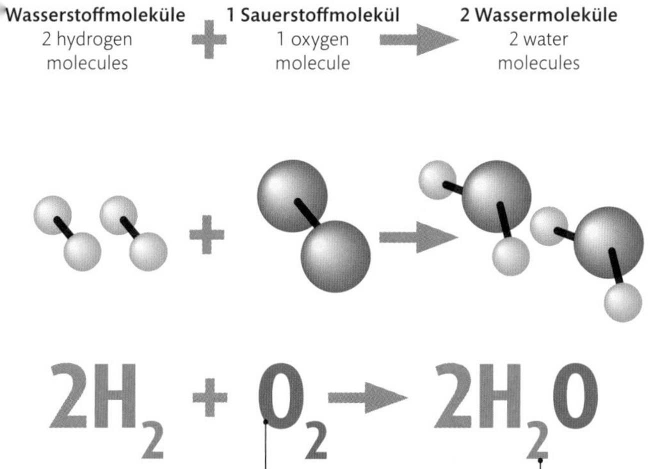


㉙ **das chemische Symbol**
chemical symbol

㉚ **das tiefgestellte Zeichen**
subscript

㉘ **die Reaktionsgleichung**
chemical equation

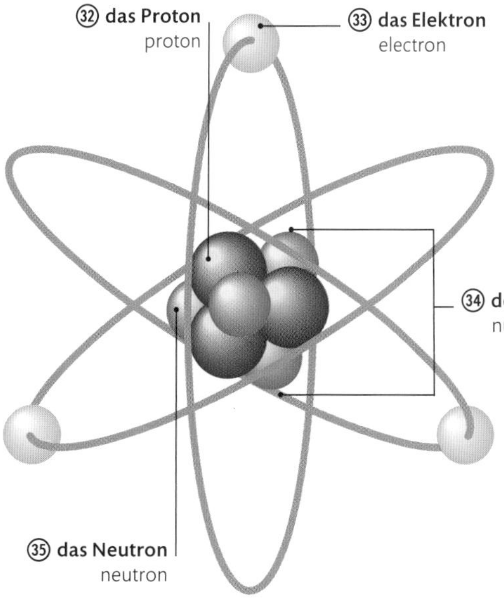

㉜ **das Proton**
proton

㉝ **das Elektron**
electron

㉞ **der Kern**
nucleus

㉟ **das Neutron**
neutron

㉛ **das Atom**
atom

㊱ **die chemische Formel**
chemical formula

㊲ **das Element**
elements

㊳ **das Molekül**
molecule

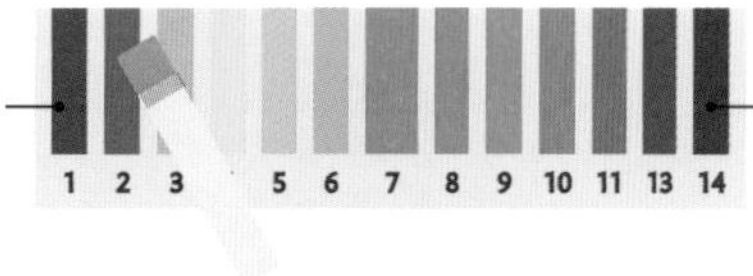


㊵ **die Sauer**
acid

㊶ **das Basisch**
alkali

㊴ **der pH-Wert**
pH level

㊷ **die Reaktion**
reaction

㊸ **die Reaktionsrichtung**
reaction direction

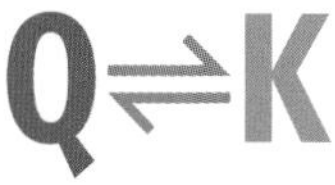


㊹ **die umkehrbare Reaktion**
reversible direction

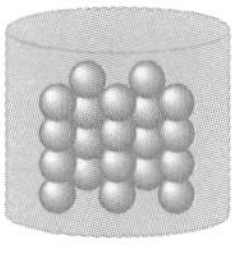

㊺ **der Feststoff**
solid

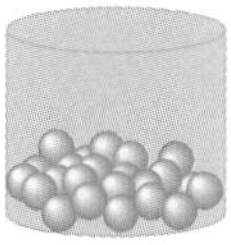

㊻ **die Flüssigkeit**
liquid

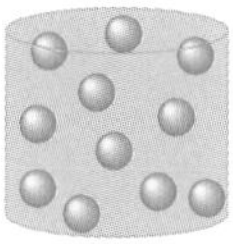

㊼ **das Gas**
gas

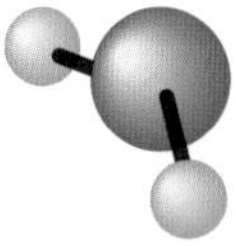

㊽ **die Verbindung**
compound

㊾ **die Base**
base

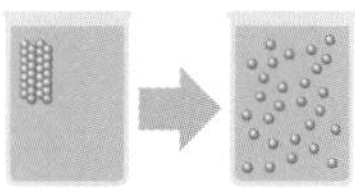

㊿ **die Diffusion**
diffusion

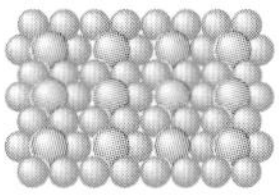

(51) **die Legierung**
alloy

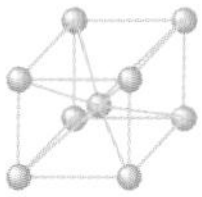

(52) **der Kristall**
crystal

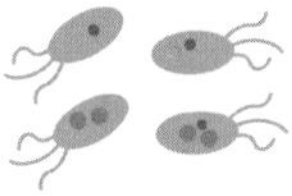

(53) **die Biochemie**
biochemistry

# 77 Biologie
## Biology

### 77.1 BIOLOGIE · BIOLOGY

① **der Biologe** *m*
**die Biologin** *f*
biologist

② **die Mikrobiologie**
microbiology

③ **der Mikrobiologe** *m*
**die Mikrobiologin** *f*
microbiologist

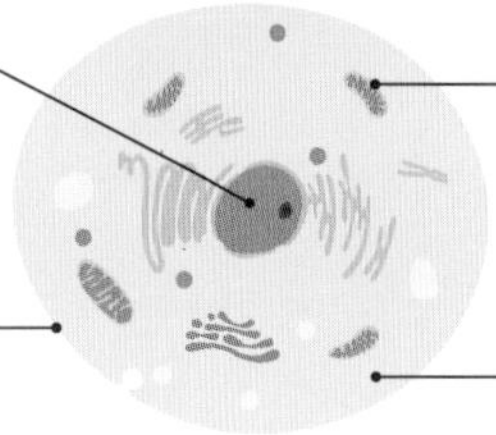

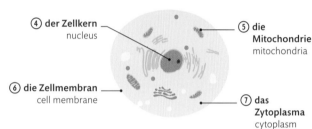

④ **der Zellkern**
nucleus

⑤ **die Mitochondrie**
mitochondria

⑥ **die Zellmembran**
cell membrane

⑦ **das Zytoplasma**
cytoplasm

⑧ **die tierische Zelle**
animal cell

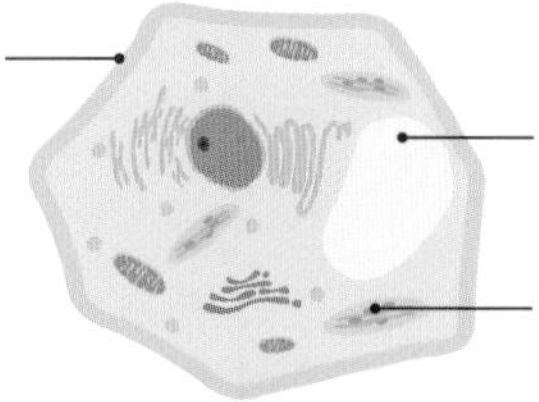

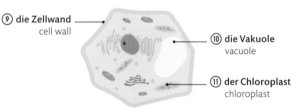

⑨ **die Zellwand**
cell wall

⑩ **die Vakuole**
vacuole

⑪ **der Chloroplast**
chloroplast

⑫ **die pflanzliche Zelle**
plant cell

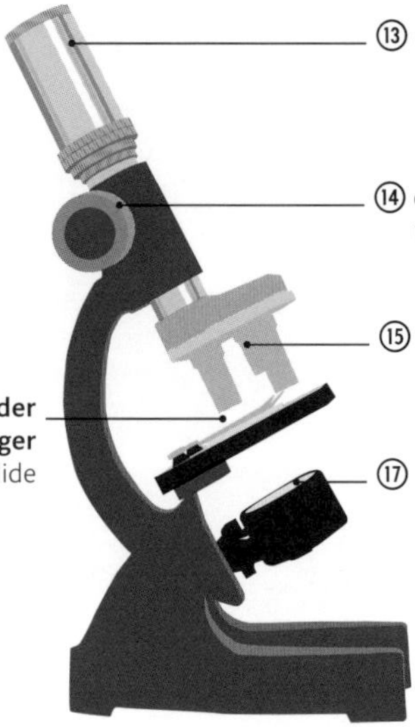

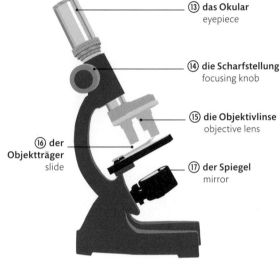

⑬ **das Okular**
eyepiece

⑭ **die Scharfstellung**
focusing knob

⑮ **die Objektivlinse**
objective lens

⑯ **der Objektträger**
slide

⑰ **der Spiegel**
mirror

⑱ **das Mikroskop**
microscope

⑲ **das rote Blutkörperchen**
red blood cell

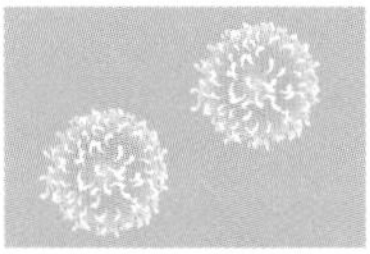

⑳ **das weiße Blutkörperchen**
white blood cell

㉒ **das Ge**
gene

㉑ **das Chromosom**
chromosome

㉓ **die DNS**
DNA

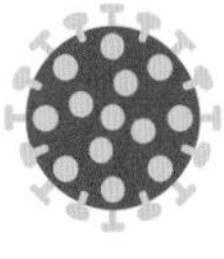

㉔ **das Virus**
virus

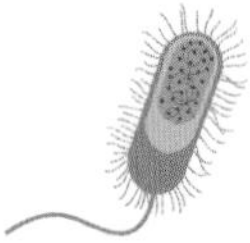

㉕ **die Bakterie**
bacteria

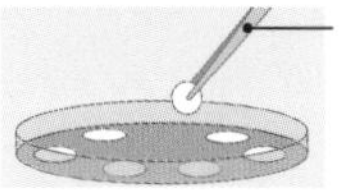

㉗ **die Pinzette**
tweezers

㉖ **die Petrischale**
petri dish

㉘ **das Skalpell**
scalpel

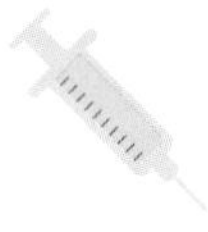

㉙ **die Spritze**
syringe

㉚ **die Zoologie**
zoology

㉛ **der Zoologe** *m*
**die Zoologin** *f*
zoologist

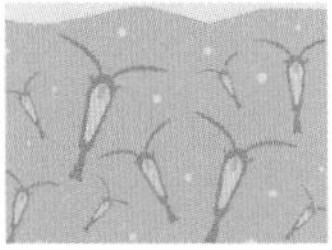

㉜ **das Plankton**
plankton

㉝ **das wirbellose Tier**
invertebrate

㉞ **das Wirbeltier**
vertebrate

㉟ **die Art**
species

See also
**157** Die Naturgeschichte • Natural history **158-159** Säugetiere • Mammals **160-161** Vögel • Birds
**162** Insekten und Käfer • Insects and bugs **163** Amphibien und Reptilien • Amphibians and reptiles
**166** Leben im Ozean • Ocean life **167-169** Pflanzen und Bäume • Plants and trees **170** Pilze • Fungi

㊱ **das Ökosystem**
ecosystem

㊲ **das Exoskelett**
exoskeleton

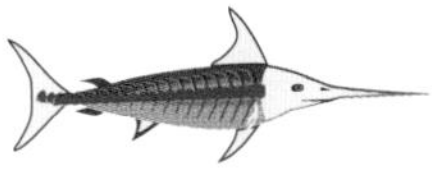

㊳ **das Endoskelett**
endoskeleton

㊴ **die Vermehrung**
reproduction

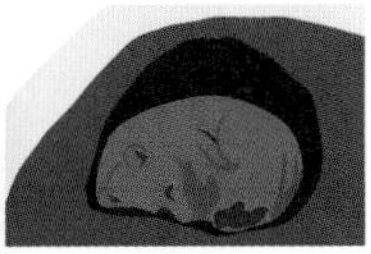

㊵ **der Winterschlaf**
hibernation

㊶ **die Botanik**
botany

㊷ **der Botaniker** *m*
**die Botanikerin** *f*
botanist

㊸ **die Pflanze**
plant

㊹ **der Pilz**
fungi

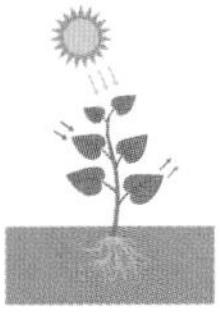

㊺ **die Fotosynthese**
photosynthesis

㊻ **der Paläontologe** *m*
**die Paläontologin** *f*
paleontologist

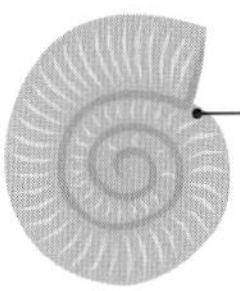

㊼ **das Fossil**
fossil

㊽ **die Evolution**
evolution

## 77.2 METAMORPHOSE • METAMORPHOSIS

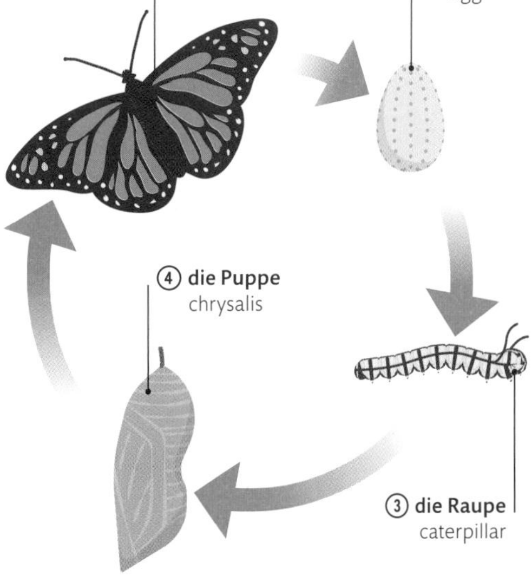

① **der Schmetterling**
butterfly

② **das Ei**
egg

③ **die Raupe**
caterpillar

④ **die Puppe**
chrysalis

⑤ **der Lebenszyklus eines Schmetterlings**
life cycle of a butterfly

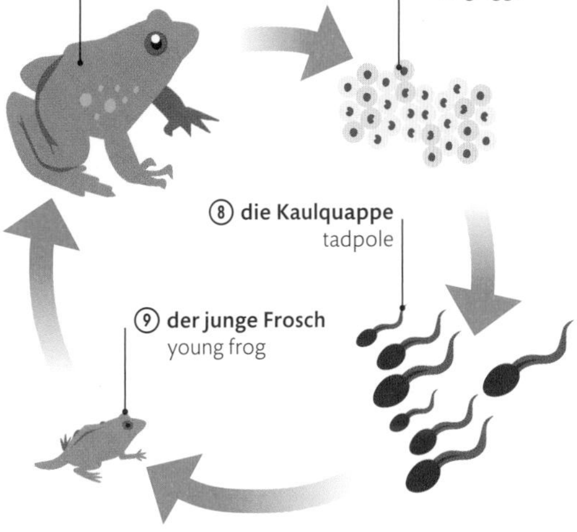

⑥ **der ausgewachsene Frosch**
adult frog

⑦ **der Froschlaich**
frog eggs

⑧ **die Kaulquappe**
tadpole

⑨ **der junge Frosch**
young frog

⑩ **der Lebenszyklus eines Froschs**
life cycle of a frog

# 78 Das Periodensystem
## The periodic table

### 78.1 DAS PERIODENSYSTEM DER ELEMENTE • THE PERIODIC TABLE

- (119) **Alkalimetalle** *n, pl* alkali metals
- (120) **Erdalkalimetalle** *n, pl* alkaline earth metals
- (121) **Übergangsmetalle** *n, pl* transition metals
- (122) **Lanthanoide** *n, pl* lanthanide series
- (124) **Metalle** *n, pl* other metals
- (125) **Halbmetalle** *n, pl* semimetals
- (126) **Nichtmetalle** *n, pl* nonmetals
- (127) **Halogene** *n, pl* halogens

| | | | | | | | | |
|---|---|---|---|---|---|---|---|---|
| ① H<br>**Wasserstoff** *m*<br>hydrogen | | | | | | | | |
| ③ Li<br>**Lithium** *n*<br>lithium | ④ Be<br>**Beryllium** *n*<br>beryllium | | | | | | | |
| ⑪ Na<br>**Natrium** *n*<br>sodium | ⑫ Mg<br>**Magnesium** *n*<br>magnesium | | | | | | | |
| ⑲ K<br>**Kalium** *n*<br>potassium | ⑳ Ca<br>**Kalzium** *n*<br>calcium | ㉑ Sc<br>**Skandium** *n*<br>scandium | ㉒ Ti<br>**Titan** *n*<br>titanium | ㉓ V<br>**Vanadium** *n*<br>vanadium | ㉔ Cr<br>**Chrom** *n*<br>chromium | ㉕ Mn<br>**Mangan** *n*<br>manganese | ㉖ Fe<br>**Eisen** *n*<br>iron | ㉗ Co<br>**Kobalt** *n*<br>cobalt |
| ㊲ Rb<br>**Rubidium** *n*<br>rubidium | ㊳ Sr<br>**Strontium** *n*<br>strontium | ㊴ Y<br>**Yttrium** *n*<br>yttrium | ㊵ Zr<br>**Zirkonium** *n*<br>zirconium | ㊶ Nb<br>**Niob** *n*<br>niobium | ㊷ Mo<br>**Molybdän** *n*<br>molybdenum | ㊸ Tc<br>**Technetium** *n*<br>technetium | ㊹ Ru<br>**Ruthenium** *n*<br>ruthenium | ㊺ Rh<br>**Rhodium** *n*<br>rhodium |
| (55) Cs<br>**Cäsium** *n*<br>cesium | (56) Ba<br>**Barium** *n*<br>barium | La-Lu | (72) Hf<br>**Hafnium** *n*<br>hafnium | (73) Ta<br>**Tantal** *n*<br>tantalum | (74) W<br>**Wolfram** *n*<br>tungsten | (75) Re<br>**Rhenium** *n*<br>rhenium | (76) Os<br>**Osmium** *n*<br>osmium | (77) Ir<br>**Iridium** *n*<br>iridium |
| (87) Fr<br>**Francium** *n*<br>francium | (88) Ra<br>**Radium** *n*<br>radium | Ac-Lr | (104) Rf<br>**Rutherfordium** *n*<br>rutherfordium | (105) Db<br>**Dubnium** *n*<br>dubnium | (106) Sg<br>**Seaborgium** *n*<br>seaborgium | (107) Bh<br>**Bohrium** *n*<br>bohrium | (108) Hs<br>**Hassium** *n*<br>hassium | (109) Mt<br>**Meitnerium** *n*<br>meitnerium |

| | | | | | |
|---|---|---|---|---|---|
| (57) La<br>**Lanthan** *n*<br>lanthanum | (58) Ce<br>**Cer** *n*<br>cerium | (59) Pr<br>**Praseodym** *n*<br>praseodymium | (60) Nd<br>**Neodym** *n*<br>neodymium | (61) Pm<br>**Promethium** *n*<br>promethium | (62) Sm<br>**Samarium** *n*<br>samarium |
| (89) Ac<br>**Actinium** *n*<br>actinium | (90) Th<br>**Thorium** *n*<br>thorium | (91) Pa<br>**Protactinium** *n*<br>protactinium | (92) U<br>**Uran** *n*<br>uranium | (93) Np<br>**Neptunium** *n*<br>neptunium | (94) Pu<br>**Plutonium** *n*<br>plutonium |

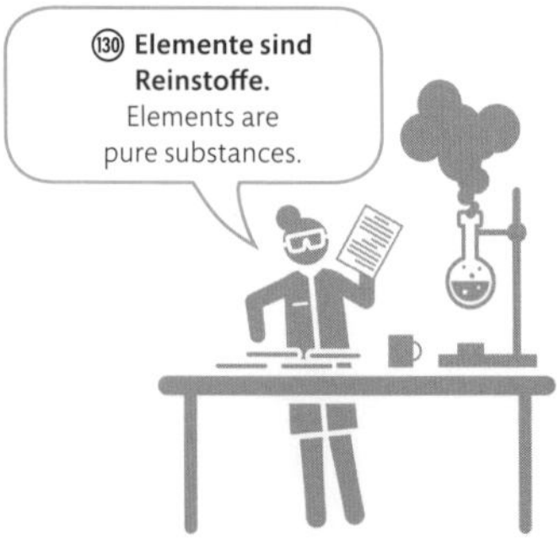

(130) Elemente sind Reinstoffe.
Elements are pure substances.

See also
**73** In der Schule • At school **75** Physik • Physics **76** Chemie • Chemistry
**156** Gesteine und Mineralien • Rocks and minerals

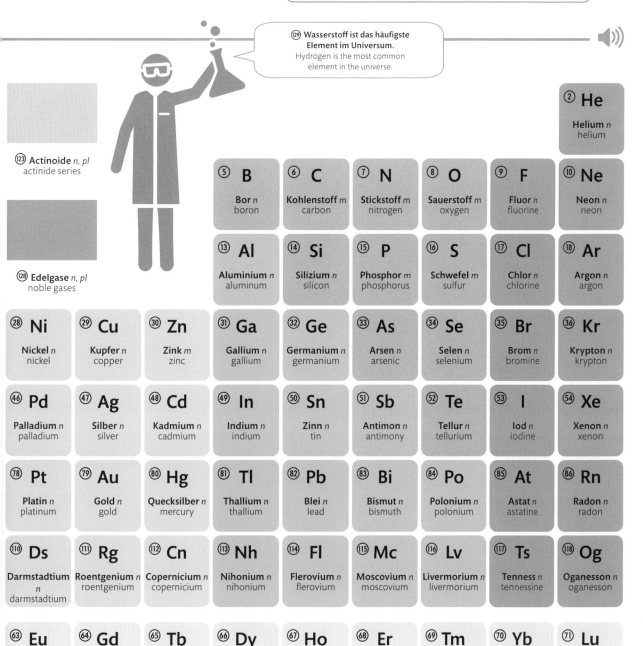

(129) **Wasserstoff ist das häufigste Element im Universum.**
Hydrogen is the most common element in the universe.

(123) **Actinoide** *n, pl*
actinide series

(128) **Edelgase** *n, pl*
noble gases

| | | | | | | | | |
|---|---|---|---|---|---|---|---|---|
| | | | | | | | | (2) **He**<br>**Helium** *n*<br>helium |
| | | | (5) **B**<br>**Bor** *n*<br>boron | (6) **C**<br>**Kohlenstoff** *m*<br>carbon | (7) **N**<br>**Stickstoff** *m*<br>nitrogen | (8) **O**<br>**Sauerstoff** *m*<br>oxygen | (9) **F**<br>**Fluor** *n*<br>fluorine | (10) **Ne**<br>**Neon** *n*<br>neon |
| | | | (13) **Al**<br>**Aluminium** *n*<br>aluminum | (14) **Si**<br>**Silizium** *n*<br>silicon | (15) **P**<br>**Phosphor** *m*<br>phosphorus | (16) **S**<br>**Schwefel** *m*<br>sulfur | (17) **Cl**<br>**Chlor** *n*<br>chlorine | (18) **Ar**<br>**Argon** *n*<br>argon |
| (28) **Ni**<br>**Nickel** *n*<br>nickel | (29) **Cu**<br>**Kupfer** *n*<br>copper | (30) **Zn**<br>**Zink** *m*<br>zinc | (31) **Ga**<br>**Gallium** *n*<br>gallium | (32) **Ge**<br>**Germanium** *n*<br>germanium | (33) **As**<br>**Arsen** *n*<br>arsenic | (34) **Se**<br>**Selen** *n*<br>selenium | (35) **Br**<br>**Brom** *n*<br>bromine | (36) **Kr**<br>**Krypton** *n*<br>krypton |
| (46) **Pd**<br>**Palladium** *n*<br>palladium | (47) **Ag**<br>**Silber** *n*<br>silver | (48) **Cd**<br>**Kadmium** *n*<br>cadmium | (49) **In**<br>**Indium** *n*<br>indium | (50) **Sn**<br>**Zinn** *n*<br>tin | (51) **Sb**<br>**Antimon** *n*<br>antimony | (52) **Te**<br>**Tellur** *n*<br>tellurium | (53) **I**<br>**Iod** *n*<br>iodine | (54) **Xe**<br>**Xenon** *n*<br>xenon |
| (78) **Pt**<br>**Platin** *n*<br>platinum | (79) **Au**<br>**Gold** *n*<br>gold | (80) **Hg**<br>**Quecksilber** *n*<br>mercury | (81) **Tl**<br>**Thallium** *n*<br>thallium | (82) **Pb**<br>**Blei** *n*<br>lead | (83) **Bi**<br>**Bismut** *n*<br>bismuth | (84) **Po**<br>**Polonium** *n*<br>polonium | (85) **At**<br>**Astat** *n*<br>astatine | (86) **Rn**<br>**Radon** *n*<br>radon |
| (110) **Ds**<br>**Darmstadtium** *n*<br>darmstadtium | (111) **Rg**<br>**Roentgenium** *n*<br>roentgenium | (112) **Cn**<br>**Copernicium** *n*<br>copernicium | (113) **Nh**<br>**Nihonium** *n*<br>nihonium | (114) **Fl**<br>**Flerovium** *n*<br>flerovium | (115) **Mc**<br>**Moscovium** *n*<br>moscovium | (116) **Lv**<br>**Livermorium** *n*<br>livermorium | (117) **Ts**<br>**Tenness** *n*<br>tennessine | (118) **Og**<br>**Oganesson** *n*<br>oganesson |
| (63) **Eu**<br>**Europium** *n*<br>europium | (64) **Gd**<br>**Gadolinium** *n*<br>gadolinium | (65) **Tb**<br>**Terbium** *n*<br>terbium | (66) **Dy**<br>**Dysprosium** *n*<br>dysprosium | (67) **Ho**<br>**Holmium** *n*<br>holmium | (68) **Er**<br>**Erbium** *n*<br>erbium | (69) **Tm**<br>**Thulium** *n*<br>thulium | (70) **Yb**<br>**Ytterbium** *n*<br>ytterbium | (71) **Lu**<br>**Lutetium** *n*<br>lutetium |
| (95) **Am**<br>**Americium** *n*<br>americium | (96) **Cm**<br>**Curium** *n*<br>curium | (97) **Bk**<br>**Berkelium** *n*<br>berkelium | (98) **Cf**<br>**Californium** *n*<br>californium | (99) **Es**<br>**Einsteinium** *n*<br>einsteinium | (100) **Fm**<br>**Fermium** *n*<br>fermium | (101) **Md**<br>**Mendelevium** *n*<br>mendelevium | (102) **No**<br>**Nobelium** *n*<br>nobelium | (103) **Lr**<br>**Lawrencium** *n*<br>lawrencium |

# 79 Geschichte
## History

### 79.1 KRIEG UND WAFFEN · WAR AND WEAPONS

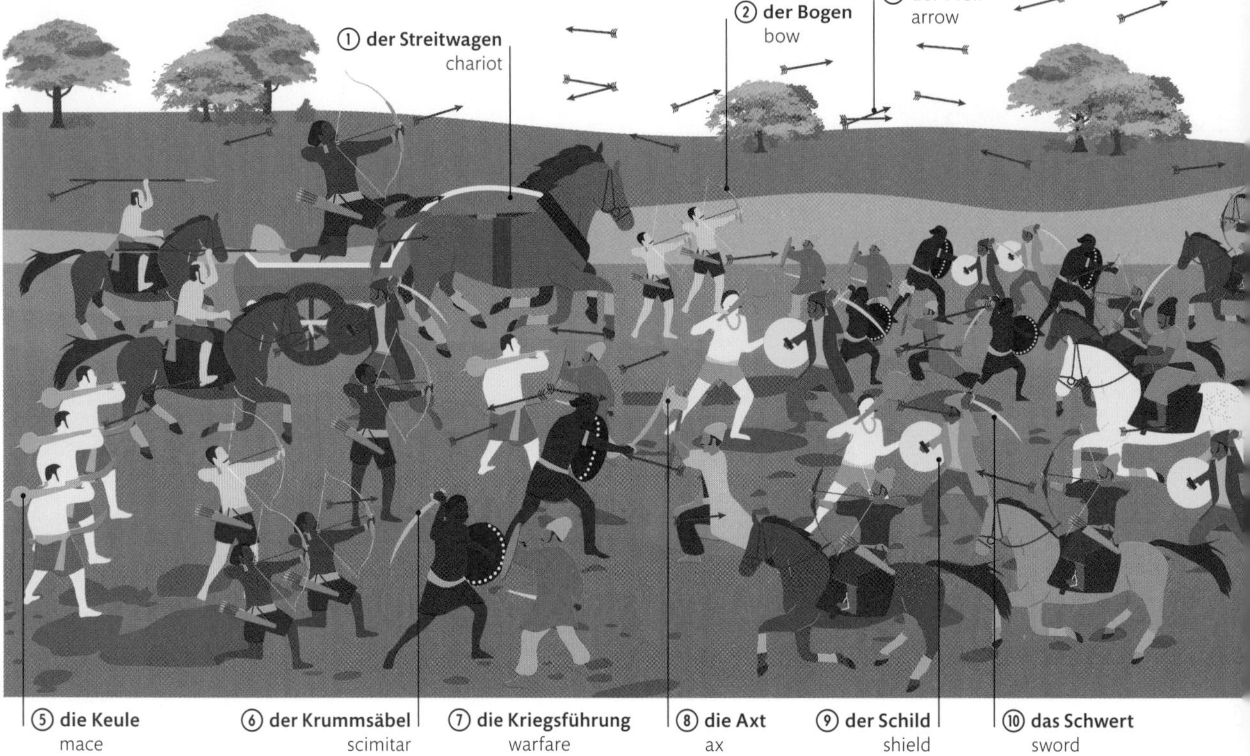


### 79.2 DER MENSCH IM WANDEL DER ZEIT · PEOPLE THROUGH TIME

See also
**44** Gebäude und Architektur • Buildings and architecture **73** In der Schule • At school
**80** An der Universität • At college **88** Das Militär • Military

⑪ **das Schlachtross**
warhorse

⑫ **der Kriegselefant**
war elephant

⑬ **die Schlacht**
battle

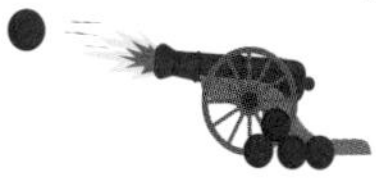

⑭ **die Kanone**
cannon

⑮ **das Katapult**
catapult

⑯ **der Rammbock**
battering ram

⑰ **der Ritter**
knight

⑱ **die Rüstung**
armor

⑲ **der Krieger** *m*
**die Kriegerin** *f*
warrior

⑧ **der Schmied** *m*
**die Schmiedin** *f*
blacksmith

⑨ **die Bauernschaft**
peasants

⑩ **das Königreich**
kingdom

⑪ **das Kaiserreich**
empire

⑱ **der Adelsherr** *m*
**die Dame** *f*
lord / lady

⑲ **der Minnesänger** *m*
**die Minnesängerin** *f*
minstrel

⑳ **der Narr** *m*
**die Närrin** *f*
jester

㉑ **der Schreiber** *m*
**die Schreiberin** *f*
scribe

㉖ **die technologische Revolution**
the Technological Revolution

㉗ **das Informationszeitalter**
the Information Age

## 79.3 DIE ERFORSCHUNG DER VERGANGENHEIT
## STUDYING THE PAST

① **der Historiker** *m*
**die Historikerin** *f*
historian

② **das Archiv**
archive

③ **die Quelle**
sources

④ **die Schriftrolle**
scroll

⑤ **das Dokument**
document

⑥ **die Archäologie**
archeology

⑦ **der Archäologe** *m*
**die Archäologin** *f*
archeologist

⑧ **die Ausgrabung**
dig / excavation

⑨ **die Überreste** *m, pl*
remains

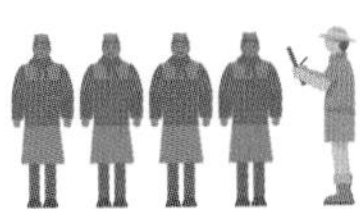

⑪ **das Fundstück**
finds

⑫ **das Grab**
tomb

⑬ **die historische Stätte**
historical site

# 80 An der Universität
## At college

### 80.1 DIE UNIVERSITÄT · COLLEGE

① **der Campus**
campus

② **der Hörsaal**
auditorium

③ **der Dozent** *m* / **die Dozentin** *f*
lecturer

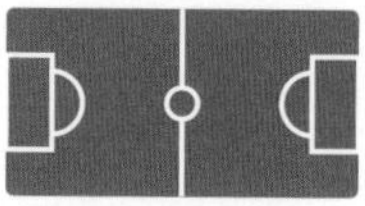

④ **der Sportplatz**
sports field

⑤ **die Mensa**
dining hall

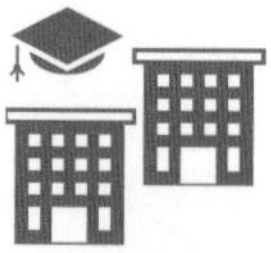

⑥ **das Studentenwohnheim**
dorms

⑦ **das Stipendium**
scholarship

⑧ **die Aufnahme**
admissions

⑨ **der Bachelorstudent** *m*
**die Bachelorstudentin** *f*
undergraduate

⑩ **das Diplom**
diploma

⑪ **die Bachelorarbeit**
dissertation

⑫ **der Abschluss**
degree

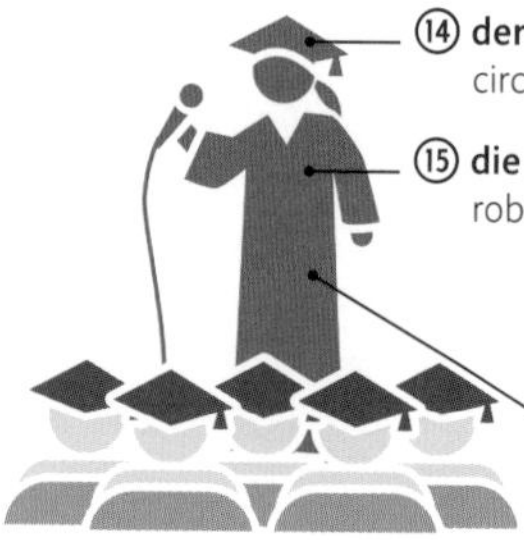

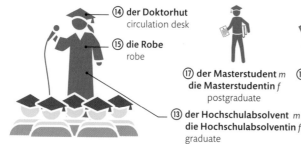

⑭ **der Doktorhut**
circulation desk

⑮ **die Robe**
robe

⑬ **der Hochschulabsolvent** *m*
**die Hochschulabsolventin** *f*
graduate

⑯ **die Abschlussfeier**
graduation ceremony

⑰ **der Masterstudent** *m*
**die Masterstudentin** *f*
postgraduate

⑱ **die Masterarbeit**
thesis

⑲ **der Masterabschluss**
master's degree

⑳ **der Doktortitel**
doctorate

### 80.2 FACHBEREICHE · DEPARTMENTS AND SCHOOLS

① **Geisteswissenschaften** *f, pl*
humanities

② **Politik** *f*
politics

③ **Literatur** *f*
literature

④ **Sprachen** *f, pl*
languages

⑤ **Wirtschaft** *f*
economics

⑥ **Philosophie** *f*
philosophy

⑦ **Geschichte** *f*
history

⑧ **Sozialwissenschaften** *f, pl*
social sciences

⑨ **Soziologie** *f*
sociology

⑩ **Jura**
law

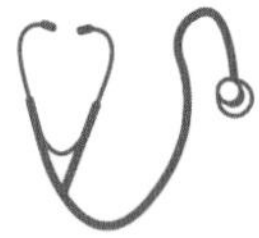

⑪ **Medizin** *f*
medicine

⑫ **Krankenpflege** *f*
nursing

See also
**73** In der Schule • At school **74** Mathematik • Mathematics **75** Physik • Physics
**76** Chemie • Chemistry **77** Biologie • Biology **79** Geschichte • History
**85** Recht • Law **138** Bücher und Lesen • Books and reading

## 80.3 IN DER BIBLIOTHEK • LIBRARY

① **der Lesesaal**
reading room

② **die Literaturliste**
reading list

③ **ausleihen**
to borrow

④ **verlängern**
to renew

⑤ **zurückgeben**
to return

⑥ **reservieren**
to reserve

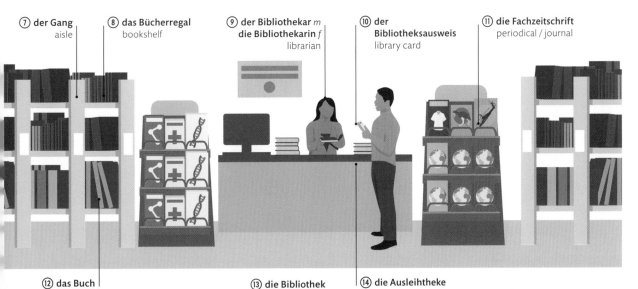

⑦ **der Gang**
aisle

⑧ **das Bücherregal**
bookshelf

⑨ **der Bibliothekar** *m*
**die Bibliothekarin** *f*
librarian

⑩ **der Bibliotheksausweis**
library card

⑪ **die Fachzeitschrift**
periodical / journal

⑫ **das Buch**
book

⑬ **die Bibliothek**
library

⑭ **die Ausleihtheke**
circulation desk

⑭ **Ich habe Fördergelder für wissenschaftliche Forschungen erhalten.**
I received a grant to do scientific research.

⑬ **Naturwissenschaften** *f, pl*
sciences

⑮ **Chemie** *f*
chemistry

⑯ **Physik** *f*
physics

⑰ **Biologie** *f*
biology

⑱ **Maschinenbau** *m*
engineering

⑲ **Zoologie** *f*
zoology

⑳ **Musikschule** *f*
music school

㉑ **Tanzschule** *f*
dance school

㉒ **Kunstakademie** *f*
art college / school

# 81 Auf der Arbeit
## At work

### 81.1 BÜROARBEIT · OFFICE WORK

① **das Unternehmen**
company

② **die Niederlassung**
branch

③ **die Anstellung**
employment

④ **verdienen**
to earn

⑤ **unbefristet**
permanent

⑥ **befristet**
temporary

⑩ **der Bürojob**
nine-to-five job

⑪ **Teilzeit arbeiten**
to work part-time

⑫ **die Schichtarbeit**
to work shifts

⑬ **der Urlaub**
vacation

⑭ **einen Tag freinehmen**
to have a day off

⑮ **in Elternzeit gehen**
to go on maternity leave

⑲ **sich krank melden**
to call in sick

⑳ **kündigen**
to hand in your notice

㉑ **gekündigt werden**
to get fired

㉒ **entlassen werden**
to be laid off

㉓ **arbeitslos sein**
to be unemployed

㉔ **das Arbeitslosengel**
unemployment benefit

㉝ **der Vorstandsvorsitzende** *m*
**die Vorstandsvorsitzende** *f*
CEO (chief executive officer)

㉞ **der Geschäftsmann**
businessman

㊴ **der Manager** *m*
**die Managerin** *f*
manager

㉙ **der Firmensitz**
headquarters

㉚ **der Rezeptionist** *m*
**die Rezeptionistin** *f*
receptionist

㊳ **der Auszubildende** *m*
**die Auszubildende** *f*
apprentice

㊵ **der Assistent** *m*
**die Assistentin**
PA (persona
assistant

㊶ **die Führungsperson**
leader

㉛ **der Wartebereich**
waiting area

㉟ **der Geschäftsabschluss**
business deal

㊱ **die Geschäftsfrau**
businesswoman

㊷ **der Kunde** *m*
**die Kundin** *f*
clients

㉘ **der Empfang**
office reception

㉜ **das Vorstandszimmer**
CEO's office

㊲ **die Besprechung**
meeting

See also
**82** Im Büro • In the office **89-90** Berufe • Jobs **91** Branchen und Abteilungen • Industries and departments **92** Bewerbungen • Applying for a job **93** Nützliche Fähigkeiten für den Arbeitsplatz • Workplace skills **95** Besprechen and präsentieren • Meeting and presenting

⑦ **die Gleitzeit**
flextime

⑧ **im Homeoffice arbeiten**
to work from home

⑨ **Vollzeit arbeiten**
to work full-time

⑯ **befördert werden**
to be promoted

⑰ **kündigen**
to resign

⑱ **in Rente gehen**
to retire

㉕ **die Geschäftsreise**
business trip

㉖ **der Termin**
appointment

㉗ **das Geschäftsessen**
business lunch

## 81.2 ENTLOHNUNG • PAY

① **der Stundensatz**
hourly rate

② **die Überstunde**
overtime

③ **das Gehalt**
salary

④ **der Lohn**
wages

⑤ **die Lohnabrechnung**
pay slip

⑥ **die Prämie**
bonus

⑦ **Zusatzleistungen**
benefits

⑧ **die Gehaltserhöhung**
raise

⑨ **die Gehaltskürzung**
pay cut

㊹ **der Interviewer** *m*
**die Interviewerin** *f*
interviewer

㊺ **der Bewerber** *m*
**die Bewerberin** *f*
applicant

㊽ **der Mitarbeiter** *m*
**die Mitarbeiterin** *f*
worker

㊾ **der Kollege** *m*
**die Kollegin** *f*
co-worker / colleague

㊿ **der Arbeitnehmer** *m*
**die Arbeitnehmerin** *f*
employee

(51) **die Führungskraft**
supervisor

(52) **der Praktikant** *m*
**die Praktikantin** *f*
intern

㊻ **der Arbeitgeber** *m* / **die Arbeitgeberin** *f*
employer

㊸ **das Vorstellungsgespräch**
interview

㊼ **das Personal**
staff

(53) **die Büroleitung**
office manager

# 82 Im Büro

## In the office

### 82.1 DAS BÜRO · OFFICE

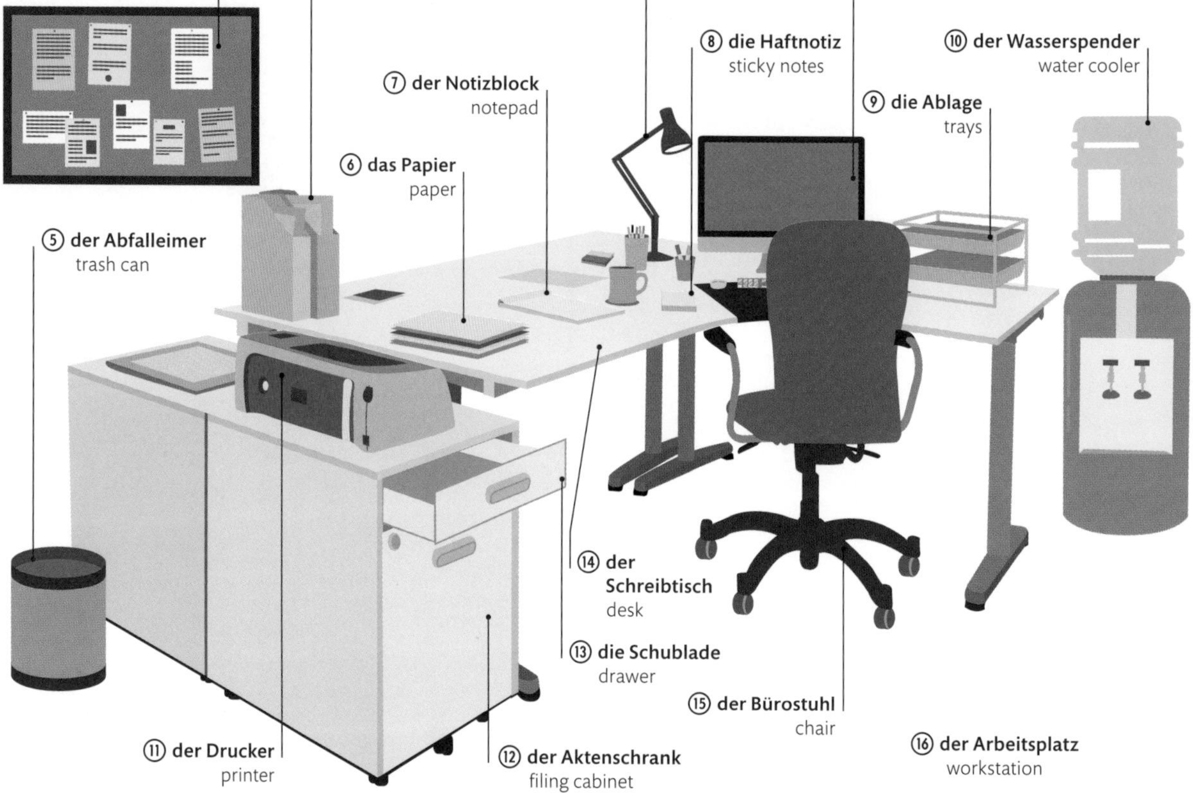


### 82.2 DIE AUSSTATTUNG DES BESPRECHUNGSZIMMERS · MEETING-ROOM EQUIPMENT

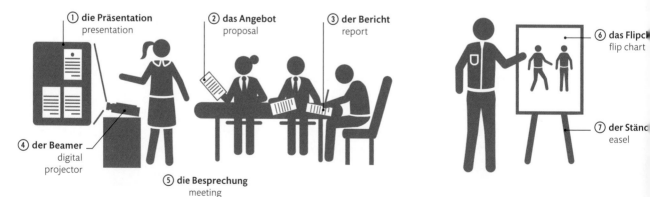

See also
**81** Auf der Arbeit • At work **83** Computer und Technologie • Computers and technology **91** Branchen und Abteilungen • Industries and departments **92** Bewerbungen • Applying for a job **93** Nützliche Fähigkeiten für den Arbeitsplatz • Workplace skills **95** Besprechen and präsentieren • Meeting and presenting

## 82.3 BÜROMATERIAL UND BÜROZUBEHÖR • OFFICE EQUIPMENT

① **der Kopierer**
photocopier

② **der Scanner**
scanner

③ **das Telefon**
telephone / phone

④ **der Laptop**
laptop

⑤ **der Beamer**
projector

⑥ **das Headset**
headset

⑦ **der Schredder**
shredder

⑧ **das Handy**
cell phone

⑨ **die Fußbank**
footrest

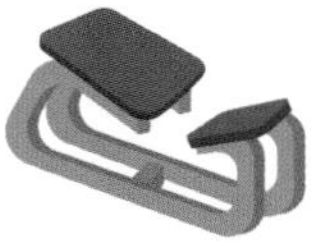
⑩ **der Kniestuhl**
kneeling chair

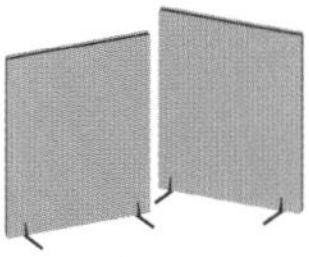
⑪ **die bewegliche Wand**
movable panel

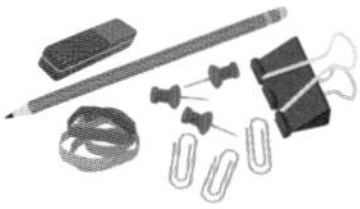
⑫ **das Büromaterial**
stationery

⑬ **der Brief**
letter

⑭ **der Umschlag**
envelope

⑮ **der Kalender**
calendar

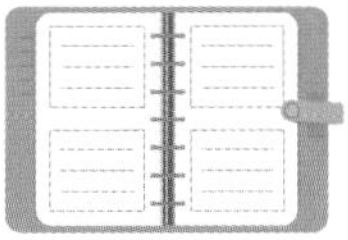
⑯ **der Planer**
planner

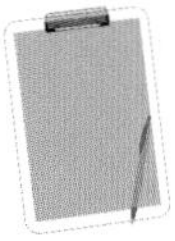
⑰ **das Klemmbrett**
clipboard

⑱ **der Locher**
hole punch

⑲ **das Gummiband**
rubber bands

⑳ **die Vielzweckklemme**
binder clip

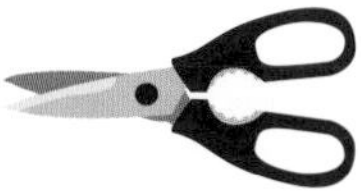
㉑ **die Schere**
scissors

㉒ **der Spitzer**
pencil sharpener

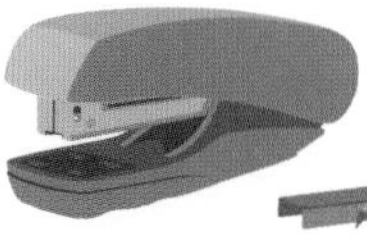
㉓ **der Hefter**
stapler

㉔ **die Heftklammern** *f, pl*
staples

㉕ **die Korrekturflüssigkeit**
correction fluid

㉖ **das Protokoll**
minutes

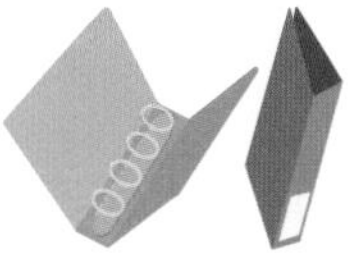
㉗ **das Ringbuch**
ring binder

㉘ **der Textmarker**
highlighter

㉙ **der Kleber**
glue

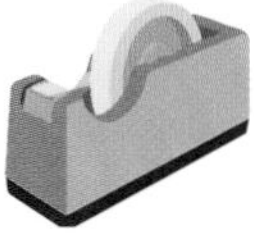
㉚ **der Tesafilm**
tape

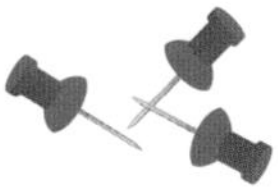
㉛ **die Reißzwecke**
thumbtack

㉜ **der Bleistift**
pencil

㉝ **der Kugelschreiber**
pen

㉞ **die Büroklammer**
paper clips

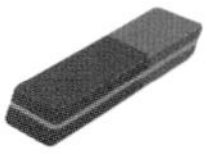
㉟ **der Radiergummi**
eraser

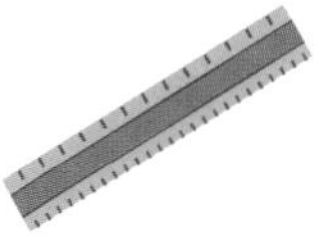
㊱ **das Lineal**
ruler

# 83 Computer und Technologie
## Computers and technology

### 83.1 GERÄTE UND TECHNOLOGIE · GADGETS AND TECHNOLOGY

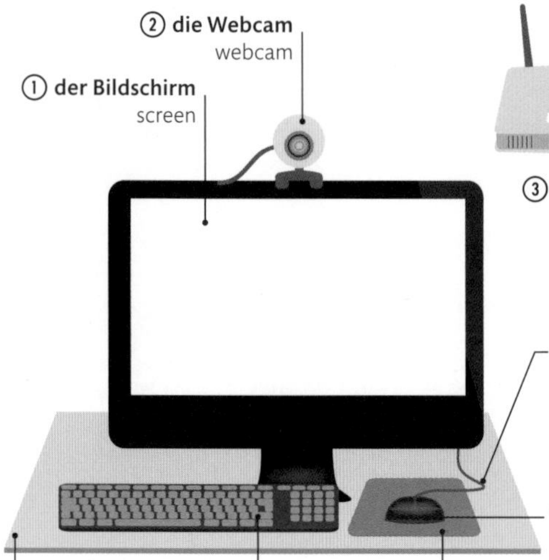

① **der Bildschirm**
screen

② **die Webcam**
webcam

⑦ **das Kabel**
wire

⑧ **die Maus**
mouse

⑨ **der Computertisch**
computer desk

⑩ **die Tastatur**
keyboard

⑪ **das Mauspad**
mouse pad

⑫ **der Desktop-Computer**
desktop computer

③ **der Router**
router

④ **das WLAN**
Wi-Fi

⑤ **der E-Reader**
e-reader

⑥ **das Tablet**
tablet

⑬ **der Laptop**
laptop

⑭ **die Kamera**
camera

⑮ **die Smartwatch**
smartwatch

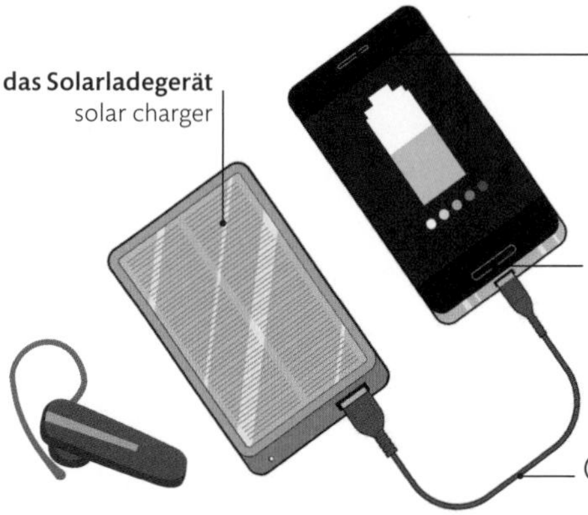

⑯ **das Solarladegerät**
solar charger

⑰ **das Smartphone**
smartphone

⑱ **die Home-Tast**
home button

⑲ **das Ladekabel**
charging cable

㉓ **das Bluetooth-Headset**
Bluetooth headset

⑳ **die Lautsprecher**
*m, pl*
speakers

㉑ **der Camcorder**
camcorder

㉒ **drahtlos**
wireless

㉔ **die Batterie / der Akku**
battery

㉕ **der USB-Stick**
USB drive

㉖ **das Diktiergerät**
voice recorder

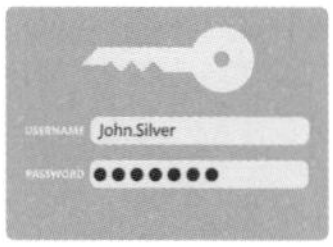


㉗ **das Passwort**
password

㉘ **die Speicherkarte**
memory card

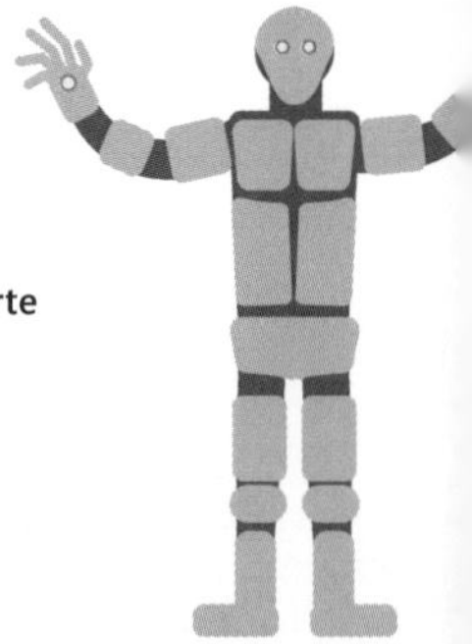

㉙ **die Festplatte**
hard drive

㉚ **der Stecker**
plug

㉛ **das Stromkabel**
power cord

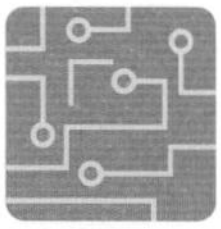

㉜ **der Stromkreis**
circuit

㉝ **die Fernbedienung**
remote control

㉞ **die künstliche Intelligenz**
artificial intelligence

See also
**73** In der Schule • At school **80** An der Universität • At college
**81** Auf der Arbeit • At work **82** Im Büro • In the office **95** Besprechen
and präsentieren • Meeting and presenting **140** Spiele • Games

## 83.2 ONLINE-KOMMUNIKATION • ONLINE COMMUNICATION

① **einschalten**
to turn on

② **ausschalten**
to turn off

③ **sich anmelden**
to log in

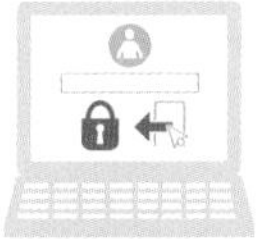

④ **sich abmelden**
to log out

⑤ **herunterladen**
to download

⑥ **hochladen**
to upload

⑦ **sichern**
to back up

⑧ **klicken**
to click

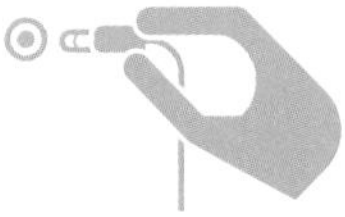

⑨ **einstecken**
to plug in

⑩ **löschen**
to delete

⑪ **ausdrucken**
to print

⑫ **der Kontakt**
contact

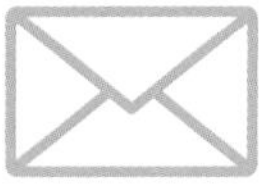

⑬ **die E-Mail**
email

⑭ **antworten**
to reply

⑮ **allen antworten**
to reply to all

⑯ **senden**
to send

⑰ **weiterleiten**
to forward

⑱ **der Entwurf**
draft

⑲ **der Posteingang**
inbox

⑳ **der Postausgang**
outbox

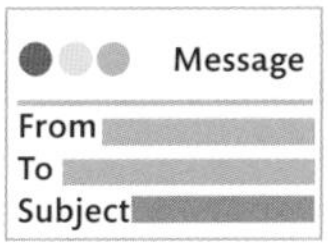
Message
From
To
Subject

㉑ **der Betreff**
subject

㉒ **der Spam**
junk mail / spam

㉓ **der Papierkorb**
trash

㉔ **der Anhang**
attachment

㉕ **der Chat**
chat

㉖ **der Videochat**
video chat

㉗ **die Unterschrift**
signature

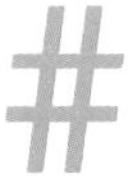

㉘ **das Hashtag**
hashtag

㉙ **das At-Zeichen**
at sign / at symbol

㉚ **Sie müssen Ihr Mikrofon einschalten, Liz.**
You need to turn on your microphone, Liz.

㉛ **die Videokonferenz**
video conference

# 84 Medien
## Media

### 84.1 DAS FERNSEHSTUDIO • TELEVISION STUDIO

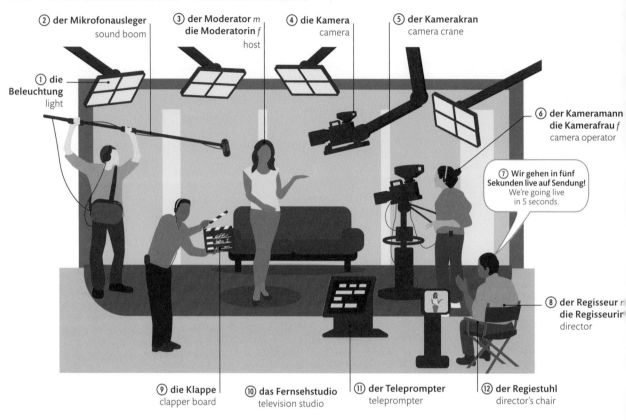

### 84.2 RADIO • RADIO

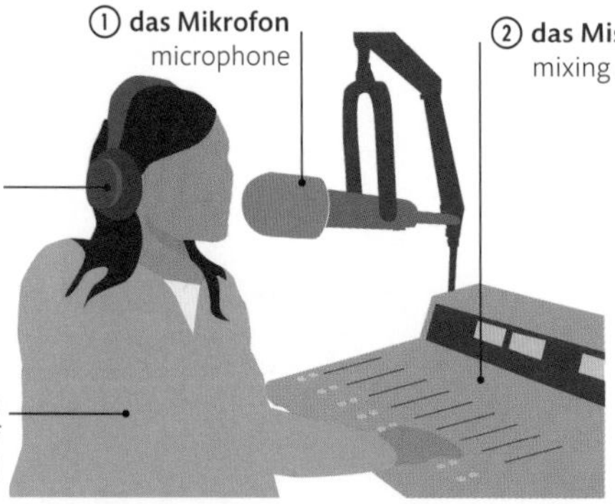


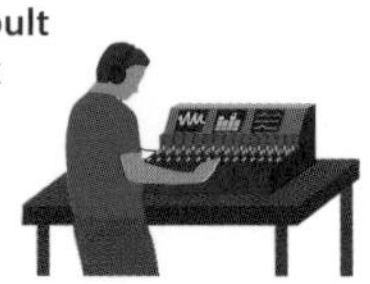

⑥ **der Tontechniker** *m*
**die Tontechnikerin** *f*
sound technician

⑦ **der Radiosender**
radio station

⑧ **senden**
to broadcast

⑨ **digital**
digital

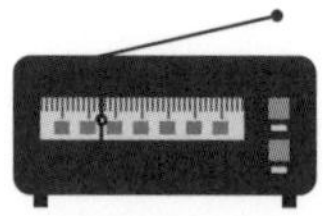

⑩ **das UKW-Radio**
FM

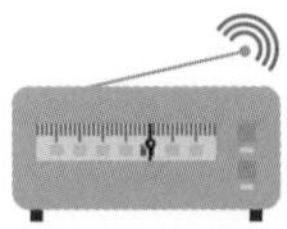

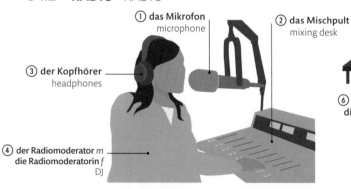

⑪ **die Frequenz**
frequency

See also
**83** Computer und Technologie • Computers and technology **128-129** Musik • Music
**136** Unterhaltung zu Hause • Home entertainment **137** Fernsehen • Television

## 84.3 SOZIALE UND ONLINE-MEDIEN
SOCIAL AND ONLINE MEDIA

① **folgen**
to follow

② **liken**
to like

③ **viral werden**
to go viral

④ **trenden**
to trend

⑤ **der Avatar**
avatar

⑥ **der Videoblog**
vlog

⑦ **der Vlogger** *m*
**die Vloggerin** *f*
vlogger

⑧ **der Blog**
blog

⑨ **Mein Blog hat über 500 Follower.**
My blog has over 500 followers.
⑩ **der Blogger** *m* **/ die Bloggerin** *f*
blogger

⑪ **teilen**
to share

⑫ **blockieren**
to block

⑬ **posten**
to post

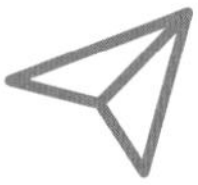
⑭ **jemandem eine Direktnachricht schreiben**
to DM someone

⑮ **der Influencer** *m*
**die Influencerin** *f*
influencer

⑯ **der Follower** *m*
**die Followerin** *f*
follower

⑰ **der Podcast**
podcast

⑱ **das Emoji**
emoji

⑲ **das Hashtag**
hashtag

⑳ **der Thread**
thread

㉑ **der Feed**
newsfeed

㉒ **das Statusupdate**
status update

㉓ **das CMS (Content-Management-System)**
CMS (content management system)

㉔ **die Plattform**
platform

㉕ **das Cookie**
cookie

㉖ **das Pop-up**
pop-up

㉗ **die Nachrichtenseite**
news website

㉘ **die Zeitschriftenseite**
magazine website

㉙ **die Community-Seite**
community website

㉚ **das Trolling**
trolling

## 85 Recht
Law

### 85.1 DAS RECHTSSYSTEM · THE LEGAL SYSTEM

⑧ Das Urteil lautet: unschuldig.
The verdict is not guilty.

① der Anwalt *m* / die Anwältin *f* – lawyer

② der Gerichtsbeamte *m* / die Gerichtsbeamtin *f* – court officer

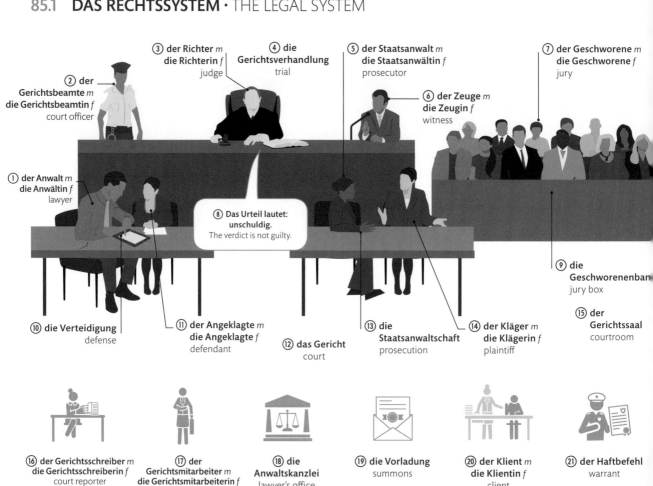

③ der Richter *m* / die Richterin *f* – judge

④ die Gerichtsverhandlung – trial

⑤ der Staatsanwalt *m* / die Staatsanwältin *f* – prosecutor

⑥ der Zeuge *m* / die Zeugin *f* – witness

⑦ der Geschworene *m* / die Geschworene *f* – jury

⑨ die Geschworenenban[k] – jury box

⑩ die Verteidigung – defense

⑪ der Angeklagte *m* / die Angeklagte *f* – defendant

⑫ das Gericht – court

⑬ die Staatsanwaltschaft – prosecution

⑭ der Kläger *m* / die Klägerin *f* – plaintiff

⑮ der Gerichtssaal – courtroom

⑯ der Gerichtsschreiber *m* / die Gerichtsschreiberin *f* – court reporter

⑰ der Gerichtsmitarbeiter *m* / die Gerichtsmitarbeiterin *f* – court official

⑱ die Anwaltskanzlei – lawyer's office

⑲ die Vorladung – summons

⑳ der Klient *m* / die Klientin *f* – client

㉑ der Haftbefehl – warrant

㉒ das Schriftstück – writ

㉓ die Gebühr – charge

㉔ die Rechtsberatung – legal advice

㉕ die Aussage – statement

㉖ der Gerichtstermin – court date

㉗ der Fall – court case

㉘ das Urteil – verdict

㉙ verurteilen – to sentence

㉚ die Geschworenenberatung – jury deliberation

㉛ der Sprecher *m* / die Sprecherin *f* – foreperson

㉜ abstimmen – vote

See also
**50** Die Rettungsdienste • Emergency services
**91** Branchen und Abteilungen • Industries and departments

㉝ **das Phantombild**
composite

㉞ **die Beweise** *m, pl*
evidence

㉟ **der Verdächtige** *m*
**die Verdächtige** *f*
suspect

㊱ **das Vorstrafenregister**
criminal record

㊲ **der Straftäter** *m*
**die Straftäterin** *f*
criminal

㊳ **der Beschuldigte** *m*
**die Beschuldigte** *f*
accused

㊴ **plädieren**
to plead

㊵ **unschuldig**
innocent

㊶ **schuldig**
guilty

㊷ **in Berufung gehen**
to appeal

㊸ **der Strafgefangene** *m*
**die Strafgefangene** *f*
prisoners

㊹ **der Gefängniswärter** *m*
**die Gefängniswärterin** *f*
prison guards

㊺ **das Gefängnis**
prison

㊻ **die Zelle**
cell

㊼ **die Kaution**
bail

㊽ **die Bewährung**
parole

㊾ **die Strafe**
fine

㊿ **freigesprochen werden**
to be acquitted

## 85.2 VERBRECHEN • CRIME

① **der Überfall / der Einbruch**
robbery / burglary

② **der Raubüberfall**
mugging

③ **der Autodiebstahl**
car theft

④ **der Krawall**
hooliganism

⑤ **der Vandalismus**
vandalism

⑥ **das Schmuggeln**
smuggling

⑦ **der Betrug**
fraud

⑧ **das Hacken**
hacking

⑨ **der Taschendiebstahl**
pickpocketing

⑩ **die Bestechung**
bribery

⑪ **die Geschwindigkeitsübertretung**
speeding

⑫ **der Drogenhandel**
drug dealing

⑬ **das Graffiti**
graffiti

⑭ **der Ladendiebstahl**
shoplifting

# 86 Landwirtschaft
## Farming

### 86.1 AUF DEM BAUERNHOF · ON THE FARM

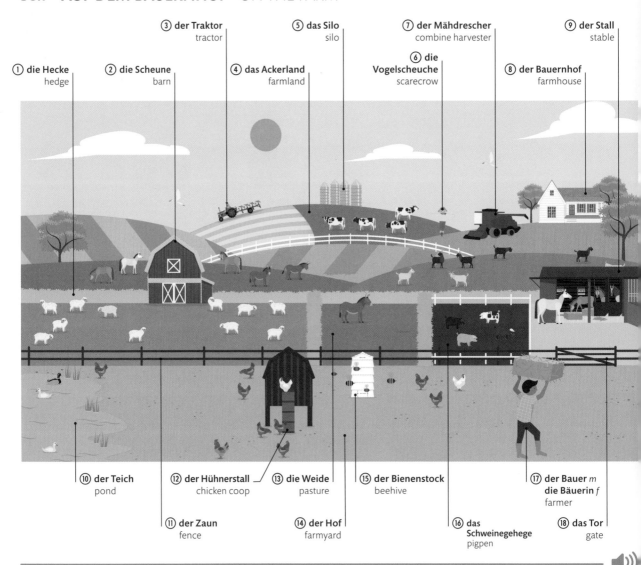

1. **die Hecke** hedge
2. **die Scheune** barn
3. **der Traktor** tractor
4. **das Ackerland** farmland
5. **das Silo** silo
6. **die Vogelscheuche** scarecrow
7. **der Mähdrescher** combine harvester
8. **der Bauernhof** farmhouse
9. **der Stall** stable
10. **der Teich** pond
11. **der Zaun** fence
12. **der Hühnerstall** chicken coop
13. **die Weide** pasture
14. **der Hof** farmyard
15. **der Bienenstock** beehive
16. **das Schweinegehege** pigpen
17. **der Bauer** *m* **die Bäuerin** *f* farmer
18. **das Tor** gate

### 86.2 LANDWIRTSCHAFTLICHE VERBEN · FARMING VERBS

1. **pflügen** to plow
2. **säen** to sow
3. **melken** to milk
4. **füttern** to feed
5. **anpflanzen** to plant
6. **ernten** to harvest

See also
**53** Fleisch • Meat **55-56** Gemüse • Vegetables **57** Obst • Fruit **58** Obst und Nüsse Fruit and nuts **61** Milchprodukte • Dairy produce **165** Bauernhoftiere • Farm animals

## 86.3 LANDWIRTSCHAFTLICHE BEGRIFFE • FARMING TERMS

① **der Ackerbaubetrieb**
crop farm

② **der Milchbetrieb**
dairy farm

③ **die Schafzucht**
sheep farm

④ **die Hühnerzucht**
poultry farm

⑤ **die Schweinezucht**
pig farm

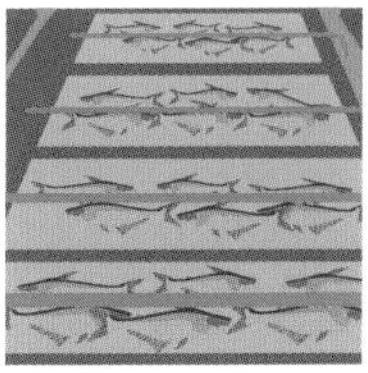

⑥ **die Fischzucht**
fish farm

⑦ **die Herde**
herd

⑧ **die Obstplantage**
fruit farm

⑨ **der Weinberg**
vineyard

⑩ **der Gemüsegarten**
vegetable garden

⑪ **der Unkrautvernichter**
herbicide

⑫ **das Pestizid**
pesticide

## 86.4 FELDFRÜCHTE • CROPS

① **der Weizen**
wheat

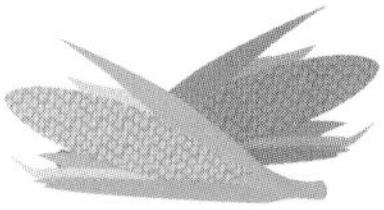

② **der Mais**
corn

③ **die Gerste**
barley

④ **der Raps**
rapeseed

⑤ **die Sonnenblume**
sunflowers

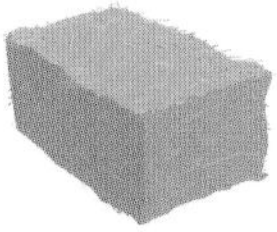

⑥ **das Heu**
hay

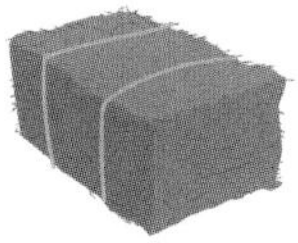

⑦ **die Alfalfa**
alfalfa

⑧ **der Tabak**
tobacco

⑨ **der Reis**
rice

⑩ **der Tee**
tea

⑪ **der Kaffee**
coffee

⑫ **das Zuckerrohr**
sugar cane

⑬ **der Flachs**
flax

⑭ **die Baumwolle**
cotton

⑮ **die Kartoffel**
potatoes

⑯ **die Yamswurzel**
yams

⑰ **die Hirse**
millet

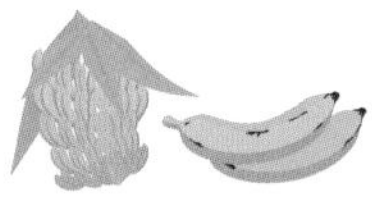

⑱ **die Kochbanane**
plantains

# 87 Der Bau
## Construction

### 87.1 **DIE BAUSTELLE** · BUILDING SITE

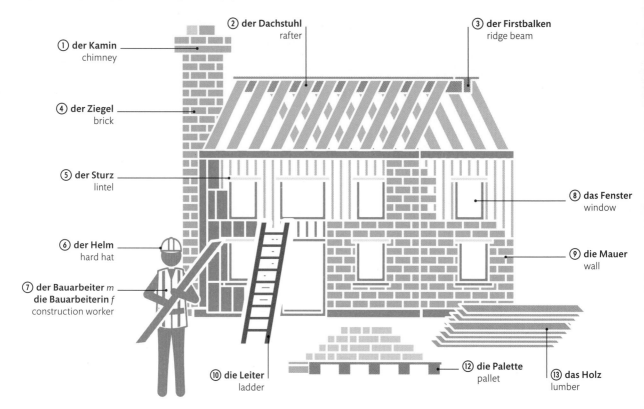

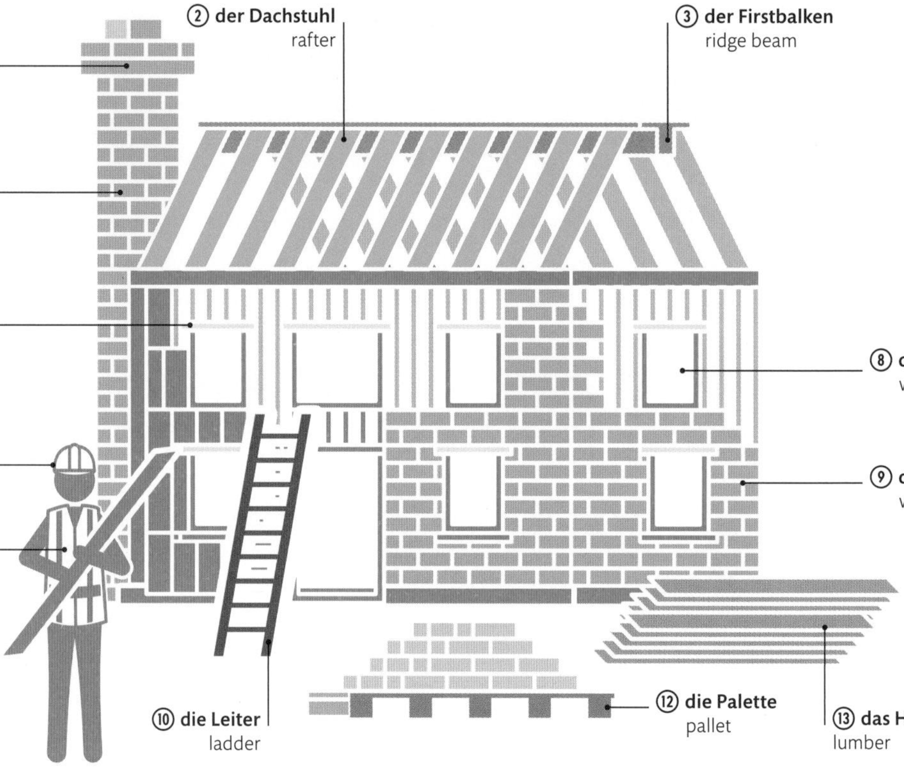


⑪ **die Baustelle**
construction site

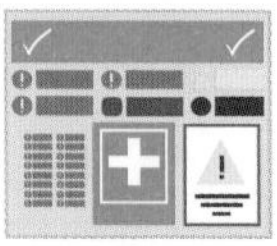

⑭ **der Aushang mit Sicherheitshinweisen**
safety notice board

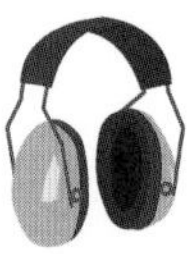

⑮ **der Ohrschutz**
ear protectors

⑯ **die Warnweste**
high-visibility vest

⑰ **die Schutzhandschuhe** *m, pl*
safety gloves

⑱ **die Schutzbrille**
safety glasses

⑲ **der Werkzeuggürtel**
tool belt

⑳ **der Träger**
girder

㉑ **das Rohr**
pipe

㉒ **der Zement / der Mörtel**
cement / mortar

㉓ **der Formstein**
cinder block

㉔ **die Schindel**
shingles

㉕ **bauen**
to build

See also
**25** Ein Ort zum Leben • A place to live **32** Haus und Heim • House and home **33** Elektrizität und Sanitärtechnik • Electrics and plumbing **35** Heimwerken • Home improvements **36** Werkzeuge • Tools **37** Wohnraumverschönerung • Renovating

## 87.2 MASCHINEN • MACHINERY

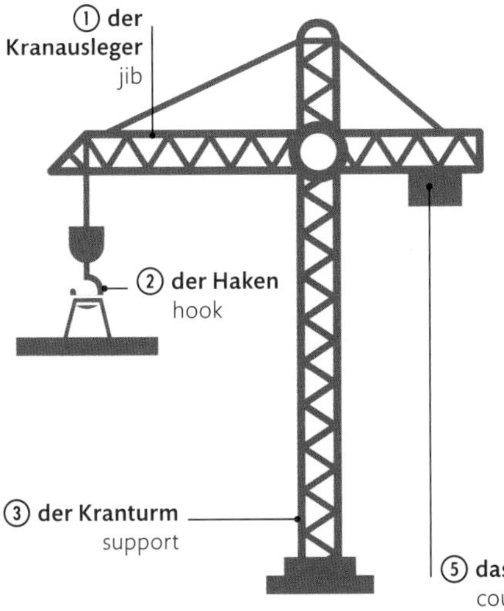

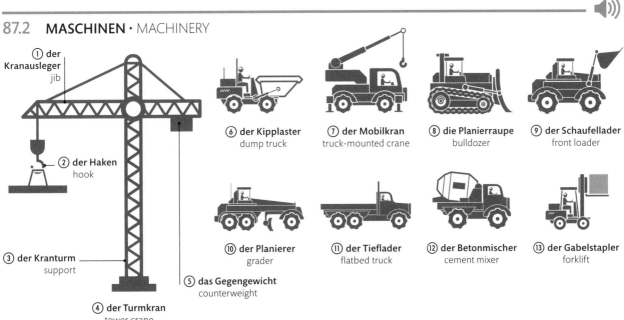

① **der Kranausleger**
jib

② **der Haken**
hook

③ **der Kranturm**
support

④ **der Turmkran**
tower crane

⑤ **das Gegengewicht**
counterweight

⑥ **der Kipplaster**
dump truck

⑦ **der Mobilkran**
truck-mounted crane

⑧ **die Planierraupe**
bulldozer

⑨ **der Schaufellader**
front loader

⑩ **der Planierer**
grader

⑪ **der Tieflader**
flatbed truck

⑫ **der Betonmischer**
cement mixer

⑬ **der Gabelstapler**
forklift

## 87.3 WERKZEUGE UND STRASSENBAUARBEITEN
TOOLS AND ROADWORKS

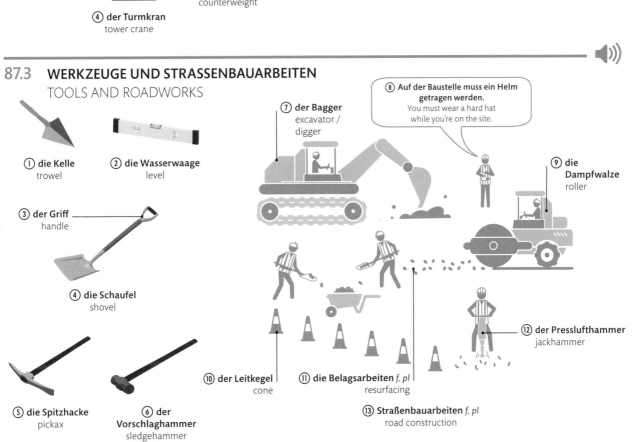

① **die Kelle**
trowel

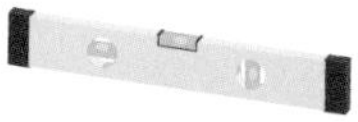

② **die Wasserwaage**
level

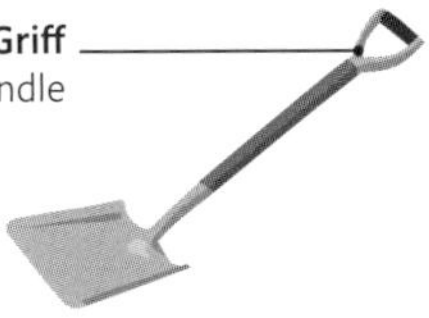

③ **der Griff**
handle

④ **die Schaufel**
shovel

⑤ **die Spitzhacke**
pickax

⑥ **der Vorschlaghammer**
sledgehammer

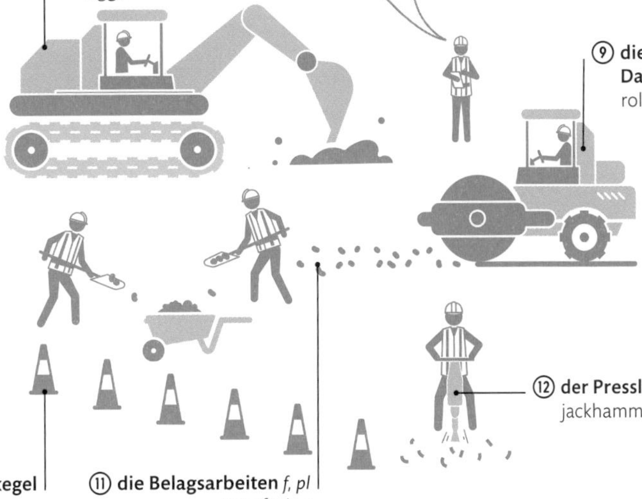

⑦ **der Bagger**
excavator / digger

⑧ **Auf der Baustelle muss ein Helm getragen werden.**
You must wear a hard hat while you're on the site.

⑨ **die Dampfwalze**
roller

⑩ **der Leitkegel**
cone

⑪ **die Belagsarbeiten** *f, pl*
resurfacing

⑫ **der Presslufthammer**
jackhammer

⑬ **Straßenbauarbeiten** *f, pl*
road construction

# 88 Das Militär
## Military

### 88.1 DIE STREITKRÄFTE
ARMED FORCES

① **die Armee**
army

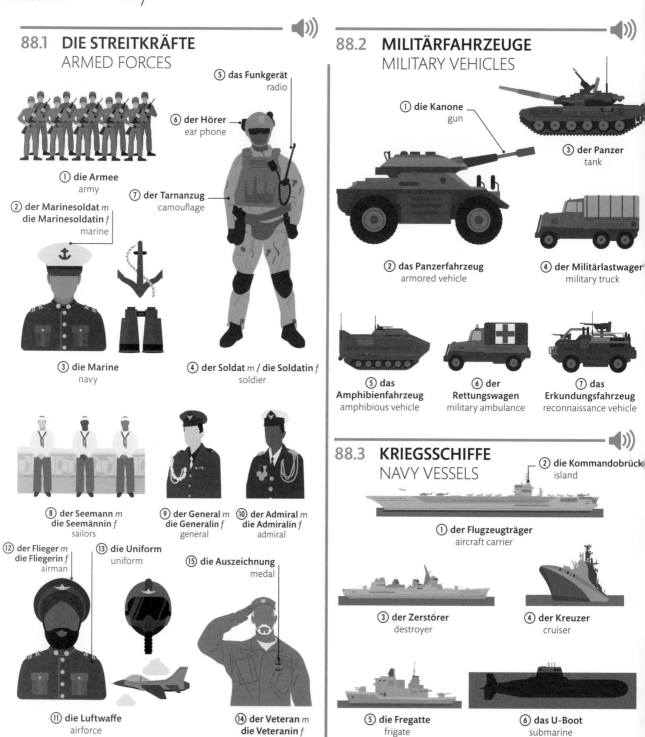

⑤ **das Funkgerät**
radio

⑥ **der Hörer**
ear phone

⑦ **der Tarnanzug**
camouflage

④ **der Soldat** *m* / **die Soldatin** *f*
soldier

② **der Marinesoldat** *m*
**die Marinesoldatin** *f*
marine

③ **die Marine**
navy

⑧ **der Seemann** *m*
**die Seemännin** *f*
sailors

⑨ **der General** *m*
**die Generalin** *f*
general

⑩ **der Admiral** *m*
**die Admiralin** *f*
admiral

⑫ **der Flieger** *m*
**die Fliegerin** *f*
airman

⑬ **die Uniform**
uniform

⑪ **die Luftwaffe**
airforce

⑮ **die Auszeichnung**
medal

⑭ **der Veteran** *m*
**die Veteranin** *f*
veteran

### 88.2 MILITÄRFAHRZEUGE
MILITARY VEHICLES

③ **der Panzer**
tank

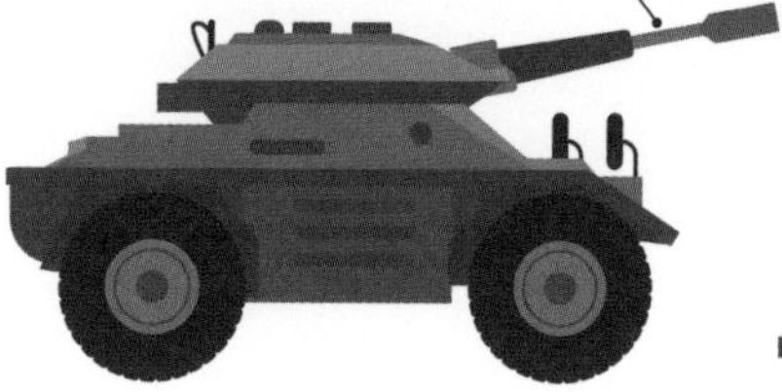

① **die Kanone**
gun

② **das Panzerfahrzeug**
armored vehicle

④ **der Militärlastwagen**
military truck

⑤ **das Amphibienfahrzeug**
amphibious vehicle

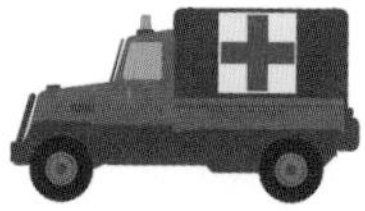

⑥ **der Rettungswagen**
military ambulance

⑦ **das Erkundungsfahrzeug**
reconnaissance vehicle

### 88.3 KRIEGSSCHIFFE
NAVY VESSELS

② **die Kommandobrück**
island

① **der Flugzeugträger**
aircraft carrier

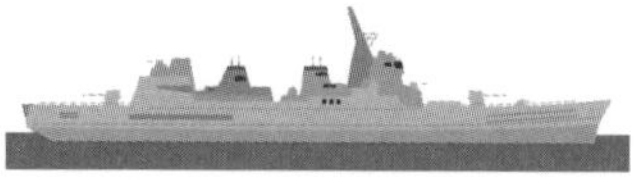

③ **der Zerstörer**
destroyer

④ **der Kreuzer**
cruiser

⑤ **die Fregatte**
frigate

⑥ **das U-Boot**
submarine

See also
**79** Geschichte • History **148** Karten und Richtungsangaben Maps and directions **149-151** Länder • Countries

## 88.4 KAMPFFLUGZEUGE • COMBAT AIRCRAFT

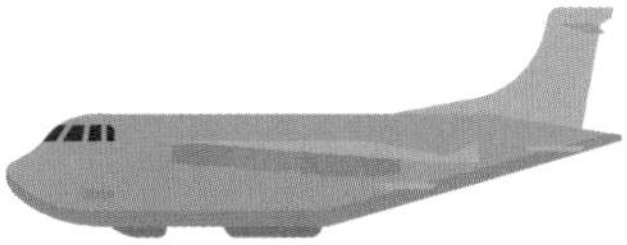

① **das militärische Transportflugzeug**
military transport aircraft

② **das Bombenflugzeug**
bomber

③ **der Kampfhubschrauber**
attack helicopter

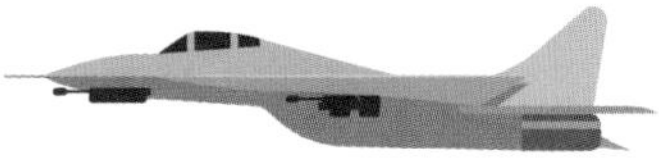

④ **das Kampfflugzeug**
fighter

⑤ **der Aufklärer**
reconnaissance aircraft

⑥ **der Lastenhubschrauber**
transport helicopter

## 88.5 KRIEG UND WAFFEN • WAR AND WEAPONS

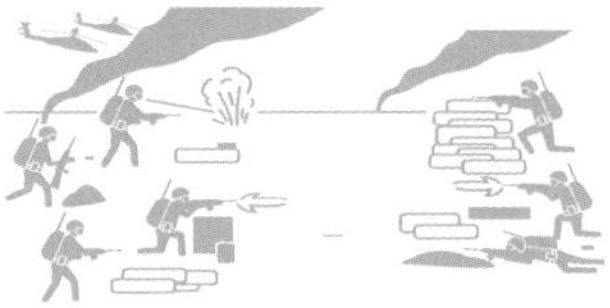

① **die Schlacht**
battle

② **die Front**
front

③ **das Geschützfeuer**
gunfire

④ **der Verwundete** *m*
**die Verwundete** *f*
casualty

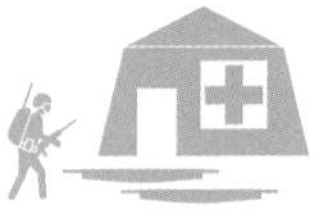

⑤ **das Feldlazarett**
field hospital

⑥ **die Kantine**
mess

⑦ **die Feuerwaffe**
guns

⑧ **das Maschinengewehr**
machine gun

⑨ **die Pistole**
pistol

⑩ **die Schrotflinte**
shotgun

⑪ **das Gewehr**
rifle

⑬ **die Granate**
grenade

⑫ **der Granatwerfer**
grenade launcher

⑭ **die Boden-Luft-Rakete**
surface-to-air missile

⑮ **die ballistische Rakete**
ballistic missile

⑯ **das tragbare Luftabwehrsystem**
shoulder-launched missile

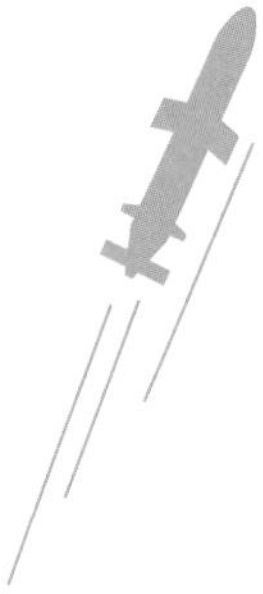

⑰ **der Marschflugkörper**
cruise missile

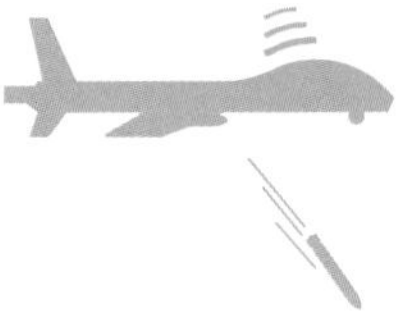

⑱ **die bewaffnete Drohne**
armed drone

# 89 Berufe
Jobs

## 89.1 BERUFSBEZEICHNUNGEN · OCCUPATIONS

① **der Schauspieler** *m*
**die Schauspielerin** *f*
actor

② **der Soziologe** *m*
**die Soziologin** *f*
sociologist

③ **der Friseur** *m*
**die Friseurin** *f*
barber

④ **der Lektor** *m*
**die Lektorin** *f*
editor

⑤ **der Bartender** *m*
**die Bartenderin** *f*
bartender

⑥ **der Fischer** *m*
**die Fischerin** *f*
fisherman

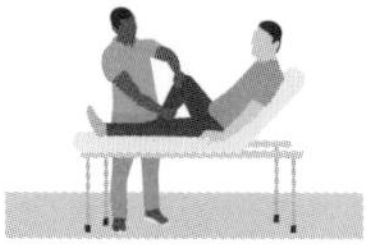
⑦ **der Physiotherapeut** *m*
**die Physiotherapeutin** *f*
physical therapist

⑧ **der Optiker** *m*
**die Optikerin** *f*
optician

⑩ **Dieses Rohr leckt.**
This pipe has
sprung a leak.
⑨ **der Klempner** *m* / **die Klempnerin** *f*
plumber

⑪ **der Schreiner** *m*
**die Schreinerin** *f*
carpenter

⑫ **der Schiffskapitän** *m*
**die Schiffskapitänin** *f*
ship's captain

⑬ **der Dozent** *m*
**die Dozentin** *f*
lecturer

⑭ **der Komiker** *m*
**die Komikerin** *f*
comedian

⑮ **der Tänzer** *m*
**die Tänzerin** *f*
dancer

⑯ **der Clown** *m*
**die Clownin** *f*
clown

⑰ **die Reinigungskraft**
cleaner

⑱ **der Arzt** *m*
**die Ärztin** *f*
doctor

⑲ **der Fahrlehrer** *m*
**die Fahrlehrerin** *f*
driving instructor

⑳ **der Maler** *m*
**die Malerin** *f*
painter

㉑ **der Elektriker** *m*
**die Elektrikerin** *f*
electrician

㉒ **der Designer** *m*
**die Designerin** *f*
designer

㉓ **der Barista** *m*
**die Barista** *f*
barista

㉔ **der Feuerwehrmann** *m*
**die Feuerwehrfrau** *f*
firefighter

㉕ **der App-Entwickler** *m*
**die App-Entwicklerin** *f*
app developer

㉖ **der Spion** *m*
**die Spionin** *f*
spy

㉗ **der Florist** *m*
**die Floristin** *f*
florist

㉘ **der Grundstückspfleg**
**die Grundstückspflegeri**
ground maintenance

㉙ **der Gärtner** *m*
**die Gärtnerin** *f*
gardener

㉚ **der Gemüsehändler** *m*
**die Gemüsehändlerin** *f*
grocer

㉛ **der Bergarbeiter** *m*
**die Bergarbeiterin** *f*
miner

㉜ **der IT-Manager** *m*
**die IT-Managerin** *f*
IT manager

㉝ **der Juwelier** *m*
**die Juwelierin** *f*
jeweler

㉞ **der Zahnarzt** *m*
**die Zahnärztin** *f*
dentist

See also
**81** Auf der Arbeit • At work **82** Im Büro • In the office **90** Berufe (Fortsetzung) • Jobs continued **91** Branchen und Abteilungen • Industries and departments **92** Bewerbungen • Applying for a job **93** Nützliche Fähigkeiten für den Arbeitsplatz • Workplace skills **95** Besprechen and präsentieren • Meeting and presenting

**35 die Haushaltshilfe**
maid / housekeeper

**36 der Friseur / Stylist** *m*
**die Friseurin / Stylistin** *f*
hairdresser / stylist

**37 der Mechaniker** *m*
**die Mechanikerin** *f*
mechanic

**38 der Dolmetscher** *m*
**die Dolmetscherin** *f*
interpreter

**39 der Kurator** *m*
**die Kuratorin** *f*
museum curator

**40 der Privatdetektiv** *m*
**die Privatdetektivin** *f*
private investigator

**41 der Bauleiter** *m*
**die Bauleiterin** *f*
site manager

**42 der Kieferorthopäde** *m*
**die Kieferorthopädin** *f*
orthodontist

**43 der Nachrichtensprecher** *m*
**die Nachrichtensprecherin** *f*
broadcaster

**44 der Apotheker** *m*
**die Apothekerin** *f*
pharmacist

**45 der Metzger** *m*
**die Metzgerin** *f*
butcher

**46 der Fotograf** *m*
**die Fotografin** *f*
photographer

**47 der Polizeibeamte** *m*
**die Polizeibeamtin** *f*
police officer

**48 der Krankenpfleger** *m*
**die Krankenschwester** *f*
nurse

**49 der Seemann** *m*
**die Seefrau** *f*
sailor

**50 der Verkäufer** *m*
**die Verkäuferin** *f*
sales assistant

**51 die Kellnerin**
server / waitress

**52 der Kellner**
server / waiter

**53 der Bildhauer** *m*
**die Bildhauerin** *f*
sculptor

**54 der Wachmann** *m*
**die Wachfrau** *f*
security guard

**55 der Schneider** *m*
**die Schneiderin** *f*
tailor

**56 der Skilehrer** *m*
**die Skilehrerin** *f*
ski instructor

**57 der Soldat** *m*
**die Soldatin** *f*
soldier

**58 der Bauer** *m*
**die Bäuerin** *f*
farmer

**59 der Sportler** *m*
**die Sportlerin** *f*
athlete / sportsperson

**60 der Fischhändler** *m*
**die Fischhändlerin** *f*
fishmonger

**61 der Sänger** *m*
**die Sängerin** *f*
singer

**62 der Makler** *m*
**die Maklerin** *f*
real estate agent

**63 der Marktforscher** *m*
**die Marktforscherin** *f*
market researcher

**65 Ihr Hund hat nun alle nötigen Impfungen.**
Your dog is up to date with its vaccinations.

**64 der Tierarzt** *m* **/ die Tierärztin** *f*
vet

# 90 Berufe (Fortsetzung)
Jobs continued

## 90.1 BERUFSBEZEICHNUNGEN · OCCUPATIONS

① **der Security-Mitarbeiter** *m*
**die Security-Mitarbeiterin** *f*
security guard

② **der Fensterputzer** *m*
**die Fensterputzerin** *f*
window cleaner

③ **der Künstler** *m*
**die Künstlerin** *f*
artist

④ **der Leibwächter** *m*
**die Leibwächterin** *f*
bodyguard

⑤ **der Psychologe** *m*
**die Psychologin** *f*
psychologist

⑥ **der Geschäftsmann**
businessman

⑦ **die Geschäftsfrau**
businesswoman

⑧ **der Steuerberater** *m*
**die Steuerberaterin** *f*
accountant

⑨ **der Koch** *m*
**die Köchin** *f*
chef

⑩ **der Bauarbeiter** *m*
**die Bauarbeiterin** *f*
construction worker

⑪ **der Radiomoderator** *m*
**die Radiomoderatorin** *f*
radio DJ

⑫ **der Techniker** *m*
**die Technikerin** *f*
engineer

⑬ **der Modedesigner** *m*
**die Modedesignerin** *f*
fashion designer

⑭ **der Rockstar** *m / f*
rock star

⑮ **der Fluglehrer** *m*
**die Fluglehrerin** *f*
flight instructor

⑯ **der Hausmeister** *m*
**die Hausmeisterin** *f*
janitor

⑰ **der Touristenführer** *m*
**die Touristenführerin** *f*
tour guide

⑱ **der Postbote** *m*
**die Postbotin** *f*
mail carrier

⑲ **der Assistent** *m*
**die Assistentin** *f*
personal assistant (PA)

⑳ **der Bibliothekar** *m*
**die Bibliothekarin** *f*
librarian

㉑ **der Schlosser** *m*
**die Schlosserin** *f*
locksmith

㉒ **der Rettungssanitäter** *m*
**die Rettungssanitäterin** *f*
paramedic

㉓ **der Musiklehrer** *m*
**die Musiklehrerin** *f*
teacher

㉔ **der Erzieher** *m*
**die Erzieherin** *f*
childcare provider

㉕ **der Küchenmonteur** *m*
**die Küchenmonteurin** *f*
kitchen installer

㉖ **der Taxifahrer** *m*
**die Taxifahrerin** *f*
taxi driver

㉗ **der Tierpfleger** *m*
**die Tierpflegerin** *f*
zookeeper

㉙ **Man sollte viel Erfahrung im Gericht sammeln, bevor man Richter wird.**
You should have a lot of courtroom experience before you become a judge.

㉘ **der Richter** *m* / **die Richterin** *f*
judge

See also
**81** Auf der Arbeit • At work **82** Im Büro • In the office **91** Branchen und Abteilungen Industries and departments **92** Bewerbungen • Applying for a job **93** Nützliche Fähigkeiten für den Arbeitsplatz • Workplace skills **95** Besprechen and präsentieren • Meeting and presenting

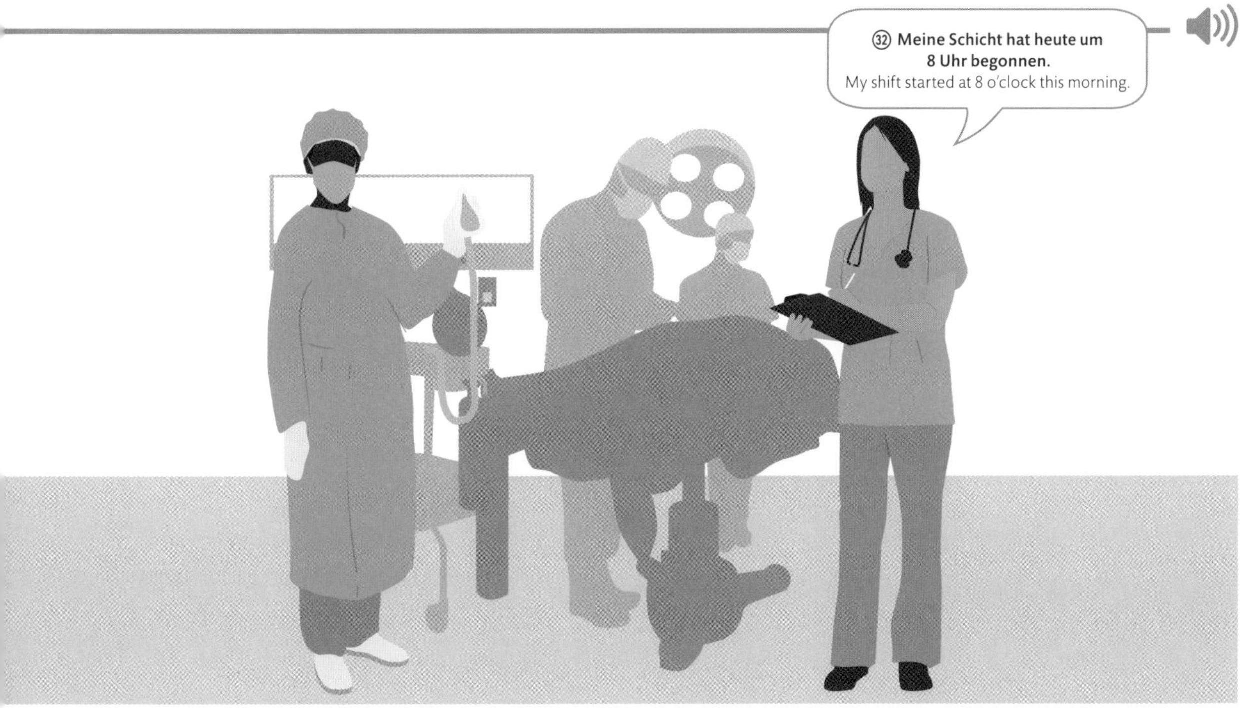
32 **Meine Schicht hat heute um 8 Uhr begonnen.**
My shift started at 8 o'clock this morning.

30 **der Anästhesiologe** *m* **/ die Anästhesiologin** *f*
anesthesiologist

31 **der Chirurg** *m* **/ die Chirurgin** *f*
surgeon

33 **der Chauffeur** *m*
**die Chauffeurin** *f*
driver

34 **der Sekretär** *m*
**die Sekretärin** *f*
secretary

35 **der Rezeptionist** *m*
**die Rezeptionistin** *f*
receptionist

36 **der Flugbegleiter** *m*
**die Flugbegleiterin** *f*
flight attendant

37 **der Wissenschaftler** *m*
**die Wissenschaftlerin** *f*
scientist

38 **der Busfahrer** *m*
**die Busfahrerin** *f*
bus driver

39 **der Musiker** *m*
**die Musikerin** *f*
musician

40 **der Landvermesser** *m*
**die Landvermesserin** *f*
surveyor

41 **der Anwalt** *m*
**die Anwältin** *f*
lawyer

42 **der Lehrer** *m*
**die Lehrerin** *f*
teacher

43 **der Journalist** *m*
**die Journalistin** *f*
journalist

44 **der Zugführer** *m*
**die Zugführerin** *f*
train driver

5 **der Reiseberater** *m*
**die Reiseberaterin** *f*
travel agent

46 **der Lastwagenfahrer** *m*
**die Lastwagenfahrerin** *f*
truck driver

47 **der Architekt** *m*
**die Architektin** *f*
architect

48 **der Schriftsteller** *m*
**die Schriftstellerin** *f*
writer

49 **der Yogalehrer** *m*
**die Yogalehrerin** *f*
yoga teacher

50 **der Pilot** *m*
**die Pilotin** *f*
pilot

# 91 Branchen und Abteilungen

## Industries and departments

### 91.1 BRANCHEN · INDUSTRIES

(1) **die Werbung**
advertising

(2) **personenbezogene Dienstleistungen** *f, pl*
personal services

(3) **die Landwirtschaft**
agriculture / farming

(4) **das Militär**
military

(5) **die Immobilienwirtschaft**
real estate

(6) **die Automobilindustrie**
automotiveindustry

ate Bank

(10) **das Bankwesen**
banking

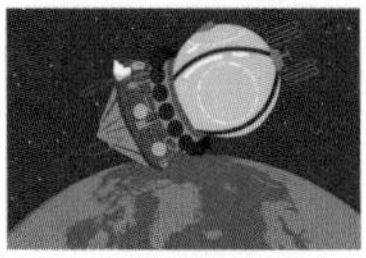

(11) **die Luft- und Raumfahrt**
aerospace

(12) **die Ölbranche**
petroleum engineering

(13) **die Chemie**
chemical industry

(14) **die Kunst**
arts

(15) **die Lehre**
education

(19) **die Gaming-Industrie**
gaming

(20) **die Energieversorgung**
energy

(21) **die Wissenschaft**
research

(22) **die Mode**
fashion

(23) **die Recyclingwirtschaft**
recycling

(24) **die Unterhaltung**
entertainment

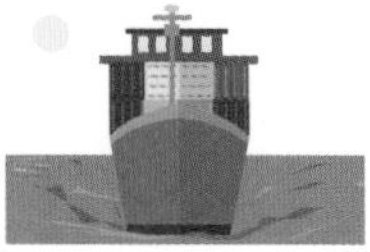

(28) **die Logistik**
shipping

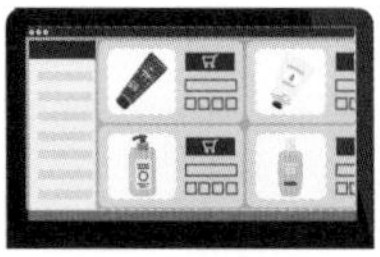

(29) **der Online-Handel**
online retail

(30) **der Journalismus**
journalism

(31) **die Textilindustrie**
textiles

(32) **die Medienbranche**
media

(33) **das Gastgewerbe**
hospitality

(37) **der Lieferdienst**
online delivery

(38) **die Wasserwirtschaft**
water

(39) **die darstellenden Künste** *f, pl*
performing arts

(40) **die Biotechnologie**
biotechnology

(42) Unsere Aktien sind dramatisch abgestürzt.
Our stocks have fallen dramatically.

(41) **das Finanzwesen**
finance

See also
**81** Auf der Arbeit • At work **82** Im Büro • In the office **89-90** Berufe • Jobs **92** Bewerbungen
Applying for a job **93** Nützliche Fähigkeiten für den Arbeitsplatz • Workplace skills

⑧ **Hier sehen Sie eines unserer berühmtesten Gebäude.**
This is one of our most famous buildings.

⑦ **die Tourismusbranche**
tourism

⑨ **die Veterinärversorgung**
pet services

⑯ **das Catering / die Lebensmittelindustrie**
catering / food

⑰ **die Pharmaindustrie**
pharmaceuticals

⑱ **das Bauwesen**
construction

㉕ **die Fischerei**
fishing

㉖ **die Elektronikbranche**
electronics

㉗ **der Einzelhandel**
retail

㉞ **das Gesundheitswesen**
healthcare

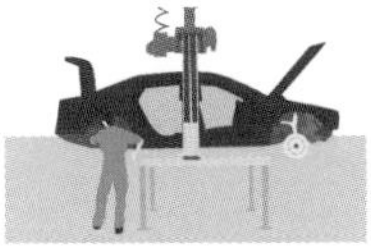

㉟ **die Produktionsindustrie**
manufacturing

㊱ **der Bergbau**
mining

㊸ **das Transportwesen**
transportation

## 91.2 ABTEILUNGEN • DEPARTMENTS

① **die Buchhaltung**
accounts / finance

② **die Fertigung**
production

CONTRACT

③ **die Rechtsabteilung**
legal

④ **das Marketing**
marketing

⑤ **die IT**
information technology (IT)

⑥ **die Büroverwaltung und Anlagenverwaltung**
facilities / office services

⑦ **der Vertrieb**
sales

⑧ **die Verwaltung**
administration

⑨ **Public Relations**
public relations (PR)

⑩ **der Einkauf**
purchasing

⑪ **die Personalabteilung**
human resources (HR)

⑬ **Diese Ideen für das neue Projekt gefallen mir.**
I love these ideas for the new project.

⑫ **Forschung und Entwicklung (F&E)**
research and development (R&D)

# 92 Bewerbungen
## Applying for a job

### 92.1 BEWERBUNGEN · JOB APPLICATIONS

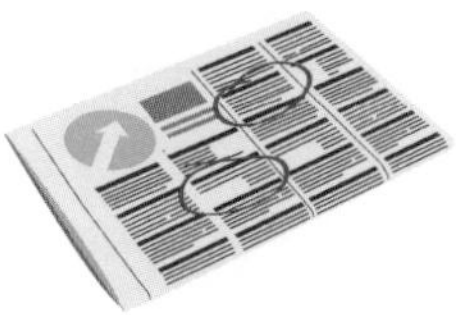

① **die Stellenanzeige**
job ads

② **das Bewerbungsformular**
application form

③ **das Anschreiben**
cover letter

④ **das Portfolio**
portfolio

⑤ **der Lebenslauf**
résumé

⑧ **Nach welcher Art Job sehen Sie sich derzeit um?**
What kind of work are you looking for?

⑦ **ein Formular ausfüllen**
to fill out a form

⑥ **die Personalvermittlung**
recruiter

### 92.2 SICH BEWERBEN · APPLYING FOR A JOB

② **die Stellenausschreibung**
vacancies

① **sich um eine Stelle bewerben**
to apply for a job

④ **Was macht Sie zur perfekten Kandidatin für diese Stelle?**
What makes you the perfect candidate for this job?
⑤ **Ich bin sehr fleißig und arbeite gerne im Team.**
I'm hardworking and I'm a team player.

③ **ein Bewerbungsgespräch haben**
to have an interview

See also
**81** Auf der Arbeit • At work **89-90** Berufe • Jobs **91** Branchen und Abteilungen Industries and departments **93** Nützliche Fähigkeiten für den Arbeitsplatz Workplace skills **95** Besprechen and präsentieren • Meeting and presenting

## 92.3 TEAMARBEIT • TEAMWORK

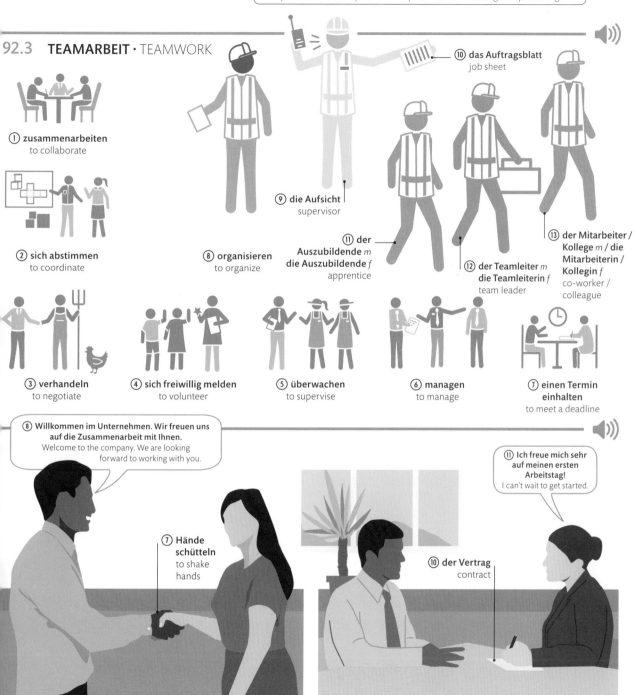

① **zusammenarbeiten**
to collaborate

② **sich abstimmen**
to coordinate

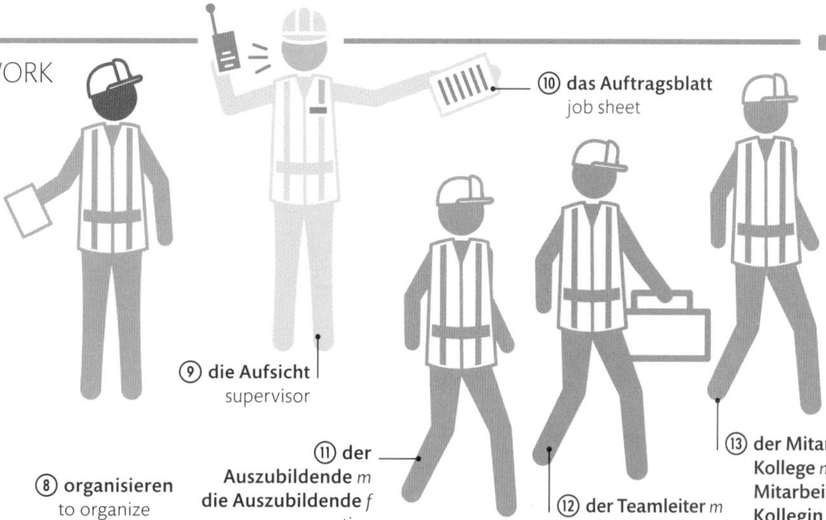

⑧ **organisieren**
to organize

⑨ **die Aufsicht**
supervisor

⑩ **das Auftragsblatt**
job sheet

⑪ **der Auszubildende** *m* **die Auszubildende** *f*
apprentice

⑫ **der Teamleiter** *m* **die Teamleiterin** *f*
team leader

⑬ **der Mitarbeiter / Kollege** *m* **/ die Mitarbeiterin / Kollegin** *f*
co-worker / colleague

③ **verhandeln**
to negotiate

④ **sich freiwillig melden**
to volunteer

⑤ **überwachen**
to supervise

⑥ **managen**
to manage

⑦ **einen Termin einhalten**
to meet a deadline

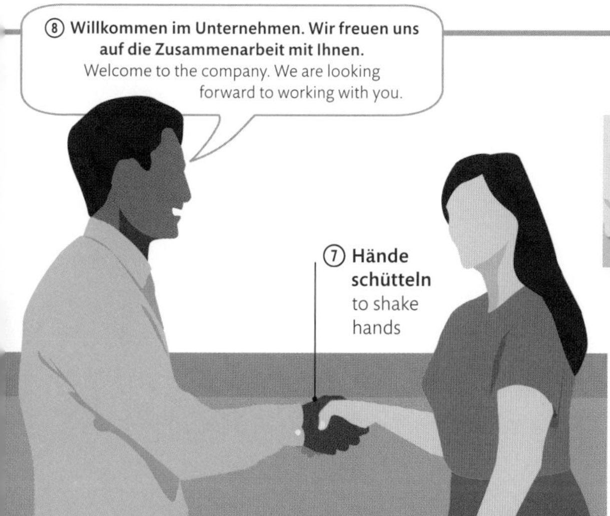
⑧ Willkommen im Unternehmen. Wir freuen uns auf die Zusammenarbeit mit Ihnen.
Welcome to the company. We are looking forward to working with you.
⑦ Hände schütteln
to shake hands

⑥ **eine Stelle bekommen**
to get the job

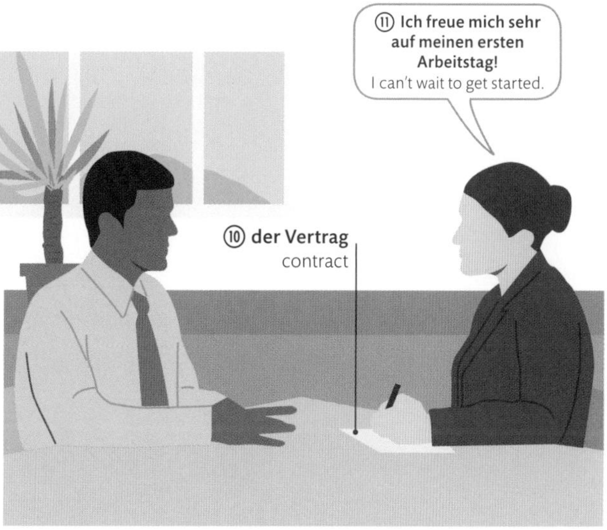
⑪ Ich freue mich sehr auf meinen ersten Arbeitstag!
I can't wait to get started.
⑩ der Vertrag
contract

⑨ **einen Vertrag unterschreiben**
to sign a contract

# 93 Nützliche Fähigkeiten für den Arbeitsplatz
## Workplace skills

### 93.1 WICHTIGE EIGENSCHAFTEN FÜR DEN BERUF • PROFESSIONAL ATTRIBUTES

① **gut organisiert**
organized

② **geduldig**
patient

③ **kreativ**
creative

④ **ehrlich**
honest

⑤ **praktisch veranlagt**
practical

⑥ **professionell**
professional

⑦ **anpassungsfähig**
adaptable

⑧ **ehrgeizig**
ambitious

⑨ **ruhig**
calm

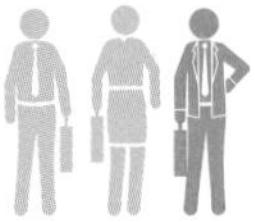
⑩ **selbstbewusst**
confident

⑪ **pünktlich**
punctual

⑫ **zuverlässig**
reliable

⑬ **kundenorientiert**
customer-focused

⑭ **unabhängig**
independent

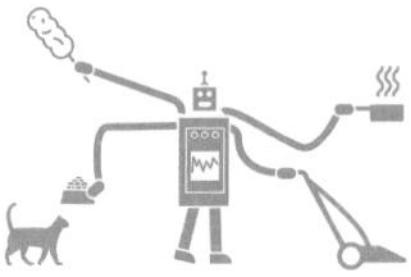
⑮ **effizient**
efficient

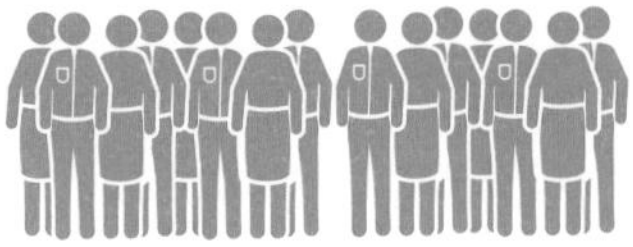
⑯ **ein Teamplayer** *m* / **eine Teamplayerin** *f*
team player

⑰ **verantwortungsbewusst**
responsible

⑱ **innovativ**
innovative

⑲ **motiviert**
motivated

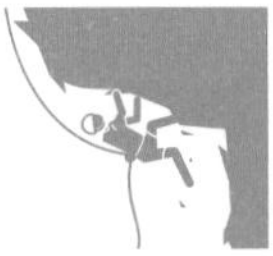
⑳ **entschlossen**
determined

㉑ **energiegeladen**
energetic

㉓ **Carlo ist der fleißigste Koch, den ich kenne.**
Carlo is the hardest-working chef I've ever met.

㉒ **fleißig**
hard-working

㉔ **Freude am Wettkampf haben**
competitive

㉕ **durchsetzungsfähig**
assertive

㉖ **einfallsreich**
imaginative

㉗ **neugierig**
curious

㉘ **originell**
original

㉙ **genau**
accurate

㉚ **ein guter Zuhörer** *m*
**eine gute Zuhörerin** *f*
good listener

㉛ **flexibel**
flexible

See also
**10** Eigenschaften • Personality traits **11** Fähigkeiten und Handlungen Abilities and actions **81** Auf der Arbeit • At work **82** Im Büro • In the office

## 93.2 BERUFLICHE FÄHIGKEITEN • PROFESSIONAL EXPERTISE

① **die Organisation**
organization

② **die Softwarekenntnis**
computer literacy

③ **das Computing**
computing

④ **die Problemlösungskompetenz**
problem-solving

⑤ **die Analyse**
analytics

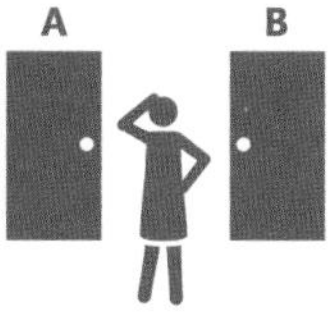


⑥ **die Entscheidungsfindung**
decision-making

⑦ **die Teamarbeit**
teamwork

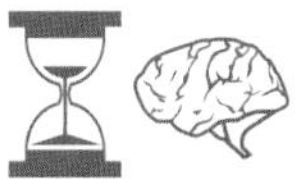

⑧ **eine schnelle Auffassungsgabe haben**
being a fast learner

⑨ **detailorientiert arbeiten**
paying attention to detail

⑩ **der Kundenservice**
customer service

⑪ **die Führungskompetenz**
leadership

⑫ **die Forschung**
research

⑬ **die Fremdsprachenkenntnisse** *f, pl*
fluent in languages

⑭ **die Technologiekenntnisse** *f, pl*
technology literate

⑮ **das Halten von Vorträgen**
public speaking

⑯ **die Verhandlung**
negotiating

⑰ **die schriftliche Kommunikation**
written communication

⑱ **die Initiative**
initiative

⑲ **der freundliche Umgang am Telefon**
telephone manner

⑳ **gut unter Druck arbeiten können**
working well under pressure

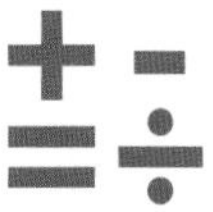

㉑ **die Rechenkenntnis**
numeracy

㉒ **der Führerscheinbesitz**
ability to drive

㉓ **hochqualifiziert**
well-qualified

㉔ **das Selbstmanagement**
self management

㉕ **die Serviceorientiertheit**
service focused

㉖ **die Einflussnahme**
influencer

㉜ **Sie müssen dringend an Ihrem Zeitmanagement arbeiten, der Bericht ist überfällig!**
You must improve your time management! This report is late.

㉛ **das Zeitmanagement**
time management

㉗ **die geschäftliche Einstellung**
businesslike attitude

㉘ **die zwischenmenschliche Kompetenz**
interpersonal skills

㉙ **das Projektmanagement**
project management

㉚ **die Verwaltung**
administration

# 94 Geld und Finanzen

## Money and finance

### 94.1 DAS GELD · MONEY

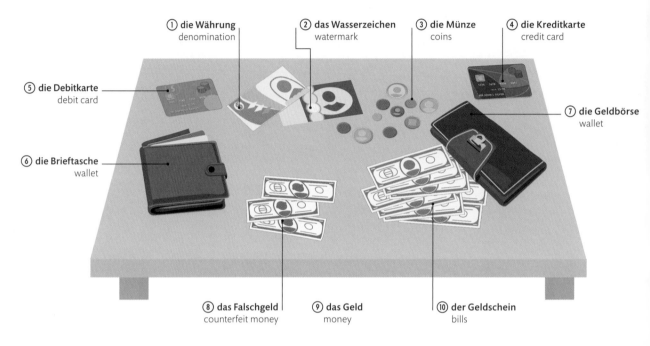

① **die Währung** denomination
② **das Wasserzeichen** watermark
③ **die Münze** coins
④ **die Kreditkarte** credit card
⑤ **die Debitkarte** debit card
⑥ **die Brieftasche** wallet
⑦ **die Geldbörse** wallet
⑧ **das Falschgeld** counterfeit money
⑨ **das Geld** money
⑩ **der Geldschein** bills

⑪ **die digitale Brieftasche**
digital wallet

⑫ **die digitale Währung**
digital currency

⑬ **die Bank**
bank

⑭ **das Online-Banking**
online banking

⑮ **das Mobile Banking**
mobile banking

⑯ **das Telefon-Banking**
telephone banking

⑰ **der Beleg**
receipt

⑱ **die Währung**
currency

Invoice

⑲ **die Rechnung**
invoice

⑳ **der Scheck**
check

㉑ **die Kasse**
cash register

㉒ **mit der Karte zahlen**
to pay by card

㉔ Nehmen Sie auch Bargeld?
Do you accept cash here?

㉓ **bar zahlen**
to pay with cash

See also
**45** Bank und Post • The bank and post office **91** Branchen und Abteilungen • Industries and departments

## 94.2 **FINANZEN** • FINANCE

① **der Aktienbroker** *m*
**die Aktienbrokerin** *f*
stockbroker

② **die Börse**
stock exchange

③ **die Anteile** *m, pl*
shares

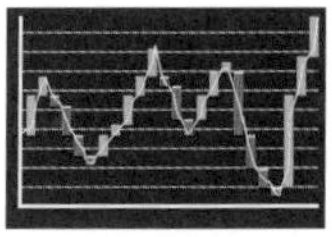

④ **der Aktienpreis**
share price

⑤ **die Dividenden** *f, pl*
dividends

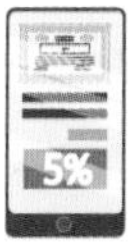


⑥ **die Provision**
commission

⑦ **das Kapital**
equity

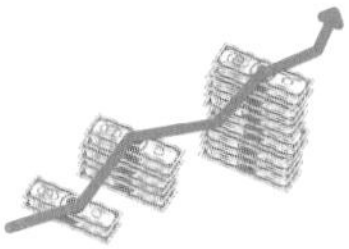

⑧ **die Investition**
investment

⑨ **das Portfolio**
portfolio

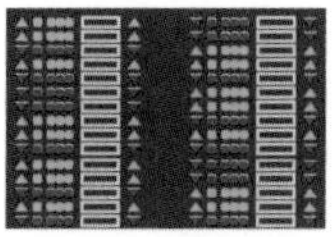

⑩ **die Aktien** *f, pl*
stocks

⑪ **der Wechselkurs**
exchange rate

⑫ **das Einkommen**
income

⑬ **das Budget**
budget

⑭ **Schulden machen**
to get into debt

⑮ **einen Gewinn machen**
to make a profit

⑯ **einen Verlust machen**
to take a loss

⑰ **die Kosten decken**
to break even

⑱ **pleite gehen**
to go out of business

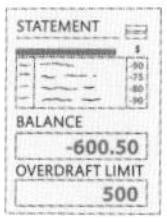


⑲ **der Dispo**
overdraft

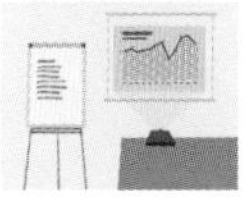

⑳ **die Ausgabe**
expenditure / outlay

㉑ **die Rezession**
economic downturn

㉒ **der Buchhalter** *m*
**die Buchhalterin** *f*
accountant

㉔ **Ich kann Sie dazu beraten, wie Sie Ihr Geld anlegen sollten.**
I can advise you where to invest your money.

㉓ **der Finanzberater** *m*
**die Finanzberaterin** *f*
financial advisor

# 95 Besprechen and präsentieren
## Meeting and presenting

### 95.1 BESPRECHEN · MEETING

② **Was steht heute auf der Tagesordnung, Maria?**
What's on the agenda today, Maria?

③ **Wir wollten über die Präsentationen kommende Woche sprechen.**
We're discussing the presentations for next week.

① **an einer Besprechung teilnehmen**
to attend a meeting

④ **eine Telefonkonferenz abhalten**
to have a conference call

⑤ **Protokoll führen**
to take minutes

⑥ **Fragen beantworten**
to take questions

⑦ **abwesend sein**
to be absent

⑧ **stören**
to interrupt

⑨ **sich einigen**
to reach a consensus

⑩ **einstimmig**
unanimous vote

⑪ **der Aktionspunkt**
action points

⑫ **per Handzeichen** *n*
show of hands

⑬ **sonstige Anliegen** *n, pl*
any other business

⑭ **das Aufsichtsratszimmer**
boardroom

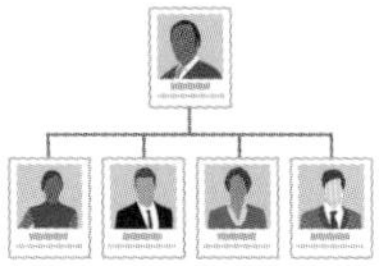

⑮ **der Aufsichtsrat**
board of directors

⑯ **sich einigen**
to reach an agreement

⑰ **die Jahreshauptversammlung**
annual general meeting (AGM)

⑱ **eine Besprechung beenden**
to wrap up the meeting

⑲ **das Whiteboard**
whiteboard

⑳ **das Notizbuch**
notebook

㉑ **die Tagesordnung**
agenda

See also
**81** Auf der Arbeit • At work **82** Im Büro • In the office
**83** Computer und Technologie • Computers and technology **84** Medien • Media

## 95.2 **PRÄSENTIEREN** • PRESENTING

① **anfangen**
to commence

② **zusammenfassen**
to sum up

③ **keine Zeit mehr haben**
to run out of time

④ **die Folie**
slide

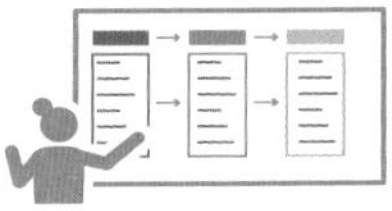

⑤ **die Roadmap**
roadmap

⑥ **eine Präsentation halten**
to give a presentation

⑦ **der Beamer**
projector

⑧ **der Timer**
timer

⑨ **das HDMI-Kabel**
HDMI cable

⑩ **der tragbare Lautsprecher**
portable speakers

⑪ **das Handout**
handouts

⑫ **die Notizen** *f, pl*
notes

⑬ **der Smartpen**
smartpen

⑭ **das Mikrofon**
microphone

⑮ **die Kopfhörer**
headphones

⑯ **das Flipchart**
flip chart

⑰ **den Bildschirm teilen**
to share your screen

⑱ **die Fernbedienung**
presenter remote

⑲ **die Konferenz**
conference

⑳ **der Gastredner** *m* / **die Gastrednerin** *f*
guest speaker

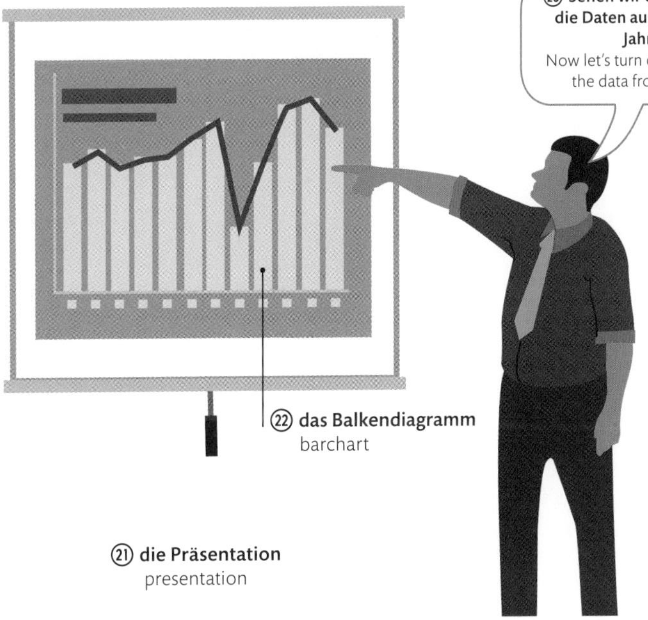

㉓ **Sehen wir uns nun einmal die Daten aus dem letzten Jahr an.**
Now let's turn our attention to the data from last year.

㉒ **das Balkendiagramm**
barchart

㉑ **die Präsentation**
presentation

# 96 Straßen
Roads

## 96.1 AUF DER STRASSE • ON THE ROAD

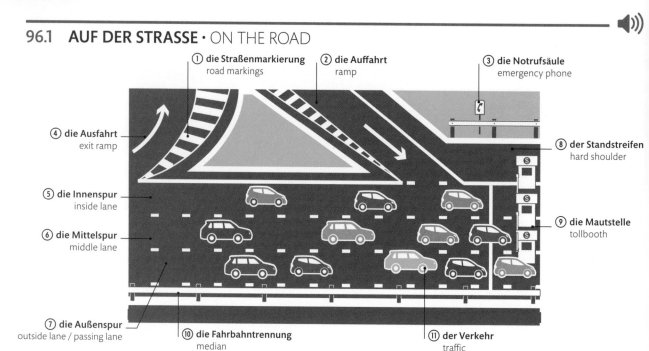

① **die Straßenmarkierung** road markings
② **die Auffahrt** ramp
③ **die Notrufsäule** emergency phone
④ **die Ausfahrt** exit ramp
⑤ **die Innenspur** inside lane
⑥ **die Mittelspur** middle lane
⑦ **die Außenspur** outside lane / passing lane
⑧ **der Standstreifen** hard shoulder
⑨ **die Mautstelle** tollbooth
⑩ **die Fahrbahntrennung** median
⑪ **der Verkehr** traffic

⑫ **die Autobahn** highway

⑭ **die Leitplanke** divider

⑬ **die doppelspurige Schnellstraße** divided highway

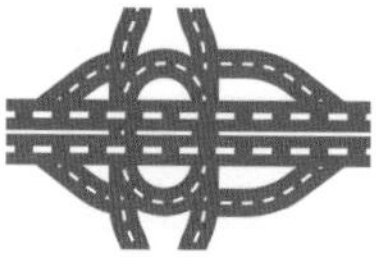

⑮ **das Autobahnkreuz** junction

⑯ **der Kreisverkehr** roundabout

⑰ **die Überführung** flyover

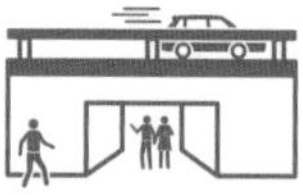

⑱ **die Unterführung** underpass

⑲ **die Absperrung** traffic barrier

⑳ **die Umleitung** detour

㉑ **der Blitzer** speed camera

㉒ **die Ampel** stop light

㉓ **der Stau** traffic jam

㉔ **die Einbahnstraße** one-way street

㉕ **der Fußgängerüberweg** pedestrian crossing

㉖ **die Straßenbauarbeiten** *f, pl* road construction

㉗ **der Behindertenparkplatz** disabled parking

㉘ **der Parkplatzwächter** *m* **die Parkplatzwächterin** *f* parking attendant

㉙ **die Parkuhr** parking meter

See also
**42-43** In der Stadt • In town **97-98** Autos • Cars **99** Autos und Busse • Cars and buses **100** Motorräder • Motorcycles **101** Radfahren • Cycling **123** Motorsport Motorsports **148** Karten und Richtungsangaben • Maps and directions

## 96.2 **VERKEHRSSCHILDER** • ROAD SIGNS

① **Einfahrt verboten**
no entry

② **Geschwindigkeitsbegrenzung** *f*
speed limit

③ **Gefahrenstelle** *f*
hazard

④ **rechts abbiegen verboten**
no right turn

⑤ **umdrehen verboten**
no U-turn

⑥ **Rechtskurve** *f*
right bend

⑦ **Vorfahrt gewähren**
yield

⑧ **Vorfahrt** *f*
right of way

⑨ **überholen verboten**
no passing

⑩ **Achtung, Schulkinder**
school zone

⑪ **unebene Fahrbahn**
bumps

⑫ **Wildwechsel** *m*
deer crossing

⑬ **hier entlang**
direction to follow

⑭ **Baustelle** *f*
construction ahead

⑮ **Ampel** *f*
stop light ahead

⑯ **keine Einfahrt für Fahrräder**
closed to bicycles

⑰ **kein Zutritt für Fußgänger**
closed to pedestrians

## 96.3 **VERKEHRSVERBEN** • VERBS FOR DRIVING

① **fahren**
to drive

② **rückwärts fahren**
to reverse

③ **anhalten**
to stop

⑤ **der Verkehrspolizist** *m* / **die Verkehrspolizistin** *f*
parking enforcement officer

④ **abschleppen**
to tow away

⑥ **links abbiegen**
to turn left

⑦ **rechts abbiegen**
to turn right

⑧ **geradeaus fahren**
to go straight ahead

⑨ **die erste Abzweigung links nehmen**
to take the first left

⑩ **die zweite Abzweigung rechts nehmen**
to take the second right

# 97 Autos
## Cars

### 97.1 DAS AUTO VON AUSSEN • CAR EXTERIOR

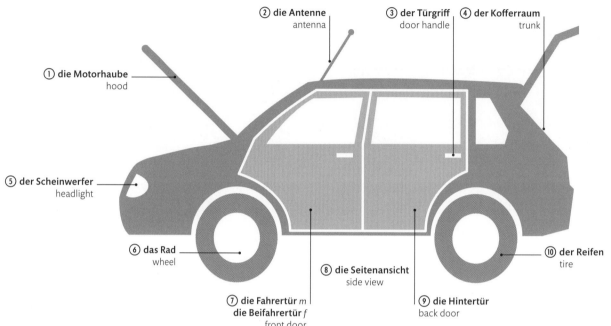

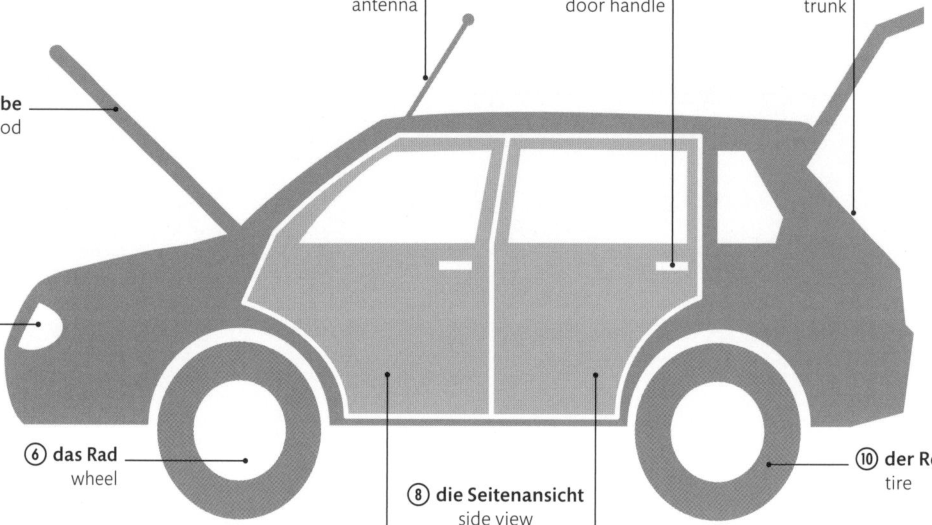


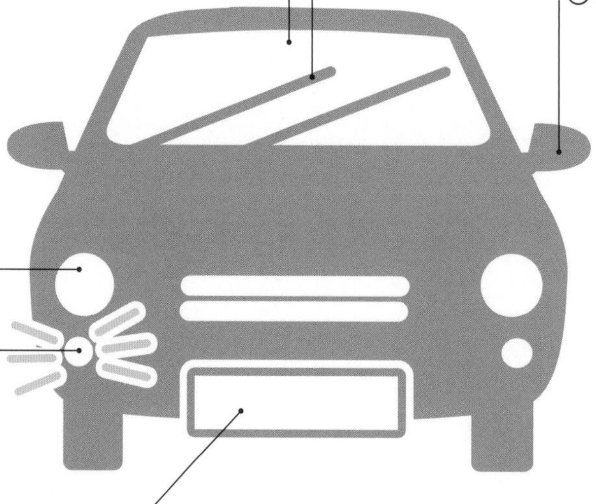

⑱ **die Stoßstange**
bumper

⑲ **die Winterreifen**
snow tires

⑳ **der Dachträger**
roof rack

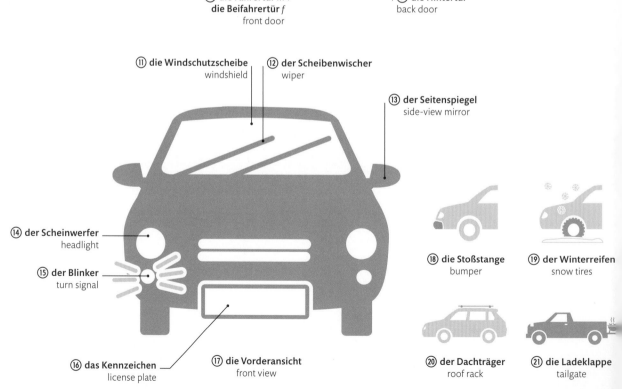

㉑ **die Ladeklappe**
tailgate

See also
**42-43** In der Stadt • In town **96** Straßen • Roads **98** Autos (Fortsetzung) • Cars continued
**99** Autos und Busse • Cars and buses **100** Motorräder • Motorcycles **123** Motorsport • Motorsports

## 97.2 AUTOTYPEN • TYPES OF CARS

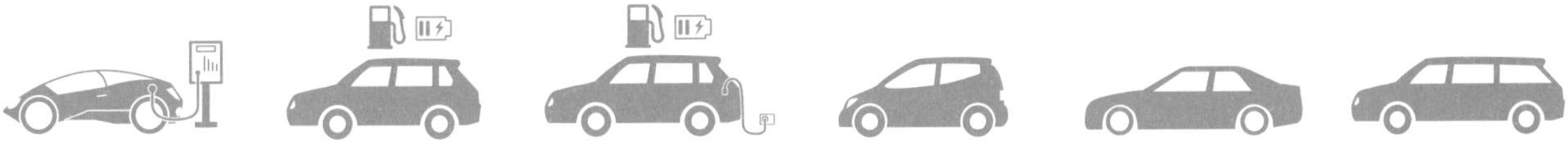

① **das Elektroauto** electric car
② **der Hybrid** hybrid
③ **der Plug-in-Hybrid** plug-in hybrid
④ **das Steilheck** hatchback
⑤ **die Limousine** sedan
⑥ **der Kombi** station wagon

⑦ **das Allradfahrzeug** four-wheel drive
⑧ **der Minivan** minivan
⑨ **die Stretch-Limousine** limousine

⑪ **der Spoiler** spoiler

⑩ **der Sportwagen** sports car

⑮ **der Überrollbügel** roll bar

⑫ **das Cabrio** convertible
⑬ **der Oldtimer** vintage car
⑭ **der Strandbuggy** dune buggy

⑱ **der Heckflügel** rear wing

⑰ **der Vorderkotflügel** front wing
⑯ **der Rennwagen** race car

## 97.3 DIE TANKSTELLE • GAS STATION

① **die Zapfsäule** gas pump
② **die Überdachung** canopy
③ **die Ladestelle** EV charging station
④ **der Scheibenreiniger** washer fluid
⑤ **das Gefrierschutzmittel** antifreeze

⑥ **das Benzin** gasoline
⑦ **bleifrei** unleaded
⑧ **bleihaltig** leaded
⑨ **der Diesel** diesel
⑩ **das Öl** oil
⑪ **die Autowaschanlage** car wash

# 98 Autos (Fortsetzung)
Cars continued

## 98.1 PANNENHILFE · BREAKDOWN ASSISTANCE

① **die Autowerkstatt**
auto repair shop

② **der Mechatroniker** *m*
**die Mechatronikerin** *f*
mechanic

③ **der Abschleppwagen**
tow truck

④ **der Ersatzreifen**
spare tire

⑤ **der Platten**
flat tire

## 98.2 DIE MECHANIK · MECHANICS

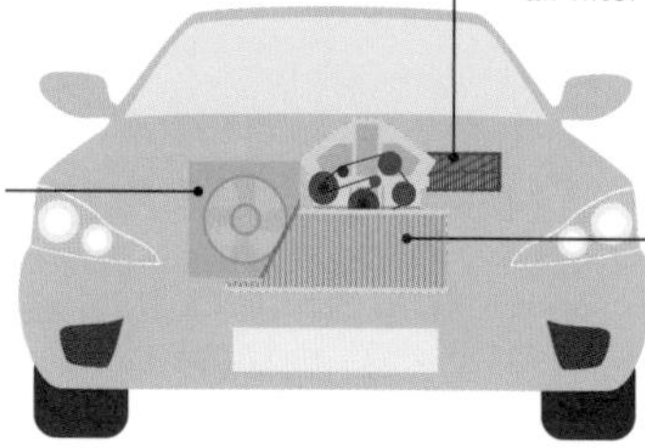

① **der Keilriemen**
fan belt

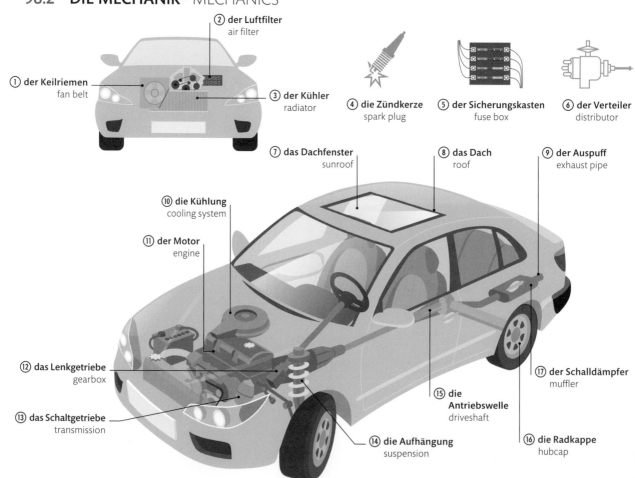

② **der Luftfilter**
air filter

③ **der Kühler**
radiator

④ **die Zündkerze**
spark plug

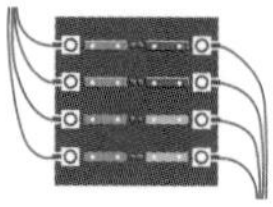

⑤ **der Sicherungskasten**
fuse box

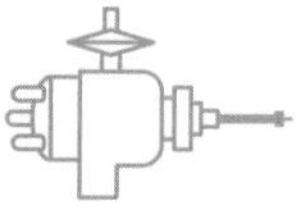

⑥ **der Verteiler**
distributor

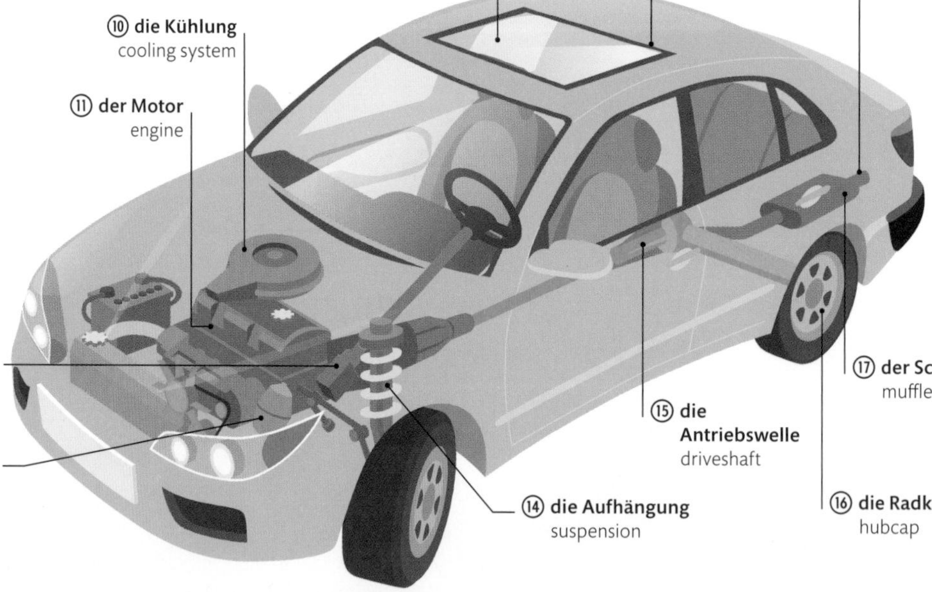

⑦ **das Dachfenster**
sunroof

⑧ **das Dach**
roof

⑨ **der Auspuff**
exhaust pipe

⑩ **die Kühlung**
cooling system

⑪ **der Motor**
engine

⑫ **das Lenkgetriebe**
gearbox

⑬ **das Schaltgetriebe**
transmission

⑭ **die Aufhängung**
suspension

⑮ **die Antriebswelle**
driveshaft

⑯ **die Radkappe**
hubcap

⑰ **der Schalldämpfer**
muffler

See also
**42-43** In der Stadt • In town **96** Straßen • Roads **99** Autos und Busse • Cars and buses
**100** Motorräder • Motorcycles **123** Motorsport • Motorsports

**der Schraubschlüssel**
wrench

⑦ **die Radmutter**
lug nuts

⑧ **der Wagenheber**
jack

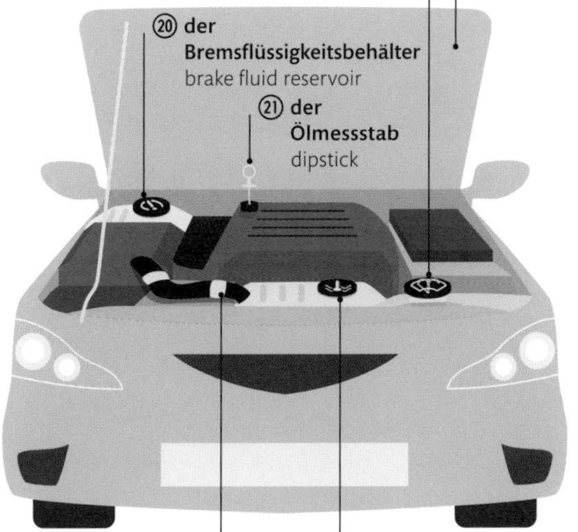

㉔ **die Batterie**
battery

㉕ **die Karosserie**
bodywork

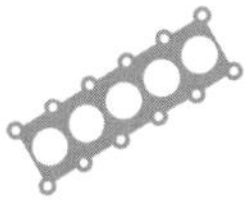

㉖ **der Zylinderkopf**
cylinder head

## 98.3 **AUTOVERBEN** • VERBS FOR DRIVING

① **tanken**
to fill up

② **den Ölstand prüfen**
to check the oil

③ **den Reifendruck prüfen**
to check the tires

④ **das Auto warten**
to service the car

⑤ **parken**
to park

⑥ **losfahren**
to take off

⑦ **blinken**
to signal

⑧ **bremsen**
to brake

⑨ **abbremsen**
to slow down

⑩ **beschleunigen**
to speed up

⑪ **jemanden mitnehmen**
to pick someone up

⑫ **jemanden absetzen**
to drop someone off

⑬ **einen Autounfall haben**
to have a car accident

⑭ **liegenbleiben**
to break down

⑮ **überholen**
to pass

# 99 Autos und Busse
## Cars and buses

### 99.1 DER AUTOINNENRAUM · CAR INTERIOR

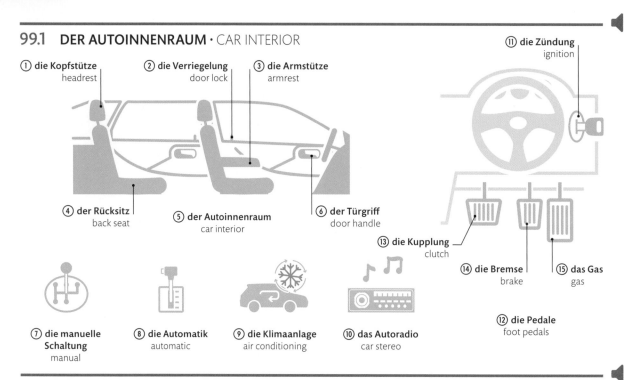

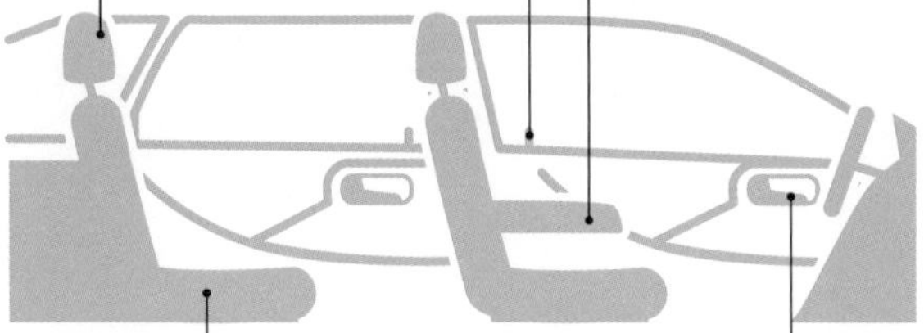

⑦ die manuelle Schaltung
manual

⑧ die Automatik
automatic

⑨ die Klimaanlage
air conditioning

⑩ das Autoradio
car stereo

### 99.2 DAS ARMATURENBRETT UND BEDIENELEMENTE · DASHBOARD AND CONTROLS

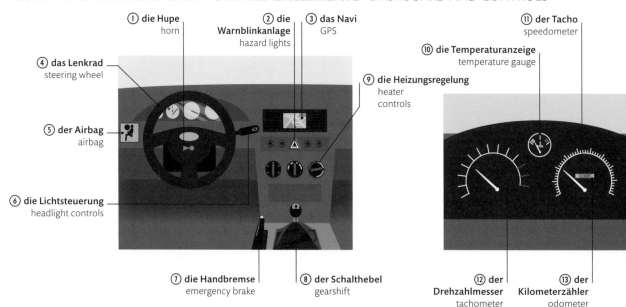

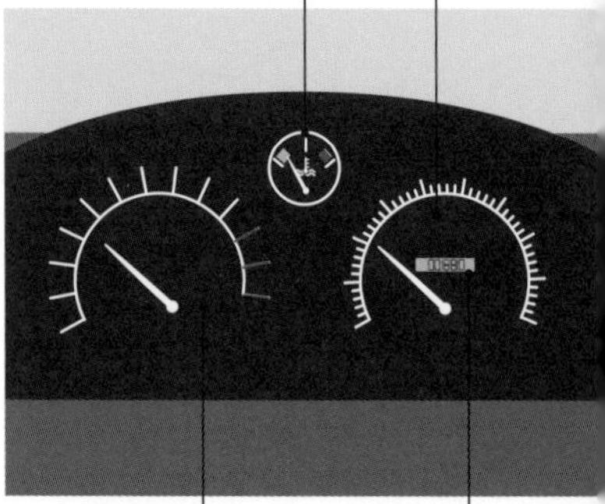

See also
**42-43** In der Stadt • In town **96** Straßen • Roads **97-98** Autos • Cars
**100** Motorräder • Motorcycles **123** Motorsport • Motorsports

## 99.3 DER BUS • BUS

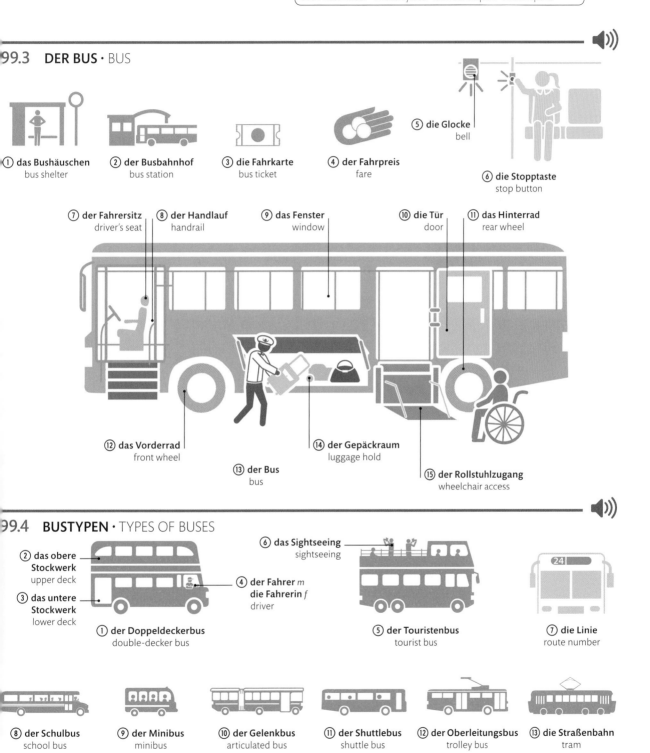

① **das Bushäuschen**
bus shelter

② **der Busbahnhof**
bus station

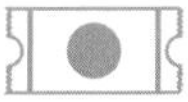

③ **die Fahrkarte**
bus ticket

④ **der Fahrpreis**
fare

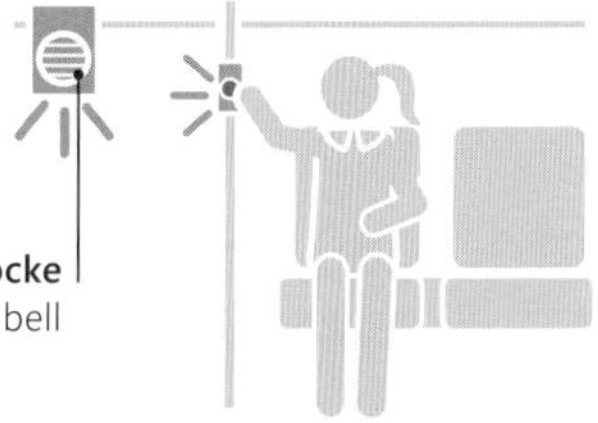

⑤ **die Glocke**
bell

⑥ **die Stopptaste**
stop button

⑦ **der Fahrersitz**
driver's seat

⑧ **der Handlauf**
handrail

⑨ **das Fenster**
window

⑩ **die Tür**
door

⑪ **das Hinterrad**
rear wheel

⑫ **das Vorderrad**
front wheel

⑬ **der Bus**
bus

⑭ **der Gepäckraum**
luggage hold

⑮ **der Rollstuhlzugang**
wheelchair access

## 99.4 BUSTYPEN • TYPES OF BUSES

② **das obere Stockwerk**
upper deck

③ **das untere Stockwerk**
lower deck

④ **der Fahrer** *m*
**die Fahrerin** *f*
driver

① **der Doppeldeckerbus**
double-decker bus

⑥ **das Sightseeing**
sightseeing

⑤ **der Touristenbus**
tourist bus

⑦ **die Linie**
route number

⑧ **der Schulbus**
school bus

⑨ **der Minibus**
minibus

⑩ **der Gelenkbus**
articulated bus

⑪ **der Shuttlebus**
shuttle bus

⑫ **der Oberleitungsbus**
trolley bus

⑬ **die Straßenbahn**
tram

# Motorräder
## Motorcycles

### 100.1 DAS MOTORRAD · MOTORCYCLE

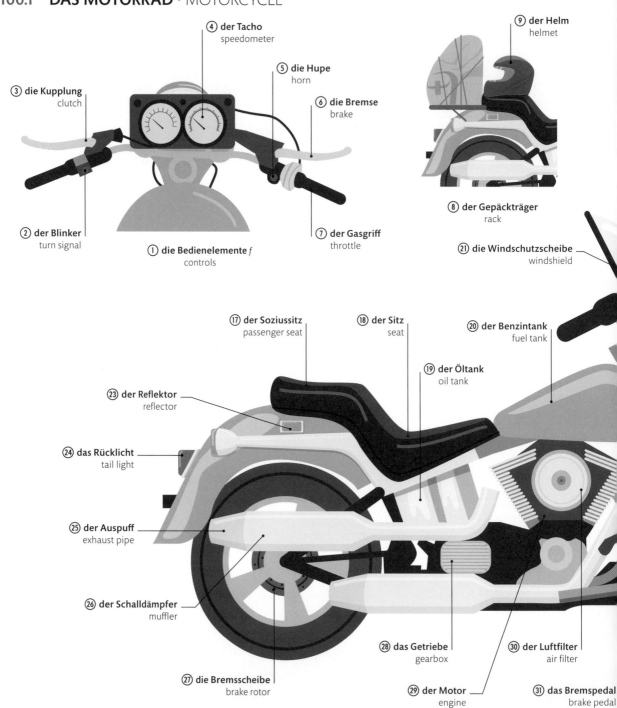

① die Bedienelemente *f*
controls
② der Blinker
turn signal
③ die Kupplung
clutch
④ der Tacho
speedometer
⑤ die Hupe
horn
⑥ die Bremse
brake
⑦ der Gasgriff
throttle

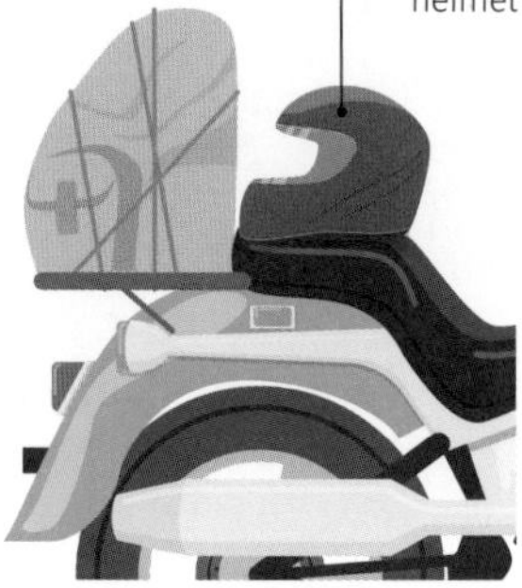

⑧ der Gepäckträger
rack
⑨ der Helm
helmet

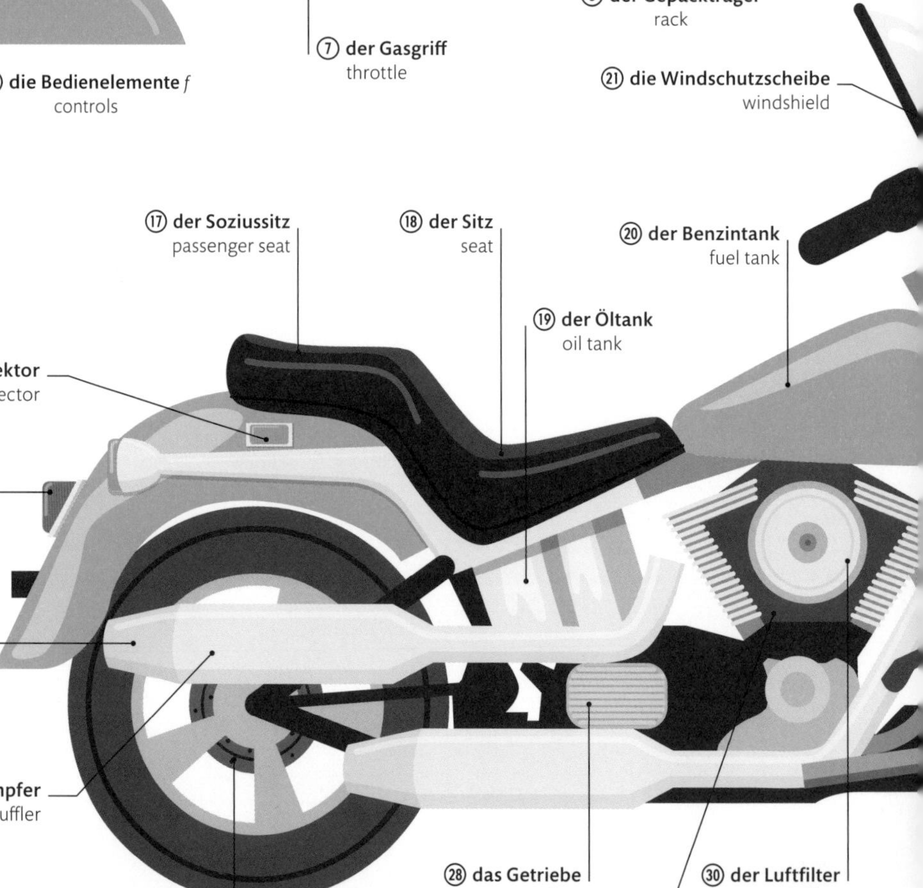

⑰ der Soziussitz
passenger seat
⑱ der Sitz
seat
⑲ der Öltank
oil tank
⑳ der Benzintank
fuel tank
㉑ die Windschutzscheibe
windshield
㉓ der Reflektor
reflector
㉔ das Rücklicht
tail light
㉕ der Auspuff
exhaust pipe
㉖ der Schalldämpfer
muffler
㉗ die Bremsscheibe
brake rotor
㉘ das Getriebe
gearbox
㉙ der Motor
engine
㉚ der Luftfilter
air filter
㉛ das Bremspedal
brake pedal

See also
**42-43** In der Stadt • In town **96** Straßen • Roads
**97-98** Autos • Cars **123** Motorsport • Motorsports

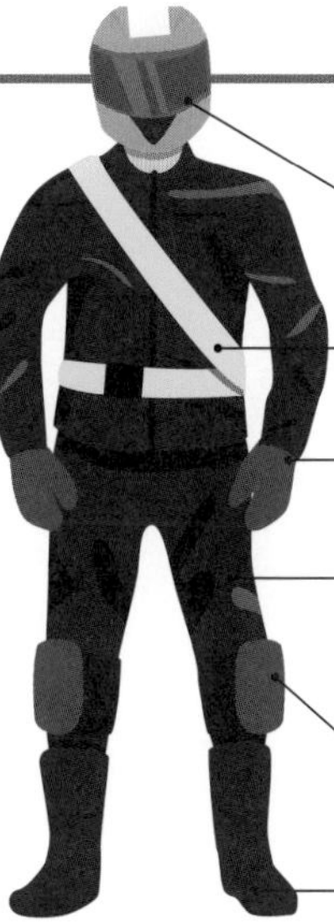

⑪ **das Visier**
visor

⑫ **das Reflektorband**
reflector strap

⑬ **der Handschuh**
glove

⑭ **die Lederkombi**
leather suit

⑮ **der Knieschoner**
knee pad

⑯ **der Stiefel**
boot

⑩ **die Motorradkleidung**
clothing

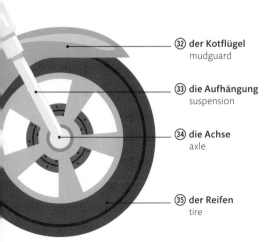

㉒ **der Scheinwerfer**
headlight

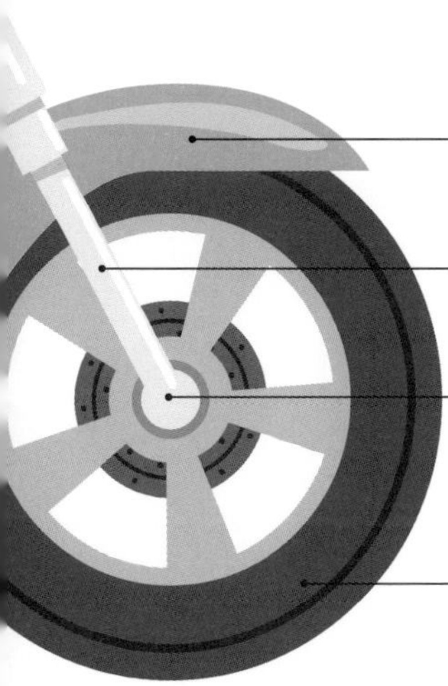

㉜ **der Kotflügel**
mudguard

㉝ **die Aufhängung**
suspension

㉞ **die Achse**
axle

㉟ **der Reifen**
tire

## 100.2 MOTORRADTYPEN • TYPES OF MOTORCYCLES

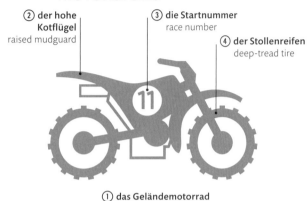

② **der hohe Kotflügel**
raised mudguard

③ **die Startnummer**
race number

④ **der Stollenreifen**
deep-tread tire

① **das Geländemotorrad**
off-road motorcycle

⑤ **das Rennmotorrad**
racing bike

⑥ **das Tourenmotorrad**
tourer

⑦ **das Quad**
all-terrain vehicle / quad bike

⑧ **der Beiwagen**
side car

⑨ **das elektrische Motorrad**
electric motorcycle

⑩ **der Elektroroller**
electric scooter

⑪ **das Dreirad**
three-wheeler

⑫ **der Motorroller**
motor scooter

⑬ **der Fahrer** *m*
**die Fahrerin** *f*
rider

⑭ **auf dem Beifahrersitz mitfahren**
to ride passenger

⑮ **aufsteigen**
to get on / mount

⑯ **absteigen**
to get off / dismount

# 101 Radfahren
Cycling

## 101.1 DAS FAHRRAD · BICYCLE

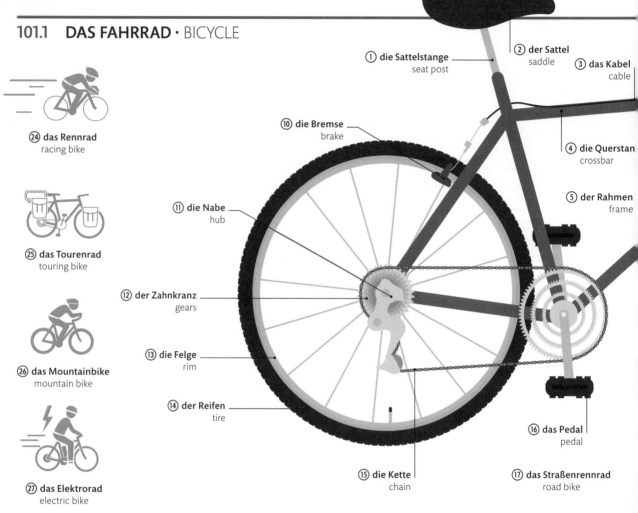

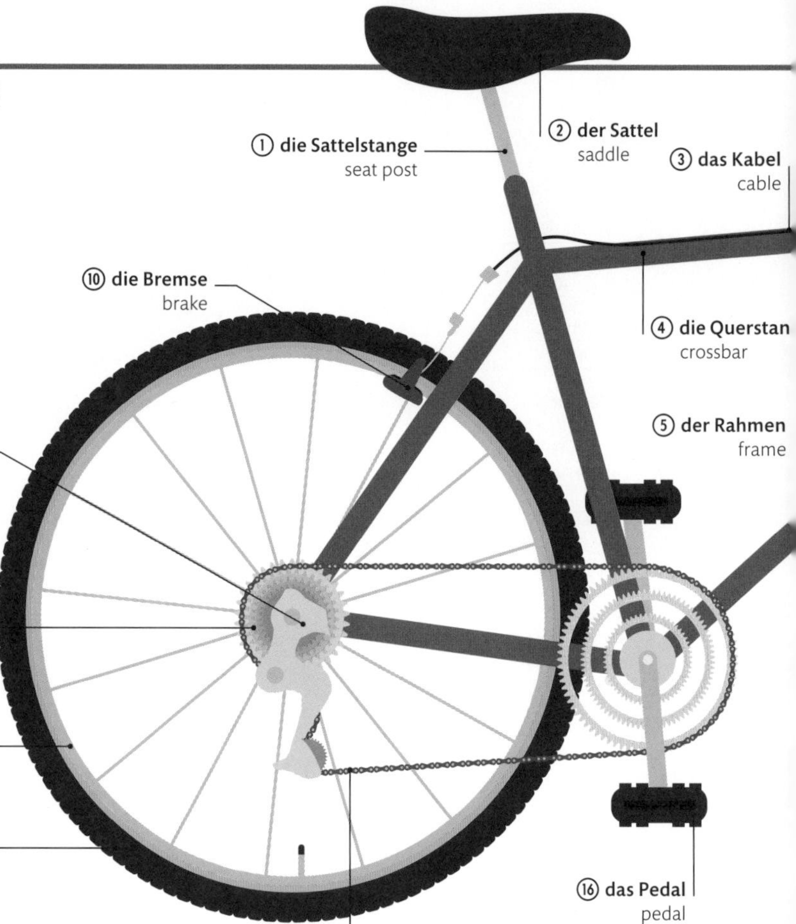

**㉔ das Rennrad**
racing bike

**㉕ das Tourenrad**
touring bike

**㉖ das Mountainbike**
mountain bike

**㉗ das Elektrorad**
electric bike

**㉘ das Tandem**
tandem

**㉙ der Korb**
basket

**㉚ der Kindersitz**
child seat

**㉛ der Radständer**
kickstand

**㉜ die Bremsbacke**
brake pad

**㉝ das Stützrad**
training wheels

**㉞ das Einrad**
unicycle

**㉟ der Pedalhaken**
toe clip

**㊱ der Fußriemen**
toe strap

**㊲ die Lampe**
lamp

**㊳ das Rücklicht**
rear light

**㊴ der Schlauch**
inner tube

See also
**42-43** In der Stadt • In town **96** Straßen • Roads **100** Motorräder Motorcycles **133** Aktivitäten im Freien • Outdoor activities

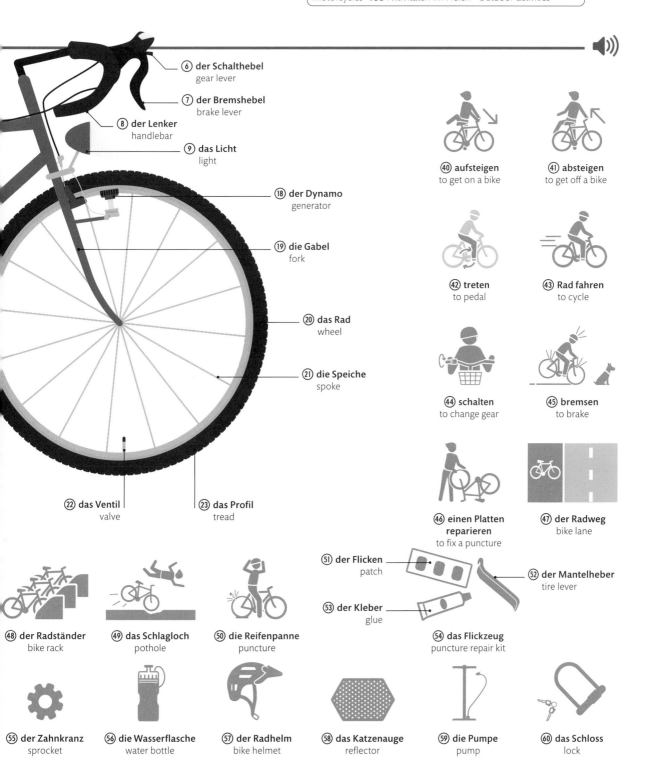

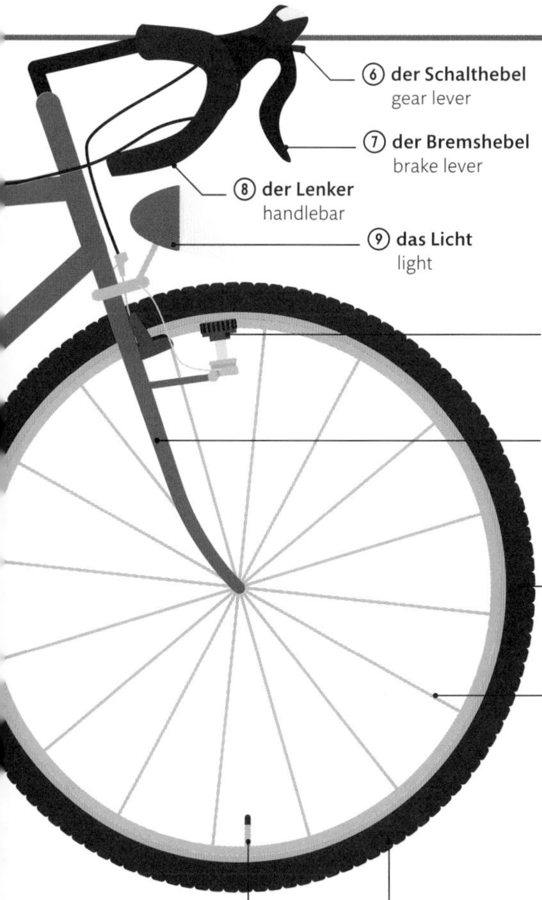

㊵ **aufsteigen**
to get on a bike

㊶ **absteigen**
to get off a bike

㊷ **treten**
to pedal

㊸ **Rad fahren**
to cycle

㊹ **schalten**
to change gear

㊺ **bremsen**
to brake

㊻ **einen Platten reparieren**
to fix a puncture

㊼ **der Radweg**
bike lane

㊽ **der Radständer**
bike rack

㊾ **das Schlagloch**
pothole

㊿ **die Reifenpanne**
puncture

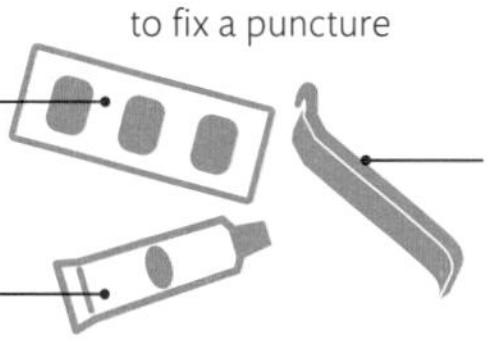

54 **das Flickzeug**
puncture repair kit

55 **der Zahnkranz**
sprocket

56 **die Wasserflasche**
water bottle

57 **der Radhelm**
bike helmet

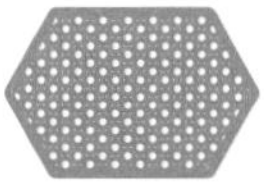
58 **das Katzenauge**
reflector

59 **die Pumpe**
pump

60 **das Schloss**
lock

# 102 Züge
Trains

## 102.1 DER BAHNHOF · TRAIN STATION

① **der Zug**
train

② **die Bahnsteignummer**
platform number

③ **der Wartebereich**
waiting room

④ **der Kartenschalter**
ticket office

⑤ **Ich hätte gerne eine Fahrkarte nach Dublin.**
Can I have a ticket to Dublin, please?

⑥ **der Bahnsteig**
platform

⑦ **die Fahrgäste** *m, pl*
passengers

⑧ **der Gepäckwagen**
cart

⑨ **das Gepäckfach**
luggage storage

⑩ **das Fundbüro**
lost property office

⑪ **die Fahrkarte**
ticket

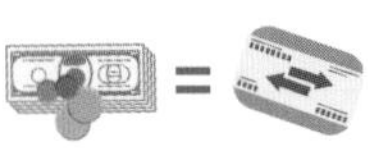

⑫ **der Fahrpreis**
fare

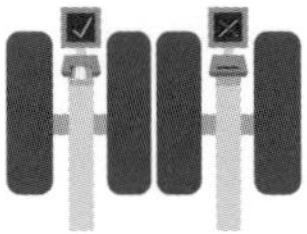

⑬ **die Sperre**
ticket barrier

⑭ **der Querbahnsteig**
concourse

⑮ **die Abfahrtstafel**
departures board

⑯ **die Lautsprechanlage**
public address system

㉒ **der Pendler** *m*
**die Pendlerin** *f*
commuters

⑰ **das Zugnetz**
rail network

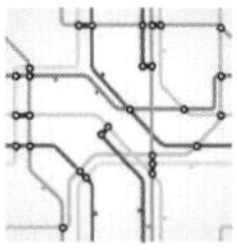

⑱ **der Netzplan**
subway map

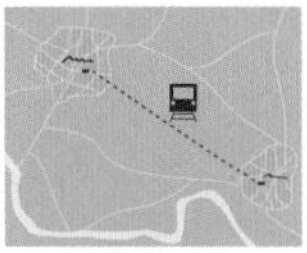

⑲ **der Intercity**
intercity train

⑳ **die Verspätung**
delay

㉑ **der Berufsverkehr**
rush hour

㉓ **einen Zug nehmen**
to catch a train

See also
**42-43** In der Stadt • In town **131** Reise und Unterkunft • Travel and accommodation

㉗ **die Stromschiene**
live rail

㉔ **den Zug verpassen**
to miss a train

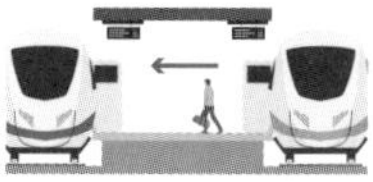

㉕ **umsteigen**
to change trains

㉖ **das Gleis**
track

㉘ **die Oberleitung**
electric lines

㉙ **die Unterführung**
underpass

㉚ **die Überführung**
overpass

㉞ **das Fenster**
window

㉟ **die Tür**
door

㉝ **die Gepäckablage**
luggage rack

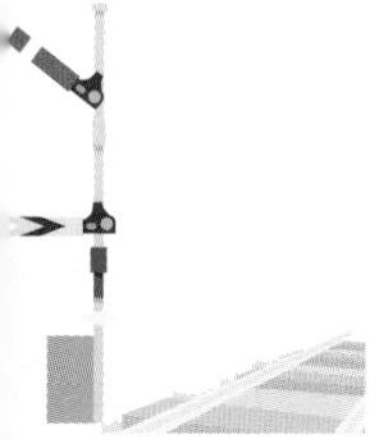

㉛ **das Signal**
signal

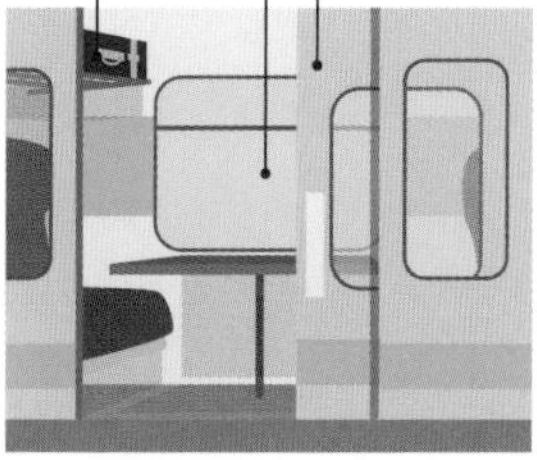

㉜ **das Abteil**
compartment

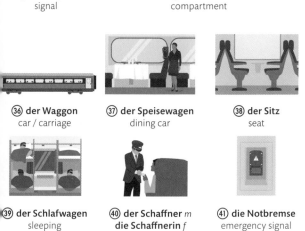

㊱ **der Waggon**
car / carriage

㊲ **der Speisewagen**
dining car

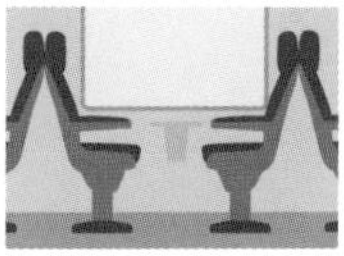

㊳ **der Sitz**
seat

㊴ **der Schlafwagen**
sleeping compartment

㊵ **der Schaffner** *m*
**die Schaffnerin** *f*
conductor

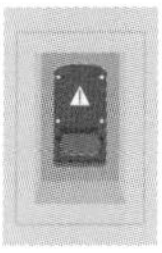

㊶ **die Notbremse**
emergency signal

## 102.2 **ZUGTYPEN** • TYPES OF TRAINS

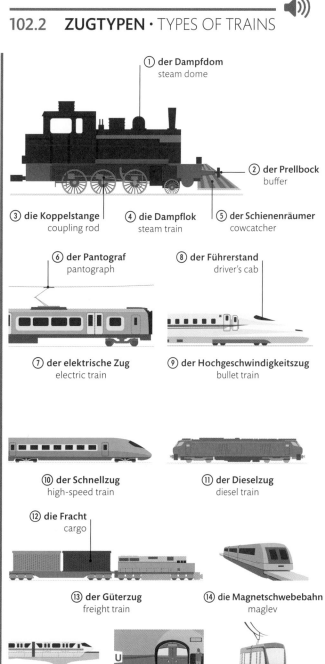

① **der Dampfdom**
steam dome

② **der Prellbock**
buffer

③ **die Koppelstange**
coupling rod

④ **die Dampflok**
steam train

⑤ **der Schienenräumer**
cowcatcher

⑥ **der Pantograf**
pantograph

⑧ **der Führerstand**
driver's cab

⑦ **der elektrische Zug**
electric train

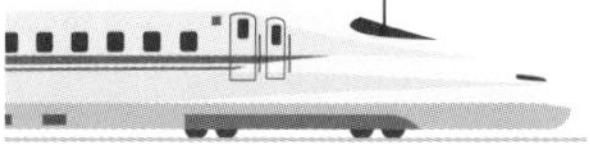

⑨ **der Hochgeschwindigkeitszug**
bullet train

⑩ **der Schnellzug**
high-speed train

⑪ **der Dieselzug**
diesel train

⑫ **die Fracht**
cargo

⑬ **der Güterzug**
freight train

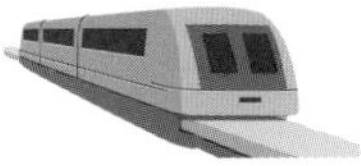

⑭ **die Magnetschwebebahn**
maglev

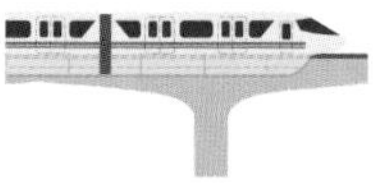

⑮ **die Einschienenbahn**
monorail

⑯ **die U-Bahn**
subway train

⑰ **die Straßenbahn**
tram

# 103 Luftfahrzeuge

## Aircraft

## 103.1 DAS PASSAGIERFLUGZEUG · PASSENGER AIRPLANE

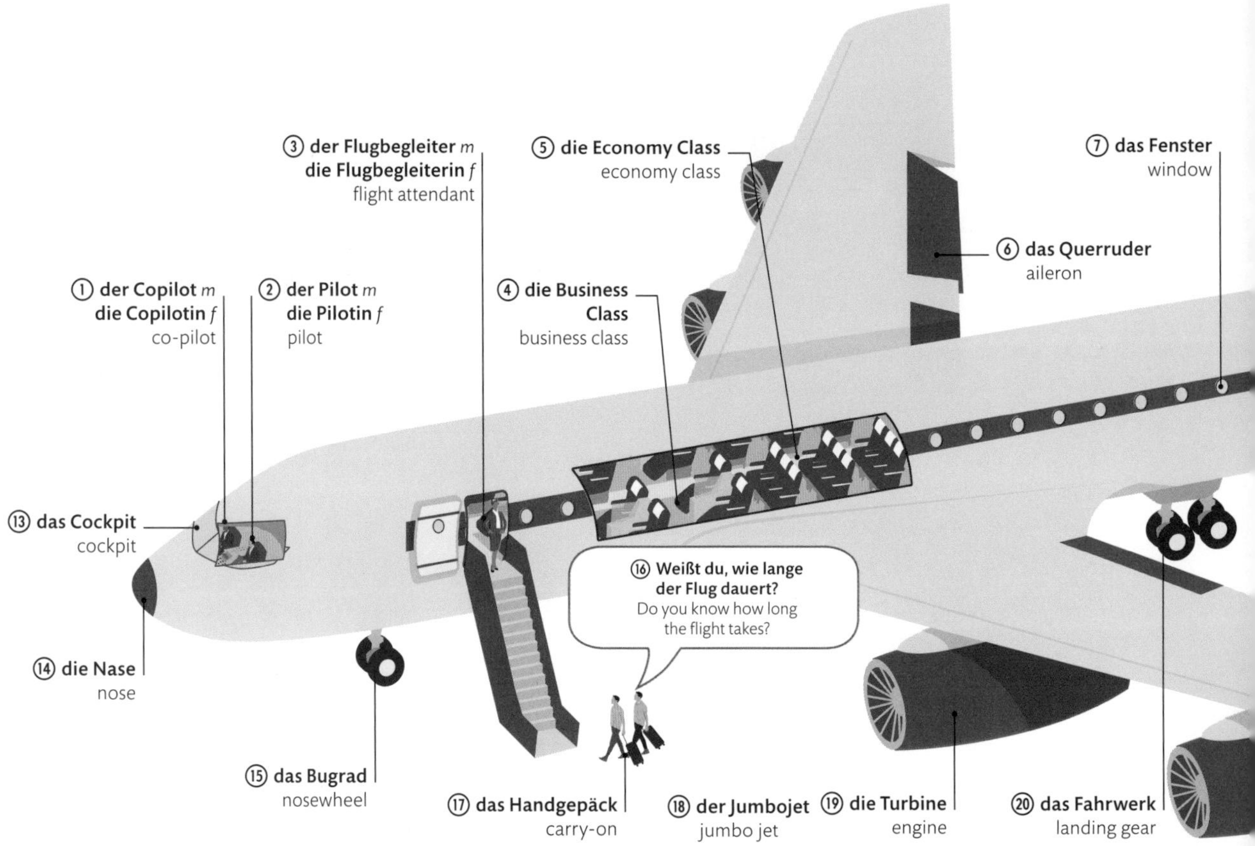


## 103.3 LUFTFAHRZEUGE · TYPES OF AIRCRAFT

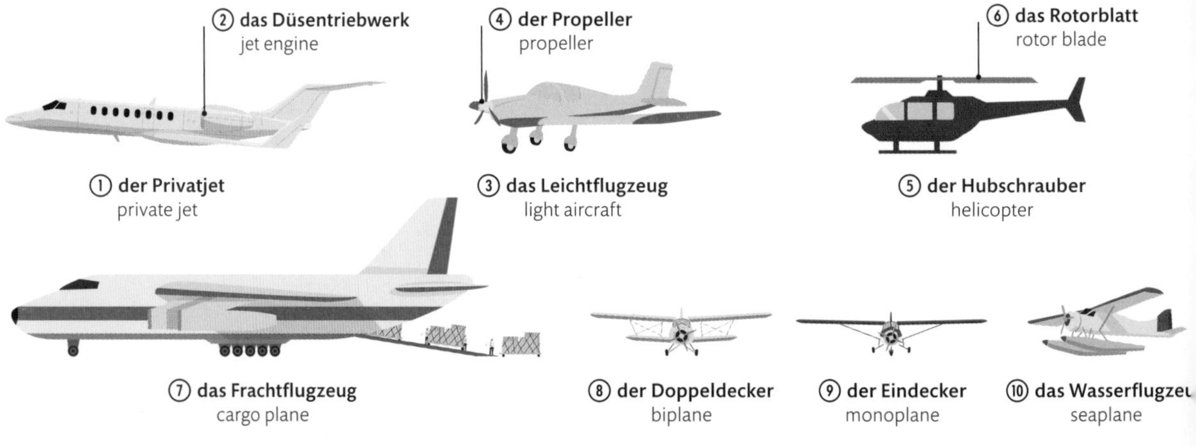

See also
**42-43** In der Stadt • In town **104** Am Flughafen • At the airport
**131** Reise und Unterkunft • Travel and accommodation

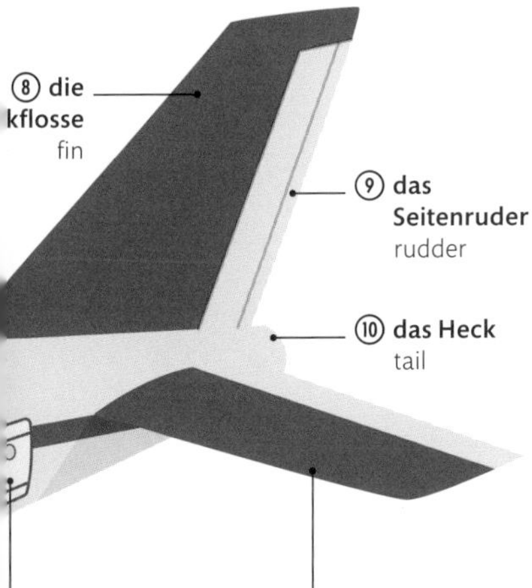

## 103.2 DIE KABINE • CABIN

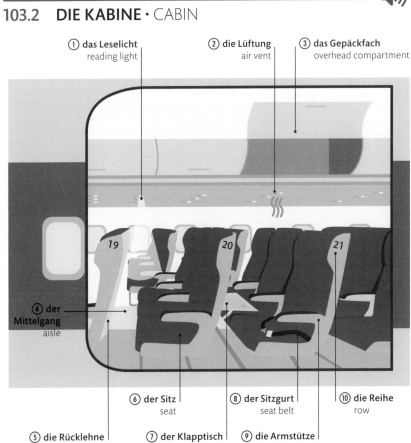

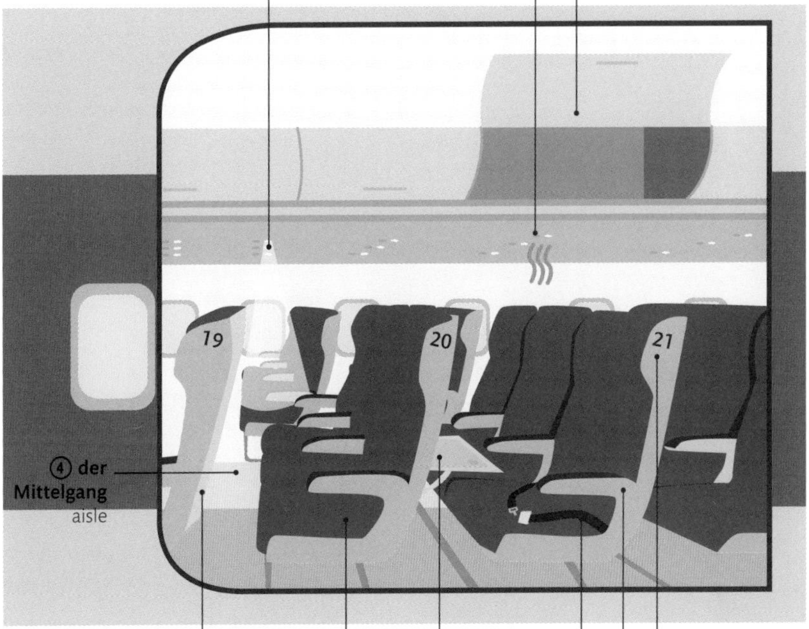


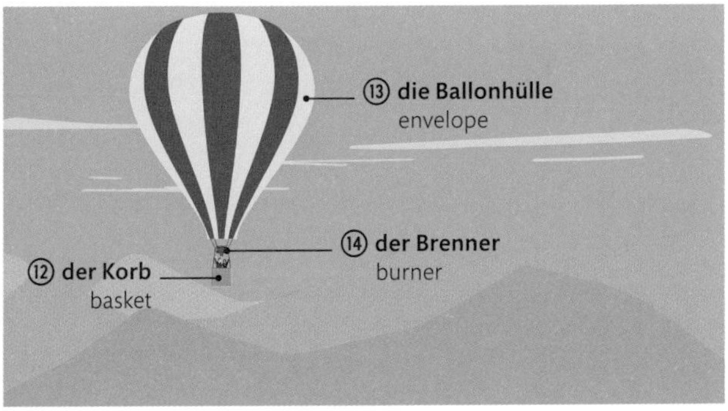


⑪ **der Heißluftballon**
hot-air balloon

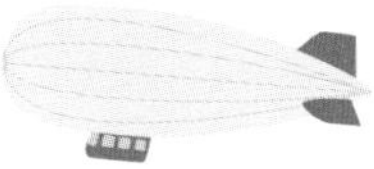

⑮ **der Zeppelin**
airship

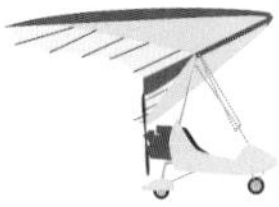

⑯ **das Ultraleichtflugzeug**
microlight

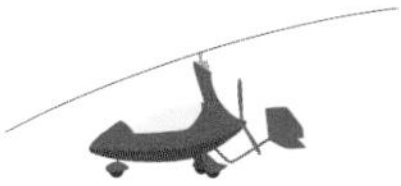

⑰ **der Tragschrauber**
gyrocopter

⑱ **das Gleitflugzeug**
glider

⑲ **der Motorschirm**
paramotor

# 104 Am Flughafen

At the airport

## 104.1 AM TERMINAL · AT THE TERMINAL

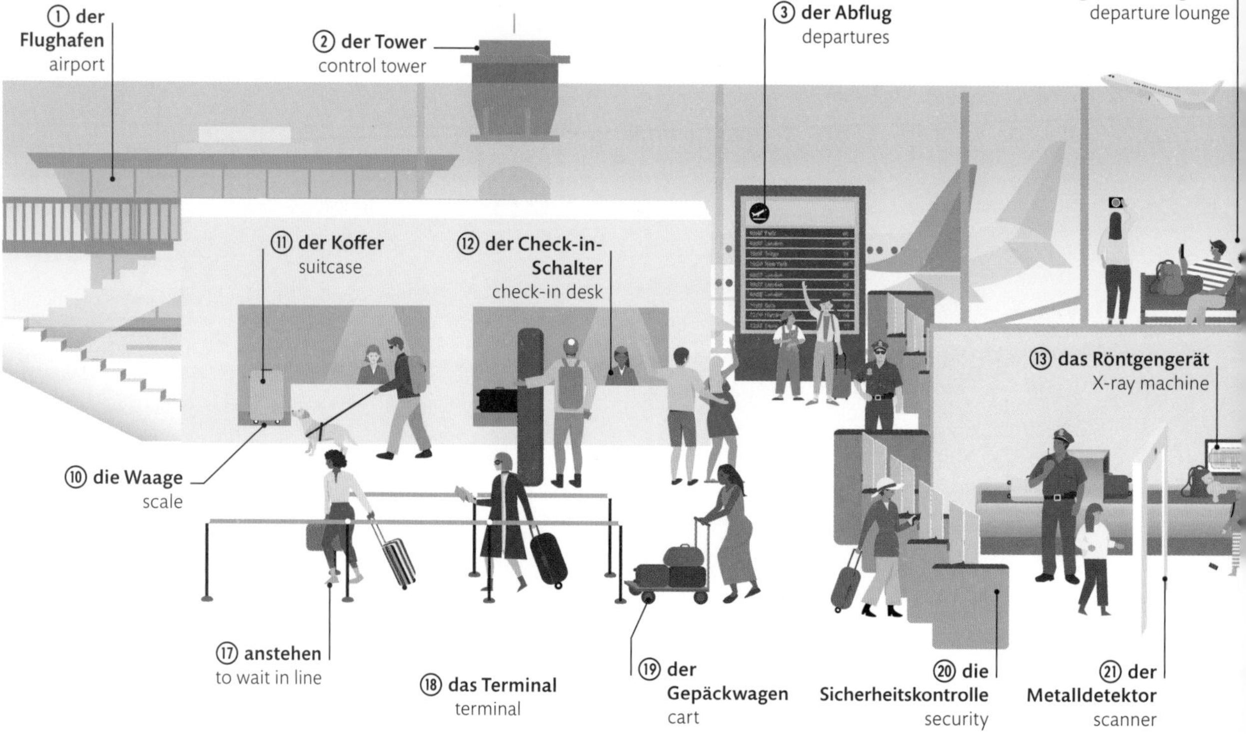

㉘ **der Pass**
passport

㉙ **der biometrische Pass**
biometric passport

㉚ **das Visum**
visa

㉛ **das Ticket**
ticket

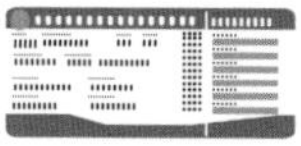

㉜ **die Bordkarte**
boarding pass

㉝ **der Online-Check-in**
online check-in

㊵ **der Urlaub**
vacation

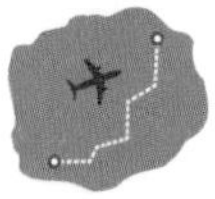

㊶ **der Inlandsflug**
domestic flight

㊷ **der internationale Flug**
international flight

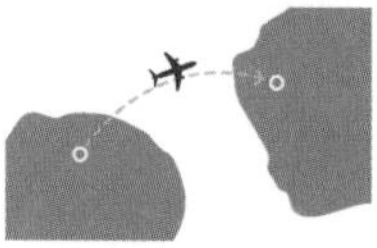

㊸ **ins Ausland gehen**
to go abroad

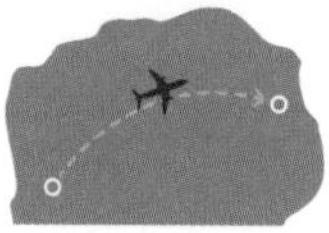

㊹ **der Direktflug**
direct flight

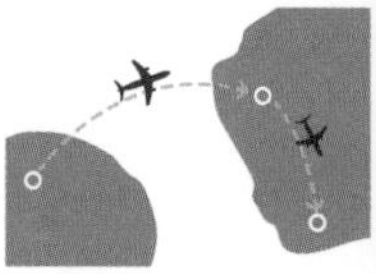

㊺ **der Anschlussflug**
connection

51 **das Übergepäck**
excess baggage

52 **die Passkontrolle**
passport control

53 **die Wechselstube**
currency exchange

54 **das zollfreie Geschäft**
duty-free shop

55 **das Fundbüro**
lost and found

56 **Verspätung haben**
to be delayed

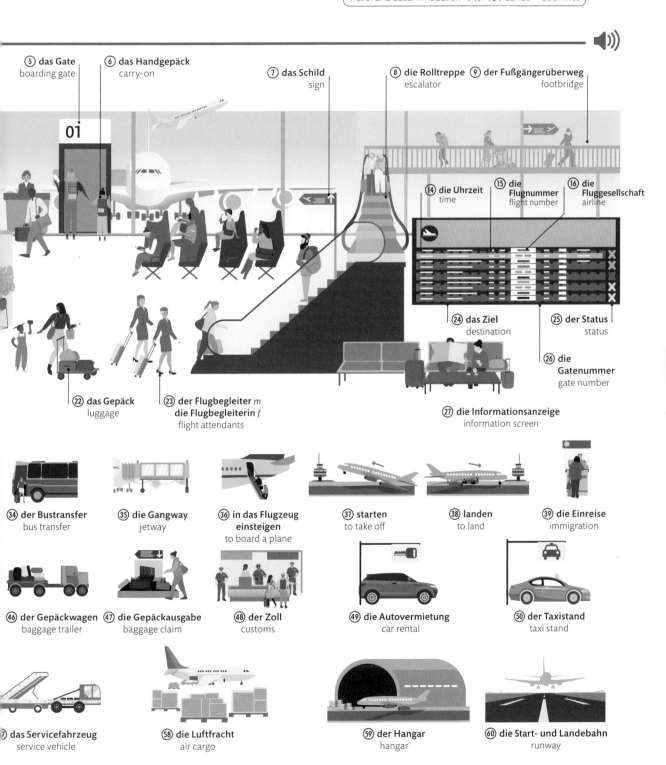

See also
**103** Luftfahrzeuge • Aircraft **131** Reise und Unterkunft Travel and accommodation **149-151** Länder • Countries

(5) **das Gate** boarding gate

(6) **das Handgepäck** carry-on

(7) **das Schild** sign

(8) **die Rolltreppe** escalator

(9) **der Fußgängerüberweg** footbridge

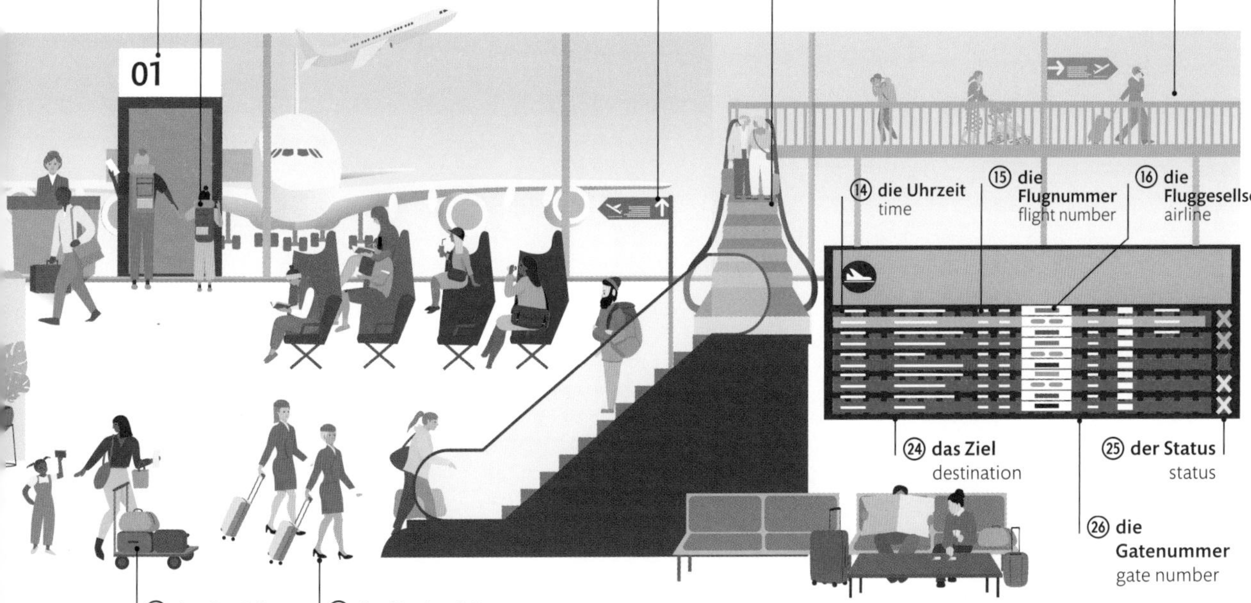


(14) **die Uhrzeit** time

(15) **die Flugnummer** flight number

(16) **die Fluggesellschaft** airline

(22) **das Gepäck** luggage

(23) **der Flugbegleiter** *m* **die Flugbegleiterin** *f* flight attendants

(24) **das Ziel** destination

(25) **der Status** status

(26) **die Gatenummer** gate number

(27) **die Informationsanzeige** information screen

(34) **der Bustransfer** bus transfer

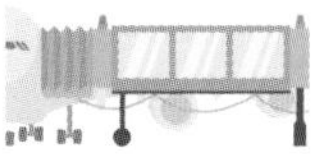
(35) **die Gangway** jetway

(36) **in das Flugzeug einsteigen** to board a plane

(37) **starten** to take off

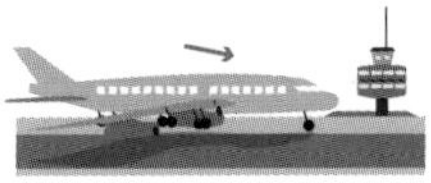
(38) **landen** to land

(39) **die Einreise** immigration

(46) **der Gepäckwagen** baggage trailer

(47) **die Gepäckausgabe** baggage claim

(48) **der Zoll** customs

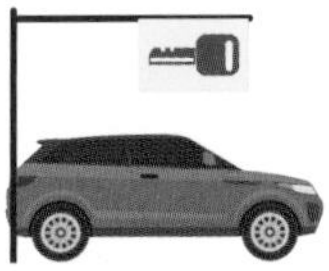
(49) **die Autovermietung** car rental

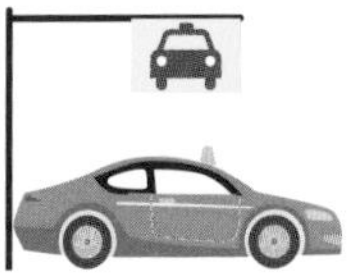
(50) **der Taxistand** taxi stand

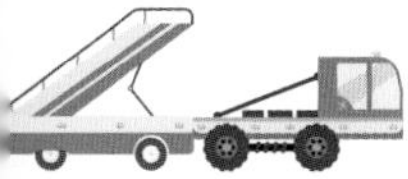
57 **das Servicefahrzeug** service vehicle

(58) **die Luftfracht** air cargo

(59) **der Hangar** hangar

(60) **die Start- und Landebahn** runway

# 105 Seefahrzeuge
## Sea vessels

### 105.1 DAS SCHIFF · SHIP

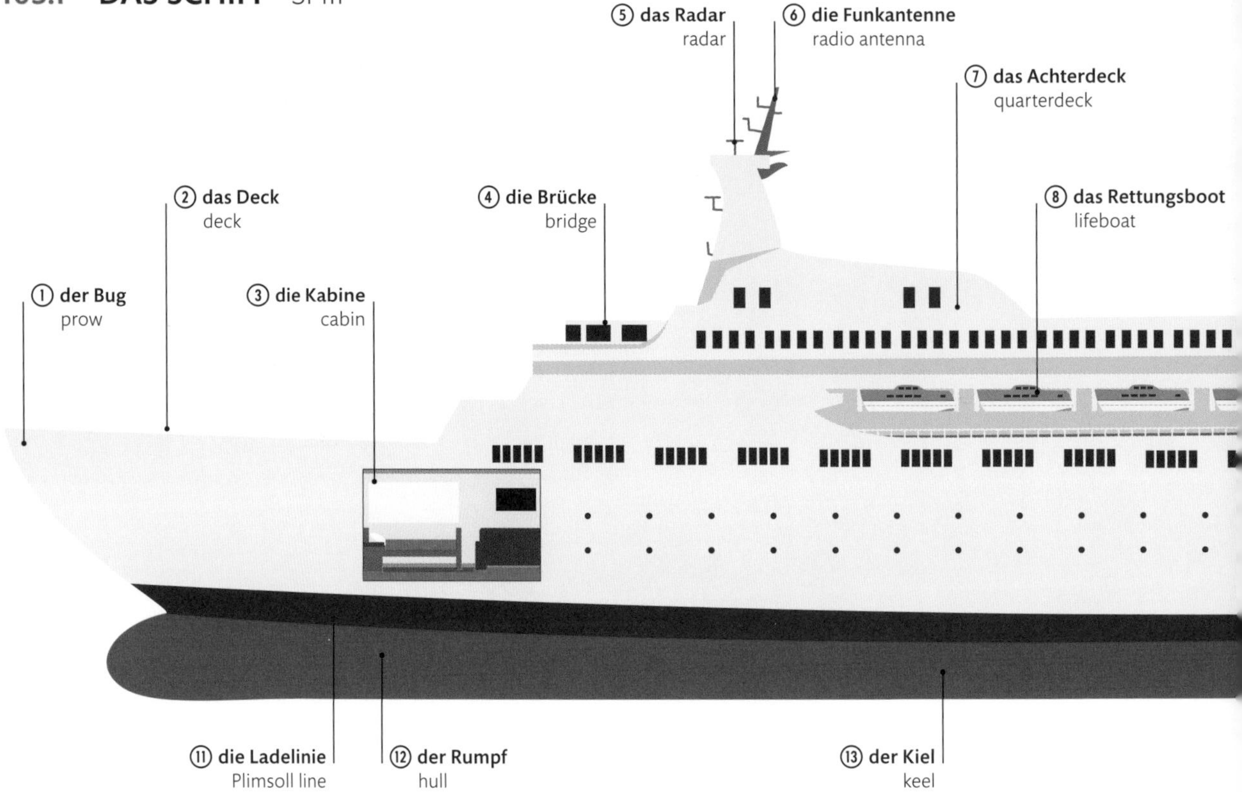


### 105.2 WEITERE BOOTE UND SCHIFFE · OTHER BOATS AND SHIPS

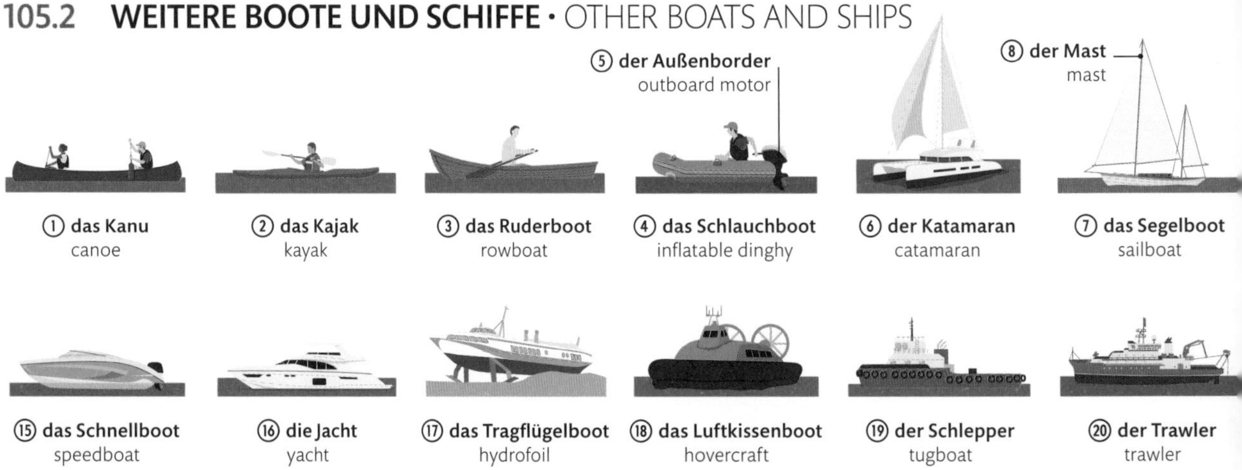

See also
**106** Der Hafen • The port **119** Segeln und Wassersport • Sailing and watersports **131** Reise und Unterkunft • Travel and accommodation

⑨ **der Schornstein**
funnel

⑩ **das Heck**
stern

⑭ **die Kombüse**
galley

⑮ **der Maschinenraum**
engine room

⑯ **der Propeller**
propeller

⑰ **der Kapitän** *m*
**die Kapitänin** *f*
captain

⑱ **der Rettungsring**
life preserver

⑲ **die Schwimmweste**
life jacket

⑳ **der Anker**
anchor

㉑ **die Gangway**
gangway

㉒ **der Poller**
bollard

㉓ **die Winsch**
windlass

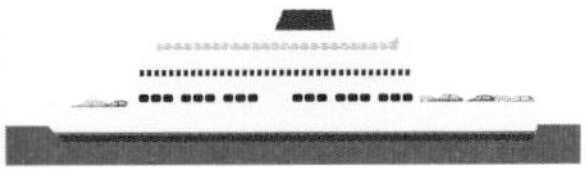

⑨ **die Fähre**
ferry

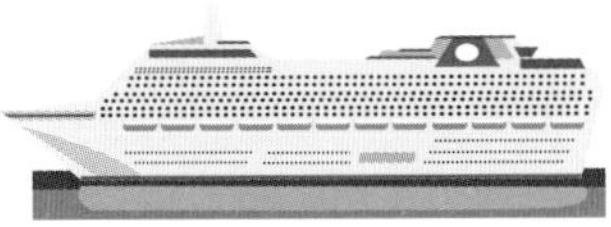

⑩ **das Kreuzfahrtschiff**
cruise ship

⑫ **der Container**
container

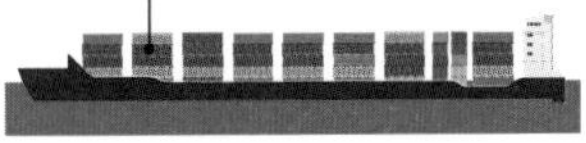

⑪ **das Containerschiff**
container ship

⑭ **die Fracht**
freight

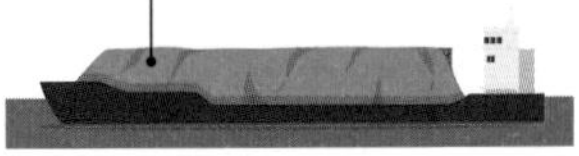

⑬ **der Frachter**
freighter

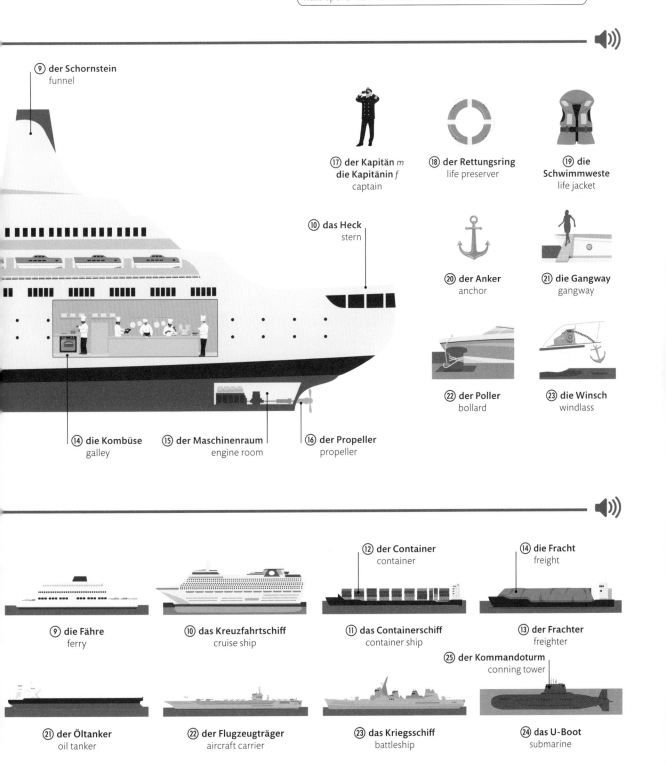

㉑ **der Öltanker**
oil tanker

㉒ **der Flugzeugträger**
aircraft carrier

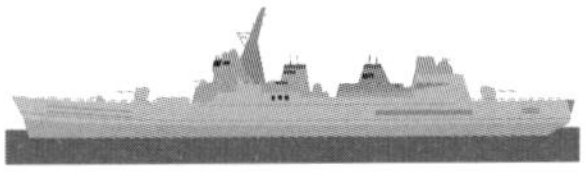

㉓ **das Kriegsschiff**
battleship

㉕ **der Kommandoturm**
conning tower

㉔ **das U-Boot**
submarine

# 106 Der Hafen
## The port

### 106.1 AM DOCK · AT THE DOCKS

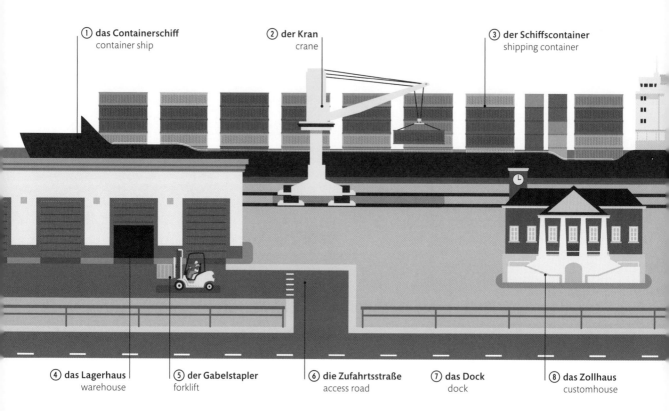

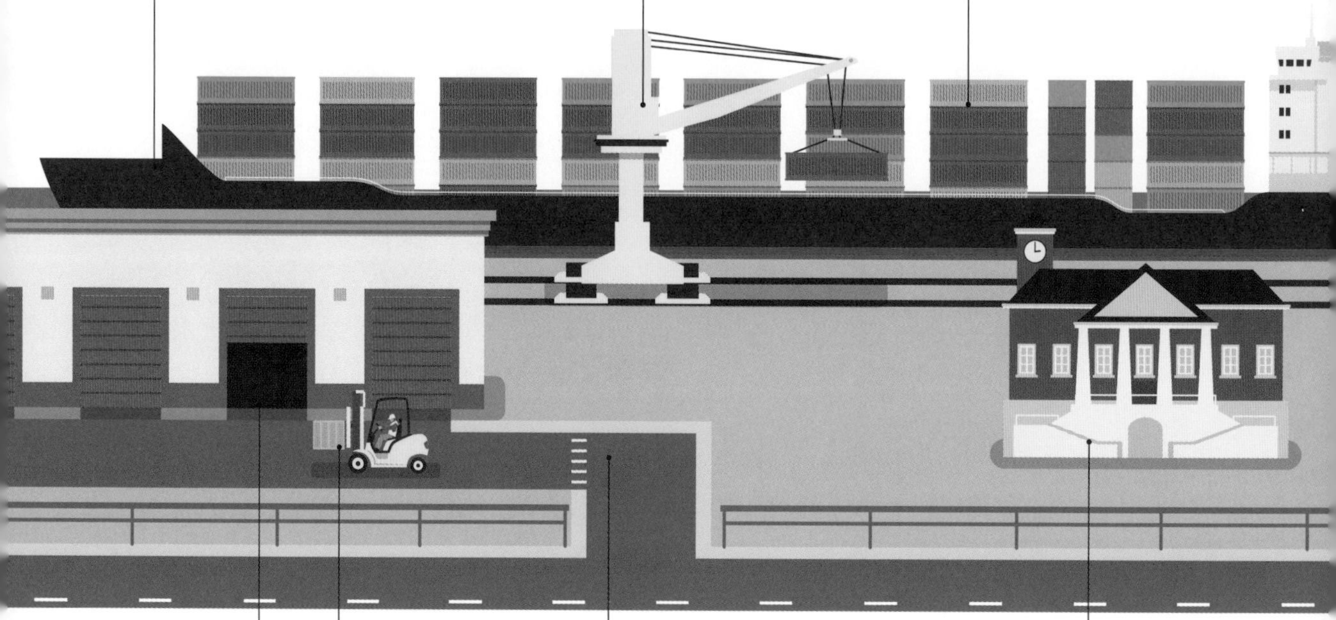


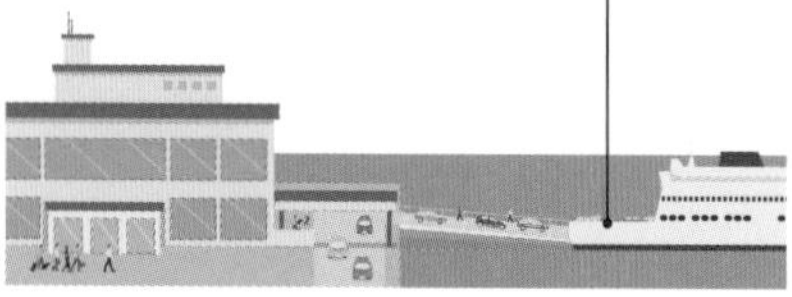


⑰ **der Fährhafen**
ferry terminal

⑲ **der Passagierhafen**
passenger port

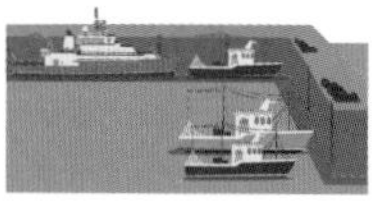

㉑ **der Fischereihafen**
fishing port

㉒ **der Fahrkartenschalter**
ticket office

㉗ **der Liegeplatz**
mooring

㉘ **der Hafen**
harbor

㉙ **die Marina**
marina

㉚ **der Pier**
pier

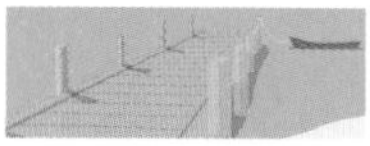

㉛ **der Steg**
jetty

㉜ **das Werftgelände**
shipyard

See also
**96** Straßen • Roads **102** Züge • Trains
**105** Seefahrzeuge • Sea vessels

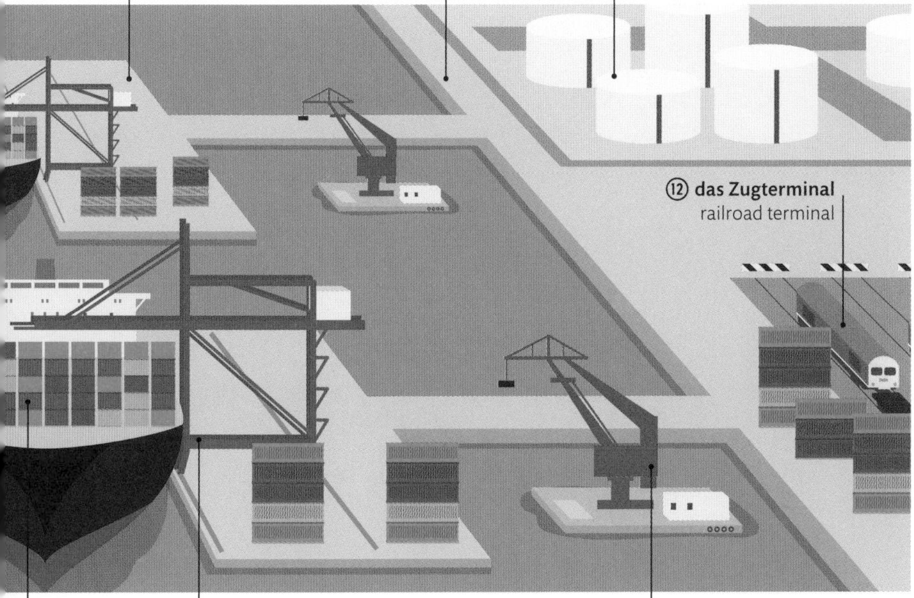

⑨ **der Kai**
quay

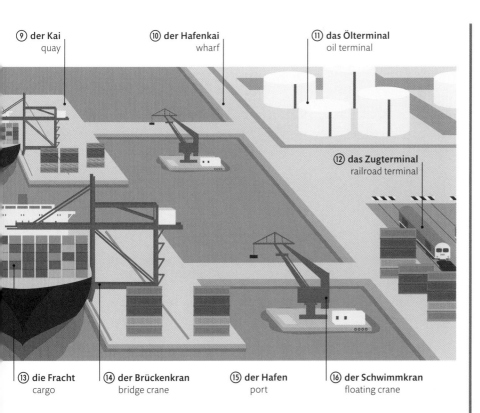

⑩ **der Hafenkai**
wharf

⑪ **das Ölterminal**
oil terminal

⑫ **das Zugterminal**
railroad terminal

⑬ **die Fracht**
cargo

⑭ **der Brückenkran**
bridge crane

⑮ **der Hafen**
port

⑯ **der Schwimmkran**
floating crane

㉓ **das Trockendock**
dry dock

㉔ **die Boje**
buoy

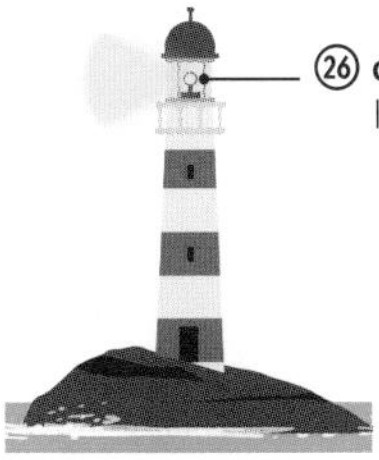

㉖ **die Laterne**
lamp

㉕ **der Leuchtturm**
lighthouse

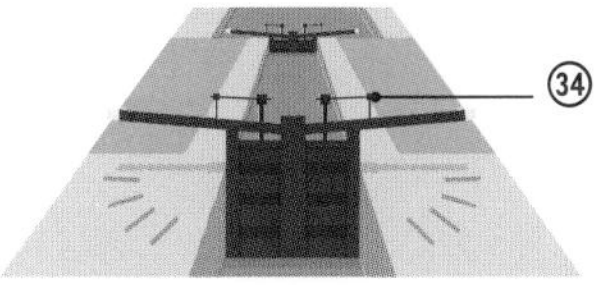

㉞ **das Schleusentor**
gate

㉝ **die Schleuse**
lock

㉟ **die Küstenwache**
coastguard

㊱ **der Hafenmeister** *m*
**die Hafenmeisterin** *f*
harbor master

## 106.2 VERBEN
VERBS

① **an Bord gehen**
to board

② **anlegen**
to moor

③ **von Bord gehen**
to disembark

④ **den Anker werfen**
to drop anchor

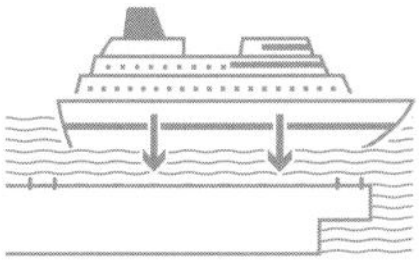

⑤ **anlanden**
to dock

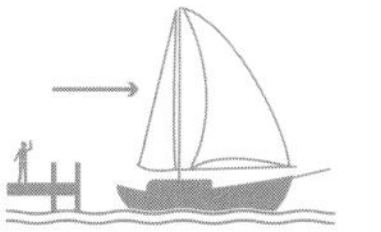

⑥ **die Segel setzen**
to set sail

# 107 American Football

## American football

### 107.1 AMERICAN FOOTBALL · AMERICAN FOOTBALL

① **der Left Cornerback** *m* **/ die Left Cornerback** *f*
left cornerback

② **der Outside Linebacker** *m* **die Outside Linebacker** *f*
outside linebacker

③ **der Left Defensive End** *m* **/ die Left Defensive End** *f*
left defensive end

④ **der Left Safety** *m* **die Left Safety** *f*
left safety

⑤ **der Left Defensive Tackle** *m* **/ die Left Defensive Tackle** *f*
left defensive tackle

⑥ **der Middle Linebacker** *m* **/ die Middle Linebacker** *f*
middle linebacker

⑦ **der Right Defensive Tackle** *m* **/ die Right Defensive Tackle** *f*
right defensive tackle

⑧ **der Right Safety** *m* **die Right Safety** *f*
right safety

⑨ **der Right Defensive End** *m* **die Right Defensive End** *f*
right defensive end

⑩ **der Outside Linebacker** *m* **/ die Outside Linebacker** *f*
outside linebacker

⑪ **der Right Cornerback** *m* **/ die Right Cornerback** *f*
right cornerback

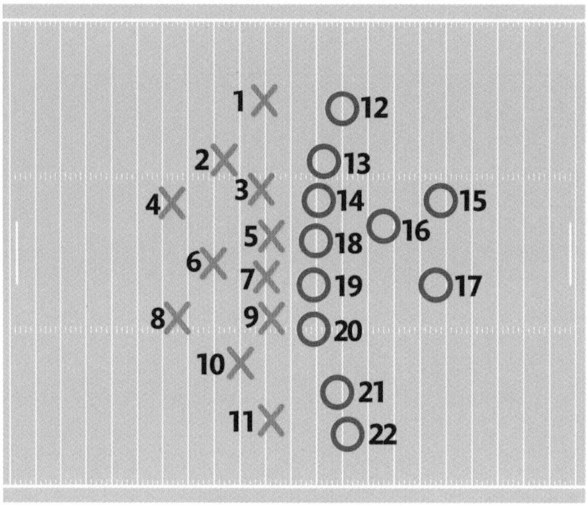


㉔ **die Verteidigung**
defense

㉓ **die Aufstellung im American Football**
American football positions

㉕ **der Angriff**
offense

⑫ **der Wide Receiver** *m* **/ die Wide Receiver** *f*
wide receiver

⑬ **der Right Tackle** *m* **die Right Tackle** *f*
right tackle

⑭ **der Right Guard** *m* **die Right Guard** *f*
right guard

⑮ **der Running Back / Halfback** *m* **/ die Running Back / Halfback** *f*
running back / halfback

⑯ **der Fullback** *m* **die Fullback** *f*
fullback

⑰ **der Quarterbac die Quarterback**
quarterback

⑱ **der Center** *m* **die Center** *f*
center

⑲ **der Left Guard die Left Guard** *f*
left guard

⑳ **der Left Tackle die Left Tackle** *f*
left tackle

㉑ ㉒ **der Wide Receiver** *m* **/ di Wide Receiver**
wide receiver

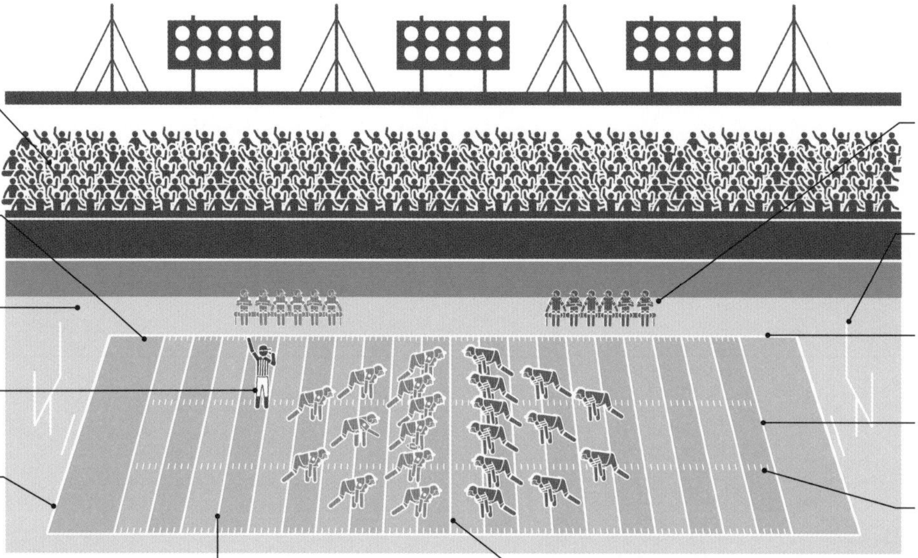

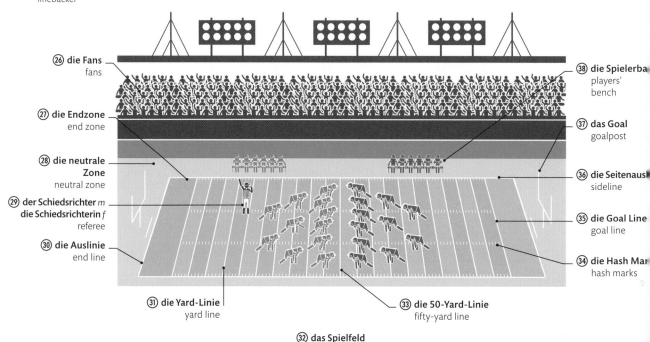

㉖ **die Fans**
fans

㉗ **die Endzone**
end zone

㉘ **die neutrale Zone**
neutral zone

㉙ **der Schiedsrichter** *m* **die Schiedsrichterin** *f*
referee

㉚ **die Auslinie**
end line

㉛ **die Yard-Linie**
yard line

㉜ **das Spielfeld**
field

㉝ **die 50-Yard-Linie**
fifty-yard line

㉞ **die Hash Mar**
hash marks

㉟ **die Goal Line**
goal line

㊱ **die Seitenaus**
sideline

㊲ **das Goal**
goalpost

㊳ **die Spielerba**
players' bench

See also
**108** Rugby • Rugby **109** Fußball • Soccer
**110** Hockey und Lacrosse • Hockey and lacrosse

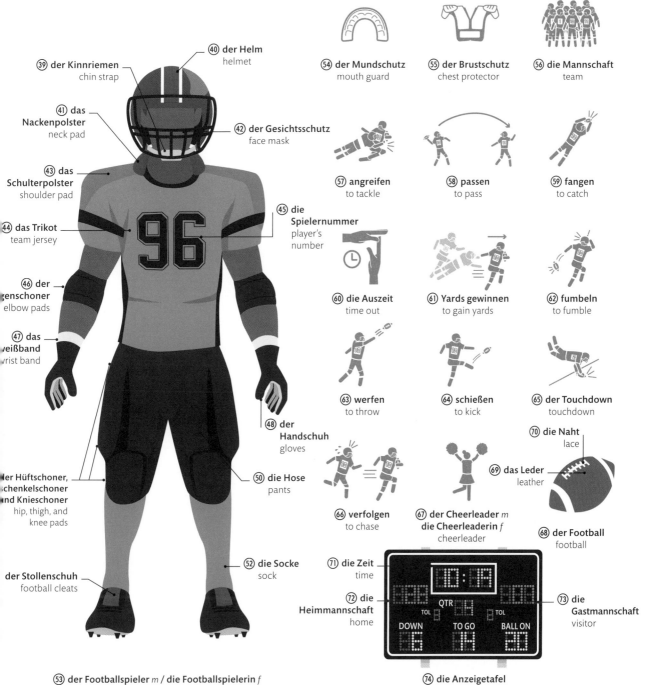

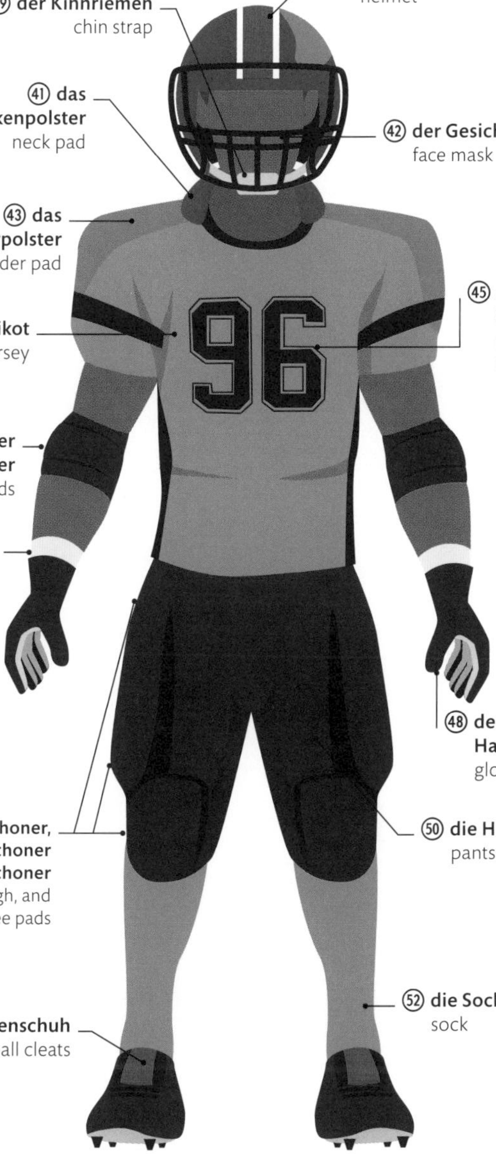


㊴ **der Kinnriemen**
chin strap

㊵ **der Helm**
helmet

㊶ **das Nackenpolster**
neck pad

㊷ **der Gesichtsschutz**
face mask

㊸ **das Schulterpolster**
shoulder pad

㊹ **das Trikot**
team jersey

㊺ **die Spielernummer**
player's number

㊻ **der**
**enschoner**
elbow pads

㊼ **das**
**eißband**
rist band

㊽ **der Handschuh**
gloves

**er Hüftschoner,**
**chenkelschoner**
**nd Knieschoner**
hip, thigh, and knee pads

㊿ **die Hose**
pants

**der Stollenschuh**
football cleats

(52) **die Socke**
sock

(53) **der Footballspieler** *m* / **die Footballspielerin** *f*
football player

(54) **der Mundschutz**
mouth guard

(55) **der Brustschutz**
chest protector

(56) **die Mannschaft**
team

(57) **angreifen**
to tackle

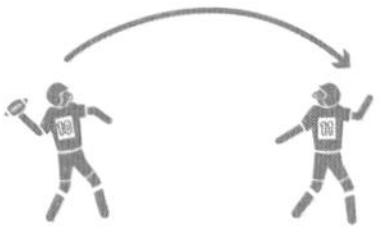

(58) **passen**
to pass

(59) **fangen**
to catch

(60) **die Auszeit**
time out

(61) **Yards gewinnen**
to gain yards

(62) **fumbeln**
to fumble

(63) **werfen**
to throw

(64) **schießen**
to kick

(65) **der Touchdown**
touchdown

(66) **verfolgen**
to chase

(67) **der Cheerleader** *m*
**die Cheerleaderin** *f*
cheerleader

(70) **die Naht**
lace

(69) **das Leder**
leather

(68) **der Football**
football

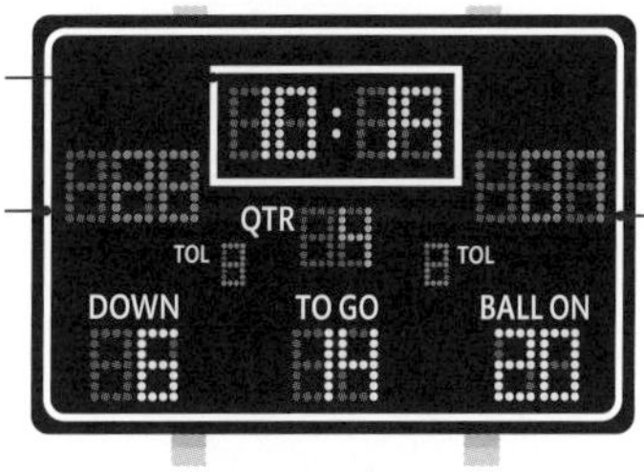


(71) **die Zeit**
time

(72) **die Heimmannschaft**
home

(73) **die Gastmannschaft**
visitor

(74) **die Anzeigetafel**
scoreboard

# 108 Rugby
Rugby

## 108.1 RUGBY · RUGBY

① **der linke Pfeiler** *m*
**die linke Pfeilerin** *f*
loosehead prop

② **der Hakler** *m*
**die Haklerin** *f*
hooker

③ **der rechte Pfeiler** *m*
**die rechte Pfeilerin** *f*
tighthead prop

④ **der Zweite-Reihe-Stürmer** *m*
**die Zweite-Reihe-Stürmerin** *f*
second row

⑤ **der Zweite-Reihe-Stürmer** *m*
**die Zweite-Reihe-Stürmerin** *f*
second row

⑥ **der linke Flügelstürmer** *m*
**die linke Flügelstürmerin** *f*
blindside flanker

⑦ **der rechte Flügelstürmer** *m*
**die rechte Flügelstürmerin** *f*
openside flanker

⑧ **die Nummer Acht**
number eight

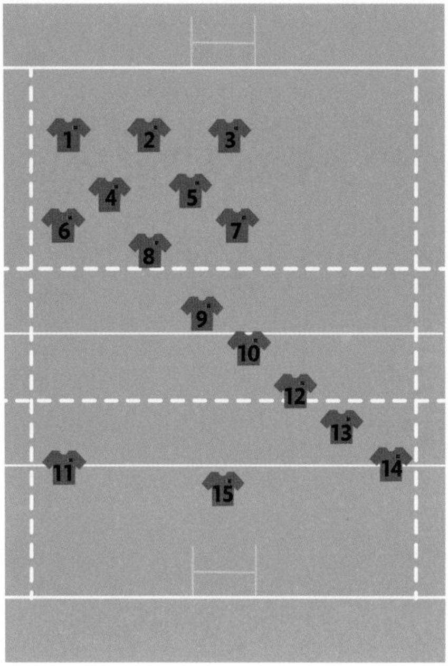


⑯ **die Aufstellung im Rugby**
rugby positions

⑨ **der Gedrängehalb** *m*
**die Gedrängehalb** *f*
scrum-half

⑩ **der Verbindungshalb** *m*
**die Verbindungshalb** *f*
fly-half

⑪ **der linke Außendreiviertel** *m*
**die linke Außendreiviertel** *f*
left-wing

⑫ **der erste Innendreiviertel** *m*
**die erste Innendreiviertel** *f*
inside center

⑬ **der zweite Innendreiviertel** *m*
**die zweite Innendreiviertel** *f*
outside center

⑭ **der rechte Außendreiviertel** *m*
**die rechte Außendreiviertel** *f*
right wing

⑮ **der Schlussmann** *m*
**die Schlussfrau** *f*
full back

㊱ **das Rollstuhl-Rugby**
wheelchair rugby

⑰ **der Spieler** *m*
**die Spielerin** *f*
player

⑱ **der Rugby-Ball**
rugby ball

⑲ **das Trikot**
rugby shirt

⑳ **das Rugby-Jersey**
rugby jersey

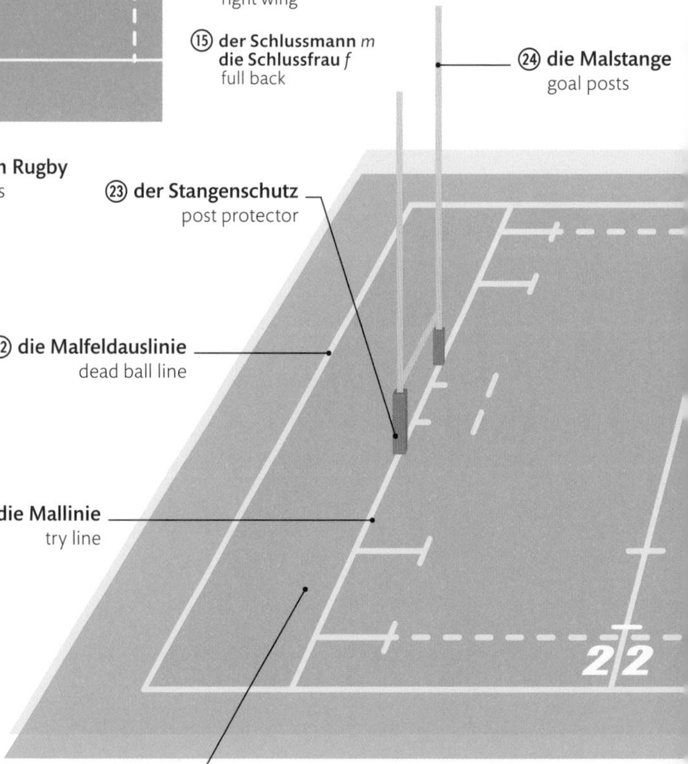


㉔ **die Malstange**
goal posts

㉓ **der Stangenschutz**
post protector

㉒ **die Malfeldauslinie**
dead ball line

㉑ **die Mallinie**
try line

㉚ **die Spielanlage**
playing surface

㉛ **das Rugby-Spielfeld**
rugby pitch

See also
**107** American Football • American football **109** Fußball • Soccer **110** Hockey und Lacrosse • Hockey and lacrosse **112** Basketball und Volleyball • Basketball and volleyball

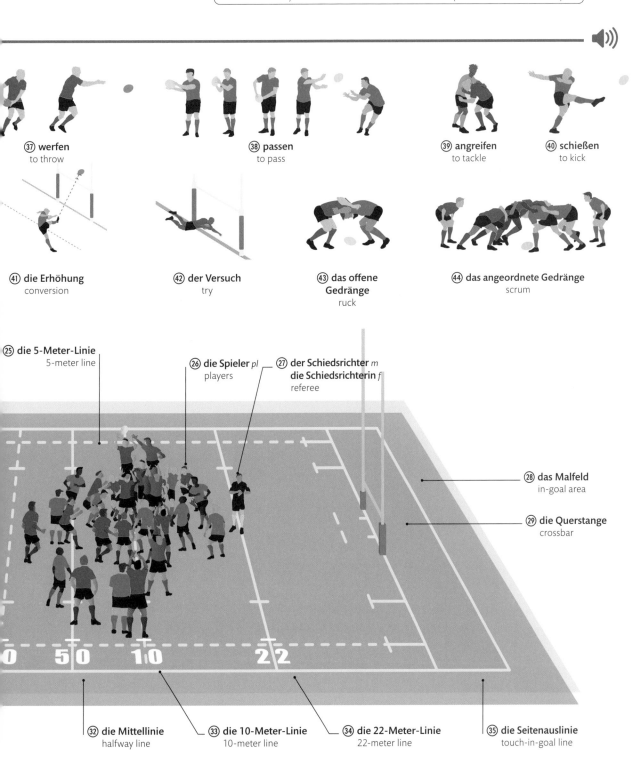

㊲ **werfen**
to throw

㊳ **passen**
to pass

㊴ **angreifen**
to tackle

㊵ **schießen**
to kick

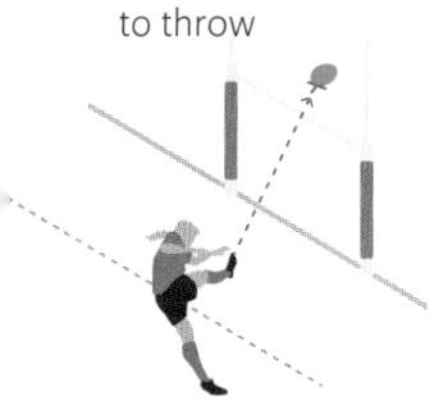

㊶ **die Erhöhung**
conversion

㊷ **der Versuch**
try

㊸ **das offene Gedränge**
ruck

㊹ **das angeordnete Gedränge**
scrum

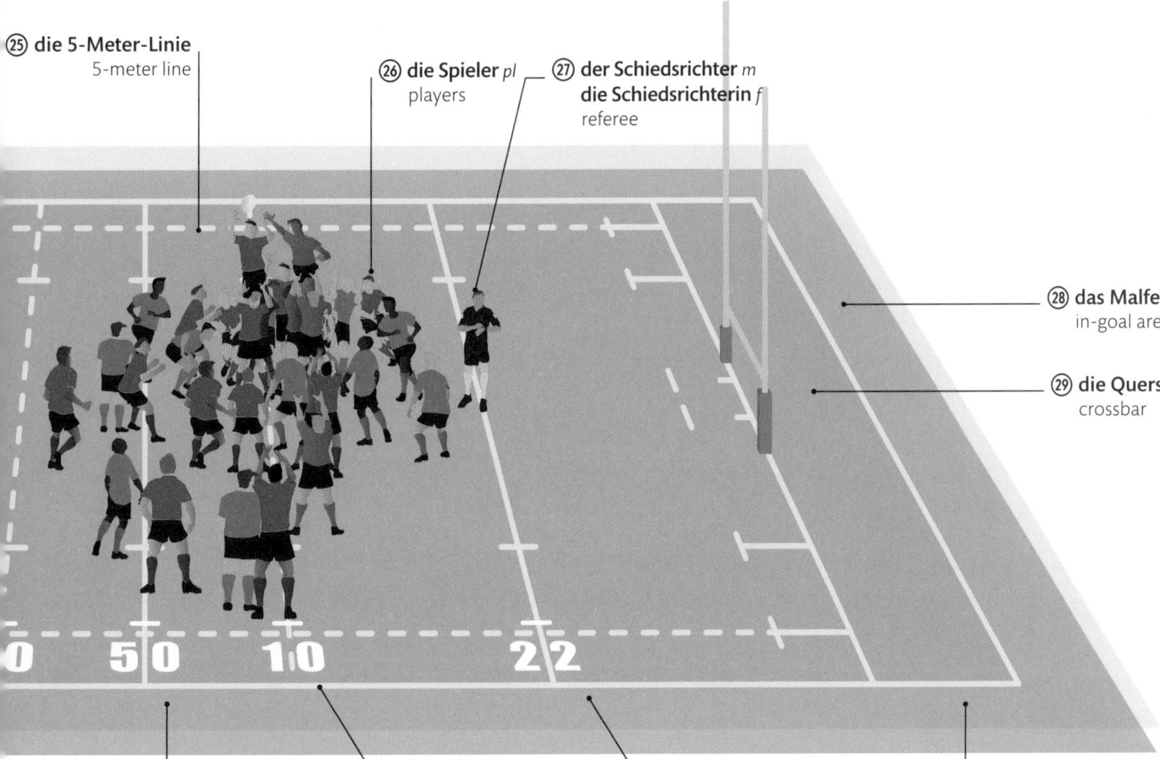


㉕ **die 5-Meter-Linie**
5-meter line

㉖ **die Spieler** *pl*
players

㉗ **der Schiedsrichter** *m*
**die Schiedsrichterin** *f*
referee

㉘ **das Malfeld**
in-goal area

㉙ **die Querstange**
crossbar

㉜ **die Mittellinie**
halfway line

㉝ **die 10-Meter-Linie**
10-meter line

㉞ **die 22-Meter-Linie**
22-meter line

㉟ **die Seitenauslinie**
touch-in-goal line

# 109 Fußball
Soccer

## 109.1 DAS FUSSBALLSPIEL · SOCCER GAME

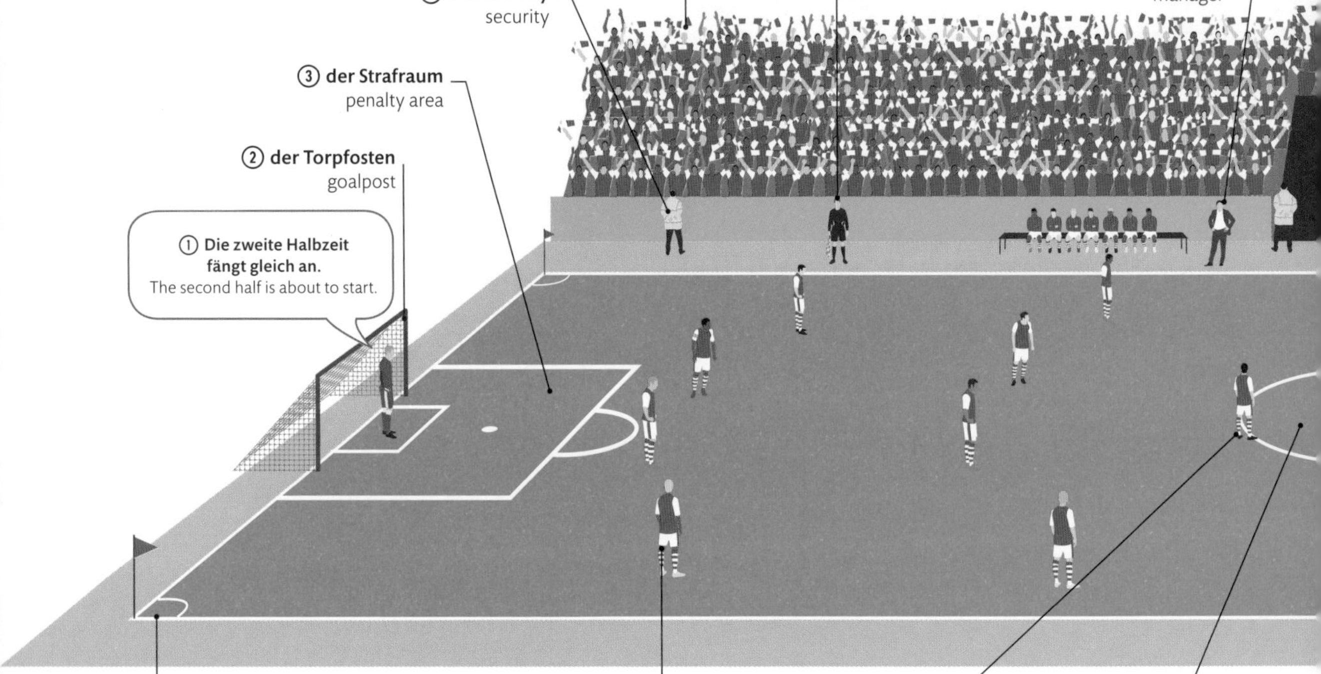
① Die zweite Halbzeit fängt gleich an.
The second half is about to start.

② **der Torpfosten**
goalpost

③ **der Strafraum**
penalty area

④ **die Security**
security

⑤ **die Fans** *m, pl*
fans

⑥ **der Linienrichter** *m*
**die Linienrichterin** *f*
linesman

⑦ **der Trainer** *m*
**die Trainerin** *f*
manager

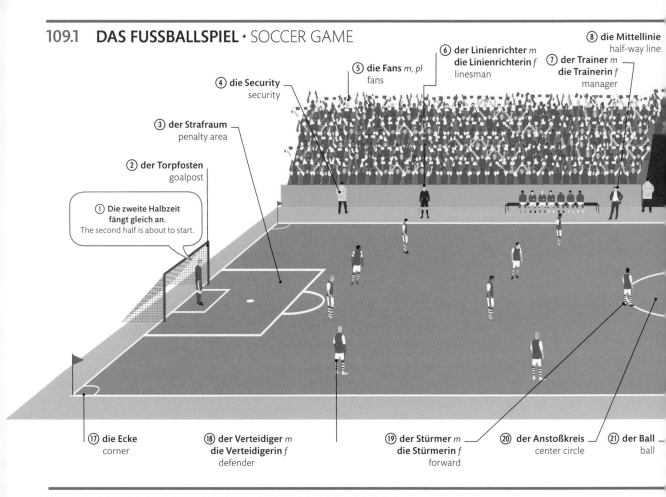

⑧ **die Mittellinie**
half-way line

⑰ **die Ecke**
corner

⑱ **der Verteidiger** *m*
**die Verteidigerin** *f*
defender

⑲ **der Stürmer** *m*
**die Stürmerin** *f*
forward

⑳ **der Anstoßkreis**
center circle

㉑ **der Ball**
ball

## 109.2 ZEITEN UND REGELN · TIMING AND RULES

00:00

① **der Anstoß**
kickoff

45:00

② **die Halbzeit**
half time

90:00

③ **das Spielzeitende**
full time

④ **der Einwurf**
throw-in

⑤ **der Abpfiff**
final whistle

⑥ **die Nachspielzeit**
stoppage time

⑨ **der Eckstoß**
corner kick

⑩ **die gelbe Karte**
yellow card

⑪ **die rote Karte**
red card

⑫ **einen Platzverweis erhalten**
to be sent off

00
00

⑬ **unentschieden spielen**
to tie

00
05

⑭ **verlieren**
to lose

See also
**107** American Football • American football **108** Rugby • Rugby **110** Hockey und Lacrosse • Hockey and lacrosse **112** Basketball und Volleyball • Basketball and volleyball

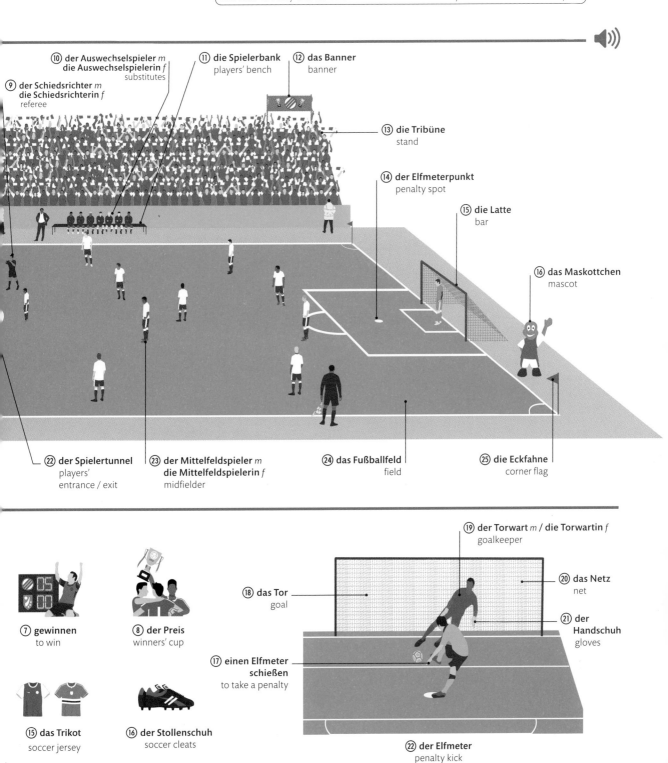

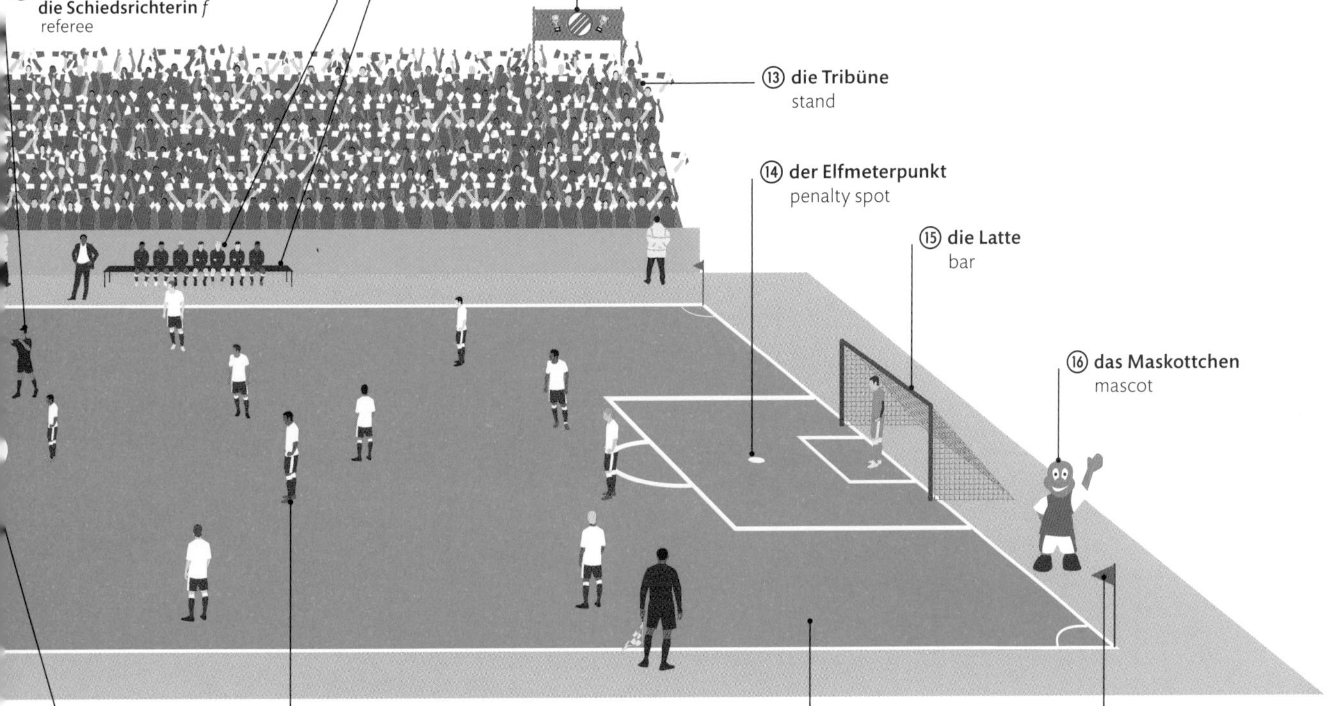

⑦ **gewinnen**
to win

⑧ **der Preis**
winners' cup

⑮ **das Trikot**
soccer jersey

⑯ **der Stollenschuh**
soccer cleats

㉒ **der Elfmeter**
penalty kick

# 110 Hockey und Lacrosse
## Hockey and lacrosse

### 110.1 EISHOCKEY • ICE HOCKEY

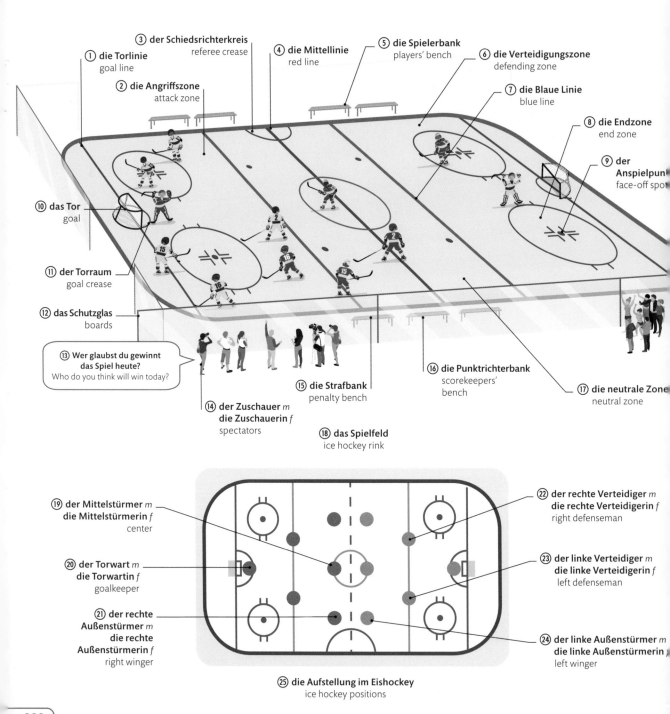

⑱ das Spielfeld
ice hockey rink

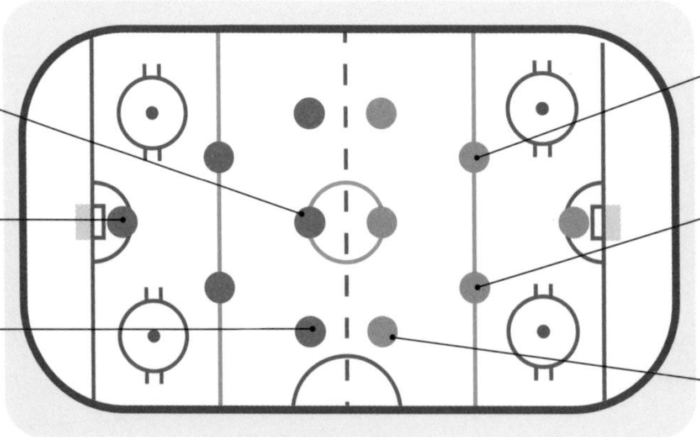


㉕ die Aufstellung im Eishockey
ice hockey positions

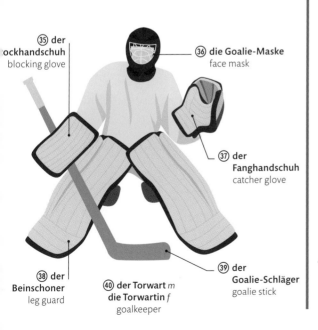

See also
**107** American Football • American football **111** Kricket • Cricket **112** Basketball und Volleyball • Basketball and volleyball **113** Baseball • Baseball **114** Tennis • Tennis

㉖ **eislaufen**
to skate

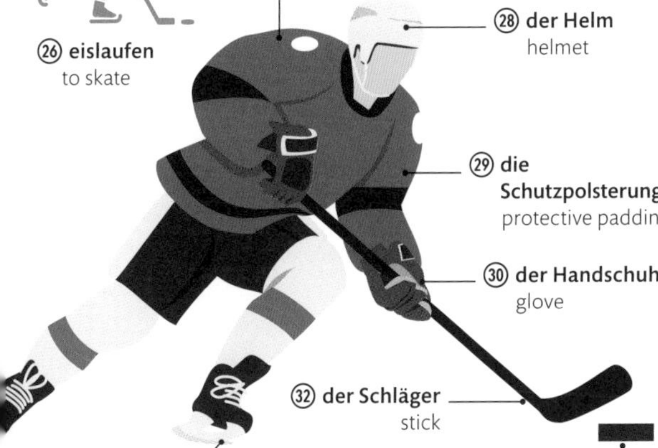

㉗ **das Schulterpolster**
shoulder pad

㉘ **der Helm**
helmet

㉙ **die Schutzpolsterung**
protective padding

㉚ **der Handschuh**
glove

㉜ **der Schläger**
stick

**der Schlittschuh**
ice skate

㉝ **der Puck**
puck

㉞ **der Eishockeyspieler** *m*
**die Eishockeyspielerin** *f*
ice hockey player

㉟ **der**
**ockhandschuh**
blocking glove

㊱ **die Goalie-Maske**
face mask

㊲ **der Fanghandschuh**
catcher glove

㊳ **der Beinschoner**
leg guard

㊵ **der Torwart** *m*
**die Torwartin** *f*
goalkeeper

㊴ **der Goalie-Schläger**
goalie stick

## 110.2 HOCKEY • FIELD HOCKEY

① **schlagen**
to hit

② **der Schienbeinschoner**
shin guard

③ **der Hockeyschläger**
hockey stick

⑤ **der Ball**
ball

④ **der Hockeyspieler** *m*
**die Hockeyspielerin** *f*
field hockey player

## 110.3 LACROSSE • LACROSSE

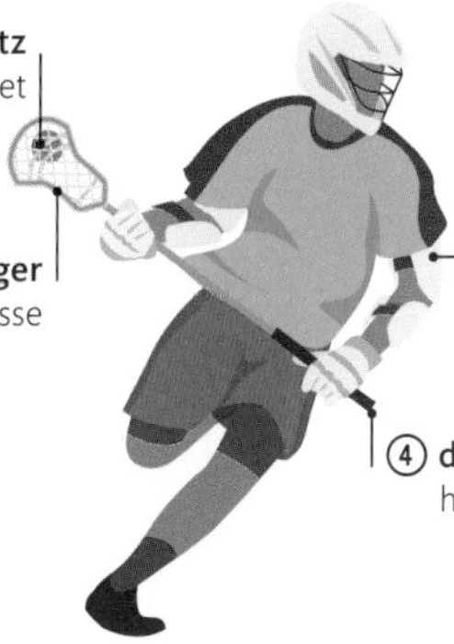

① **das Netz**
head pocket

② **der Schläger**
crosse

③ **der Armschutz**
arm protection

④ **der Griff**
handle

⑤ **der Lacrossespieler** *m*
**die Lacrossespielerin** *f*
lacrosse player

⑥ **passen**
to pass

⑦ **aufnehmen**
to scoop

⑧ **der Face-Off**
face-off

# 111 Kricket
Cricket

## 111.1 DAS KRICKETSPIELFELD UND DIE KRICKETAUFSTELLUNG
CRICKET PITCH AND POSITIONS

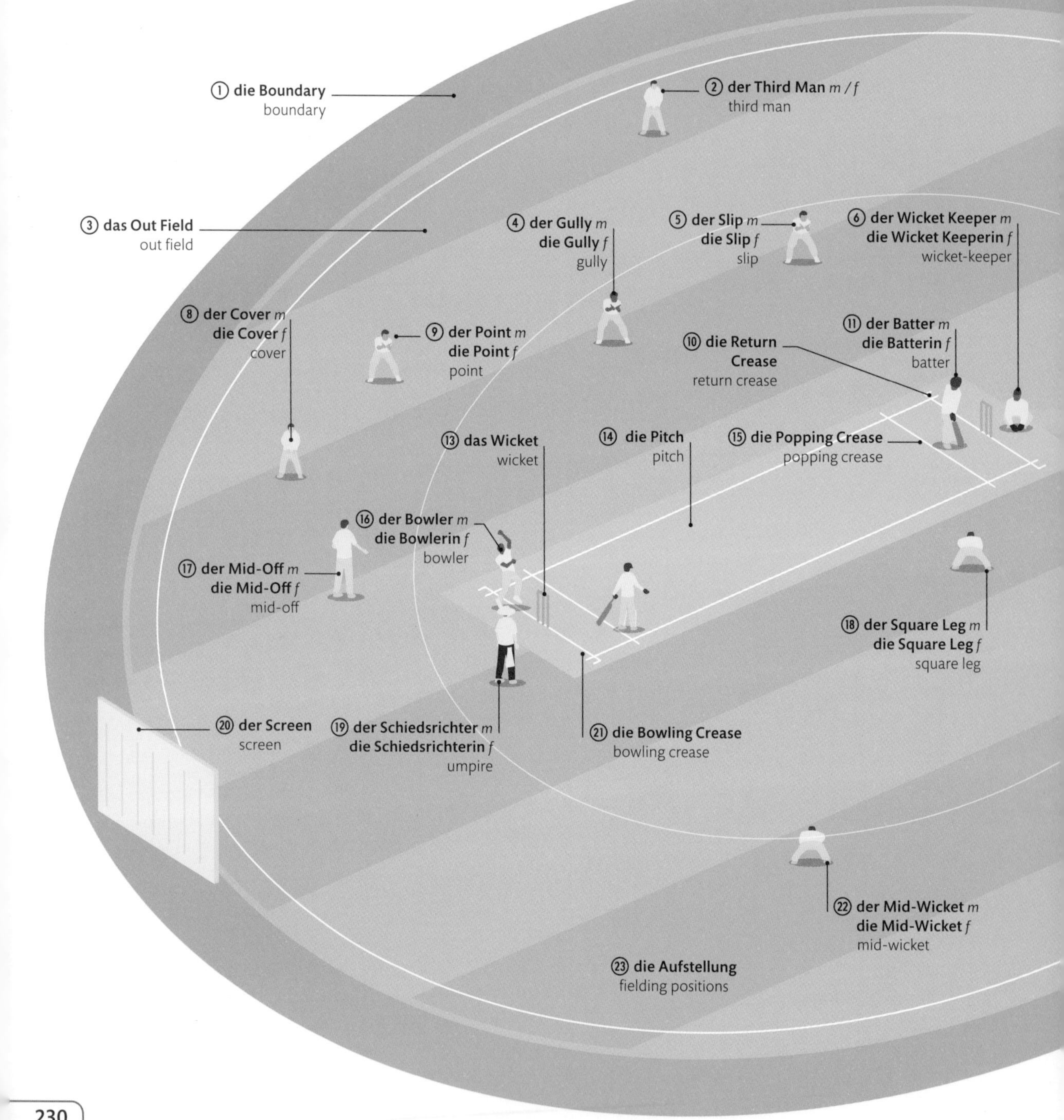

See also
**109** Fußball • Soccer **110** Hockey und Lacrosse • Hockey and lacrosse **113** Baseball • Baseball **115** Golf • Golf

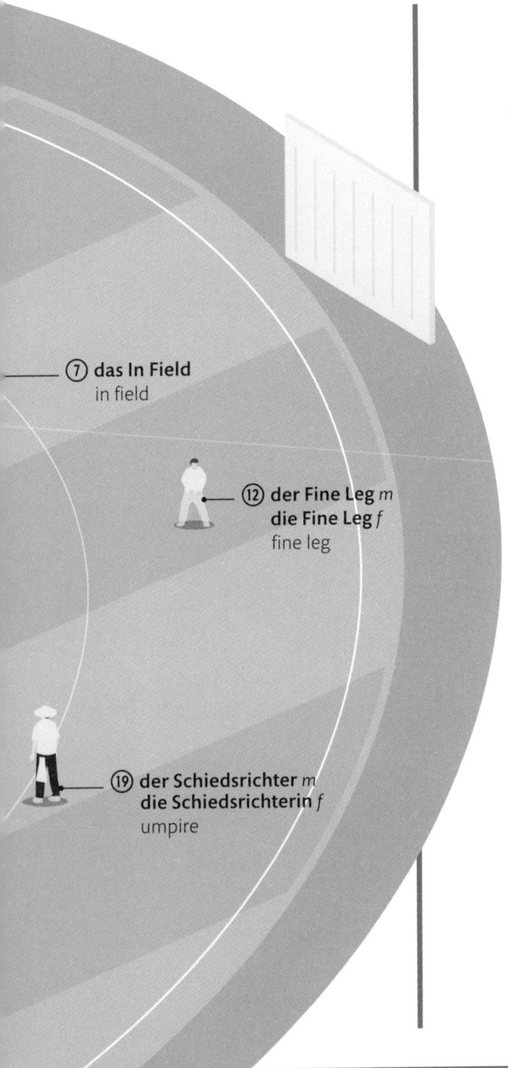


## 111.2 KRICKETAUSRÜSTUNG • CRICKET EQUIPMENT

① **der Kricketschuh**
cricket shoes

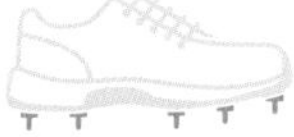

② **die Stollen** *m, pl*
studs

③ **der Kricketball**
cricket ball

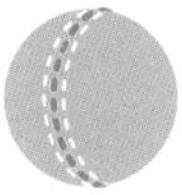

④ **die Naht**
seam

⑤ **der Stab**
stumps

⑥ **der Querstab**
bail

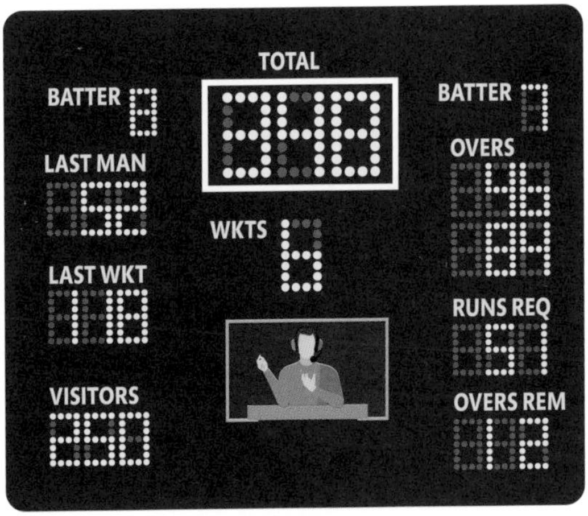


⑦ **die Anzeigetafel**
scoreboard

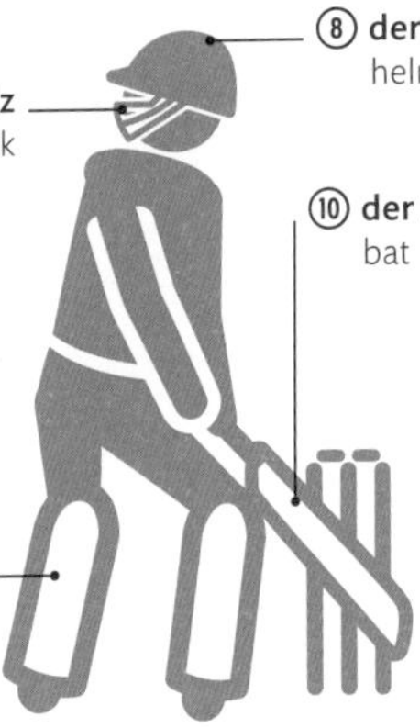

⑧ **der Helm**
helmet

⑨ **der Gesichtsschutz**
facemask

⑩ **der Schläger**
bat

⑪ **der Beinschoner**
leg pad

⑫ **der Batter** *m*
**die Batterin** *f*
batter / batsman

## 111.3 KRICKETVERBEN • CRICKET VERBS

① **laufen**
to run

② **werfen**
to bowl

③ **schlagen**
to bat

④ **fangen**
to field

⑤ **ins Aus schlagen**
to strike out

⑥ **ausschalten**
to stump

# 112 Basketball und Volleyball
## Basketball and volleyball

### 112.1 BASKETBALL · BASKETBALL

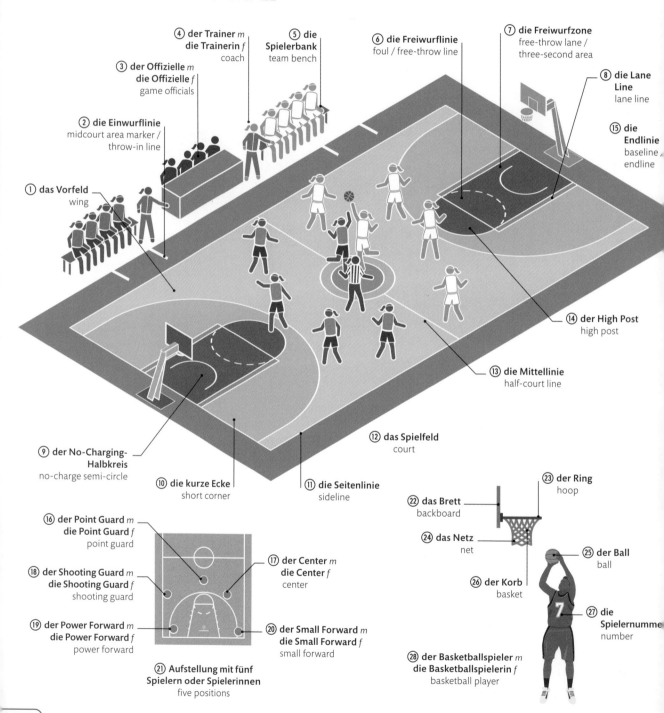

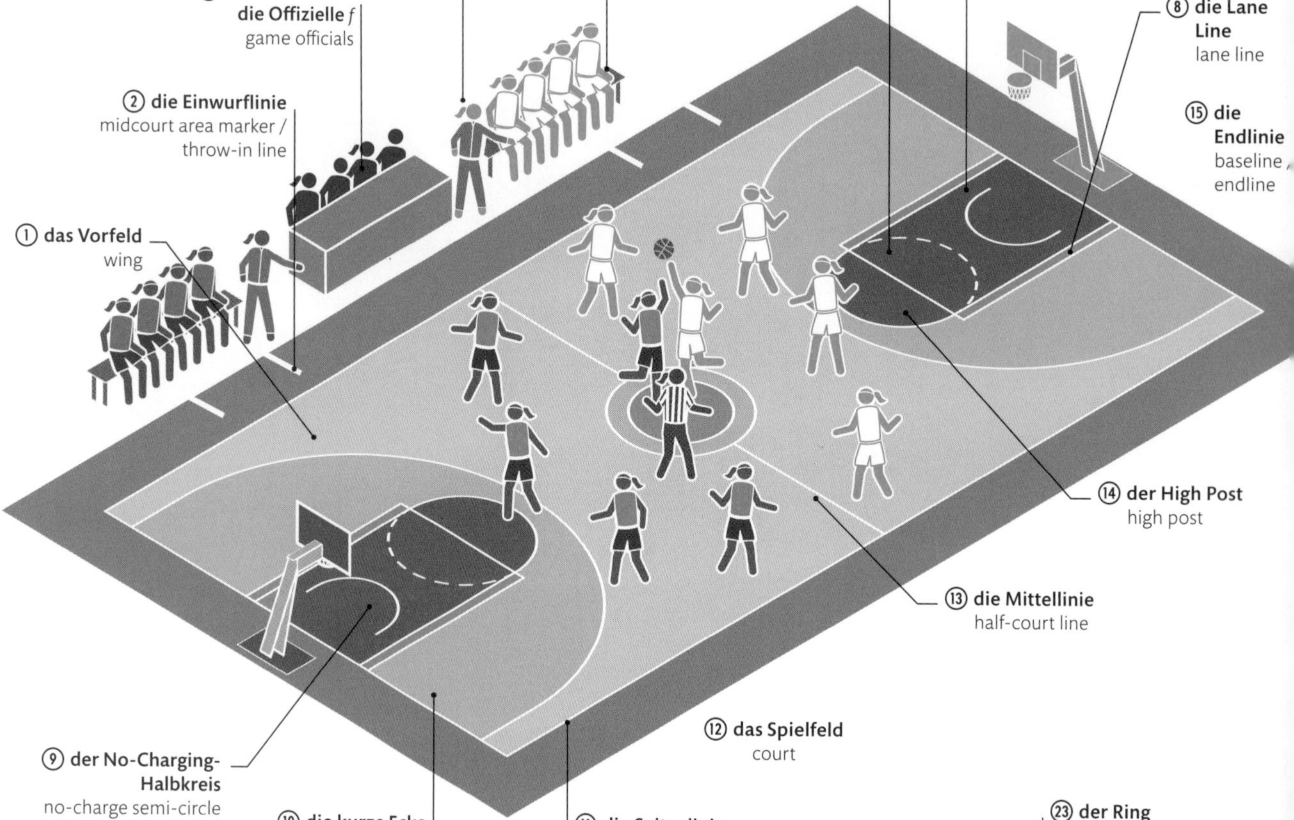


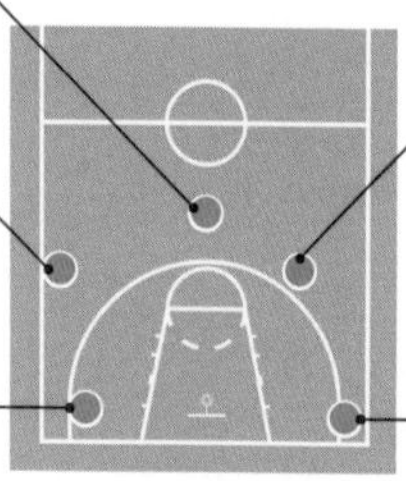


㉑ **Aufstellung mit fünf Spielern oder Spielerinnen**
five positions

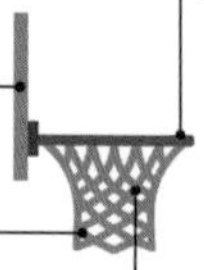

㉘ **der Basketballspieler** *m*
**die Basketballspielerin** *f*
basketball player

See also
**107** American Football • American football **108** Rugby • Rugby **109** Fußball • Soccer
**124** Im Fitnessstudio • At the gym **125** Weitere Sportarten • Other sports

㉙ **passen**
pass

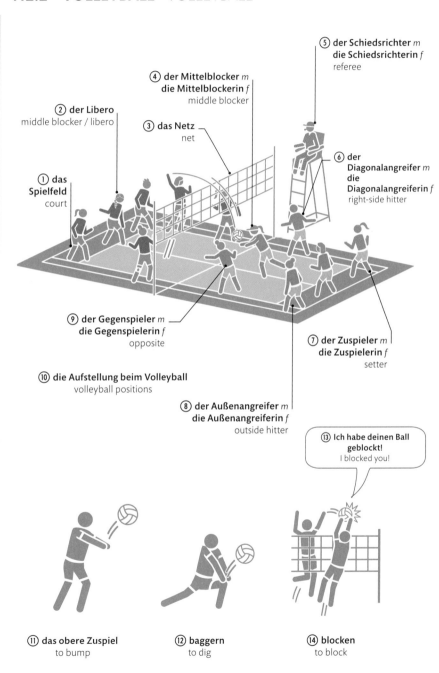

㉚ **im Aus**
out of bounds

㉛ **der Einwurf**
throw-in

㉜ **der Rebound**
rebound

㉝ **der Airball**
airball

㉞ **der Schiedsrichterball**
jump ball

㉟ **das Foul**
foul

㊱ **decken**
to mark

㊲ **dribbeln**
to bounce

㊳ **dunken**
to dunk

㊴ **werfen**
to shoot

㊵ **abwehren**
to block

## 112.2 VOLLEYBALL • VOLLEYBALL

① **das Spielfeld**
court

② **der Libero**
middle blocker / libero

③ **das Netz**
net

④ **der Mittelblocker** *m*
**die Mittelblockerin** *f*
middle blocker

⑤ **der Schiedsrichter** *m*
**die Schiedsrichterin** *f*
referee

⑥ **der Diagonalangreifer** *m*
**die Diagonalangreiferin** *f*
right-side hitter

⑦ **der Zuspieler** *m*
**die Zuspielerin** *f*
setter

⑧ **der Außenangreifer** *m*
**die Außenangreiferin** *f*
outside hitter

⑨ **der Gegenspieler** *m*
**die Gegenspielerin** *f*
opposite

⑩ **die Aufstellung beim Volleyball**
volleyball positions

⑪ **das obere Zuspiel**
to bump

⑫ **baggern**
to dig

⑬ Ich habe deinen Ball geblockt!
I blocked you!

⑭ **blocken**
to block

# 113 Baseball

## Baseball

### 113.1 DAS BASEBALLSPIEL · BASEBALL GAME

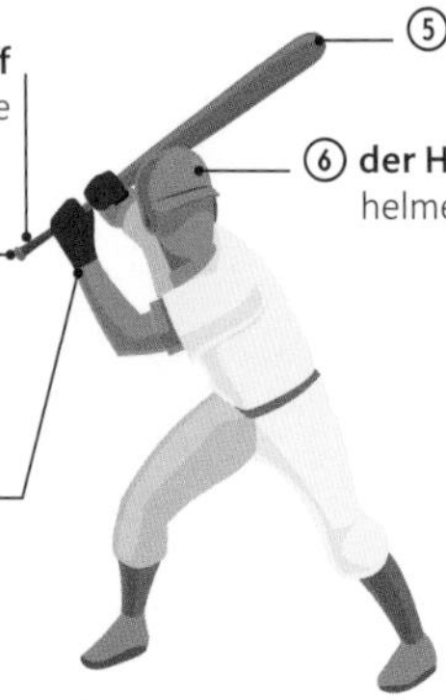

① **der Griff** handle

② **der Knauf** knob

③ **der Handschuh** batting glove

④ **der Batter** *m* **die Batterin** *f* batter

⑤ **der Schläger** bat

⑥ **der Helm** helmet

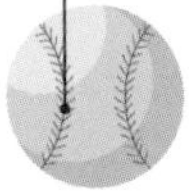

⑦ **die Naht** stitches

⑧ **der Baseball** baseball

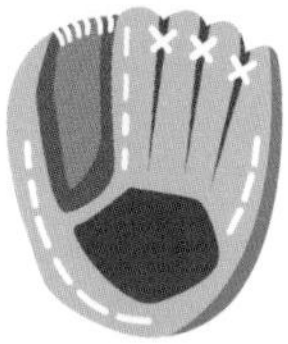

⑨ **der Baseballhandschuh** mitt

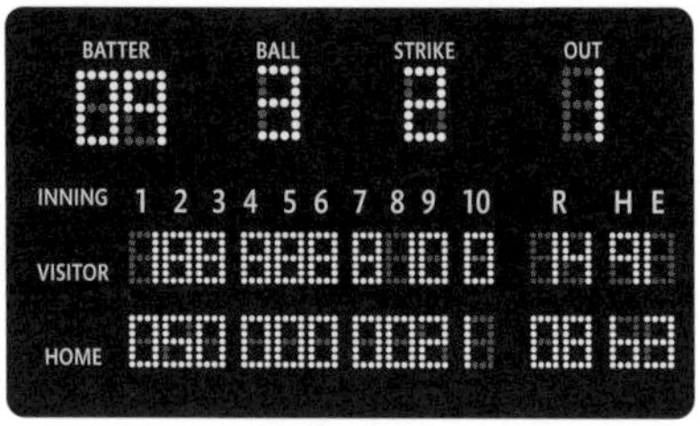


⑩ **das Inning** inning

⑪ **die Gesichtsmaske** mask

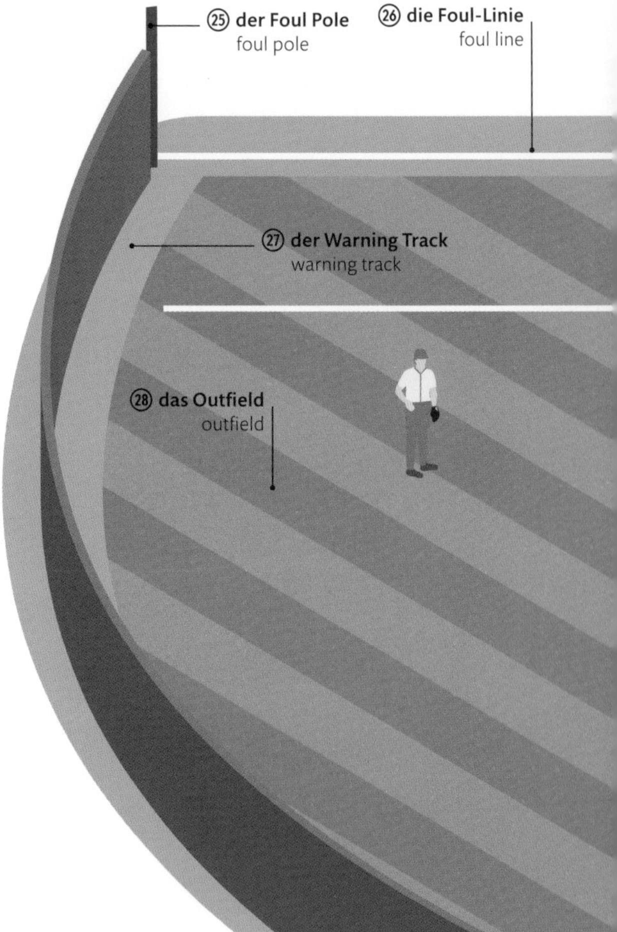

㉕ **der Foul Pole** foul pole

㉖ **die Foul-Linie** foul line

㉗ **der Warning Track** warning track

㉘ **das Outfield** outfield

⑫ **treffen** strike

⑬ **das Aus** out

⑭ **der Foul Ball** foul ball

⑮ **safe** safe

⑯ **spielen** to play

⑰ **werfen** to throw

⑱ **fangen** to catch

⑲ **schlagen** to bat

⑳ **schlittern** to slide

㉑ **werfen** to pitch

㉒ **laufen** to run

㉓ **taggen** to tag

㉔ **abfangen** to field

See also
**107** American Football • American football **110** Hockey und Lacrosse • Hockey and lacrosse
**111** Kricket • Cricket **112** Basektball und Volleyball • Basketball and volleyball

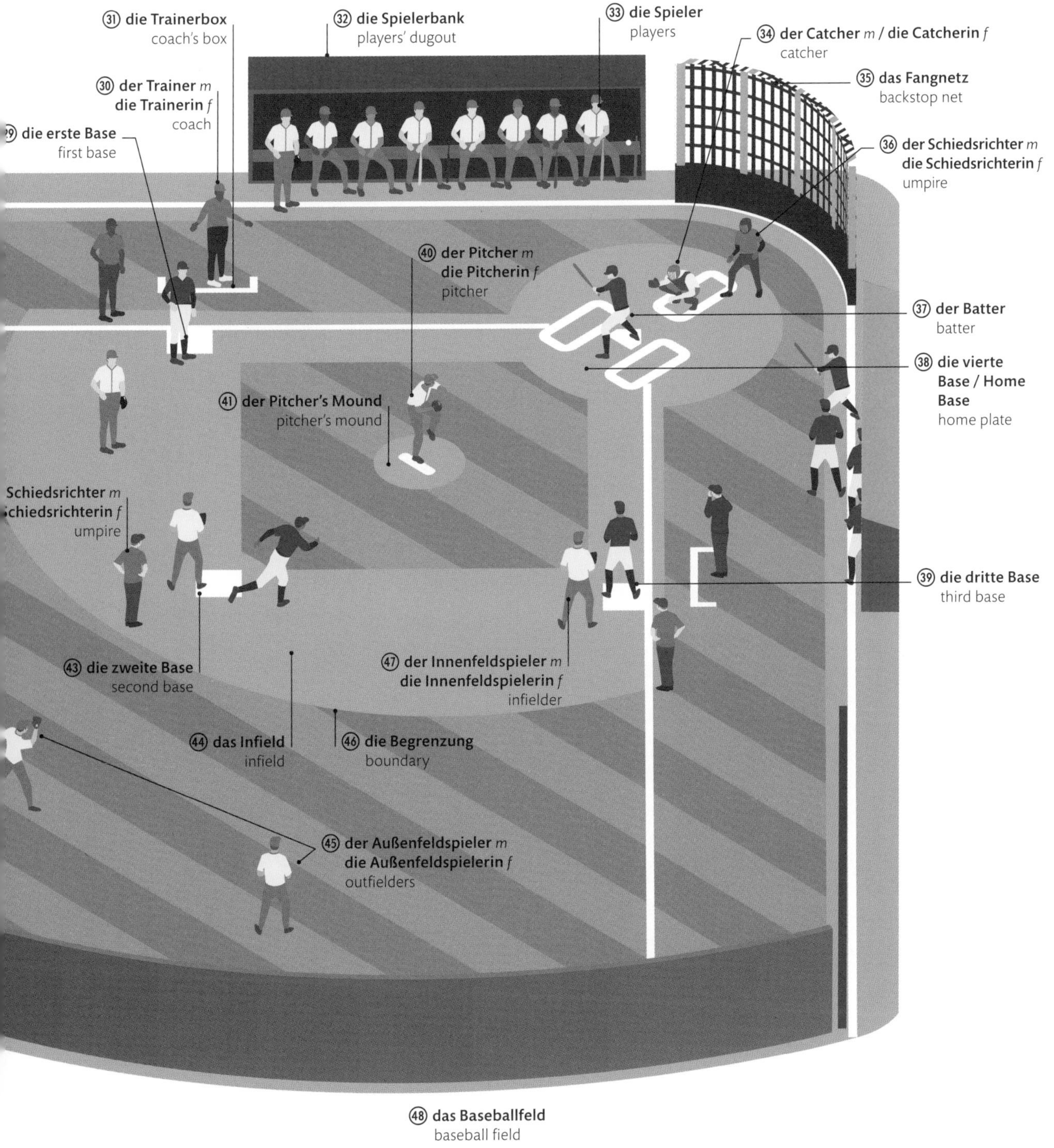

# 114 Tennis
Tennis

## 114.1 DAS TENNISMATCH · TENNIS MATCH

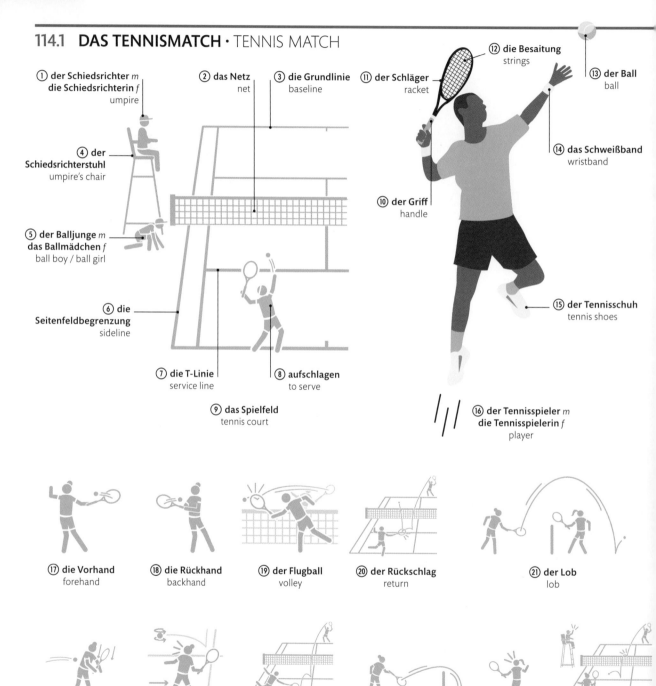

① **der Schiedsrichter** *m* **die Schiedsrichterin** *f*
umpire

② **das Netz**
net

③ **die Grundlinie**
baseline

④ **der Schiedsrichterstuhl**
umpire's chair

⑤ **der Balljunge** *m* **das Ballmädchen** *f*
ball boy / ball girl

⑥ **die Seitenfeldbegrenzung**
sideline

⑦ **die T-Linie**
service line

⑧ **aufschlagen**
to serve

⑨ **das Spielfeld**
tennis court

⑩ **der Griff**
handle

⑪ **der Schläger**
racket

⑫ **die Besaitung**
strings

⑬ **der Ball**
ball

⑭ **das Schweißband**
wristband

⑮ **der Tennisschuh**
tennis shoes

⑯ **der Tennisspieler** *m* **die Tennisspielerin** *f*
player

⑰ **die Vorhand**
forehand

⑱ **die Rückhand**
backhand

⑲ **der Flugball**
volley

⑳ **der Rückschlag**
return

㉑ **der Lob**
lob

㉒ **der Slice**
slice

㉓ **der Spin**
spin

㉔ **das Ass**
ace

㉕ **der Stoppball**
dropshot

㉖ **der Netzball**
let

See also
**111** Kricket • Cricket **113** Baseball • Baseball
**115** Golf • Golf **116** Leichtathletik • Athletics

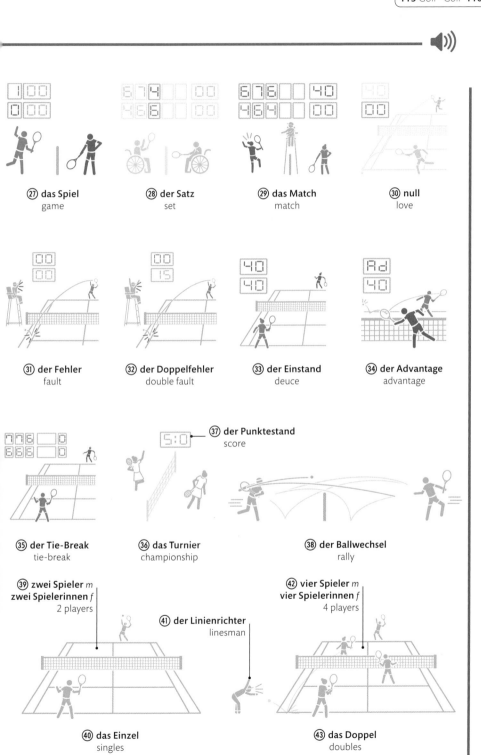

㉗ **das Spiel**
game

㉘ **der Satz**
set

㉙ **das Match**
match

㉚ **null**
love

㉛ **der Fehler**
fault

㉜ **der Doppelfehler**
double fault

㉝ **der Einstand**
deuce

㉞ **der Advantage**
advantage

㉟ **der Tie-Break**
tie-break

㊲ **der Punktestand**
score

㊱ **das Turnier**
championship

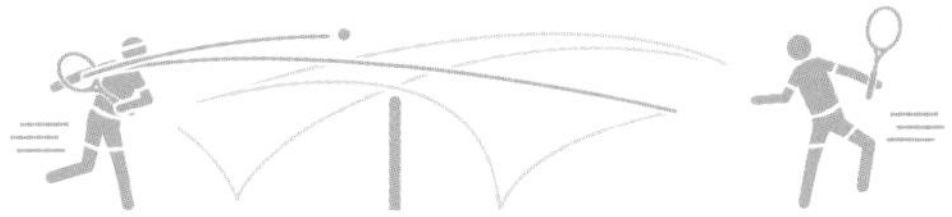

㊳ **der Ballwechsel**
rally

㊴ **zwei Spieler** *m*
**zwei Spielerinnen** *f*
2 players

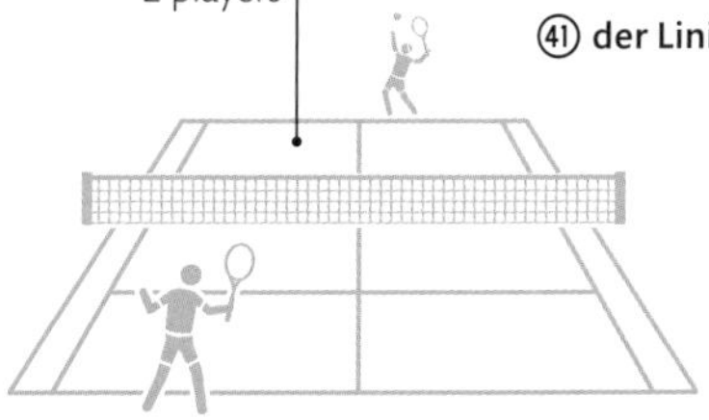

㊵ **das Einzel**
singles

㊶ **der Linienrichter**
linesman

㊷ **vier Spieler** *m*
**vier Spielerinnen** *f*
4 players

㊸ **das Doppel**
doubles

## 114.2 BALLSPORTARTEN MIT SCHLÄGER
RACKET GAMES

① **das Squash**
squash

② **der Racquetball**
racquetball

③ **das Tischtennis / Pingpong**
ping pong / table tennis

④ **der Schläger**
paddle

⑤ **das Badminton**
badminton

⑥ **der Federball**
shuttlecock

## 115.1 AUF DEM GOLFPLATZ · ON THE GOLF COURSE

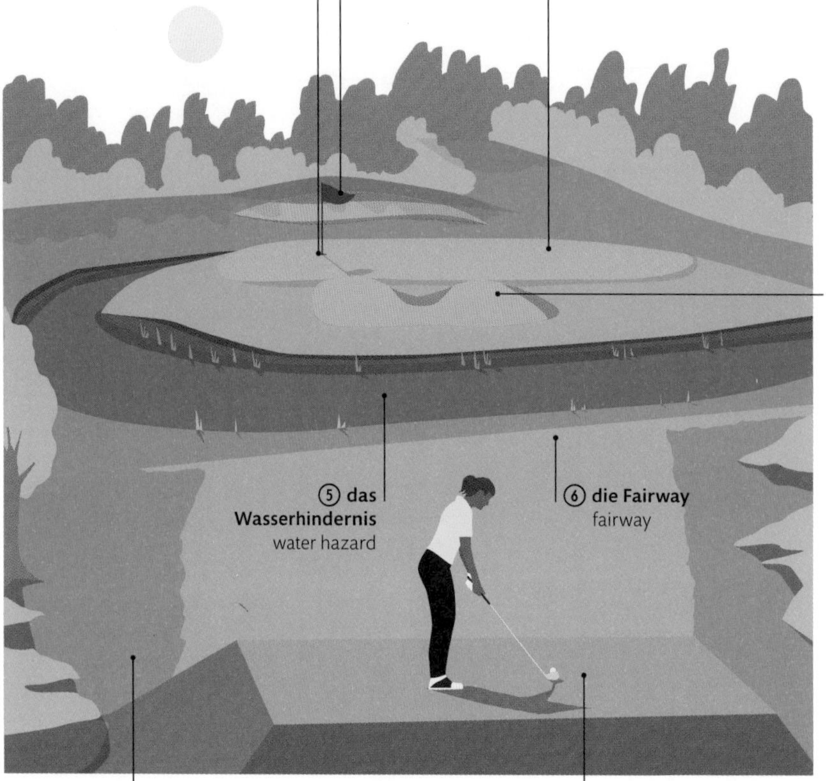

① **das Loch** hole
② **die Fahne** flag
③ **das Grün** green
④ **der Bunker** bunker
⑤ **das Wasserhindernis** water hazard
⑥ **die Fairway** fairway
⑦ **das Rough** rough
⑧ **der Golfplatz** golf course
⑨ **der Abschlagplatz** teeing ground

⑩ **der Schwung** swing
⑪ **der Stand** stance
⑫ **der Golfspieler** *m* **die Golfspielerin** *f* golfer

⑬ **das Clubhaus** clubhouse

⑭ **der Golfwagen** cart

⑮ **der Caddie** caddy

⑯ **das Par** par

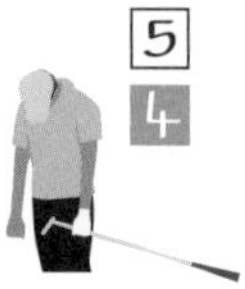


⑰ **über Par** over par

⑱ **unter Par** under par

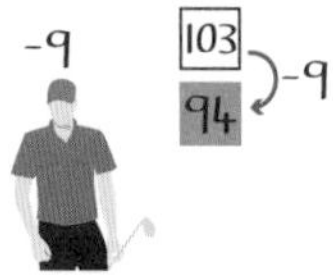


⑲ **das Handicap** handicap

⑳ **die Ziellinie** line of play

㉑ **der Probeschwung** practice swing

㉒ **der Rückschwung** backswing

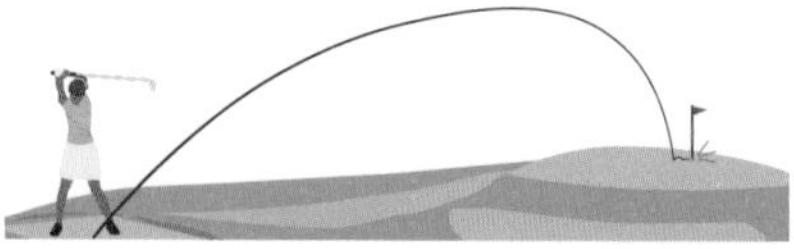

㉓ **das Hole-in-One** hole in one

㉔ **das Turnier** tournament

㉕ **der Zuschauer** *m* **die Zuschauerin** *f* spectators

See also
**111** Kricket • Cricket **113** Baseball
Baseball **114** Tennis • Tennis

## 115.2 GOLFAUSSTATTUNG
GOLF EQUIPMENT

① **die Golfkappe**
golf cap

② **der Golfball**
golf ball

③ **das Tee**
tee

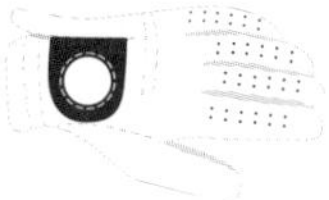

④ **der Handschuh**
glove

⑤ **der Golfschuh**
golf shoe

⑥ **der Stollen**
spikes

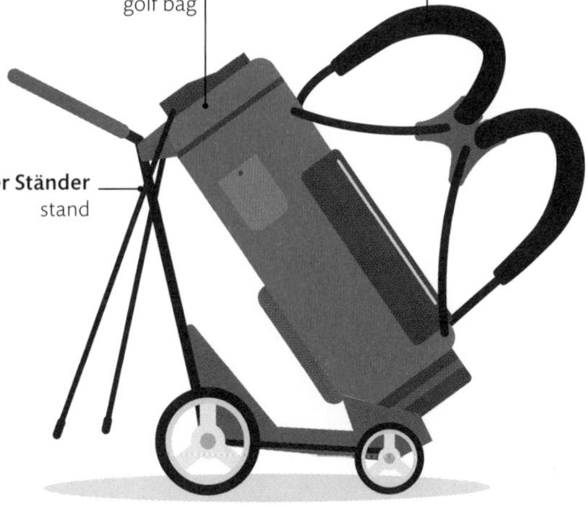

⑦ **die Golftasche**
golf bag

⑧ **der Träger**
harness

**der Ständer**
stand

⑩ **der Trolley**
golf push cart

## 115.3 GOLFSCHLÄGER • GOLF CLUBS

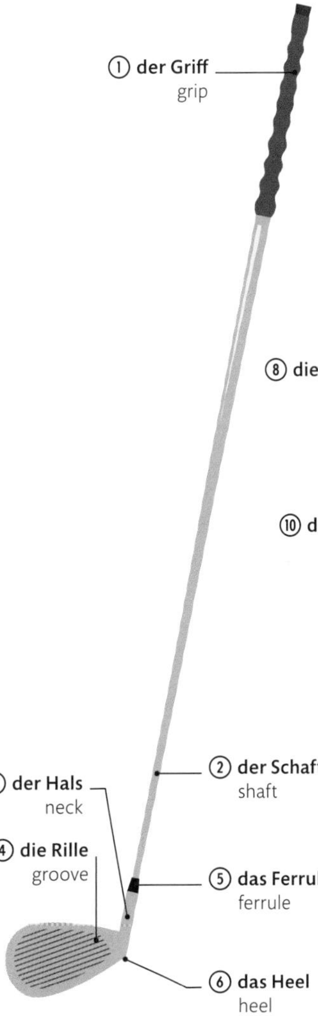

① **der Griff**
grip

② **der Schaft**
shaft

③ **der Hals**
neck

④ **die Rille**
groove

⑤ **das Ferrule**
ferrule

⑥ **das Heel**
heel

⑦ **der Putter**
putter

⑧ **die Sohle**
sole

⑨ **das Holz**
wood

⑩ **der Toe**
toe

⑪ **der Wedge**
wedge

⑫ **das Eisen**
iron

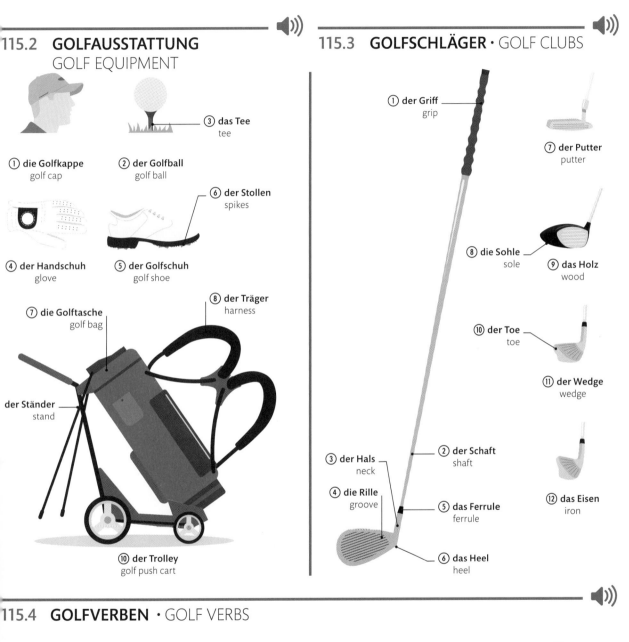

## 115.4 GOLFVERBEN • GOLF VERBS

① **abschlagen**
to tee off

② **driven**
to drive

③ **schwingen**
to swing

④ **putten**
to putt

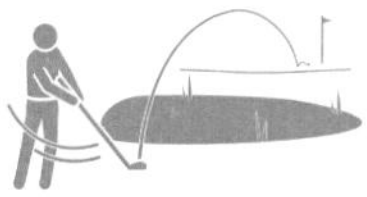

⑤ **chippen**
to chip

⑥ **gewinnen**
to win

# 116 Leichtathletik
## Athletics

### 116.1 DIE LAUFBAHN · ATHLETICS TRACK

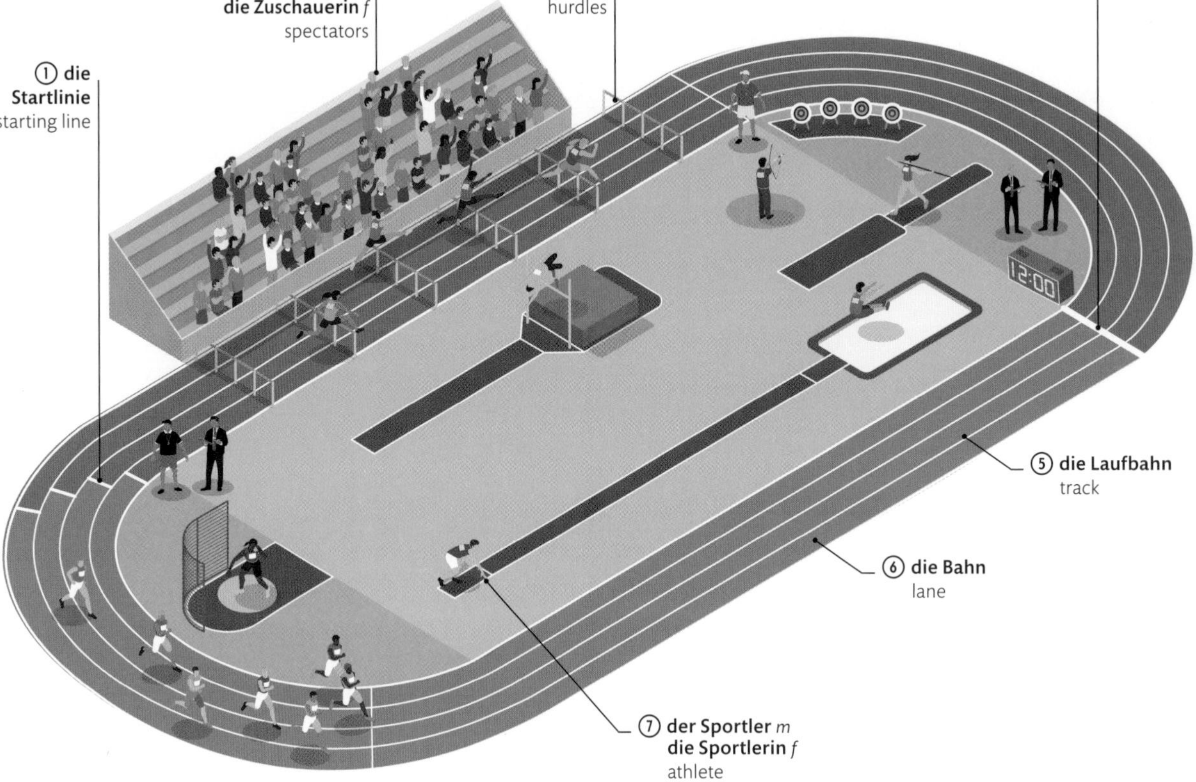


### 116.2 WETTLÄUFE · RACING EVENTS

① **der Wettlauf**
race

② **der Startblock**
starting block

③ **der Sprinter** *m*
**die Sprinterin** *f*
sprinter

④ **der Wettlauf für Sehbehinderte**
T11 (visual impairment) race

⑤ **das Rollstuhlrennen**
wheelchair race

⑥ **die Staffel**
relay race

⑦ **der Staffelstab**
baton

⑧ **der Marathon**
marathon

⑨ **das Fotofinish**
photo finish

See also
117 Kampfsportarten • Combat sports 118 Schwimmen • Swimming 119 Segeln und Wassersport • Sailing and watersports 120 Reiten • Horseback riding 122 Wintersport Winter sports 124 Im Fitnessstudio • At the gym 125 Weitere Sportarten • Other sports

## 116.3 DISZIPLINEN • FIELD EVENTS

① **der Diskuswurf**
discus

② **das Kugelstoßen**
shot put

③ **der Hammerwurf**
hammer

④ **das Speerwerfen**
javelin

⑤ **der Stabhochsprung**
pole vault

⑥ **der Weitsprung**
long jump

⑦ **der Hochsprung**
high jump

⑧ **der Dreisprung**
triple jump

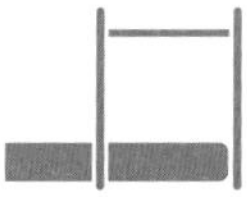
⑨ **die Latte**
crossbar

⑩ **der Laser-Run**
laser run

⑪ **das Fechten**
fencing

## 116.4 AUF DEM PODEST • ON THE PODIUM

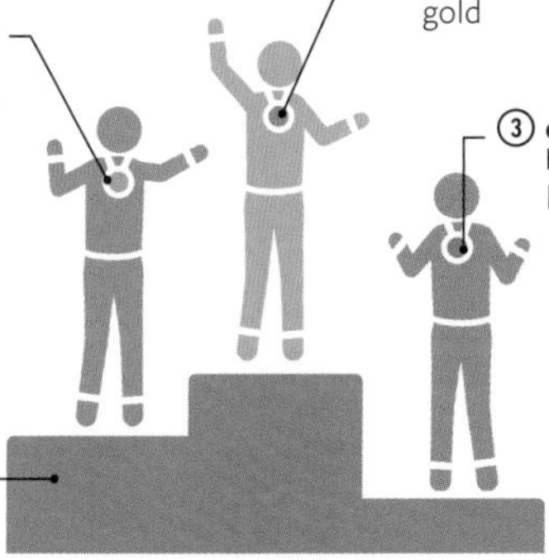
① **die Goldmedaille**
gold

② **die Silbermedaille**
silver

③ **die Bronzemedaille**
bronze

**Siegerpodest**
podium

④ **Medaillen** *f, pl*
medals

## 116.5 MEHRKÄMPFE COMBINED EVENTS

① **der Triathlon**
triathlon

② **der moderne Fünfkampf**
modern pentathlon

③ **der Damen-Siebenkampf**
women's heptathlon

④ **der Herren-Zehnkampf**
men's decathlon

# 117 Kampfsportarten
## Combat sports

### 117.1 DER KAMPFSPORT · MARTIAL ARTS

① **der Leistenschutz** groin protector
② **der Handschuh** glove
③ **der Gurt** belt
④ **der Kopfschutz** head guard
⑤ **der Brustschutz** chest protection
⑥ **Taekwondo** *n* taekwondo

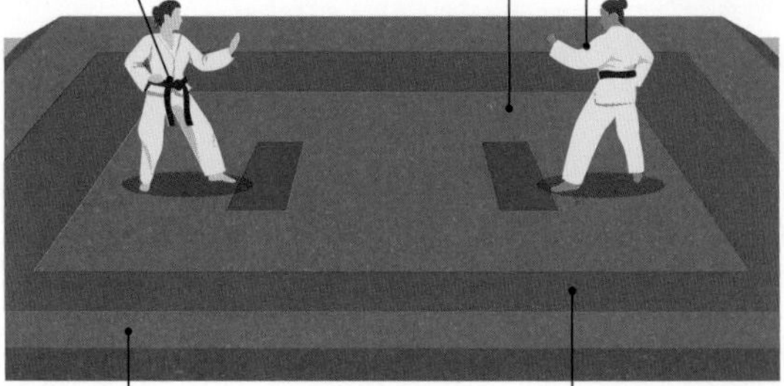

⑦ **der Schwarzgurt** black belt
⑧ **die Karatematte** karate mat
⑨ **der Gegner** *m* **die Gegnerin** *f* opponent
⑩ **die Sicherheitszone** safety area
⑪ **Karate** *n* karate
⑫ **die Gefahrenzor** danger area

⑬ **Judo** *n* judo

⑭ **Aikido** *n* aikido
⑮ **der Hakama** hakama

⑯ **Kung-Fu** *n* kung fu

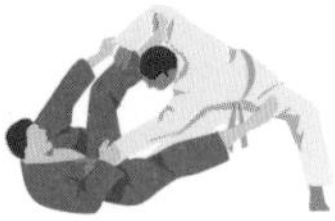

⑰ **Jiu-Jitsu** *n* jujitsu

⑱ **Capoeira** *f* capoeira

⑲ **Kickboxen** *n* kickboxing

⑳ **Tai-Chi** *n* tai chi

㉑ **Wrestling** *n* wrestling

㉒ **Sumoringen** *n* sumo wrestling

㉓ **die Maske** mask
㉔ **das Schwer** sword
㉕ **Kendo** *n* kendo

### 117.2 HANDLUNGEN · ACTIONS

① **fallen** to fall

② **festhalten** to hold

③ **werfen** to throw

④ **niederhalten** to pin

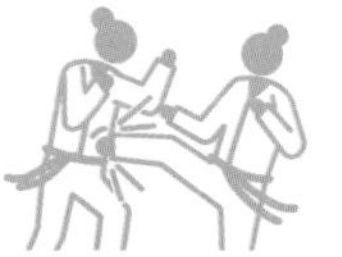

⑤ **der Front-Kick** front kick

⑥ **der Sprungtritt** flying kick

See also
**116** Leichtathletik • Athletics **124** Im Fitnessstudio At the gym **125** Weitere Sportarten • Other sports

## 117.3 BOXEN • BOXING

① **der Ring** boxing ring

② **das Seil** ropes

③ **der Boxkampf** boxing match

④ **die Runde** round

⑤ **der Knock-out** knock out

⑥ **der Boxhandschuh** boxing gloves

⑦ **der Mundschutz** mouth guard

⑧ **der Sandsack** punching bag

## 117.4 FECHTEN • FENCING

① **einen Ausfallschritt machen** to lunge

② **parieren** to parry

③ **das Heft** hilt

⑤ **die Klinge** blade

④ **das Florett** foil

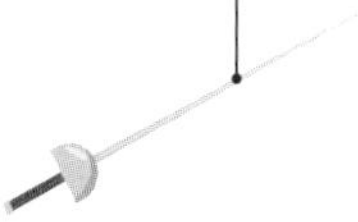

⑥ **der Degen** épée

⑦ **der Säbel** saber

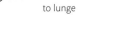

⑦ **schlagen** to punch

⑧ **treffen** to strike

⑨ **blocken** to block

⑩ **springen** to jump

⑪ **zerschlagen** to chop

# 118 Schwimmen
## Swimming

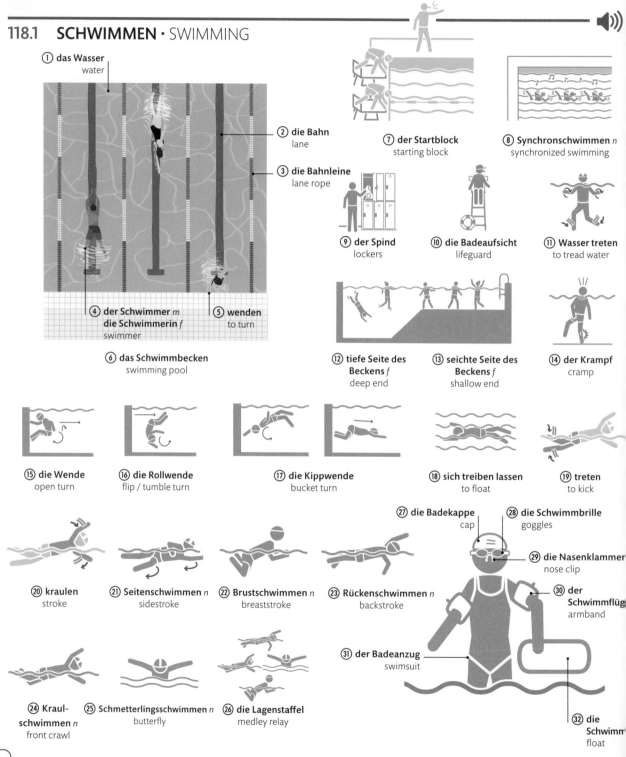

### 118.1 SCHWIMMEN · SWIMMING

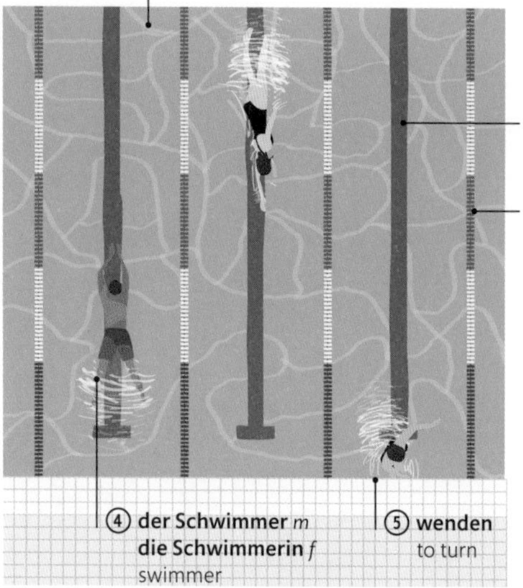

① **das Wasser** water

② **die Bahn** lane

③ **die Bahnleine** lane rope

④ **der Schwimmer** *m* **die Schwimmerin** *f* swimmer

⑤ **wenden** to turn

⑥ **das Schwimmbecken** swimming pool

⑦ **der Startblock** starting block

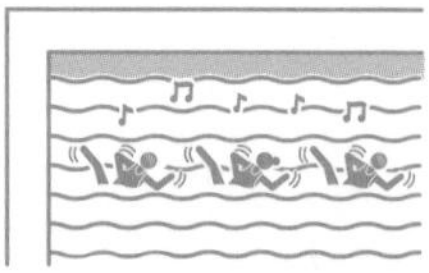

⑧ **Synchronschwimmen** *n* synchronized swimming

⑨ **der Spind** lockers

⑩ **die Badeaufsicht** lifeguard

⑪ **Wasser treten** to tread water

⑫ **tiefe Seite des Beckens** *f* deep end

⑬ **seichte Seite des Beckens** *f* shallow end

⑭ **der Krampf** cramp

⑮ **die Wende** open turn

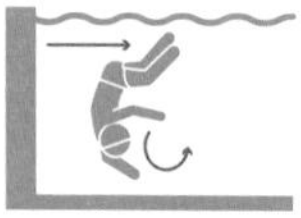

⑯ **die Rollwende** flip / tumble turn

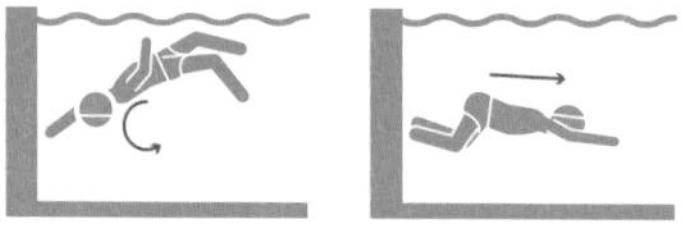

⑰ **die Kippwende** bucket turn

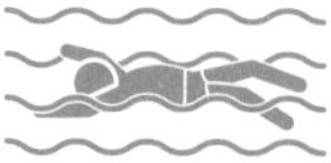

⑱ **sich treiben lassen** to float

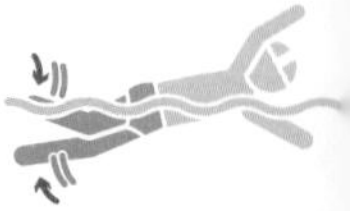

⑲ **treten** to kick

⑳ **kraulen** stroke

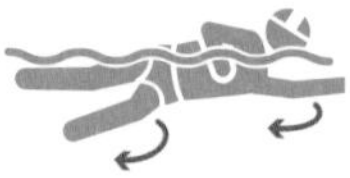

㉑ **Seitenschwimmen** *n* sidestroke

㉒ **Brustschwimmen** *n* breaststroke

㉓ **Rückenschwimmen** *n* backstroke

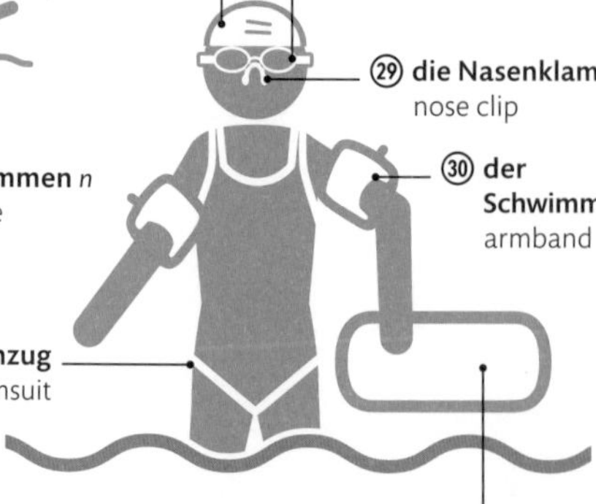

㉗ **die Badekappe** cap

㉘ **die Schwimmbrille** goggles

㉙ **die Nasenklammer** nose clip

㉚ **der Schwimmflüg** armband

㉛ **der Badeanzug** swimsuit

㉜ **die Schwimm** float

㉔ **Kraul-schwimmen** *n* front crawl

㉕ **Schmetterlingsschwimmen** *n* butterfly

㉖ **die Lagenstaffel** medley relay

See also
**119** Segeln und Wassersport • Sailing and watersports
**134** Am Strand • On the beach **166** Leben im Ozean • Ocean life

## 118.2 TURMSPRINGEN DIVING

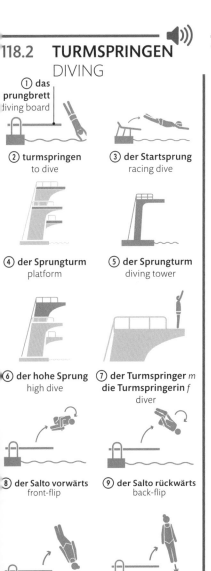

① **das prungbrett**
iving board

② **turmspringen**
to dive

③ **der Startsprung**
racing dive

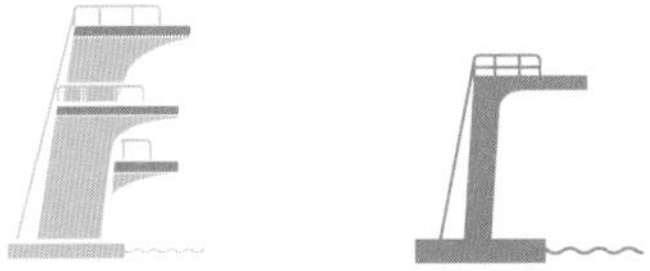

④ **der Sprungturm**
platform

⑤ **der Sprungturm**
diving tower

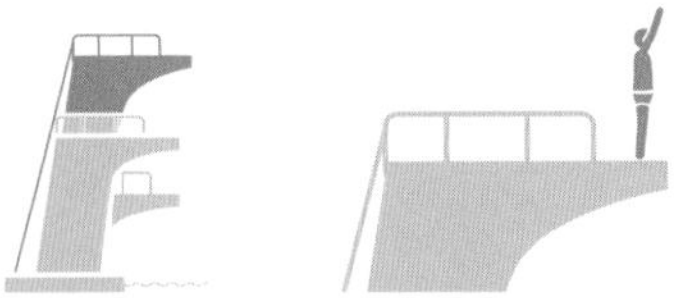

⑥ **der hohe Sprung**
high dive

⑦ **der Turmspringer** *m*
**die Turmspringerin** *f*
diver

**Salto vorwärts**
front-flip

⑨ **der Salto rückwärts**
back-flip

⑩ **der Kopfsprung**
head-first

⑪ **mit den Füßen voraus**
feet-first

⑫ **das Sprungbrett**
springboard

## 118.3 TAUCHEN • UNDERWATER DIVING

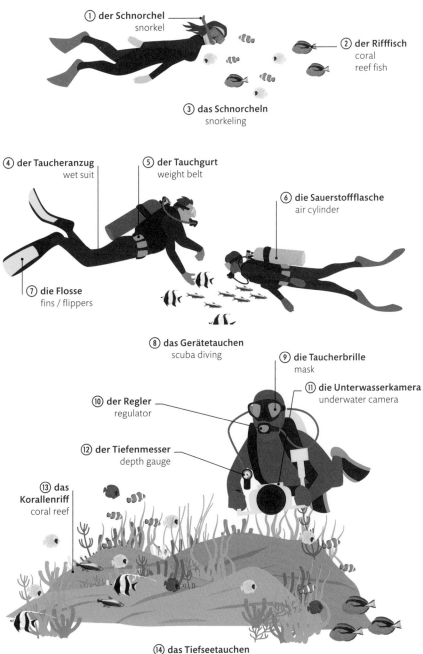

① **der Schnorchel**
snorkel

② **der Rifffisch**
coral reef fish

③ **das Schnorcheln**
snorkeling

④ **der Taucheranzug**
wet suit

⑤ **der Tauchgurt**
weight belt

⑥ **die Sauerstoffflasche**
air cylinder

⑦ **die Flosse**
fins / flippers

⑧ **das Gerätetauchen**
scuba diving

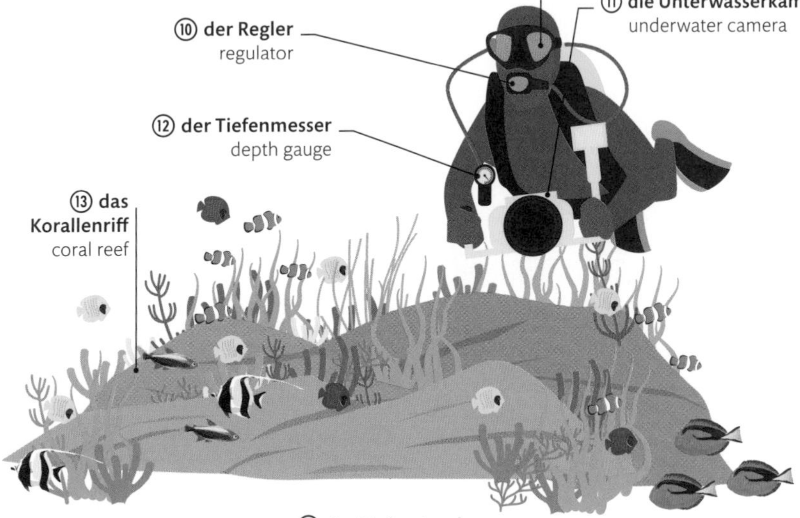

⑨ **die Taucherbrille**
mask

⑩ **der Regler**
regulator

⑪ **die Unterwasserkamera**
underwater camera

⑫ **der Tiefenmesser**
depth gauge

⑬ **das Korallenriff**
coral reef

⑭ **das Tiefseetauchen**
deep diving

# 119 Segeln und Wassersport
## Sailing and watersports

### 119.1 SEGELN · SAILING

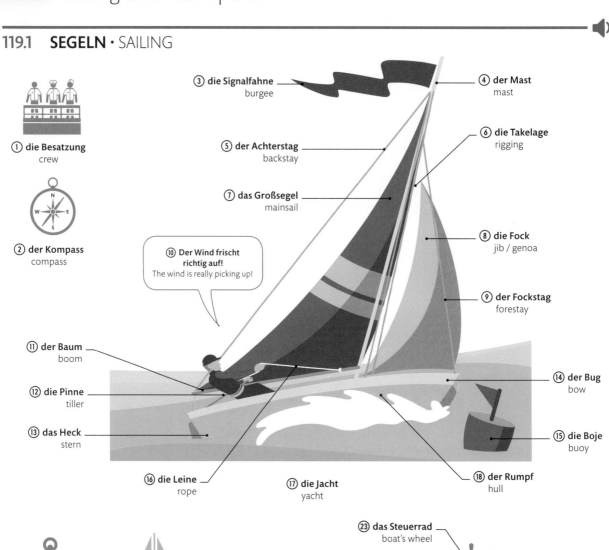

① **die Besatzung**
crew

② **der Kompass**
compass

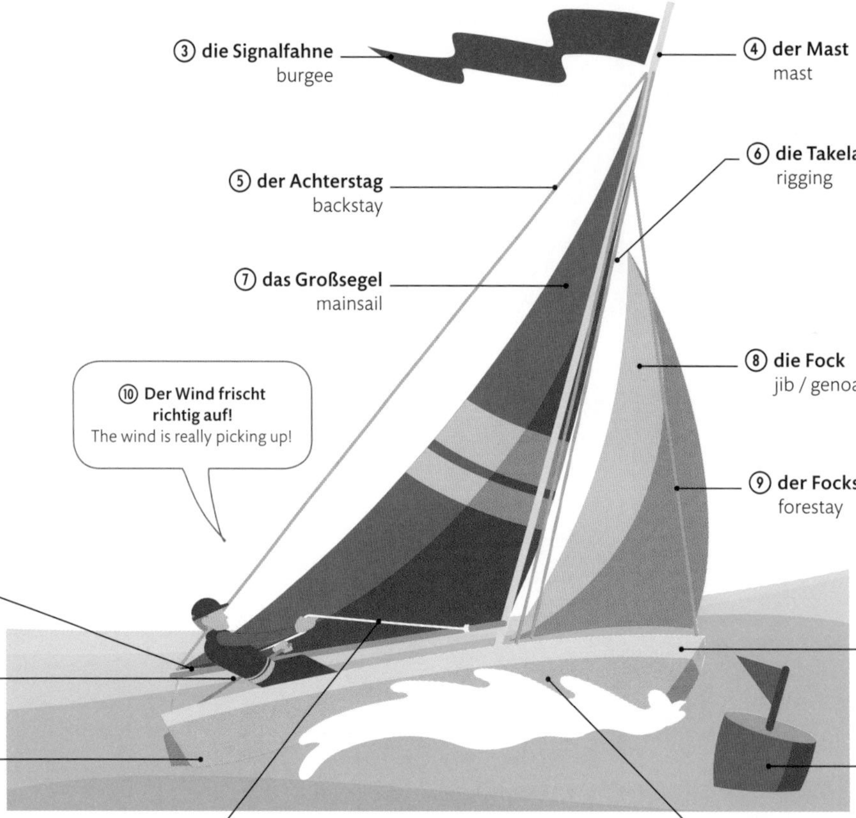

⑲ **der Anker**
anchor

⑳ **die Schot**
sheet

㉑ **die Klampe**
cleat

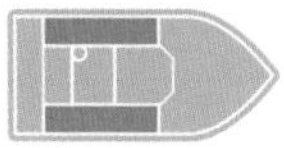

㉒ **das Seitendeck**
sidedeck

㉔ **das Steuer**
helm

㉕ **das Kielschwer**
centerboard

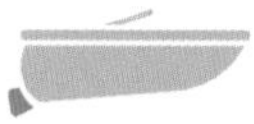

㉖ **das Ruder**
rudder

㉗ **der Kiel**
keel

㉘ **die Leuchtfackel**
flare

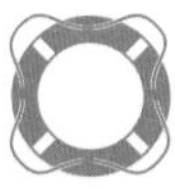

㉙ **der Rettungsring**
life preserver

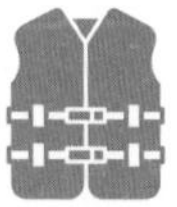

㉚ **die Schwimmweste**
life jacket

㉛ **das Rettungsboo**
life raft

See also
**105** Seefahrzeuge • Sea vessels **106** Der Hafen • The port **118** Schwimmen • Swimming
**121** Fischen • Fishing **134** Am Strand • On the beach

## 119.2 WASSERSPORT • WATERSPORTS

**Ruderer** *m*
**ie Ruderin** *f*
rower

③ **das Ruder**
oar

② **Rudern** *n*
rowing

④ **das Kajak**
kayak

⑥ **das Paddel**
paddle

⑤ **Kajakfahren** *n*
kayaking

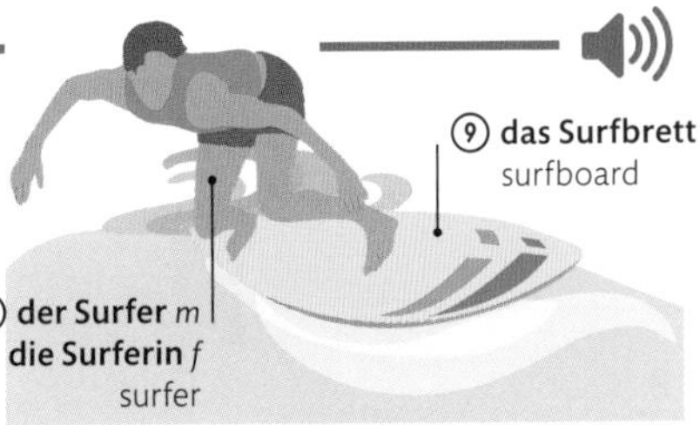

⑨ **das Surfbrett**
surfboard

⑦ **der Surfer** *m*
**die Surferin** *f*
surfer

⑧ **Surfen** *n*
surfing

⑩ **das**
**oogiebrett**
ogie board

⑪ **Bodyboarding** *n*
bodyboarding

⑫ **Paddleboarding** *n*
paddleboarding

⑬ **Parasailing** *n*
parasailing

⑭ **Kitesurfen** *n*
kite surfing

⑳ **der Ski**
ski

㉑ **der Wasserskifahrer** *m*
**die Wasserskifahrerin** *f*
water skier

⑲ **Wasserskifahren** *n*
water skiing

⑮ **Sportbootfahren** *n*
speed boating

⑯ **Rafting** *n*
rafting

⑰ **Jetskifahren** *n*
jet skiing

⑱ **Wasserball** *n*
water polo

㉒ **kentern**
to capsize

㉓ **navigieren**
to navigate

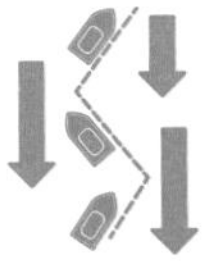

㉔ **kreuzen**
to tack

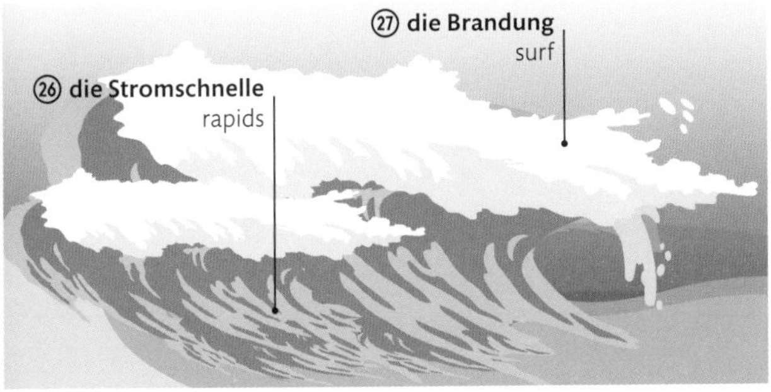

㉗ **die Brandung**
surf

㉖ **die Stromschnelle**
rapids

㉕ **die Welle**
wave

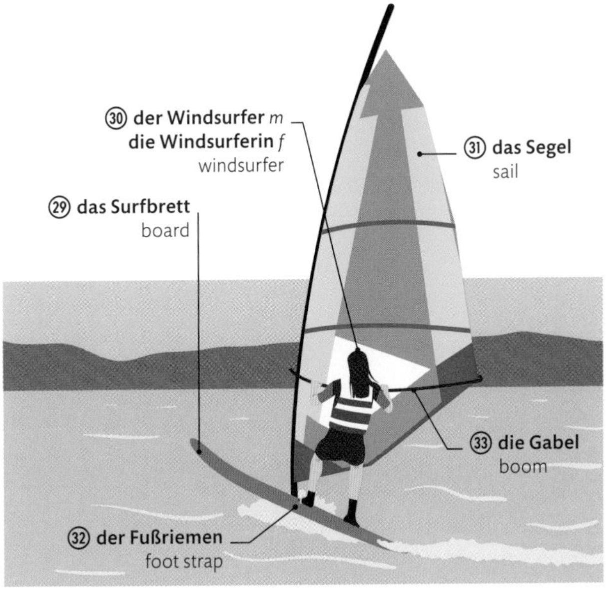

㉚ **der Windsurfer** *m*
**die Windsurferin** *f*
windsurfer

㉛ **das Segel**
sail

㉙ **das Surfbrett**
board

㉝ **die Gabel**
boom

㉜ **der Fußriemen**
foot strap

㉘ **Windsurfen** *n*
windsurfing

# 120 Reiten
## Horseback riding

### 120.1 REITEN · HORSEBACK RIDING

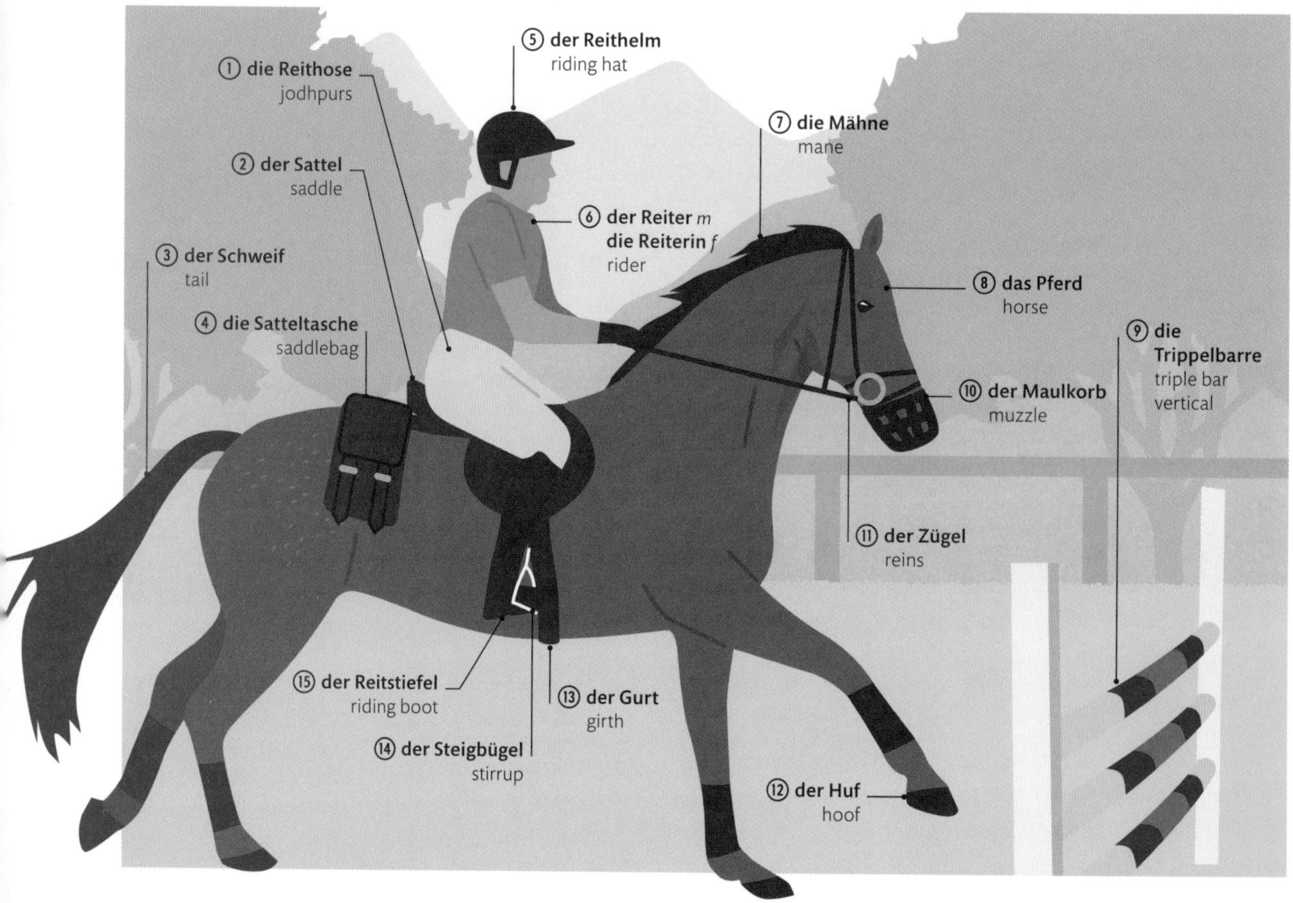

(16) **das Hufeisen**
horseshoe

(17) **das Halfter**
halter

(18) **der Nasenriemen**
noseband

(19) **das Gebiss**
bit

(20) **der Stirnriemen**
browband

(21) **das Zaumzeug**
bridle

(22) **der Vorderzwiesel**
pommel

(23) **der Sitz**
seat

(24) **die Gerte**
riding crop

(25) **der Jockey**
jockey

(26) **das Rennpferd**
racehorse

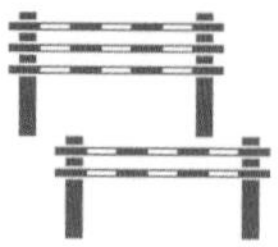
(27) **das Hindernis**
verticals

See also
**116** Leichtathletik • Athletics **125** Weitere Sportarten • Other sports
**133** Aktivitäten im Freien • Outdoor activities

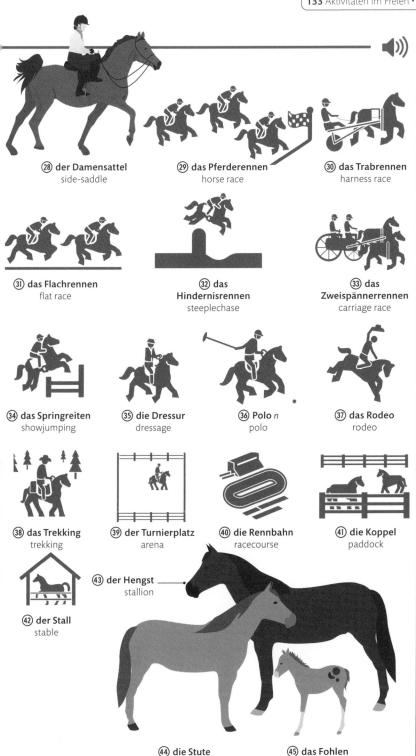

(28) **der Damensattel**
side-saddle

(29) **das Pferderennen**
horse race

(30) **das Trabrennen**
harness race

(31) **das Flachrennen**
flat race

(32) **das Hindernisrennen**
steeplechase

(33) **das Zweispännerrennen**
carriage race

(34) **das Springreiten**
showjumping

(35) **die Dressur**
dressage

(36) **Polo** *n*
polo

(37) **das Rodeo**
rodeo

(38) **das Trekking**
trekking

(39) **der Turnierplatz**
arena

(40) **die Rennbahn**
racecourse

(41) **die Koppel**
paddock

(42) **der Stall**
stable

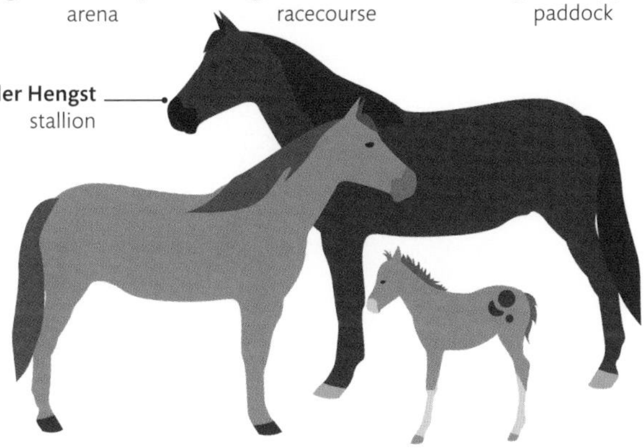

(43) **der Hengst**
stallion

(44) **die Stute**
mare

(45) **das Fohlen**
foal

## 120.2 VERBEN • VERBS

(1) **striegeln**
to groom

(2) **im Schritt reiten**
to walk

(3) **traben**
to trot

(4) **im leichten Galopp reiten**
to canter

(5) **galoppieren**
to gallop

(6) **springen**
to jump

(7) **züchten**
to breed

(8) **ausmisten**
to muck out

# 121 Fischen
## Fishing

### 121.1 ANGLER · ANGLER

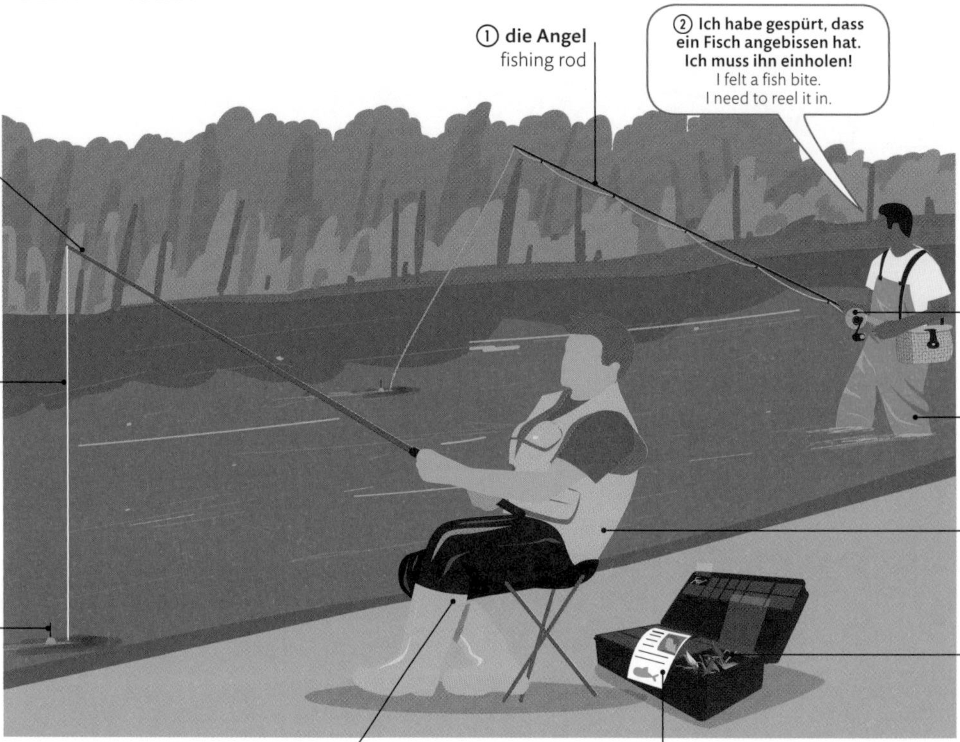

② Ich habe gespürt, dass ein Fisch angebissen hat. Ich muss ihn einholen!
I felt a fish bite. I need to reel it in.

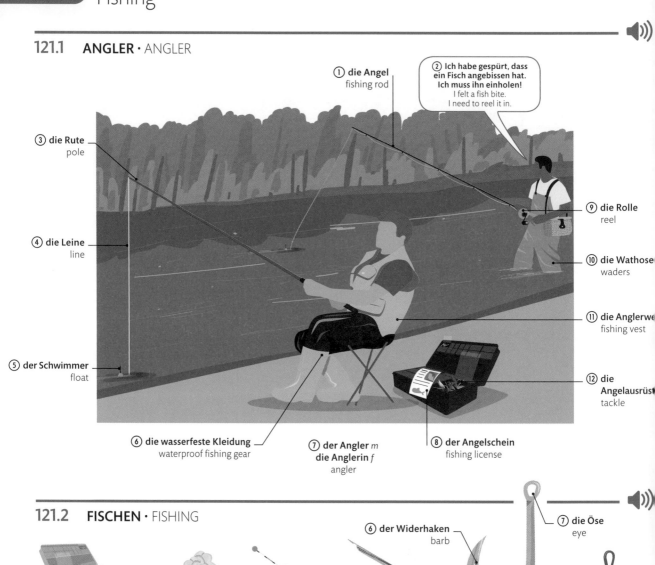

① **die Angel** fishing rod

③ **die Rute** pole

④ **die Leine** line

⑤ **der Schwimmer** float

⑥ **die wasserfeste Kleidung** waterproof fishing gear

⑦ **der Angler** *m* **die Anglerin** *f* angler

⑧ **der Angelschein** fishing license

⑨ **die Rolle** reel

⑩ **die Wathose** waders

⑪ **die Anglerwe** fishing vest

⑫ **die Angelausrüs** tackle

### 121.2 FISCHEN · FISHING

① **der Angelkasten** tackle box

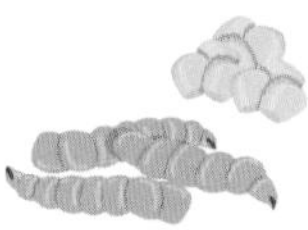

② **der Naturköder** bait

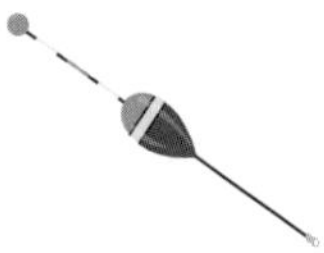

③ **der Schwimmer** float

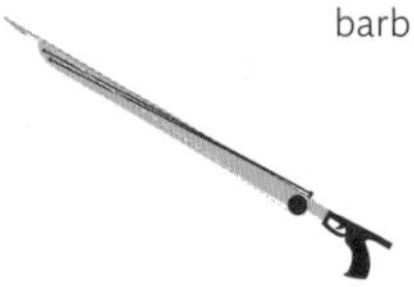

④ **die Harpune** harpoon

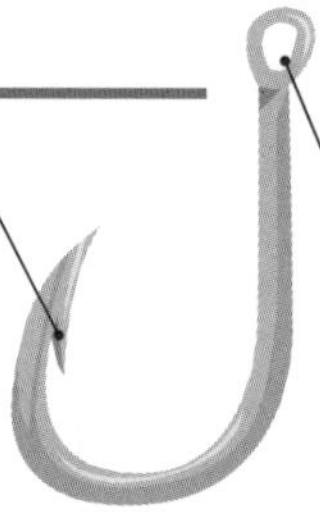

⑤ **der Angelhaken** fishhook

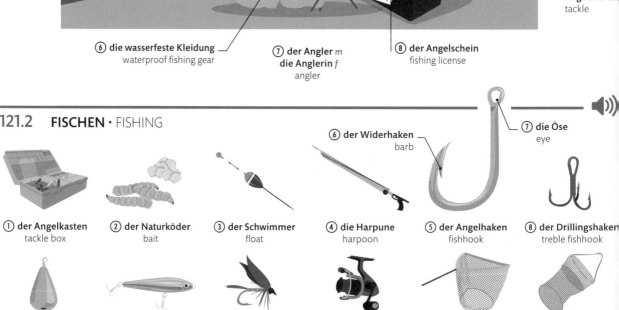

⑥ **der Widerhaken** barb

⑦ **die Öse** eye

⑧ **der Drillingshaken** treble fishhook

⑨ **das Gewicht** weight

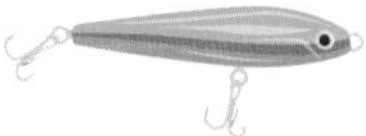

⑩ **der Kunstköder** lure

⑪ **die Fliege** fly

⑫ **die Rolle** reel

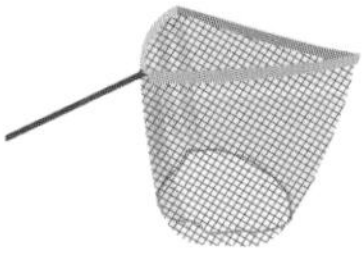

⑬ **der Kescher** landing net

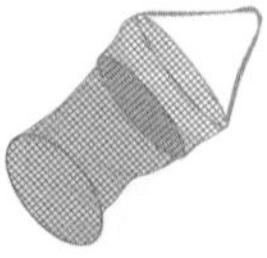

⑭ **der Setzkescher** keep net

See also
**54** Fisch und Meeresfrüchte • Fish and seafood **119** Segeln und Wassersport
Sailing and watersports **166** Leben im Ozean • Ocean life

## 121.3 FISCHEREIDISZIPLINEN
TYPES OF FISHING

① **die Fliegenfischerei**
fly fishing

② **die Süßwasserfischerei**
freshwater fishing

③ **die Seefischerei**
marine fishing

④ **die Tiefseefischerei**
deep sea fishing

⑤ **die Sportfischerei**
sport fishing

⑥ **die Unterwasserfischerei**
spearfishing

⑦ **die Eisfischerei**
ice fishing

⑧ **der Ständer**
stand

⑨ **das Brandungsangeln**
surfcasting

## 121.4 FISCHEREIVERBEN • FISHING VERBS

① **ködern**
to bait

② **auswerfen**
to cast

③ **anbeißen**
to bite

④ **fangen**
to catch

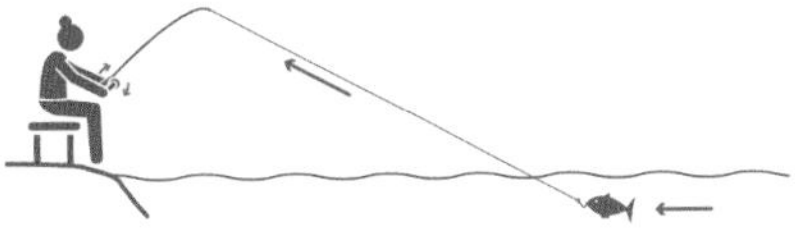

⑤ **einholen**
to reel in

⑥ **mit dem Netz fangen**
to net

⑦ **freilassen**
to release

## 121.5 KNOTEN • KNOTS

① **der Clinchknoten**
clinch knot

② **der Blutknoten**
blood knot

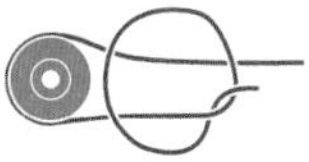

③ **der Arborknoten**
arbor knot

④ **der Snell-Knoten**
snell knot

⑤ **der Turle-Knoten**
turle knot

⑥ **der Palomar-Knoten**
palomar knot

# 122 Wintersport
## Winter sports

### 122.1 **SKIFAHREN** · SKIING

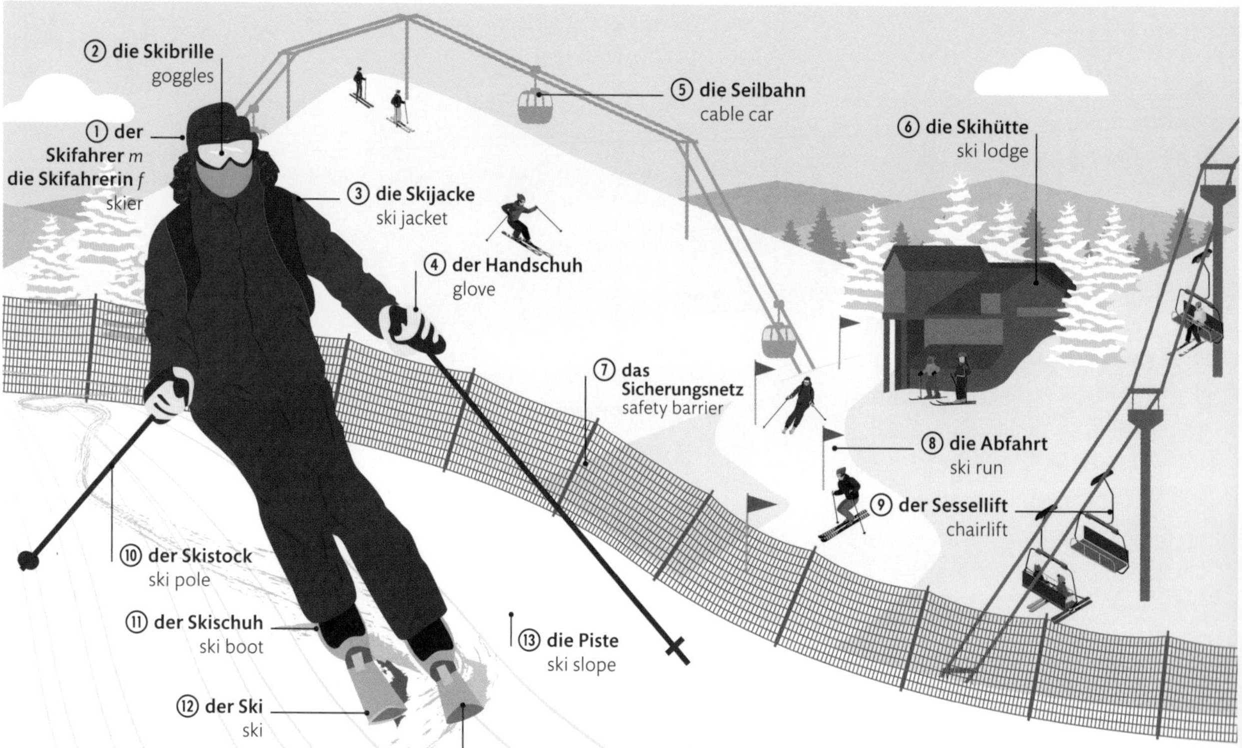


**⑭ die Spitze**
tip

**⑮ das Skigebiet**
ski resort

**⑯ Ski fahren**
to ski

**⑰ die Abfahrt**
downhill skiing

**⑱ der Slalom**
slalom

**⑲ der Riesenslalom**
giant slalom

**⑳ der Skilanglauf**
cross-country skiing

**㉑ abseits der Piste**
off-piste

**㉒ der Biathlon**
biathlon

**㉓ die Lawine**
avalanche

**㉔ die Aufsprungbahn**
landing hill

**㉕ das Tor**
gate

**㉖ der Skisprung**
ski jump

**㉗ die Sprungschanze**
jumping ramp

See also
**116** Leichtathletik • Athletics **124** Im Fitnessstudio • At the gym
**125** Weitere Sportarten • Other sports

## 122.2 WEITERE WINTERSPORTARTEN • OTHER WINTER SPORTS

① **Wintersport** *m*
winter sports

② **der Schlittschuh**
skate

③ **Eislaufen** *n*
ice-skating

④ **Eisschnelllauf** *m*
speed skating

⑤ **Eiskunstlauf** *m*
figure skating

⑥ **Snowboardfahren** *n*
snowboarding

⑦ **Rodeln** *n*
luge

⑧ **Skeleton** *m*
skeleton

⑨ **Schlittenfahren** *n*
sledding

⑩ **Bobfahren** *n*
bobsled

⑬ **Eisklettern** *n*
ice climbing

⑭ **das Schneemobil**
snowmobile

⑮ **Para-Eishockey** *n*
para ice hockey

⑯ **Rollstuhlcurling** *n*
wheelchair curling

⑰ **Curling** *n*
curling

㉔ **das Schlittenhunderennen**
dog sledding

㉕ **die Olympischen Winterspiele** *pl*
Winter Olympics

# 123 Motorsport
## Motorsports

### 123.1 DER RENNWAGEN · RACE CAR

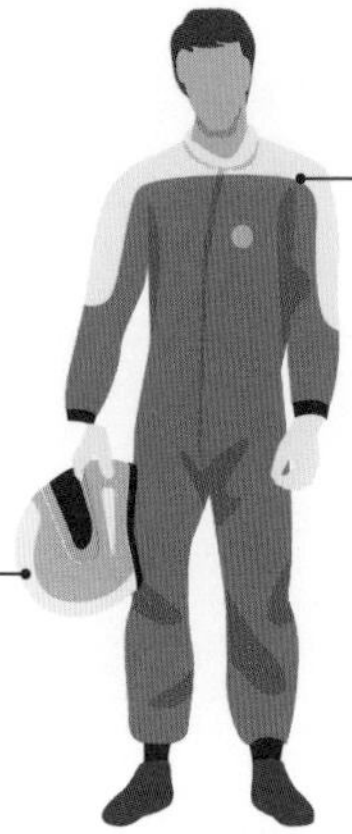

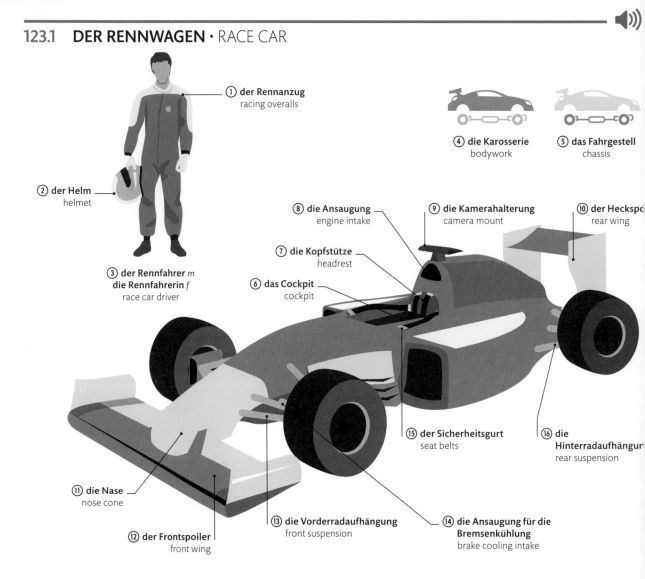

① **der Rennanzug**
racing overalls

② **der Helm**
helmet

③ **der Rennfahrer** *m*
**die Rennfahrerin** *f*
race car driver

④ **die Karosserie**
bodywork

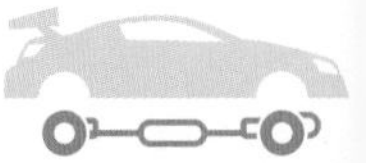

⑤ **das Fahrgestell**
chassis

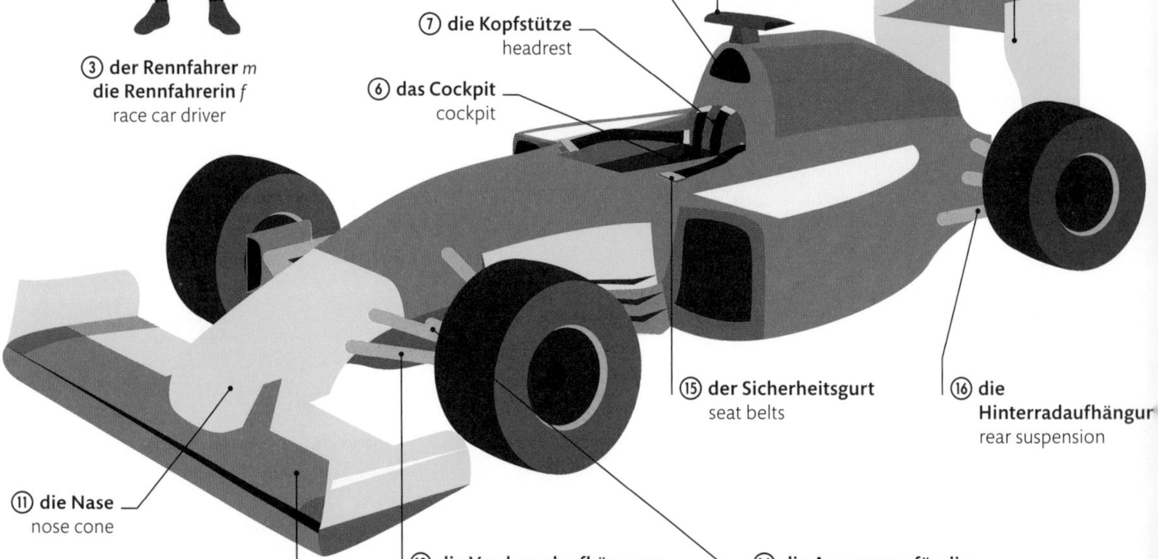

⑥ **das Cockpit**
cockpit

⑦ **die Kopfstütze**
headrest

⑧ **die Ansaugung**
engine intake

⑨ **die Kamerahalterung**
camera mount

⑩ **der Heckspo**
rear wing

⑪ **die Nase**
nose cone

⑫ **der Frontspoiler**
front wing

⑬ **die Vorderradaufhängung**
front suspension

⑭ **die Ansaugung für die Bremsenkühlung**
brake cooling intake

⑮ **der Sicherheitsgurt**
seat belts

⑯ **die Hinterradaufhängun**
rear suspension

### 123.2 MOTORSPORTDISZIPLINEN · TYPES OF MOTORSPORTS

① **das Autorennen**
auto racing

② **die Rallye**
rally driving

③ **das Dragracing**
drag racing

See also
**96** Straßen • Roads **97-98** Autos • Cars **99** Autos und Busse
Cars and buses **100** Motorräder • Motorcycles

## 123.3 DIE RENNSTRECKE • RACE TRACK

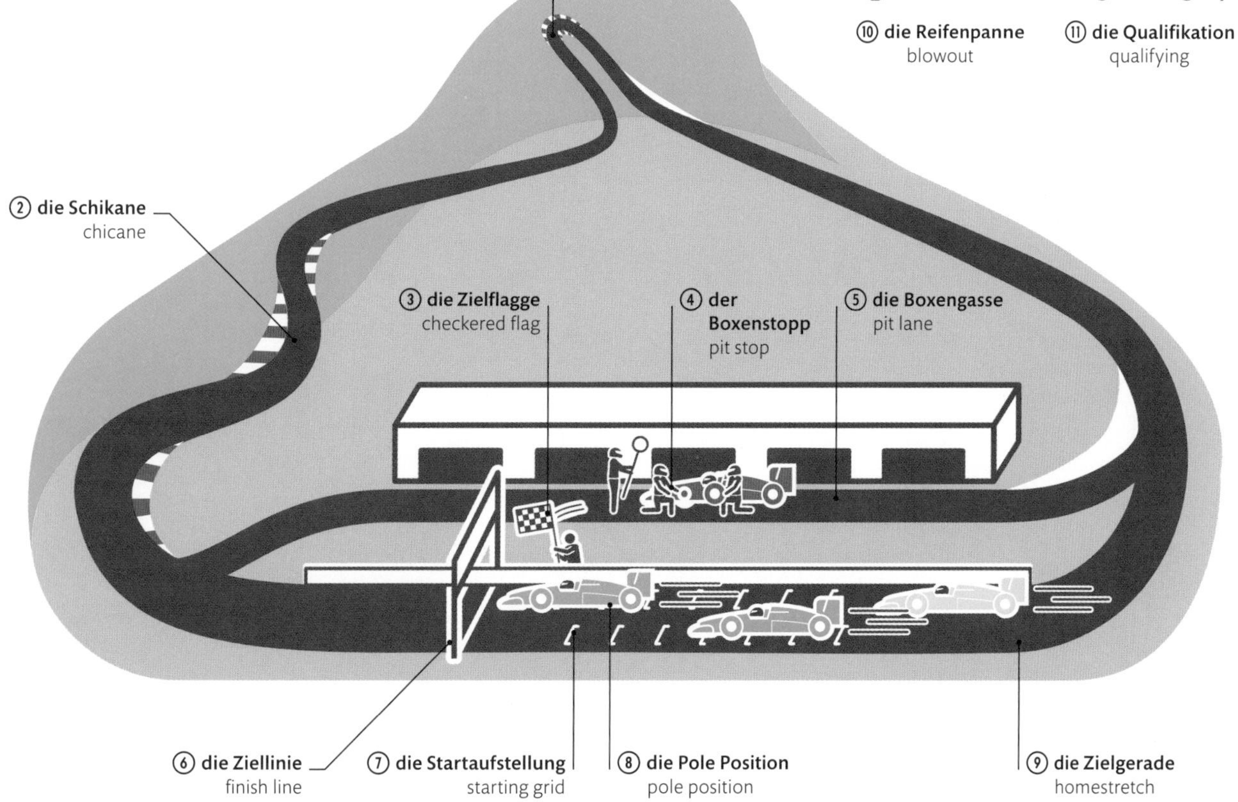

**⑩ die Reifenpanne**
blowout

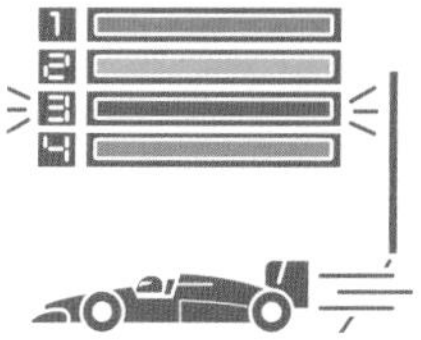

**⑪ die Qualifikation**
qualifying

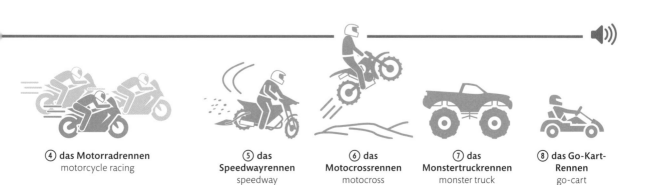

**④ das Motorradrennen**
motorcycle racing

**⑤ das Speedwayrennen**
speedway

**⑥ das Motocrossrennen**
motocross

**⑦ das Monstertruckrennen**
monster truck

**⑧ das Go-Kart-Rennen**
go-cart

# 124 Im Fitnessstudio

At the gym

## 124.1 SPORT TREIBEN · WORKING OUT

② Ich mache dreimal die Woche Sport.
I exercise three times a week.
① Wie oft treibst du Sport?
How often do you work out?
③ der Cross-Trainer
elliptical
⑤ das Rudergerät
rowing machine
④ Sport treiben
working out
⑥ der Heimtrainer
exercise bike
⑫ die Fitnessgeräte n, pl
gym machines

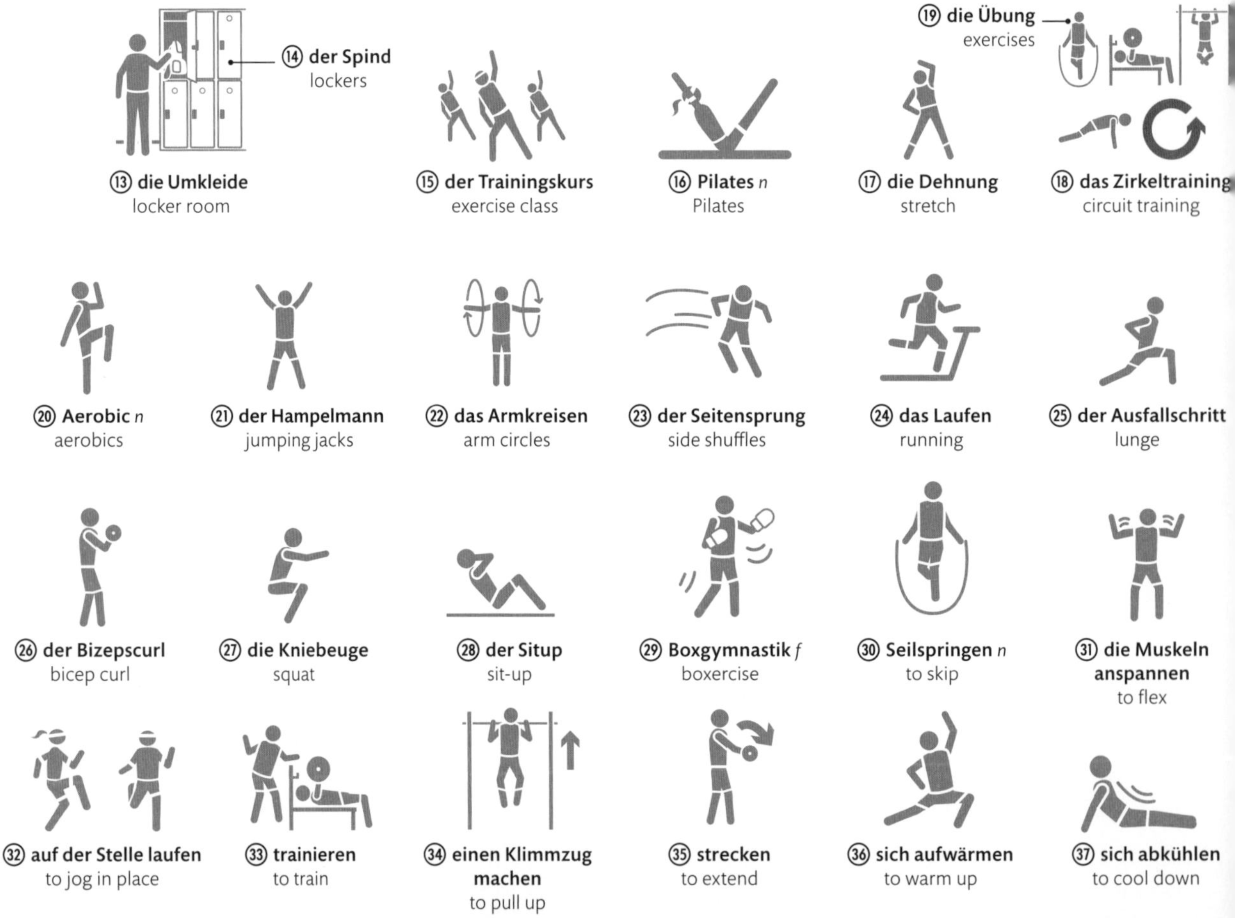
⑲ die Übung
exercises
⑭ der Spind
lockers
⑬ die Umkleide
locker room
⑮ der Trainingskurs
exercise class
⑯ Pilates n
Pilates
⑰ die Dehnung
stretch
⑱ das Zirkeltraining
circuit training
⑳ Aerobic n
aerobics
㉑ der Hampelmann
jumping jacks
㉒ das Armkreisen
arm circles
㉓ der Seitensprung
side shuffles
㉔ das Laufen
running
㉕ der Ausfallschritt
lunge
㉖ der Bizepscurl
bicep curl
㉗ die Kniebeuge
squat
㉘ der Situp
sit-up
㉙ Boxgymnastik f
boxercise
㉚ Seilspringen n
to skip
㉛ die Muskeln anspannen
to flex
㉜ auf der Stelle laufen
to jog in place
㉝ trainieren
to train
㉞ einen Klimmzug machen
to pull up
㉟ strecken
to extend
㊱ sich aufwärmen
to warm up
㊲ sich abkühlen
to cool down

See also
**116** Leichtathletik • Athletics **117** Kampfsportarten • Combat sports **118** Schwimmen • Swimming
**122** Wintersport • Winter sports **125** Weitere Sportarten • Other sports

㊳ **die Mitgliedschaft**
membership

㊴ **das Fitnessgerät**
gym equipment

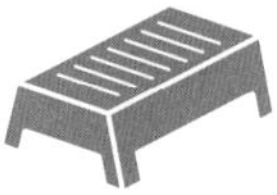

㊵ **der Aerobic-Stepper**
aerobics step

㊶ **die Hantel**
dumbbell

㊷ **der Handgriff**
hand grips

㊸ **die Hantelstange**
barbell

㊹ **die Stange**
bar

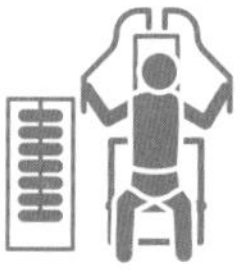

㊺ **das Brustdrücken**
chest press

㊻ **das Springseil**
jump rope

㊼ **der Gymnastikball**
exercise ball

㊽ **die Drehstange**
twist bar

㊾ **die Gewichtsmanschette**
ankle weights / wrist weights

㊿ **die Beinpresse**
leg press

(51) **der Brustexpander**
chest expander

(52) **das Ab Wheel**
ab wheel

(53) **das Laufband**
running machine

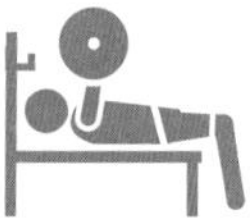

(54) **die Bank**
bench

(55) **der Puls**
heart rate

(56) **die Sauna**
sauna

(57) **der Whirlpool**
hot tub

(58) **der Personal Trainer** *m*
**die Personal Trainerin** *f*
personal trainer

# 125 Weitere Sportarten
## Other sports

### 125.1 TURNEN · GYMNASTICS

1. **die Bodenmatte** floor mat
2. **der Reifen** hoop
3. **das Band** ribbon
4. **der Barren** horizontal bar
5. **der Sprungtisch** vault
6. **der Stufenbarren** uneven bars
7. **der Schwebebalken** beam
8. **das Pferd** pommel horse
9. **die Ringe** *m, pl* rings
10. **der Parallelbarren** parallel bars
11. **das Sprungbrett** springboard

### 125.2 WEITERE SPORTARTEN · OTHER SPORTS

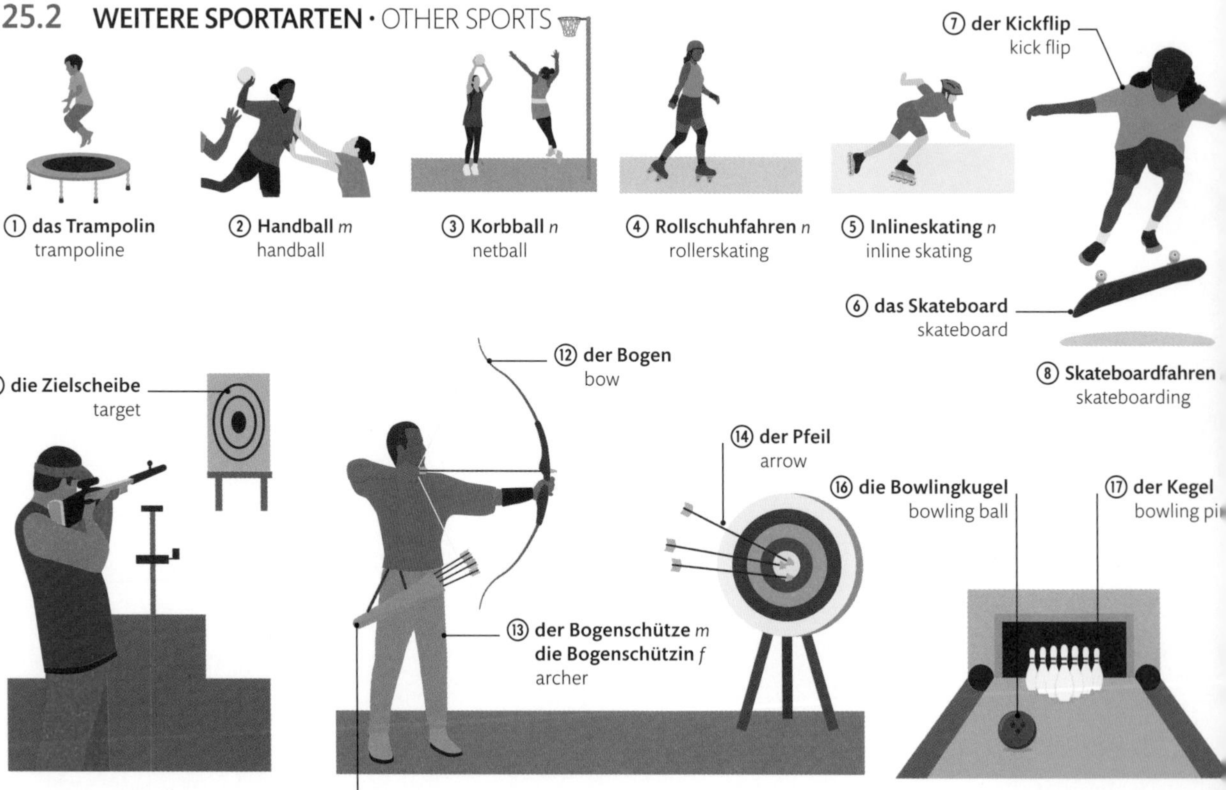

1. **das Trampolin** trampoline
2. **Handball** *m* handball
3. **Korbball** *n* netball
4. **Rollschuhfahren** *n* rollerskating
5. **Inlineskating** *n* inline skating
6. **das Skateboard** skateboard
7. **der Kickflip** kick flip
8. **Skateboardfahren** skateboarding
9. **die Zielscheibe** target
10. **Sportschießen** *n* target shooting
11. **der Köcher** quiver
12. **der Bogen** bow
13. **der Bogenschütze** *m* **die Bogenschützin** *f* archer
14. **der Pfeil** arrow
15. **Bogenschießen** *n* archery
16. **die Bowlingkugel** bowling ball
17. **der Kegel** bowling pi
18. **Bowling** *n* bowling

See also
116 Leichtathletik • Athletics 117 Kampfsportarten • Combat sports 118 Schwimmen • Swimming
120 Reiten • Horseback riding 122 Wintersport • Winter sports 124 Im Fitnessstudio • At the gym

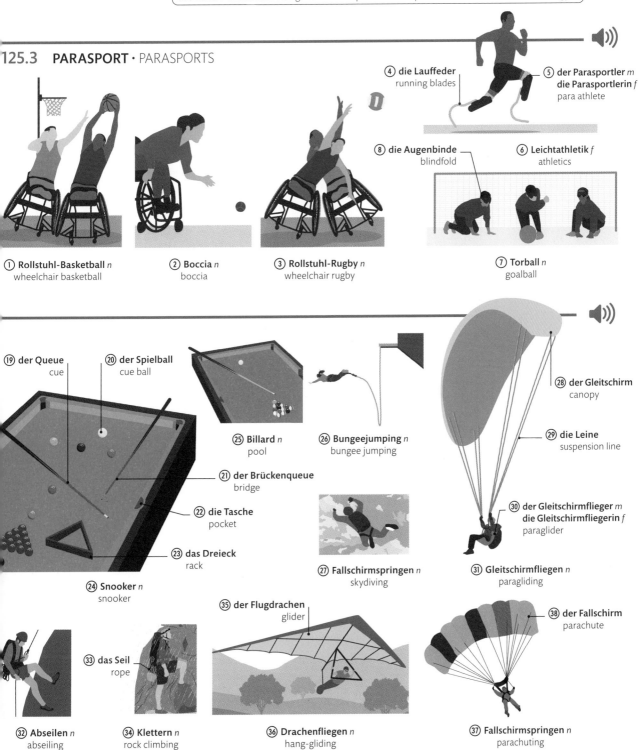

## 125.3 PARASPORT • PARASPORTS

① **Rollstuhl-Basketball** *n*
wheelchair basketball

② **Boccia** *n*
boccia

③ **Rollstuhl-Rugby** *n*
wheelchair rugby

④ **die Lauffeder**
running blades

⑤ **der Parasportler** *m*
**die Parasportlerin** *f*
para athlete

⑥ **Leichtathletik** *f*
athletics

⑧ **die Augenbinde**
blindfold

⑦ **Torball** *n*
goalball

---

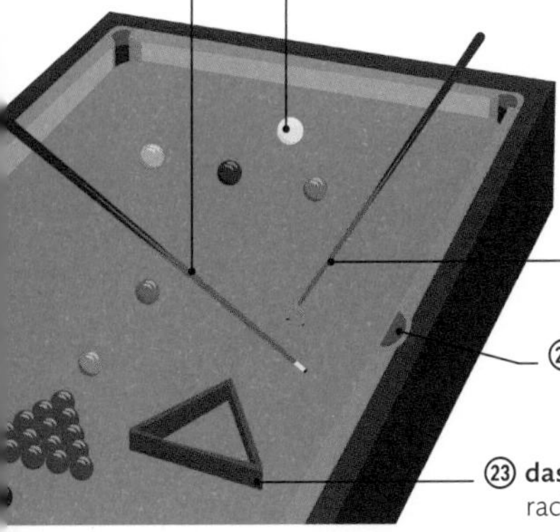

⑲ **der Queue**
cue

⑳ **der Spielball**
cue ball

㉑ **der Brückenqueue**
bridge

㉒ **die Tasche**
pocket

㉓ **das Dreieck**
rack

㉔ **Snooker** *n*
snooker

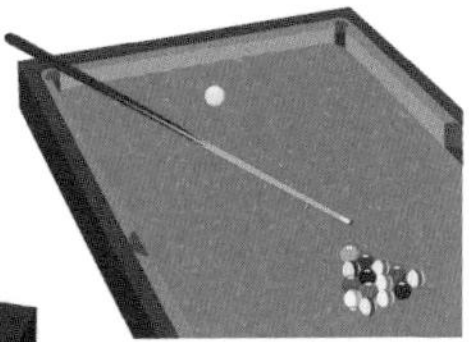

㉕ **Billard** *n*
pool

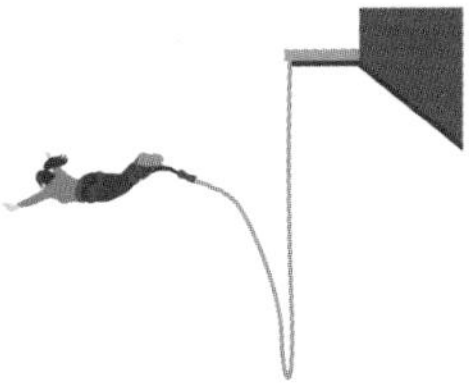

㉖ **Bungeejumping** *n*
bungee jumping

㉗ **Fallschirmspringen** *n*
skydiving

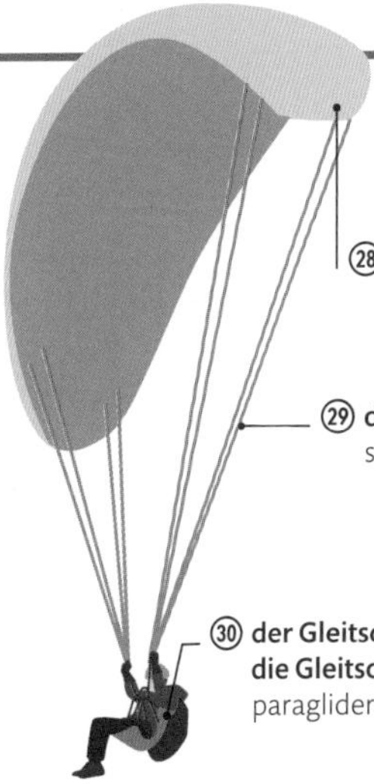

㉘ **der Gleitschirm**
canopy

㉙ **die Leine**
suspension line

㉚ **der Gleitschirmflieger** *m*
**die Gleitschirmfliegerin** *f*
paraglider

㉛ **Gleitschirmfliegen** *n*
paragliding

㉜ **Abseilen** *n*
abseiling

㉝ **das Seil**
rope

㉞ **Klettern** *n*
rock climbing

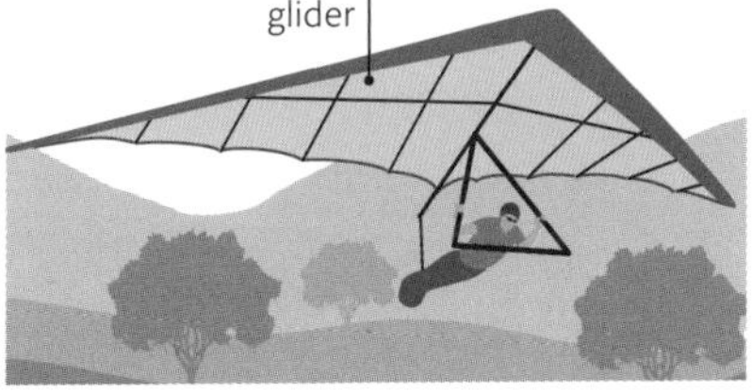

㉟ **der Flugdrachen**
glider

㊱ **Drachenfliegen** *n*
hang-gliding

㊳ **der Fallschirm**
parachute

㊲ **Fallschirmspringen** *n*
parachuting

# 126 Auf der Bühne
## On stage

### 126.1 DAS THEATER • THEATER

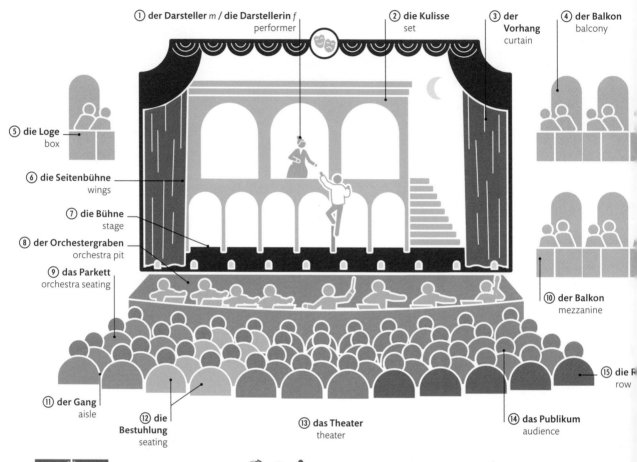

**16 das Theaterstück**
play

**17 das Kostüm**
costumes

**18 die Requisite**
props

**19 das Bühnenbild**
sets

**20 der Hintergrund**
backdrop

**21 das Textbuch**
script

**22 der Produzent** *m*
**die Produzentin** *f*
producer

**23 der Regisseur** *m*
**die Regisseurin** *f*
director

**24 der Schauspieler** *m*
**die Schauspielerin** *f*
actor

**25 die Besetzung**
cast

**26 die Premiere**
opening night

**27 die Pause**
intermission

See also
**127** Filme • Movies **128-129** Musik • Music
**139** Fantasy und Mythologie • Fantasy and myth

## 126.2 BALLETT • BALLET

④ **eine Pirouette machen / sich drehen**
to pirouette / to turn

⑤ **einen Plié machen / die Beine beugen**
to plié / to bend

⑥ **der Balletttänzer**
male ballet dancer

⑦ **die Ballerina**
ballerina

⑧ **das Tütü**
tutu

⑨ **das Balletttrikot**
ballet leotard

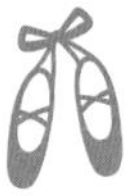

⑩ **der Ballettschuh**
ballet slippers

⑪ **die Aufführung**
performance

⑫ **die Zugabe**
encore

⑬ **der Beifall**
applause

## 126.3 DIE OPER • OPERA

① **der Bass**
bass

② **der Bariton**
baritone

③ **der Tenor**
tenor

④ **das Opernhaus**
opera house

⑤ **der Alt**
alto

⑥ **der Mezzosopran**
mezzo-soprano

⑦ **der Sopran**
soprano

⑧ **die Primadonna**
prima donna

⑨ **das Libretto**
libretto

㉘ **das Programm**
program

**der Platzanweiser** *m*
**e Platzanweiserin** *f*
usher

㉚ **die Tragödie**
tragedy

㉛ **die Komödie**
comedy

㉜ **das Musical**
musical

㉝ **der Stehbeifall**
standing ovation

# 127 Filme
## Movies

### 127.1 IM KINO · AT THE MOVIES

① **das Drama**
drama

② **das Musical**
musical

③ **der Science-Fiction-Film**
science fiction

④ **der Thriller**
thriller

⑤ **die Komödie**
comedy

⑥ **der Actionfilm**
action movie

⑦ **der Horrorfilm**
horror

⑧ **der Animationsfilm**
animation

⑨ **die romantische Komödie**
romantic comedy

⑩ **der Krimi**
crime drama

⑪ **der Western**
western

⑫ **das Historiendram**
historical drama

⑬ **der Fantasyfilm**
fantasy

⑭ **der Kampfsportfilm**
martial arts

⑮ **der Spezialeffekt**
special effects

⑯ **die Kasse**
box office

⑰ **das Multiplexkino**
multiplex

⑱ **das Popcorn**
popcorn

⑲ **der Filmstar**
movie star

⑳ **die Leinwand**
screen

㉑ **das Publikum**
audience

㉒ **das Kino**
movie theater

㉓ **die Hauptfigur**
main character

㉔ **der Held** *m*
**die Heldin** *f*
hero

㉕ **der Bösewicht**
villain

See also
**126** Auf der Bühne • On stage **136** Unterhaltung zu Hause
Home entertainment **137** Fernsehen • Television

## 127.2 **DAS FILMSTUDIO** • FILM STUDIO

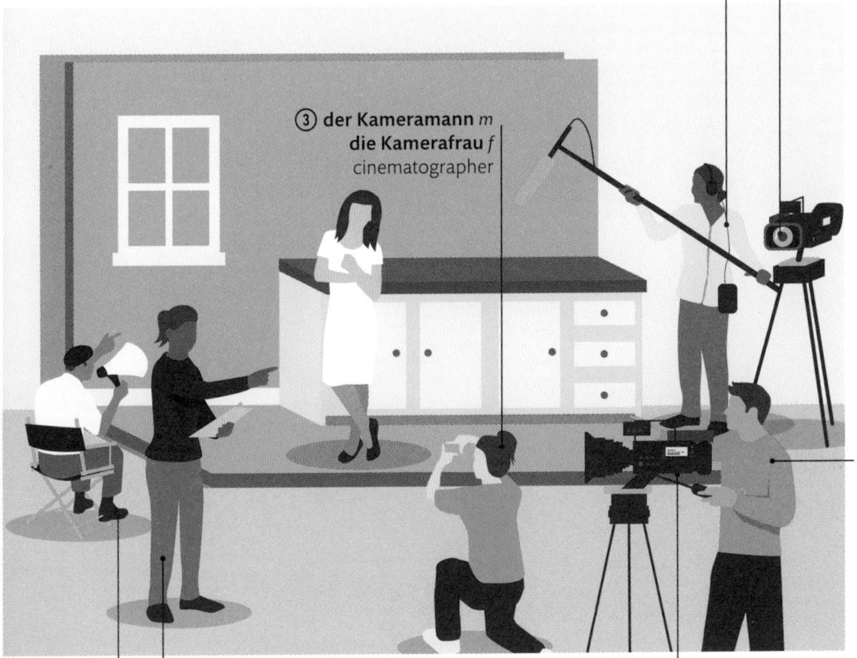

① **der Tontechniker** *m*
**die Tontechnikerin** *f*
sound engineer

② **das Objektiv**
lens

③ **der Kameramann** *m*
**die Kamerafrau** *f*
cinematographer

④ **der Kameraassistent** *m*
**die Kameraassistentin** *f*
camera operator

**r Regisseur** *m*
**Regisseurin** *f*
director

⑥ **der Produzent** *m*
**die Produzentin** *f*
producer

⑦ **die Filmkamera**
movie camera

⑧ **das Filmset**
film set

⑨ **die Paparazzi** *m, pl*
paparazzi

⑩ **der rote Teppich**
red carpet

⑪ **der Star**
celebrity

⑫ **die Premiere**
premiere

⑬ **das Vorsprechen**
audition

⑭ **die Besetzung**
cast

⑮ **der Statist** *m*
**die Statistin** *f*
extras

⑯ **der Stunt**
stunt

⑰ **die Requisite**
props

⑱ **das Drehbuch**
screenplay

⑲ **das Kostüm**
costumes

⑳ **der Soundtrack**
soundtrack

㉑ **der Drehbuchautor** *m*
**die Drehbuchautorin** *f*
screenwriter

# Musik
Music

## 128.1 ORCHESTERINSTRUMENTE · ORCHESTRAL INSTRUMENTS

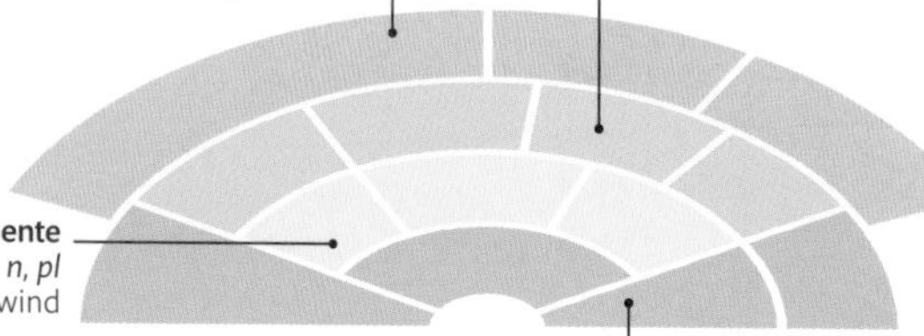

① **Holzblasinstrumente** *n, pl*
woodwind

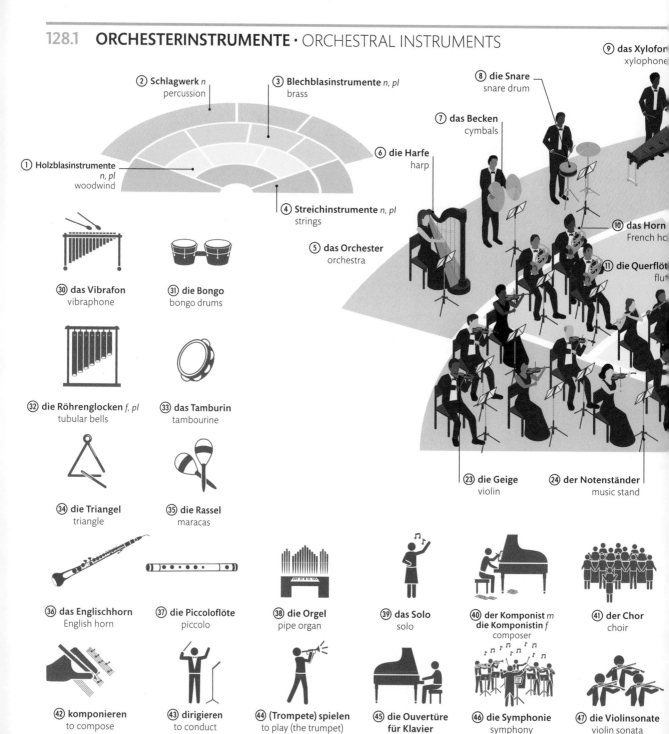

② **Schlagwerk** *n*
percussion

③ **Blechblasinstrumente** *n, pl*
brass

④ **Streichinstrumente** *n, pl*
strings

⑤ **das Orchester**
orchestra

⑥ **die Harfe**
harp

⑦ **das Becken**
cymbals

⑧ **die Snare**
snare drum

⑨ **das Xylofon**
xylophone

⑩ **das Horn**
French ho

⑪ **die Querflöt**
flu

㉓ **die Geige**
violin

㉔ **der Notenständer**
music stand

㉚ **das Vibrafon**
vibraphone

㉛ **die Bongo**
bongo drums

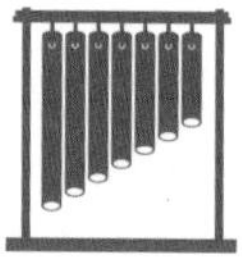

㉜ **die Röhrenglocken** *f, pl*
tubular bells

㉝ **das Tamburin**
tambourine

㉞ **die Triangel**
triangle

㉟ **die Rassel**
maracas

㊱ **das Englischhorn**
English horn

㊲ **die Piccoloflöte**
piccolo

㊳ **die Orgel**
pipe organ

㊴ **das Solo**
solo

㊵ **der Komponist** *m*
**die Komponistin** *f*
composer

㊶ **der Chor**
choir

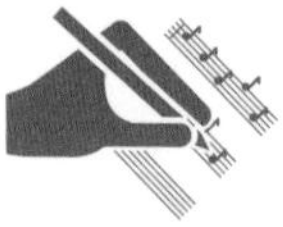

㊷ **komponieren**
to compose

㊸ **dirigieren**
to conduct

㊹ **(Trompete) spielen**
to play (the trumpet)

㊺ **die Ouvertüre für Klavier**
piano overture

㊻ **die Symphonie**
symphony

㊼ **die Violinsonate**
violin sonata

See also
**126** Auf der Bühne • On stage **127** Filme • Movies **129** Musik (Fortsetzung) Music continued **136** Unterhaltung zu Hause • Home entertainment

## 128.2 PARTITUR, NOTEN UND NOTENSCHRIFT • SCORE, NOTES, AND NOTATION

⑤ **die Partitur**
score

⑥ **der Akkord**
chord

⑦ **die Tonleiter**
scale

⑩ **die Tonlage**
pitch

♯

⑪ **das Kreuzvorzeichen**
sharp

♭

⑫ **das b-Vorzeichen**
flat

# 129 Musik (Fortsetzung)
## Music continued

### 129.1 **POPMUSIK** · POPULAR MUSIC

⑫ **der Plattenspieler** turntable

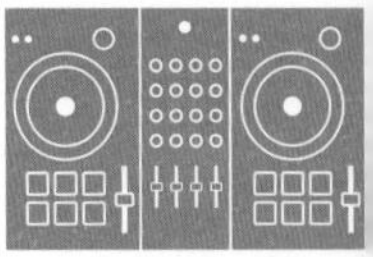
⑬ **das Mischpult** DJ console

⑭ **die Schallplatte** vinyl records

⑮ **der Begleitsänger** *m* **die Begleitsängerin** *f* backup singers

⑯ **das Lied** song

⑰ **die Melodie** melody

⑱ **der Takt** beat

⑲ **die Band** band

⑳ **das Album** album

㉑ **der Jazz** jazz

㉒ **der Blues** the blues

㉓ **der Punk** punk

㉔ **die Folk-Musik** folk

㉕ **der Pop** pop

㉖ **der K-Pop** K-pop

㉗ **der Heavy Metal** heavy metal

㉘ **der Hiphop** hip-hop

㉙ **die Countrymusik** country

㉚ **der Rock** rock

㉛ **der Soul** soul

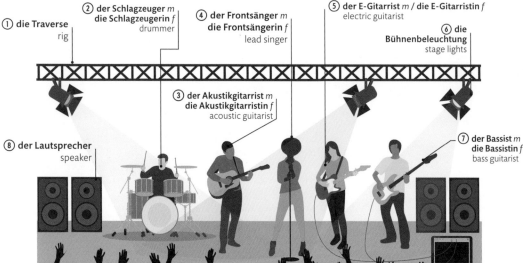

㉜ **die lateinamerikanische Musik** Latin

See also
126 Auf der Bühne • On stage 127 Filme • Movies
136 Unterhaltung zu Hause • Home entertainment

## 129.2 WEITERE INSTRUMENTE • MORE INSTRUMENTS

(33) der Tanz
dance

(34) der Bhangra
bhangra

(35) der Reggae
reggae

(36) die Oper
opera

(37) die klassische Musik
classical music

(38) der Gospel
gospel

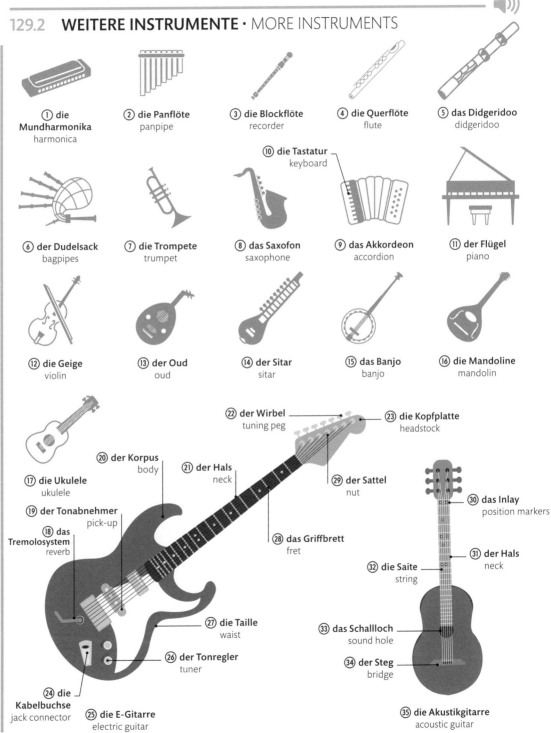

(1) die Mundharmonika
harmonica

(2) die Panflöte
panpipe

(3) die Blockflöte
recorder

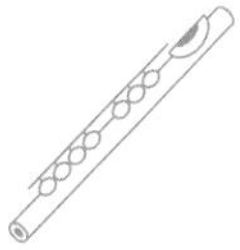
(4) die Querflöte
flute

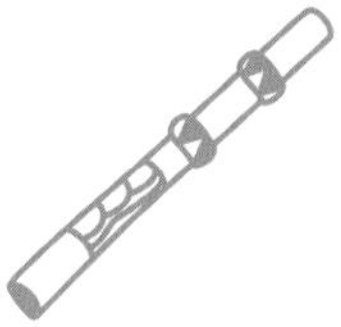
(5) das Didgeridoo
didgeridoo

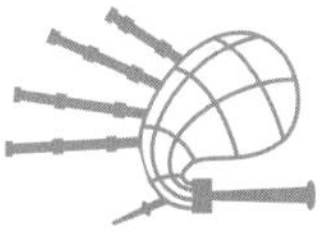
(6) der Dudelsack
bagpipes

(7) die Trompete
trumpet

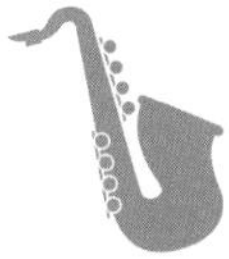
(8) das Saxofon
saxophone

(10) die Tastatur
keyboard

(9) das Akkordeon
accordion

(11) der Flügel
piano

(12) die Geige
violin

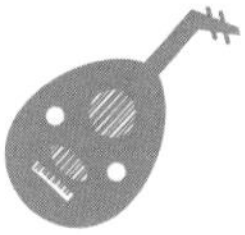
(13) der Oud
oud

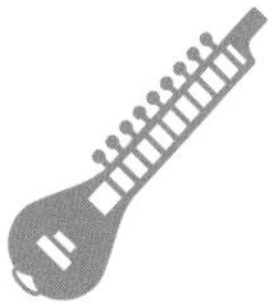
(14) der Sitar
sitar

(15) das Banjo
banjo

(16) die Mandoline
mandolin

(17) die Ukulele
ukulele

(18) das Tremolosystem
reverb

(19) der Tonabnehmer
pick-up

(20) der Korpus
body

(21) der Hals
neck

(22) der Wirbel
tuning peg

(23) die Kopfplatte
headstock

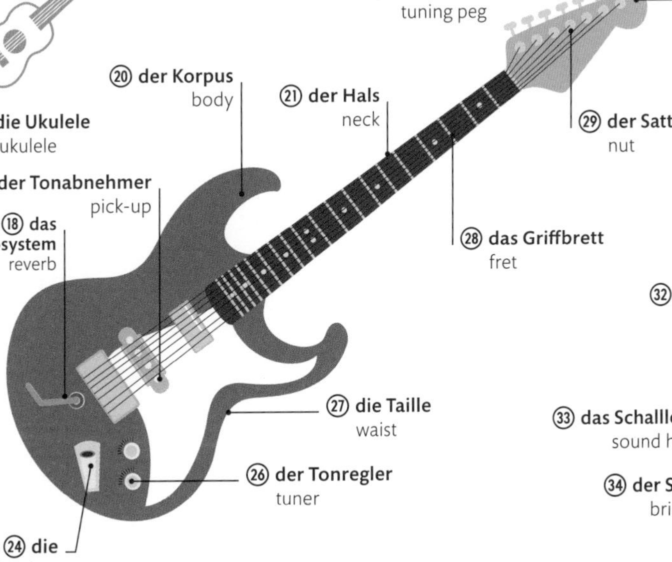

(24) die Kabelbuchse
jack connector

(25) die E-Gitarre
electric guitar

(26) der Tonregler
tuner

(27) die Taille
waist

(28) das Griffbrett
fret

(29) der Sattel
nut

(30) das Inlay
position markers

(31) der Hals
neck

(32) die Saite
string

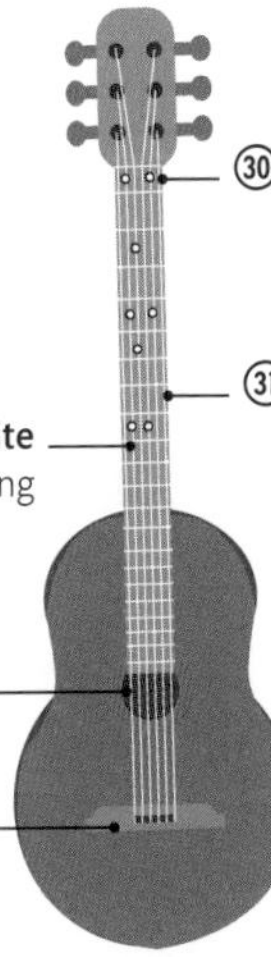

(33) das Schallloch
sound hole

(34) der Steg
bridge

(35) die Akustikgitarre
acoustic guitar

# 130 Museen und Kunstgalerien

## Museums and galleries

### 130.1 IM MUSEUM UND IN DER KUNSTGALERIE • AT THE MUSEUM AND ART GALLERY

① **die Galerie**
gallery

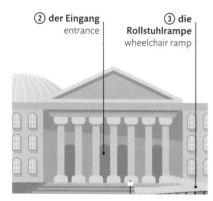

② **der Eingang**
entrance

③ **die Rollstuhlrampe**
wheelchair ramp

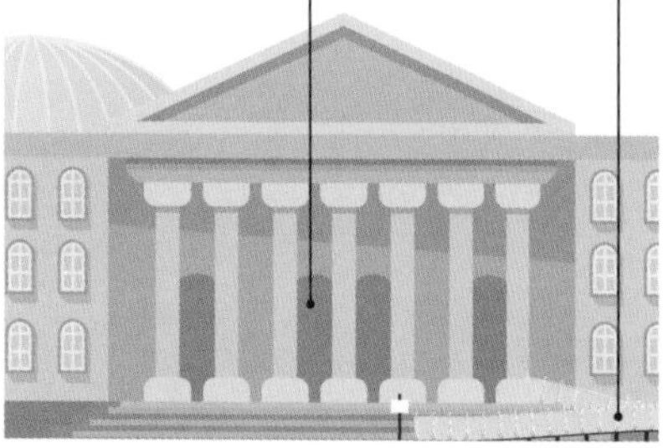

④ **das Museum**
museum

⑤ **die Toilette**
restrooms

⑥ **die Garderobe**
cloakroom

⑦ **der Eintritt**
admission fee

⑧ **die Karte**
ticket

⑨ **der Kartenverkauf**
ticket office

⑩ **die Spende**
donation

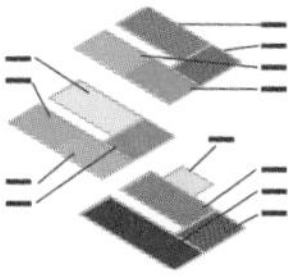

⑪ **der Gebäudeplan**
floor plan

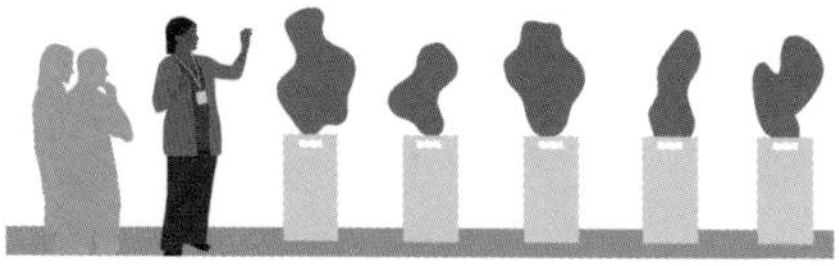

⑫ **der Kurator** *m* **/ die Kuratorin** *f*
curator

⑭ **das Ausstellungsstüc**
exhibit

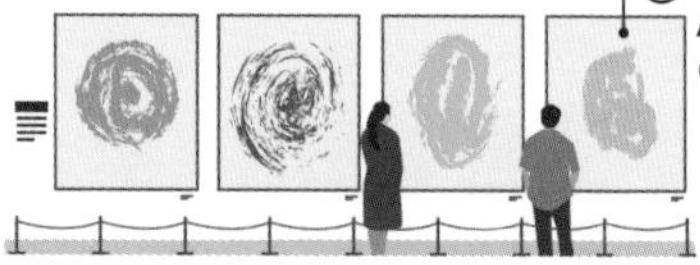

⑬ **die Ausstellung**
exhibition

⑮ **die Dauerausstellung**
permanent exhibition

⑰ **die Installation**
installation

⑯ **die Sonderausstellung**
temporary exhibition

⑱ **die Sammlung**
collection

⑲ **die Restaurierung**
conservation

⑳ **der Museumsführer** *m*
**die Museumsführerin** *f*
tour guide

㉑ **der Audioguide**
audio guide

㉒ **fotografieren verboten**
no photography

㉓ **der Geschenkeladen**
gift shop

See also
**42-43** In der Stadt • In town **132** Sightseeing • Sightseeing
**141-142** Kunst und Handwerk • Arts and crafts

**㉔ die Skulptur**
sculpture

**㉕ die Überwachungskamera**
surveillance camera

**㉙ Dieses Meisterwerk ist unbezahlbar!**
This masterpiece is priceless!

**㉖ das Schild**
label

**㉗ das Meisterwerk**
masterpiece

**㉘ der Museumswächter** *m*
**die Museumswächterin** *f*
security guard

**㉚ der Rahmen**
frame

**㉛ das Gemälde**
painting

**㉜ das Ölgemälde**
oil painting

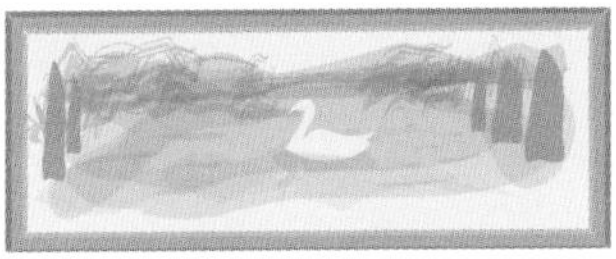

**㉝ das Aquarell**
watercolor

**㉞ der Klassizismus**
Classicism

**㉟ der Impressionismus**
Impressionism

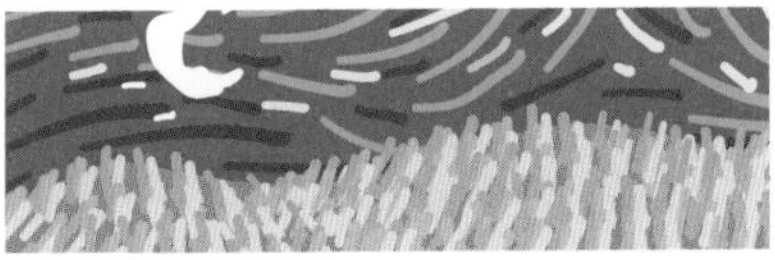

**㊱ der Postimpressionismus**
Post-Impressionism

**㊶ das Art-déco**
Art Deco

**㊷ der Jugendstil**
Art Nouveau

**㊲ der Kubismus**
Cubism

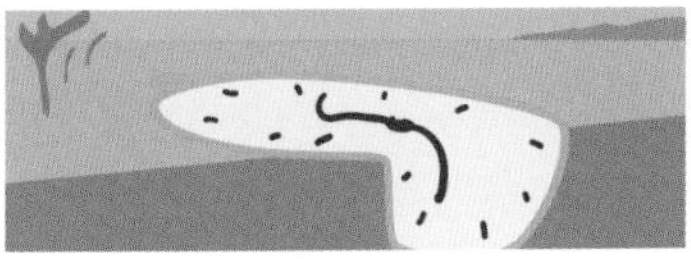

**㊳ der Surrealismus**
Surrealism

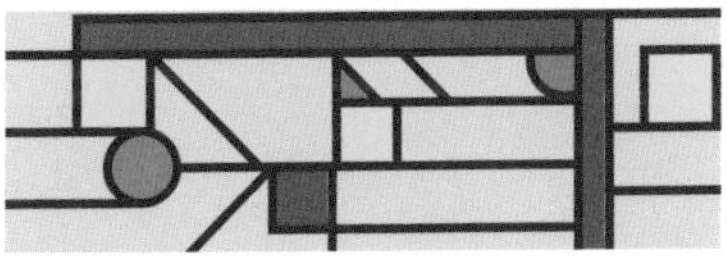

**㊴ das Bauhaus**
Bauhaus

**㊵ die Pop-Art**
Pop Art

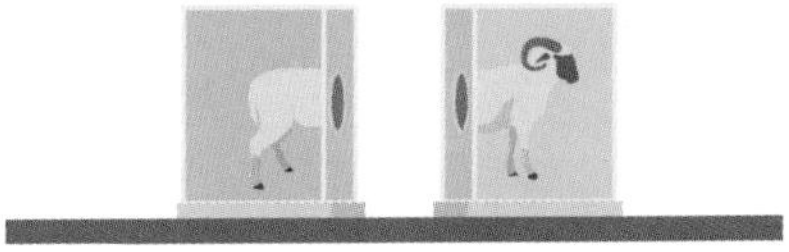

**㊸ die Konzeptkunst**
conceptual art

# 131 Reise und Unterkunft

## Travel and accommodation

### 131.1 REISEN · TRAVEL

① **der Reiseführer**
guidebook

② **das Wörterbuch mit praktischen Redewendungen**
phrasebook

③ **der Einzelfahrschein**
one-way ticket

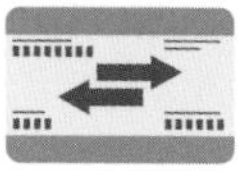
④ **die Hin- und Rückfahrkarte**
round-trip

⑤ **einen Urlaub buchen**
to book a vacation

⑥ **den Koffer packen**
to pack your bags

⑦ **in den Urlaub fahren**
to go on a vacation

⑧ **eine Kreuzfahrt machen**
to go on a cruise

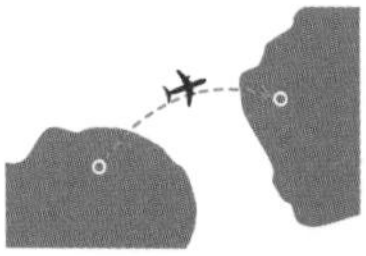
⑨ **ins Ausland gehen**
to go abroad

⑩ **reservieren**
to make a reservation

⑪ **ein Ferienhaus mieten**
to rent a cottage

⑫ **eine Rucksacktour machen**
to go backpacking

⑬ **einchecken**
to check in

⑭ **auschecken**
to check out

⑮ **im Hotel übernachten**
to stay in a hotel

### 131.2 UNTERKÜNFTE · ACCOMMODATION

① **das Hotel**
hotel

② **die Wohnung**
apartment

③ **das Hostel**
hostel

⑨ **das Gasthaus**
guest house

⑩ **die Übernachtung mit Frühstück**
bed and breakfast

⑪ **die Villa**
villa

⑱ **der Aufzug**
elevator

⑲ **die Gäste** *pl*
guests

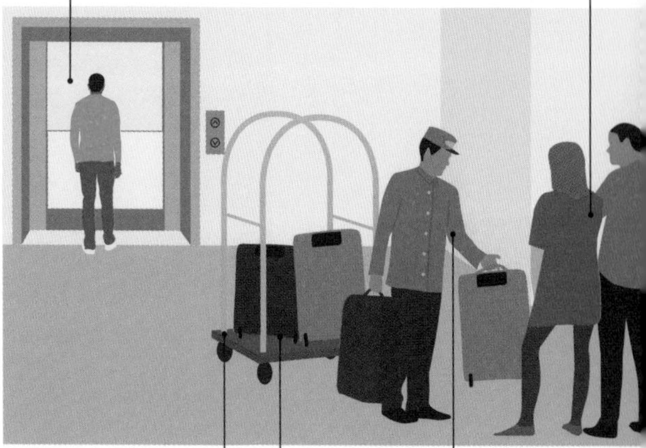

㉔ **der Gepäckwagen**
trolley

㉕ **das Gepäck**
luggage

㉖ **der Hotelpage** *m* **die Pförtnerin** *f*
porter

### 131.3 LEISTUNGEN · SERVICES

① **das Restaurant**
restaurant

② **das Fitnessstudio**
gym

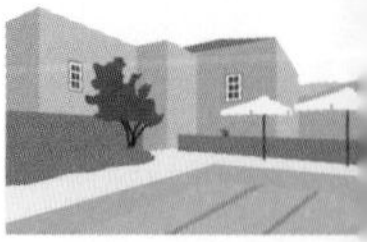
③ **das Schwimmbecken**
swimming pool

See also
**104** Am Flughafen • At the airport **132** Sightseeing • Sightseeing
**133** Aktivitäten im Freien • Outdoor activities **134** Am Strand • On the beach

④ **die Skihütte**
chalet

⑤ **die Hütte**
cabin

⑥ **der Ökotourismus**
ecotourism

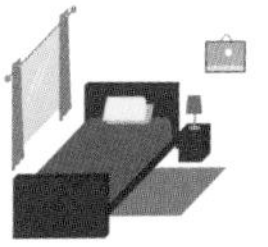

⑦ **das Einzelzimmer**
single room

⑧ **das Zweibettzimmer**
twin room

⑫ **das Doppelzimmer**
double room

⑬ **das private Badezimmer**
private bathroom

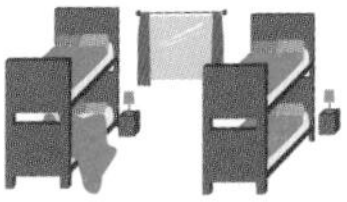

⑭ **der Schlafsaal**
dorm

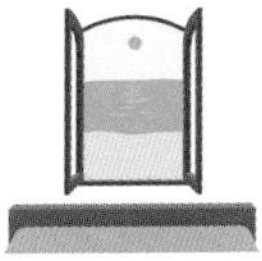

⑮ **das Zimmer mit Ausblick**
room with a view

⑯ **Zimmer frei**
vacancies

⑰ **alle Zimmer besetzt**
no vacancies

⑳ **der Rezeptionist** *m*
**die Rezeptionistin** *f*
receptionist

㉑ **die Rezeption**
front desk

㉒ **die Toilette**
restrooms

㉓ **der Notausgang**
emergency exit

㉗ **der Tresen**
counter

㉘ **die Lobby**
hotel lobby

⑤ **das Frühstückstablett**
breakfast tray

④ **der Zimmerservice**
room service

⑥ **der Wäscheservice**
laundry service

⑦ **die Zimmerreinigung**
maid service

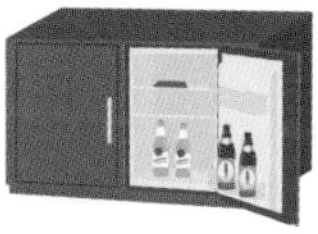

⑧ **die Minibar**
minibar

⑨ **der Tresor**
safe

# 132 Sightseeing
Sightseeing

## 132.1 DIE TOURISTENATTRAKTION • TOURIST ATTRACTION

① **der Touristenbus**
tour bus

② **einen Ausflug machen**
to go on an excursion

③ **die Führung**
guided tour

⑥ **eine Führung machen**
to go on a tour

⑦ **der Tourist** *m*
**die Touristin** *f*
tourist

⑧ **der Fremdenführer** *m*
**die Fremdenführerin** *f*
tour guide

⑨ **das Sightseeing**
sightseeing

## 132.2 SEHENSWÜRDIGKEITEN • ATTRACTIONS

① **die Kunstgalerie**
art gallery

② **das Museum**
museum

③ **das Denkmal**
monument

④ **das Schloss**
palace

⑤ **das historische Gebäude**
historic building

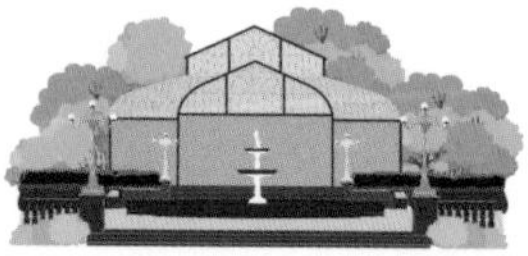

⑥ **der botanische Garten**
botanical gardens

⑧ **die Landschaft**
landscape

⑨ **malerisch**
scenic

⑦ **der Nationalpark**
national park

See also
**99** Autos und Busse • Cars and buses **130** Museen und Kunstgalerien • Museums and galleries
**131** Reise und Unterkunft • Travel and accommodation **149-151** Länder • Countries

⑤ Müssen wir für den Eintritt bezahlen?
Do we have to pay an admission fee?

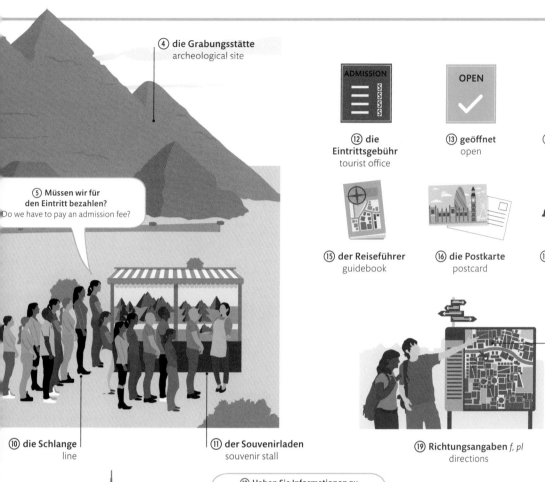

④ **die Grabungsstätte**
archeological site

⑩ **die Schlange**
line

⑪ **der Souvenirladen**
souvenir stall

ADMISSION

⑫ **die Eintrittsgebühr**
tourist office

OPEN

⑬ **geöffnet**
open

CLOSED

⑭ **geschlossen**
closed

⑮ **der Reiseführer**
guidebook

⑯ **die Postkarte**
postcard

⑰ **das Souvenir**
souvenir

⑱ **die Karte**
tourist map

⑲ **Richtungsangaben** *f, pl*
directions

⑩ **das Ufer**
waterfront

⑪ **der Kunstmarkt**
craft market

⑬ **Haben Sie Informationen zu lokalen Sehenswürdigkeiten?**
Can I have some information on the local sights?

⑫ **die Touristeninformation**
tourist office

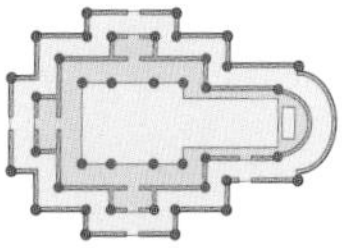

⑭ **der Gebäudeplan**
floor plan

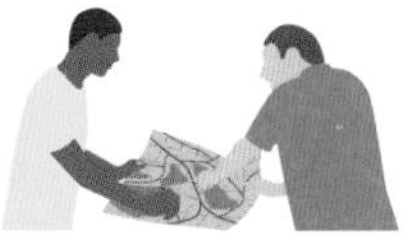

⑮ **die Karte**
map

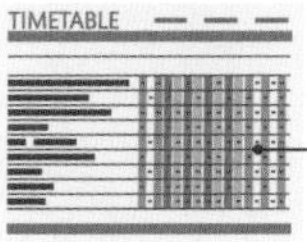
TIMETABLE

⑯ **der Zeitplan**
timetable

⑰ **die Öffnungszeiten** *f, pl*
opening times

# 133 Aktivitäten im Freien
## Outdoor activities

### 133.1 AKTIVITÄTEN AN DER FRISCHEN LUFT • OPEN-AIR ACTIVITIES

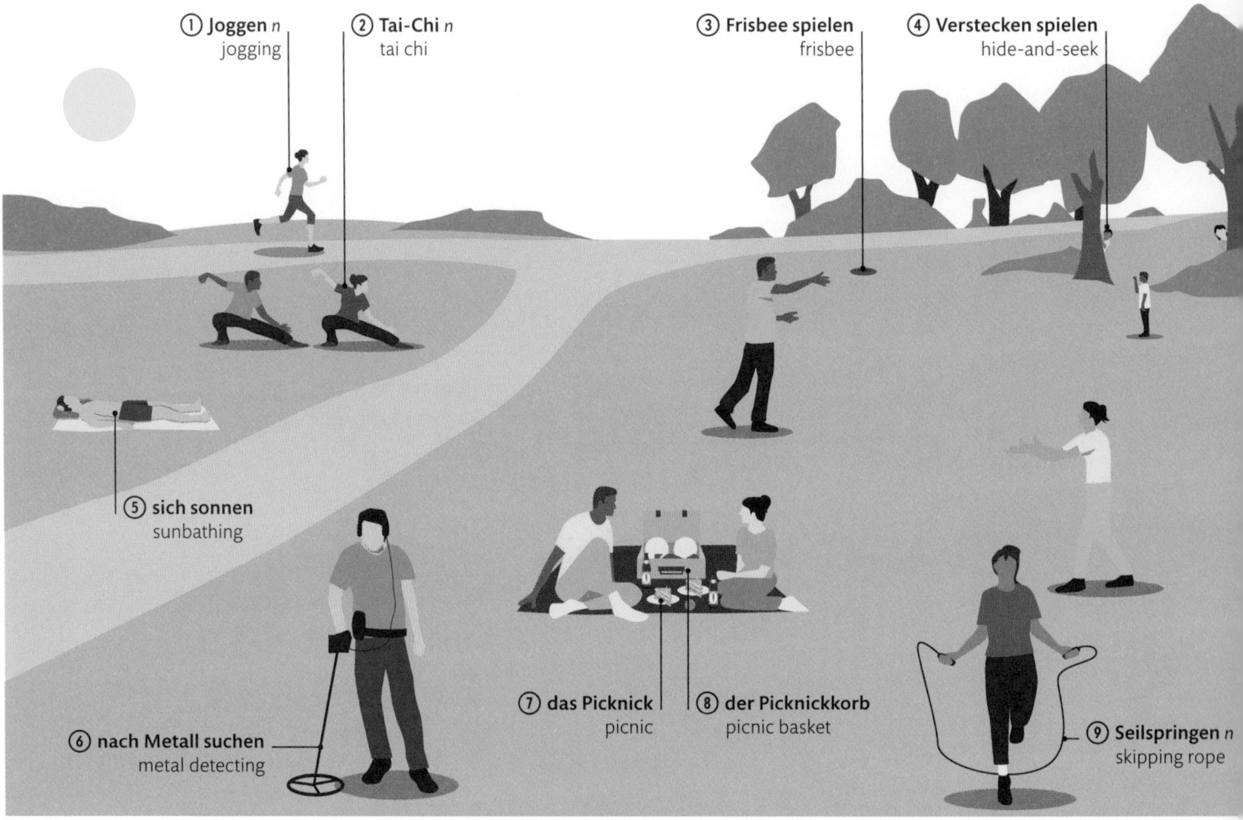


⑩ **der Park** park

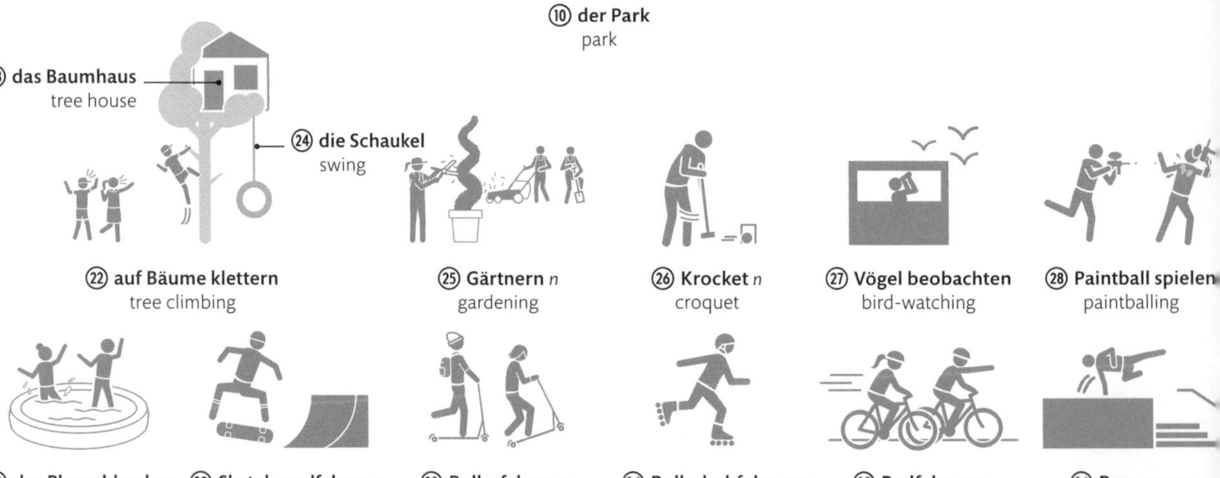

See also
**11** Fähigkeiten und Handlungen • Abilities and actions **134** Am Strand • On the beach
**135** Camping • Camping **148** Karten und Richtungsangaben • Maps and directions

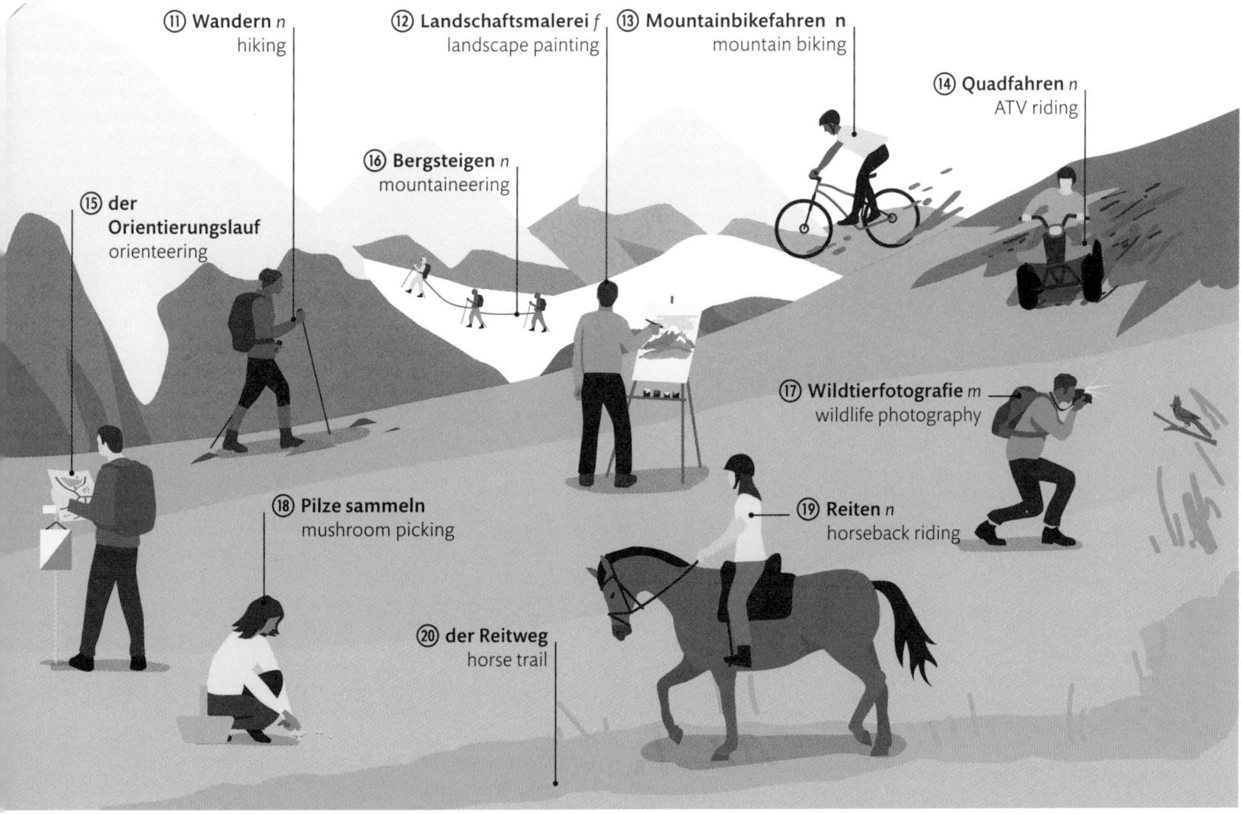


㉑ **der Nationalpark**
national park

㉙ **der Safaripark**
safari park

㉚ **das Naturschutzgebiet**
nature reserve

㊲ **der Tierpark**
zoo

㊳ **der Abenteuerspielplatz**
adventure playground

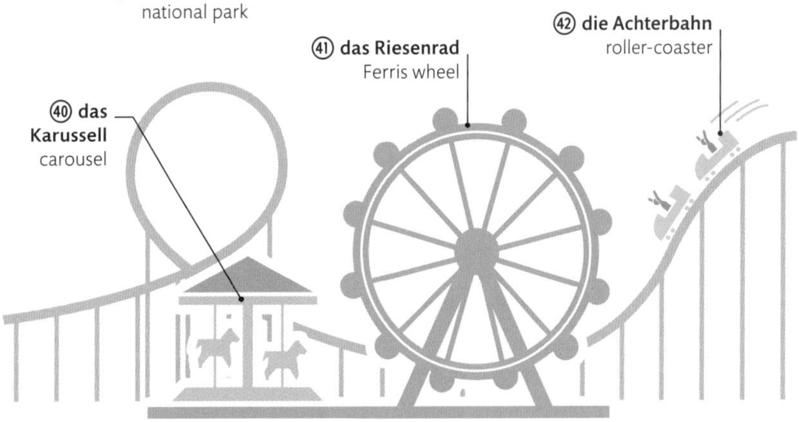


㊴ **der Erlebnispark**
theme park

# 134 Am Strand
## On the beach

### 134.1 DER STRAND · THE BEACH

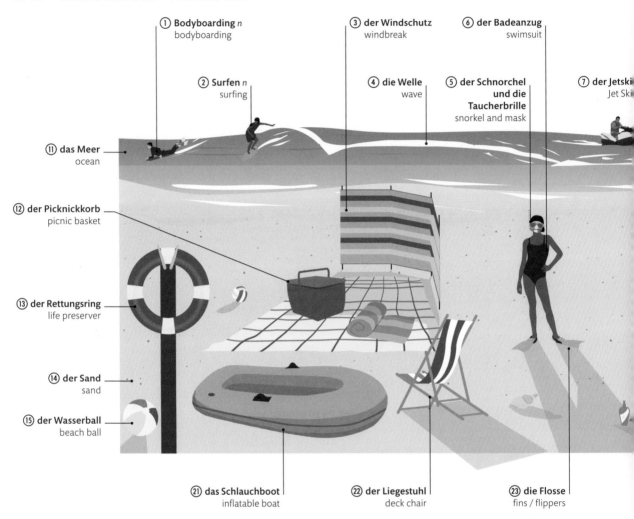

① **Bodyboarding** *n*
bodyboarding

② **Surfen** *n*
surfing

③ **der Windschutz**
windbreak

④ **die Welle**
wave

⑤ **der Schnorchel und die Taucherbrille**
snorkel and mask

⑥ **der Badeanzug**
swimsuit

⑦ **der Jetski**
Jet Ski

⑪ **das Meer**
ocean

⑫ **der Picknickkorb**
picnic basket

⑬ **der Rettungsring**
life preserver

⑭ **der Sand**
sand

⑮ **der Wasserball**
beach ball

㉑ **das Schlauchboot**
inflatable boat

㉒ **der Liegestuhl**
deck chair

㉓ **die Flosse**
fins / flippers

㉕ **das Segel**
sail

㉖ **die Jacht**
yacht

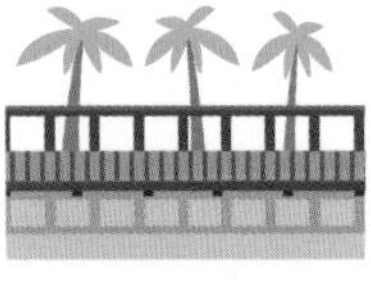

㉗ **der Bohlenweg**
boardwalk

㉘ **die Strandpromenade**
promenade

㉙ **das Strandhäusche**
beach hut

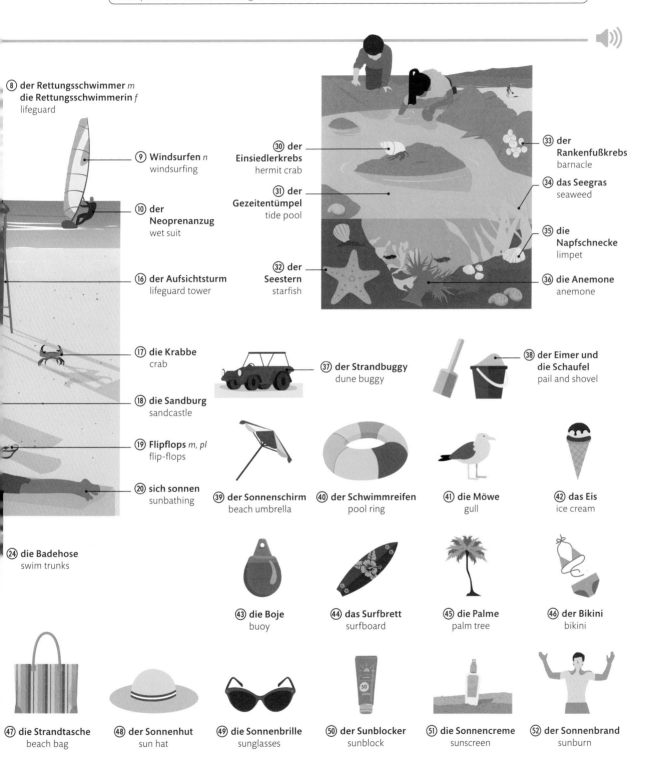

See also
**105** Seefahrzeuge • Sea vessels **118** Schwimmen • Swimming **119** Segeln und Wassersport • Sailing and watersports **121** Fischen • Fishing **133** Aktivitäten im Freien • Outdoor activities **166** Leben im Ozean • Ocean life

⑧ **der Rettungsschwimmer** *m*
**die Rettungsschwimmerin** *f*
lifeguard

⑨ **Windsurfen** *n*
windsurfing

⑩ **der Neoprenanzug**
wet suit

⑯ **der Aufsichtsturm**
lifeguard tower

⑰ **die Krabbe**
crab

⑱ **die Sandburg**
sandcastle

⑲ **Flipflops** *m, pl*
flip-flops

⑳ **sich sonnen**
sunbathing

㉚ **der Einsiedlerkrebs**
hermit crab

㉛ **der Gezeitentümpel**
tide pool

㉜ **der Seestern**
starfish

㉝ **der Rankenfußkrebs**
barnacle

㉞ **das Seegras**
seaweed

㉟ **die Napfschnecke**
limpet

㊱ **die Anemone**
anemone

㊲ **der Strandbuggy**
dune buggy

㊳ **der Eimer und die Schaufel**
pail and shovel

㊴ **der Sonnenschirm**
beach umbrella

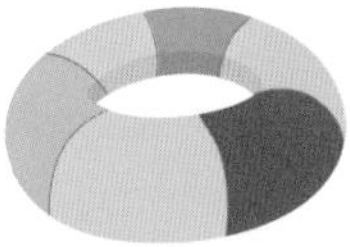

㊵ **der Schwimmreifen**
pool ring

㊶ **die Möwe**
gull

㊷ **das Eis**
ice cream

㉔ **die Badehose**
swim trunks

㊸ **die Boje**
buoy

㊹ **das Surfbrett**
surfboard

㊺ **die Palme**
palm tree

㊻ **der Bikini**
bikini

㊼ **die Strandtasche**
beach bag

㊽ **der Sonnenhut**
sun hat

㊾ **die Sonnenbrille**
sunglasses

㊿ **der Sunblocker**
sunblock

(51) **die Sonnencreme**
sunscreen

(52) **der Sonnenbrand**
sunburn

# 135 Camping
## Camping

### 135.1 CAMPINGAUSRÜSTUNG UND ZUBEHÖR · CAMPING EQUIPMENT AND FACILITIES

① **campen**
to camp

② **ein Zelt aufstellen**
to pitch a tent

③ **das Zweipersonenzelt**
two-person tent

④ **der Stellplatz**
site

⑤ **freie Stellplätze**
sites available

⑥ **alles besetzt**
full

⑧ **der Stromanschluss**
electric hook-up

⑨ **der Anhänger**
trailer

⑩ **das Wohnmobil**
motor home

⑪ **die Hängematte**
hammock

⑫ **das Lagerfeuer**
campfire

⑬ **Feuer machen**
to light a fire

⑮ **die Kohle**
charcoal

⑯ **der Grill**
barbecue

⑰ **der Gaskocher**
single-burner camping stove

⑱ **der Campingkocher mit zwei Herdplatten**
double-burner camping stove

⑲ **der Faltrost**
folding grill

⑳ **die Picknickbank**
picnic bench

㉒ **das Duschhaus**
shower block

㉓ **das Toilettenhaus**
toilet block

㉔ **die Abfallsammelstelle**
waste disposal

㉕ **das Campingbüro**
site manager's office

㉖ **der Rucksack**
backpack

㉗ **die Taschenlampe**
flashlight

㉙ **der Kompass**
compass

㉚ **die Thermounterwäsche**
thermals

㉛ **die Wanderschuhe** *m, pl*
walking boots

㉜ **die Regenjacke**
rain gear

㉝ **das Mehrzweckmesser**
multi-purpose knife

㉞ **das Insektenschutzmitte**
insect repellent

㊱ **der Schlafsack**
sleeping bag

㊲ **die Isomatte**
sleeping mat

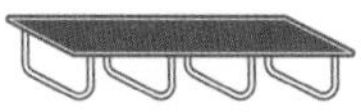

㊳ **das Campingbett**
camp bed

㊴ **die selbst aufblasende Matratze**
self-inflating mattress

㊵ **die Luftmatratze**
air bed / air mattress

㊶ **die Luftpumpe**
air pump

See also
**131** Reise und Unterkunft • Travel and accommodation **133** Aktivitäten im Freien • Outdoor activities **146-147** Geografie • Geography

## 135.2 DER CAMPINGPLATZ • CAMPGROUND

⑦ **der Wohnwagen**
camper

⑭ **der Anzünder**
firestarter

㉑ **die Wasserflasche**
water bottles

㉘ **die Stirnlampe**
headlamp

㉟ **das Mückennetz**
mosquito net

㊷ **die elektrische Pumpe**
electric pump

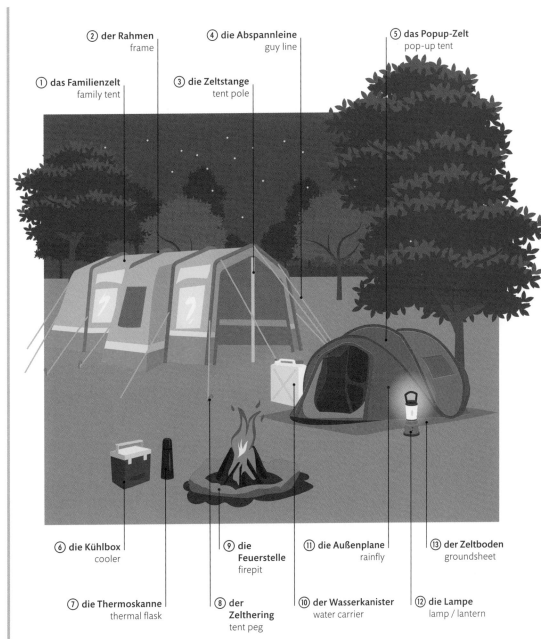

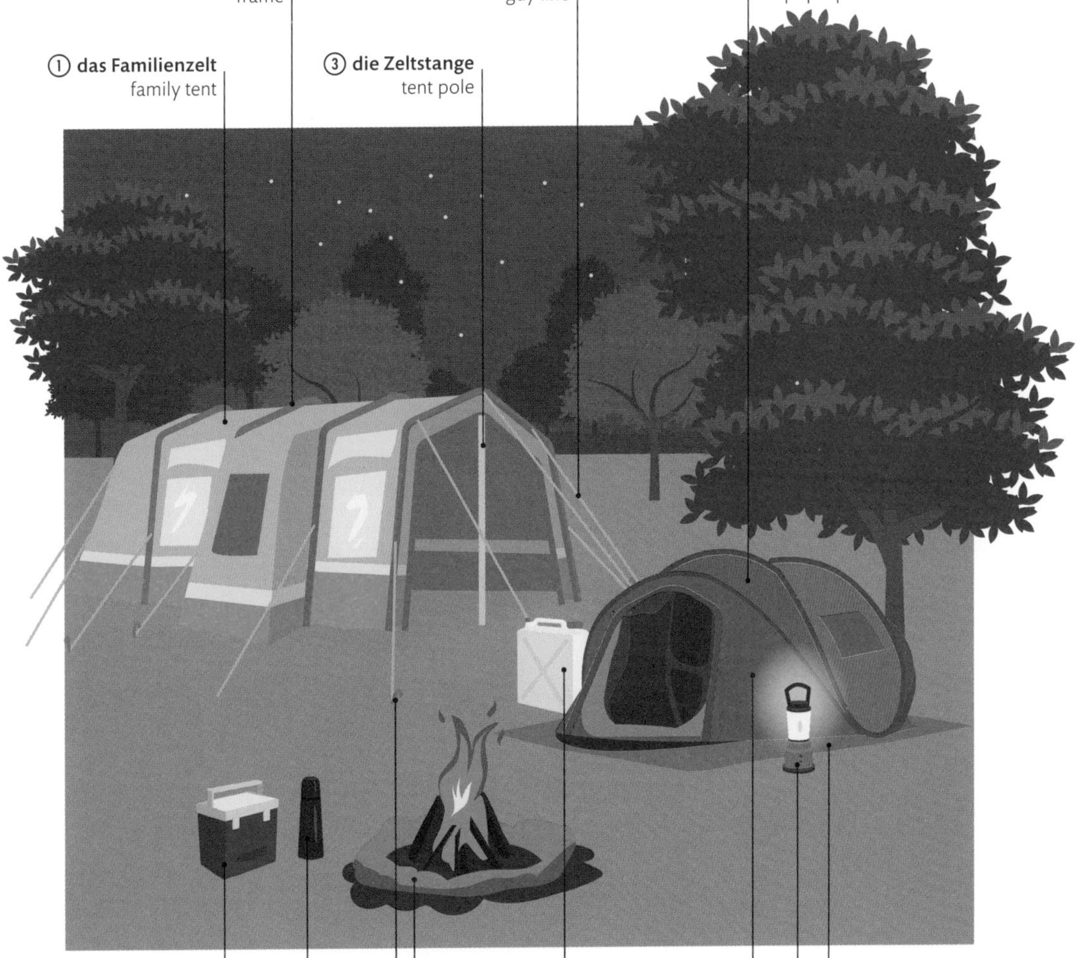

# Unterhaltung zu Hause
## Home entertainment

### 136.1 FERNSEHER UND LAUTSPRECHER · TELEVISION AND AUDIO

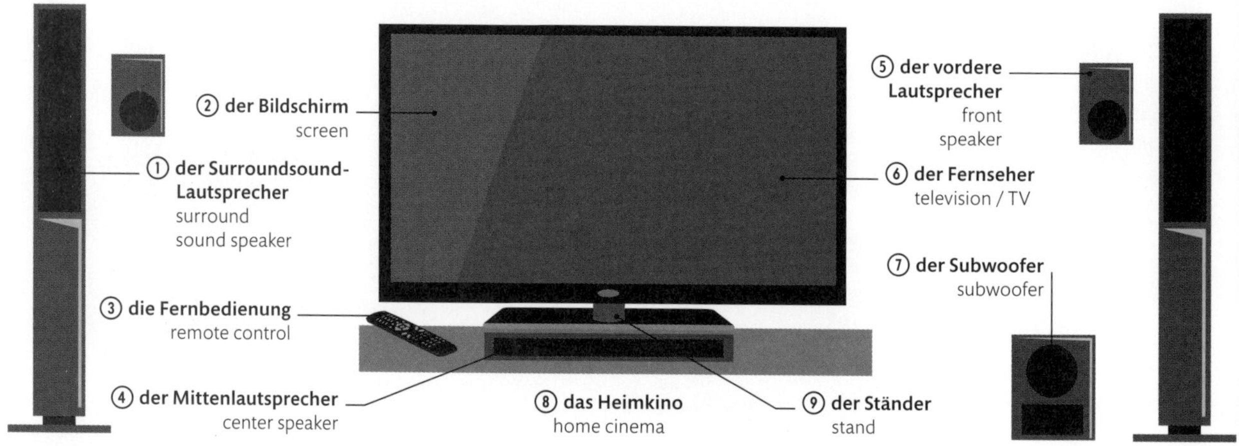


⑧ **das Heimkino**
home cinema

⑩ **die Soundbar**
sound bar

⑪ **die CD**
CD

⑫ **die DVD**
DVD

⑮ **das Radio**
radio

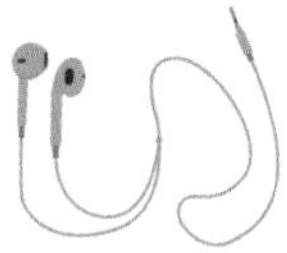

⑯ **die Ohrhörer** *m, pl*
earphones

⑰ **der Kopfhörer**
headphones

⑱ **der kabellose Kopfhörer**
wireless headphones

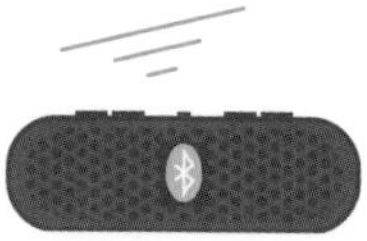

⑲ **der Regler**
Bluetooth speaker

⑳ **der Plattenspieler**
record player

㉑ **die Schallplatte**
records

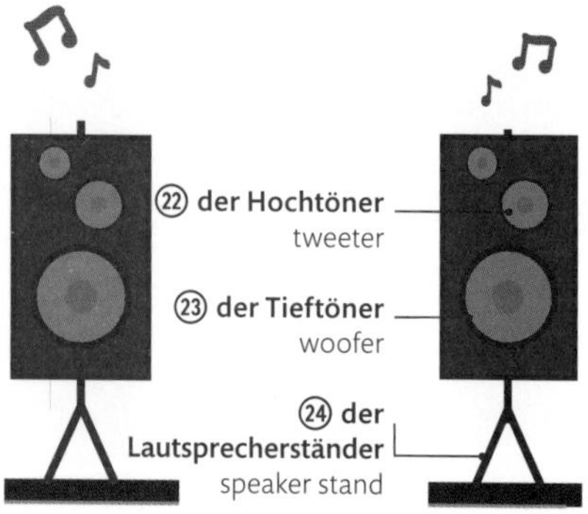


㉕ **der Lautsprecher**
loudspeakers

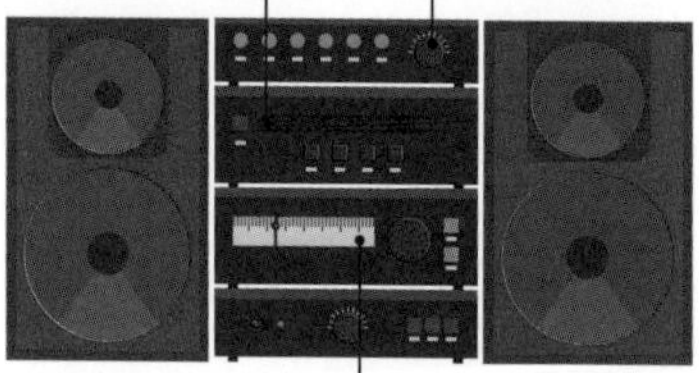


㉙ **die Hi-Fi-Anlage**
hi-fi system

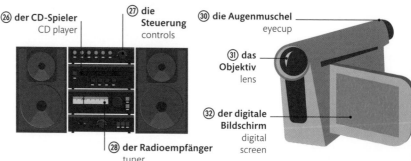

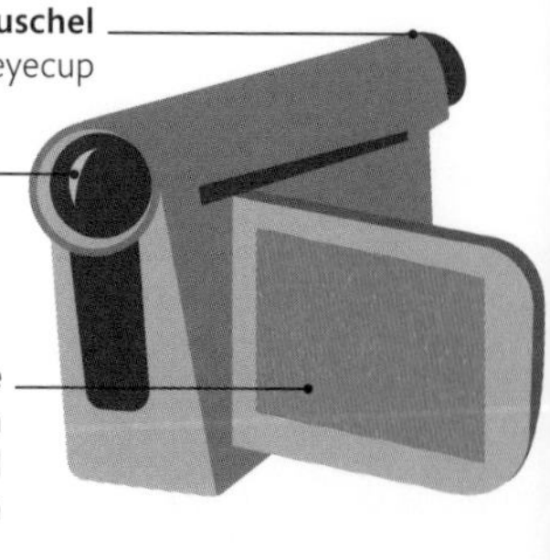


㉝ **der Camcorder**
camcorder

See also
**127** Filme • Movies **128-129** Musik • Music
**137** Fernsehen • Television **140** Spiele • Games

(34) **stereo**
stereo

(35) **mono**
mono

(36) **den Sender einstellen**
to tune in

(37) **die Lautstärke**
volume

(38) **lauter machen**
to turn up

(39) **leiser machen**
to turn down

(40) **die Satellitenschüssel**
satellite dish

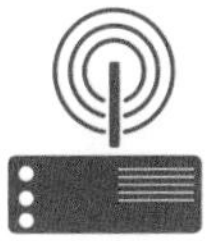
(41) **der Digitalempfänger**
digital box

(42) **das Mikrofon**
microphone

(43) **Karaoke** *n*
karaoke

## 136.2 VIDEOSPIELE • VIDEO GAMES

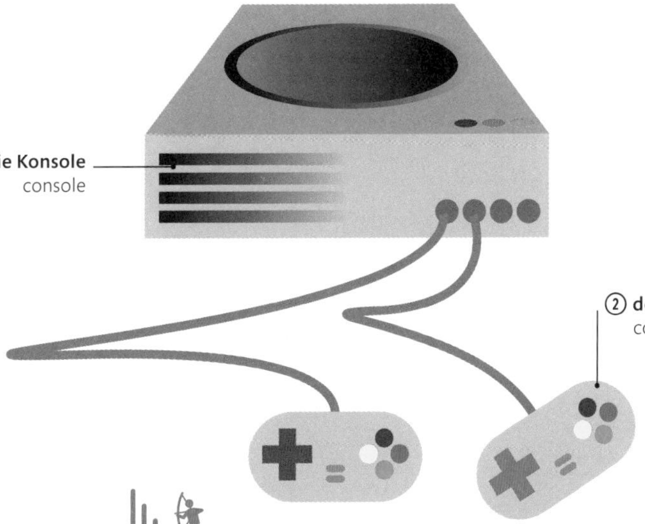
(1) **die Konsole**
console

(2) **der Controller**
controller

(3) **das Strategiespiel**
strategy game

(4) **das Wissensquiz**
trivia game

(5) **das Plattformspiel**
platform game

(6) **das Abenteuerspiel**
adventure game

(7) **das Rollenspiel**
role-playing game

(8) **das Actionspiel**
action game

(9) **das Spiel für mehrere Spieler**
multiplayer game

(10) **das Simulationsspiel**
simulation game

(11) **das Sportspiel**
sports game

(12) **das Blockpuzzle**
puzzle game

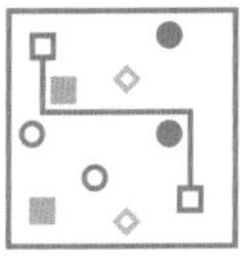
(13) **das Logikspiel**
logic game

# Fernsehen
## Television

### 137.1 FERNSEHEN · WATCHING TELEVISION

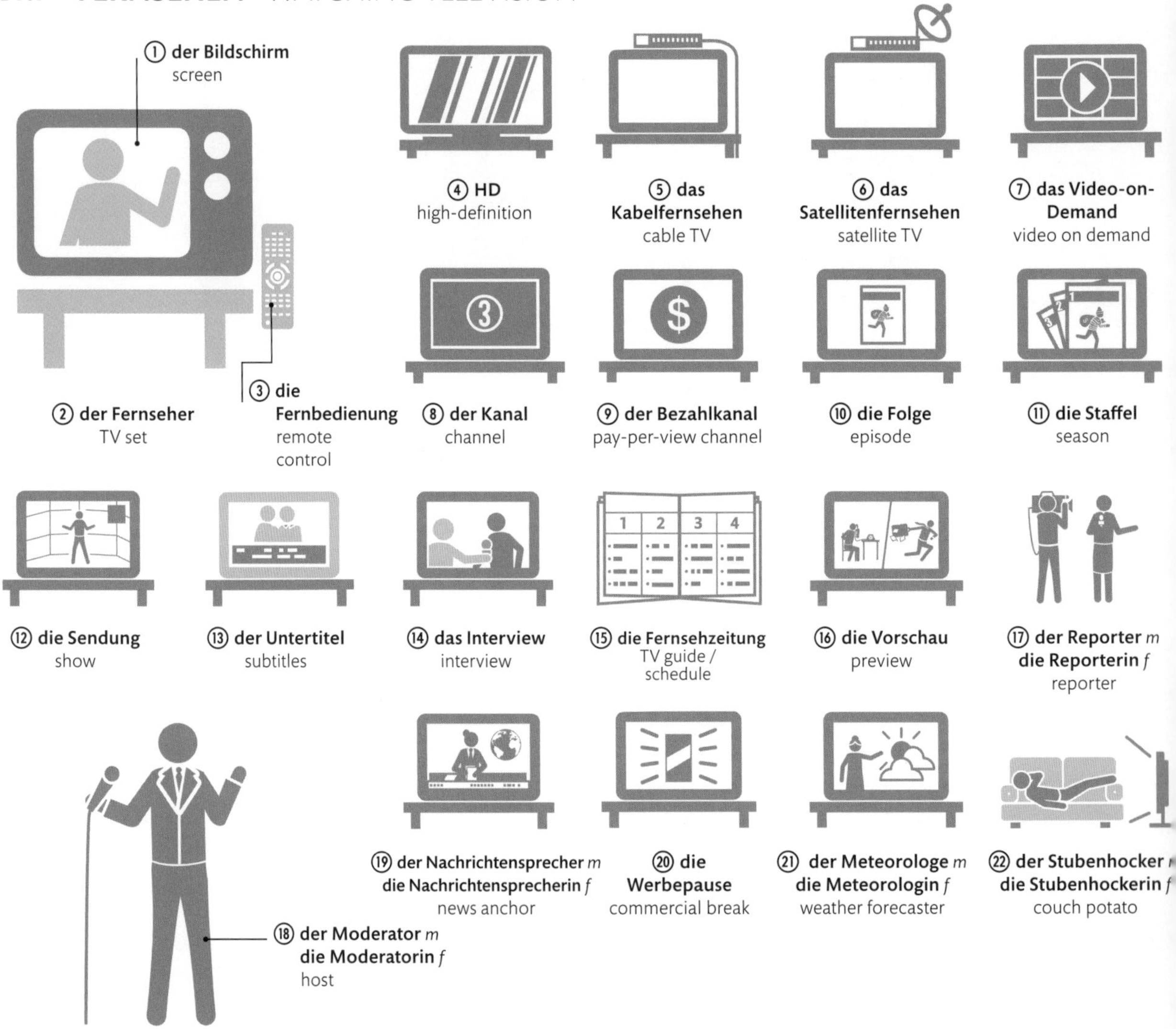

① der Bildschirm
screen
② der Fernseher
TV set
③ die Fernbedienung
remote control
④ HD
high-definition
⑤ das Kabelfernsehen
cable TV
⑥ das Satellitenfernsehen
satellite TV
⑦ das Video-on-Demand
video on demand
⑧ der Kanal
channel
⑨ der Bezahlkanal
pay-per-view channel
⑩ die Folge
episode
⑪ die Staffel
season
⑫ die Sendung
show
⑬ der Untertitel
subtitles
⑭ das Interview
interview
⑮ die Fernsehzeitung
TV guide / schedule
⑯ die Vorschau
preview
⑰ der Reporter *m*
die Reporterin *f*
reporter
⑱ der Moderator *m*
die Moderatorin *f*
host
⑲ der Nachrichtensprecher *m*
die Nachrichtensprecherin *f*
news anchor
⑳ die Werbepause
commercial break
㉑ der Meteorologe *m*
die Meteorologin *f*
weather forecaster
㉒ der Stubenhocker *m*
die Stubenhockerin *f*
couch potato

### 137.2 FERNSEHVERBEN · TELEVISION VERBS

① einschalten
to turn on
② ausschalten
to turn off
③ lauter machen
to turn up the volume
④ leiser machen
to turn down the volume
⑤ umschalten
to change the channel
⑥ streamen
to stream

See also
**26** Das Wohnzimmer und das Esszimmer • Living room and dining room **84** Medien Media **127** Filme • Movies **136** Unterhaltung zu Hause • Home entertainment

## 137.3 FERNSEHSENDUNGEN UND KANÄLE • TV SHOWS AND CHANNELS

① **die Kochsendung**
cooking show

② **die Talkshow**
talk show

③ **der Sport**
sports

④ **die Dokumentation**
documentary

⑤ **die Naturdokumentation**
nature documentary

⑥ **das Historiendrama**
period drama / costume drama

⑦ **die Sitcom**
sitcom

⑧ **die Quizshow**
quiz show

⑨ **das Tagesgeschehen** *n, pl*
current affairs

⑩ **die Nachrichten** *pl*
news

⑪ **das Wetter**
weather

⑫ **die Seifenoper**
soap opera

⑬ **die Gameshow**
game show

⑭ **die Komödie**
comedy

⑮ **der Cartoon**
cartoon

⑯ **der Krimi**
crime

⑰ **der Thriller**
thriller

⑱ **die Satire**
satire

⑲ **die Kindersendung**
children's show

⑳ **das Frühstücksfernsehen**
morning show

㉑ **die Realityshow**
reality TV

㉒ **die TV-Mediathek**
catch-up TV

㉓ **der Shoppingkanal**
shopping channel

㉔ **der Musikkanal**
music channel

⑦ **abspielen**
to play

⑧ **anhalten**
to stop

⑨ **unterbrechen**
to pause

⑩ **zurückspulen**
to rewind

⑪ **vorspulen**
to fast forward

⑫ **aufzeichnen**
to record

# 138 Bücher und Lesen
## Books and reading

### 138.1 BÜCHER · BOOKS

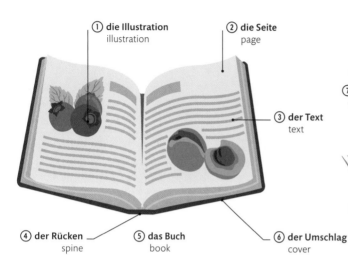

① die Illustration
illustration

② die Seite
page

③ der Text
text

④ der Rücken
spine

⑤ das Buch
book

⑥ der Umschlag
cover

⑦ der Schriftsteller *m*
die Schriftstellerin *f*
author

⑧ das Taschenbuch
paperback

⑨ das gebundene Buch
hardback

⑬ die Rezension
review

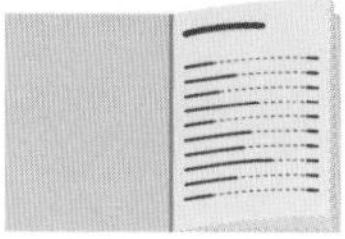

⑭ der Inhalt
contents

⑮ das Kapitel
chapter

### 138.2 LESEN UND GENRES · READING AND GENRES

① das Sachbuch
nonfiction

② das Wörterbuch
dictionary

③ das Lexikon
encyclopedia

④ das Gartenbuch
gardening book

⑤ die Fernsehzeitung
TV guide

⑥ der Ratgeber
self-help

⑦ die Autobiografie
autobiography

⑧ die Biografie
biography

⑨ das Kochbuch
cookbook

⑩ der Reiseführer
guidebook

⑪ das Natursachbuch
nature writing

⑫ das Kursbuch
textbook / course book

⑬ die Erzählliteratur
fiction

⑭ der Roman
novel

⑮ das Science-Fiction-Buch
science fiction

⑯ das Fantasy-Buch
fantasy

⑰ der Comic
comic

⑱ der Reisebericht
travel writing

See also
**127** Filme • Movies **136** Unterhaltung zu Hause • Home entertainment
**139** Fantasy und Mythologie • Fantasy and myth **175** Schreiben • Writing

**⑳ Ich liebe diesen Krimi. Ich kann ihn gar nicht aus der Hand legen.**
I love this crime novel. It's a real page-turner.

**㉑ Ich hasse diesen Fantasy-Roman. Die Handlung ist lächerlich.**
I hate this fantasy novel. The plot is ridiculous.

**⑩ der Titel**
title

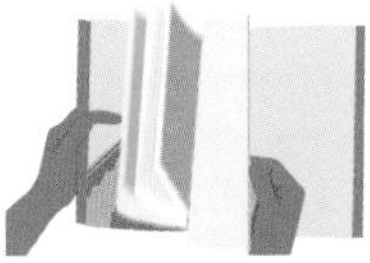

**⑪ durchblättern**
to flip through

**⑫ der E-Reader**
e-reader

**⑯ das Literaturverzeichnis**
bibliography

**⑰ das Glossar**
glossary

**⑱ das Wortverzeichnis**
index

**⑲ das Lesen**
reading

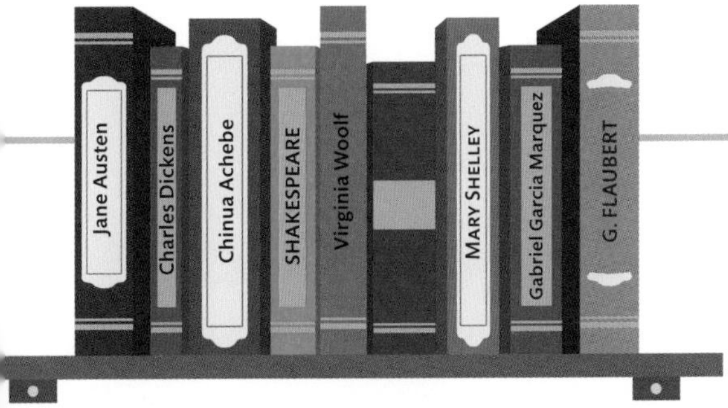


**⑲ die Belletristik**
literary fiction

**㉑ die Figur**
character

**⑳ das Kinderbuch**
children's book

**㉒ das Malbuch**
coloring book

**㉓ das Märchen**
fairy tale

**㉔ die Romanze**
romance

**㉕ der Krimi**
crime fiction

**㉖ die Unterhaltungsliteratur**
humor

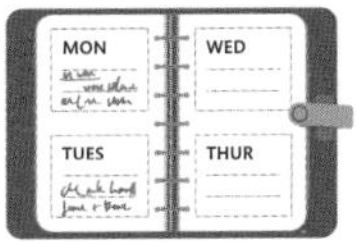


**㉗ der Kalender**
planner

**㉝ die Schlagzeile**
headline

**㉞ der Artikel**
article

**㉜ die Zeitung**
newspaper

**㉘ der Bestseller**
bestseller

**㉙ das Horoskop**
horoscope

**㉚ das Klatschmagazin**
gossip magazine

**㉛ das Rätselbuch**
puzzles

# Fantasy und Mythologie

## Fantasy and myth

### 139.1 MYTHEN, GESCHICHTEN UND FABELWESEN · MYTHS, STORIES, AND FANTASTIC CREATURES

② **Es war einmal, in einem weit entfernten Land...**
Once upon a time in a land far away...

① **das Märchen**
fairy tale

③ **das Einhorn**
unicorn

⑥ **zaubern**
to cast a spell

⑤ **der Zauberstab**
wand

④ **das Zauberbuch**
spell book

⑧ **der Zaubertrank**
witches' brew

⑦ **der Kessel**
cauldron

⑨ **die Kristallkugel**
crystal ball

⑩ **der Zaubertrank**
potion

⑪ **die Kerzenmagie**
candle magic

⑱ **der Stab**
staff

⑰ **der Zauberer**
wizard

⑭ **der Held** *m*
**die Heldin** *f*
hero

⑬ **der Minotaurus**
Minotaur

⑫ **die griechische Mythologie**
Greek mythology

⑮ **das Elixier**
elixir

⑯ **das Amulett**
amulet

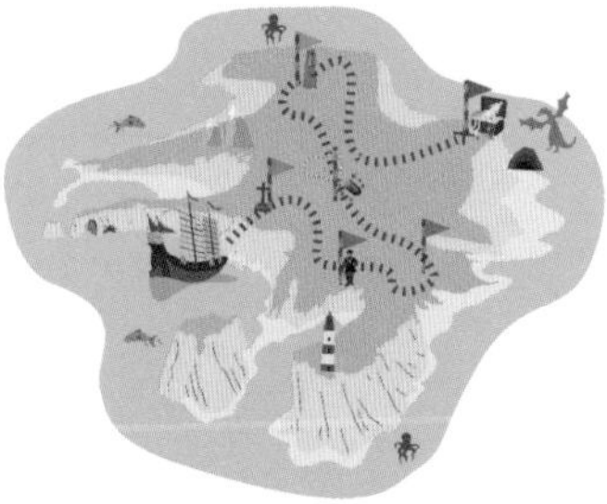

⑲ **die Aufgabe**
quest

⑳ **der Schatz**
treasure

㉑ **der fliegende Teppich**
flying carpet

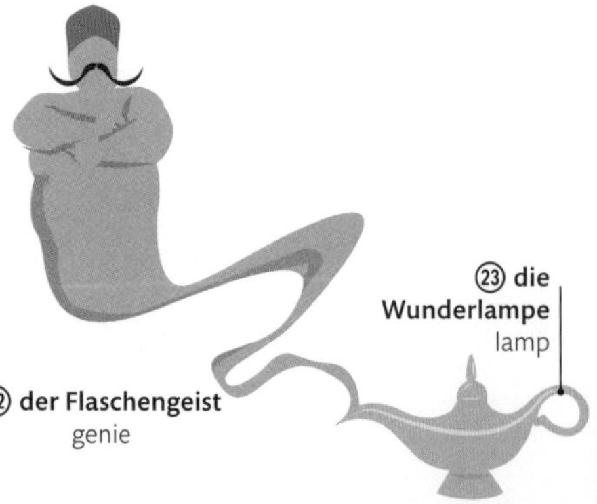

㉒ **der Flaschengeist**
genie

㉓ **die Wunderlampe**
lamp

See also
**127** Filme • Movies **137** Fernsehen • Television
**138** Bücher und Lesen • Books and reading

㉔ **die Seeschlange**
sea serpent

㉕ **Hugin und Munin**
Hugin and Munin

㉖ **die Disen** *pl*
the Disir

㉗ **das Monster**
monster

㉘ **der Zombie**
zombie

㉙ **der Werwolf**
werewolf

㉚ **der Vampir**
vampire

㉛ **das Gespenst**
ghost

㉜ **die Kürbisfratze**
jack-o'-lantern

㉝ **der Drache**
dragon

㉞ **der Ritter**
knight

㊱ **der Besen**
broomstick

㉟ **die Hexe**
witch

㊲ **die Fee**
fairy

㊳ **die Elfe**
pixie

㊴ **der Faun**
faun

㊵ **der Zwerg**
gnome

㊶ **der Kobold**
leprechaun

㊷ **der Gremlin**
gremlin

㊸ **der Goblin**
goblin

㊹ **der Troll**
troll

㊺ **der Oger**
ogre

㊻ **der Ork**
orc

㊼ **der Riese**
giant

㊽ **der Elf**
elf

㊾ **der Zwerg**
dwarf

㊿ **die Meerjungfrau**
mermaid

(51) **der Meermann**
merman

(52) **der Phönix**
phoenix

(53) **der Greif**
griffin

(54) **die Hydra**
hydra

(55) **der Zentaur**
centaur

(56) **die Sphinx**
sphinx

(57) **Kerberos**
Cerberus

(58) **der böse Roboter**
bad robot

(59) **der Außerirdische**
alien

# 140 Spiele
Games

## 140.1 SCHACH · CHESS

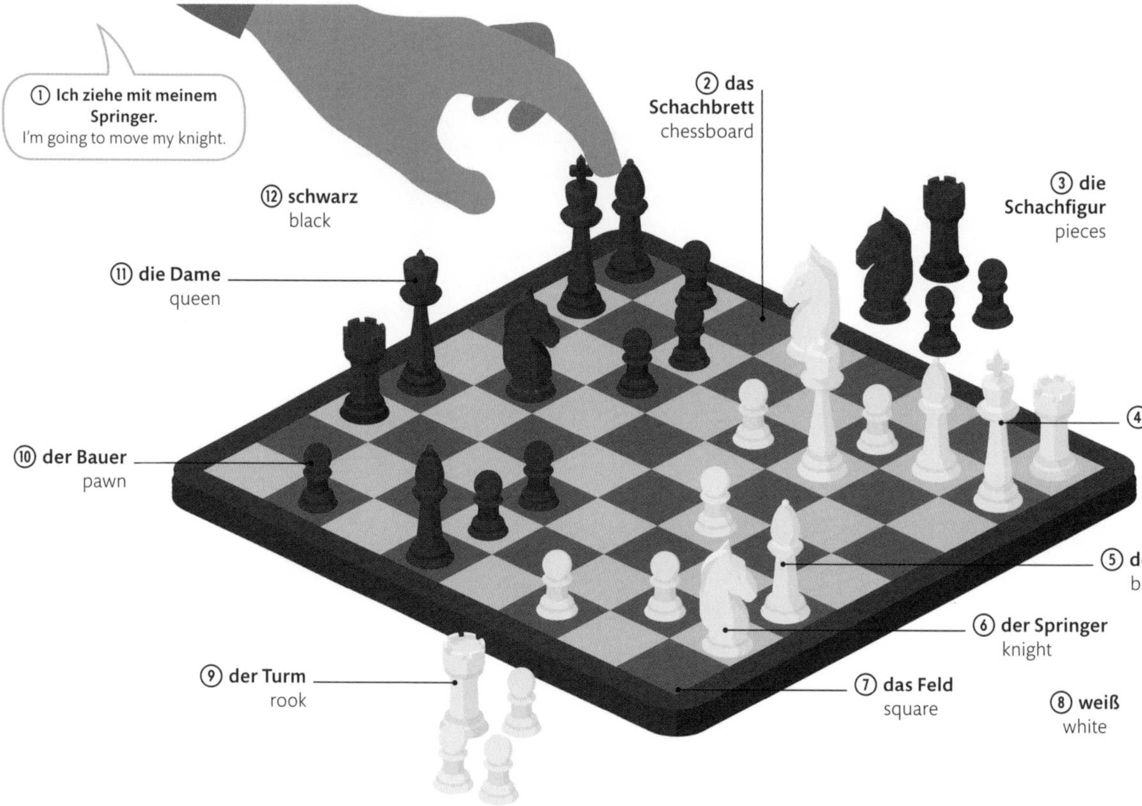


## 140.3 SPIELE · GAMES

① **das Brettspiel**
board games

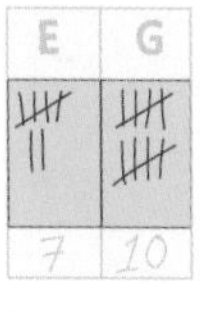


② **der Punkt**
points

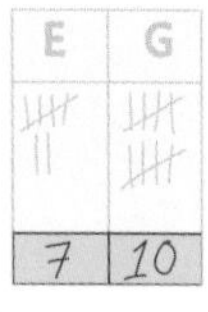


③ **das Ergebnis**
score

④ **Tic-Tac-Toe** *n*
tic-tac-toe

⑤ **der Würfel**
dice

⑥ **Solitär** *n*
solitaire

⑦ **die Figur**
pieces

⑧ **das Puzzle**
jigsaw puzzle

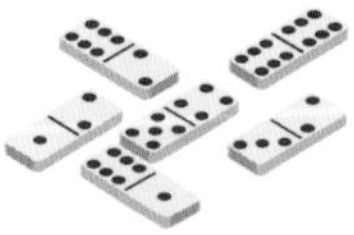

⑨ **Domino** *n*
dominoes

⑩ **der Dartpfeil**
darts

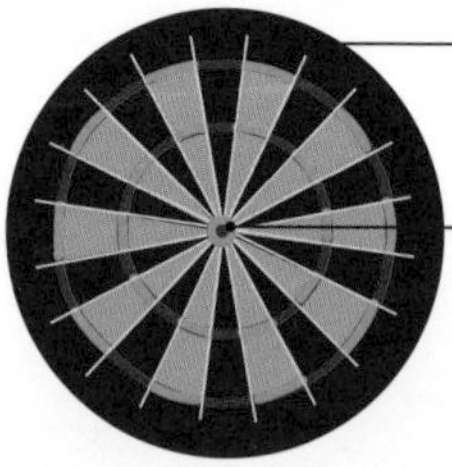

See also
**136** Unterhaltung zu Hause • Home entertainment **138** Bücher und Lesen • Books and reading **141-142** Kunst und Handwerk • Arts and crafts

## 140.2 **SPIELKARTEN** • PLAYING CARDS

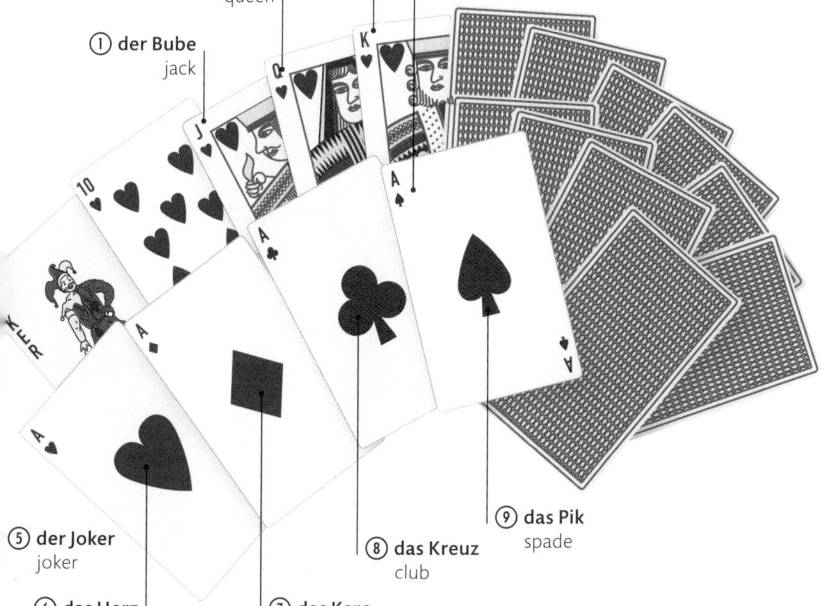

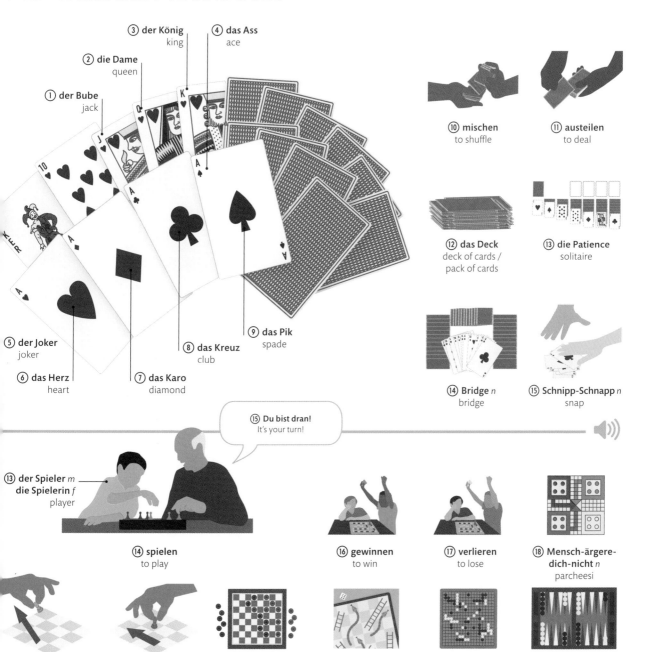

① **der Bube** jack
② **die Dame** queen
③ **der König** king
④ **das Ass** ace
⑤ **der Joker** joker
⑥ **das Herz** heart
⑦ **das Karo** diamond
⑧ **das Kreuz** club
⑨ **das Pik** spade

⑩ **mischen** to shuffle

⑪ **austeilen** to deal

⑫ **das Deck** deck of cards / pack of cards

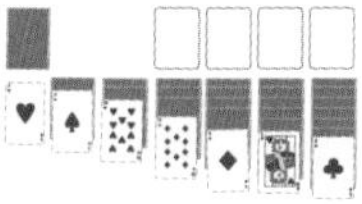

⑬ **die Patience** solitaire

⑭ **Bridge** *n* bridge

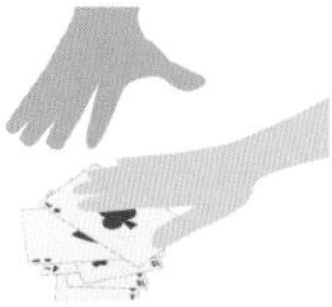

⑮ **Schnipp-Schnapp** *n* snap

⑮ **Du bist dran!**
It's your turn!

⑬ **der Spieler** *m* **die Spielerin** *f* player

⑭ **spielen** to play

⑯ **gewinnen** to win

⑰ **verlieren** to lose

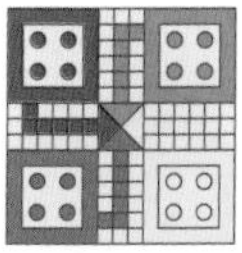

⑱ **Mensch-ärgere-dich-nicht** *n* parcheesi

⑲ **nehmen** to take

⑳ **ziehen** to move

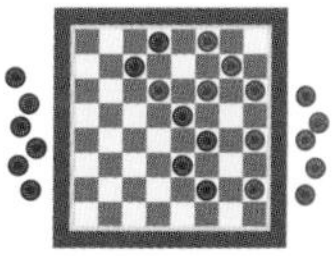

㉑ **Dame** *n* checkers

㉒ **Leiterspiel** *n* chutes and ladders

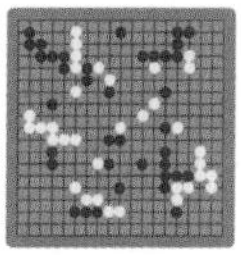

㉓ **Go** *n* go

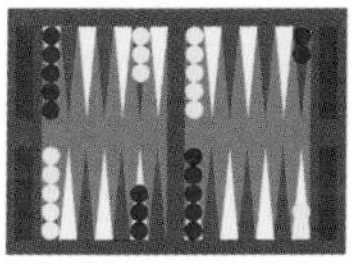

㉔ **Backgammon** *n* backgammon

# 141 Kunst und Handwerk

## Arts and crafts

### 141.1 DAS MALEN · PAINTING

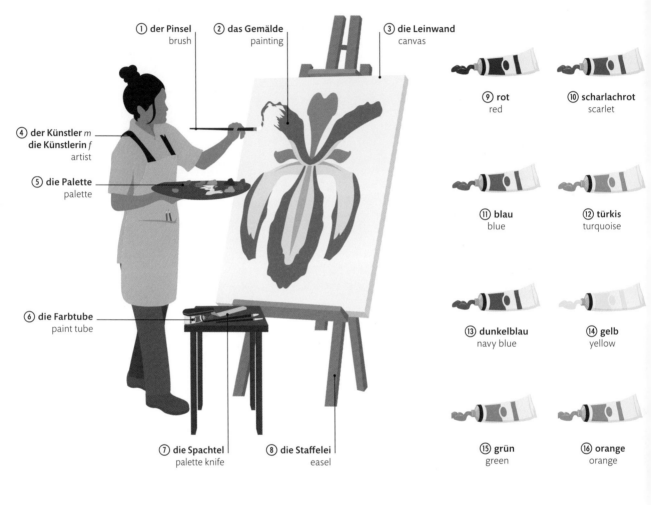

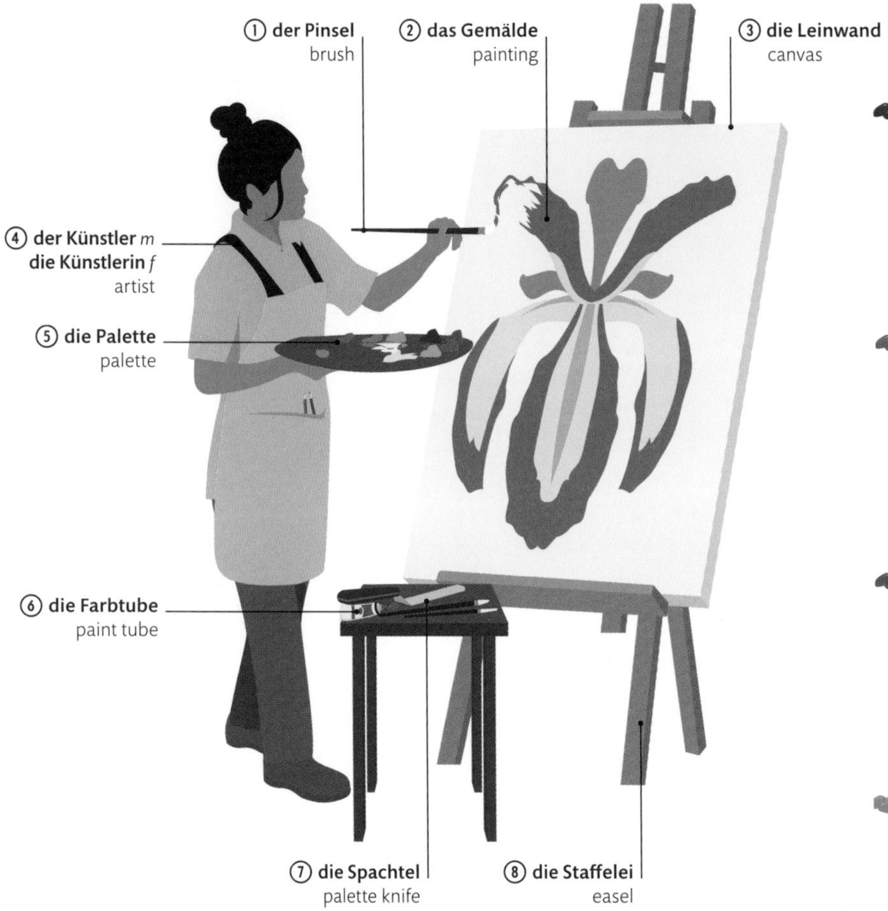

⑨ **rot**
red

⑩ **scharlachrot**
scarlet

⑪ **blau**
blue

⑫ **türkis**
turquoise

⑬ **dunkelblau**
navy blue

⑭ **gelb**
yellow

⑮ **grün**
green

⑯ **orange**
orange

⑰ **violett**
purple

⑱ **indigoblau**
indigo

⑲ **pink**
pink

⑳ **braun**
brown

㉑ **grau**
gray

㉒ **schwarz**
black

㉓ **weiß**
white

㉔ **die Ölfarbe**
oil paints

㉕ **die Wasserfarbe**
watercolors

㉖ **der Pastellstift**
pastels

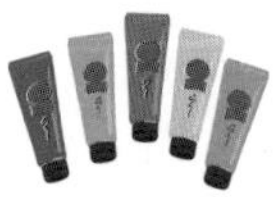

㉗ **die Acrylfarbe**
acrylic paints

㉘ **die Plakatfarbe**
poster paint

See also
**37** Wohnraumverschönerung • Renovating **130** Museen und Kunstgalerien • Museums and galleries **142** Kunst und Handwerk (Fortsetzung) • Arts and crafts continued

## 141.2 ANDERE KUNST- UND HANDWERKSARTEN • OTHER ARTS AND CRAFTS

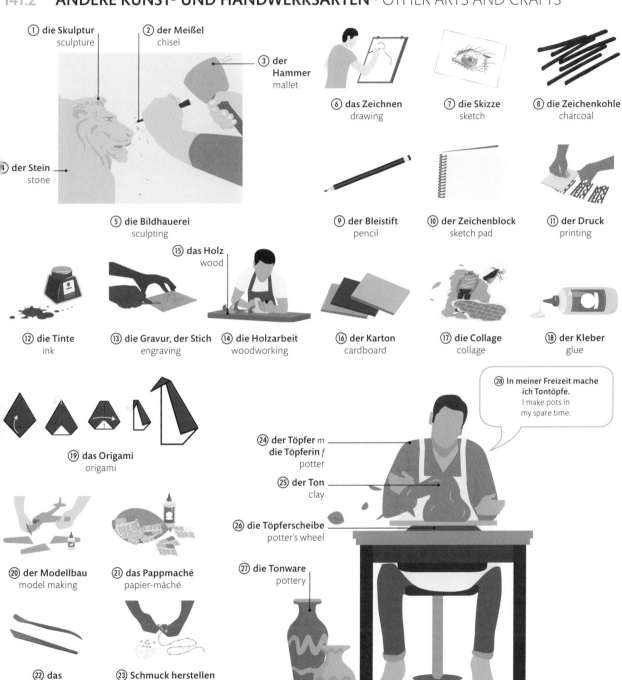

① **die Skulptur**
sculpture

② **der Meißel**
chisel

③ **der Hammer**
mallet

④ **der Stein**
stone

⑤ **die Bildhauerei**
sculpting

⑥ **das Zeichnen**
drawing

⑦ **die Skizze**
sketch

⑧ **die Zeichenkohle**
charcoal

⑨ **der Bleistift**
pencil

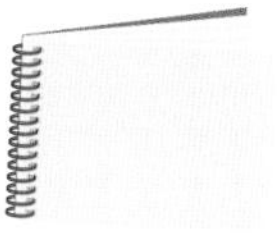

⑩ **der Zeichenblock**
sketch pad

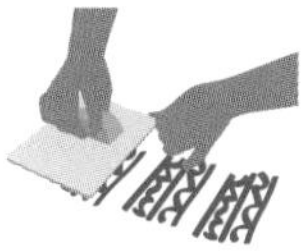

⑪ **der Druck**
printing

⑫ **die Tinte**
ink

⑬ **die Gravur, der Stich**
engraving

⑮ **das Holz**
wood

⑭ **die Holzarbeit**
woodworking

⑯ **der Karton**
cardboard

⑰ **die Collage**
collage

⑱ **der Kleber**
glue

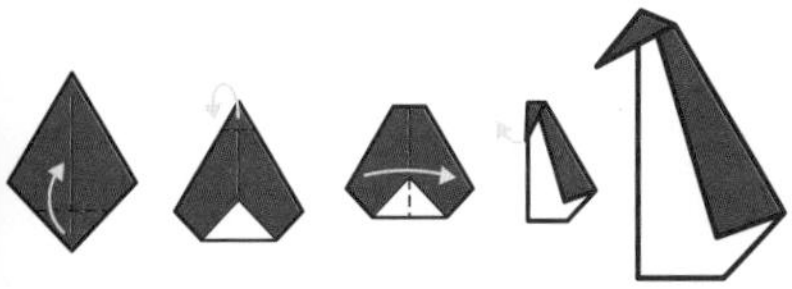

⑲ **das Origami**
origami

⑳ **der Modellbau**
model making

㉑ **das Pappmaché**
papier-mâché

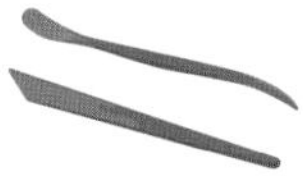

㉒ **das Modellierwerkzeug**
modeling tool

㉓ **Schmuck herstellen**
making jewelry

㉘ **In meiner Freizeit mache ich Tontöpfe.**
I make pots in my spare time.

㉔ **der Töpfer** *m*
**die Töpferin** *f*
potter

㉕ **der Ton**
clay

㉖ **die Töpferscheibe**
potter's wheel

㉗ **die Tonware**
pottery

# 142 Kunst und Handwerk (Fortsetzung)

## Arts and crafts continued

### 142.1 NÄHEN · SEWING

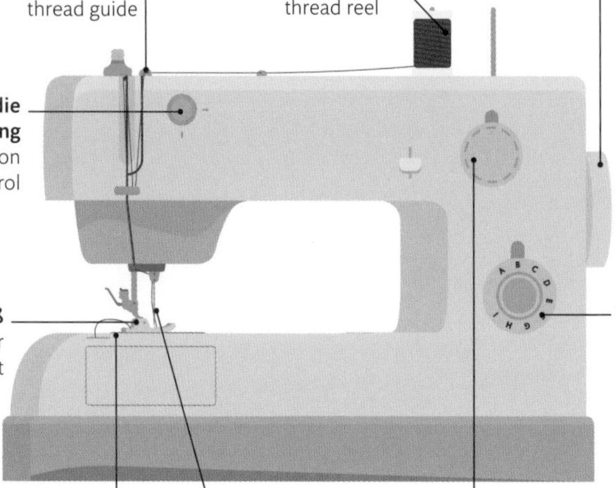

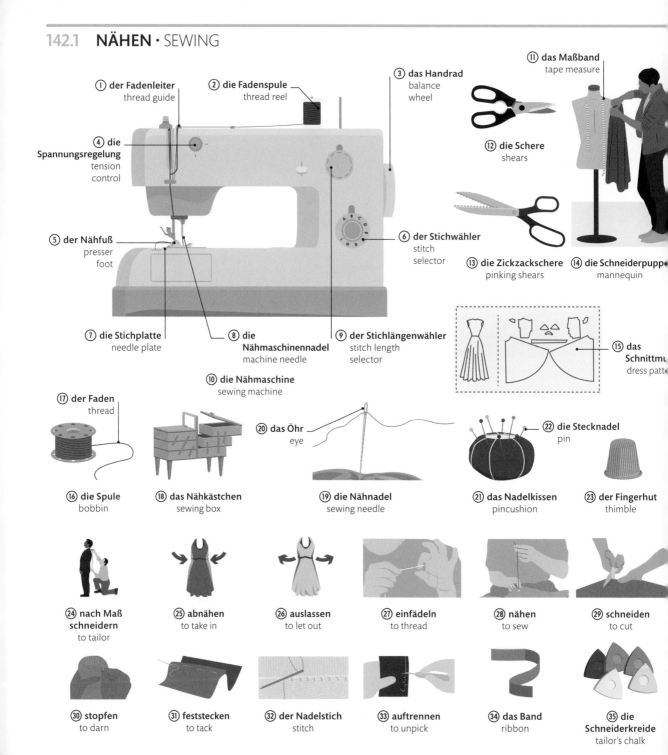

① **der Fadenleiter**
thread guide

② **die Fadenspule**
thread reel

③ **das Handrad**
balance wheel

④ **die Spannungsregelung**
tension control

⑤ **der Nähfuß**
presser foot

⑥ **der Stichwähler**
stitch selector

⑦ **die Stichplatte**
needle plate

⑧ **die Nähmaschinennadel**
machine needle

⑨ **der Stichlängenwähler**
stitch length selector

⑩ **die Nähmaschine**
sewing machine

⑪ **das Maßband**
tape measure

⑫ **die Schere**
shears

⑬ **die Zickzackschere**
pinking shears

⑭ **die Schneiderpupp**
mannequin

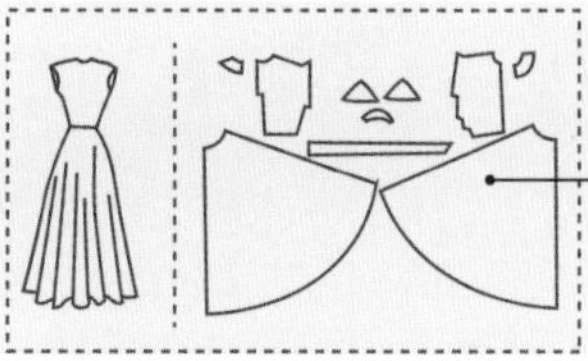

⑮ **das Schnittm**
dress patt

⑰ **der Faden**
thread

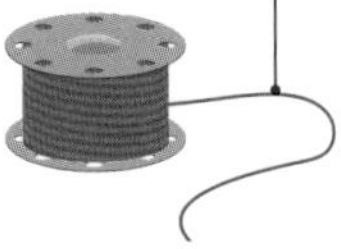

⑯ **die Spule**
bobbin

⑱ **das Nähkästchen**
sewing box

⑳ **das Öhr**
eye

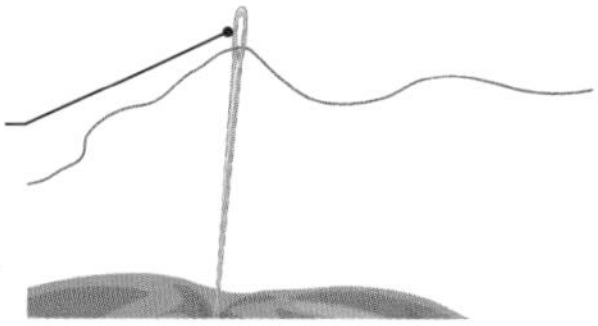

⑲ **die Nähnadel**
sewing needle

㉒ **die Stecknadel**
pin

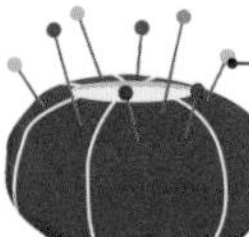

㉑ **das Nadelkissen**
pincushion

㉓ **der Fingerhut**
thimble

㉔ **nach Maß schneidern**
to tailor

㉕ **abnähen**
to take in

㉖ **auslassen**
to let out

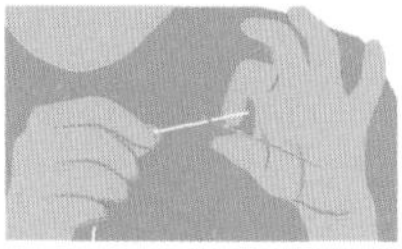

㉗ **einfädeln**
to thread

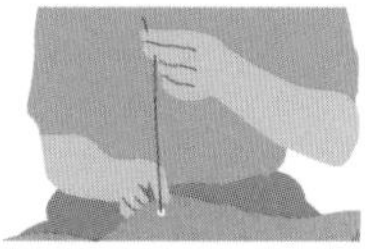

㉘ **nähen**
to sew

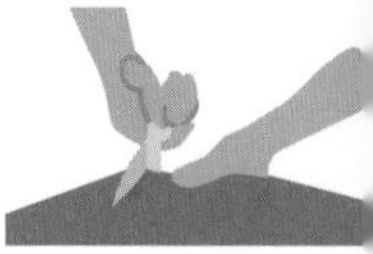

㉙ **schneiden**
to cut

㉚ **stopfen**
to darn

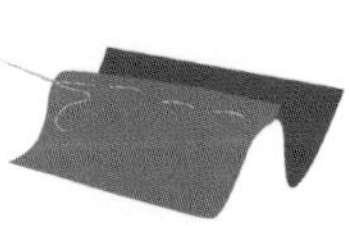

㉛ **feststecken**
to tack

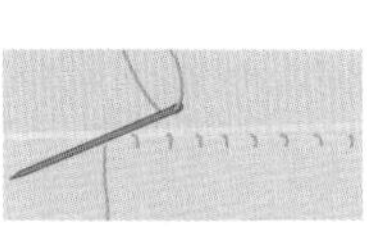

㉜ **der Nadelstich**
stitch

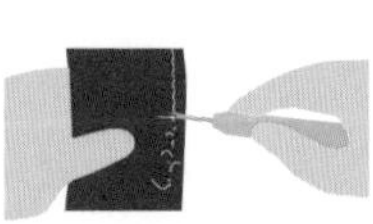

㉝ **auftrennen**
to unpick

㉞ **das Band**
ribbon

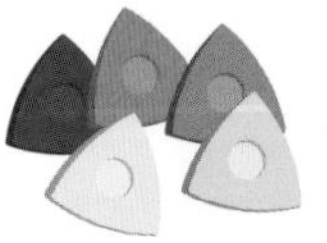

㉟ **die Schneiderkreide**
tailor's chalk

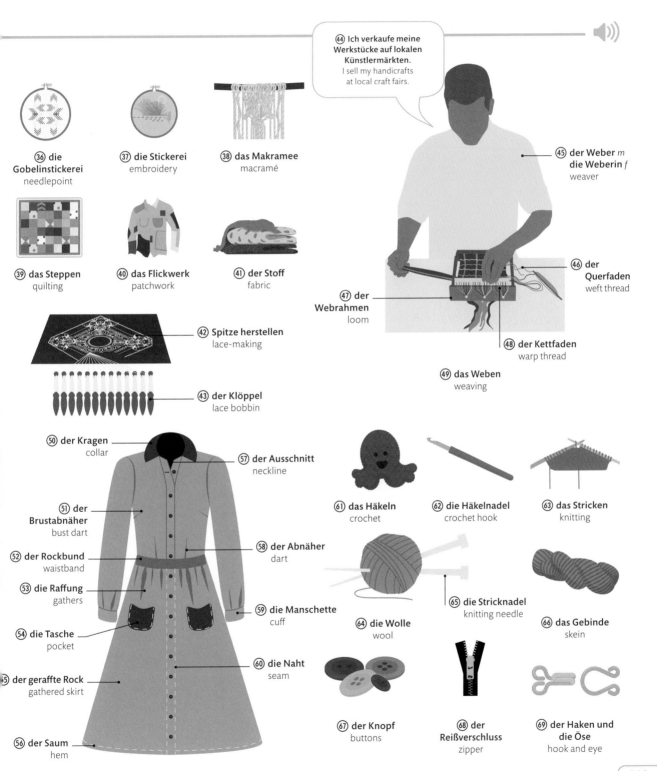

See also
**11** Fähigkeiten und Handlungen • Abilities and actions **13-15** Kleidung • Clothes
**37** Wohnraumverschönerung • Renovating **39** Gartenarbeit • Practical gardening

(36) **die Gobelinstickerei**
needlepoint

(37) **die Stickerei**
embroidery

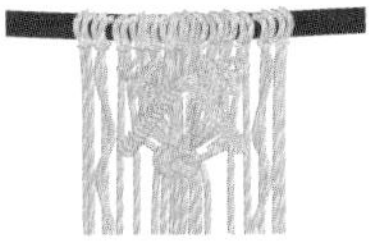

(38) **das Makramee**
macramé

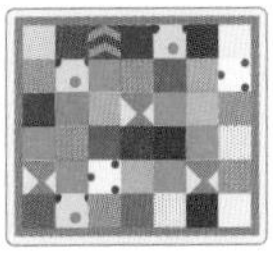

(39) **das Steppen**
quilting

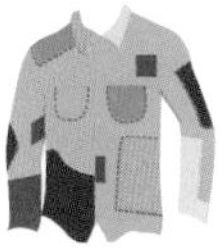

(40) **das Flickwerk**
patchwork

(41) **der Stoff**
fabric

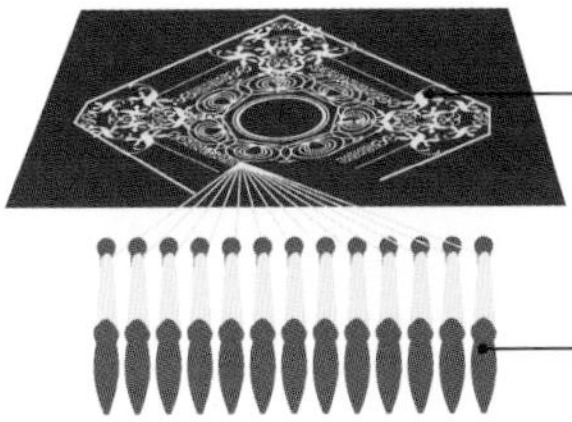

(42) **Spitze herstellen**
lace-making

(43) **der Klöppel**
lace bobbin

(44) **Ich verkaufe meine Werkstücke auf lokalen Künstlermärkten.**
I sell my handicrafts at local craft fairs.

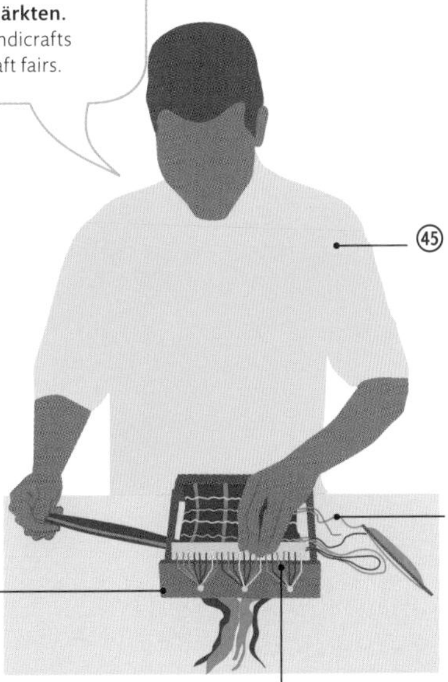

(45) **der Weber** *m* **die Weberin** *f*
weaver

(46) **der Querfaden**
weft thread

(47) **der Webrahmen**
loom

(48) **der Kettfaden**
warp thread

(49) **das Weben**
weaving

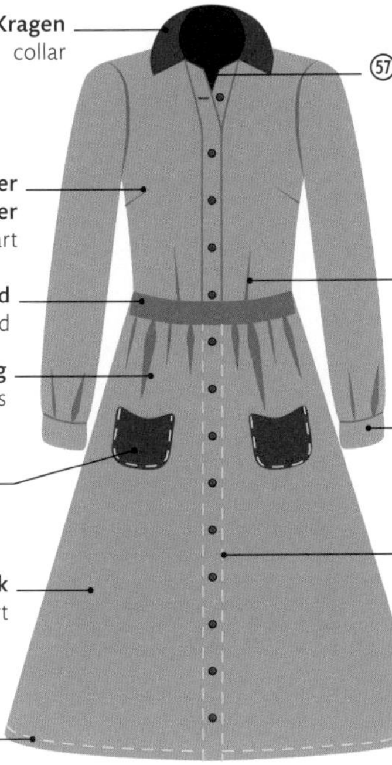

(50) **der Kragen**
collar

(51) **der Brustabnäher**
bust dart

(52) **der Rockbund**
waistband

(53) **die Raffung**
gathers

(54) **die Tasche**
pocket

(55) **der geraffte Rock**
gathered skirt

(56) **der Saum**
hem

(57) **der Ausschnitt**
neckline

(58) **der Abnäher**
dart

(59) **die Manschette**
cuff

(60) **die Naht**
seam

(61) **das Häkeln**
crochet

(62) **die Häkelnadel**
crochet hook

(63) **das Stricken**
knitting

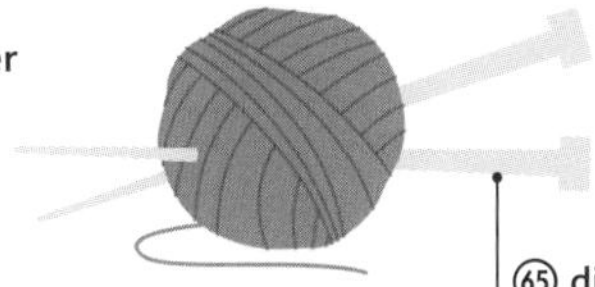

(64) **die Wolle**
wool

(65) **die Stricknadel**
knitting needle

(66) **das Gebinde**
skein

(67) **der Knopf**
buttons

(68) **der Reißverschluss**
zipper

(69) **der Haken und die Öse**
hook and eye

# 143 Der Weltraum
## Space

### 143.1 DAS SONNENSYSTEM • THE SOLAR SYSTEM

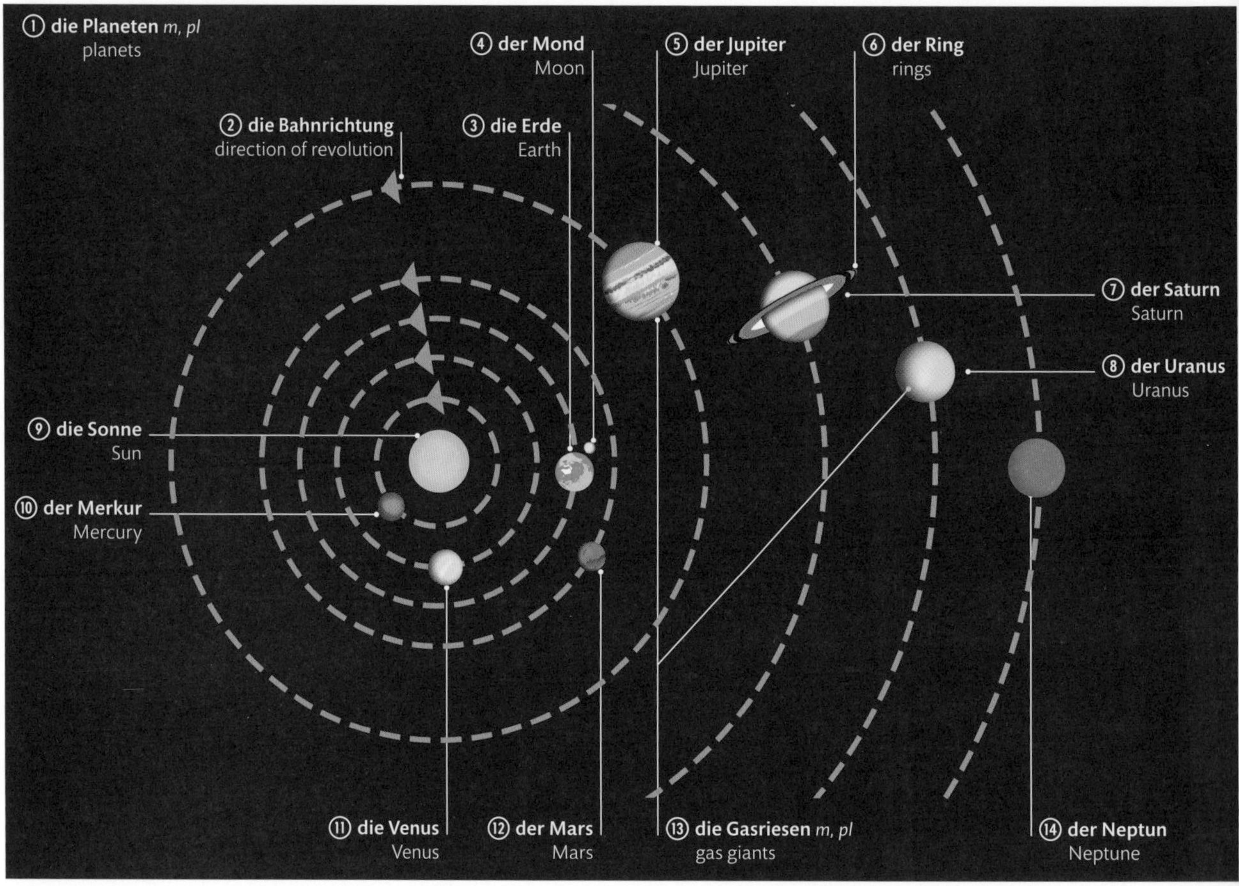

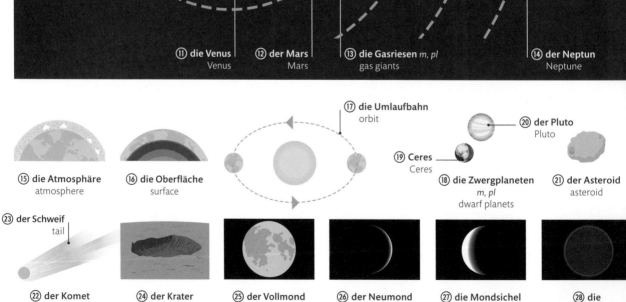

⑮ **die Atmosphäre**
atmosphere

⑯ **die Oberfläche**
surface

⑰ **die Umlaufbahn**
orbit

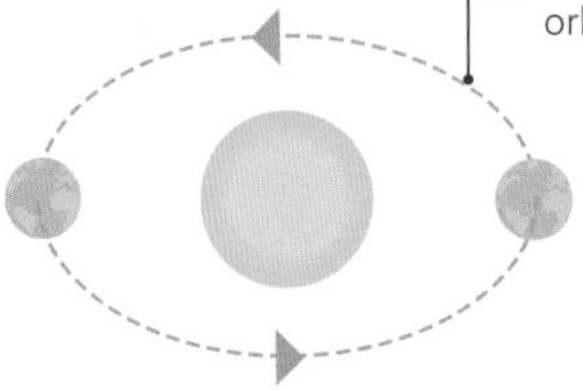

⑳ **der Pluto**
Pluto

⑲ **Ceres**
Ceres

⑱ **die Zwergplaneten** *m, pl*
dwarf planets

㉑ **der Asteroid**
asteroid

㉓ **der Schweif**
tail

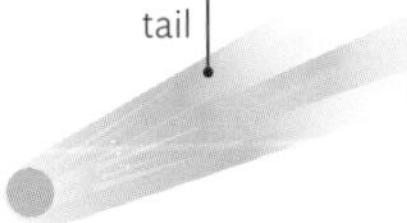

㉒ **der Komet**
comet

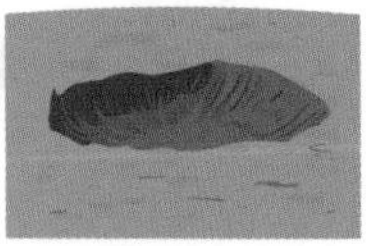

㉔ **der Krater**
crater

㉕ **der Vollmond**
full moon

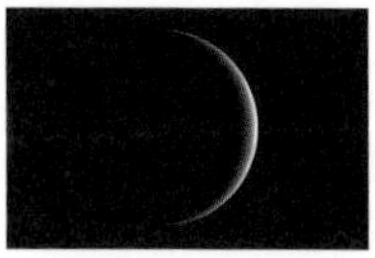

㉖ **der Neumond**
new moon

㉗ **die Mondsichel**
crescent moon

㉘ **die Mondfinsternis**
lunar eclipse

See also
**74** Mathematik • Mathematics **75** Physik • Physics **83** Computer und Technologie • Computers and technology **144** Der Weltraum (Fortsetzung) • Space continued **145** Der Planet Erde • Planet Earth **156** Gesteine und Mineralien • Rocks and minerals

## 143.2 DIE ERKUNDUNG DES WELTRAUMS • SPACE EXPLORATION

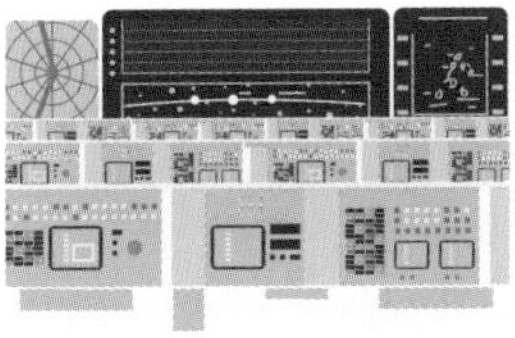

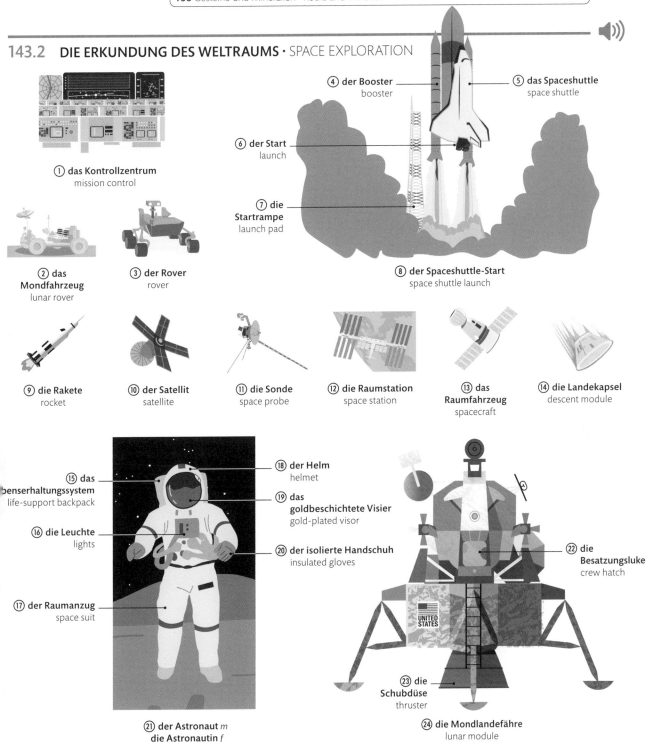

① **das Kontrollzentrum**
mission control

② **das Mondfahrzeug**
lunar rover

③ **der Rover**
rover

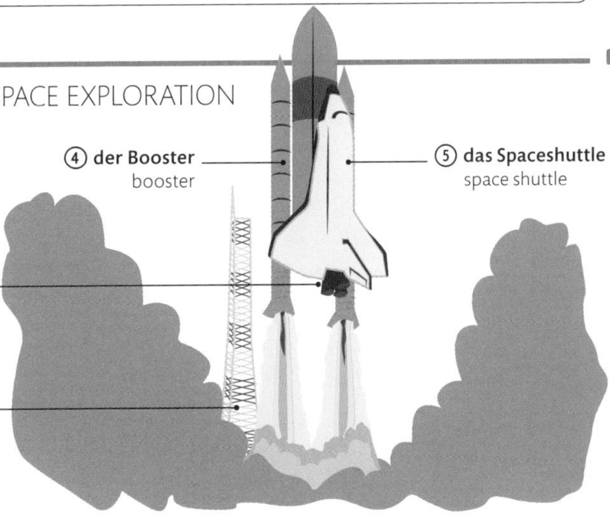

④ **der Booster**
booster

⑤ **das Spaceshuttle**
space shuttle

⑥ **der Start**
launch

⑦ **die Startrampe**
launch pad

⑧ **der Spaceshuttle-Start**
space shuttle launch

⑨ **die Rakete**
rocket

⑩ **der Satellit**
satellite

⑪ **die Sonde**
space probe

⑫ **die Raumstation**
space station

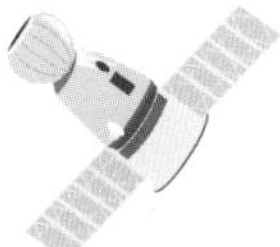

⑬ **das Raumfahrzeug**
spacecraft

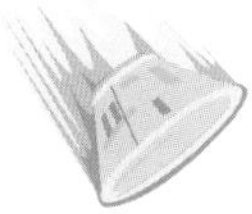

⑭ **die Landekapsel**
descent module

⑮ **das benserhaltungssystem**
life-support backpack

⑯ **die Leuchte**
lights

⑰ **der Raumanzug**
space suit

⑱ **der Helm**
helmet

⑲ **das goldbeschichtete Visier**
gold-plated visor

⑳ **der isolierte Handschuh**
insulated gloves

㉑ **der Astronaut** *m*
**die Astronautin** *f*
astronaut

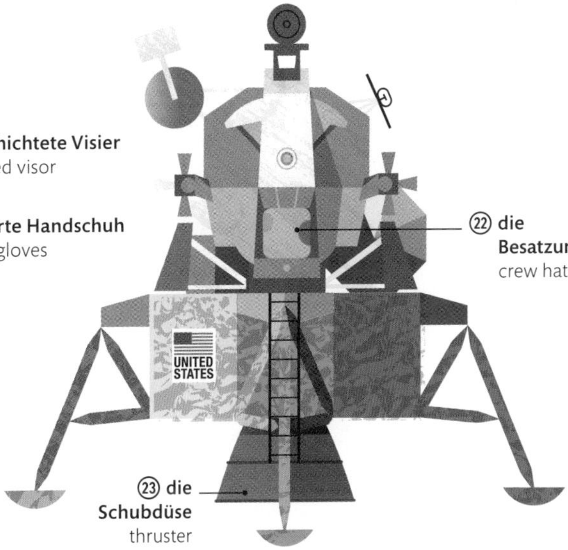


㉒ **die Besatzungsluke**
crew hatch

㉓ **die Schubdüse**
thruster

㉔ **die Mondlandefähre**
lunar module

# 144 Der Weltraum (Fortsetzung)
Space continued

## 144.1 ASTRONOMIE · ASTRONOMY

① **das Fernglas**
binoculars

② **das Linsenteleskop (Fernrohr)**
refractor telescope

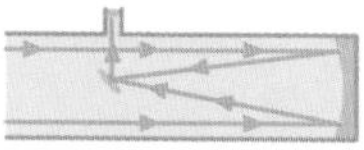
③ **das Spiegelteleskop**
reflector telescope

④ **das Radioteleskop**
radio telescope

⑤ **das Observatorium**
observatory

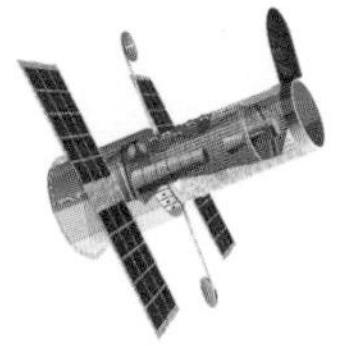
⑥ **das Weltraumteleskop**
space telescope

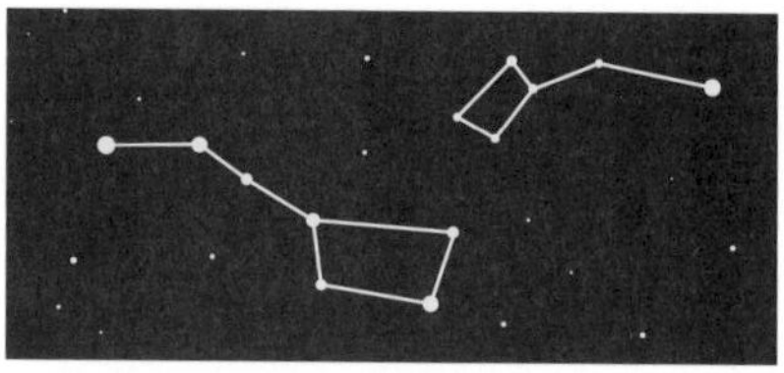
⑦ **das Sternbild**
constellation

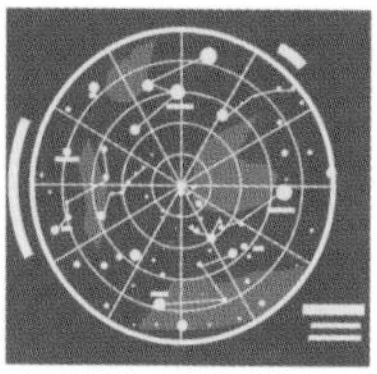
⑧ **die Sternkarte**
star chart

⑨ Ich habe eben einen Kometen entdeckt!
I've just spotted a comet.

⑩ **das Okular**
eyepiece

⑪ **das Suchfernrohr**
finderscope

⑫ **der Komet**
comet

⑬ **das Stativ**
tripod

⑭ **die Fokussierung**
focusing knob

⑮ **das Teleskop**
telescope

## 144.2 STERNE UND STERNBILDER · STARS AND CONSTELLATIONS

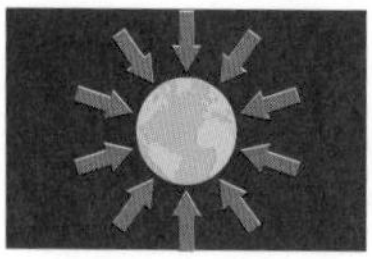
① **die Schwerkraft**
gravity

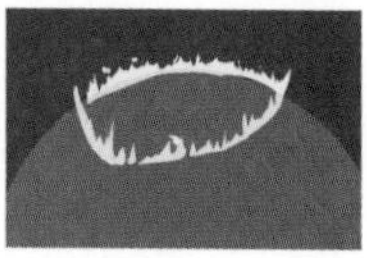
② **das Polarlicht**
aurora

③ **der Stern**
star

④ **die Sonneneruption**
flare

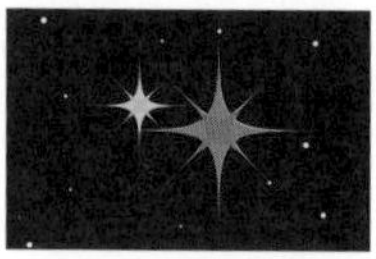
⑤ **der Doppelstern**
double star

⑥ **der Neutronenstern**
neutron star

⑬ **der Polarstern / Polaris**
the Pole Star / Polaris

⑭ **der Große Wagen**
the Big Dipper

⑮ **das Kreuz des Südens**
the Southern Cross

⑯ **der Orion**
Orion

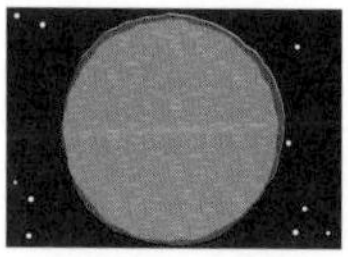
⑰ **der rote Riese**
red giant

⑱ **der weiße Zwerg**
white dwarf

See also
**74** Mathematik • Mathematics **75** Physik • Physics **83** Computer und Technologie • Computers and technology **145** Der Planet Erde • Planet Earth **156** Gesteine und Mineralien • Rocks and minerals

## 144.3 DER TIERKREIS • THE ZODIAC

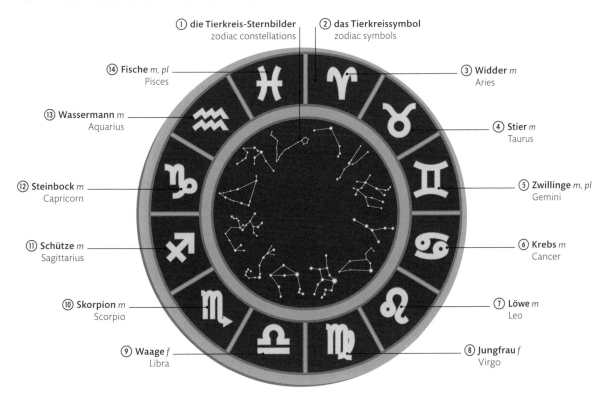

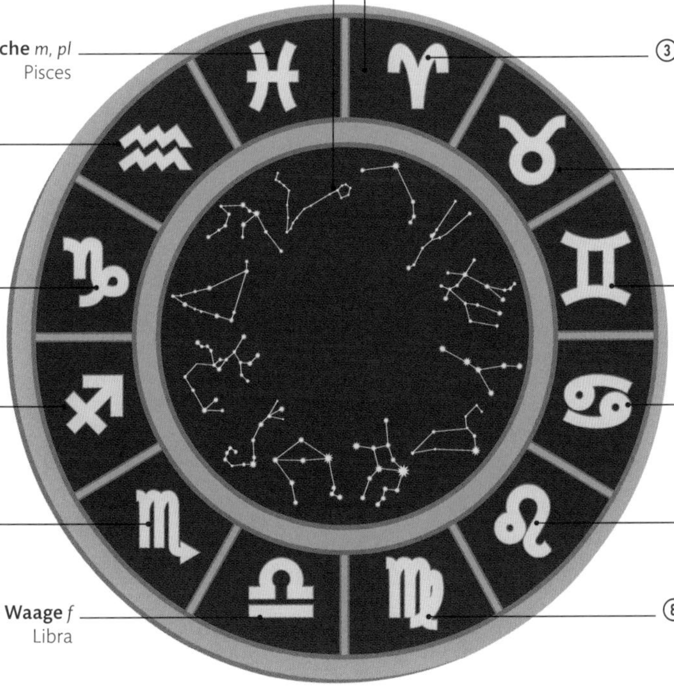

⑦ **die Supernova** supernova

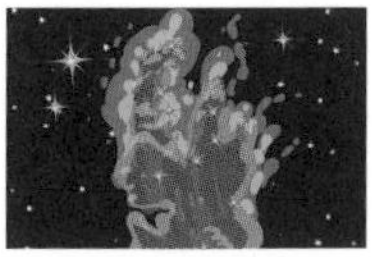
⑧ **der Nebel** nebula

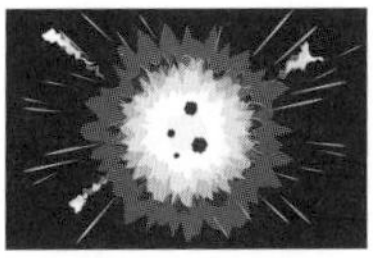
⑨ **der Urknall** the Big Bang

⑩ **der Sternhaufen** star cluster

⑪ **die elliptische Galaxie** elliptical galaxy

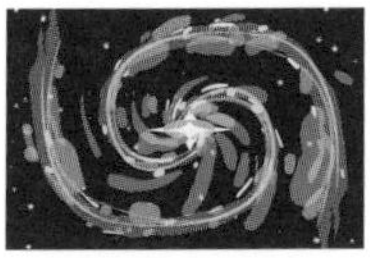
⑫ **die Spiralgalaxie** spiral galaxy

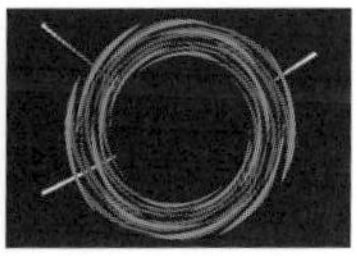
⑲ **das Schwarze Loch** black hole

⑳ **der Meteor** meteor

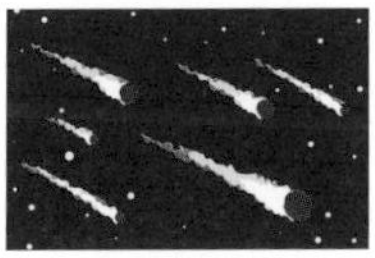
㉑ **der Meteorschauer** meteor shower

㉒ **die Milchstraße** the Milky Way

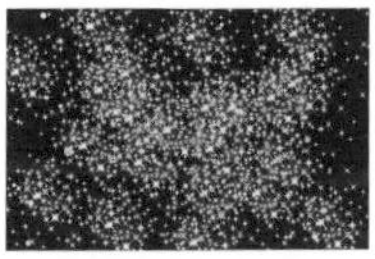
㉓ **das Universum** the universe

# 145 Der Planet Erde
Planet Earth

## 145.1 DIE ERDE · THE EARTH

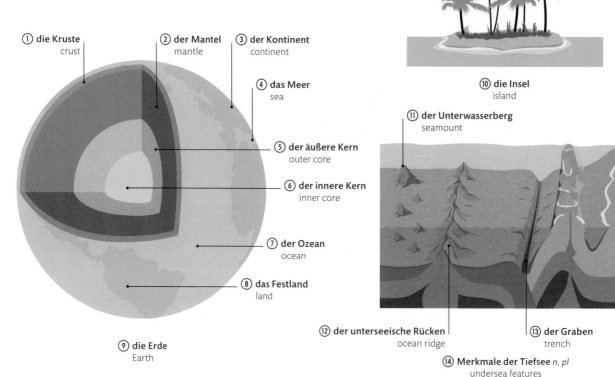

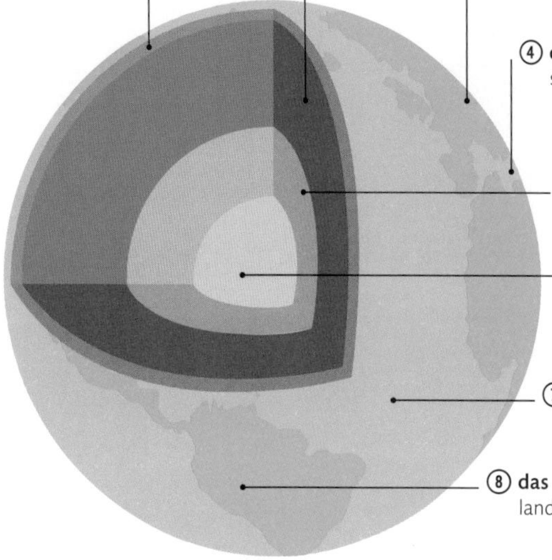


⑨ die Erde
Earth

⑩ die Insel
island

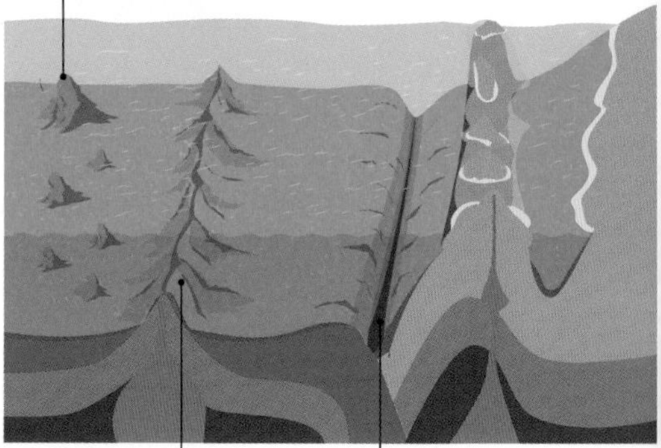


⑭ Merkmale der Tiefsee *n, pl*
undersea features

## 145.2 DIE PLATTENTEKTONIK · PLATE TECTONICS

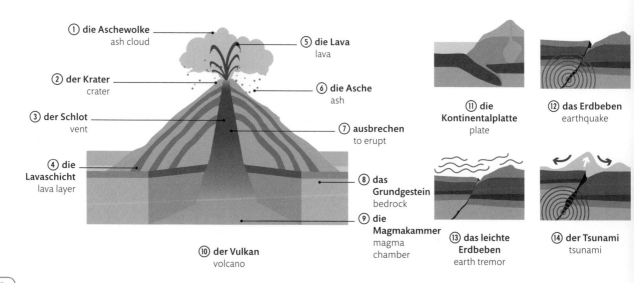

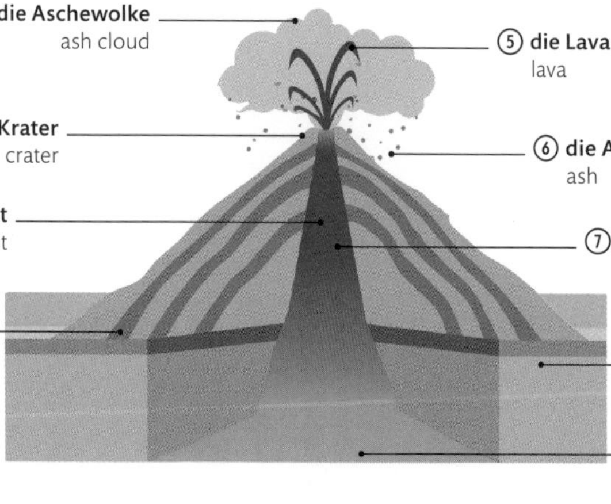


⑩ der Vulkan
volcano

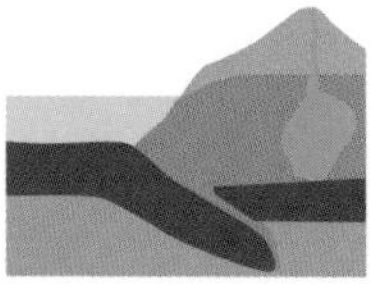

⑪ die Kontinentalplatte
plate

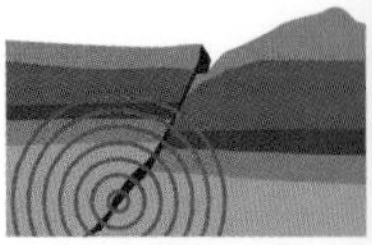

⑫ das Erdbeben
earthquake

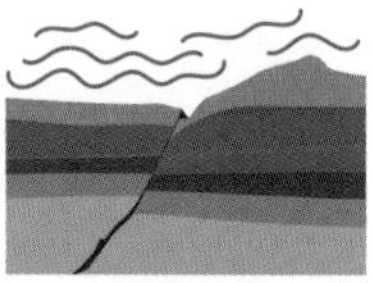

⑬ das leichte Erdbeben
earth tremor

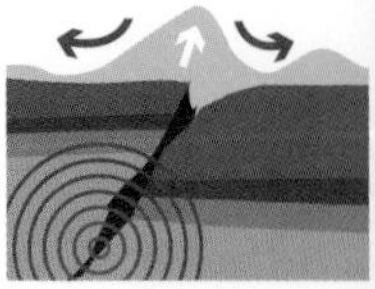

⑭ der Tsunami
tsunami

See also
**143-144** Der Weltraum • Space **146-147** Geografie • Geography **148** Karten und Richtungsangaben • Maps and directions **149-151** Länder • Countries

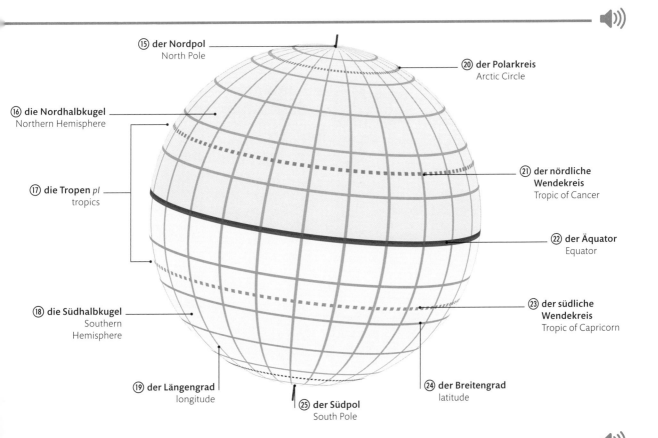

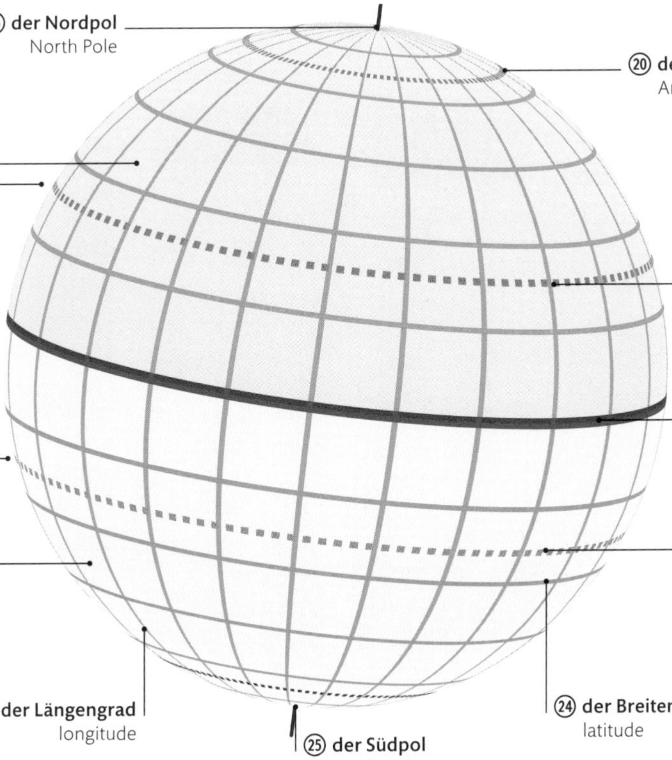


## 145.3 GEWÄSSER UND WASSERPHÄNOMENE • WATER FEATURES AND PHENOMENA

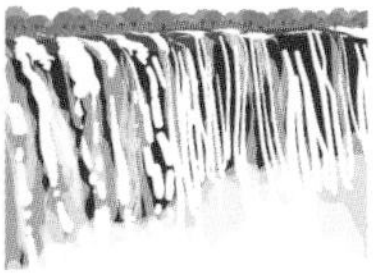
① **die Viktoriafälle**
Victoria Falls

② **die Hang-Son-Doong-Höhle**
Hang Son Doong

③ **der Amazonas**
the Amazon

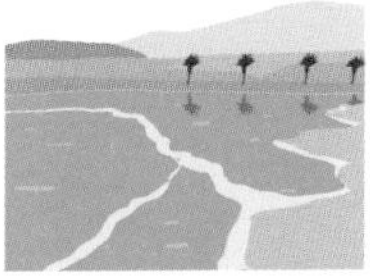
④ **das Tote Meer**
the Dead Sea

⑤ **der Cano Cristales**
Caño Cristales

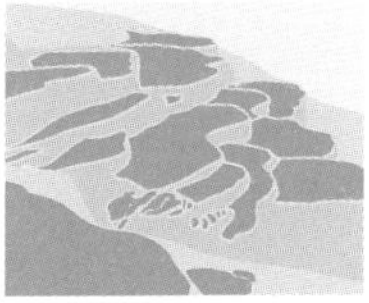
⑥ **Pamukkale**
Pamukkale

⑦ **das Great Barrier Reef**
the Barrier Reef

⑧ **der Ganges**
the Ganges

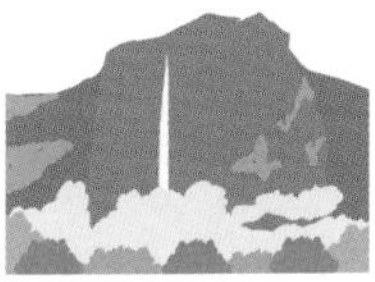
⑨ **der Salto Angel**
Angel Falls

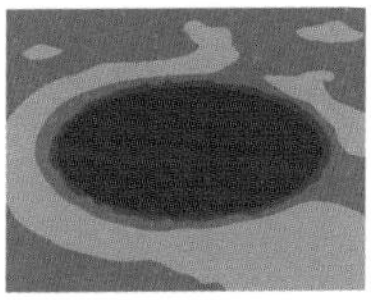
⑩ **das Great Blue Hole**
the Great Blue Hole

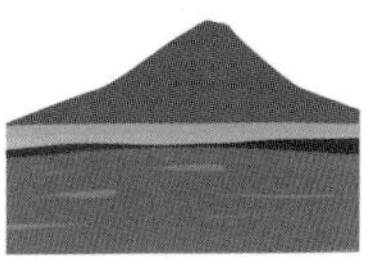
⑪ **der Natronsee**
Lake Natron

⑫ **der Spotted Lake**
Spotted Lake

# 146 Geografie
## Geography

### 146.1 GEOGRAFISCHE MERKMALE UND LANDSCHAFTEN · GEOGRAPHICAL FEATURES AND LANDSCAPE

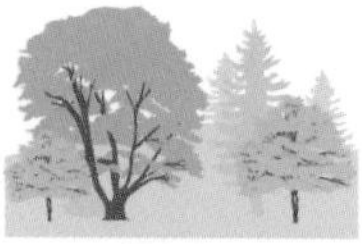

① **der Wald**
woods

② **der Regenwald**
rain forest

③ **der Nadelwald**
coniferous forest

④ **der Laubwald**
deciduous forest

⑨ **der Wasserfall**
waterfall

⑤ **die Stromschnelle**
rapids

⑥ **die Landschaft**
countryside

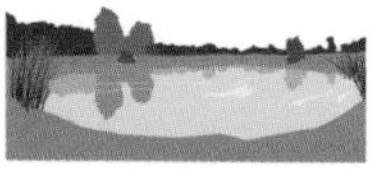

⑦ **der See**
lake

⑧ **der Sumpf**
swamp

⑩ **das Feld**
field

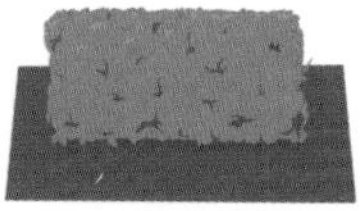

⑪ **die Hecke**
hedge

⑫ **das Tal**
valley

⑬ **das Ackerland**
farmland

⑭ **das Feuchtgebiet**
wetlands

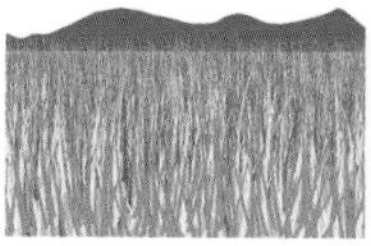

⑮ **das Grasland**
grassland

⑯ **die Prärie**
prairie

⑰ **die Steppe**
steppe

⑱ **der Tafelberg**
mesa

⑲ **das Hochland**
highland

⑳ **der Grat**
ridge

㉑ **das Gebirge**
mountain range

㉒ **die Savanne**
savannah

㉓ **die Gebirgskette**
mountain chain

㉔ **der Geysir**
geyser

㉕ **die Ebene**
plain

㉖ **die Oase**
oasis

㉗ **die Wüste**
desert

㉘ **die Sanddüne**
sand dune

See also
**133** Aktivitäten im Freien • Outdoor activites **145** Der Planet Erde • Planet Earth **147** Geografie (Fortsetzung) • Geography continued **148** Karten und Richtungsangaben • Maps and directions **149-151** Länder • Countries

㉙ **der Canyon**
canyon

㉚ **der Eisberg**
iceberg

㉛ **die Schlammlawine**
mudslide

㉜ **der Erdrutsch**
landslide

㊱ **der Gletscher**
glacier

㉝ **die Hochebene**
plateau

㉞ **die Polarregion**
polar region

㉟ **die Tundra**
tundra

## 146.2 HÖHLEN UND HÖHLENWANDERN · CAVES AND CAVING

# 147 Geografie (Fortsetzung)

Geography continued

## 147.1 **KÜSTENMERKMALE** · COASTAL FEATURES

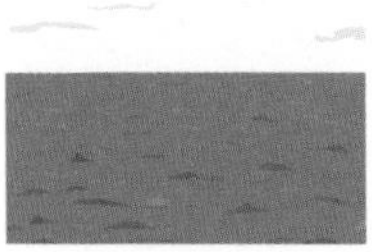

① **der Ozean**
ocean

② **die Welle**
wave

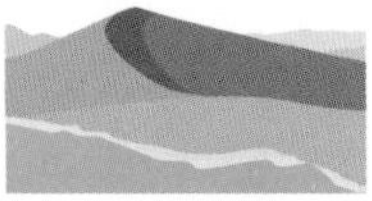

③ **die Düne**
dune

④ **die Insel**
island

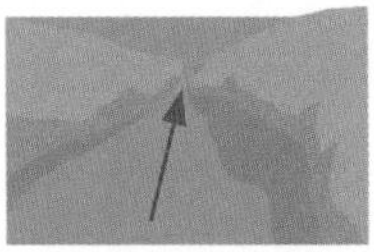

⑤ **die Meerenge**
strait

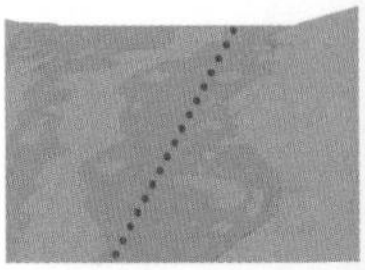

⑥ **der Kanal**
channel

⑦ **die Flut**
high tide

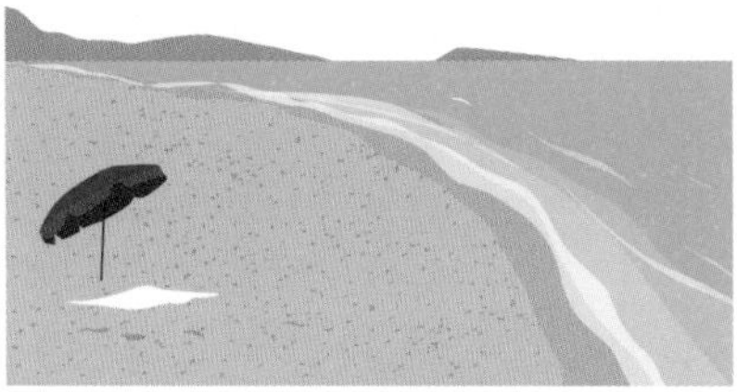

⑧ **die Ebbe**
low tide

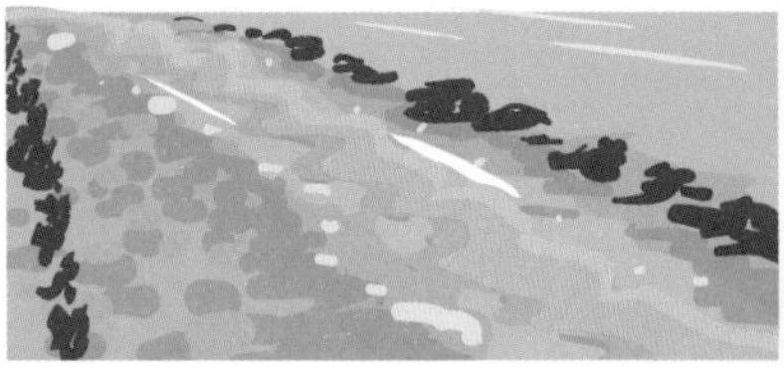

⑨ **das Riff**
reef

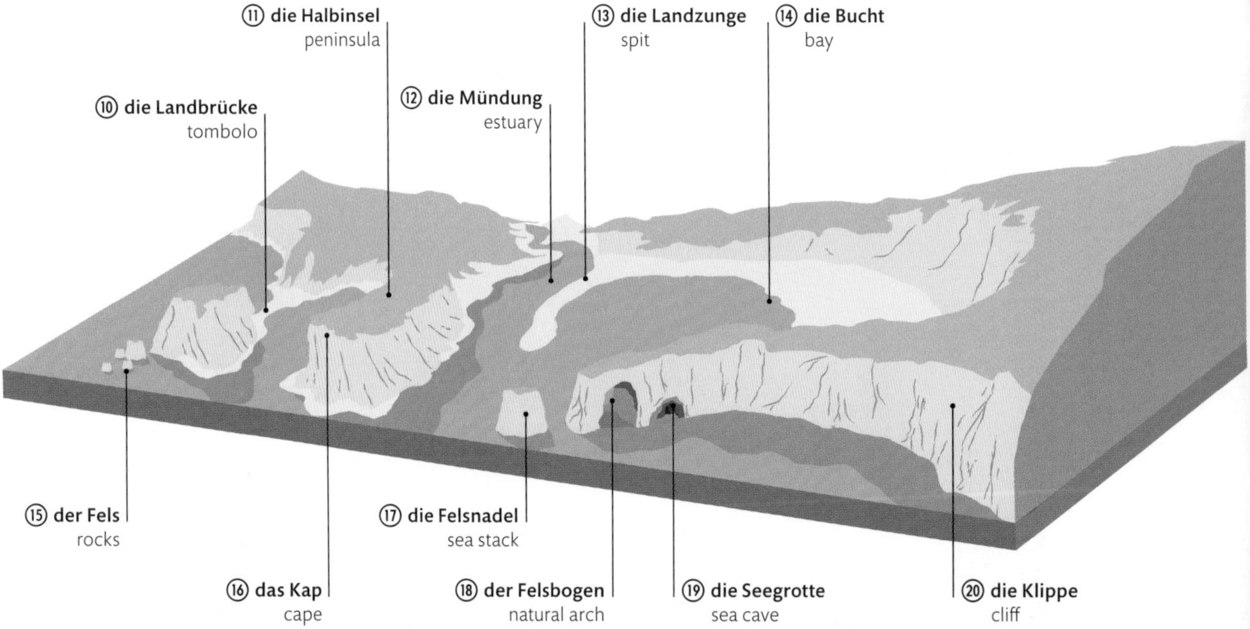

See also
**133** Aktivitäten im Freien • Outdoor activities **145** Der Planet Erde • Planet Earth
**148** Karten und Richtungsangaben • Maps and directions **149-151** Länder • Countries

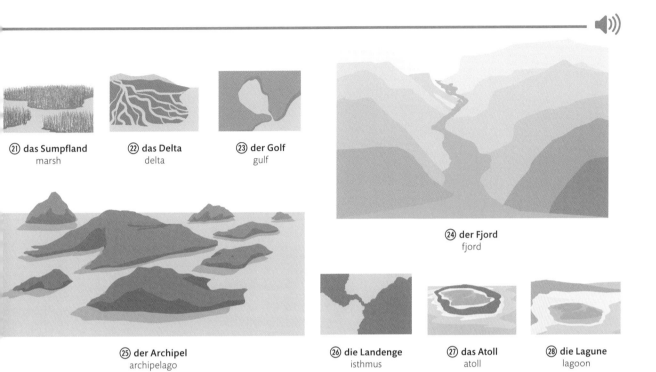

㉑ **das Sumpfland**
marsh

㉒ **das Delta**
delta

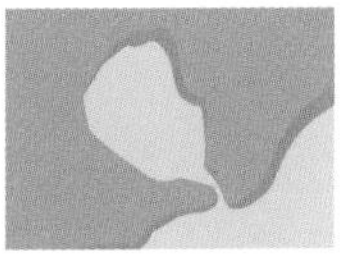

㉓ **der Golf**
gulf

㉔ **der Fjord**
fjord

㉕ **der Archipel**
archipelago

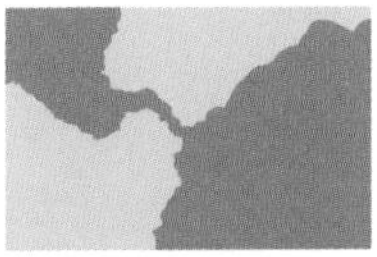

㉖ **die Landenge**
isthmus

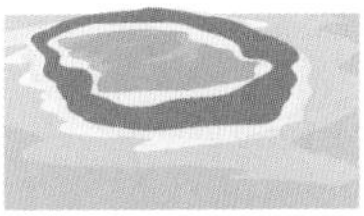

㉗ **das Atoll**
atoll

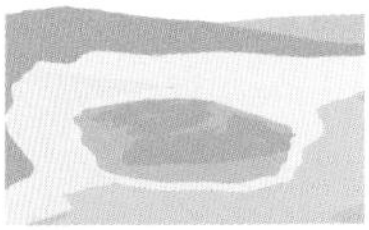

㉘ **die Lagune**
lagoon

## 147.2 MERKMALE VON FLÜSSEN • RIVER FEATURES

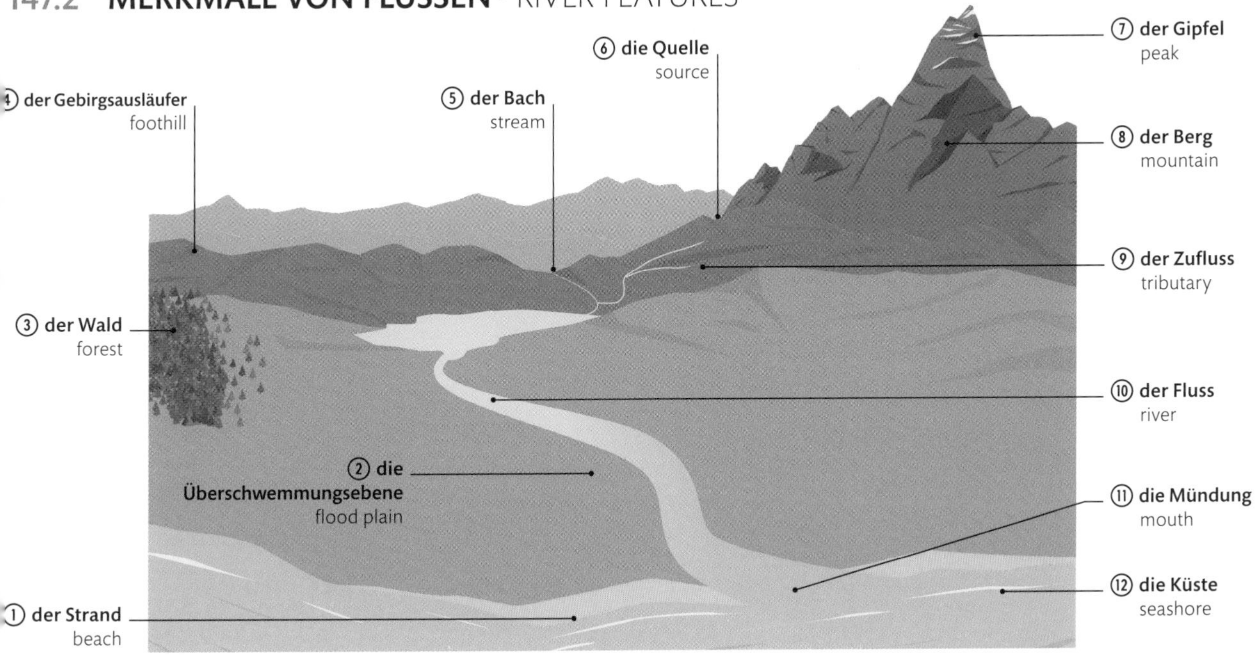

# 148 Karten und Richtungsangaben

## Maps and directions

### 148.1 KARTEN LESEN · READING A MAP

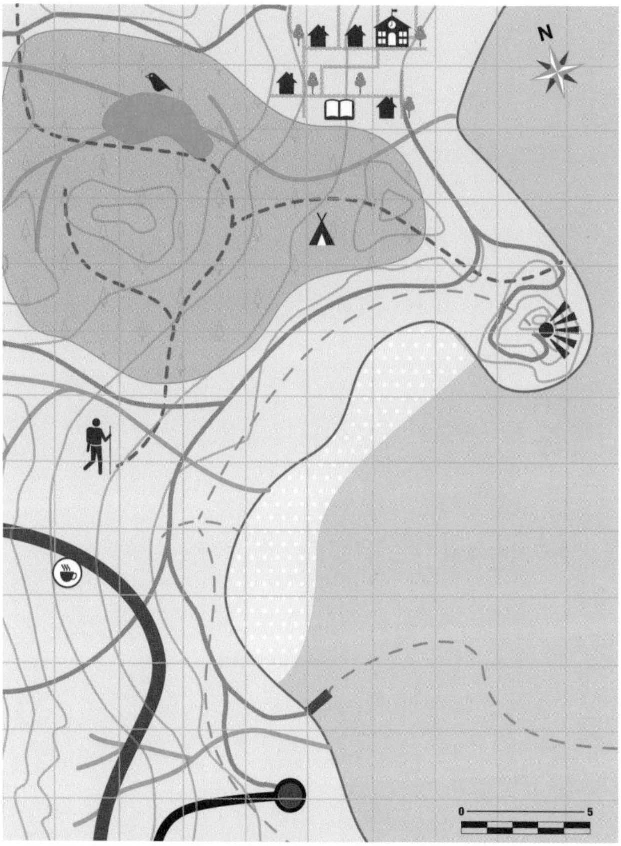


① **die Landkarte**
map

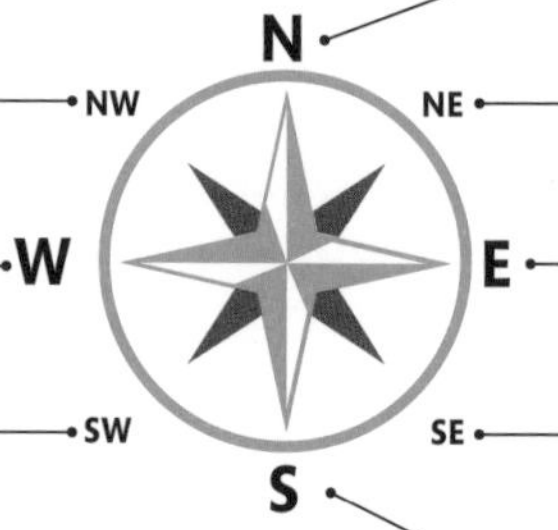


③ **der Norden**
north

④ **der Nordoste**
northeast

⑩ **der Nordwesten**
northwest

⑨ **der Westen**
west

⑤ **der Osten**
east

⑧ **der Südwesten**
southwest

⑥ **der Südosten**
southeast

⑦ **der Süden**
south

② **der Kompass**
compass

⑪ **die Hauptverkehrsstraße**
main road

⑫ **die Nebenstraße**
secondary road

⑬ **der öffentliche Fußweg**
public footpath

⑭ **die Bahnlinie**
railroad

⑮ **der Bahnhof**
train station

⑯ **der Campingplatz**
campground

⑰ **der Rastplatz**
rest stop

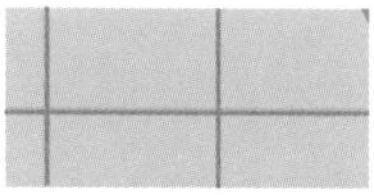

⑱ **die Gitternetzlinien** *f, pl*
grid lines

⑲ **das Naturschutzgebiet**
nature reserve

⑳ **der Aussichtspunkt**
viewpoint

㉑ **der Wanderweg**
walking trail

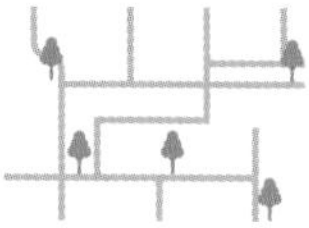

㉒ **die Stadt**
town

㉓ **das Haus / das Gebäude**
house / building

㉔ **die Schule**
school

㉕ **die Bibliothek**
library

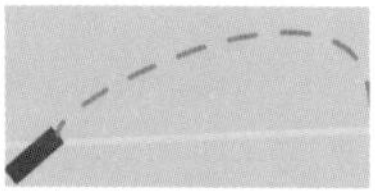

㉖ **die Fährverbindung**
ferry route

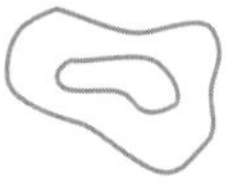

㉗ **die Höhenlinie**
contours

㉘ **der Fluss**
river

㉙ **der See**
lake

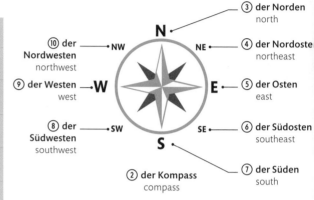

㉚ **der Wald**
forest



㉛ **der Strand**
beach

See also
**96** Straßen • Roads **133** Aktivitäten im Freien • Outdoor activities **145** Der Planet Erde • Planet Earth **146-147** Geografie • Geography **149-151** Länder • Countries

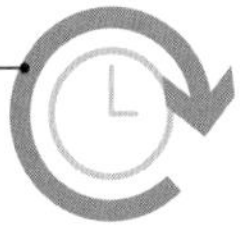

**㉜ im Uhrzeigersinn**
clockwise

**㉝ gegen den Uhrzeigersinn**
counterclockwise

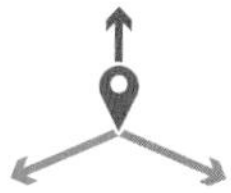

**㉞ die Koordinaten** *f, pl*
coordinates

**㉟ der Orientierungslauf**
orienteering

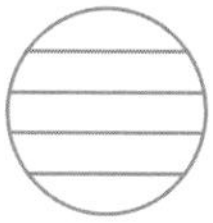

**㊱ der Breitengrad**
latitude

**㊲ der Längengrad**
longitude

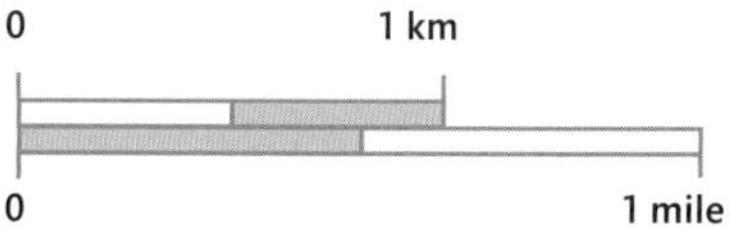


**㊳ der Maßstab**
scale

**㊴ der Kartograf** *m*
**die Kartografin** *f*
cartographer

**㊵ die Online-Karte**
online map

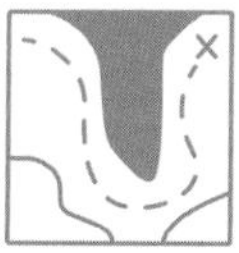

**㊶ die Wanderkarte**
trail map

**㊷ die Straßenkarte**
roadmap

## 148.2 ORTSANGABEN • PREPOSITIONS OF PLACE

**① neben**
next to / beside

**② gegenüber**
across from

**③ zwischen**
between

**④ an der Kreuzung**
on the corner

**⑤ vor**
in front of

**⑥ hinter**
behind

**⑦ links von**
on the left

**⑧ rechts von**
on the right

## 148.3 RICHTUNGSVERBEN • DIRECTION VERBS

**① links abbiegen**
to go left / to turn left

**② rechts abbiegen**
to go right / to turn right

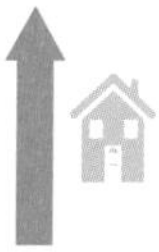

**③ geradeaus gehen / fahren**
to go straight ahead

**④ umkehren**
to go back

**⑤ an (dem Restaurant) vorbei gehen / fahren**
to go past (the restaurant)

**⑥ die erste Abzweigung links abbiegen**
to take the first left

**⑦ die zweite Abzweigung rechts abbiegen**
to take the second right

**⑧ (am Hotel) halten**
to stop at (the hotel)

**⑨ die Route planen**
to plan your route

**⑩ sich verlaufen**
to lose your way

**⑪ die Landkarte lesen**
to read a map

**⑫ nach dem Weg fragen**
to ask directions

# 149 Länder
## Countries

### 149.1 AFRIKA · AFRICA

① **Marokko**
Morocco

② **Mauretanien**
Mauritania

③ **Kap Verde**
Cape Verde

④ **Senegal**
Senegal

⑤ **Gambia**
Gambia

⑥ **Guinea-Bissau**
Guinea-Bissau

⑦ **Guinea**
Guinea

⑧ **Sierra Leone**
Sierra Leone

⑨ **Liberia**
Liberia

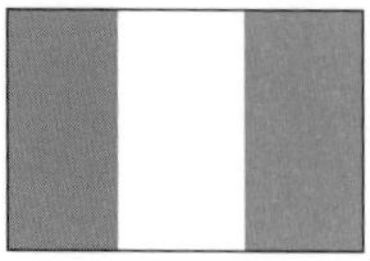

⑩ **Elfenbeinküste** *f*
Ivory Coast

⑪ **Burkina Faso**
Burkina Faso

⑫ **Mali**
Mali

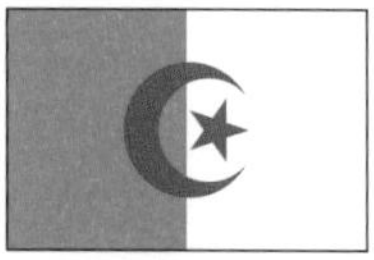

⑬ **Algerien**
Algeria

⑭ **Tunesien**
Tunisia

⑮ **Libyen**
Libya

⑯ **Niger**
Niger

⑰ **Ghana**
Ghana

⑱ **Togo**
Togo

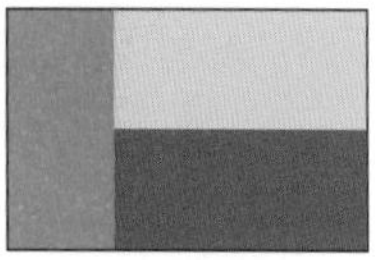

⑲ **Benin**
Benin

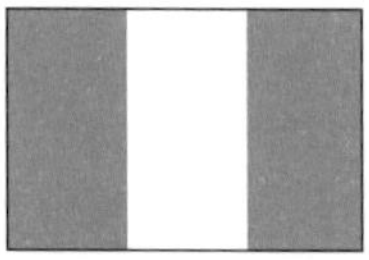

⑳ **Nigeria**
Nigeria

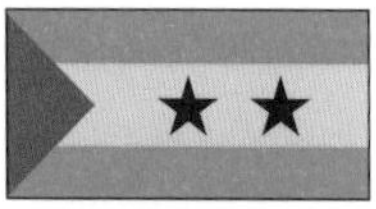

㉑ **São Tomé und Príncipe**
São Tomé and Príncipe

㉒ **Äquatorialguinea**
Equatorial Guinea

㉓ **Gabun**
Gabon

㉔ **Kamerun**
Cameroon

㉕ **Tschad**
Chad

㉖ **Ruanda**
Rwanda

㉗ **Burundi**
Burundi

㉘ **Tansania**
Tanzania

㉙ **Mosambik**
Mozambique

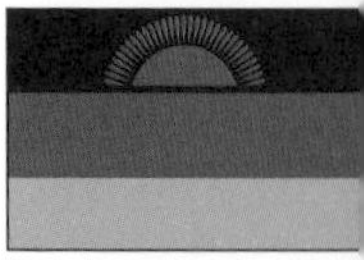

㉚ **Malawi**
Malawi

㉛ **Republik Kongo** *f*
Republic of the Congo

㉜ **Demokratische Republik Kongo** *f*
Democratic Republic of the Congo

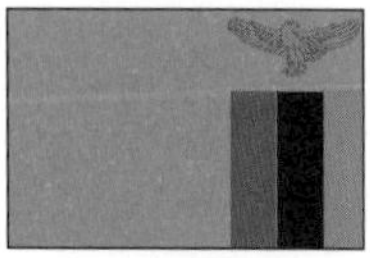

㉝ **Sambia**
Zambia

㉞ **Angola**
Angola

㉟ **Namibia**
Namibia

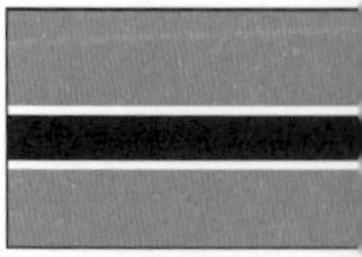

㊱ **Botsuana**
Botswana

See also
**145** Der Planet Erde • Planet Earth **146-147** Geografie • Geography **148** Karten und Richtungsangaben • Maps and directions **150-151** Länder (Fortsetzung) • Countries continued **152-153** Staatsangehörigkeiten • Nationalities

**37 Simbabwe**
Zimbabwe

**38 Südafrika**
South Africa

**39 Lesotho**
Lesotho

**40 die Komoren** *pl*
Comoros

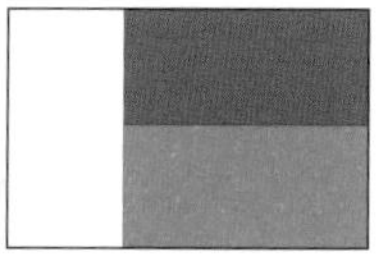

**41 Madagaskar**
Madagascar

**42 Ägypten**
Egypt

**43 Sudan**
Sudan

**44 Südsudan**
South Sudan

**45 Äthiopien**
Ethiopia

**46 Eritrea**
Eritrea

**47 Somalia**
Somalia

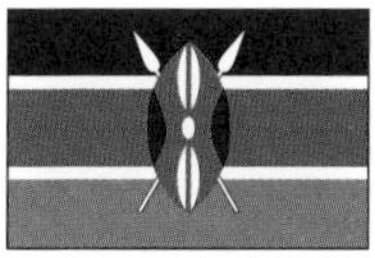

**48 Kenia**
Kenya

**49 Uganda**
Uganda

**50 Dschibuti**
Djibouti

**51 die Seychellen** *pl*
Seychelles

**52 Mauritius**
Mauritius

**53 Zentralafrikanische Republik** *f*
Central African Republic

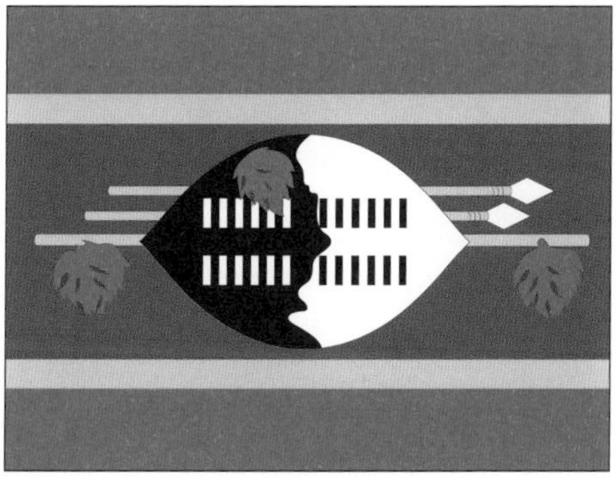

**54 Eswatini**
Eswatini

## 149.2 SÜDAMERIKA
SOUTH AMERICA

**1 Venezuela**
Venezuela

**2 Kolumbien**
Colombia

**3 Brasilien**
Brazil

**4 Bolivien**
Bolivia

**5 Ecuador**
Ecuador

**6 Peru**
Peru

**7 Chile**
Chile

**8 Argentinien**
Argentina

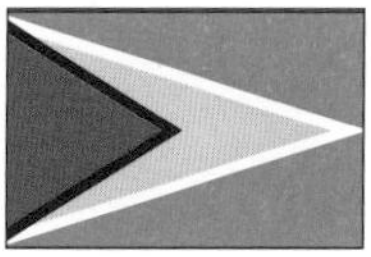

**9 Guyana**
Guyana

**10 Suriname**
Suriname

**11 Paraguay**
Paraguay

**12 Uruguay**
Uruguay

# 150 Länder (Fortsetzung)
## Countries continued

### 150.1 NORD- UND MITTELAMERIKA UND DIE KARIBIK
NORTH AND CENTRAL AMERICA AND THE CARIBBEAN

① **Kanada**
Canada

② **die USA** *pl*
United States of America

③ **Mexiko**
Mexico

④ **Guatemala**
Guatemala

⑤ **Belize**
Belize

⑥ **El Salvador**
El Salvador

⑧ **Honduras**
Honduras

⑨ **Nicaragua**
Nicaragua

⑩ **Costa Rica**
Costa Rica

⑪ **Panama**
Panama

⑫ **Kuba**
Cuba

⑬ **die Bahamas** *pl*
Bahamas

⑮ **Jamaika**
Jamaica

⑯ **Haiti**
Haiti

⑰ **Dominikanische Republik** *f*
Dominican Republic

⑱ **Barbados**
Barbados

⑲ **Trinidad und Tobago**
Trinidad and Tobago

⑳ **St. Kitts und Nevis**
St. Kitts and Nevis

㉒ **Dominica**
Dominica

㉓ **Antigua und Barbuda**
Antigua and Barbuda

### 150.2 OZEANIEN · OCEANIA

① **Papua-Neuguinea**
Papua New Guinea

② **Australien**
Australia

③ **Neuseeland**
New Zealand

④ **die Marshallinseln** *pl*
Marshall Islands

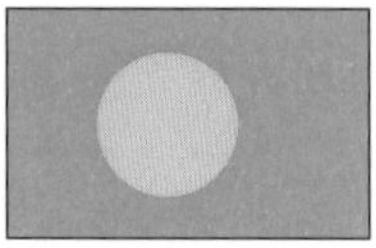

⑤ **Palau**
Palau

⑥ **Mikronesien**
Micronesia

⑧ **Nauru**
Nauru

⑨ **Kiribati**
Kiribati

⑩ **Tuvalu**
Tuvalu

⑪ **Samoa**
Samoa

⑫ **Tonga**
Tonga

⑬ **Vanuatu**
Vanuatu

See also
**145** Der Planet Erde • Planet Earth **146-147** Geografie • Geography
**148** Karten und Richtungsangaben • Maps and directions
**151** Länder (Fortsetzung) • Countries continued

⑦ **Grenada**
Grenada

⑭ **St. Lucia**
St. Lucia

㉑ **St. Vincent und die Grenadinen**
St. Vincent and The Grenadines

⑦ **die Salomonen** *pl*
Solomon Islands

⑭ **Fidschi**
Fiji

## 150.3 ASIEN • ASIA

① **Türkei**
Türkiye

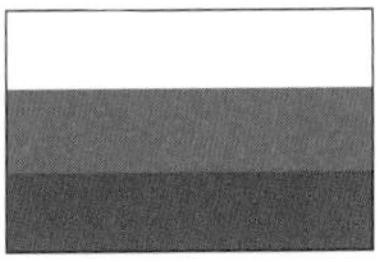

② **Russland**
Russian Federation

③ **Georgien**
Georgia

④ **Armenien**
Armenia

⑤ **Aserbaidschan**
Azerbaijan

⑥ **Irak**
Iraq

⑦ **Syrien**
Syria

⑧ **Libanon** *m*
Lebanon

⑨ **Israel**
Israel

⑩ **Jordanien**
Jordan

⑪ **Pakistan**
Pakistan

⑫ **Indien**
India

⑬ **die Malediven** *pl*
Maldives

⑭ **Sri Lanka**
Sri Lanka

⑮ **China**
China

⑯ **die Mongolei**
Mongolia

⑰ **Nordkorea**
North Korea

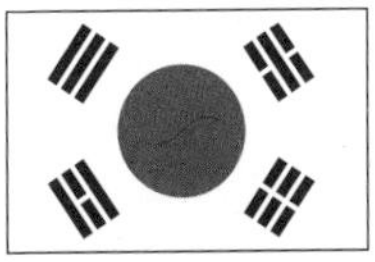

⑱ **Südkorea**
South Korea

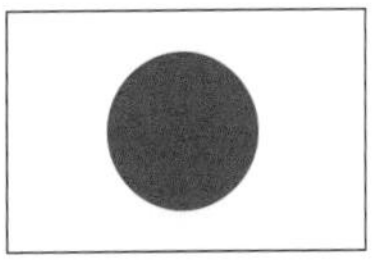

⑲ **Japan**
Japan

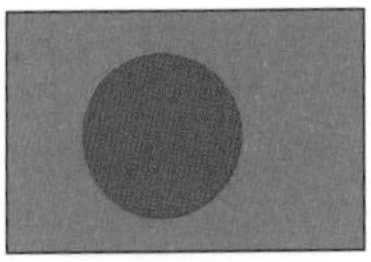

⑳ **Bangladesch**
Bangladesh

㉑ **Bhutan**
Bhutan

㉒ **Myanmar (Burma)**
Myanmar (Burma)

㉓ **Thailand**
Thailand

㉔ **Laos**
Laos

㉕ **Vietnam**
Vietnam

㉖ **Kambodscha**
Cambodia

㉗ **Nepal**
Nepal

# 151 Länder (Fortsetzung)

## Countries continued

### 151.1 **ASIEN (FORTSETZUNG)** · ASIA CONTINUED

① **Singapur**
Singapore

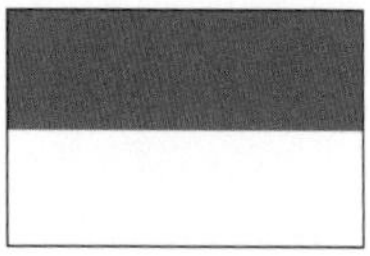

② **Indonesien**
Indonesia

③ **Brunei**
Brunei

④ **die Philippinen** *pl*
Philippines

⑤ **Osttimor**
East Timor

⑥ **Malaysia**
Malaysia

⑦ **die Vereinigten Arabischen Emirate**
United Arab Emirates

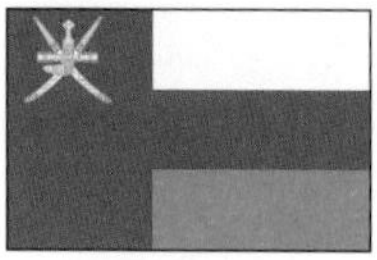

⑧ **Oman**
Oman

⑨ **Bahrain**
Bahrain

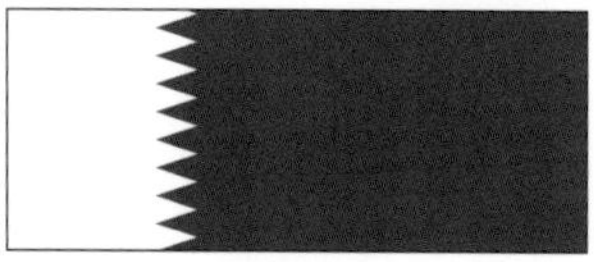

⑩ **Katar**
Qatar

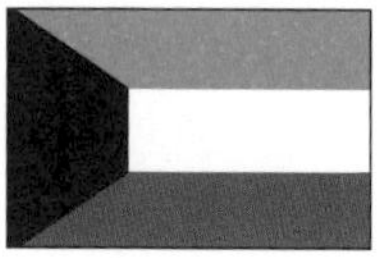

⑪ **Kuwait**
Kuwait

⑫ **Iran**
Iran

⑬ **Jemen**
Yemen

⑭ **Saudi-Arabien**
Saudi Arabia

⑮ **Usbekistan**
Uzbekistan

⑯ **Turkmenistan**
Turkmenistan

⑰ **Afghanistan**
Afghanistan

⑱ **Tadschikistan**
Tajikistan

⑲ **Kirgisistan**
Kyrgyzstan

⑳ **Kasachstan**
Kazakhstan

### 151.2 **EUROPA** · EUROPE

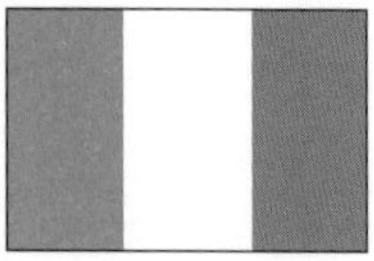

① **Irland**
Ireland

② **Vereinigtes Königreich** *n*
United Kingdom

⑨ **Belgien**
Belgium

⑩ **Niederlande** *pl*
Netherlands

⑰ **Portugal**
Portugal

⑱ **Spanien**
Spain

㉕ **Luxemburg**
Luxembourg

㉖ **Deutschland**
Germany

㉝ **Andorra**
Andorra

㉞ **Frankreich**
France

㊶ **Dänemark**
Denmark

㊷ **Norwegen**
Norway

See also
**145** Der Planet Erde • Planet Earth **146-147** Geografie • Geography **148** Karten und Richtungsangaben • Maps and directions **152-153** Staatsangehörigkeiten • Nationalities

③ **Schweden**
Sweden

④ **Finnland**
Finland

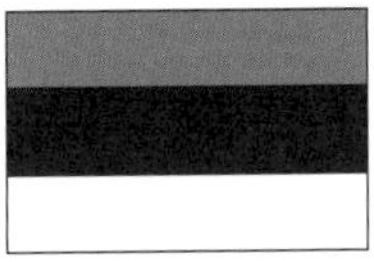
⑤ **Estland**
Estonia

⑥ **Lettland**
Latvia

⑦ **Litauen**
Lithuania

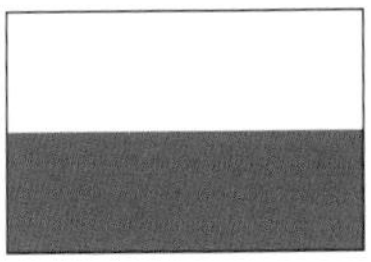
⑧ **Polen**
Poland

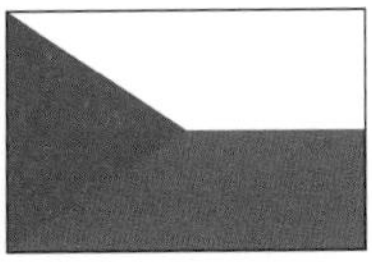
⑪ **Tschechische Republik** *f*
Czech Republic

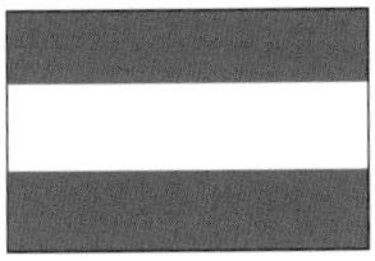
⑫ **Österreich**
Austria

⑬ **Liechtenstein**
Liechtenstein

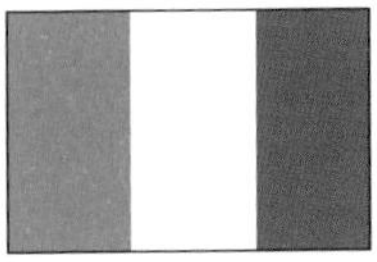
⑭ **Italien**
Italy

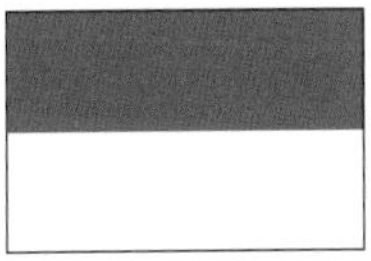
⑮ **Monaco**
Monaco

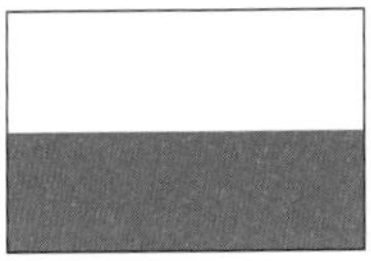
⑯ **San Marino**
San Marino

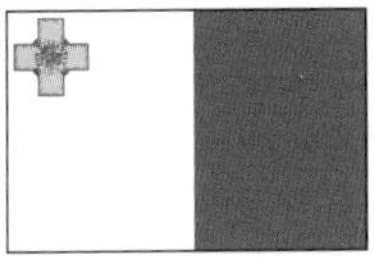
⑲ **Malta**
Malta

⑳ **Slowenien**
Slovenia

㉑ **Kroatien**
Croatia

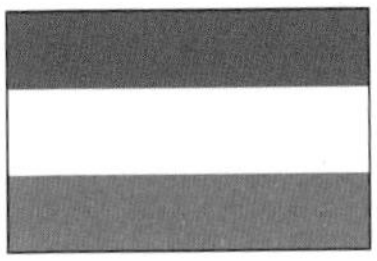
㉒ **Ungarn**
Hungary

㉓ **Slowakei** *f*
Slovakia

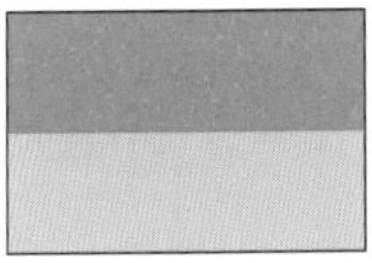
㉔ **Ukraine**
Ukraine

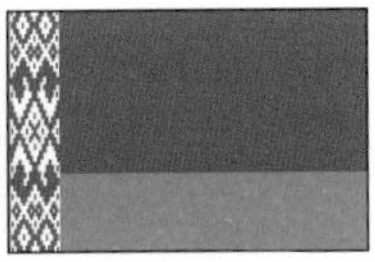
㉗ **Belarus**
Belarus

㉘ **Moldawien**
Moldova

㉙ **Rumänien**
Romania

㉚ **Serbien**
Serbia

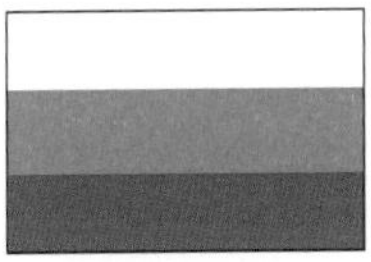
㉛ **Bulgarien**
Bulgaria

㉜ **Albanien**
Albania

㉟ **Griechenland**
Greece

㊱ **Island**
Iceland

㊲ **Zypern**
Cyprus

㊳ **Montenegro**
Montenegro

㊴ **Vatikanstaat** *m*
Vatican City

㊵ **Türkei** *f*
Türkiye

㊸ **Bosnien und Herzegowina**
Bosnia and Herzegovina

㊹ **Nordmazedonien**
North Macedonia

㊺ **Schweiz** *f*
Switzerland

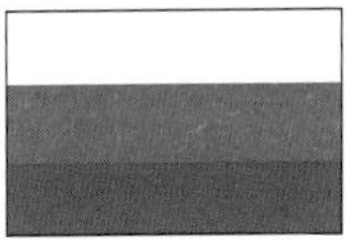
㊻ **Russland**
Russian Federation

# 152 Staatsangehörigkeiten

## Nationalities

### 152.1 AFRIKA · AFRICA

| Country | Adjective | English Adjective |
|---|---|---|
| ① **Afrika** Africa | **afrikanisch** | African |
| ② **Marokko** Morocco | **marokkanisch** | Moroccan |
| ③ **Mauretanien** Mauritania | **mauretanisch** | Mauritanian |
| ④ **Kap Verde** Cape Verde | **kapverdisch** | Cape Verdean |
| ⑤ **Senegal** Senegal | **senegalesisch** | Senegalese |
| ⑥ **Gambia** Gambia | **gambisch** | Gambian |
| ⑦ **Guinea-Bissau** Guinea-Bissau | **guinea-bissauisch** | Bissau-Guinean |
| ⑧ **Guinea** Guinea | **guineisch** | Guinean |
| ⑨ **Sierra Leone** Sierra Leone | **sierra-leonisch** | Sierra Leonean |
| ⑩ **Liberia** Liberia | **liberianisch** | Liberian |
| ⑪ **die Elfenbeinküste** Ivory Coast | **ivorisch** | Ivorian |
| ⑫ **Burkina Faso** Burkina Faso | **burkinisch** | Burkinabe |
| ⑬ **Mali** Mali | **malisch** | Malian |
| ⑭ **Algerien** Algeria | **algerisch** | Algerian |
| ⑮ **Tunesien** Tunisia | **tunesisch** | Tunisian |
| ⑯ **Libyen** Libya | **libysch** | Libyan |
| ⑰ **Niger** Niger | **nigrisch** | Nigerien |
| ⑱ **Ghana** Ghana | **ghanaisch** | Ghanaian |
| ⑲ **Togo** Togo | **togoisch** | Togolese |
| ⑳ **Benin** Benin | **beninisch** | Beninese |
| ㉑ **Nigeria** Nigeria | **nigerianisch** | Nigerian |
| ㉒ **São Tomé und Príncipe** São Tomé and Príncipe | **sao-tomeisch** | São Toméan |
| ㉓ **Äquatorialguinea** Equatorial Guinea | **äquatorialguineisch** | Equatorial Guinean |
| ㉔ **Kamerun** Cameroon | **kamerunisch** | Cameroonian |
| ㉕ **Tschad** Chad | **tschadisch** | Chadian |
| ㉖ **Ägypten** Egypt | **ägyptisch** | Egyptian |
| ㉗ **Sudan** Sudan | **sudanesisch** | Sudanese |
| ㉘ **Südsudan** South Sudan | **südsudanesisch** | South Sudanese |
| ㉙ **Eritrea** Eritrea | **eritreisch** | Eritrean |
| ㉚ **Dschibuti** Djibouti | **dschibutisch** | Djiboutian |
| ㉛ **Äthiopien** Ethiopia | **äthiopisch** | Ethiopian |
| ㉜ **Somalia** Somalia | **somalisch** | Somalian |
| ㉝ **Kenia** Kenya | **kenianisch** | Kenyan |
| ㉞ **Uganda** Uganda | **ugandisch** | Ugandan |
| ㉟ **die Zentralafrikanische Republik** Central African Republic | **zentralafrikanisch** | Central African |
| ㊱ **Gabun** Gabon | **gabunisch** | Gabonese |
| ㊲ **Republik Kongo** Republic of the Congo | **kongolesisch** | Congolese |
| ㊳ **die Demokratische Republik Kongo** Democratic Republic of the Congo | **kongolesisch** | Congolese |
| ㊴ **Ruanda** Rwanda | **ruandisch** | Rwandan |
| ㊵ **Burundi** Burundi | **burundisch** | Burundian |
| ㊶ **Tansania** Tanzania | **tansanisch** | Tanzanian |
| ㊷ **Mosambik** Mozambique | **mosambikisch** | Mozambican |
| ㊸ **Malawi** Malawi | **malaiisch** | Malawian |
| ㊹ **Sambia** Zambia | **sambisch** | Zambian |
| ㊺ **Angola** Angola | **angolanisch** | Angolan |
| ㊻ **Namibia** Namibia | **namibisch** | Namibian |
| ㊼ **Botsuana** Botswana | **botswanisch** | Botswanan |
| ㊽ **Simbabwe** Zimbabwe | **simbabwisch** | Zimbabwean |
| ㊾ **Südafrika** South Africa | **südafrikanisch** | South African |
| ㊿ **Lesotho** Lesotho | **lesothisch** | Basotho |
| (51) **Eswatini** Eswatini | **eswatinisch** | Swazi |
| (52) **die Komoren** Comoros | **komorisch** | Comoran |
| (53) **Madagaskar** Madagascar | **madagassisch** | Madagascan |
| (54) **die Seychellen** Seychelles | **seychellisch** | Seychellois |
| (55) **Mauritius** Mauritius | **mauritisch** | Mauritian |

See also
**145** Der Planet Erde • Planet Earth **146-147** Geografie • Geography
**148** Karten und Richtungsangaben • Maps and directions **149-151** Länder
Countries **153** Staatsangehörigkeiten (Fortsetzung) • Nationalities continued

## 152.2 SÜDAMERIKA • SOUTH AMERICA

| Country | Adjective | English Adjective |
|---|---|---|
| ① **Südamerika** South America | **südamerikanisch** | South American |
| ② **Venezuela** Venezuela | **venezolanisch** | Venezuelan |
| ③ **Kolumbien** Colombia | **kolumbisch** | Colombian |
| ④ **Ecuador** Ecuador | **ecuadorianisch** | Ecuadorian |
| ⑤ **Peru** Peru | **peruanisch** | Peruvian |
| ⑥ **Guyana** Guyana | **guyanisch** | Guyanese |
| ⑦ **Suriname** Suriname | **surinamisch** | Surinamese |
| ⑧ **Brasilien** Brazil | **brasilianisch** | Brazilian |
| ⑨ **Bolivien** Bolivia | **bolivianisch** | Bolivian |
| ⑩ **Chile** Chile | **chilenisch** | Chilean |
| ⑪ **Argentinien** Argentina | **argentinisch** | Argentinian |
| ⑫ **Paraguay** Paraguay | **paraguayisch** | Paraguayan |
| ⑬ **Uruguay** Uruguay | **uruguayisch** | Uruguayan |

## 152.3 NORD- UND MITTELAMERIKA UND DIE KARIBIK
NORTH AND CENTRAL AMERICA AND THE CARIBBEAN

| Country | Adjective | English Adjective |
|---|---|---|
| ① **Nord- und Mittelamerika und die Karibik** North and Central America and the Caribbean | **nordamerikanisch, mittelamerikanisch und karibisch** | North American, Central American, and Caribbean |
| ② **Kanada** Canada | **kanadisch** | Canadian |
| ③ **die USA** United States of America | **US-amerikanisch** | American |
| ④ **Mexiko** Mexico | **mexikanisch** | Mexican |
| ⑤ **Guatemala** Guatemala | **guatemaltekisch** | Guatemalan |
| ⑥ **Belize** Belize | **belizisch** | Belizean |
| ⑦ **El Salvador** El Salvador | **salvadorianisch** | Salvadoran |
| ⑧ **Honduras** Honduras | **honduranisch** | Honduran |
| ⑨ **Nicaragua** Nicaragua | **nicaraguanisch** | Nicaraguan |
| ⑩ **Costa Rica** Costa Rica | **costa-ricanisch** | Costa Rican |
| ⑪ **Panama** Panama | **costa-ricanisch** | Panamanian |
| ⑫ **Kuba** Cuba | **kubanisch** | Cuban |
| ⑬ **die Bahamas** Bahamas | **bahamaisch** | Bahamian |
| ⑭ **Jamaika** Jamaica | **jamaikanisch** | Jamaican |
| ⑮ **Haiti** Haiti | **haitianisch** | Haitian |
| ⑯ **die Dominikanische Republik** Dominican Republic | **dominikanisch** | Dominican |
| ⑰ **Barbados** Barbados | **barbadisch** | Barbadian |
| ⑱ **Trinidad und Tobago** Trinidad and Tobago | **trinidadisch** | Trinidadian or Tobagonian |
| ⑲ **St. Kitts und Nevis** St. Kitts and Nevis | **kittisch oder nevisisch** | Kittian or Nevisian |
| ⑳ **Antigua und Barbuda** Antigua and Barbuda | **antiguanisch** | Antiguan or Barbudan |
| ㉑ **Dominica** Dominica | **dominicanisch** | Dominican |
| ㉒ **St. Lucia** St. Lucia | **lucianisch** | St. Lucian |
| ㉓ **St. Vincent und die Grenadinen** St. Vincent and The Grenadines | **vincentisch** | Vincentian |
| ㉔ **Grenada** Grenada | **grenadisch** | Grenadian |

# 153 Staatsangehörigkeiten (Fortsetzung)

## Nationalities continued

### 153.1 OZEANIEN · OCEANIA

| Country | Adjective | English Adjective |
|---|---|---|
| (1) **Ozeanien** Oceania | **ozeanisch** | Oceanian |
| (2) **Papua-Neuguinea** Papua New Guinea | **papua-neuguinesisch** | Papua New Guinean |
| (3) **Australien** Australia | **australisch** | Australian |
| (4) **Neuseeland** New Zealand | **neuseeländisch** | New Zealand |
| (5) **die Marshallinseln** Marshall Islands | **marshallisch** | Marshallese |
| (6) **Palau** Palau | **palauisch** | Palauan |
| (7) **Mikronesien** Micronesia | **mikronesisch** | Micronesian |
| (8) **Nauru** Nauru | **nauruisch** | Nauruan |
| (9) **Kiribati** Kiribati | **kiribatisch** | Kiribati |
| (10) **Tuvalu** Tuvalu | **tuvaluisch** | Tuvaluan |
| (11) **Samoa** Samoa | **samoisch** | Samoan |
| (12) **Tonga** Tonga | **tongaisch** | Tongan |
| (13) **Vanuatu** Vanuatu | **vanuatuisch** | Vanuatuan |
| (14) **die Salomonen** Solomon Islands | **salomonisch** | Solomon Island |
| (15) **Fidschi** Fiji | **fidschianisch** | Fijian |

### 153.2 ASIEN · ASIA

| Country | Adjective | English Adjective |
|---|---|---|
| (1) **Asien** • Asia | **asiatisch** | Asian |
| (2) **die Türkei** Türkiye | **türkisch** | Turkish |
| (3) **Russland** Russian Federation | **russisch** | Russian |
| (4) **Georgien** Georgia | **georgisch** | Georgian |
| (5) **Armenien** Armenia | **armenisch** | Armenian |
| (6) **Aserbaidschan** Azerbaijan | **aserbaidschanisch** | Azerbaijani |
| (7) **der Iran** Iran | **iranisch** | Iranian |
| (8) **der Irak** Iraq | **irakisch** | Iraqi |
| (9) **Syrien** Syria | **syrisch** | Syrian |
| (10) **der Libanon** Lebanon | **libanesisch** | Lebanese |
| (11) **Israel** Israel | **israelisch** | Israeli |
| (12) **Jordanien** Jordan | **jordanisch** | Jordanian |
| (13) **Saudi-Arabien** Saudi Arabia | **saudi-arabisch** | Saudi |
| (14) **Kuwait** Kuwait | **kuwaitisch** | Kuwaiti |
| (15) **Bahrain** Bahrain | **bahrainisch** | Bahraini |
| (16) **Katar** Qatar | **katarisch** | Qatari |
| (17) **die Vereinigten Arabischen Emirate** United Arab Emirates | **emiratisch** | Emirati |
| (18) **der Oman** Oman | **omanisch** | Omani |
| (19) **der Jemen** Yemen | **jemenitisch** | Yemeni |
| (20) **Kasachstan** Kazakhstan | **kasachisch** | Kazakh |
| (21) **Usbekistan** Uzbekistan | **usbekisch** | Uzbek |
| (22) **Turkmenistan** Turkmenistan | **turkmenisch** | Turkmen |
| (23) **Afghanistan** Afghanistan | **afghanisch** | Afghan |
| (24) **Tadschikistan** Tajikistan | **tadschikisch** | Tajikistani |
| (25) **Kirgisistan** Kyrgyzstan | **kirgisisch** | Kyrgyz |
| (26) **Pakistan** Pakistan | **pakistanisch** | Pakistani |
| (27) **Indien** India | **indisch** | Indian |
| (28) **die Malediven** Maldives | **maledivisch** | Maldivian |
| (29) **Sri Lanka** Sri Lanka | **sri-lankisch** | Sri Lankan |
| (30) **China** China | **chinesisch** | Chinese |
| (31) **die Mongolei** Mongolia | **mongolisch** | Mongolian |
| (32) **Nordkorea** North Korea | **nordkoreanisch** | North Korean |
| (33) **Südkorea** South Korea | **südkoreanisch** | South Korean |
| (34) **Japan** Japan | **japanisch** | Japanese |
| (35) **Nepal** Nepal | **nepalesisch** | Nepalese |
| (36) **Butan** Bhutan | **bhutanisch** | Bhutanese |
| (37) **Bangladesch** Bangladesh | **bangladeschisch** | Bangladeshi |
| (38) **Myanmar (Burma)** Myanmar (Burma) | **myanmarisch** | Burmese |
| (39) **Thailand** Thailand | **thailändisch** | Thai |

See also
**145** Der Planet Erde • Planet Earth **146-147** Geografie • Geography **148** Karten und Richtungsangaben • Maps and directions **149-151** Länder • Countries

## 153.2 ASIEN (FORTSETZUNG) • ASIA CONTINUED

| Country | Adjective | English Adjective |
|---|---|---|
| 40 **Laos** Laos | **laotisch** | Laotian |
| 41 **Vietnam** Vietnam | **vietnamesisch** | Vietnamese |
| 42 **Kambodscha** Cambodia | **kambodschanisch** | Cambodian |
| 43 **Malaysia** Malaysia | **malaysisch** | Malaysian |
| 44 **Singapur** Singapore | **singapurisch** | Singaporean |
| 45 **Indonesien** Indonesia | **indonesisch** | Indonesian |
| 46 **Brunei** Brunei | **bruneiisch** | Bruneian |
| 47 **die Philippinen** Philippines | **philippinisch** | Filipino |
| 48 **Osttimor** East Timor | **timorisch** | Timorese |

## 153.3 EUROPA • EUROPE

| Country | Adjective | English Adjective |
|---|---|---|
| 1 **Europa** • Europe | **europäisch** | European |
| 2 **Irland** Ireland | **irisch** | Irish |
| 3 **das Vereinigte Königreich** United Kingdom | **britisch** | British |
| 4 **Portugal** Portugal | **portugiesisch** | Portuguese |
| 5 **Spanien** Spain | **spanisch** | Spanish |
| 6 **Andorra** Andorra | **andorranisch** | Andorran |
| 7 **Frankreich** France | **französisch** | French |
| 8 **Belgien** Belgium | **belgisch** | Belgian |
| 9 **die Niederlande** Netherlands | **niederländisch** | Dutch |
| 10 **Luxemburg** Luxembourg | **luxemburgisch** | Luxembourg |
| 11 **Deutschland** Germany | **deutsch** | German |
| 12 **Dänemark** Denmark | **dänisch** | Danish |
| 13 **Norwegen** Norway | **norwegisch** | Norwegian |
| 14 **Schweden** Sweden | **schwedisch** | Swedish |
| 15 **Finnland** Finland | **finnisch** | Finnish |
| 16 **Estland** Estonia | **estnisch** | Estonian |
| 17 **Lettland** Latvia | **lettisch** | Latvian |
| 18 **Litauen** Lithuania | **litauisch** | Lithuanian |
| 19 **Polen** Poland | **polnisch** | Polish |
| 20 **die Tschechische Republik** Czech Republic | **tschechisch** | Czech |
| 21 **Österreich** Austria | **österreichisch** | Austrian |
| 22 **Liechtenstein** Liechtenstein | **liechtensteinisch** | Liechtensteiner |
| 23 **die Schweiz** Switzerland | **schweizerisch** | Swiss |
| 24 **Italien** Italy | **italienisch** | Italian |
| 25 **Monaco** Monaco | **monegassisch** | Monacan |
| 26 **San Marino** San Marino | **san-marinesisch** | Sammarinese |
| 27 **Malta** Malta | **maltesisch** | Maltese |
| 28 **Slowenien** Slovenia | **slowenisch** | Slovenian |
| 29 **Kroatien** Croatia | **kroatisch** | Croatian |
| 30 **Ungarn** Hungary | **ungarisch** | Hungarian |
| 31 **die Slowakei** Slovakia | **slowakisch** | Slovakian |
| 32 **die Ukraine** Ukraine | **ukrainisch** | Ukrainian |
| 33 **Belarus** Belarus | **belarussisch** | Belarusian |
| 34 **Moldawien** Moldova | **moldawisch** | Moldovan |
| 35 **Rumänien** Romania | **rumänisch** | Romanian |
| 36 **Serbien** Serbia | **serbisch** | Serbian |
| 37 **Bosnien und Herzegowina** Bosnia and Herzegovina | **bosnisch und herzegowinisch** | Bosnian or Herzegovinia |
| 38 **Albanien** Albania | **albanisch** | Albanian |
| 39 **Nordmazedonien** North Macedonia | **nordmazedonisch** | North Macedonian |
| 40 **Bulgarien** Bulgaria | **bulgarisch** | Bulgarian |
| 41 **Griechenland** Greece | **griechisch** | Greek |
| 42 **Montenegro** Montenegro | **montenegrinisch** | Montenegrin |
| 43 **Island** Iceland | **isländisch** | Icelandic |
| 44 **Zypern** Cyprus | **zyprisch** | Cypriot |
| 45 **die Türkei** Türkiye | **türkisch** | Turkish |
| 46 **Russland** Russian Federation | **russisch** | Russian |

# 154 Das Wetter
## Weather

### 154.1 DAS WETTER · WEATHER

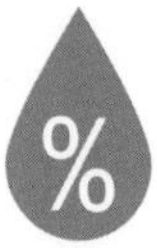
① die Luftfeuchtigkeit
humidity

② die Hitzewelle
heat wave

③ die Dürre
drought

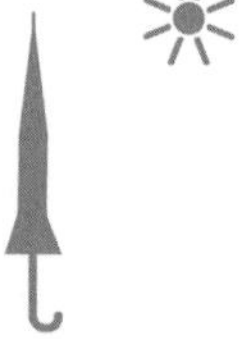
④ trocken
dry

⑤ nass
wet

⑥ bewölkt
overcast

⑦ der Smog
smog

⑧ der Regentropfen
raindrop

⑨ der leichte Schauer
light shower

⑩ der Nieselregen
drizzle

⑪ der Wolkenbruch
downpour

⑫ die Überschwemmung
flood

⑬ der Sandsturm
sandstorm

⑭ der Sturm
gale

⑮ das Gewitter
storm

⑯ der Donner
thunder

⑰ der Blitz
lightning

⑱ der Regenbogen
rainbow

⑲ der Schneeregen
sleet

⑳ die Schneeflocke
snowflake

㉑ die Schneeverwehung
snowdrift

㉒ der Blizzard
blizzard

㉓ der Schneesturm
snowstorm

㉔ der Hagel
hailstone

㉕ der Hurrikan
hurricane

㉖ der Tornado
tornado

㉘ Heute gießt es wie aus Eimern.
It's raining cats and dogs today.
㉗ die Pfütze
puddle

See also
**145** Der Planet Erde • Planet Earth **146-147** Geografie • Geography
**155** Klima und Umwelt • Climate and the environment

## 154.2 DIE TEMPERATUR • TEMPERATURE

① **eiskalt** freezing
② **kalt** cold
③ **kühl** chilly
④ **warm** warm
⑤ **heiß** hot
⑥ **stickig** stifling

⑦ **der Gefrierpunkt** freezing point
⑧ **der Siedepunkt** boiling point
⑨ **minus 10 Grad** minus 10
⑩ **25 Grad** 25 degrees

⑪ **Celsius** Celsius
⑫ **Fahrenheit** Fahrenheit
⑬ **kühl** cool
⑭ **mild** mild

⑯ **Es ist kochend heiß. Ich muss unbedingt in den Schatten!**
It's boiling! I need to find some shade

⑮ **kochend heiß** boiling

## 154.3 WETTERADJEKTIVE • WEATHER ADJECTIVES

① **die Sonne → sonnig** sun → sunny
② **die Wolke → wolkig** cloud → cloudy
③ **der Nebel → neblig** fog → foggy
④ **der Regen → regnerisch** rain → rainy
⑤ **der Schnee → verschneit** snow → snowy
⑥ **das Eis → eisig** ice → icy

⑦ **der Frost → frostig** frost → frosty
⑧ **der Wind → windig** wind → windy
⑨ **der Sturm → stürmisch** storm → stormy
⑩ **der Donner → gewittrig** thunder → thundery
⑪ **der Nebel → neblig** mist → misty
⑫ **die Brise → windig** breeze → breezy

# 155 Klima und Umwelt
## Climate and the environment

### 155.1 DIE ATMOSPHÄRE · ATMOSPHERE

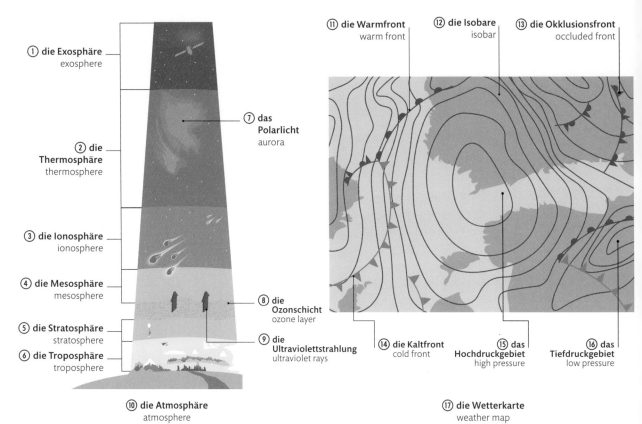

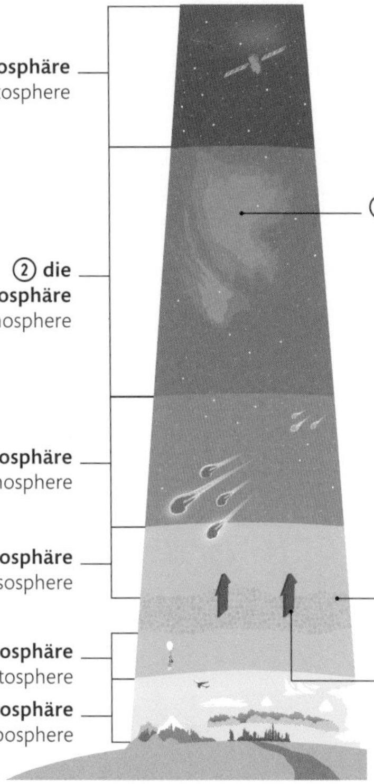


⑩ **die Atmosphäre**
atmosphere

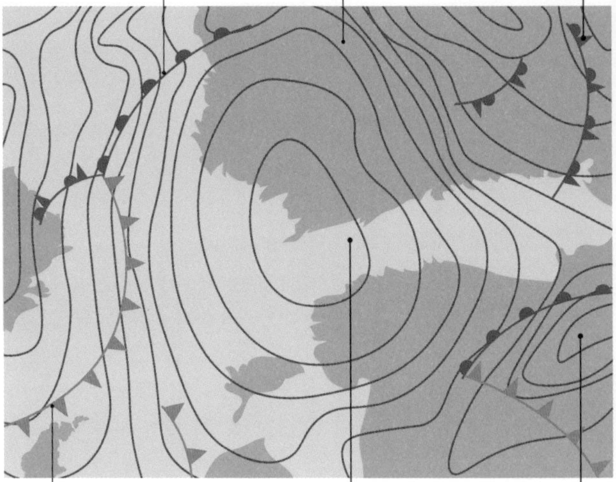


⑰ **die Wetterkarte**
weather map

### 155.2 UMWELTGEFÄHRDUNGEN · ENVIRONMENTAL ISSUES

① **die Abholzung**
deforestation

② **die Zerstörung von Lebensräumen**
habitat loss

③ **die gefährdete Art**
endangered species

④ **der Plastikmüll**
plastic waste

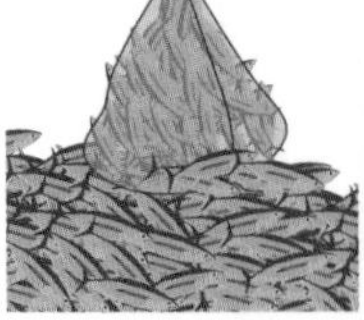

⑤ **die Überfischung**
overfishing

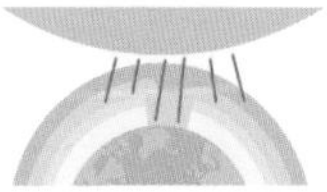

⑥ **der Abbau der Ozonschicht**
ozone depletion

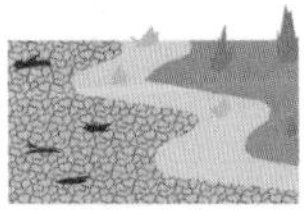

⑦ **die Verwüstung**
desertification

⑧ **der Ölteppich**
oil slick

⑨ **der saure Regen**
acid rain

See also
**145** Der Planet Erde • Planet Earth **146-147** Geografie Geography **154** Das Wetter • Weather

## 155.3 DER KLIMAWANDEL • CLIMATE CHANGE

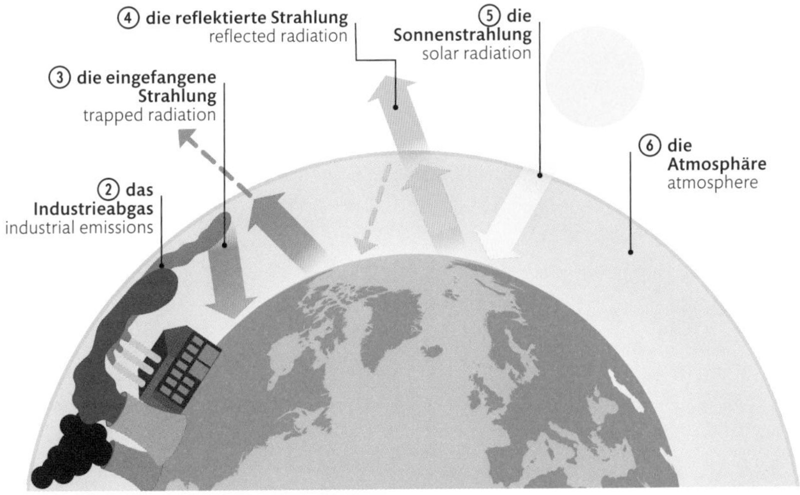

④ **die reflektierte Strahlung** reflected radiation

⑤ **die Sonnenstrahlung** solar radiation

③ **die eingefangene Strahlung** trapped radiation

② **das Industrieabgas** industrial emissions

⑥ **die Atmosphäre** atmosphere

① **der Treibhauseffekt** greenhouse effect

⑧ **das Kohlendioxid, $CO_2$** carbon dioxide

⑨ **das Methan, $CH_4$** methane

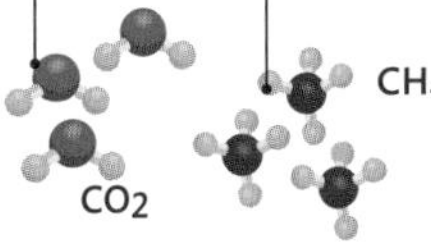


⑦ **das Treibhausgas** greenhouse gases

⑩ **die fossilen Brennstoffe** *m, pl* fossil fuels

⑪ **die Emissionen** *f, pl* emissions

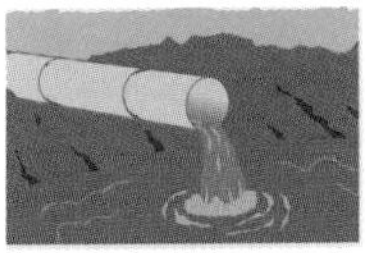

⑫ **die Umweltverschmutzung** pollution

⑬ **das Ökosystem** ecosystem

⑭ **kohlenstofffrei** zero carbon

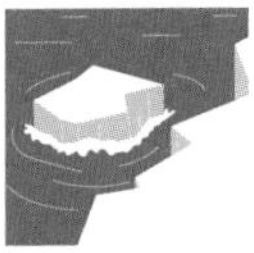

⑮ **der abschmelzende Gletscher** shrinking glaciers

⑯ **der abschmelzende Eisschild** melting ice caps

## 155.4 ABFALL UND RECYCLING • WASTE AND RECYCLING

② **Ich versuche, so viel Kunststoff und Papier wie möglich zu recyceln.** I try to recycle plastic and paper as much as possible.

① **den Müll trennen** to sort your trash

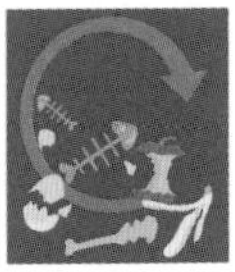

③ **die Speisereste** *m, pl* food waste

④ **das Papier** paper

⑤ **der Kunststoff** plastic

⑥ **das Glas** glass

⑦ **das Metall** metal

⑧ **der kompostierbare Müllbeutel** compostable bags

⑨ **die Mülldeponie** landfill

# 156 Gesteine und Mineralien
## Rocks and minerals

### 156.1 GESTEINE · ROCKS

① **das Sediment**
sedimentary

② **der Sandstein**
sandstone

③ **der Kalkstein**
limestone

④ **die Kreide**
chalk

⑤ **der Feuerstein**
flint

⑥ **das Konglomerat**
conglomerate

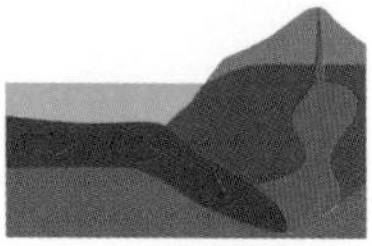
⑦ **das metamorphe Gestein**
metamorphic

⑧ **der Schiefer**
slate

⑨ **der Schiefer**
schist

⑩ **der Gneis**
gneiss

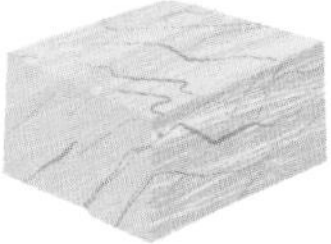
⑪ **der Marmor**
marble

⑫ **der Quarzit**
quartzite

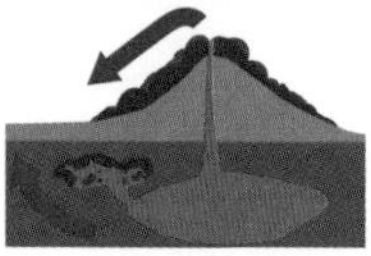
⑬ **das Eruptivgestein**
igneous

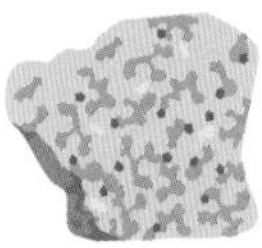
⑭ **der Granit**
granite

⑮ **der Obsidian**
obsidian

⑯ **der Basalt**
basalt

⑰ **der Tuffstein**
tuff

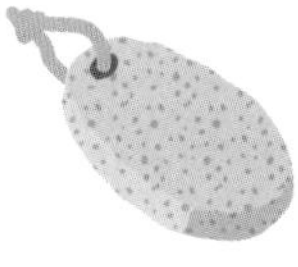
⑱ **der Bimsstein**
pumice

### 156.2 MINERALIEN · MINERALS

① **der Quarz**
quartz

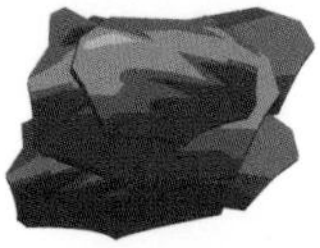
② **der Glimmer**
mica

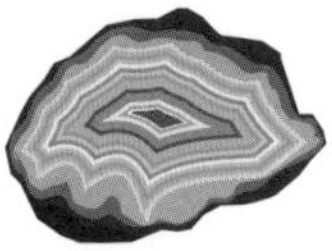
③ **der Achat**
agate

④ **der Hämatit**
hematite

⑤ **der Kalzit**
calcite

⑥ **der Malachit**
malachite

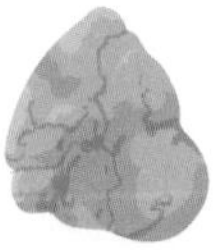
⑦ **der Türkis**
turquoise

⑧ **der Onyx**
onyx

⑨ **der Schwefel**
sulfur

⑩ **der Grafit**
graphite

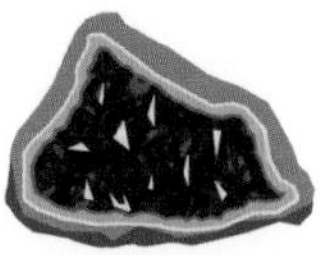
⑪ **die Geode**
geode

⑫ **die Sandrose**
sand rose

See also
**76** Chemie • Chemistry **78** Das Periodensystem • The periodic table
**145** Der Planet Erde • Planet Earth **146-147** Geografie • Geography

## 156.3 EDELSTEINE • GEMS

① **der Diamant**
diamond

② **der Saphir**
sapphire

③ **der Smaragd**
emerald

④ **der Rubin**
ruby

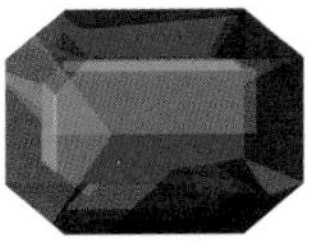
⑤ **der Amethyst**
amethyst

⑥ **der Topas**
topaz

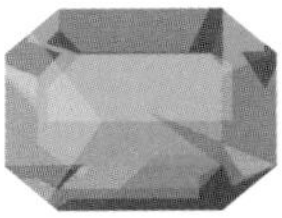
⑦ **der Aquamarin**
aquamarine

⑧ **der Mondstein**
moonstone

⑨ **der Opal**
opal

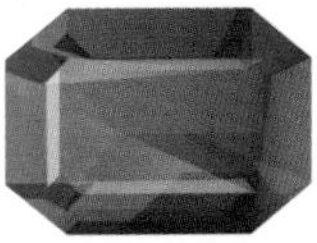
⑩ **der Turmalin**
tourmaline

⑪ **der Granat**
garnet

⑫ **der Citrin**
citrine

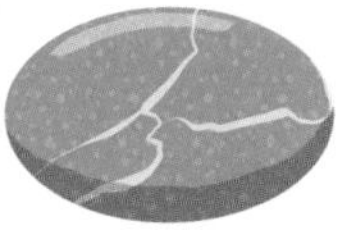
⑬ **die Jade**
jade

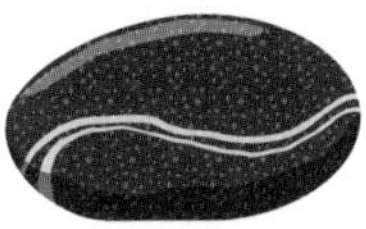
⑭ **der Gagat**
jet

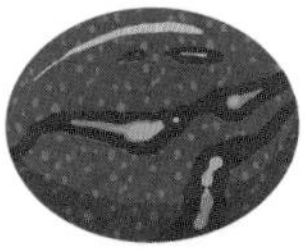
⑮ **der Lapislazuli**
lapis lazuli

⑯ **der Jaspis**
jasper

⑰ **das Tigerauge**
tiger's eye

⑱ **der Karneol**
carnelian

## 156.4 METALLE • METALS

① **das Gold**
gold

② **das Silber**
silver

③ **das Platin**
platinum

④ **das Magnesium**
magnesium

⑤ **das Eisen**
iron

⑥ **das Kupfer**
copper

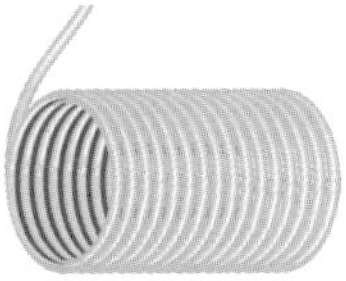
⑦ **das Zinn**
tin

⑧ **das Aluminium**
aluminum

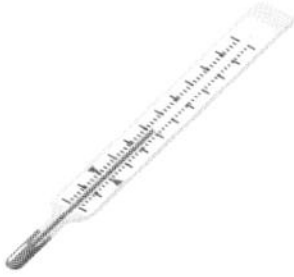
⑨ **das Quecksilber**
mercury

⑩ **das Nickel**
nickel

⑪ **das Zink**
zinc

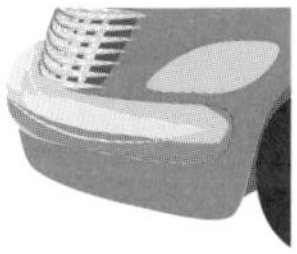
⑫ **das Chrom**
chromium

# 157 Die Naturgeschichte
Natural history

## 157.1 GEOLOGISCHE ZEITALTER · GEOLOGICAL PERIODS

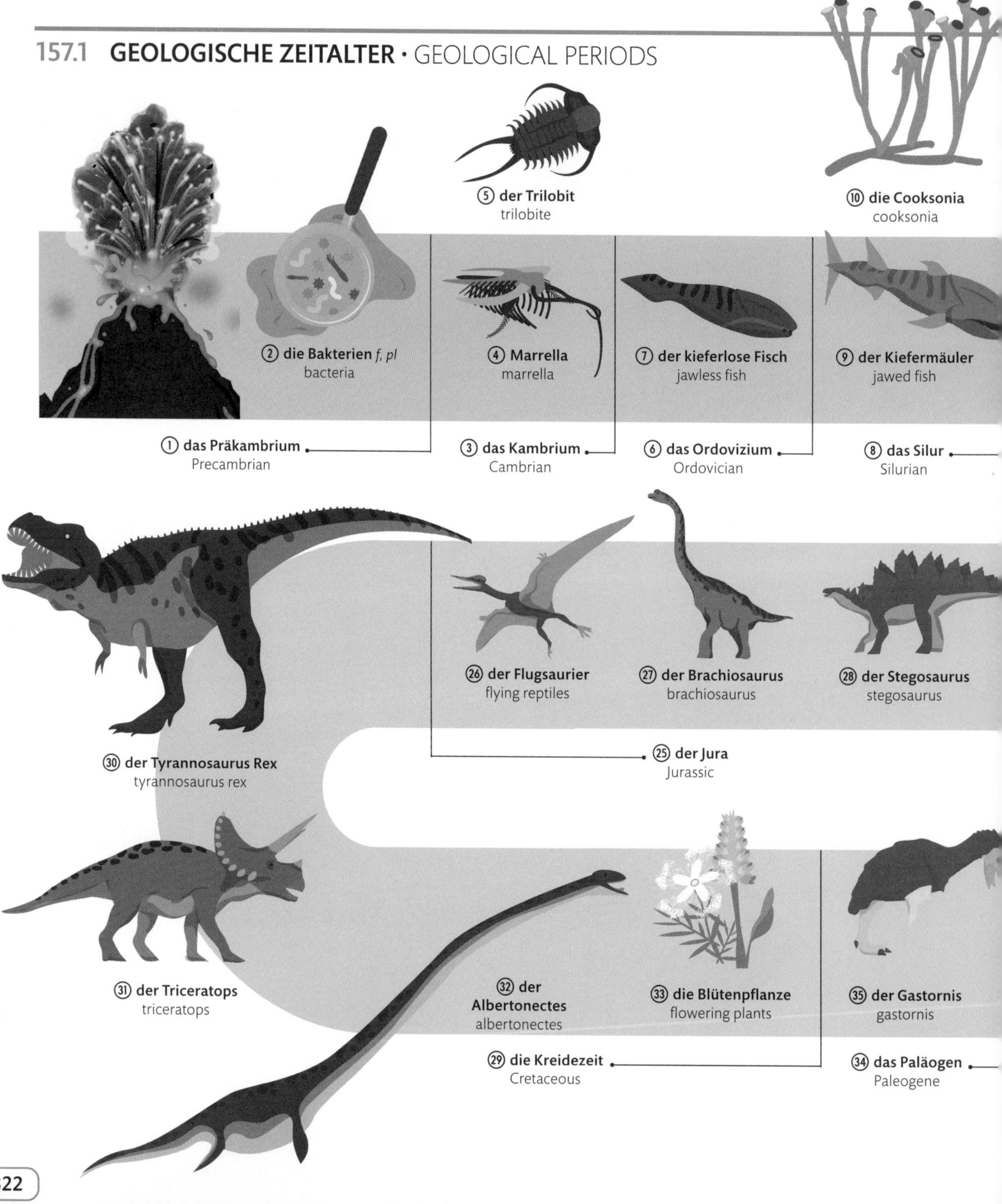

See also
**145** Der Planet Erde • Planet Earth **158-159** Säugetiere • Mammals **160-161** Vögel • Birds **162** Insekten und Käfer • Insects and bugs **163** Amphibien und Reptilien • Amphibians and reptiles **166** Leben im Ozean • Ocean life **167-169** Pflanzen und Bäume • Plants and trees

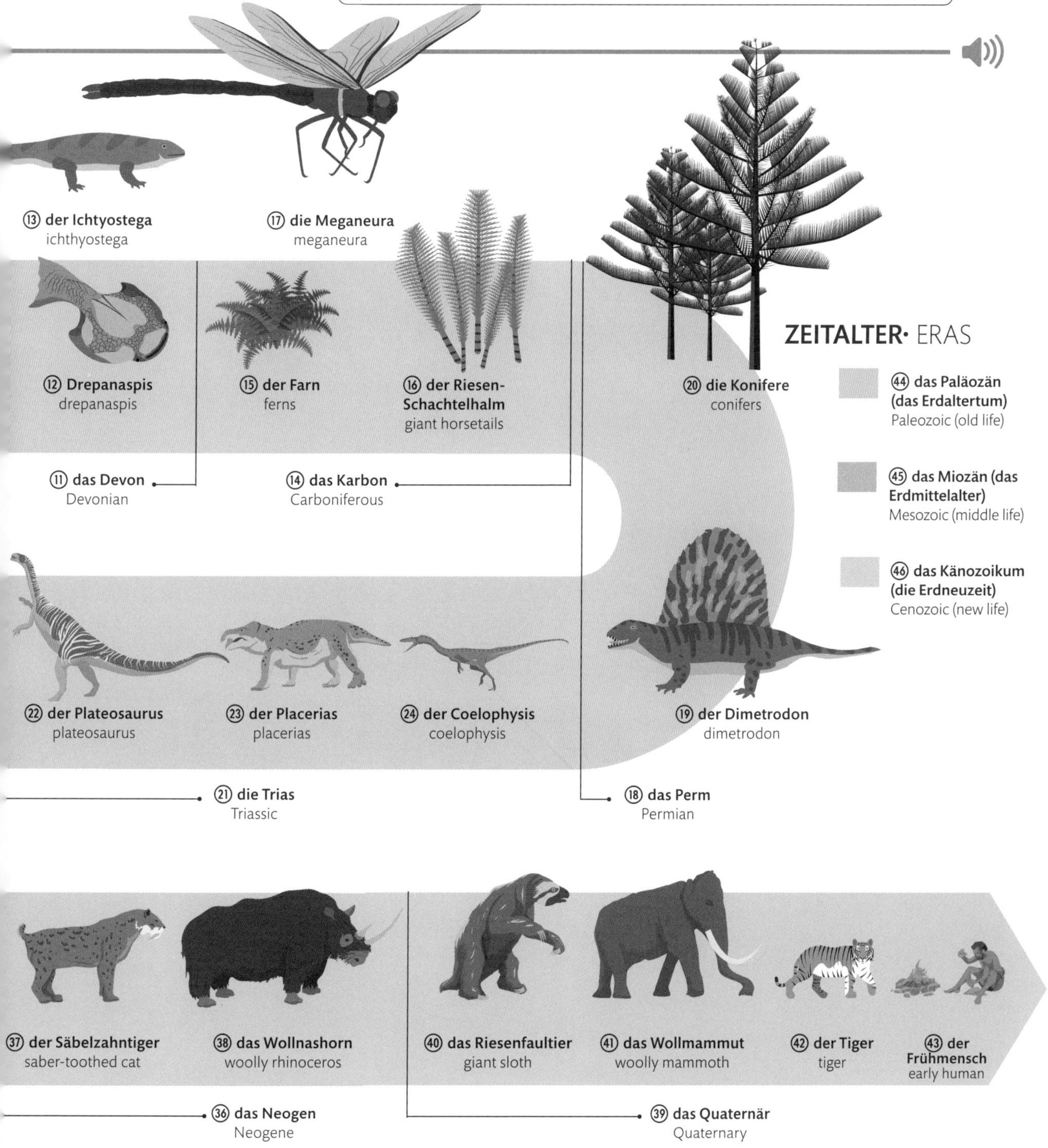

# 158 Säugetiere
## Mammals

### 158.1 SÄUGETIERARTEN · SPECIES OF MAMMALS

① die Impala
impala
② der Pavian
baboon
③ das Erdferkel
aardvark
④ das Nashorn
rhinoceros
⑧ der Gepard
cheetah
⑨ der Löwe
lion
⑩ die Löwin
lioness
⑪ die Hyäne
hyena
⑫ die Savanne
savannah

⑰ das Schnabeltier
platypus
⑱ der Ameisenigel
echidna
⑲ der Tasmanische Teufel
Tasmanian devil
⑳ der Wombat
wombat
㉒ das Kängurujunge
joey
㉓ der Beute
pouch
㉑ das Känguru
kangaroo
㉔ der Koala
koala
㉕ das Kaninchen
rabbit
㉘ die Schnurrhaare n, pl
whiskers
㉖ der Hamster
hamster
㉗ die Maus
mouse
㉙ die Ratte
rat
㉚ der Schwanz
tail
㉛ das Stachelschwein
porcupine
㉜ das Eichhörnchen
squirrel
㉝ der Igel
hedgehog
㉞ das Flughörnchen
flying squirrel
㉟ die Fledermaus
bat
㊱ der Flughund
fruit bat

See also
**157** Die Naturgeschichte • Natural history **159** Säugetiere (Fortsetzung) • Mammals continued
**164** Haustiere • Pets **165** Bauernhoftiere • Farm animals **166** Leben im Ozean • Ocean life

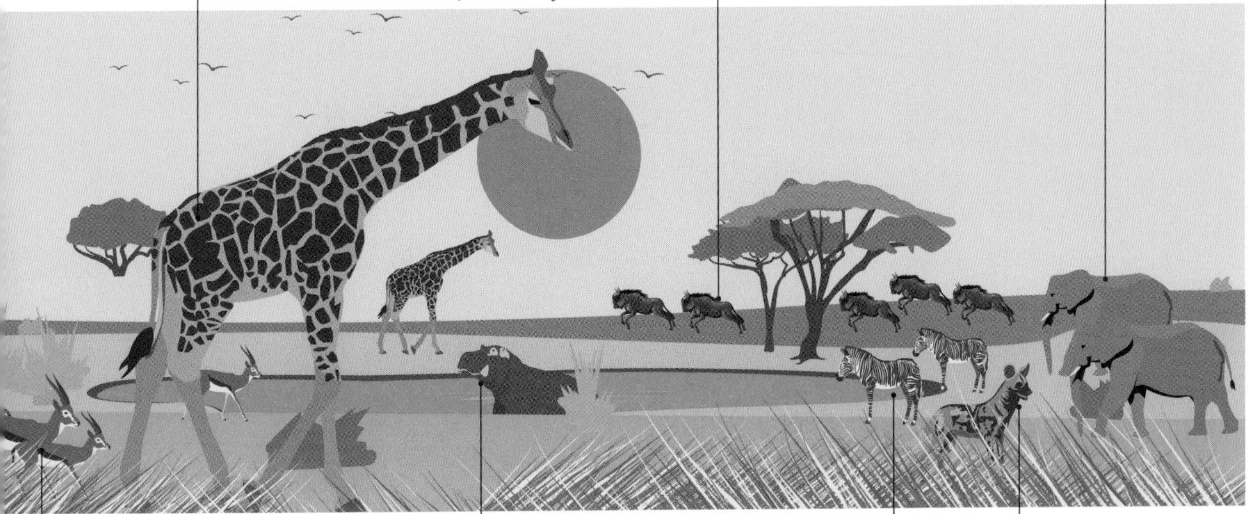

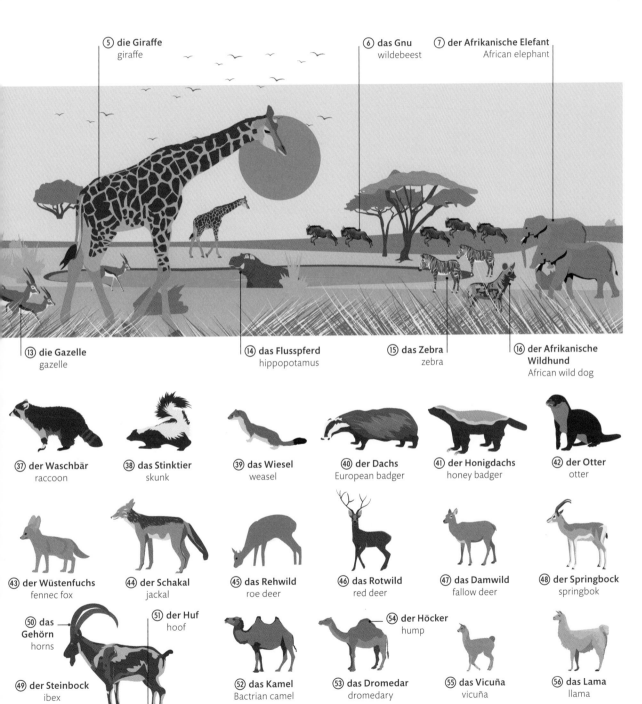

⑤ **die Giraffe**
giraffe

⑥ **das Gnu**
wildebeest

⑦ **der Afrikanische Elefant**
African elephant

⑬ **die Gazelle**
gazelle

⑭ **das Flusspferd**
hippopotamus

⑮ **das Zebra**
zebra

⑯ **der Afrikanische Wildhund**
African wild dog

㊲ **der Waschbär**
raccoon

㊳ **das Stinktier**
skunk

㊴ **das Wiesel**
weasel

㊵ **der Dachs**
European badger

㊶ **der Honigdachs**
honey badger

㊷ **der Otter**
otter

㊸ **der Wüstenfuchs**
fennec fox

㊹ **der Schakal**
jackal

㊺ **das Rehwild**
roe deer

㊻ **das Rotwild**
red deer

㊼ **das Damwild**
fallow deer

㊽ **der Springbock**
springbok

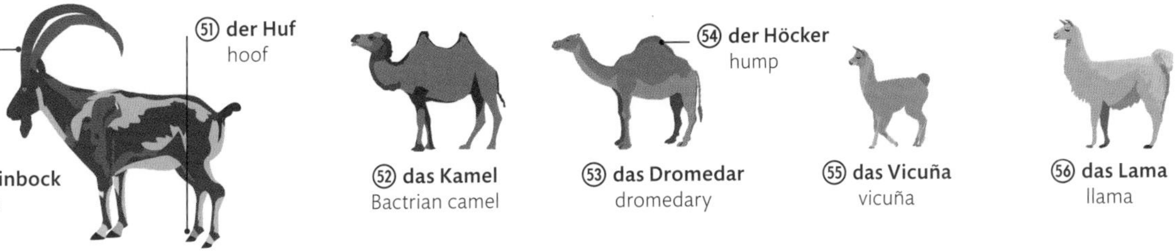

㊿ **das Gehörn**
horns

(51) **der Huf**
hoof

㊾ **der Steinbock**
ibex

(52) **das Kamel**
Bactrian camel

(54) **der Höcker**
hump

(53) **das Dromedar**
dromedary

(55) **das Vicuña**
vicuña

(56) **das Lama**
llama

# 159 Säugetiere (Fortsetzung)
## Mammals continued

### 159.1 SÄUGETIERARTEN • SPECIES OF MAMMALS

① das Rentier
reindeer
② das Karibu
caribou
③ der Polarwolf
Arctic wolf
④ der Polarfuchs
Arctic fox
⑤ der Moschusochse
musk ox
⑥ der Eisbär
polar bear
⑦ der Schneehase
Arctic hare
⑧ die Robbe
seal
⑨ die Arktis
Arctic
⑩ der Braunbär
brown bear
⑪ der Fuchs
red fox
⑮ der Laubwald
broadleaf forest
㉓ der Asiatische Elefant
Asian elephant
㉔ der Rüssel
trunk
㉕ der Ameisenbär
anteater
㉖ der Tiger
tiger
㉗ das Junge
cub
㉘ der Leopard
leopard
㉙ die Wildkatze
wildcat
㉚ der Rotluchs
bobcat
㉛ der Schneeleopard
snow leopard
㉜ der Katta
ring-tailed lemur
㉝ das Kapuzineräffchen
capuchin monkey
㉞ der Klammeraffe
spider monkey
㉟ der Schwanz
tail
㊱ der Nasenaffe
proboscis monkey
㊲ die gurkenförmige Nase
pendulous nose
㊳ der Makake
macaque
㊴ der Mandrill
mandrill
㊵ der Seidenaffe
marmoset
㊶ der Orang-Utan
orangutan
㊷ der Schimpanse
chimpanzee
㊸ der Gibbon
gibbon
㊹ der Gorilla
gorilla
㊺ der Panda
panda

See also
**157** Die Naturgeschichte • Natural history **164** Haustiere • Pets
**165** Bauernhoftiere • Farm animals **166** Leben im Ozean • Ocean life

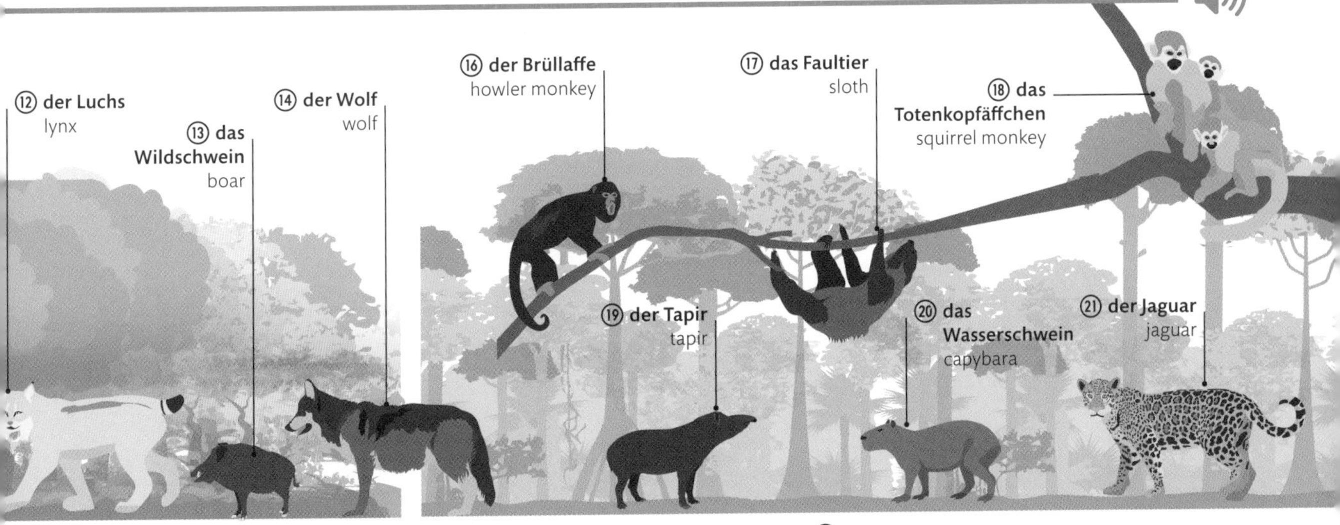


㉒ der Regenwald
rain forest

# 160 Vögel
Birds

## 160.1 VOGELARTEN · SPECIES OF BIRDS

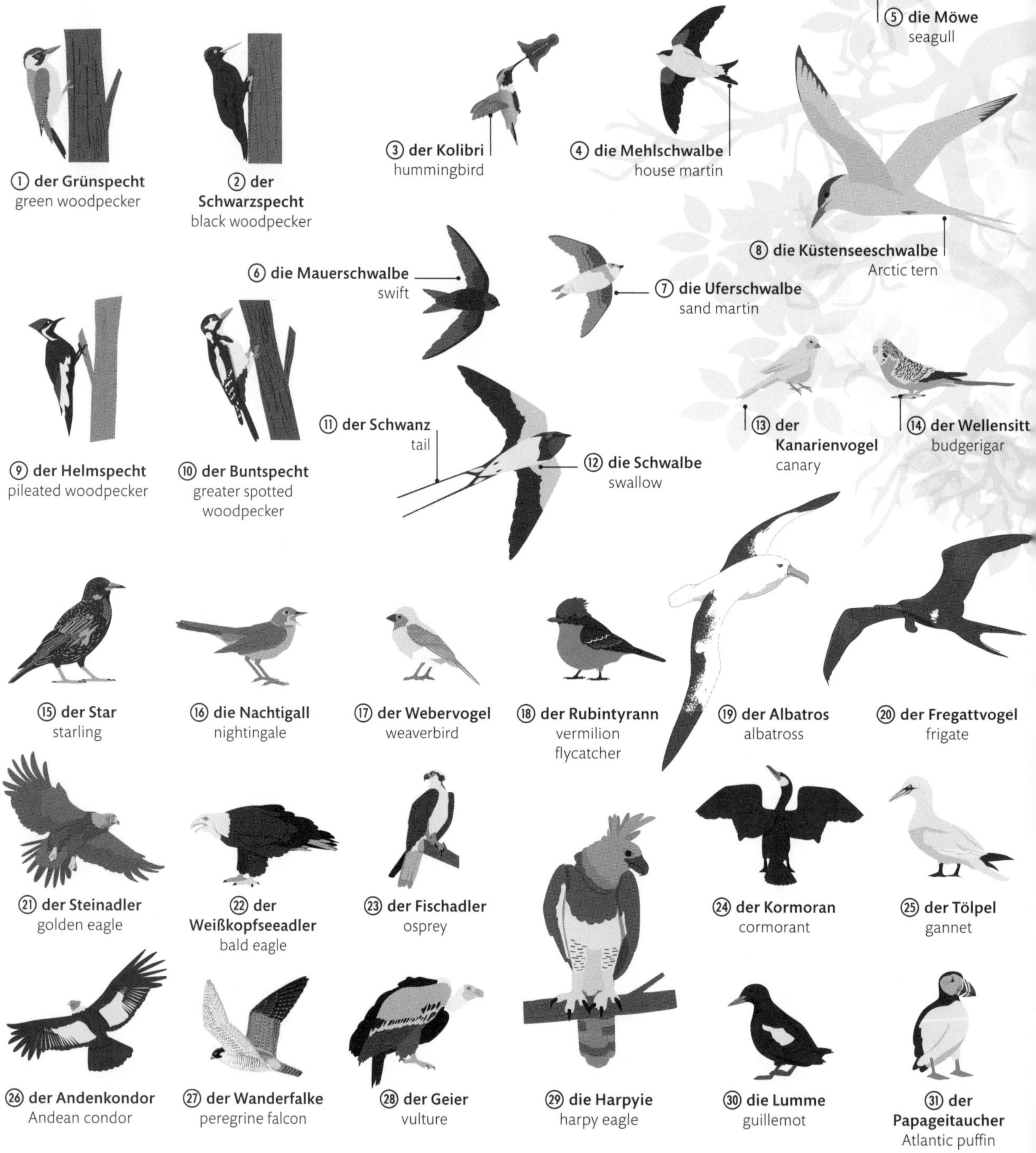

① der Grünspecht
green woodpecker
② der Schwarzspecht
black woodpecker
③ der Kolibri
hummingbird
④ die Mehlschwalbe
house martin
⑤ die Möwe
seagull
⑥ die Mauerschwalbe
swift
⑦ die Uferschwalbe
sand martin
⑧ die Küstenseeschwalbe
Arctic tern
⑨ der Helmspecht
pileated woodpecker
⑩ der Buntspecht
greater spotted woodpecker
⑪ der Schwanz
tail
⑫ die Schwalbe
swallow
⑬ der Kanarienvogel
canary
⑭ der Wellensitt
budgerigar
⑮ der Star
starling
⑯ die Nachtigall
nightingale
⑰ der Webervogel
weaverbird
⑱ der Rubintyrann
vermilion flycatcher
⑲ der Albatros
albatross
⑳ der Fregattvogel
frigate
㉑ der Steinadler
golden eagle
㉒ der Weißkopfseeadler
bald eagle
㉓ der Fischadler
osprey
㉔ der Kormoran
cormorant
㉕ der Tölpel
gannet
㉖ der Andenkondor
Andean condor
㉗ der Wanderfalke
peregrine falcon
㉘ der Geier
vulture
㉙ die Harpyie
harpy eagle
㉚ die Lumme
guillemot
㉛ der Papageitaucher
Atlantic puffin

See also
**157** Die Naturgeschichte • Natural history **161** Vögel (Fortsetzung) Birds continued **165** Bauernhoftiere • Farm animals

# 161 Vögel (Fortsetzung)
Birds continued

## 161.1 VOGELARTEN · SPECIES OF BIRDS

① **der Rosakakadu**
galah

② **der Edelpapagei**
eclectus parrot

③ **der Sittich**
rose-ringed parakeet

④ **der Scharlachara**
scarlet macaw

⑤ **der Regenbogenlori**
lorikeet

⑩ **die Schneeeule**
snowy owl

⑪ **der Uhu**
eagle owl

⑫ **der Bartkauz**
great gray owl

⑬ **der Haubenkauz**
crested owl

⑭ **die Schleiereule**
barn owl

⑮ **rufen**
to hoot

㉒ **der Höckerschwan**
mute swan

㉓ **der Trauerschwan**
black swan

㉔ **der Singschwan**
whooper swan

㉕ **das Blässhuhn**
coot

㉖ **die Stockente**
mallard

㉗ **die Mandarinente**
mandarin duck

㉘ **der Haubentaucher**
grebe

㉙ **die Brautente**
wood duck

㉚ **die Wasserralle**
water rail

㉛ **der Brachvogel**
curlew

㉜ **der Fasan**
pheasant

㉝ **der Truthahn**
turkey

㉞ **der Pfau**
peacock

㉟ **ein Rad schlagen**
feathers displayed

㊱ **der Hals**
neck

See also
157 Die Naturgeschichte • Natural history
165 Bauernhoftiere • Farm animals

⑥ **der Kakadu**
cockatoo

⑦ **der Graupapagei**
African gray parrot

⑨ **Ich habe gerade einen Steinadler entdeckt!**
I've just spotted a golden eagle!

⑧ **der Vogelbeobachter** *m*
**die Vogelbeobachterin** *f*
bird-watcher

⑯ **der Waldkauz**
tawny owl

⑰ **der Elfenkauz**
elf owl

⑱ **das Küken**
hatchling

⑲ **die Eierschale**
eggshell

㉑ **die weiche Daunenfeder**
soft down feathers

⑳ **der Jungvogel**
fledgling

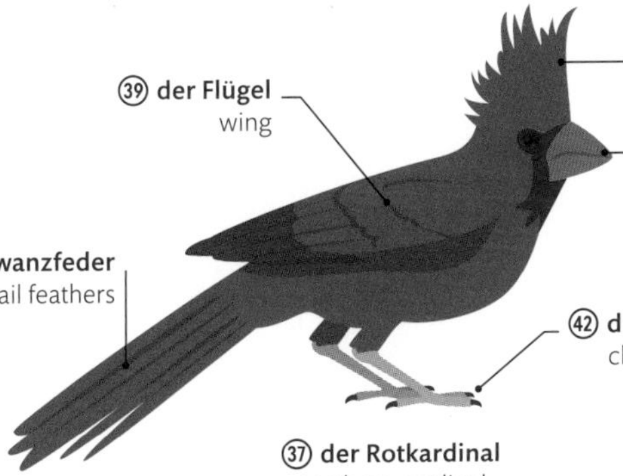

㊴ **der Flügel**
wing

㊵ **der Schopf**
crest

㊶ **der Schnabel**
bill / beak

㊳ **die Schwanzfeder**
tail feathers

㊷ **die Klaue**
claw

㊲ **der Rotkardinal**
northern cardinal

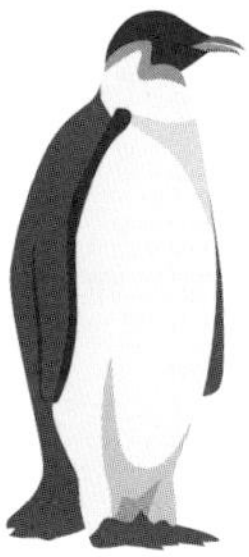

㊸ **der Kaiserpinguin**
emperor penguin

㊹ **der Felsenpinguin**
rockhopper penguin

㊺ **der Humboldtpinguin**
Humboldt penguin

㊻ **der Eselspinguin**
Gentoo penguin

㊼ **der Australische Zwergpinguin**
Australian little penguin

## 161.2 VERBEN
VERBS

① **schlüpfen**
to hatch

② **(in den Süden / Norden) ziehen**
to migrate

③ **(mit den Flügeln) schlagen**
to flap

④ **gleiten**
to glide

⑤ **einen Sturzflug machen**
to swoop

# 162 Insekten und Käfer
## Insects and bugs

### 162.1 **SCHMETTERLINGE UND FALTER** · BUTTERFLIES AND MOTHS

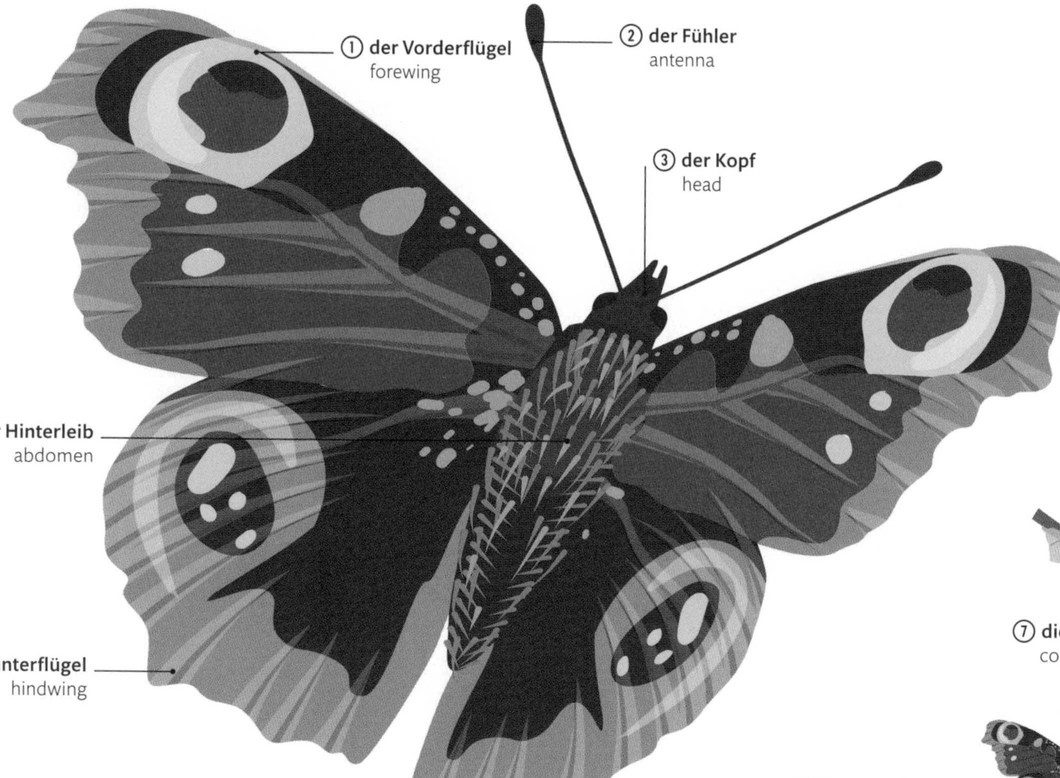


⑥ **der Schmetterling**
butterfly

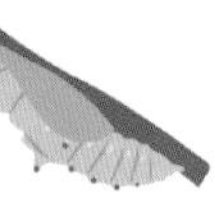

⑦ **die Puppe**
cocoon

⑧ **die Raupe**
caterpillar

⑨ **das Pfauenauge**
peacock butterfly

⑩ **der Monarchfalter**
monarch butterfly

⑪ **der Distelfalter**
painted lady butterfly

⑫ **der Schwalbenschwanz**
swallowtail butterfly

⑬ **der Glasflügelfalter**
glasswing butterfly

⑭ **der Kohlweißling**
cabbage white butterfly

⑮ **der Birkenspanner**
peppered moth

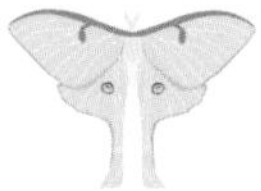

⑯ **die Lunamotte**
luna moth

⑰ **das Karpfenschwänzchen**
hummingbird hawksmoth

⑱ **das Kleine Nachtpfauenauge**
emperor moth

⑲ **der Atlasspinner**
atlas moth

⑳ **die Kleidermotte**
clothes moth

㉑ **der Fledermausschwärmer**
hawk moth

See also
**157** Die Naturgeschichte • Natural history **158-159** Säugetiere • Mammals
**160-161** Vögel • Birds **163** Amphibien und Reptilien • Amphibians and reptiles

## 162.2 **WEITERE KÄFER UND WIRBELLOSE** • OTHER BUGS AND INVERTEBRATES

① **der Nashornkäfer**
rhinoceros beetle

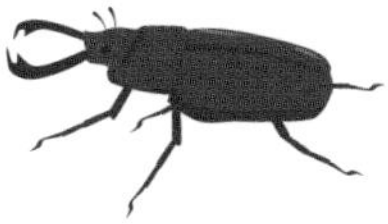
② **der Hirschkäfer**
stag beetle

③ **der Rüsselkäfer**
weevil

④ **die Kakerlake**
cockroach

⑤ **der Marienkäfer**
ladybug

⑥ **die Fliege**
fly

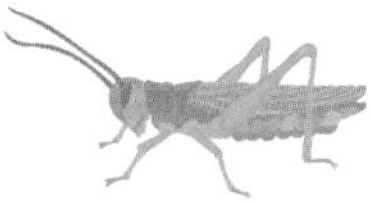
⑦ **der Grashüpfer**
grasshopper

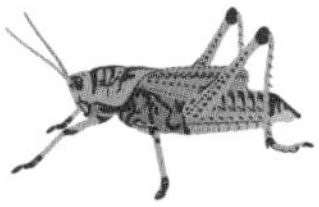
⑧ **die Heuschrecke**
locust

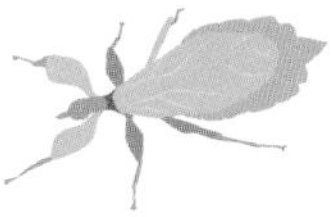
⑨ **die Gespenstschrecke**
leaf insect

⑩ **die Gottesanbeterin**
praying mantis

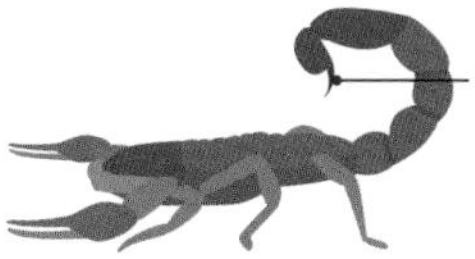
⑫ **der Stachel**
sting

⑪ **der Skorpion**
scorpion

⑬ **die Grille**
cricket

⑭ **der Hundertfüßer**
centipede

⑮ **der Tausendfüßer**
millipede

⑯ **die Libelle**
dragonfly

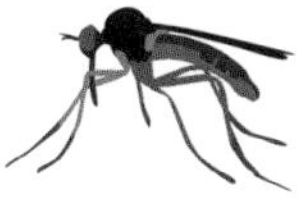
⑰ **die Mücke**
mosquito

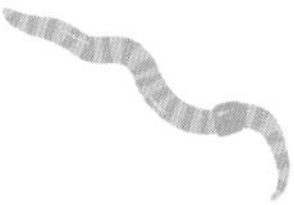
⑱ **der Wurm**
worm

⑲ **die Tarantel**
tarantula

⑳ **die Schwarze Witwe**
black widow spider

㉑ **die Springspinne**
jumping spider

㉒ **die Sektorspinne**
orb weaver

㉓ **die Nacktschnecke**
slug

㉔ **die Schnecke**
snail

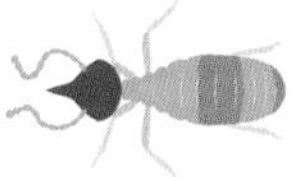
㉕ **die Termite**
termite

㉖ **die Ameise**
ant

㉗ **die Hummel**
bumble bee

㉘ **die Wespe**
wasp

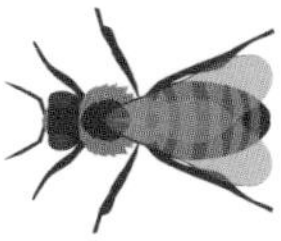
㉙ **die Honigbiene**
honey bee

㉚ **stechen**
to sting

㉛ **fliegen**
to fly

㉜ **brummen**
to buzz

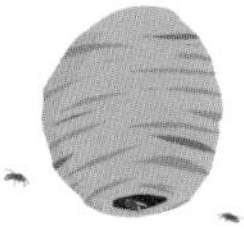
㉝ **das Wespennest**
wasp nest

㉞ **der Bienenstock**
beehive

㉟ **der Schwarm**
swarm

# 163 Amphibien und Reptilien

## Amphibians and reptiles

### 163.1 AMPHIBIEN · AMPHIBIANS

① **der Grasfrosch**
European common frog

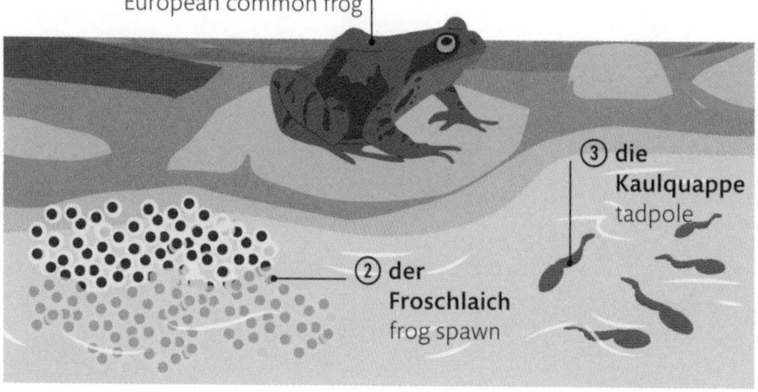

② **der Froschlaich**
frog spawn

③ **die Kaulquappe**
tadpole

④ **der Wallace-Flugfrosch**
Wallace's flying frog

⑤ **der Pfeilgiftfrosch**
poison dart frog

⑥ **der Darwin-Nasenfrosch**
Darwin's frog

⑦ **der Rotaugenlaubfrosch**
red-eyed tree frog

⑧ **die Gemeine Kröte**
common toad

⑨ **der Afrikanische Ochsenfrosch**
African bullfrog

⑩ **die Chinesische Rotbauchunke**
Oriental fire-bellied toad

⑪ **die Präriekröte**
Great Plains toad

⑫ **der Feuersalamander**
fire salamander

⑬ **der Olm**
olm

⑭ **das Axolotl**
Mexican axolotl

⑮ **der Kammmolch**
great crested newt

⑯ **der Rotsalamander**
red salamander

### 163.2 REPTILIEN · REPTILES

② **der Panzer**
shell

① **die Galapagosschildkröte**
Galápagos turtle

③ **die Strahlenschildkröte**
radiated tortoise

④ **die Matamata**
matamata

⑤ **die Diamantschildkröte**
diamond back terrapin

⑥ **die Australische Schlangenhalsschildkröte**
common snake-necked turtle

⑦ **die Grüne Meeresschildkröte**
green sea turtle

⑧ **die Lederschildkröte**
leatherback sea turtle

⑨ **das Parsons-Chamäleon**
parson's chameleon

⑩ **das Pantherchamäleon**
panther chameleon

⑪ **das Dreihornchamäleon**
Jackson's chameleon

⑫ **der Komodowaran**
Komodo dragon

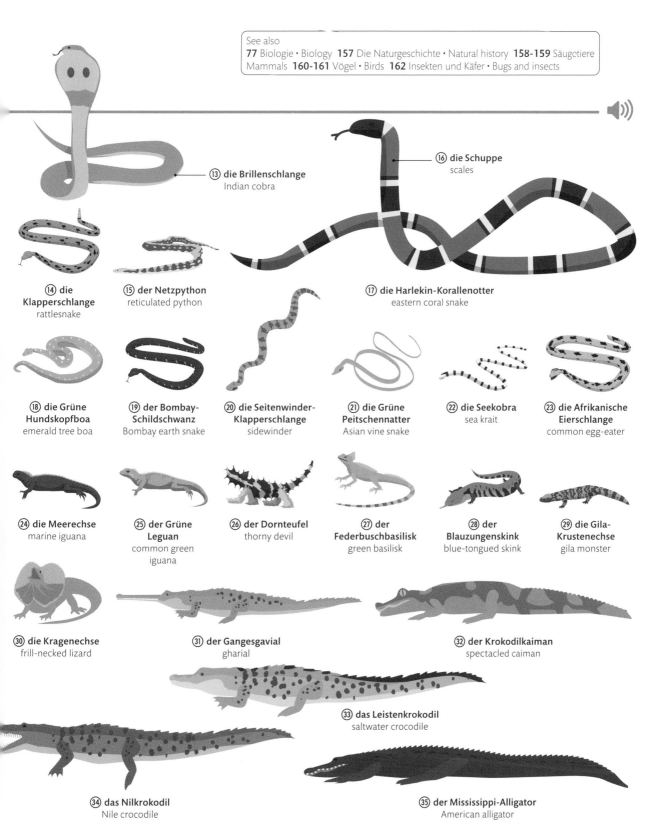

See also
**77** Biologie • Biology **157** Die Naturgeschichte • Natural history **158-159** Säugetiere Mammals **160-161** Vögel • Birds **162** Insekten und Käfer • Bugs and insects

⑬ **die Brillenschlange**
Indian cobra

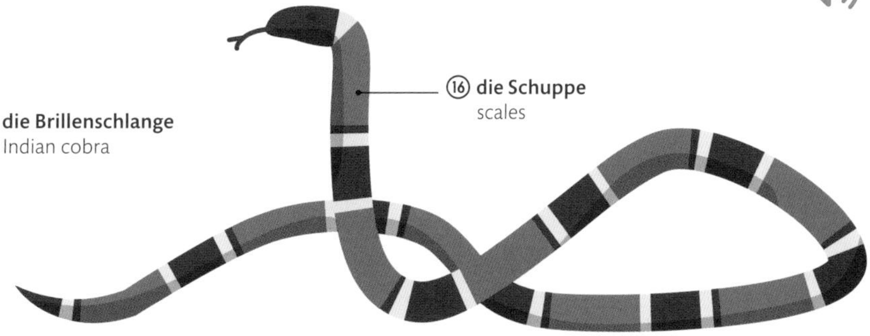

⑯ **die Schuppe**
scales

⑭ **die Klapperschlange**
rattlesnake

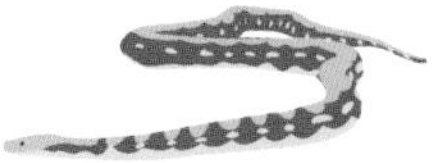

⑮ **der Netzpython**
reticulated python

⑰ **die Harlekin-Korallenotter**
eastern coral snake

⑱ **die Grüne Hundskopfboa**
emerald tree boa

⑲ **der Bombay-Schildschwanz**
Bombay earth snake

⑳ **die Seitenwinder-Klapperschlange**
sidewinder

㉑ **die Grüne Peitschennatter**
Asian vine snake

㉒ **die Seekobra**
sea krait

㉓ **die Afrikanische Eierschlange**
common egg-eater

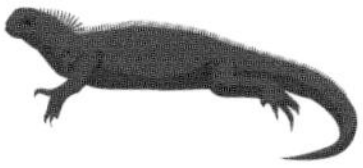

㉔ **die Meerechse**
marine iguana

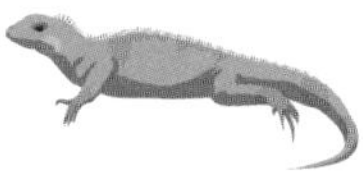

㉕ **der Grüne Leguan**
common green iguana

㉖ **der Dornteufel**
thorny devil

㉗ **der Federbuschbasilisk**
green basilisk

㉘ **der Blauzungenskink**
blue-tongued skink

㉙ **die Gila-Krustenechse**
gila monster

㉚ **die Kragenechse**
frill-necked lizard

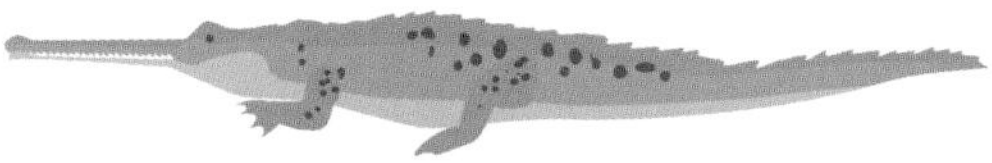

㉛ **der Gangesgavial**
gharial

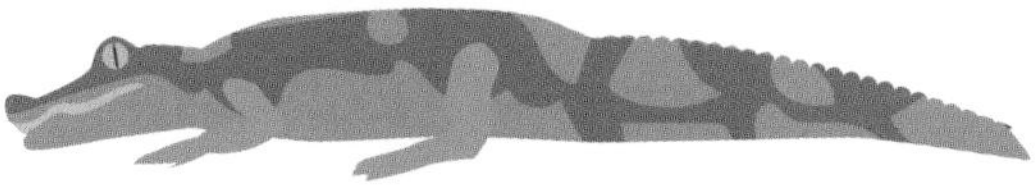

㉜ **der Krokodilkaiman**
spectacled caiman

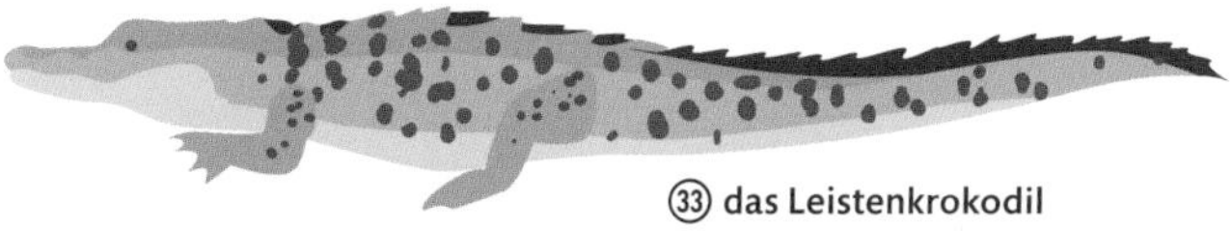

㉝ **das Leistenkrokodil**
saltwater crocodile

㉞ **das Nilkrokodil**
Nile crocodile

㉟ **der Mississippi-Alligator**
American alligator

# 164 Haustiere
## Pets

### 164.1 KATZENRASSEN · CAT BREEDS

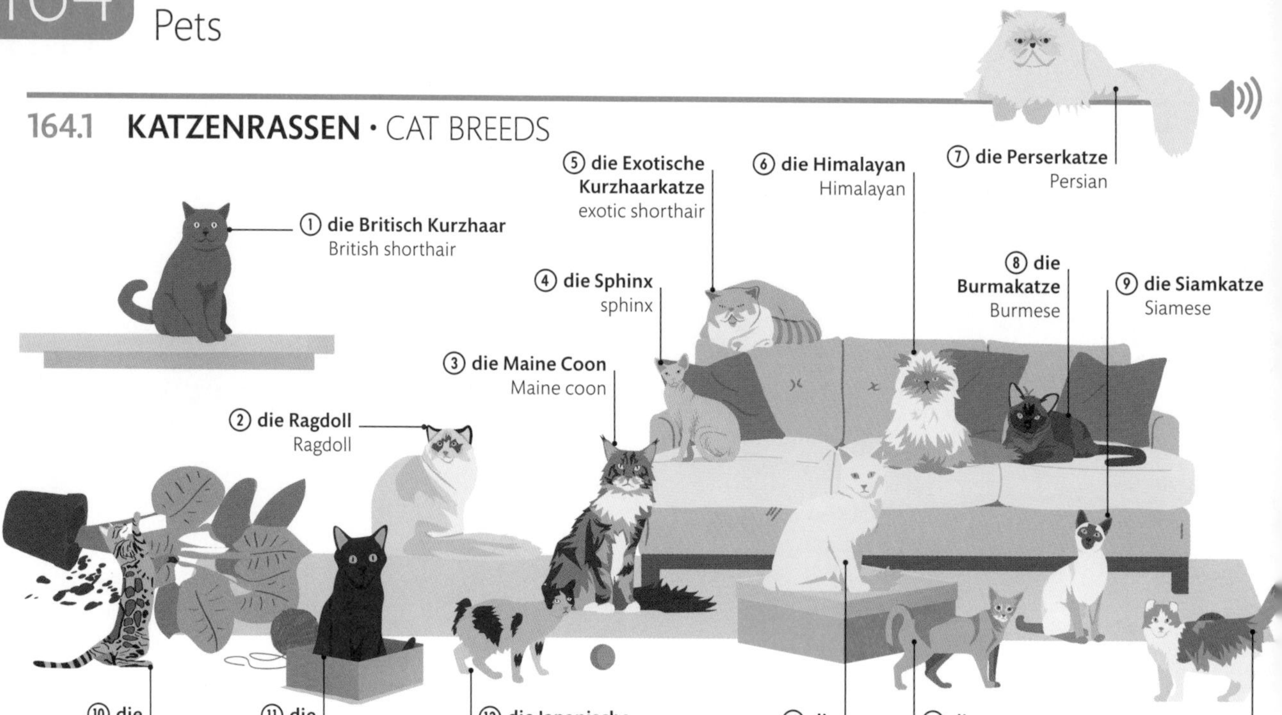

① **die Britisch Kurzhaar**
British shorthair

② **die Ragdoll**
Ragdoll

③ **die Maine Coon**
Maine coon

④ **die Sphinx**
sphinx

⑤ **die Exotische Kurzhaarkatze**
exotic shorthair

⑥ **die Himalayan**
Himalayan

⑦ **die Perserkatze**
Persian

⑧ **die Burmakatze**
Burmese

⑨ **die Siamkatze**
Siamese

⑩ **die Bengalkatze**
Bengal

⑪ **die Bombaykatze**
Bombay

⑫ **die Japanische Stummelschwanzkatze**
Japanese bobtail

⑬ **die Angorakatze**
Angora

⑭ **die Abessinierkatze**
Abyssinian

⑮ **die American Curl**
American curl

⑯ **miauen**
to meow

⑰ **schnurren**
to purr

⑱ **sich verstecken**
to hide

⑲ **haaren**
to molt

⑳ **das Kätzchen**
kitten

### 164.3 WEITERE HAUSTIERE · OTHER PETS

① **der Hamster**
hamster

② **die Rennmaus**
gerbil

③ **die Maus**
mouse

④ **piepsen**
to squeak

⑤ **das Meerschweinchen**
guinea pig

⑥ **das Kaninchen**
rabbit

⑦ **hüpfen**
to hop

⑧ **das Frettchen**
ferret

⑨ **der Fisch**
fish

⑩ **die Eidechse**
lizard

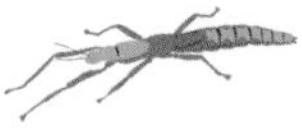

⑪ **das Stabinsekt**
stick insect

⑫ **die Schildkröte**
tortoise

⑬ **der Wellensittich**
budgerigar / budgie

⑭ **der Nymphensittich**
cockatiel

See also
**158-159** Säugetiere • Mammals **160-161** Vögel • Birds **162** Insekten und Käfer Insects and bugs **163** Amphibien und Reptilien • Amphibians and reptiles

## 164.2 HUNDERASSEN • DOG BREEDS

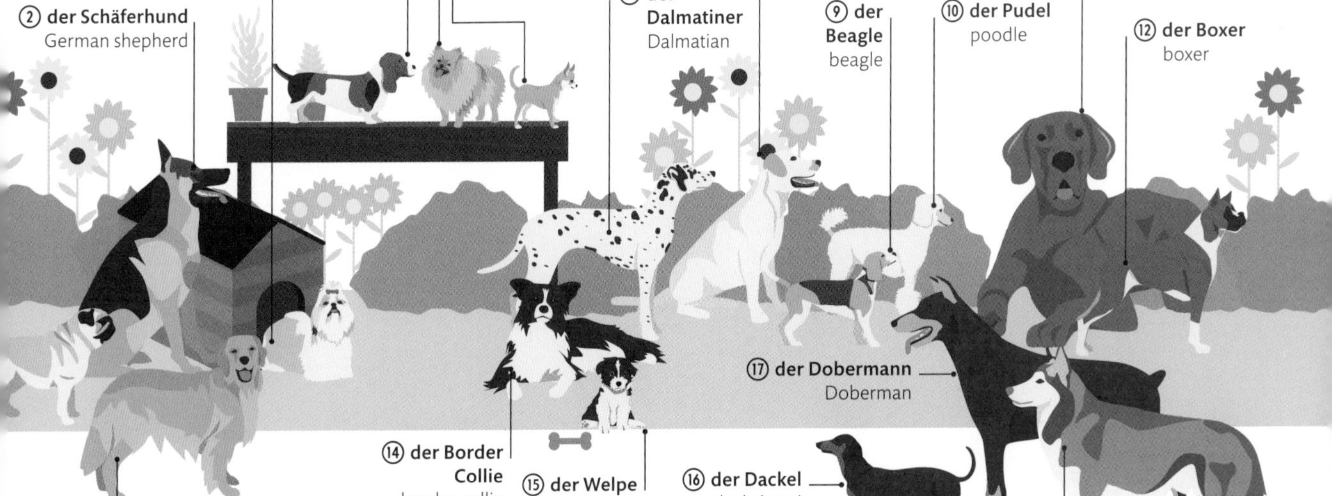

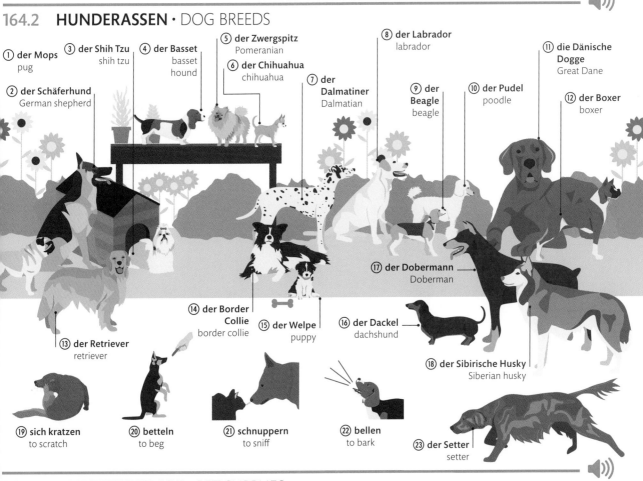

1. **der Mops** pug
2. **der Schäferhund** German shepherd
3. **der Shih Tzu** shih tzu
4. **der Basset** basset hound
5. **der Zwergspitz** Pomeranian
6. **der Chihuahua** chihuahua
7. **der Dalmatiner** Dalmatian
8. **der Labrador** labrador
9. **der Beagle** beagle
10. **der Pudel** poodle
11. **die Dänische Dogge** Great Dane
12. **der Boxer** boxer
13. **der Retriever** retriever
14. **der Border Collie** border collie
15. **der Welpe** puppy
16. **der Dackel** dachshund
17. **der Dobermann** Doberman
18. **der Sibirische Husky** Siberian husky

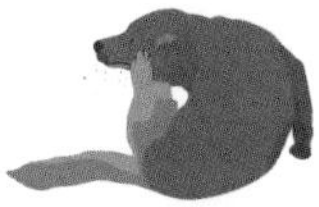

19. **sich kratzen** to scratch

20. **betteln** to beg

21. **schnuppern** to sniff

22. **bellen** to bark

23. **der Setter** setter

## 164.4 HAUSTIERBEDARF • PET SUPPLIES

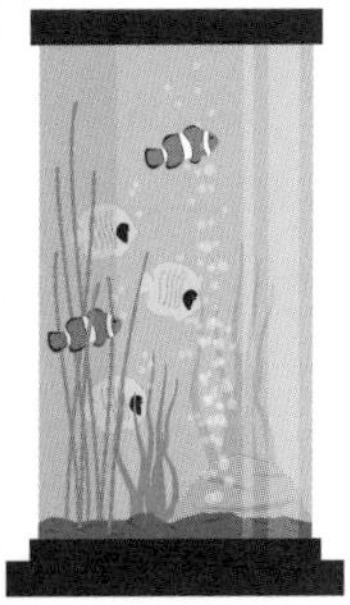

1. **das Aquarium** fish tank / aquarium

2. **der Korb** basket

3. **die Hundehütte** doghouse

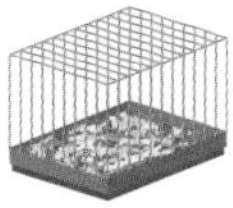

4. **der Käfig** cage

5. **der Kaninchenstall** rabbit hutch

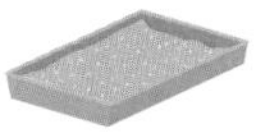

6. **das Katzenklo** litterbox

7. **die Leine** leash

8. **das Vivarium** vivarium

9. **das Vogelfutter** birdseed

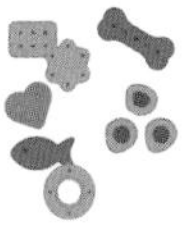

10. **das Leckerli** treats

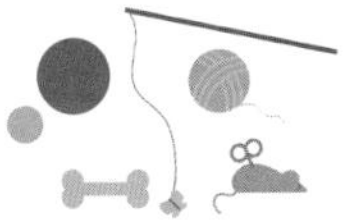

11. **das Spielzeug** toys

# 165 Bauernhoftiere
## Farm animals

### 165.1 AUF DEM BAUERNHOF • ON THE FARM

⑭ **der Hahn**
rooster

⑮ **die Henne**
hen

⑯ **der Truthahn**
turkey

⑰ **das Geflügel**
poultry

㉑ **die Biene**
bee

⑳ **der Bienenstock**
hive

㉒ **die Schafsherde**
flock of sheep

⑱ **der Bock**
ram

⑲ **die Au**
ewe

㉓ **die Kuhherde**
herd of cows

㉔ **der Bulle**
bull

㉕ **das Kalb**
calf

㉖ **die Rinder** *n, pl*
cattle

㉗ **der Esel**
donkey

See also
**53** Fleisch • Meat **86** Landwirtschaft • Farming
**158-159** Säugetiere • Mammals **164** Haustiere • Pets

⑦ **das Pferd**
horse

⑧ **die Gans**
goose

⑨ **das Küken**
gosling

⑩ **das Schwein**
pig

⑪ **das Ferkel**
piglet

⑫ **die Ente**
duck

⑬ **das Entlein**
duckling

㉘ **der Hengst**
stallion

㉙ **die Stute**
mare

㉚ **das Fohlen**
foal

㉛ **die Ziege**
goat

㉜ **das Zicklein**
kid

㉝ **der Strauß**
ostrich

㉞ **das Lama**
llama

㉟ **das Alpaka**
alpaca

㊱ **scheren**
to shear

㊲ **traben**
to trot

㊳ **galoppieren**
to gallop

㊴ **auf jemanden zulaufen**
to charge

㊵ **krähen**
to crow

㊶ **mähen**
to bleat

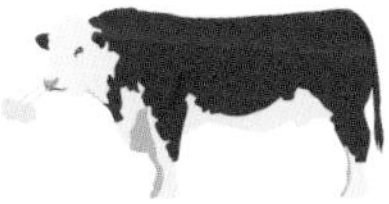

㊷ **schnauben**
to snort

㊸ **grunzen**
to grunt

㊹ **iahen**
to bray

㊺ **quaken**
to quack

# Leben im Ozean
## Ocean life

### 166.1 MEERESTIERE · MARINE SPECIES

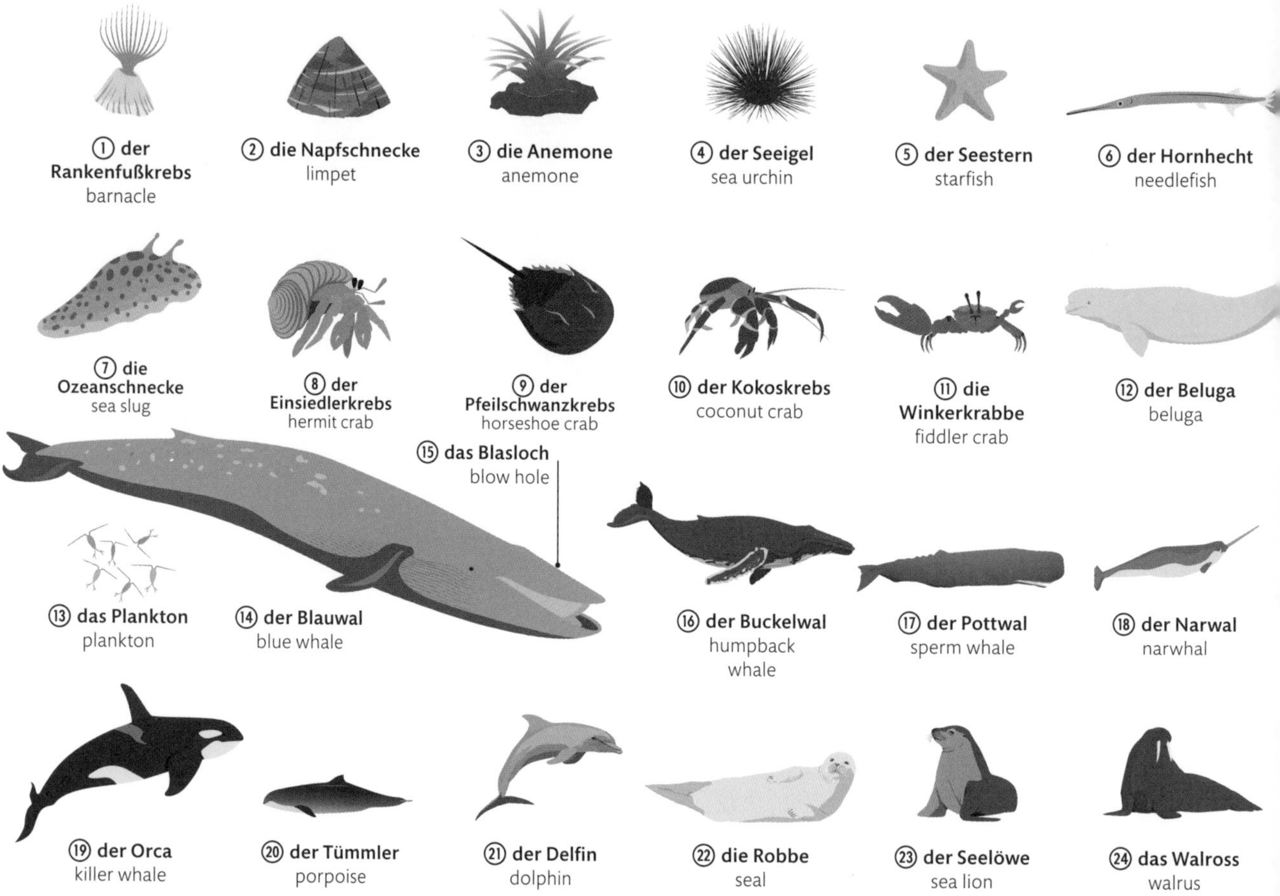
① der Rankenfußkrebs
barnacle
② die Napfschnecke
limpet
③ die Anemone
anemone
④ der Seeigel
sea urchin
⑤ der Seestern
starfish
⑥ der Hornhecht
needlefish
⑦ die Ozeanschnecke
sea slug
⑧ der Einsiedlerkrebs
hermit crab
⑨ der Pfeilschwanzkrebs
horseshoe crab
⑩ der Kokoskrebs
coconut crab
⑪ die Winkerkrabbe
fiddler crab
⑫ der Beluga
beluga
⑬ das Plankton
plankton
⑭ der Blauwal
blue whale
⑮ das Blasloch
blow hole
⑯ der Buckelwal
humpback whale
⑰ der Pottwal
sperm whale
⑱ der Narwal
narwhal
⑲ der Orca
killer whale
⑳ der Tümmler
porpoise
㉑ der Delfin
dolphin
㉒ die Robbe
seal
㉓ der Seelöwe
sea lion
㉔ das Walross
walrus

### 166.2 DAS KORALLENRIFF · CORAL REEF

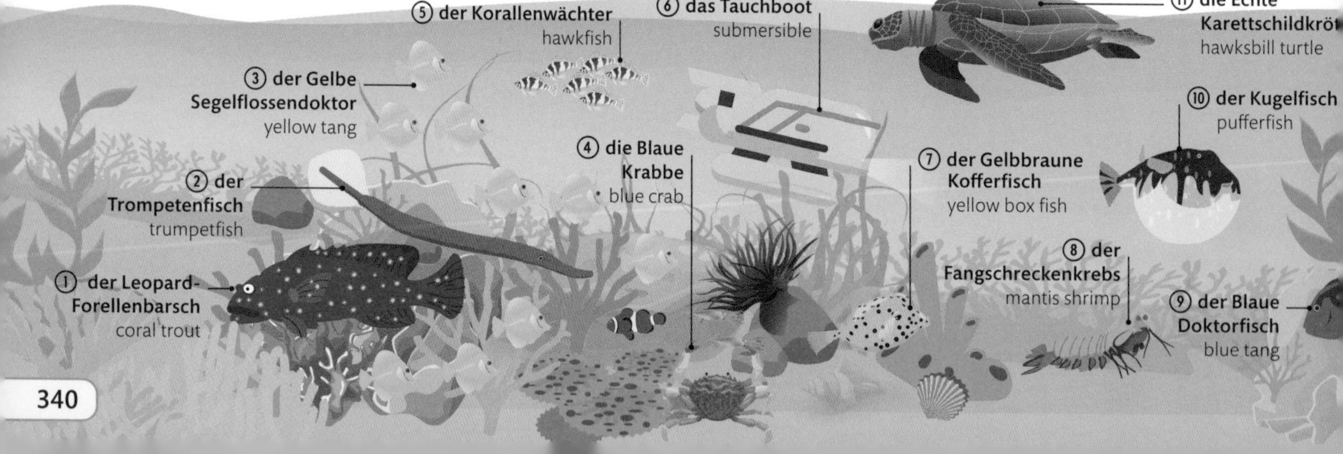
① der Leopard-Forellenbarsch
coral trout
② der Trompetenfisch
trumpetfish
③ der Gelbe Segelflossendoktor
yellow tang
④ die Blaue Krabbe
blue crab
⑤ der Korallenwächter
hawkfish
⑥ das Tauchboot
submersible
⑦ der Gelbbraune Kofferfisch
yellow box fish
⑧ der Fangschreckenkrebs
mantis shrimp
⑨ der Blaue Doktorfisch
blue tang
⑩ der Kugelfisch
pufferfish
⑪ die Echte Karettschildkrö
hawksbill turtle

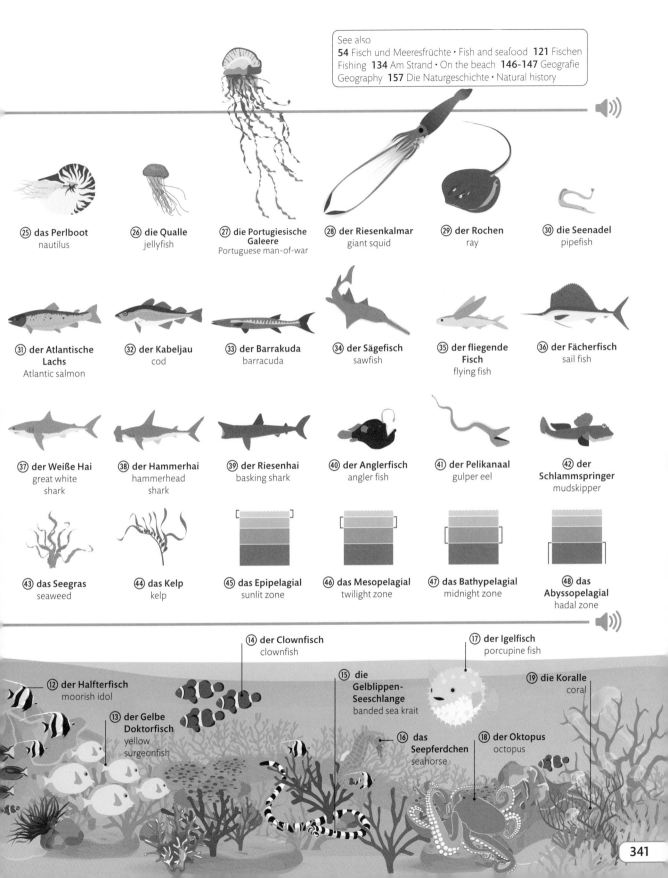

See also
**54** Fisch und Meeresfrüchte • Fish and seafood **121** Fischen Fishing **134** Am Strand • On the beach **146-147** Geografie Geography **157** Die Naturgeschichte • Natural history

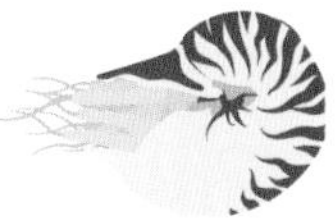
㉕ **das Perlboot**
nautilus

㉖ **die Qualle**
jellyfish

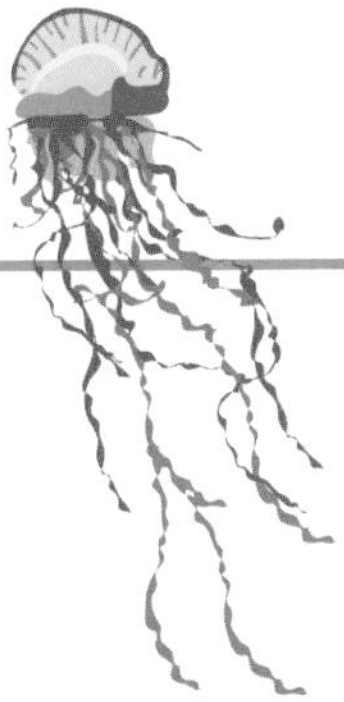
㉗ **die Portugiesische Galeere**
Portuguese man-of-war

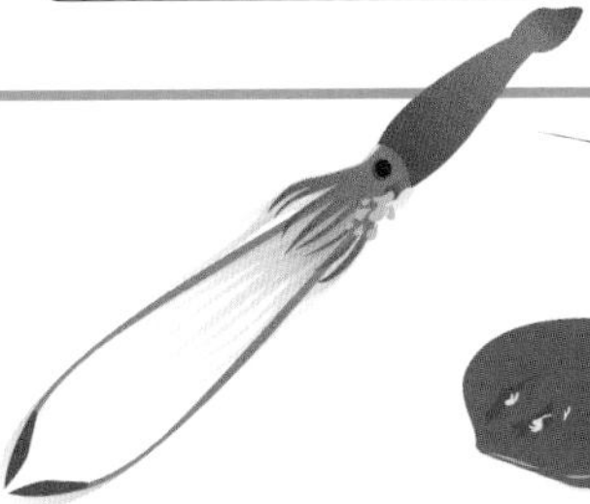
㉘ **der Riesenkalmar**
giant squid

㉙ **der Rochen**
ray

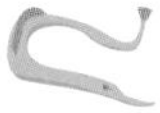
㉚ **die Seenadel**
pipefish

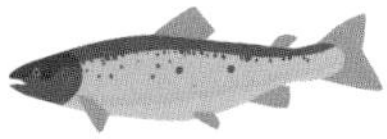
㉛ **der Atlantische Lachs**
Atlantic salmon

㉜ **der Kabeljau**
cod

㉝ **der Barrakuda**
barracuda

㉞ **der Sägefisch**
sawfish

㉟ **der fliegende Fisch**
flying fish

㊱ **der Fächerfisch**
sail fish

㊲ **der Weiße Hai**
great white shark

㊳ **der Hammerhai**
hammerhead shark

㊴ **der Riesenhai**
basking shark

㊵ **der Anglerfisch**
angler fish

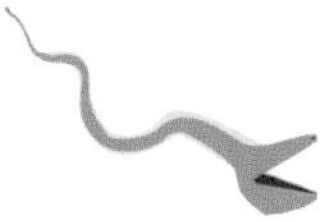
㊶ **der Pelikanaal**
gulper eel

㊷ **der Schlammspringer**
mudskipper

㊸ **das Seegras**
seaweed

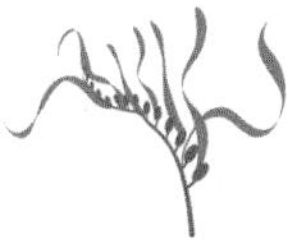
㊹ **das Kelp**
kelp

㊺ **das Epipelagial**
sunlit zone

㊻ **das Mesopelagial**
twilight zone

㊼ **das Bathypelagial**
midnight zone

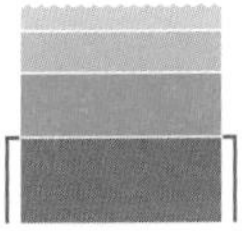
㊽ **das Abyssopelagial**
hadal zone

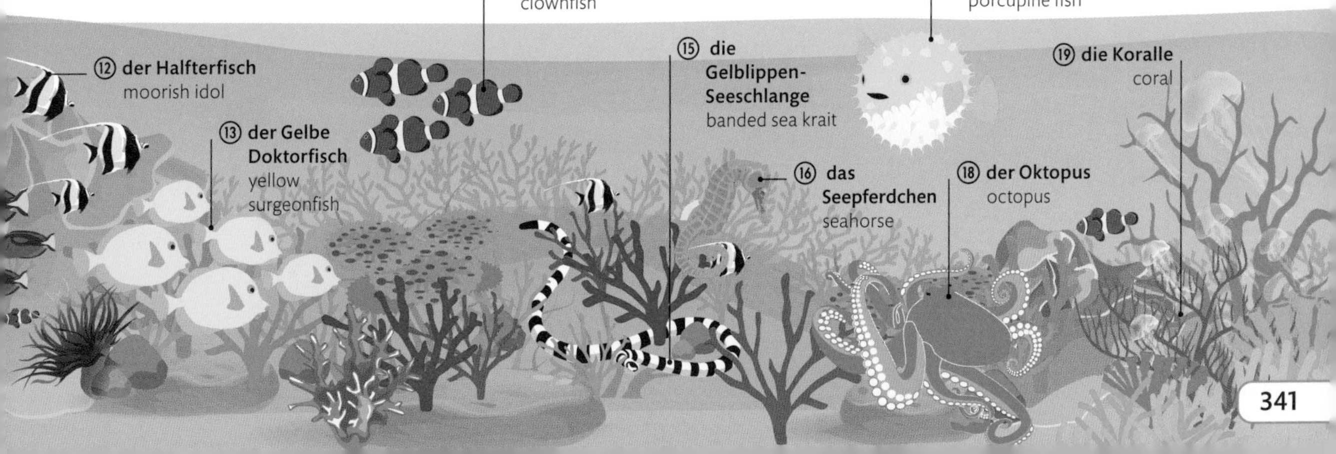

# 167 Pflanzen und Bäume

## Plants and trees

### 167.1 PFLANZEN UND BÄUME · PLANTS AND TREES

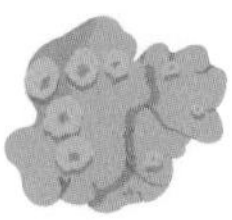
① **das Lebermoos**
liverwort

② **das Moos**
moss

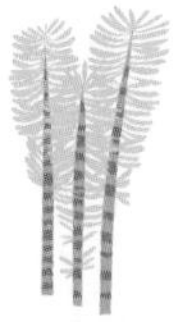
③ **der Schachtelhalm**
horsetail

④ **der Farn**
fern

⑤ **der Brotpalmfarn**
cycad

⑥ **der Ginkgo**
ginkgo

⑦ **die Fichte**
spruce

⑧ **die Tanne**
fir

⑨ **die Andentanne**
monkey puzzle

⑩ **die Eibe**
yew

⑪ **der Nadelbaum**
conifers

⑫ **die Lärche**
larch

⑬ **die Libanonzeder**
cedar of Lebanon

⑭ **die Pinie**
umbrella pine

⑮ **die Seerose**
water lily

⑯ **die Magnolie**
magnolia

⑰ **der Avocadobaum**
avocado tree

⑱ **der Lorbeerbaum**
laurel

⑲ **die Calla**
arum lily

⑳ **der Riesenmammutbaum**
giant sequoia

㉑ **der Josuabaum**
Joshua tree

㉒ **die Amaryllis**
amaryllis

㉓ **die Schusterpalme**
cast-iron plant

㉔ **der Drachenbaum**
dragon tree

㉕ **der Blaustern**
English bluebell

㉖ **das Schneeglöckchen**
snowdrop

㉗ **der Krokus**
crocus

See also
**38** Gartenpflanzen und Zimmerpflanzen • Garden plants and houseplants **57** Obst • Fruit
**58** Obst und Nüsse • Fruit and nuts **157** Die Naturgeschichte • Natural history
**168-169** Pflanzen und Bäume (Fortsetzung) • Plants and trees continued **170** Pilze • Fungi

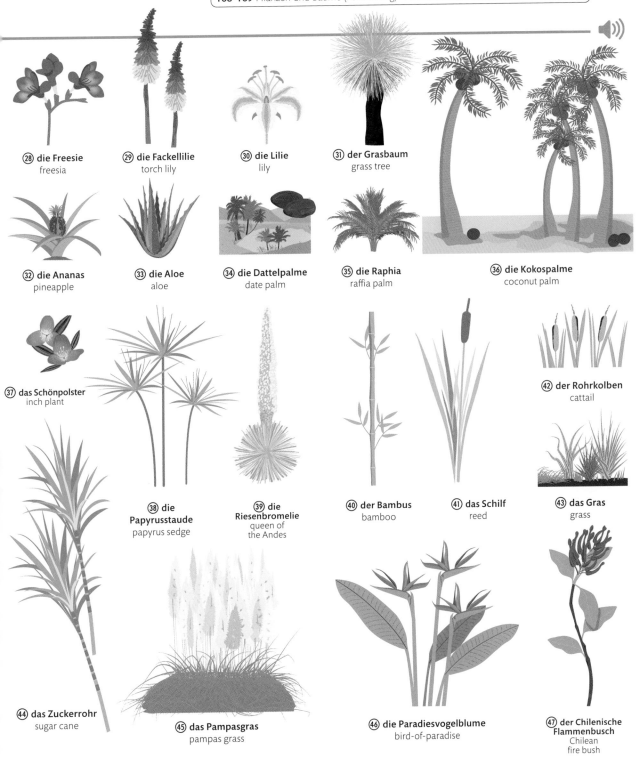

㉘ **die Freesie**
freesia

㉙ **die Fackellilie**
torch lily

㉚ **die Lilie**
lily

㉛ **der Grasbaum**
grass tree

㉜ **die Ananas**
pineapple

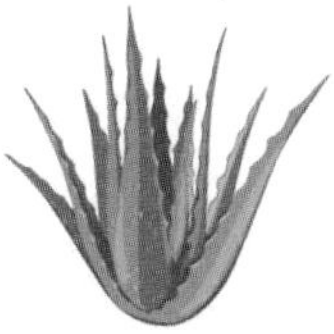

㉝ **die Aloe**
aloe

㉞ **die Dattelpalme**
date palm

㉟ **die Raphia**
raffia palm

㊱ **die Kokospalme**
coconut palm

㊲ **das Schönpolster**
inch plant

㊳ **die Papyrusstaude**
papyrus sedge

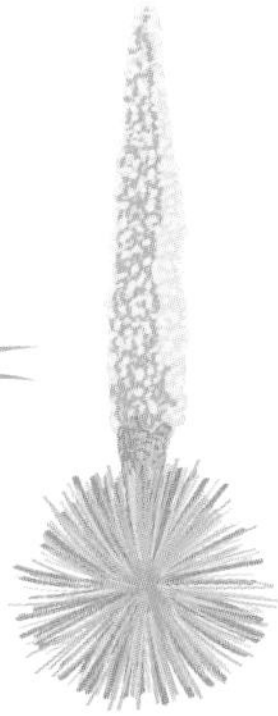

㊴ **die Riesenbromelie**
queen of the Andes

㊵ **der Bambus**
bamboo

㊶ **das Schilf**
reed

㊷ **der Rohrkolben**
cattail

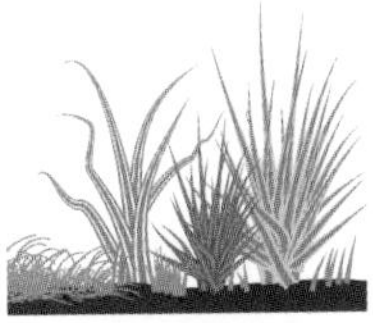

㊸ **das Gras**
grass

㊹ **das Zuckerrohr**
sugar cane

㊺ **das Pampasgras**
pampas grass

㊻ **die Paradiesvogelblume**
bird-of-paradise

㊼ **der Chilenische Flammenbusch**
Chilean fire bush

# Pflanzen und Bäume (Fortsetzung)

Plants and trees continued

## 168.1 PFLANZEN UND BÄUME · PLANTS AND TREES

① **das Schöllkraut**
celandine

② **der Klatschmohn**
common poppy

③ **die Berberitze**
barberry

④ **die Gemeine Platane**
London plane

⑤ **die Butterblume**
buttercup

⑥ **der Blaumohn**
opium poppy

⑦ **der Baum der Reisenden**
traveler's tree

⑧ **die Macadamia**
macadamia

⑨ **der Goldwein**
golden guinea vine

⑩ **das Mammutblatt**
gunnera

⑪ **die Akelei**
columbine

⑫ **die Frithia pulchra**
fairy elephant's feet

⑬ **die Lebenden Steine** *m, pl*
living stones

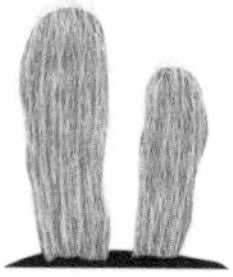

⑭ **das Greisenhaupt**
old man cactus

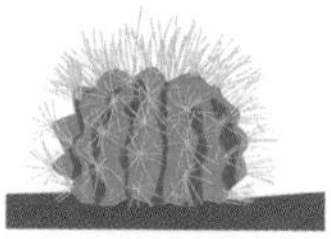

⑮ **der Kugelkaktus**
barrel cactus

⑯ **die Kaktusfeige**
prickly pear

⑰ **die Lichtnelke**
campion

⑱ **der Thelocactus bicolor**
glory of Texas

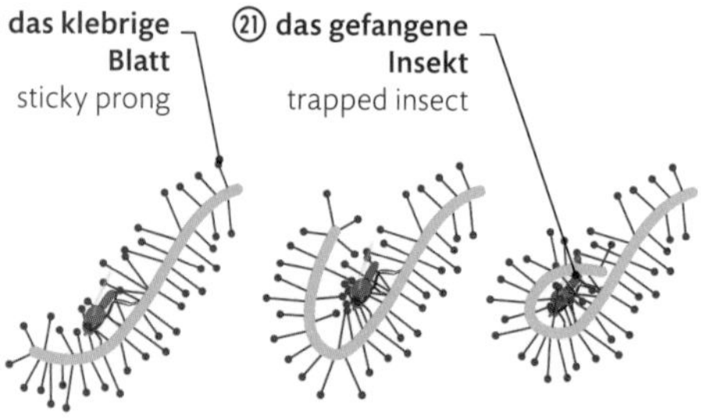


⑲ **der Sonnentau**
sundew

㉒ **die Venusfliegenfalle**
Venus fly-trap

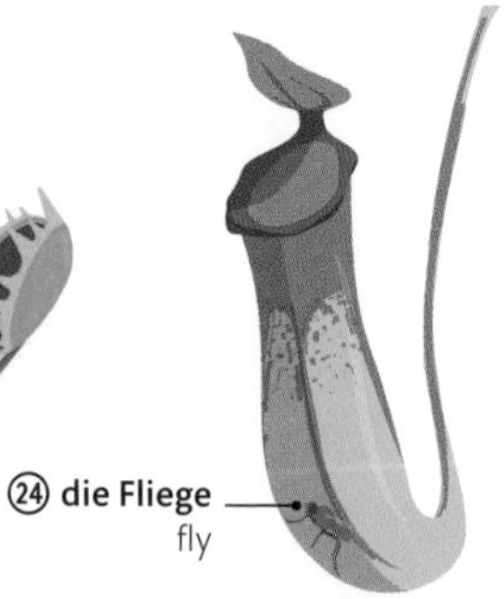


㉓ **die Kannenpflanze**
pitcher plant

See also
**38** Gartenpflanzen und Zimmerpflanzen • Garden plants and houseplants **57** Obst
Fruit **58** Obst und Nüsse • Fruit and nuts **157** Die Naturgeschichte • Natural history
**169** Pflanzen und Bäume (Fortsetzung) • Plants and trees continued **170** Pilze • Fungi

**㉕ die Bougainville**
bougainvillea

**㉖ der Flammenbaum**
fire tree

**㉗ die Mistel**
mistletoe

**㉘ die Alpen-Hauswurz**
common houseleek

**㉙ der Wein**
grapevine

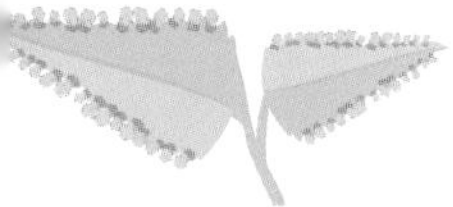

**㉚ das Brutblatt**
mother of thousands

**㉛ die Pfingstrose**
peony

**㉜ der Wilde Wein**
Virginia creeper

**㉝ die Myrte**
myrtle

**㉞ der Granatapfelbaum**
pomegranate

**㉟ der Braune Weiderich**
purple loosestrife

**㊱ die Henna**
henna

**㊲ der Zwergflaschenputzer**
Tonghi bottlebrush

**㊳ die Guave**
guava

**㊴ die Fuchsie**
fuchsia

**㊵ die Mimose**
mimosa

**㊶ die Seidenakazie**
silk tree

**㊷ die Hainbuche**
hornbeam

**㊹ der Samen**
seed

**㊸ die Haselnuss**
hazel

**㊺ der Walnussbaum**
walnut

**㊻ die Edelkastanie**
Spanish chestnut

**㊼ der Pekannussbaum**
pecan

**㊽ die Buche**
beech

**㊾ die Birke**
birch

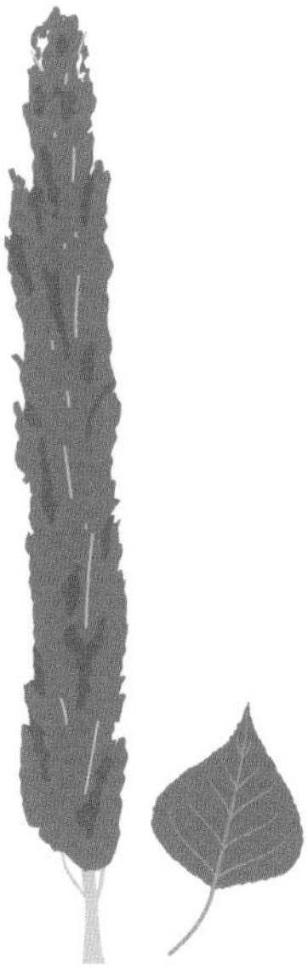

**㊿ die Pappel**
poplar

# 169 Pflanzen und Bäume (Fortsetzung)

Plants and trees continued

## 169.1 PFLANZEN UND BÄUME · PLANTS AND TREES

② **die Eichel**
acorn

① **die Eiche**
oak

③ **das Wüsteneisenholz**
desert ironwood tree

④ **der Wunderbaum**
castor oil plant

⑤ **die Weide**
willow

⑥ **der Mangrovenbaum**
mangrove

⑦ **der Gummibaum**
rubber tree

⑧ **die Passionsblume**
passion flower

⑨ **die Aschweide**
grey willow

⑩ **der Sanddorn**
sea buckthorn

⑱ **die Blüte**
blossom

⑰ **der Zweig**
branch

⑯ **die Kirsche**
cherries

⑪ **die Birne**
pear

⑫ **der Johannisapfel**
crab apple

⑬ **die Pflaume**
plum

⑭ **die Feige**
fig

⑮ **der Kirschbaum**
cherry

⑲ **die Ölweide**
oleaster

⑳ **der Hanf**
hemp

㉑ **der Hopfen**
hop

㉒ **die Hagebutte**
dog rose

See also
**38** Gartenpflanzen und Zimmerpflanzen • Garden plants and houseplants **57** Obst • Fruit
**58** Obst und Nüsse • Fruit and nuts **157** Die Naturgeschichte • Natural history **170** Pilze • Fungi

㉓ **die Zwergmispel**
cotoneaster

㉔ **die Eberesche**
mountain ash

㉕ **die Mispel**
medlar

㉖ **der Weißdorn**
hawthorn

㉗ **die Ulme**
elm

㉘ **die Nessel**
nettle

㉙ **die Kapuzinerkresse**
nasturtium

㉚ **das Mauerblümchen**
wallflower

㉛ **der Hibiskus**
Chinese hibiscus

㉜ **der Kakaobaum**
cocoa

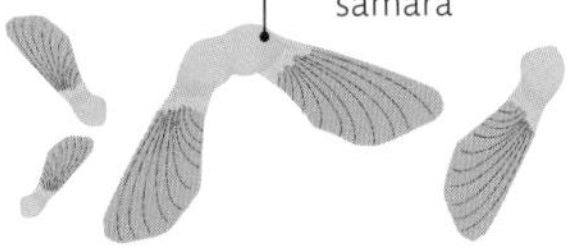

㊸ **die Samara**
samara

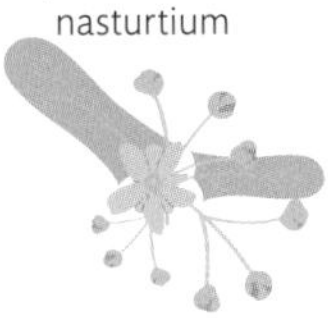

㉝ **die Linde**
lime / linden

㉞ **die Schlüsselblume**
cowslip

㉟ **der Chinesische Surenbaum**
Chinese mahogany

㊱ **der Affenbrotbaum**
baobab tree

㊷ **das Sommerblatt**
summer leaf

㊶ **der Bergahorn**
sycamore

㊹ **das Herbstblatt**
fall leaf

㊲ **der Ahorn**
maple

㊳ **die Rosskastanie**
horse chestnut

㊴ **der Oleander**
oleander

㊵ **die Olive**
olive

㊺ **die Ackerwinde**
morning glory

㊻ **die Belladonna**
deadly nightshade

㊼ **der Schierling**
hemlock

㊽ **die Distel**
thistle

㊾ **der Efeu**
ivy

㊿ **die Lampionblume**
Chinese lantern

# Pilze
## Fungi

### 170.1 PILZARTEN · SPECIES OF FUNGI

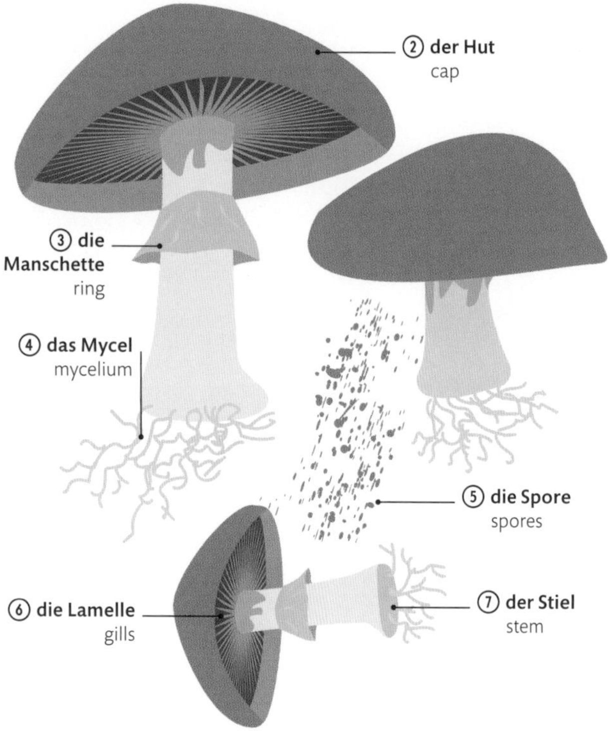


① **die Pilze** *m, pl*
mushrooms

㉑ **die Zuchtpilze** *m, pl*
cultivated mushrooms

㉒ **die Giftpilze** *m, pl*
toadstools

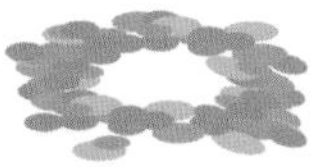

㉓ **der Hexenring**
fairy ring

㉔ **der Austernpilz**
oyster mushroom

㉕ **die Laubwaldrotkappe**
orange-cap boletus

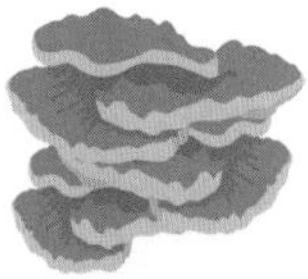

㉖ **der Schwefelporling**
chicken of the woods

㉗ **der Semmelstoppelpilz**
hedgehog mushroom

㉘ **der Igelstachelbart**
bear's head tooth

㉙ **die Totentrompete**
black trumpet

㉚ **der Spargelpilz**
shaggy mane mushroom

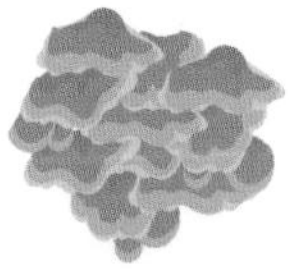

㉛ **der Kastanienschwamm**
hen of the wood

㉜ **der Schimmel**
mold

See also
**55-56** Gemüse • Vegetables **133** Aktivitäten im Freien • Outdoor activities **167-169** Pflanzen und Bäume • Plants and trees

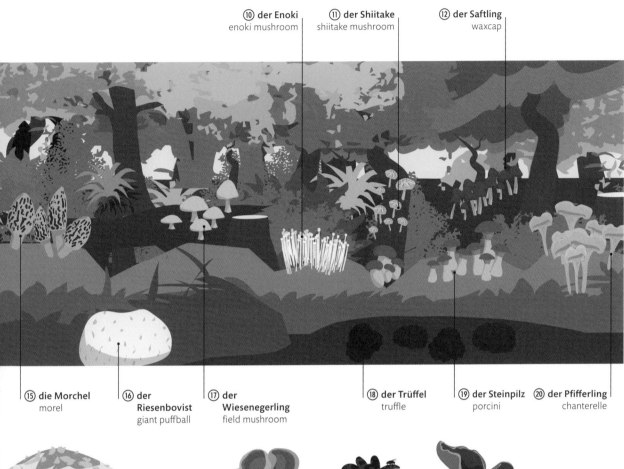

(10) **der Enoki**
enoki mushroom

(11) **der Shiitake**
shiitake mushroom

(12) **der Saftling**
waxcap

(15) **die Morchel**
morel

(16) **der Riesenbovist**
giant puffball

(17) **der Wiesenegerling**
field mushroom

(18) **der Trüffel**
truffle

(19) **der Steinpilz**
porcini

(20) **der Pfifferling**
chanterelle

(33) **der Knollenblätterpilz**
death cap

(34) **Amanita ocreata**
death angel

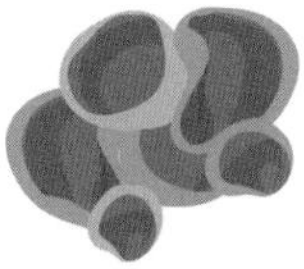

(35) **der Orangerote Becherpilz**
orange peel fungus

(36) **die Stinkmorchel**
stinkhorn

(37) **das Hasenohr**
hare's ear

(38) **der Dunkle Ölbaumtrichterling**
jack-o'-lantern

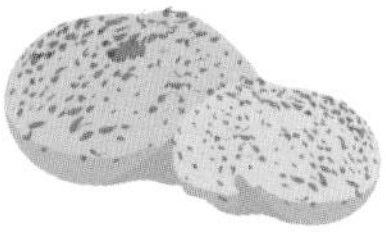

(39) **der Gemeine Kartoffelbovist**
common earthball

(40) **das Milchweiße Samthäuptchen**
milky conecap

(41) **der Fliegenpilz**
fly agaric

# 171 Die Zeit

Time

## 171.1 DIE ZEIT ABLESEN • TELLING THE TIME

① Wie viel Uhr ist es?
What time is it?
② Es ist drei Uhr.
It's three o'clock.

③ **ein Uhr**
one o'clock

④ **fünf nach eins**
five past one

⑤ **zehn nach eins**
ten past one

⑥ **Viertel nach eins**
quarter past one

⑦ **zwanzig nach eins**
twenty past one

⑧ **fünf vor halb zwei**
twenty-five past one

⑨ **halb zwei**
one thirty / half past one

⑩ **fünf nach halb zwei**
twenty-five to two

⑪ **zwanzig vor zwei**
twenty to two

⑫ **Viertel vor zwei**
quarter to two

⑬ **zehn vor zwei**
ten to two

⑭ **fünf vor zwei**
five to two

⑮ **zwei Uhr**
two o'clock

⑯ **die Sekunde**
second

⑰ **die Minute**
minute

⑱ **die Viertelstunde**
quarter of an hour

## 171.2 DIE TAGESZEITEN • PARTS OF THE DAY

① **die Morgendämmerung**
dawn

② **der Sonnenaufgang**
sunrise

③ **der Vormittag**
morning

④ **der Mittag**
midday

⑤ **der Nachmittag**
afternoon

See also
**172** Der Kalender • The calendar **173** Zahlen • Numbers
**174** Gewichte und Maße • Weights and measures

⑲ **zwanzig Minuten**
twenty minutes

⑳ **die halbe Stunde**
half an hour

㉑ **vierzig Minuten**
forty minutes

㉒ **eine Stunde**
an hour

㉓ **jetzt**
now

㉔ **zu früh**
early

㉕ **pünktlich**
on time

㉖ **zu spät**
late

㉗ **später**
later

㉘ **stündlich**
hourly

㉙ **immer**
always

㉚ **nie**
never

㉜ der Minutenzeiger
minute hand
㉝ die Uhr
clock
㉛ der Sekundenzeiger
second hand
㉞ der Stundenzeiger
hour hand
㉟ Wann geht es los?
What time does it start?
㊱ Um 18 Uhr. Wir kommen zu spät!
At 6pm. We're going to be late!

㊲ **spät dran sein**
to be late

⑥ **der Abend**
evening

⑦ **der Sonnenuntergang**
sunset

⑧ **die Abenddämmerung**
dusk

⑨ **Mitternacht**
midnight

⑩ **die Nacht**
night

⑪ **der Tag**
day

# 172 Der Kalender
## The calendar

### 172.1 KALENDER UND JAHRESZEITEN · CALENDAR AND SEASONS

① **der Tag**
day

② **die Woche**
week

③ **zwei Wochen** *f, pl*
two weeks

④ **das Wochenende**
weekend

⑤ **der Monat**
month

⑥ **das Jahr**
year

⑦ **das Jahrzehnt**
decade

⑧ **das Jahrhundert**
century

⑨ **das Jahrtausend**
millennium

⑩ **Montag** *m*
Monday

⑪ **Dienstag** *m*
Tuesday

⑫ **Mittwoch** *m*
Wednesday

⑬ **Donnerstag** *m*
Thursday

⑭ **Freitag** *m*
Friday

⑮ **Samstag** *m*
Saturday

⑯ **Sonntag** *m*
Sunday

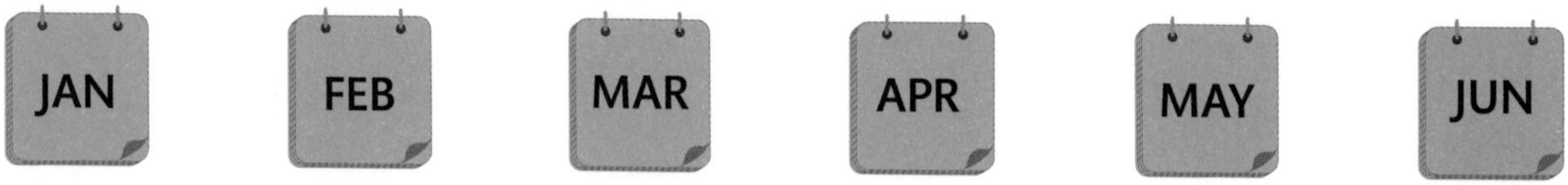


⑰ **Januar** *m*
January

⑱ **Februar** *m*
February

⑲ **März** *m*
March

⑳ **April** *m*
April

㉑ **Mai** *m*
May

㉒ **Juni** *m*
June

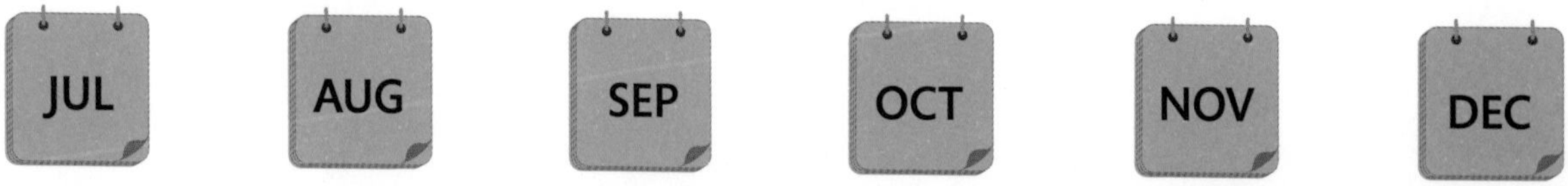


㉓ **Juli** *m*
July

㉔ **August** *m*
August

㉕ **September** *m*
September

㉖ **Oktober** *m*
October

㉗ **November** *m*
November

㉘ **Dezember** *m*
December

See also
**171** Die Zeit • Time
**173** Zahlen • Numbers

(29) **neunzehnhundert**
nineteen hundred

(30) **neunzehnhunderteins**
nineteen-oh-one

(31) **neunzehnhundertzehn**
nineteen ten

(32) **zweitausend**
two thousand

(33) **zweitausendeins**
two thousand and one

(34) **zweitausenddreiunddreißig**
twenty thirty-three

(35) **einmal in der Woche**
once a week

(36) **zweimal in der Woche**
twice a week

(37) **dreimal in der Woche**
three times a week

(38) **täglich**
every day

(39) **alle zwei Tage**
every other day

(40) **nur an Wochenenden**
only weekends

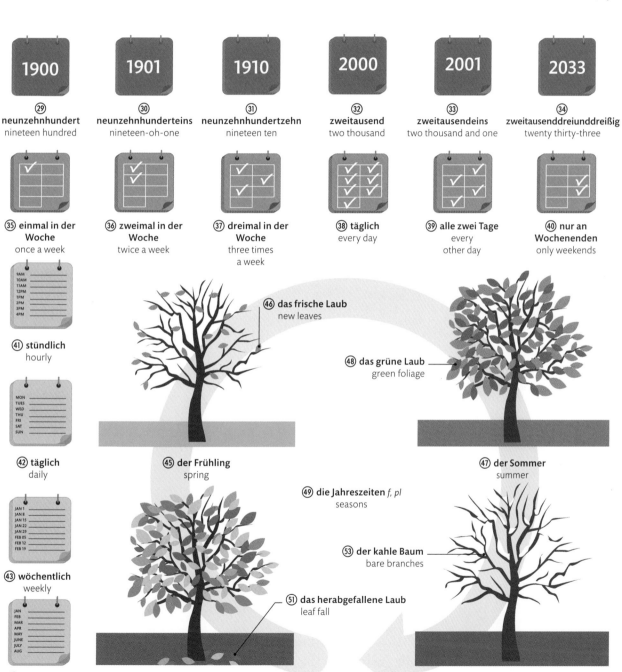

(41) **stündlich**
hourly

(42) **täglich**
daily

(43) **wöchentlich**
weekly

(44) **monatlich**
monthly

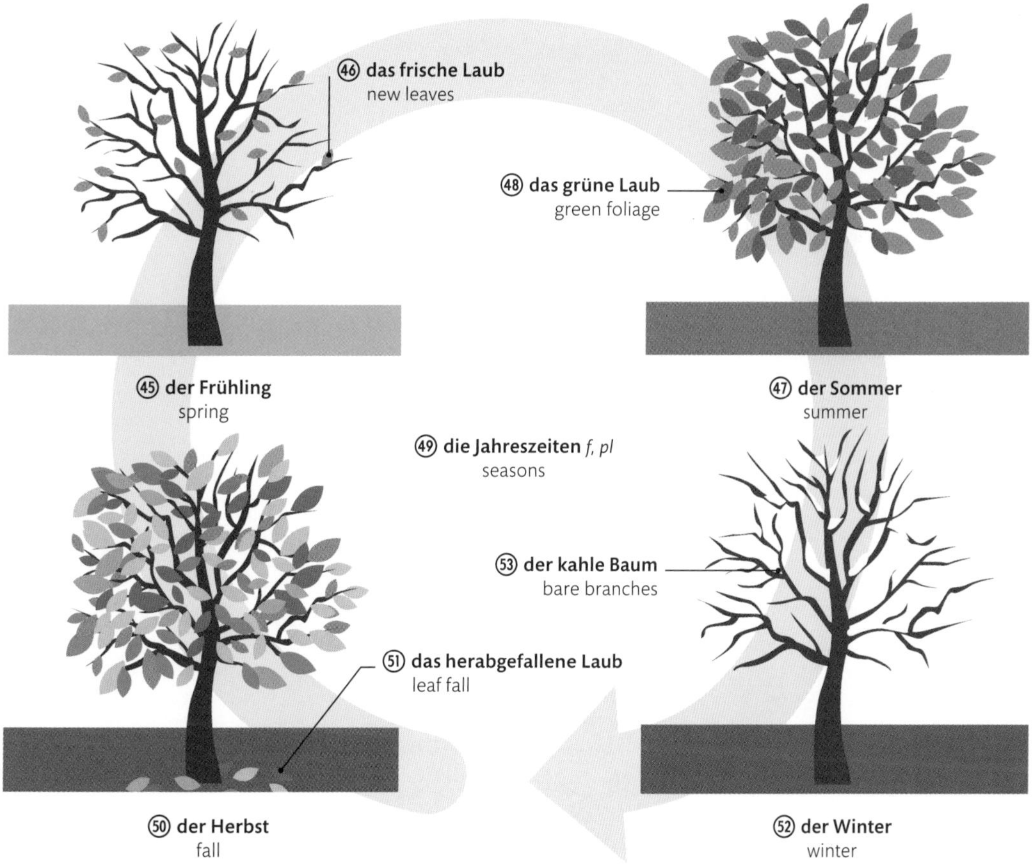

(46) **das frische Laub**
new leaves

(45) **der Frühling**
spring

(48) **das grüne Laub**
green foliage

(47) **der Sommer**
summer

(49) **die Jahreszeiten** *f, pl*
seasons

(53) **der kahle Baum**
bare branches

(51) **das herabgefallene Laub**
leaf fall

(50) **der Herbst**
fall

(52) **der Winter**
winter

# 173 Zahlen

## Numbers

### 173.1 GRUNDZAHLEN · CARDINAL NUMBERS

**1** ① **eins** one

**2** ② **zwei** two

**3** ③ **drei** three

**4** ④ **vier** four

**5** ⑤ **fünf** five

**6** ⑥ **sechs** six

**7** ⑦ **sieben** seven

**8** ⑧ **acht** eight

**9** ⑨ **neun** nine

**10** ⑩ **zehn** ten

**11** ⑪ **elf** eleven

**12** ⑫ **zwölf** twelve

**13** ⑬ **dreizehn** thirteen

**14** ⑭ **vierzehn** fourteen

**15** ⑮ **fünfzehn** fifteen

**16** ⑯ **sechzehn** sixteen

**17** ⑰ **siebzehn** seventeen

**18** ⑱ **achtzehn** eighteen

**19** ⑲ **neunzehn** nineteen

**20** ⑳ **zwanzig** twenty

**21** ㉑ **einundzwanzig** twenty-one

**22** ㉒ **zweiundzwanzig** twenty-two

**30** ㉓ **dreißig** thirty

**40** ㉔ **vierzig** forty

**50** ㉕ **fünfzig** fifty

**60** ㉖ **sechzig** sixty

**70** ㉗ **siebzig** seventy

**80** ㉘ **achtzig** eighty

**90** ㉙ **neunzig** ninety

**100** ㉚ **hundert** one hundred

**0** ㉛ **null** zero

### 173.2 ORDINALZAHLEN · ORDINAL NUMBERS

**1st** ① **erster / erste / erstes** *m / f / n* first

**2nd** ② **zweiter / zweite / zweites** *m / f / n* second

**3rd** ③ **dritter / dritte / drittes** *m / f / n* third

**4th** ④ **vierter / vierte / viertes** *m / f / n* fourth

**5th** ⑤ **fünfter / fünfte / fünftes** *m / f / n* fifth

**6th** ⑥ **sechster / sechste / sechstes** *m / f / n* sixth

**7th** ⑦ **siebter / siebte / siebtes** *m / f / n* *seventh*

**8th** ⑧ **achter / achte / achtes** *m / f / n* eighth

**9th** ⑨ **neunter / neunte / neuntes** *m / f / n* ninth

**10th** ⑩ **zehnter / zehnte / zehntes** *m / f / n* tenth

**20th** ⑪ **zwanzigster / zwanzigste / zwanzigstes** *m / f / n* twentieth

**21st** ⑫ **einundzwanzigster / einundzwanzigste / einundzwanzigstes** *m / f / n* twenty-first

See also
**74** Mathematik • Mathematics **171** Die Zeit • Time **172** Der Kalender
The calendar **174** Gewichte und Maße • Weights and measures

## 173.3 GROSSE ZAHLEN • LARGE NUMBERS

**200**
① **zweihundert**
two hundred

**250**
② **zweihundertfünfzig**
two hundred and fifty

**500**
③ **fünfhundert**
five hundred

**750**
④ **siebenhundertfünfzig**
seven hundred and fifty

**1,000**
⑤ **eintausend**
one thousand

**1,200**
⑥ **eintausendzweihundert**
one thousand two hundred

**10,000**
⑦ **zehntausend**
ten thousand

**100,000**
⑧ **hunderttausend**
one hundred thousand

**1,000,000**
⑨ **eine Million**
one million

**5,000,000**
⑩ **fünf Millionen**
five million

**500,000,000**
⑪ **fünfhundert Millionen**
**eine halbe Milliarde**
five hundred million / half a billion

**1,000,000,000**
⑫ **eine Milliarde**
one billion

**3,846**
⑬ **dreitausendachthundertsechsundvierzig**
three thousand, eight hundred and forty-six

**82,043**
⑭ **zweiundachtzigtausenddreiundvierzig**
eighty-two thousand and forty-three

⑮ Ich habe mich verzählt!
I've lost count!

**234,407**
⑯ **zweihundertvierunddreißigtausend-vierhundertundsieben**
two hundred and thirty-four thousand, four hundred and seven

**3,089,342**
⑰ **drei Millionen neunundachtzigtausenddreihundertzweiundvierzig**
three million, eighty-nine thousand, three hundred and forty-two

## 173.4 BRÜCHE, DEZIMALZAHLEN UND PROZENTANGABEN
FRACTIONS, DECIMALS, AND PERCENTAGES

**1/8**
① **ein Achtel** *n*
an eighth

**1/4**
② **ein Viertel** *n*
a quarter

**1/3**
③ **ein Drittel** *n*
a third

**1/2**
④ **einhalb**
a half

**3/5**
⑤ **drei Fünftel** *n*
three-fifths

**7/8**
⑥ **sieben Achtel** *n*
seven-eighths

**0.5**
⑦ **null Komma fünf**
zero point five

**1.7**
⑧ **eins Komma sieben**
one point seven

**3.97**
⑨ **drei Komma neun sieben**
three point nine seven

**1%**
⑩ **ein Prozent** *n*
one percent

**99%**
⑪ **neunundneunzig Prozent**
ninety-nine percent

**100%**
⑫ **hundert Prozent**
one hundred percent

# 174 Gewichte und Maße

## Weights and measures

### 174.1 **GEWICHTE** · WEIGHT

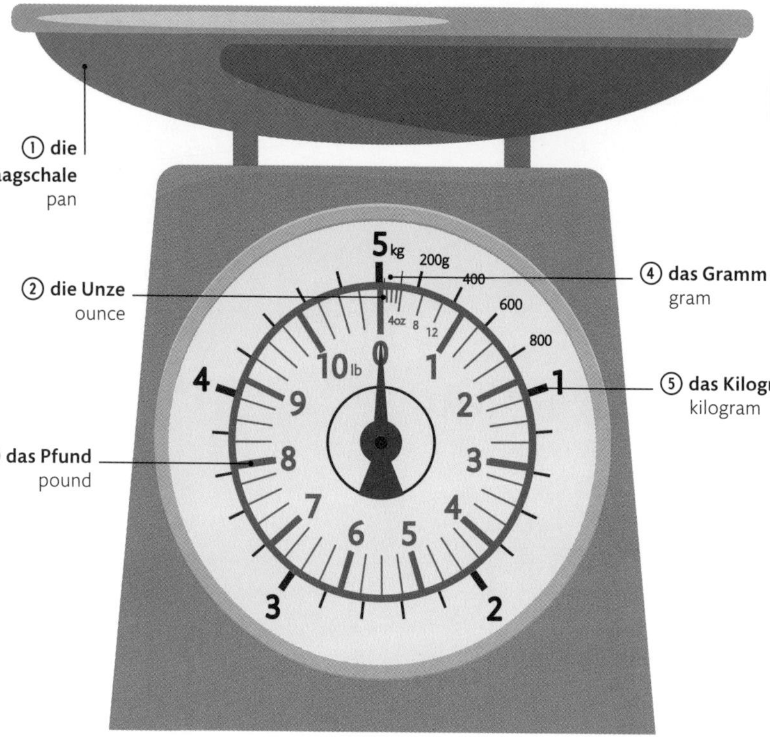

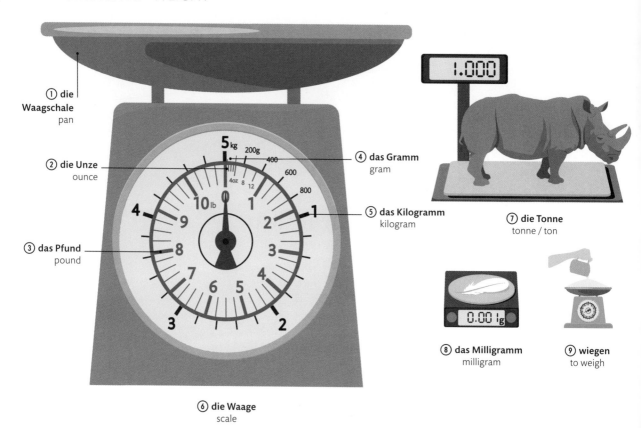

① **die Waagschale**
pan

② **die Unze**
ounce

③ **das Pfund**
pound

④ **das Gramm**
gram

⑤ **das Kilogramm**
kilogram

⑥ **die Waage**
scale

⑦ **die Tonne**
tonne / ton

⑧ **das Milligramm**
milligram

⑨ **wiegen**
to weigh

### 174.2 **ENTFERNUNGEN, FLÄCHEN UND LÄNGEN** · DISTANCE, AREA, AND LENGTH

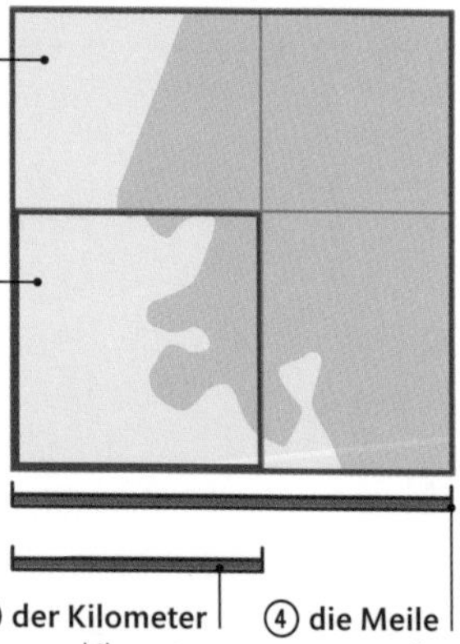

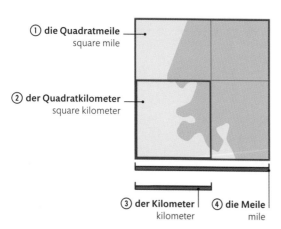

① **die Quadratmeile**
square mile

② **der Quadratkilometer**
square kilometer

③ **der Kilometer**
kilometer

④ **die Meile**
mile

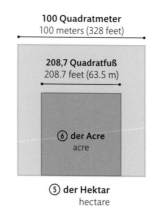

**100 Quadratmeter**
100 meters (328 feet)

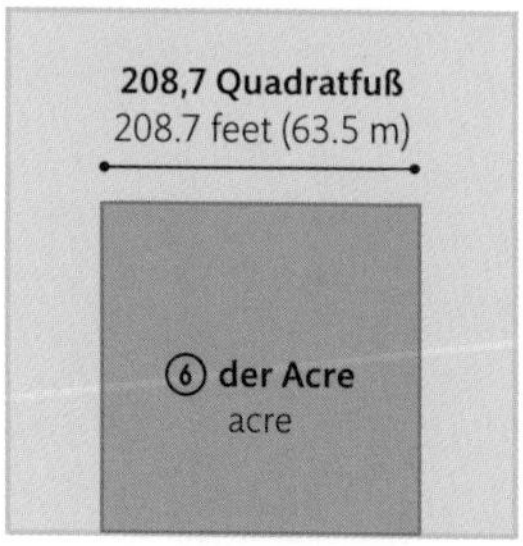

**208,7 Quadratfuß**
208.7 feet (63.5 m)

⑥ **der Acre**
acre

⑤ **der Hektar**
hectare

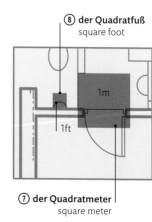

⑧ **der Quadratfuß**
square foot

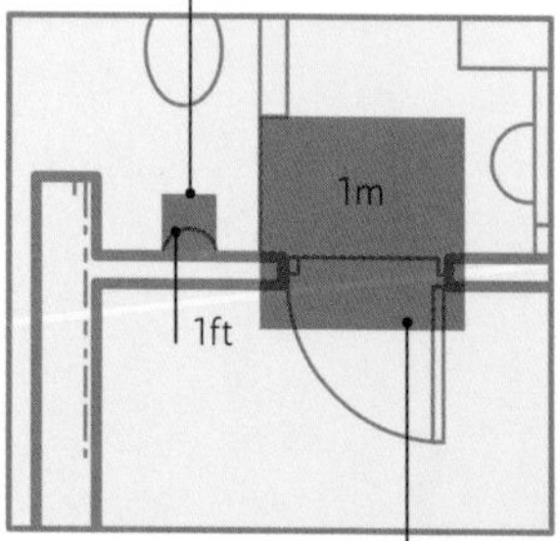


⑦ **der Quadratmeter**
square meter

See also
**29** Kochen • Cooking **35** Heimwerken • Home improvements
**74** Mathematik • Mathematics **173** Zahlen • Numbers

## 174.3 **DAS VOLUMEN** • LIQUID MEASUREMENTS / VOLUME

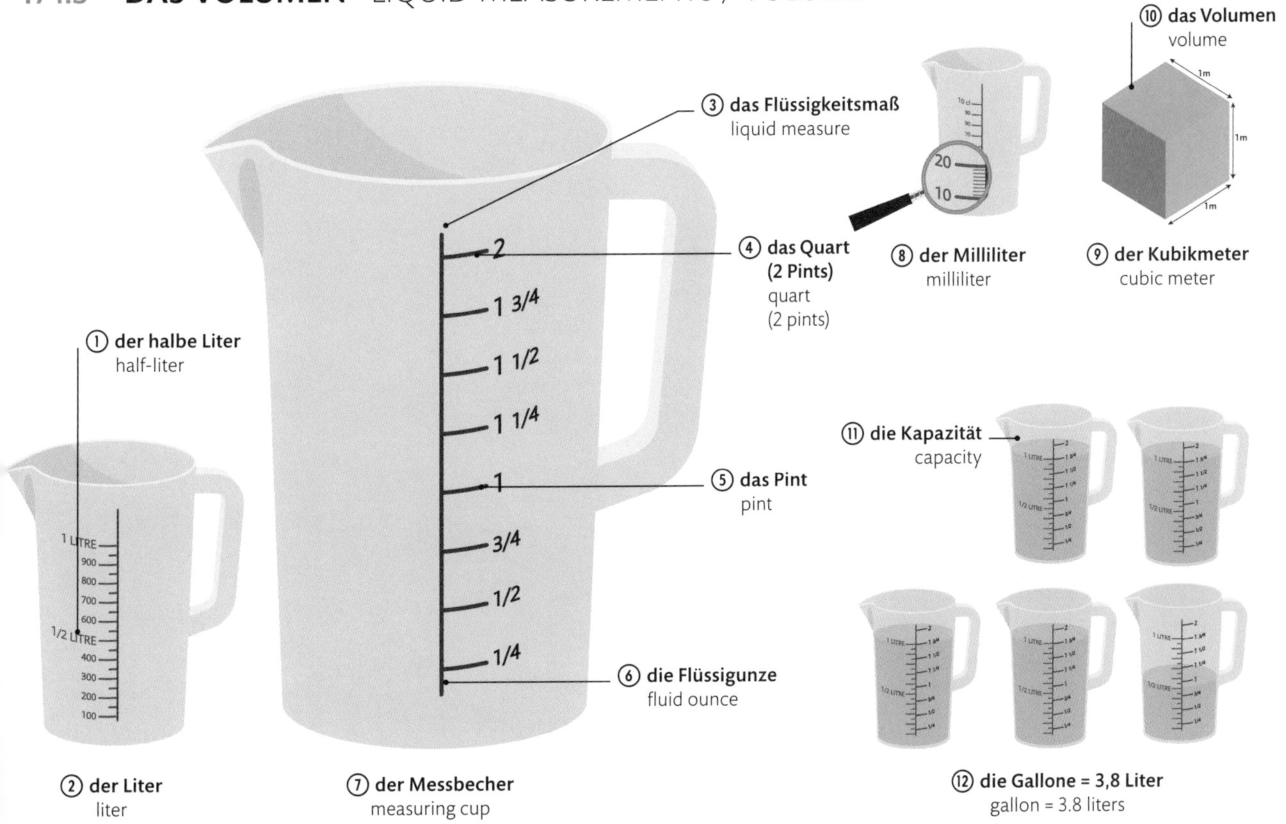


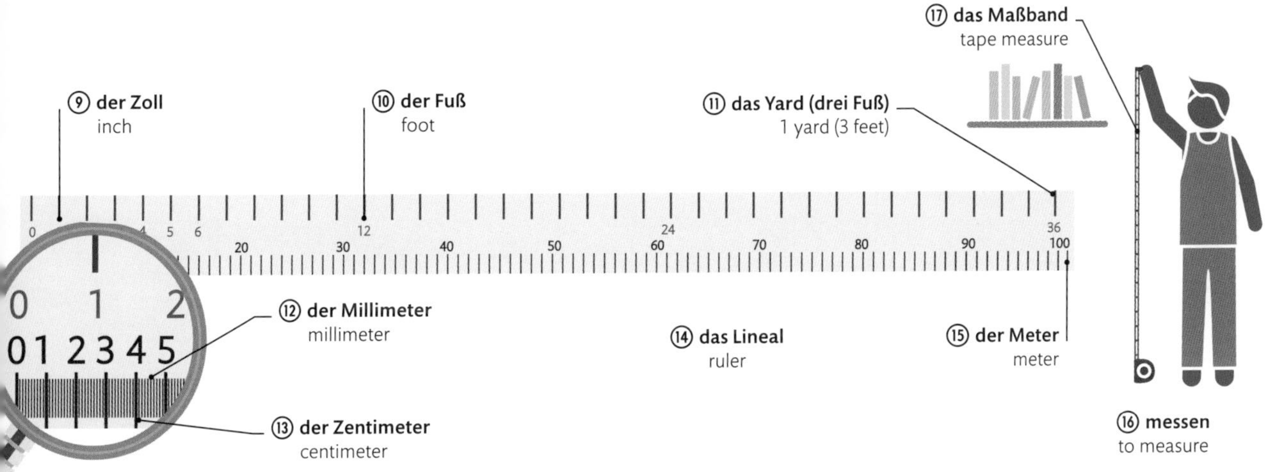

# 175 Schreiben
## Writing

### 175.1 SCHREIBEN UND SCHREIBUTENSILIEN • WRITING AND WRITING EQUIPMENT

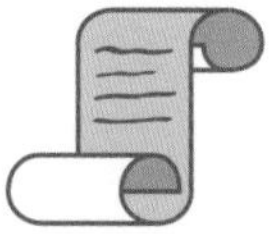

⑩ **das Pergament**
parchment

⑪ **der Ausdruck**
printing

⑫ **das Emoji**
emojis

abcdefghijk
lmnopqrst
uvwxyz

⑬ **die Schriftart**
typeface

| Aa | ABC | abc | **abc** | *abc* | 123 |
|---|---|---|---|---|---|
| ⑭ **der Buchstabe** letters | ⑮ **der Großbuchstabe** uppercase / capital letters | ⑯ **der Kleinbuchstabe** lowercase | ⑰ **fett** bold | ⑱ **kursiv** italic | ⑲ **die Ziffer** numerals |

| ft | . | - | — | _ | , |
|---|---|---|---|---|---|
| ⑳ **der Buchstabenverbund** ligature | ㉑ **der Punkt** period | ㉒ **der Bindestrich** hyphen | ㉓ **der Gedankenstrich** dash | ㉔ **der Unterstrich** underscore | ㉕ **das Komma** comma |

See also
**73** In der Schule • At school
**138** Bücher und Lesen • Books and reading

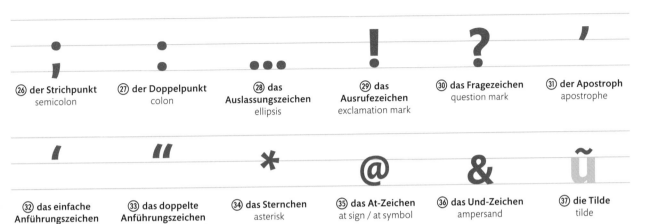

;
(26) **der Strichpunkt**
semicolon

:
(27) **der Doppelpunkt**
colon

...
(28) **das Auslassungszeichen**
ellipsis

!
(29) **das Ausrufezeichen**
exclamation mark

?
(30) **das Fragezeichen**
question mark

’
(31) **der Apostroph**
apostrophe

‘
(32) **das einfache Anführungszeichen**
single quotation mark

“
(33) **das doppelte Anführungszeichen**
double quotation mark

*
(34) **das Sternchen**
asterisk

@
(35) **das At-Zeichen**
at sign / at symbol

&
(36) **das Und-Zeichen**
ampersand

ũ
(37) **die Tilde**
tilde

é
(38) **der Accent aigu**
acute accent

è
(39) **der Accent grave**
grave accent

ü
(40) **der Umlaut**
umlaut

ĉ
(41) **der Accent circonflexe**
circumflex

ç
(42) **die Cedille**
cedilla

©
(43) **das Copyright-Zeichen**
copyright

®
(44) **das eingetragene Warenzeichen**
registered trademark

( )
(45) **die Klammer**
brackets

#
(46) **das Hashtag**
hashtag

cat
(47) **das lateinische Alphabet**
Latin alphabet

Γάτα
(48) **das griechische Alphabet**
Greek alphabet

кошка
(49) **das kyrillische Alphabet**
Cyrillic alphabet

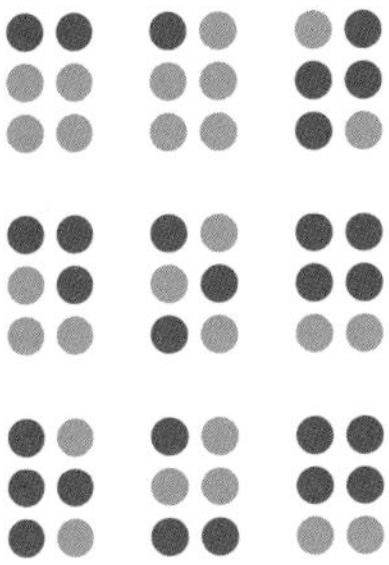
(50) **die Blindenschrift**
Braille

قط
شجرة
ماء
(51) **die arabische Schrift**
Arabic script

市
車 両
道
(52) **die japanischen Schriftzeichen** *n, pl*
Japanese characters

桃
橘子
柠檬
(53) **die chinesischen Schriftzeichen** *n, pl*
Chinese characters

खेत
घोड़ा
नदी
(54) **Dewanagari** *f*
Devanagari script

(55) **die altägyptischen Hieroglyphen** *f, pl*
Ancient Egyptian hieroglyphs

# 176 Dinge beschreiben

## Describing things

### 176.1 MATERIALIEN · MATERIALS

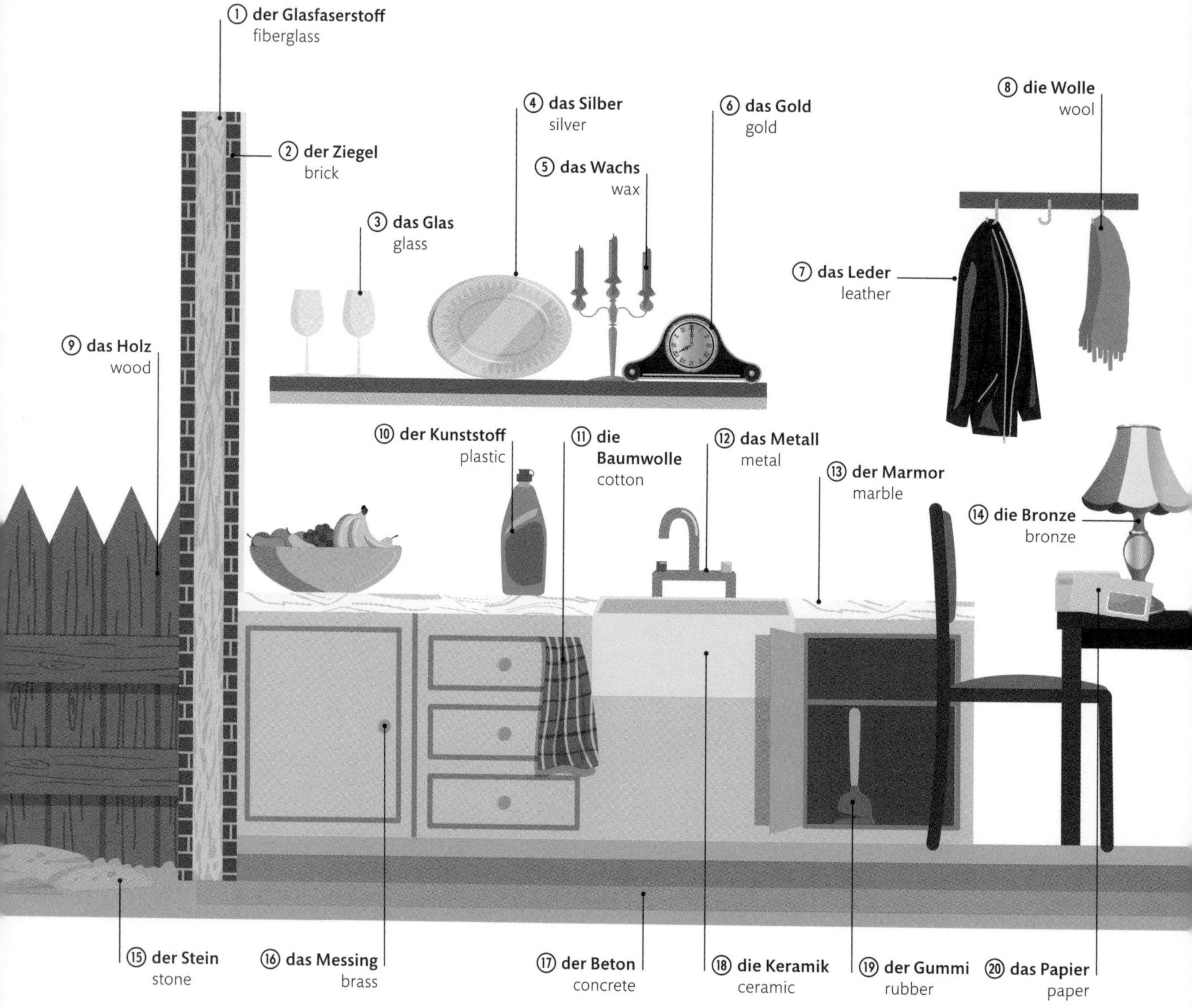

See also
**32** Haus und Heim • House and home **35** Heimwerken • Home improvements
**37** Wohnraumverschönerung • Renovating **87** Der Bau • Construction
**177** Dinge beschreiben (Fortsetzung) • Describing things continued

## 176.2 ADJEKTIVE • ADJECTIVES

① **groß**
big / large

② **klein**
small / little

③ **breit**
wide

④ **schmal / eng**
narrow

⑤ **tief**
deep

⑥ **seicht**
shallow

⑦ **hoch**
high

⑧ **niedrig**
low

⑨ **schwer**
heavy

⑩ **leicht**
light

⑪ **sauber**
clean

⑫ **schmutzig**
dirty

⑬ **heiß**
hot

⑭ **kalt**
cold

⑮ **lang**
long

⑯ **kurz**
short

⑰ **locker**
loose

⑱ **fest**
tight

⑲ **dünn**
thin

⑳ **dick**
thick

㉑ **nahe**
near

㉒ **fern**
far

㉓ **langsam**
slow

㉔ **schnell**
fast

㉕ **neu**
new

㉖ **alt**
old

㉗ **leer**
empty

㉘ **voll**
full

㉙ **laut**
noisy

㉚ **leise**
quiet

㉛ **richtig**
correct

㉜ **falsch**
incorrect

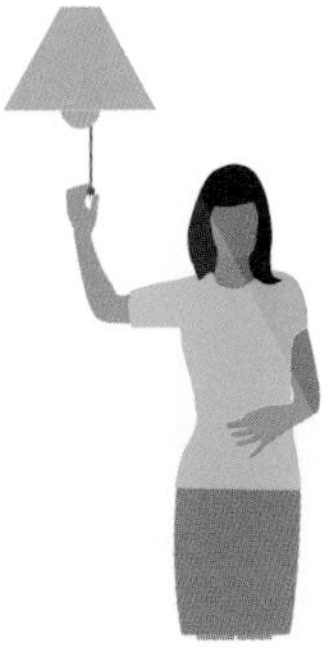

㉝ **hell**
light

㉞ **dunkel**
dark

# 177 Dinge beschreiben (Fortsetzung)

## Describing things continued

### 177.1 ANSICHTEN · OPINIONS

② **Was für eine atemberaubende Aussicht!**
The view here is absolutely breathtaking.

① **atemberaubend**
breathtaking

③ **aufregend**
exciting

④ **schön**
beautiful

⑤ **spannend**
thrilling

⑥ **spaßig**
fun

⑦ **romantisch**
romantic

⑧ **beeindruckend**
stunning

⑨ **toll**
great

10
10
10

⑩ **unglaublich**
incredible

⑪ **wichtig**
important

⑫ **süß**
cute

⑬ **respektvoll**
respectful

⑭ **besonders**
special

⑮ **elegant**
graceful

⑯ **bemerkenswert**
remarkable

⑰ **herausragend**
outstanding

⑱ **urkomisch**
hilarious

⑲ **lustig**
funny

⑳ **außergewöhnlich**
extraordinary

㉑ **wundervoll**
wonderful

㉒ **harmlos**
harmless

㉓ **altmodisch**
old-fashioned

See also
**06** Gefühle und Stimmung • Feelings and moods **10** Eigenschaften Personality traits **11** Fähigkeiten und Handlungen • Abilities and actions
**93** Nützliche Fähigkeiten für den Arbeitsplatz • Workplace skills

**24 gut**
good

**25 schlecht**
bad

**26 fantastisch**
fantastic

**27 furchtbar**
terrible

**28 angenehm**
pleasant

**29 unangenehm**
unpleasant

**30 brillant**
brilliant

**31 schrecklich**
dreadful

**32 praktisch**
useful

**33 nutzlos**
useless

**34 wohlschmeckend**
delicious

**35 ekelerregend**
disgusting

**36 hübsch**
pretty

**37 hässlich**
ugly

**38 interessant**
interesting

**39 langweilig**
boring

**40 entspannend**
relaxing

**41 anstrengend**
exhausting

**42 hervorragend**
superb

**43 entsetzlich**
awful

**44 nett**
nice

**45 gemein**
nasty

**46 verblüffend**
amazing

**47 durchschnittlich**
mediocre

**48 beängstigend**
frightening

**49 angsteinflößend**
terrifying

**50 seltsam**
strange / odd

**51 schockierend**
shocking

**52 ärgerlich**
annoying

**53 fürchterlich**
horrible

**54 ein Desaster**
disastrous

**55 verwirrend**
confusing

**56 ermüdend**
tiring

**57 lästig**
irritating

**58 grässlich**
dire

**59 enttäuschend**
disappointing

# 178 Geläufige Verben

## Common phrasal verbs

### 178.1 **ALLTAGSVERBEN** · VERBS FOR DAILY LIFE

① **sich beruhigen**
to calm down

② **sich entspannen**
to chill out

③ **suchen**
to look for

④ **erwachsen werden**
to grow up

⑤ **jemanden anrufen**
to call up

⑥ **etwas anziehen**
to put on

⑦ **sich herausputzen**
to dress up

⑧ **angeben**
to show off

⑨ **anhäufen**
to pile up

⑩ **zurückgeben**
to give back

⑪ **einnicken**
to doze off

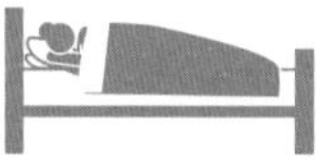

⑫ **ausschlafen**
to sleep in

⑬ **aufstehen**
to get up

⑭ **nach oben gehen**
to go up

⑮ **nach unten gehen**
to go down

⑯ **einholen**
to catch up

⑰ **Unsinn machen**
to mess around

⑱ **aufhängen**
to hang up

⑲ **hereinlassen**
to let in

⑳ **herausreißen**
to rip out

㉑ **etwas geht aus**
to run out (of)

㉒ **auslösen**
to set off

㉓ **über etwas stolpern**
to trip over

㉔ **abmessen**
to measure

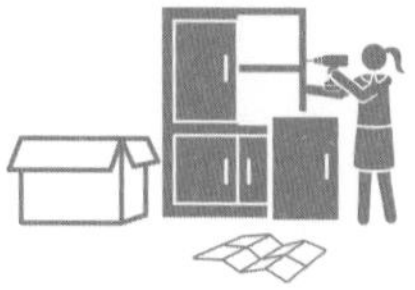

㉕ **zusammenbauen**
to put together

㉖ **renovieren**
to fix up

㉗ **aufräumen**
to put away

㉙ **Ich warte schon die ganze Nacht auf euch!**
I've been waiting up all night!

㉘ **warten**
to wait up

㉚ **ausfüllen**
to fill out

㉛ **sich anmelden**
to log in

㉜ **sich abmelden**
to log out

See also
**09** Die Alltagsroutine • Daily routines **11** Fähigkeiten und Handlungen
Abilities and actions **179-180** Nützliche Ausdrücke • Useful expressions

(33) **aufwachen**
to wake up

(34) **abwiegen**
to weigh

(35) **einschalten**
to turn on

(36) **ausschalten**
to turn off

(37) **lauter machen**
to turn up

(38) **leiser machen**
to turn down

(39) **eine Panne haben**
to break down

(40) **tanken**
to fill up

(41) **einchecken**
to check in

(42) **auschecken**
to check out

(43) **essen gehen**
to eat out

(44) **servieren**
to wait on

(45) **einsteigen**
to get on

(46) **aussteigen**
to get off

(47) **in Strömen regnen**
to pour down

(48) **wegfahren**
to go away / to get away

(49) **auf etwas hinweisen**
to point out

(50) **sich kümmern**
to care for

(51) **beobachten**
to look at

(52) **schenken**
to give away

(53) **verteilen**
to give out

(54) **aufgeben**
to give up

(60) **Hallo! Schön, dass ihr kommen konntet!**
Hi! So glad you could join us!

(59) **sich treffen**
to get together

(55) **sich trennen**
to break up

(56) **etwas absagen**
to call off

(57) **sich versöhnen**
to make up

(58) **sich treffen**
to meet up

(61) **austeilen**
to hand out

(62) **aufputzen**
to clean up

(63) **aufheben**
to pick up

(64) **wegwerfen**
to throw away

(65) **weglaufen**
to run away

(66) **abfliegen**
to take off

# 179 Nützliche Ausdrücke

## Useful expressions

### 179.1 DIE BEGRÜSSUNG · GREETINGS

② Hallo.
Hi!
③ Hi!
Hello.

① sich treffen
to meet

⑥ Guten Morgen.
Good morning.

⑦ Guten Tag.
Good afternoon.

⑤ Guten Abend.
Good evening.

④ sich (förmlich) begrüßen
to greet (formal)

⑧ Gute Nacht.
Good night!

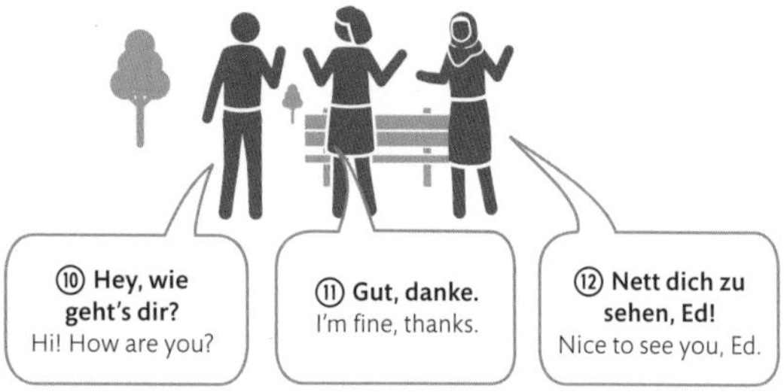

⑩ Hey, wie geht's dir?
Hi! How are you?
⑪ Gut, danke.
I'm fine, thanks.
⑫ Nett dich zu sehen, Ed!
Nice to see you, Ed.

⑨ sich (informell) begrüßen
to greet (informal)

⑭ Auf Wiedersehen!
Goodbye!
⑮ Bis später!
See you later!

⑬ gehen
to leave

### 179.2 JEMANDEN KENNENLERNEN · GETTING TO KNOW SOMEONE

① Wie heißt du?
What's your name?
② Ich bin Sally.
My name is Sally.

③ Wie alt bist du?
How old are you?
④ Ich bin 25.
I'm 25 years old.

⑤ Wo wohnst du?
Where do you live?
⑥ Ich wohne in Edinburgh.
I live in Edinburgh.

See also
**07** Lebensereignisse • Life events **09** Die Alltagsroutine • Daily routines **46** Einkaufen • Shopping **180** Nützliche Ausdrücke (Fortsetzung) • Useful expressions continued

## 179.3 EINKAUFEN • SHOPPING

① **Wie viel kostet das?**
How much is this?

② **15 Dollar.**
It's 15 dollars

③ **Kann ich bei Ihnen zahlen?**
Can I pay here?

④ **Könnten Sie mir bitte die rote Tasse geben?**
Could you get the red cup for me, please?

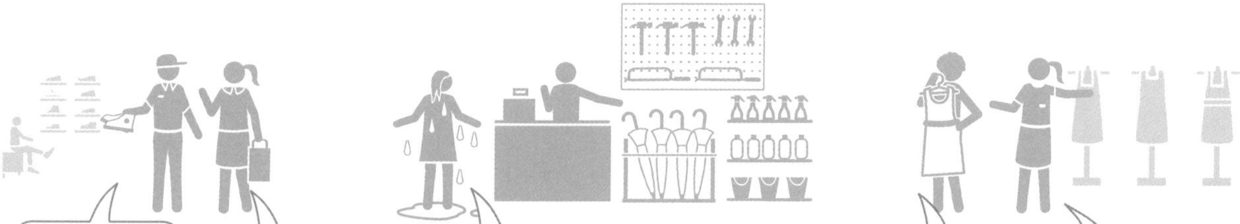

⑤ **Kann ich Ihnen behilflich sein?**
Can I help you?

⑥ **Ich sehe mich nur um, danke.**
I'm just browsing, thanks.

⑦ **Verkaufen Sie auch Regenschirme?**
Do you sell umbrellas?

⑧ **Haben Sie das eine Größe kleiner?**
Do you have this in a smaller size?

⑨ **Lassen Sie mich kurz nachsehen.**
Let me check for you.

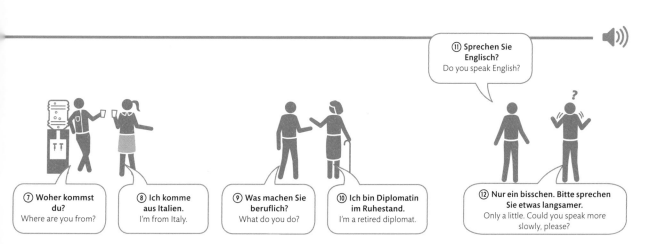

⑪ **Sprechen Sie Englisch?**
Do you speak English?

⑦ **Woher kommst du?**
Where are you from?

⑧ **Ich komme aus Italien.**
I'm from Italy.

⑨ **Was machen Sie beruflich?**
What do you do?

⑩ **Ich bin Diplomatin im Ruhestand.**
I'm a retired diplomat.

⑫ **Nur ein bisschen. Bitte sprechen Sie etwas langsamer.**
Only a little. Could you speak more slowly, please?

# Nützliche Ausdrücke (Fortsetzung)

Useful expressions continued

## 180.1 WEGBESCHREIBUNGEN · DIRECTIONS

① Können Sie mir helfen? Can you help me, please?
② Ja, natürlich! Yes, of course.
③ Wo finde ich den Bahnhof? Where is the train station?
④ Dahin brauchen Sie zu Fuß 15 Minuten. Biegen Sie am Supermarkt links ab. It's a 15-minute walk. Turn left at the supermarket.

⑤ Wie weit ist es bis zum Hotel? How far is it to the hotel?

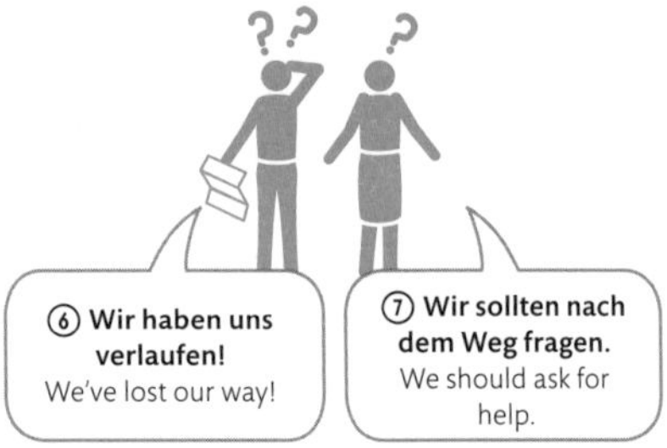
⑥ Wir haben uns verlaufen! We've lost our way!
⑦ Wir sollten nach dem Weg fragen. We should ask for help.

⑧ Können Sie uns den Weg zum See zeigen? Can you show us the way to the lake?

⑨ Wie kommen wir denn zum Strand? How do we get to the beach?
⑩ Einfach geradeaus! It's straight ahead!

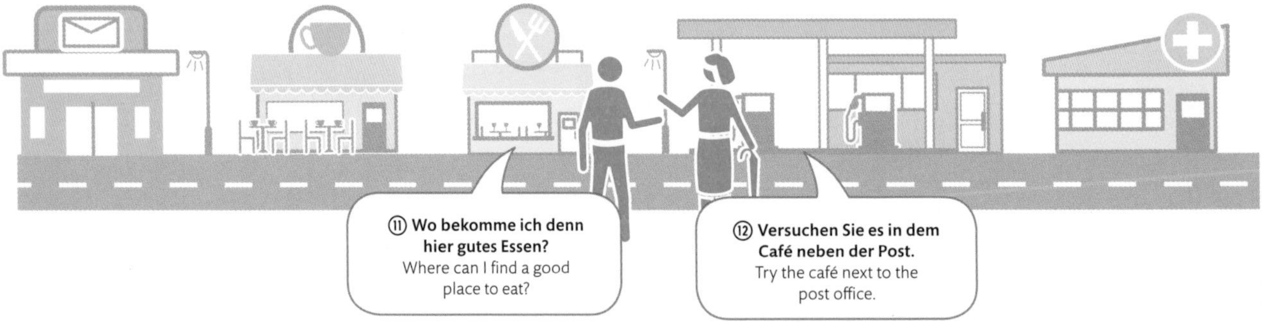
⑪ Wo bekomme ich denn hier gutes Essen? Where can I find a good place to eat?
⑫ Versuchen Sie es in dem Café neben der Post. Try the café next to the post office.

See also
**42-43** In der Stadt • In town **148** Karten und Richtungsangaben • Maps and directions

## 180.2 PRÄPOSITIONEN • PREPOSITIONS

① **innerhalb**
in

② **außerhalb**
out

③ **innen**
inside

④ **außen**
outside

⑤ **zwischen**
between

⑥ **unter**
under

⑦ **auf**
on

⑧ **neben**
next to / beside

⑨ **vor**
in front of

⑩ **hinter**
behind

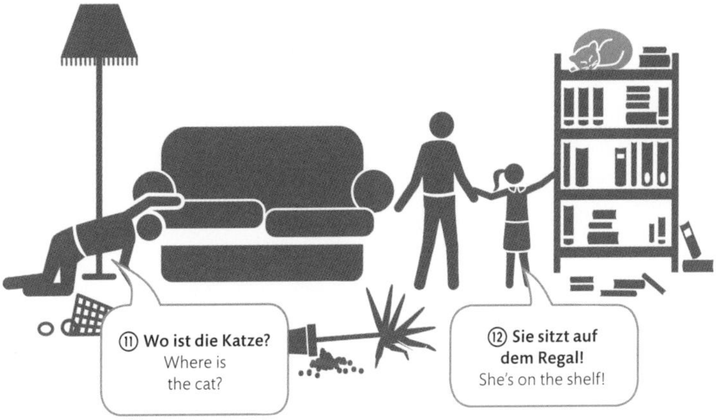
⑪ Wo ist die Katze?
Where is the cat?
⑫ Sie sitzt auf dem Regal!
She's on the shelf!

# English word list

The numbers after each word or phrase refer to the units in which they can be found.

## KEY

*adj* – adjective
*adv* – adverb
*n* – noun
*num* – number
*phr* – phrase
*prep* – preposition
*v* – verb

---

# A

à la carte menu n 69
aardvark n 158
ab wheel n 124
abandoned
   building n 44
abdomen n 01, 162
abdominals n 03
abilities n 11
ability to drive n 93
abseiling n 125
Abyssinian n 164
acacia n 47
access road n 106
accessories n 16
accident n 19
accident and
   emergency n 50
accommodation n 131
accordion n 129
account number n 45
accountant n 90, 94
accounts n 91
accurate adj 93
ace n 114, 140
ache v 20
Achilles tendon n 03
acid n 76
acid rain n 51, 155
acorn n 169
acorn squash n 56
acoustic guitar n 129

acoustic guitarist n 129
acquaintance n 07
acquitted adj 85
acre n 174
across from prep 148
acrylic paint n 141
act v 11
actinide series n 78
actinium n 78
action game n 136
action movie n 127
action points n 95
actions n 11
actor n 89, 126
acupressure n 24
acupuncture n 24
acute accent n 175
Adam's apple n 04
adaptable adj 93
add v 11, 29, 74
add to cart v 46
add to wishlist v 46
additives n 23
address n 45
adhesive
   bandage n 20
adhesive tape n 20
administration n 91, 93
admiral n 88
admission fee n 130
admissions n 80
admit v 21
adrenal gland n 04
adult frog n 77
adult teeth n 03
adults n 05
advantage n 114
adventure game n 136
adventure
   playground n 133
adventurous adj 10
advertising n 91
aerate v 39
aerobics n 124
aerobics step n 124
aerospace n 91
Afghan adj 153
Afghanistan n 151, 153
Africa n 149, 152
African adj 152
African bullfrog n 163
African daisy n 38
African elephant n 158
African gray
   parrot n 161
African wild dog n 158
Afro n 12
afternoon n 09, 171
aftershave n 18, 31

agate n 156
agbada n 15
agenda n 95
agriculture n 91
aikido n 117
aileron n 103
air ambulance n 50
air bed n 135
air cargo n 104
air conditioning n 33, 99
air control tower n 43
air cylinder n 118
air filter n 98, 100
air mattress n 135
air pump n 135
air vent n 103
airbag n 99
airball n 112
aircraft carrier n 88, 105
aircraft n 103
airforce n 88
airline n 104
airmail n 45
airman n 88
airport n 43, 104
airship n 103
airtight container n 52
aisle, aisles n 48, 80,
   103, 126
alarm n 50
alarm clock n 30
alarm goes off phr 09
Albania n 151, 153
Albanian adj 153
albatross n 160
albertonectes n 157
album n 129
alcohol-free beer n 68
ale n 68
alfalfa n 86
Algeria n 149, 152
Algerian adj 152
alien n 139
alkali n 76
alkali metals n 78
alkaline earth metals n 78
all-terrain vehicle n 100
allergic adj 23
allergy n 19
alley n 42
alligator clip n 75
alloy n 76
allspice n 59
almond milk n 61
almond oil n 60
almonds n 58, 68
aloe n 167
alpaca n 165
alpine plants n 41

alternating current n 33, 75
alto n 126
aluminum n 78, 156
always adj 171
amaryllis n 167
amazed adj 06
amazing adj 177
Amazon n 145
ambitious adj 10, 93
ambulance n 21, 50
ambulance stretcher n 50
American adj 152
American alligator n 163
American curl n 164
American
   football field n 107
American football n 107
American football
   positions n 107
americium n 78
amethyst n 156
amount n 45
amp n 33
ampersand n 175
amphibians n 163
amphibious vehicle n 88
amplifier n 129
amulet n 139
amused adj 06
analytics n 93
anchor n 105, 119
anchovies n 64
Ancient Egyptian
   hieroglyphs n 175
Ancient Greek temple n 44
ancient ruins n 44
Andean condor n 160
Andorra n 151, 153
Andorran adj 153
anemone n 134, 166
anesthesiologist n 90
Angel Falls n 145
angle n 74
angler n 121
angler fish n 166
Angola n 149, 152
Angolan adj 152
Angora n 164
angry adj 06
animal cell n 77
animation n 127
anise n 59
ankle n 01–02
ankle boots n 17
ankle strap heels n 17
ankle weights n 124
anklet n 16
anniversary n 07
annoyed adj 06
annoying adj 177
annual n 41
annual general
   meeting (AGM) n 95

anorak n 15
answer v 73
ant n 162
anteater n 159
antenna n 25, 97
antenna n 162
anther n 38
anti-inflammatory n 49
antibiotics n 49
antifreeze n 97
Antigua and
   Barbuda n 150, 152
Antiguan adj 152
antimony n 78
antiques store n 46
antiseptic n 20
antiseptic wipes n 20
antler n 159
anxious adj 06
any other business phr 95
apartment n 25
apartment n 131
apartment building n 25,
   43
apartment buzzer n 25
apex n 74
apostrophe n 175
app developer n 89
appeal n 85
appearance n 12
appendicitis n 19
appendix n 04
appetizer n 69
applause n 126
apple n 58
apple corer n 28
apple juice n 65
applicant n 81
application form n 92
apply for a job v 92
applying for a job n 92
appointment n 20, 81
appreciative adj 06
apprentice n 81, 92
approachable adj 10
apricot n 57
April n 172
apron n 13, 29
aquamarine n 156
aquarium n 164
Aquarius n 144
Arabic script n 175
arbor knot n 121
arc n 74, 112
arch n 02, 41, 44
arch window n 32
archeological
   site n 132
archeologist n 79
archeology n 79
archer n 125
archery n 125
archipelago n 147

architect n 90
architecture n 44
archive n 79
Arctic n 159
Arctic Circle n 145
Arctic fox n 159
Arctic hare n 159
Arctic tern n 160
Arctic wolf n 159
area n 74, 174
arena n 120
Argentina n 149, 152
Argentinian adj 152
argon n 78
Aries n 144
arm, arms n 01, 126
arm circles n 124
arm protection n 110
armadillo n 159
armband n 118
armchair n 26
armed drone n 88
armed forces n 88
Armenia n 150, 153
Armenian adj 153
armor n 79
armored
   vehicle n 88
armpit n 01
armrest n 99, 103
army n 88
aromatherapy n 24
arrest n 50
arrival n 43
arrive v 09
arrive early v 09
arrive home v 09
arrive late v 09
arrive on time v 09
arrogant adj 10
arrow n 79, 125
arrow slit n 44
arsenic n 78
art, arts n 73, 91, 141–142
art college n 80
Art Deco n 130
art gallery n 43, 130, 132
Art Nouveau n 130
art school n 80
art store n 46
art therapy n 24
artery n 04
artichoke heart n 56
artichoke n 56
article n 138
articulated bus n 99
artificial intelligence n 83
artisan n 79
artist n 90, 141
arugula n 55
arum lily n 167
ash n 145
ash cloud n 145

Asia n 150, 153
Asian adj 153
Asian elephant n 159
Asian vine snake n 163
ask directions v 148
asparagus n 56
asparagus tip n 56
assertive adj 10, 93
astatine n 78
asterisk n 175
asteroid n 143
asthma n 19
astigmatism n 22
astronaut n 143
astronomy n 144
at sign n 83, 175
at symbol n 83, 175
athlete n 89, 116
athletics n 116, 125
athletics track n 116
Atlantic puffin n 160
Atlantic salmon n 166
atlas moth n 162
atlas n 73
ATM n 45
ATV riding n 133
atmosphere n 143, 155
atoll n 147
atom n 76
attachment n 83
attack helicopter n 88
attack zone n 110
attend a meeting v 95
attic n 25
attractions n 132
aubergines n 56
auburn hair n 12
audience n 126, 127
audio n 136
audio guide n 130
audition n 127
auditorium n 80
August n 172
aunt n 05
aurora n 144, 155
Australia n 150, 153
Australian adj 153
Australian
   little penguin n 161
Austria n 151, 153
Austrian adj 153
author n 138
auto racing n 123
auto repair shop n 98
autobiography n 138
autocue n 84
automatic n 99
automatic toilet
   cleaner n 34
automotive industry n 91
autumn leaf n 169
avalanche n 122
avatar n 84

avenue n 43
avocado n 56
avocado toast n 71
avocado tree n 167
awful adj 177
awning n 65
ax n 36, 50, 79
axle n 100
ayran n 61
ayurveda n 24
azalea n 38
Azerbaijan n 150, 153
Azerbaijani adj 153

# B

babies' clothes n 13
baboon n 158
baby n 05
baby bath n 08
baby carriage n 08
baby changing
   facilities n 47
baby corn n 55
baby formula n 08
baby monitor n 08, 30
baby products n 48
baby teeth n 22
back adj 03
back n 26
back bacon n 53
back brush n 31
back door n 97
back seat n 99
back up v 83
back-flip n 118
backache n 19
backboard n 112
backdrop n 126
backgammon n 140
backhand n 114
backing singers n 129
backpack n 16, 135
backpack sprayer n 40
backsplash n 27
backstay n 119
backstop net n 113
backstroke n 118
backswing n 115
bacon n 53, 71
bacteria n 77, 157
Bactrian camel n 158
bad adj 52, 177
bad robot n 139

badge n 50
badminton n 114
bag, bags n 16, 52
bag store n 47
bagel n 62, 71
baggage claim n 104
baggage trailer n 104
bagpipes n 129
baguette n 62
baggy adj 13, 176
Bahamas n 150, 162
Bahamian adj 152
Bahrain n 151, 153
Bahraini adj 153
bail n 85, 111
Baisakhi n 07
bait n 121
bait v 121
bake v 29, 62–63
baked adj 72
baked beans n 71
baker n 62
bakery n 46, 48, 62–63
baking n 29
baking pan n 29
baklava n 63
balance wheel n 142
balanced diet n 23
balcony n 126
balcony n 25
bald adj 12
bald eagle n 160
ball n 02, 08, 109–110,
   112, 114
ball boy n 114
ball girl n 114
ballerina n 126
ballet n 126
ballet flats n 17
ballet leotard n 126
ballet slippers n 126
ballistic missile n 88
balloon n 08
ballpoint pen n 175
balsamic vinegar n 60
bamboo n 41, 55, 167
banana n 58
band n 129
bandage n 20, 49
banded sea krait n 166
Bangladesh n 150, 153
Bangladeshi adj 153
bangle n 16
banister n 25–26
banjo n 129
bank n 45, 94
bank loan n 45
bank statement n 45
banking n 91
banner n 109
baobab tree n 169
baptism n 07
bar, bars n 30, 68, 109, 124

bar chart n 95
bar counter n 68
bar mitzvah n 07
bar snacks n 68
bar stool n 68
bar tender n 69
barb n 121
Barbadian adj 152
Barbados n 150, 152
barbecue n 135
barbell n 124
barber n 89
barberry n 168
Barbudan adj 152
barcode n 48
bare branches n 172
bargain n 48
barista n 65, 89
baritone n 126
barium n 78
bark v 164
barley n 86
barn n 86
barn owl n 161
barnacle n 134, 166
barracuda n 166
barrel cactus n 168
Barrier Reef n 145
bartender n 68, 89
basa n 54
basalt n 156
base n 74, 76
baseball n 113
baseball cap n 16
baseball cleats n 17
baseball game n 113
baseboard n 30
baseline n 114
basement n 25, 47
basil n 59
basin n 22, 33
basket n 48, 101, 103,
   112, 164
basket of fruit n 57
basketball n 112
basketball player n 112
basking shark n 166
Basotho adj 152
bass n 126
bass clef n 128
bass drum n 128
bass guitarist n 129
basset hound n 164
bassoon n 128
bat n 111, 113–114, 158
bat v 111, 113
bat mitzvah n 07
bath towel n 31
bath toys n 31
bath tub n 31
bathmat n 31
bathrobe n 14, 31
bathroom n 31

# C

chopsticks *n* 27
chord *n* 128
chorizo *n* 53, 64
choux pastry *n* 63
christening *n* 07
Christmas *n* 07
chromium *n* 78, 156
chromosome *n* 77
chrysalis *n* 77
chrysanthemum *n* 38
chuck *n* 35
chukka boots *n* 17
church *n* 43–44
chutes and
  ladders *n* 140
chutney *n* 60, 72
cider *n* 68
cider vinegar *n* 60
cilantro *n* 59
cinder block *n* 87
cinematographer *n* 127
cinnamon *n* 59
cinnamon rolls *n* 71
cinnamon stick *n* 59
circle *n* 74
circuit *n* 83
circuit board *n* 75
circuit training *n* 124
circular saw *n* 35
circulation desk *n* 80
circumference *n* 74
circumflex *n* 175
cistern *n* 33
citrine *n* 156
citrus fruit *n* 57
clam *n* 54
clamp *n* 35, 76
clap *v* 02
clapper board *n* 84
clarinet *n* 128
class *n* 73
classical *adj* 129
Classicism *n* 130
classroom *n* 73
clavicle *n* 03
claw *n* 161
clay *n* 39, 141
clean *adj* 176
clean the bathroom *v* 34
clean the car *v* 09
clean the oven *v* 34
clean the windows *v* 34
clean up *v* 34, 178
cleaned *adj* 54
cleaner *n* 89
cleaning *n* 34
cleanser *n* 18
clear the table *v* 09, 34
cleat *n* 119
cleaver *n* 28
clementine *n* 57
click *n* 83
client, clients *n* 81, 85

cliff *n* 147
climate *n* 155
climate change *n* 155
climb *v* 11
climber *n* 41
clinch knot *n* 121
clipboard *n* 82
cloak *n* 15
cloakroom *n* 130
cloche *n* 16
clock *n* 44, 171
clock radio *n* 30
clockwise *adv* 148
clogs *n* 17
closed *adj* 48, 132
closed to bicycles *adj* 96
closed to
  pedestrians *adj* 96
closet *n* 30
cloth *n* 34
clothes *n* 13–15
clothes moth *n* 162
clothes pin *n* 34
clothesline *n* 34
clothing *n* 100
cloud, clouds *n* 51, 154
cloudy *adj* 154
cloves *n* 59
clown *n* 89
clownfish *n* 166
club *n* 140
club sandwich *n* 70
clubhouse *n* 115
clumsy *adj* 10
clutch *n* 99–100
CMS
  (content management
  system) *n* 84
co-pilot *n* 103
co-worker *n* 81
CO₂ bubbles *n* 62
coach *n* 112–113
coach's box *n* 113
coal *n* 51
coal mine *n* 51
coastal features *n* 147
coaster *n* 27, 68
coastguard *n* 106
coat hanger *n* 30
coats *n* 15
cobalt *n* 78
cobra pose *n* 24
coccyx *n* 03
cockatiel *n* 164
cockatoo *n* 161
cockle *n* 54
cockpit *n* 103, 123
cockroach *n* 162
cocktail *n* 68
cocktail glass *n* 68
cocktail shaker *n* 68
cocoa *n* 169
cocoa powder *n* 65

coconut *n* 58
coconut crab *n* 166
coconut oil *n* 60
coconut palm *n* 167
coconut shell *n* 57
coconut water *n* 58, 65
cocoon *n* 162
cod *n* 166
cod fillet *n* 54
coelophysis *n* 157
coffee *n* 52, 65, 69, 71, 86
coffee cup *n* 27
coffee machine *n* 65, 68
coffee press *n* 28
coffee shop *n* 46
coffee table *n* 26
coins *n* 45, 94
cola *n* 52
colander *n* 28
cold *adj* 154, 176
cold *n* 19
cold frame *v* 39
cold front *n* 155
cold meats *n* 71
cold water *n* 31
collaborate *v* 92
collage *n* 141
collar *n* 15, 142
collarbone *n* 03
collards *n* 55
colleague *n* 07, 81, 92
collection *n* 130
college *n* 43, 80
college departments *n* 80
college schools *n* 80
Colombia *n* 149, 152
Colombian *adj* 152
colon *n* 175
colored pencils *n* 73
coloring book *n* 138
Colosseum *n* 44
columbine *n* 168
column *n* 44, 146
comb *n* 12
combat aircraft *n* 88
combat sports *n* 117
combination *adj* 18
combine harvester *n* 86
combined events *n* 116
comedian *n* 89
comedy *n* 126–127, 137
comet *n* 143–144
comic *n* 48, 138
comma *n* 175
commence *v* 95
commercial break *n* 137
commercial district *n* 42
commis chef *n* 69
commission *n* 94
common earthball *n* 170
common egg-eater *n* 163
common green
  iguana *n* 163

common houseleek *n*
  168
common poppy *n* 168
common puffball *n* 170
common snake-necked
  turtle *n* 163
common toad *n* 163
community website *n* 84
commuters *n* 102
Comoran *adj* 152
Comoros *n* 149, 152
company *n* 81
compartment *n* 102
compass *n* 73–74, 119,
  135, 148
competitive *adj* 93
complain *v* 46
complaint *n* 50
compose *v* 128
composer *n* 128
composite *n* 85
compost *n* 40
compost bin *n* 40
compost heap *n* 41
compostable bags *n*
  155
composter *n* 40
compound *n* 76
compressed-air
  cylinder *n* 50
computer,
  computers *n* 82–83
computer desk *n* 83
computer literacy *n* 93
computing *n* 93
concave lens *n* 75
concealer *n* 18
conceptual art *n* 130
concert hall *n* 43
conchiglie *n* 64
concourse *n* 102
concrete *adj* 176
concrete *n* 35, 176
concussion *n* 19
condensed milk *n* 61
condiment,
  condiments *n*
  60, 70, 71–72
conduct *v* 128
conductor *n* 75, 102, 128
cone *n* 74, 87
conference *n* 95
confident *adj* 06, 10, 93
confused *adj* 06
confusing *adj* 177
conglomerate *n* 156
Congolese *adj* 152
coniferous forest *n* 146
conifers *n* 41, 157, 167
connection *n* 104
conning tower *n* 105
conservation *n* 130
considerate *adj* 10

console *n* 136
constellation,
  constellations *n* 144
construction *n* 87, 91
construction
  ahead *n* 96
construction site *n* 87
construction waste *n* 33
construction
  worker *n* 87, 90
contact *n* 83
contact lens,
  contact lenses *n* 22, 49
contact lens solution *n* 22
container *n* 105
container port *n* 106
container ship *n* 105–106
containers *n* 52
contents *n* 138
continent *n* 145
contours *n* 148
contract *n* 92
control tower *n* 104
controller *n* 136
controls *n* 100, 136
convenience food *n* 23, 48
conversion *n* 108
convert the attic *v* 35
convertible *n* 97
convex lens *n* 75
conveyor belt *n* 48
cook dinner *v* 09
cookbook *n* 138
cooked *adj* 56
cooked breakfast *n* 71
cooked meat *n* 53, 64
cooked vegetables *n* 72
cookie *n* 63, 84
cooking *n* 29
cooking show *n* 137
cooksonia *n* 157
cool *adj* 154
cool down *v* 124
coolant reservoir *n* 98
cooler *n* 135
cooling rack *n* 29
cooling system *n* 98
cooling tower *n* 51
coordinate *v* 92
coordinates *n* 148
coot *n* 161
copernicium *n* 78
copper *n* 78, 156
copy *v* 11
copyright *n* 175
coral *n* 166
coral reef *n* 118, 166
coral reef fish *n* 118
coral trout *n* 166
cordless drill *n* 35
core *n* 57
coriander seeds *n* 59
cork *n* 60

# D

dull *adj* 176
dumbbell *n* 124
dump truck *n* 87
dumplings *n* 70, 72
dumpster *n* 25
dune *n* 147
dune buggy *n* 97, 134
dunk *v* 112
duplex *n* 32
dusk *n* 171
dust *v* 34
dustbin *n* 25
duster *n* 34
dustpan *n* 34
dustsheet *n* 37
Dutch *adj* 153
duty belt *n* 50
duty-free shop *n* 104
duvet *n* 30
DVD *n* 136
dwarf *n* 139
dwarf planets *n* 143
dysprosium *n* 78

# E

e-reader *n* 83, 138
eagle owl *n* 161
ear *n* 01
ear phone *n* 88
ear protectors *n* 87
ear thermometer *n* 20
early *adj* 171
early *adv* 171
early human *n* 157
earn *v* 81
earphones *n* 136
earrings *n* 16
Earth *n* 143, 145
earth tremor *n* 145
earthquake *n* 145
easel *n* 82, 141
east *n* 148
East Timor *n* 151, 153
Easter *n* 07
eastern coral snake *n* 163
eat *v* 52
eat breakfast *v* 09
eat dinner *v* 09
eat in *v* 70
eat lunch *v* 09
eat out *v* 69, 178
eating *n* 52
eccentric *adj* 10
echidna *n* 158

éclair *n* 63
eclectus parrot *n* 161
economic downturn *n* 94
economics *n* 80
economy class *n* 103
ecosystem *n* 77, 155
ecotourism *n* 131
ecstatic *adj* 06
Ecuador *n* 149, 152
Ecuadorian *adj* 152
eczema *n* 19
Edam *n* 64
editor *n* 89
education *n* 91
eel *n* 54
efficient *adj* 93
egg, eggs *n* 61, 77
egg allergy *n* 23
egg cup *n* 27, 61
egg slicer *n* 28
egg timer *n* 28
egg white *n* 61, 71
eggplant *n* 56
eggshell *n* 161
Egypt *n* 149, 152
Egyptian *adj* 152
Egyptian goose *n* 160
Eid al-Fitr *n* 07
Eiffel Tower *n* 44
eight *num* 173
eighteen *num* 173
eighth *num* 173
eighty *num* 173
einsteinium *n* 78
El Salvador *n* 150, 152
elbow *n* 01
elbow pads *n* 107
elderberry *n* 57
elderly *adj* 05
electric bike *n* 101
electric blanket *n* 30
electric car *n* 97
electric drill *n* 35
electric field *n* 75
electric guitar *n* 129
electric guitarist *n* 129
electric hook-up *n* 135
electric kettle *n* 27
electric lines *n* 102
electric motorcycle *n* 100
electric pump *n* 135
electric razor *n* 31
electric scooter *n* 100
electric shock *n* 19
electric train *n* 102
electrical appliances *n* 47
electrical goods *n* 48
electrical waste *n* 33
electrician *n* 89
electricity *n* 33, 51, 75
electricity meter *n* 33
electrics *n* 33
electromagnetic

spectrum *n* 75
electron *n* 76
electronics *n* 91
electronics store *n* 46
elements *n* 76
elevator *n* 25, 47, 131
eleven *num* 173
elf *n* 139
elf owl *n* 161
elixir *n* 139
ellipsis *n* 175
elliptical *n* 124
elliptical galaxy *n* 144
elm *n* 169
email *n* 83
embarrassed *adj* 06
embroidery *n* 142
embryo *n* 08
emerald *n* 156
emerald toucan *n* 160
emerald tree boa *n* 163
emergency
    brake *n* 99
emergency
    department *n* 50
emergency exit *n* 103, 131
emergency phone *n* 96
emergency room *n* 21
emergency services *n* 50
emergency signal *n* 102
emergency vehicle
    beacon *n* 50
emigrate *v* 07
Emirati *adj* 153
emissions *n* 51, 155
emoji, emojis *n* 84, 175
empanada *n* 70
emperor *n* 79
emperor moth *n* 162
emperor penguin *n* 161
empire *n* 79
Empire State Building *n* 44
employee *n* 81
employer *n* 81
employment *adj* 81
empress *n* 79
empty *adj* 176
emu *n* 160
enamel *n* 03
encore *n* 126
encyclopedia *n* 73, 138
end line *n* 107
end zone *n* 107, 110
endangered species *n* 155
endive *n* 55
endocrine *n* 04
endocrinology *n* 21
endoskeleton *n* 77
energetic *adj* 93
energy *n* 23, 51, 91
energy drink *n* 52
engaged couple *n* 07
engine *n* 98, 100, 103

engine intake *n* 123
engine room *n* 105
engineer *n* 90
engineering *n* 80
English *n* 73
English bluebell *n* 167
English horn *n* 128
English mustard *n* 60
engraving *n* 141
Enlightenment *n* 79
enoki mushroom *n* 56, 170
ENT *n* 21
enter *v* 11
entertainment *n* 91
enthusiastic *adj* 10
entrance *n* 130
entrance fee *n* 132
entrée *n* 69
envelope *n* 45, 82, 103
environment *n* 155
environmental issues *n*
    155
épée *n* 117
epiglottis *n* 04
episode *n* 137
equals *n* 74
equation *n* 74
Equator *n* 145
Equatorial Guinea *n*
    149, 152
Equatorial Guinean *adj*
    152
equity *n* 94
eraser *n* 73, 82
erbium *n* 78
Eritrea *n* 149, 152
Eritrean *adj* 152
erupt *v* 145
escalator *n* 47, 104
esophagus *n* 04
espadrilles *n* 17
espresso *n* 65
espresso maker *n* 27
essay *n* 73
essential oils *n* 24
Estonia *n* 151, 153
Estonian *adj* 153
estuary *n* 147
Eswatini *n* 149, 152
Ethiopia *n* 149, 152
Ethiopian *adj* 152
Europe *n* 151, 153
European *adj* 153
European badger *n* 158
European common
    frog *n* 163
European robin *n* 160
europium *n* 78
EV charging
    station *n* 97
eave *n* 32, 44
evening *n* 09, 171
evening dress *n* 15

evening primrose *n* 38
evergreen *n* 41
every day *adv* 172
every other day *adv* 172
evidence *n* 50, 85
evolution *n* 77
ewe *n* 165
ex-husband *n* 05
ex-wife *n* 05
exam *n* 73
excavation *n* 79, 87
excess baggage *n* 104
exchange *v* 46
exchange rate *n* 45, 94
excited *adj* 06
exciting *adj* 177
exclamation mark *n*
    175
exercise *v* 09, 20
exercise ball *n* 124
exercise bike *n* 124
exercise book *n* 73
exercise class *n* 124
exercise mat *n* 124
exercises *n* 124
exhaust fan *n* 27
exhaust pipe *n* 98, 100
exhausted *adj* 06
exhausting *adj* 177
exhibit *n* 130
exhibition *n* 130
exit *n* 48
exit *v* 11
exit ramp *n* 96
exoskeleton *n* 77
exosphere *n* 155
exotic shorthair *n* 164
expenditure *n* 94
experiment *n* 76
expiration date *n* 49
extend *v* 124
extension cord *n* 35
extra virgin *adj* 60
extraction *n* 22
extraordinary *adj* 177
extras *n* 127
eye, eyes *n* 01, 121, 142
eye drops *n* 22
eye mask *n* 14
eyeball *n* 22
eyebrow *n* 01
eyebrow brush *n* 18
eyebrow pencil *n* 18
eyecup *n* 136
eyelashes *n* 01
eyelet *n* 17
eyelid *n* 01
eyeliner *n* 18
eyepiece *n* 77, 144
eyeshadow *n* 18

# F

# G

gingerbread man *n* 63
ginkgo *n* 167
ginkgo nuts *n* 58
giraffe *n* 158
girder *n* 87
girl *n* 05
girlfriend *n* 05
girth *n* 120
give a presentation *v* 95
give away *v* 178
give back *v* 178
give notice *v* 32
give out *v* 178
give up *v* 23, 178
glacier *n* 146
gladiator sandals *n* 17
gladiolus *n* 47
glass *adj* 176
glass, glasses *n* 27, 52, 68, 155, 176
glass baking dish *n* 28
glass bottle *n* 76
glass rod *n* 76
glasses *n* 22
glassware *n* 27
glasswing butterfly *n* 162
glaze *v* 62-63
glide *v* 161
glider *n* 103, 125
glory of Texas *n* 168
gloss *n* 37
glossary *n* 138
glove, gloves *n* 16, 100, 110, 115, 117, 122, 107, 109
glue *n* 82, 101, 141
glue gun *n* 35
gluten intolerant *adj* 23
gluten-free *adj* 23
gluten-free flour *n* 62
gluteus maximus *n* 03
gneiss *n* 156
gnocchi *n* 64
gnome *n* 139
go *n* 140
go abroad *v* 104, 141
go away *v* 178
go back *v* 148
go backpacking *v* 131
go down *v* 178
go on a cruise *v* 131
go on a diet *v* 23
go on a vacation *v* 131
go on an excursion *v* 132
go on a tour *v* 132
go on Hajj *v* 07
go on maternity leave *v* 81
go out of business *v* 94
go out with friends *v* 09
go past
   (the restaurant) *v* 148
go straight
   ahead *v* 96, 148

go to a café *v* 09
go to bed *v* 09
go to preschool *v* 07
go to school *v* 09
go to sleep *v* 09
go to work *v* 09
go up *v* 178
go viral *v* 84
go-cart *n* 123
goal *n* 108-110
goal crease *n* 110
goal line *n* 107, 110
goal posts *n* 108
goalball *n* 125
goalie stick *n* 110
goalkeeper *n* 109-110
goalpost *n* 107-09
goat *n* 53, 165
goat's cheese *n* 61
goat's milk *n* 61
goatee *n* 12
goblin *n* 139
goggles *n* 15, 118, 122
goji berry *n* 57
gold *adj* 176
gold *n* 78, 116, 156, 176
gold-plated visor *n* 143
golden eagle *n* 160
golden guinea vine *n* 168
golden raisin *n* 58
golf *n* 115
golf bag *n* 115
golf ball *n* 115
golf cap *n* 115
golf clubs *n* 115
golf course *n* 115
golf equipment *n* 115
golf push cart *n* 115
golf shoe,
   golf shoes *n* 17, 115
golfer *n* 115
gong *n* 128
good *adj* 177
good afternoon *phr* 179
good evening *phr* 179
good listener *n* 93
good morning *phr* 179
good night *phr* 179
goodbye *phr* 179
goose *n* 53, 165
goose egg *n* 61
gooseberry *n* 57
gorilla *n* 159
gosling *n* 165
gospel *n* 129
gossip magazine *n* 138
government building *n* 43
GPS *n* 99
grab bar *n* 31
graceful *adj* 177
grade *n* 73
grader *n* 87
graduate *n* 80

graduate *v* 07
graduation ceremony *n* 80
graffiti *n* 85
graft *v* 39
gram *n* 174
granddaughter *n* 05
grandfather *n* 05
grandmother *n* 05
grandparents *n* 05
grandson *n* 05
granite *n* 156
grapefruit *n* 57
grapes *n* 57
grapeseed oil *n* 60
grapevine *n* 168
graphite *n* 156
grass, grasses *n* 25, 41, 167
grass collector *n* 40
grass tree *n* 167
grasshopper *n* 162
grassland *n* 146
grate *v* 29
grated cheese *n* 61
grateful *adj* 06
grater *n* 28
grave accent *n* 175
gravel *n* 35, 40
gravity *n* 144
gray *adj* 01, 141
gray *n* 01, 141
gray hair *n* 12
gray willow *n* 169
grease *v* 29
greasy hair *n* 12
great *adj* 177
Great Blue Hole *n* 145
great crested newt *n* 163
Great Dane *n* 164
great gray owl *n* 161
Great Mosque
   of Djenné *n* 44
Great Plains toad *n* 163
great white shark *n* 166
greater spotted
   woodpecker *n* 160
grebe *n* 161
Greece *n* 151, 153
Greek *adj* 153
Greek alphabet *n* 175
Greek mythology *n* 139
Greek salad *n* 72
green *adj* 01, 141
green *n* 115, 141
green basilisk *n* 163
green beans *n* 55
green energy *n* 51
green foliage *n* 172
green olives *n* 64
green sea turtle *n* 163
green tea *n* 66
green woodpecker *n* 160
greenhouse *n* 39
greenhouse effect *n* 155
greenhouse gases *n* 155

greet *v* 179
greetings *n* 179
gremlin *n* 139
Grenada *n* 150, 152
grenade *n* 88
grenade launcher *n* 88
Grenadian *adj* 152
gray willow *n* 169
grid lines *n* 148
griffin *n* 139
grill *n* 41
grill pan *n* 28
grilled *adj* 72
grilled tomato *n* 71
grin *v* 02
grip *n* 115
grocer *n* 89
grocery store *n* 46, 56
groin *n* 01
groin protector *n* 117
groom *n* 07
groom *v* 120
groove *n* 115
ground *n* 33
ground chili *n* 59
ground cinnamon *n* 59
ground cover *n* 41
ground level *n* 47
ground maintenance *n* 89
ground meat *n* 53
ground sheet *n* 135
group therapy *n* 24
grout *n* 37
grow up *v* 178
grow your hair *v* 12
growing up *n* 05
grunt *v* 165
guarantee *n* 47
Guatemala *n* 150, 152
Guatemalan *adj* 152
guava *n* 58, 168
guest *n* 26
guest house *n* 131
guest speaker *n* 95
guests *n* 131
guidebook *n* 131-132, 138
guided tour *n* 132
guillemot *n* 160
guilty *adj* 06, 85
Guinea *n* 149, 152
guinea pig *n* 164
Guinea-Bissau *n* 149, 152
Guinean *adj* 152
gulf *n* 147
gull *n* 134
gully *n* 111
gulp *v* 52
gulper eel *n* 166
gum *n* 03
gun, guns *n* 88
gunfire *n* 88
gunnera *n* 168
gutter *n* 25, 43

guy line *n* 135
Guyana *n* 149, 152
Guyanese *adj* 152
gym *n* 124, 131
gym equipment *n* 124
gym machines *n* 124
gymnastics *n* 125
gynecology *n* 21
gypsophila *n* 47
gyrocopter *n* 103

# H

habitat loss *n* 155
hacking *n* 85
hacksaw *n* 36
hadal zone *n* 166
haddock tail *n* 54
hafnium *n* 78
haggle *v* 46
hailstone *n* 154
hair *n* 01, 12
hair dryer *n* 12
hair dye *n* 18
hair gel *n* 12
hair salon *n* 47
hair scissors *n* 12
hair spray *n* 12
hair towel wrap *n* 18
hairbrush *n* 12
hairdresser *n* 89
hairpin turn *n* 123
Haiti *n* 150, 152
Haitian *adj* 152
hakama *n* 117
halal *adj* 72
half *num* 173
half an hour *n* 171
half moon pose *n* 24
half time *n* 109
half-court line *n* 112
half-liter *n* 174
half-way line *n* 109
halfback *n* 107
halfway line *n* 108
halibut *n* 54
halloumi *n* 64
Halloween *n* 07
hallway *n* 25-26
halogens *n* 78
halter *n* 120
halter neck *n* 15
halva *n* 67
ham *n* 53, 71
hamburger *n* 70

housekeeper n 89
houseplants n 38
hovercraft n 105
howler monkey n 159
hub n 51, 101
hubcap n 98
Hugin and Munin n 139
hula hoop n 08
hull n 105, 119
human body n 01
human resources (HR) n 91
humanities n 80
Humboldt penguin n 161
humerus n 03
humidity n 154
hummingbird n 160
hummingbird
    hawksmoth n 162
hummus n 72
humor n 138
hump n 158
humpback whale n 166
Hungarian adj 153
Hungary n 151, 153
hungry adj 26
hunt v 159
hurdles n 116
hurricane n 154
hurt v 20
husband n 05
hut n 32
hybrid n 97
Hydra n 139
hydrangea n 38
hydrant n 50
hydroelectric energy n 51
hydroelectric power
    station n 51
hydrofoil n 105
hydrogen n 78
hydrotherapy n 24
hyena n 158
hyphen n 175
hypnotherapy n 24
hypotenuse n 74
hyssop n 59

I

Iberian ham n 64
ibex n 158
ice n 68, 154
ice and lemon n 68
ice bucket n 68
ice climbing n 122

ice cream n 61, 70, 134
ice cream cone n 65
ice cream scoop n 65
ice cream sundae n 63
ice fishing n 121
ice hockey n 110
ice hockey player n 110
ice hockey rink n 110
ice maker n 27
ice skate n 110
ice-skating n 122
iceberg lettuce n 55
iceberg n 146
iced adj 52
iced bun n 63
iced coffee n 65
iced tea n 52, 66
Iceland n 151, 153
Icelandic adj 153
ichthyostega n 157
icicle n 146
icing n 29, 63
icy adj 154
igloo n 32
igneous adj 156
ignition n 99
illness n 19
illustration n 138
imaginative adj 93
immature adj 10
immigration n 104
impala n 158
impatient adj 10
important adj 177
Impressionism n 130
impulsive adj 10
in brine phr 64
in credit phr 45
in debt phr 45
in field n 111
in front of prep 148, 180
in oil phr 64
in prep 180
in sauce phr 72
in the black phr 45
in the red phr 45
in town n 42
in-goal area n 108
inbox n 83
incandescent bulb n 33
inch n 174
inch plant n 167
incisors n 03
income n 94
incontinence pads n 49
incorrect adj 176
incredible adj 177
incubator n 08
independent adj 93
index n 138
index finger n 02
India n 150, 153
Indian adj 153

Indian cobra n 163
Indian pale ale (IPA) n 68
indifferent adj 06
indigo n 141
indium n 78
Indonesia n 151, 153
Indonesian adj 153
industrial emissions n 155
industrial revolution n 79
industrial zone n 42
industries n 91
infection n 19
infield n 113
infielders n 113
inflatable boat n 134
inflatable dinghy n 105
influencer n 84, 93
information age n 79
information chart n 49
information screen n 104
information technology
    (IT) n 73, 91
infrared n 75
inhaler n 20, 49
initiative n 93
injera n 62
injury n 19
ink n 141, 175
inline skating n 125
inner core n 145
inner tube n 101
inning n 113
innocent adj 85
innovative adj 93
inoculation n 20
insect repellent n 49, 135
insects n 162
insensitive adj 10
inside prep 180
inside center n 108
inside lane n 96
insoles n 17, 49
insomnia n 19, 30
inspector n 50
install v 33
install a carpet v 35
installation n 130
instep n 02
instruments n 129
insulated gloves n 143
insulating tape n 36
insulation n 35
insulin n 49
intelligent adj 10
intensive care unit n 21
intercity train n 102
intercom n 25
intercostal n 03
interdental brush n 22
interest rate n 45
interested adj 06
interesting adj 177
intermission n 126

intern n 81
internal organs n 04
international flight n 104
interpersonal skills n 93
interrogation room n 50
interrupt v 95
intersection n 43
interview n 81, 137
interviewer n 81
intolerant adj 23
intrigued adj 06
invertebrate n 77
investigation n 50
investment n 94
invoice n 94
iodine n 78
ionosphere n 155
Iran n 151, 153
Iranian adj 153
Iraq n 150, 153
Iraqi adj 153
Ireland n 151, 153
iridium n 78
iris n 01, 38
Irish adj 153
Irish coffee n 65
iron n 23, 34, 49, 78,
    115, 156
iron a shirt v 09
Iron age n 79
ironing board n 34
irritated adj 06
irritating adj 177
Islamic Golden Age n 79
island n 88, 145, 147
isobar n 155
Israel n 150, 153
Israeli adj 153
isthmus n 147
IT manager n 89
Italian adj 153
italic adj 175
italic n 175
Italy n 151, 153
IV n 21
IV pole n 21
Ivorian adj 152
Ivory Coast n 149, 152
ivy n 169

J

jack n 98, 140
jack connector n 129
jack-o'-lantern n 139, 170

jackal n 158
jacket n 15
jackfruit n 58
jackhammer n 87
Jackson's chameleon n 163
jacuzzi n 25
jade n 156
jade pothos n 38
jaguar n 159
jalapeños n 59
jam n 71
Jamaica n 150, 152
Jamaican adj 152
janitor n 90
January n 172
Japan n 150, 153
Japanese adj 153
Japanese bobtail n 164
Japanese characters n 175
jar n 27, 52, 60
jasper n 156
javelin n 116
jaw n 01, 03
jawed fish n 157
jawless fish n 157
jazz n 129
jealous adj 06
jeans n 14
jelly beans n 67
jelly donut n 63
jelly sandals n 17
jellyfish n 166
Jerusalem
    artichoke n 56
jester n 79
jet n 156
jet engine n 103
Jet Ski n 134
jet skiing n 119
jetty n 106
jetway n 104
jeweler n 46, 89
jewelry n 16
jewelry box n 16
jewelry making n 141
jib n 87, 119
jigsaw n 35
jigsaw puzzle n 08, 140
job ads n 92
job applications n 92
job sheet n 92
job skills n 92
jobs n 89–90
jockey n 120
jodhpurs n 120
joey n 158
jog in place v 124
jogging n 133
joker n 140
Jordan n 150, 153
Jordanian adj 153
Joshua tree n 167
journal n 80

librarian n 80, 90
library n 43, 80, 148
library card n 80
libretto n 126
Libya n 149, 152
Libyan adj 152
license plate n 97
lick v 02, 11
licorice n 67
lid n 28
lie down v 20
Liechtenstein n 151, 153
Liechtensteiner adj 153
life cycle n 77
life events n 07
life jacket n 105, 119
life preserver n
   105, 119, 134
life raft n 119
life-support
   backpack n 143
lifeboat n 105
lifeguard n 118, 134
lifeguard tower n 134
lift v 11
ligament n 03
ligature n 175
light adj 60, 176
light, lights n 32, 50, 84,
   101, 143
light a fire v 135
light aircraft n 103
light bulbs n 33
light cream n 61
light shower n 154
light switch n 33
lighthouse n 44, 106
lighting n 47
lightning n 154
like v 84
lilac n 38
lily n 38, 167
lily of the valley n 38
lime n 57, 169
lime pickle n 60
limestone n 156
limousine n 97
limpet n 134, 166
linden n 169
line, lines n 74, 121
line n 48, 132
line of play n 115
linen chest n 30
linesman n 109, 114
lingerie n 47
lining n 15
lining paper n 37
lintel n 87
lion n 158
lioness n 158
lip balm n 18
lip brush n 18
lip liner n 18

lips n 01
lipstick n 18
liqueur n 68
liquid n 76
liquid measure n 174
liquid measurements n
   174
liquor store n 46
listen v 11
listen to the radio v 09
liter n 174
literary fiction n 138
literature n 73, 80
lithium n 78
Lithuania n 151, 153
Lithuanian adj 153
little finger n 02
little gem n 55
little toe n 02
litterbox n 164
live n 33
live rail n 102
liver n 04, 53
livermorium n 78
liverwort n 167
living room n 26
living stones n 168
lizard n 164
llama n 158, 165
load the dishwasher v 34
loaf n 62
loafers n 17
loam n 39
lob n 114
lobster n 54
local produce n 23
lock n 101, 106
locker room n 124
lockers n 118, 124
locksmith n 90
locust n 162
log in v 83, 178
log out v 83, 178
loganberry n 57
logic game n 136
loin n 54
lollipop n 67
London plane n 168
lonely adj 06
long adj 176
long hair n 12
long jump n 116
long legs n 159
long-handled shears n 40
longitude n 145, 148
look at v 178
look for v 178
loom n 142
loose adj 13, 176
loosehead prop n 108
loppers n 40
lord n 79
lorikeet n 161

lose v 109, 140
lose weight v 20, 23
lose your way v 148
lost and found n 104
lost property office n 102
lotus n 38
loudspeakers n 136
lovage n 59
love n 114
low adj 176
low calorie adj 23
low pressure n 155
low tide n 147
lower deck n 99
lower pitch n 128
lowercase n 175
loyalty card n 47
lucky adj 06
ludo n 140
lug nuts n 98
luge n 122
luggage n 104, 131
luggage hold n 99
luggage rack n 102
luggage storage n 102
lumbar vertebrae n 03
lumber n 87
luna moth n 162
lunar eclipse n 143
lunar module n 143
lunar rover n 143
lunch n 26, 72
lunch menu n 69
lung n 04
lunge n 117, 124
lupin n 38
lure n 121
lutetium n 78
Luxembourg adj 153
Luxembourg n 151, 153
lychee n 57
lymphatic n 04
lynx n 159

# M

macadamia,
   macadamias n 58, 168
macaque n 159
macaron n 63
macaroni n 64
mace n 59, 79
machine gun n 88
machine needle n 142

machinery n 87
mackerel n 54
macramé n 142
mad adj 06
Madagascan adj 152
Madagascar n 149, 152
magazine website n 84
maglev n 102
magma chamber n 145
magnesium n 49, 78, 156
magnet n 75
magnetic field n 75
magnolia n 167
maid n 89
maid service n 131
mail carrier n 45, 90
mail slot n 25, 45
mailbox n 25, 45
main character n 127
main road n 148
main street n 46
Maine coon n 164
mainsail n 119
make v 11
make a loss v 94
make a profit v 94
make a
   reservation v 69, 131
make curtains v 35
make friends v 07
make the bed v 09, 34
make up v 178
makeup n 18
makeup bag n 18
malachite n 156
Malawi n 149, 152
Malawian adj 152
Malaysia n 151, 153
Malaysian adj 153
Maldives n 150, 153
Maldivian adj 153
male n 04
Mali n 149, 152
Malian adj 152
mallard n 161
mallet n 36, 141
malt vinegar n 60
Malta n 151, 153
Maltese adj 153
mammals n 158, 159
man n 05
manage v 92
manager n 81, 109
managing director n 81
manchego n 64
mandarin duck n 161
mandarin orange n 57
mandolin n 129
mandoline n 28
mandrill n 159
mane n 120
manganese n 78
mango n 57

mango juice n 65
mangosteen n 58
mangrove n 169
manhole n 43
manicure n 18
mannequin n 142
mansion n 32
mantis shrimp n 166
mantle n 145
mantlepiece n 26
manual n 99
manufacturing n 91
map n 132
maple n 169
maple syrup n 60
maps n 148
maracas n 128
marathon n 116
marble adj 176
marble n 156, 176
marble queen n 38
March n 172
mare n 120, 165
margarine n 61
marigold n 38
marina n 106
marinated adj 64, 72
marinated fish n 64
marine n 88
marine fishing n 121
marine iguana n 163
marine species n 166
marjoram n 59
mark v 112
marker n 175
market researcher n 89
marketing n 91
marmalade n 60, 71
marmoset n 159
marrella n 157
married adj 05
married couple n 07
marrow n 56
Mars n 143
marsh n 147
Marshall Islands n
   150, 153
Marshallese adj 153
marshmallow n 67
martial arts n 117, 127
Martini n 68
Mary Janes n 17
marzipan n 63
mascara n 18
mascot n 109
mash v 29
mashed adj 72
masher n 28
mask n 113, 117–118
masking tape n 37
Mason jar n 52
masonry bit n 36
massage n 24

mast n 105, 119
master's degree n 80
masterpiece n 130
mat n 24
matamata n 163
match n 114
materials n 35, 176
maternity n 21
maternity ward n 21
math n 73
mathematical
   equipment n 74
mathematics n 74
matte n 37
mattress n 30
mature adj 10
matzo n 62
Mauritania n 149, 152
Mauritanian adj 152
Mauritian adj 152
Mauritius n 149, 152
May n 172
mayonnaise n 60
MDF n 35
meal deal n 70
meals n 72
mean adj 10
measles n 19
measure n 68
measure v 174, 178
measurements n 74
measures n 174
measuring cup n
   27–29, 174
measuring spoon n 28,
   49
meat n 48, 53
meat hook n 53
meat pie n 72
meat pies n 64
meat tenderizer n 28
meat thermometer n 28
meatballs n 72
mechanic n 89, 98
mechanics n 98
medal n 88, 116
media n 84, 91
median n 96
medical chart n 21
medical examination n
   20
medication n 20, 49
medicine n 20, 49, 80
mediocre adj 177
meditation n 24
medium height adj 12
medlar n 169
medley relay n 118
meerkat n 159
meet v 179
meet a deadline v 92
meet up v 178
meeting n 81, 82, 95

meeting-room
   equipment n 82
meganeura n 157
megaphone n 50
meitnerium n 78
melody n 129
melons n 58
melt butter v 29
melting ice caps n 155
membership n 124
memory card n 83
mendelevium n 78
men's decathlon n 116
menswear n 47
menu n 65, 70
meow v 164
merchant n 79
Mercury n 143
mercury n 78, 156
meringue n 63
mermaid n 139
merman n 139
mesa n 146
mesosphere n 155
Mesozoic
   (middle life) adj 157
Mesozoic
   (middle life) n 157
mess n 88
mess around v 178
metacarpals n 03
metal adj 176
metal, metals n 35, 155,
   156, 176
metal bit n 36
metal detecting n 133
metamorphic adj 156
metamorphosis n 77
metatarsals n 03
meteor n 144
meteor shower n 144
meter n 174
meter line n 108
methane n 155
meticulous adj 10
Mexican adj 152
Mexican axolotl n 163
Mexico n 150, 152
mezzanine n 126
mezzo-soprano n 126
mica n 156
microbiologist n 77
microbiology n 77
microlight n 103
Micronesia n 150, 153
Micronesian adj 153
microphone n 84, 95, 136
microscope n 77
microwave v 29
microwave oven n 27
microwaves n 75
mid-off n 111
mid-wicket n 111

midcourt area
   marker n 112
midday n 171
middle blocker n 112
middle finger n 02
middle lane n 96
middle level n 47
middle linebacker n 107
middle-aged adj 12
midfielder n 109
midnight n 171
midnight zone n 166
midwife n 08
migraine n 19
migrate v 161
mild adj 154
mile n 174
military n 88, 91
military ambulance n 88
military transport
   aircraft n 88
military truck n 88
military uniform n 13
military vehicles n 88
milk n 61, 65, 71
milk v 86
milk carton n 61
milk chocolate n 67
milk products n 61
milkshake n 52, 65, 70
milky conecap n 170
Milky Way n 144
millennium n 172
millet n 86
milligram n 174
milliliter n 174
millimeter n 174
millipede n 162
mimosa n 168
minaret n 44
mince v 29
mindfulness n 24
mine shaft n 51
miner, miners n 51, 89
mineral spirits n 37
mineral water n 52, 68
minerals n 23, 156
minibar n 131
minibus n 99
mining n 91
minivan n 97
Minotaur n 139
minstrel n 79
mint n 59, 67
mint tea n 66
minus sign n 74
minute n 82, 171
minute hand n 171
mirror n 18, 30, 77
miserable adj 06
miss a train v 102
mission control n 143
mist n 154

mistletoe n 168
misty adj 154
mitochondria n 77
mitt n 113
mittens n 13
mix v 29, 62
mixing bowl n 28
mixing desk n 84
moat n 44
mobile n 30
mobile banking n 94
mobile home n 32
moccasins n 17
mochi n 63
mocktail n 68
model making n 141
modeling tool n 141
modern building n 44
modern pentathlon n 116
moisturizer n 18
molars n 03
mold n 170
molding n 26
Moldova n 151, 153
Moldovan adj 153
mole n 12, 159
molecule n 76
molt v 164
molybdenum n 78
mom n 05
Monacan adj 153
Monaco n 151, 153
monarch butterfly n 162
monastery n 44
Monday n 172
money n 45, 94
Mongolia n 150, 153
Mongolian adj 153
mongoose n 159
monkey puzzle n 167
monkey wrench n 36
monkfish n 54
mono adj 136
monocle n 22
monoplane n 103
monorail n 102
monster n 139
monster truck n 123
Montenegrin adj 153
Montenegro n 151, 153
month n 172
monthly adj 172
monthly adv 172
monument n 42, 44, 132
moods n 06
Moon n 143
moonstone n 156
moor v 106
mooring n 106
moorish idol n 166
moose n 159
mop n 34
mop the floor v 34

morel n 170
morning n 09, 171
morning glory n 169
morning show n 137
Moroccan adj 152
Morocco n 149, 152
mortar n 28, 35, 76, 87
mortar and pestle n 28
mortarboard n 80
mortgage n 32, 45
moscovium n 78
mosque n 44
mosquito n 162
mosquito net n 135
moss n 167
mother n 05
mother-in-law n 05
mother of thousands n
   168
moths n 162
motion-sickness
   medication n 49
motivated adj 93
motor home n 135
motor scooter n 100
motocross n 123
motorcycle n 100
motorcycle officer n 50
motorcycle
   racing n 123
motorsports n 123
mount v 100
mountain n 147
mountain ash n 169
mountain bike n 101
mountain biking n 133
mountain chain n 146
mountain goat n 159
mountain pose n 24
mountain range n 146
mountaineering n 133
mouse n 83, 158, 164
mouse pad n 83
mouth n 01, 147
mouth guard n 107, 117
mouthwash n 31
movable panel n 82
move v 11, 140
move in v 32
move out v 32
movie camera n 127
movie star n 127
movie
   theater n 42, 127
movies n 127
moving truck n 32
mow the lawn v 09, 39
Mozambican adj 152
Mozambique n 149, 152
mozzarella n 64
muck out v 120
mudguard n 100

mudskipper *n* 166
mudslide *n* 146
muesli *n* 71
muffin *n* 63, 70
muffin tin *n* 29
muffler *n* 98, 100
mug *n* 27
mugging *n* 85
mulberry *n* 57
mulch *v* 39
mules *n* 17
multi-purpose knife *n* 135
multi-vitamins *n* 49
multiplayer game *n* 136
multiplex *n* 127
multiplication sign *n* 74
multiply *v* 74
mumps *n* 19
muscles *n* 03
museum *n* 43, 130, 132
museum curator *n* 89
musher *n* 122
mushroom picking *n* 133
mushroom,
    mushrooms *n* 56, 170
music *n* 73, 128, 129
music channel *n* 137
music school *n* 80
music stand *n* 128
music teacher *n* 90
music therapy *n* 24
musical *n* 126, 127
musician *n* 90
musk ox *n* 159
mussel *n* 54
mustache *n* 12
mustard *n* 70
mustard allergy *n* 23
mustard seeds *n* 60
mute swan *n* 161
muzzle *n* 120
Myanmar
    (Burma) *n* 150, 153
mycelium *n* 170
myrtle *n* 168
myths *n* 139

# N

nacelle *n* 51
nachos *n* 70
nail *n* 36
nail clippers *n* 18, 49
nail file *n* 18
nail polish *n* 18

nail polish remover *n* 18
nail scissors *n* 18
Namibia *n* 149, 152
Namibian *adj* 152
napkin *n* 27, 72
napkin ring *n* 27
Napoleon *n* 63
narrow *adj* 176
narwhal *n* 166
nasal spray *n* 20
nasturtium *n* 169
nasty *adj* 177
national park *n* 132, 133
nationalities *n* 152, 153
natural arch *n* 147
natural history *n* 157
nature documentary *n* 137
nature reserve *n* 133, 148
nature therapy *n* 24
nature writing *n* 138
naturopathy *n* 24
Nauru *n* 150, 153
Nauruan *adj* 153
nausea *n* 19
nautilus *n* 166
navel *n* 01
navigate *v* 119
navy *n* 88
navy blue *n* 141
navy vessels *n* 88
near *adj* 176
nearsighted *adj* 22
nebula *n* 144
neck *n* 01, 115, 129, 161
neck brace *n* 19
neck pad *n* 107
necklace *n* 16
neckline *n* 142
nectarine *n* 57
needle *n* 20
needlefish *n* 166
needle-nose pliers *n* 36
needle plate *n* 142
needlepoint *n* 142
negative *adj* 75
negative electrode *n* 75
negotiate *v* 92
negotiating *n* 93
neighbor *n* 07
neodymium *n* 78
Neogene *adj* 157
Neogene *n* 157
neon *n* 78
Nepal *n* 150, 153
Nepalese *adj* 153
nephew *n* 05
Neptune *n* 143
neptunium *n* 78
nerve *n* 03, 22
nervous *adj* 04, 06, 10
nest *n* 160
net *n* 109, 112, 114
net *v* 121

netball *n* 125
Netherlands *n* 151, 153
nettle *n* 169
neurology *n* 21
neutral *n* 33
neutral zone *n* 107, 110
neutron *n* 76
neutron star *n* 144
never *adv* 171, 172
Nevisian *adj* 152
new *adj* 176
new leaves *n* 172
new moon *n* 143
new potato *n* 56
New Year *n* 07
New Zealand *adj* 153
New Zealand *n* 150, 153
newborn baby *n* 08
news anchor *n* 137
news *n* 137
news website *n* 84
newsboy cap *n* 16
newsfeed *n* 84
newspaper *n* 48, 138
newsstand *n* 46, 48
next to *prep* 148, 180
nib *n* 73, 175
nibble *v* 52
Nicaragua *n* 150, 152
Nicaraguan *adj* 152
nice *adj* 177
nickel *n* 78, 156
niece *n* 05
nigella seeds *n* 59
Niger *n* 149, 152
Nigeria *n* 149, 152
Nigerian *adj* 152
Nigerien *adj* 152
night *n* 171
night-light *n* 30
nightclub *n* 42
nightgown *n* 14
nightie *n* 14
nightingale *n* 160
nightmare *n* 30
nightstand *n* 30
nightwear *n* 14
nihonium *n* 78
Nile crocodile *n* 163
nine *num* 173
nine-to-five job *n* 81
nineteen *num* 173
ninety *num* 173
ninth *num* 173
niobium *n* 78
nipple *n* 01, 08
nitrogen *n* 78
no entry *n* 96
no passing *phr* 96
no photography *phr* 130
no right turn *phr* 96
no U-turn *phr* 96
no vacancies *phr* 131

no-charge
    semi-circle *n* 112
nobelium *n* 78
noble gases *n* 78
nobles *n* 79
nod *v* 02
noisy *adj* 176
non-blood relative *n* 05
non-carbonated *adj* 52
nonfiction *n* 138
nonmetals *n* 78
noodle soup *n* 72
noodles *n* 64, 70, 72
normal *adj* 18
normal hair *n* 12
north *n* 148
North America *n* 150, 152
North American *adj* 152
North Korea *n* 150, 153
North Korean *adj* 153
North
    Macedonia *n* 151, 153
North Macedonian *adj*
    153
North Pole *n* 75, 145
northeast *n* 148
northern cardinal *n* 161
Northern
    Hemisphere *n* 145
northwest *n* 148
Norway *n* 151, 153
Norwegian *adj* 153
nose *n* 01, 103
nose clip *n* 118
nose cone *n* 123
noseband *n* 120
nosebleed *n* 19
nosewheel *n* 103
nostrils *n* 01
notation *n* 128
notebook *n* 73, 95
notepad *n* 82
notes *n* 95, 128
nougat *n* 67
novel *n* 138
November *n* 172
now *adv* 171
nozzle *n* 40
nuclear energy *n* 51
nuclear power
    plant *n* 51
nuclear waste *n* 51
nucleus *n* 76, 77
number *n* 112
number eight *n* 108
numbers *n* 173
numeracy *n* 93
numerals *n* 175
numerator *n* 74
nurse *n* 20, 21, 89
nursery *n* 30
nursing *n* 80
nut allergy *n* 23

nut, nuts *n* 36, 58, 68, 129
nutmeg *n* 59
nutrition *n* 23

# O

oak *n* 169
oar *n* 119
oasis *n* 146
oatmeal *n* 70
objective lens *n* 77
obliques *n* 03
oboe *n* 128
observatory *n* 144
obsidian *n* 156
obstetrician *n* 08
occupations *n* 89–90
occluded front *n* 155
ocean *n* 134, 145, 147
ocean life *n* 166
ocean ridge *n* 145
Oceania *n* 150, 153
Oceanian *adj* 153
octagon *n* 74
October *n* 172
octopus *n* 54, 166
odd *adj* 177
odometer *n* 99
off the shoulder *adj* 15
off-piste *n* 122
off-road motorcycle *n* 100
offal *n* 53
offense *n* 107
office *n* 82
office building *n* 42
office equipment *n* 82
office manager *n* 81
office reception *n* 81
office services *n* 91
office work *n* 81
often *adv* 172
oganesson *n* 78
ogre *n* 139
oil *n* 51, 60, 64, 97
oil field *n* 51
oil painting *n* 130
oil paints *n* 141
oil slick *n* 155
oil tank *n* 100
oil tanker *n* 105
oil terminal *n* 106
oil-filled radiator *n* 33
oily *adj* 18
ointment *n* 20, 49
okra *n* 55

# P

# Q

# R

rabbit *n* 53, 158, 164
rabbit hutch *n* 164
raccoon *n* 158
race *n* 116
race car *n* 97, 123
race car driver *n* 123
race number *n* 100
race track *n* 123
racecourse *n* 120
racehorse *n* 120
racing bike *n* 100, 101
racing dive *n* 118
racing events *n* 116
racing overalls *n* 123
rack *n* 100, 125
racket *n* 114
racket games *n* 114
racquetball *n* 114
radar *n* 105
radar speed gun *n* 50
radiated tortoise *n* 163
radiator *n* 33, 98
radicchio *n* 55
radio antenna *n* 105
radio *n* 50, 84, 88, 136
radio DJ *n* 90
radio station *n* 84
radio telescope *n* 144
radio waves *n* 75
radioactivity *n* 75
radiology *n* 21
radish *n* 56
radium *n* 78
radius *n* 03, 74
radon *n* 78
raffia palm *n* 167
rafter *n* 87
rafting *n* 119
Ragdoll *n* 164
rail network *n* 102
railing *n* 65
railroad *n* 148
railroad
    terminal *n* 106
rain *n* 51, 154
rain boots *n* 17
rain forest *n* 146, 159
rain gear *n* 135
rainbow *n* 154
rainbow trout *n* 54
raincoat *n* 15
raindrop *n* 154
rainfly *n* 135
rainy *adj* 154
raise *n* 81
raise *v* 11
raised mudguard *n* 100

raisin *n* 58
rake *n* 40
rake (leaves) *v* 39
rake (soil) *v* 39
rally *n* 114
rally driving *n* 123
ram *n* 165
ramekin *n* 28
ramen *n* 64, 72
ramp *n* 96
ranch house *n* 32
rapeseed *n* 86
rapeseed oil *n* 60
rapids *n* 119, 146
ras el hanout *n* 59
rash *n* 19
raspberry *n* 57
raspberry jam *n* 60
rat *n* 158
rattle *n* 08
rattlesnake *n* 163
raven *n* 160
raw *adj* 56
raw meat *n* 53
ray *n* 166
razor blade *n* 31
razor-shell *n* 54
reach a consensus *v* 95
reach an agreement *v* 95
reaction *n* 76
reaction direction *n* 76
reactor *n* 51
read *v* 73
read a map *v* 148
read a newspaper *v* 09
reading *n* 138
reading a map *n* 148
reading glasses *n* 22, 49
reading light *n* 103
reading list *n* 80
reading room *n* 80
real estate *n* 32, 91
real estate agent 89
reality TV *n* 137
realtor *n* 32
reamer *n* 36
rear light *n* 101
rear suspension *n* 123
rear wheel *n* 99
rear wing *n* 97, 123
reasonable *adj* 10
rebound *n* 112
receipt *n* 48, 69, 94
receptacle *n* 38
receptionist *n* 81, 90, 131
reconnaissance
    aircraft *n* 88
reconnaissance
    vehicle *n* 88
record player *n* 136
record store *n* 46
record *v* 137
recorder *n* 129

recording studio *n* 84
records *n* 136
recover *v* 20
recovery room *n* 21
recruiter *n* 92
rectangle *n* 74
recycling *n* 91, 155
recycling bin *n* 33, 34
red *n* 141
red blood cell *n* 77
red cabbage *n* 55
red card *n* 109
red carpet *n* 127
red currant *n* 57
red deer *n* 158
red fox *n* 159
red giant *n* 144
red hair *n* 12
red line *n* 110
red meat *n* 53
red mullet *n* 54
red panda *n* 159
red salamander *n* 163
red wine *n* 52, 68
red-eyed tree frog *n* 163
reed *n* 167
reef *n* 147
reel *n* 121
reel in *v* 121
referee *n* 107–109, 112
referee crease *n* 110
reflected radiation *n* 155
reflection *n* 75
reflector *n* 100, 101
reflector strap *n* 100
reflector telescope *n* 144
reflexology *n* 24
refraction *n* 75
refractor telescope *n* 144
refrigerator *n* 27
refund *v* 46
reggae *n* 129
registered mail *n* 45
registered trademark *n* 175
regulator *n* 118
reiki *n* 24
reindeer *n* 159
reins *n* 120
relationships *n* 05, 07
relaxation *n* 24
relaxed *adj* 06
relaxing *adj* 177
relay race *n* 116
release *v* 121
reliable *adj* 10, 93
remains *n* 79
remarkable *adj* 177
remember *v* 11
remote *n* 137
remote
    control *n* 26, 83, 136
renew *v* 80
renewable energy *n* 51

renovating *n* 37
rent *v* 32
rent a cottage *v* 131
rent out *v* 32
renting a house *n* 32
repair *v* 11, 33
reply *v* 83
reply to all *v* 83
report *n* 82
reporter *n* 137
reproduction *n* 77
reproductive *n* 04
reproductive organs *n* 04
reptiles *n* 163
Republic of the
    Congo *n* 149, 152
research *n* 91, 93
research and
    development (R&D) *n* 91
reserve *v* 80
reservoir *n* 51
residential area *n* 32
residential buildings *n* 44
residential district *n* 42
resign *v* 81
respectful *adj* 177
respiratory *n* 04
responsible *adj* 93
rest *v* 20
rest stop *n* 148
restaurant *n* 42, 69, 131
restaurant manager *n* 69
restricted area *n* 112
restroom *n* 47, 130, 131
résumé *n* 92
resurfacing *n* 87
resuscitate *v* 20
retail *n* 91
retake *v* 73
reticulated python *n* 163
retina *n* 22
retinal camera *n* 22
retire *v* 07, 81
retriever *n* 164
return *n* 114
return *v* 46, 80
return crease *n* 111
reusable cup *n* 70
reverb *n* 129
reverse *v* 96
reversible direction *n* 76
review *n* 138
review *v* 73
rewind *v* 137
rewire the house *v* 35
rhenium *n* 78
rhinoceros *n* 158
rhinoceros beetle *n* 162
rhodium *n* 78
rhododendron *n* 38
rhombus *n* 74
rhubarb *n* 58
rib *n* 03, 53

rib cage *n* 03
ribs *n* 70
ribbon *n* 63, 125, 142
rice *n* 72, 86
rice bowl *n* 27
rice noodles *n* 64
rice pudding *n* 63
rich *adj* 52
ride *v* 11
ride passenger *v* 100
rider *n* 100, 120
ridge *n* 146
ridge beam *n* 87
riding boot *n* 17, 120
riding crop *n* 120
riding hat *n* 120
rifle *n* 88
rig *n* 129
rigging *n* 119
right angle *n* 74
right bend *n* 96
right cornerback *n* 107
right
    defenseman *n* 110
right defensive end *n* 107
right defensive tackle *n*
    107
right guard *n* 107
right of way *n* 96
right safety *n* 107
right side *n* 112
right tackle *n* 107
right wing *n* 108
right winger *n* 110
rim *n* 101
rind *n* 61, 64
ring *n* 16, 170
ring binder *n* 82
ring finger *n* 02
ring ties *n* 40
ring-tailed lemur *n* 159
rings *n* 125, 143
rinse *v* 22
rip out *v* 178
ripe *adj* 57
rise *v* 62
risotto *n* 72
river *n* 147, 148
river features *n* 147, 148
road *n* 96
road bike *n* 101
road construction *n*
    87, 96
road markings *n* 96
road signs *n* 96
roadmap *n* 95
roadmap *n* 148
roar *v* 159
roast *n* 29, 72
robbers *n* 50
robbery *n* 50, 85
robe *n* 80
rock *n* 129

ski instructor *n* 89
ski jacket *n* 122
ski jump *n* 122
ski lodge *n* 122
ski pole *n* 122
ski resort *n* 122
ski run *n* 122
ski slope *n* 122
skier *n* 122
skiing *n* 122
skillet *n* 28
skim milk *n* 61
skin *n* 01, 58
skin care *n* 49
skin type *n* 18
skip *v* 124
skipping rope *n* 133
skirt *n* 14
skull *n* 03
skunk *n* 158
skydiving *n* 125
skyscraper *n* 42
slalom *n* 122
slate *n* 156
sled *n* 122
sledding *n* 122
sledgehammer *n* 87
sleep in *v* 178
sleeping bag *n* 135
sleeping
    compartment *n* 102
sleeping mat *n* 135
sleeping pills *n* 49
sleepsuit *n* 13
sleet *n* 154
sleeve *n* 15
sleeveless *adj* 15
slice *n* 53, 114
slice *v* 29, 62
sliced bread *n* 62
slicer *n* 62
slide *n* 43, 77, 95
slide *v* 113
sliders *n* 17
sling *n* 19–20
slingback heels *n* 17
slip *n* 14, 111
slip-ons *n* 17
slippers *n* 14, 17
slit skirt *n* 15
sloth *n* 159
slotted spoon *n* 28
Slovakia *n* 151, 153
Slovakian *adj* 153
Slovenia *n* 151, 153
Slovenian *adj* 153
slow *adj* 176
slow down *v* 98
slug *n* 162
sluice gates *n* 51
small *adj* 176
small creatures *n* 162
small forward *n* 112

small intestine *n* 04
smartpen *n* 95
smartphone *n* 83
smartwatch *n* 83
smell *v* 11
smile *v* 02
smog *n* 154
smoke *n* 50
smoke alarm *n* 50
smoked *adj* 54, 72
smoked fish *n* 64
smoked haddock *n* 64
smoked mackerel *n* 64, 71
smoked meat *n* 53
smoked salmon *n* 64, 71
smooth orange juice *n* 65
smoothie *n* 52
smuggling *n* 85
snack bar *n* 48, 65
snacks *n* 65
snail *n* 162
snake plant *n* 38
snap *n* 13
snap *n* 140
snare drum *n* 128
sneaker *n* 17
sneeze *v* 02, 20
snell knot *n* 121
Snellen chart *n* 22
sniff *v* 164
snooker *n* 125
snore *v* 02, 30
snorkel *n* 118
snorkel and mask *n* 15, 134
snorkeling *n* 118
snort *v* 165
snow *n* 154
snow goose *n* 160
snow leopard *n* 159
snow peas *n* 55
snow tires *n* 97
snowboarding *n* 122
snowdrift *n* 154
snowdrop *n* 167
snowflake *n* 154
snowmobile *n* 122
snowstorm *n* 154
snowsuit *n* 13
snowy *adj* 154
snowy owl *n* 161
soap *n* 31
soap dish *n* 31
soap opera *n* 137
soccer *n* 109
soccer cleats *n* 17, 109
soccer game *n* 109
soccer jersey *n* 15, 109
social media *n* 84
social sciences *n* 80
sociologist *n* 89
sociology *n* 80
sock, socks *n* 14, 107

socket *n* 33
socket wrench *n* 36
soda *n* 70
soda bread *n* 62
sodium *n* 78
sofa bed *n* 26
soft *adj* 57, 176
soft candy *n* 67
soft cheese *n* 61
soft down feathers *n* 161
soft drink *n* 70
softwood *n* 35
soil *n* 39
soil tiller *n* 40
soil types *n* 39
solar charger *n* 83
solar energy *n* 51
solar farm *n* 51
solar panel *n* 51
solar radiation *n* 155
solar system *n* 143
solar water heating *n* 51
solder *n* 35–36
solder *v* 35
soldering iron *n* 35–36
soldier *n* 88–89
sole *n* 02, 17, 54, 115
solid, solids *n* 74, 76
solitaire *n* 140
solo *n* 128
Solomon Island *adj* 153
Solomon Islands *n* 150, 153
soluble *adj* 49
solvent *n* 37
Somalia *n* 149, 152
Somalian *adj* 152
sombrero *n* 16
sometimes *adj* 172
sommelier *n* 69
son *n* 05
son-in-law *n* 05
song *n* 129
soprano *n* 126
sore throat *n* 19
sorrel *n* 55, 59
sort your trash *v* 155
sorting unit *n* 33
soufflé *n* 72
soufflé dish *n* 28
soul *n* 129
sound bar *n* 136
sound boom *n* 84
sound engineer *n* 127
sound hole *n* 129
sound technician *n* 84
soundtrack *n* 127
soup *n* 69, 72
soup bowl *n* 27
soup spoon *n* 27
sour *adj* 52, 57
source *n* 147
sources *n* 79
sourdough bread *n* 62

sourdough starter *n* 62
south *n* 148
South Africa *n* 149, 152
South African *adj* 152
South America *n* 149, 152
South American *adj* 152
South Korea *n* 150, 153
South Korean *adj* 153
South Pole *n* 75, 145
South Sudan *n* 149, 152
South Sudanese *adj* 152
southeast *n* 148
Southern Cross *n* 144
Southern
    Hemisphere *n* 145
southwest *n* 148
souvenir *n* 132
souvenir stall *n* 132
sow *v* 39, 86
soy allergy *n* 23
soy milk *n* 61
soy sauce *n* 60
soy sauce dip *n* 72
soybean oil *n* 60
space *n* 143–144
space exploration *n* 143
space probe *n* 143
space shuttle *n* 143
space shuttle launch *n* 143
space station *n* 143
space suit *n* 143
space telescope *n* 144
spacecraft *n* 143
spackle *n* 37
spackle *v* 37
spade *n* 40, 140
spaghetti *n* 64, 72
Spain *n* 151, 153
spam *n* 83
Spanish *adj* 153
Spanish chestnut *n* 168
spare tire *n* 98
spark plug *n* 98
sparkling *adj* 52
sparkling wine *n* 68
sparrow *n* 160
spatula *n* 28, 76
speak *v* 11
speaker, speakers *n* 83, 129
speaker stand *n* 136
spear *n* 79
spearfishing *n* 121
special *adj* 177
special effects *n* 127
special offer *n* 48
specials *n* 69
species *n* 77
species of birds *n* 160–161
species of fungi *n* 170
species of
    mammals *n* 158–159
spectacled caiman *n* 163
spectators *n* 110, 115–116

speed boating *n* 119
speed camera *n* 96
speed limit *n* 96
speed skating *n* 122
speed up *v* 98
speedboat *n* 105
speeding *n* 85
speedometer *n* 99–100
speedway *n* 123
spell *v* 11, 73
spell book *n* 139
sperm whale *n* 166
sphere *n* 74
sphinx *n* 139, 164
spices *n* 59
spicy *adj* 52, 56
spicy sausage *n* 64
spider monkey *n* 159
spider plant *n* 38
spikes *n* 115
spin *n* 114
spinach *n* 55
spinal cord *n* 04
spine *n* 03, 138
spiral galaxy *n* 144
spirit dispenser *n* 68
spit *n* 147
spleen *n* 04
splinter *n* 19
split the check *v* 69
spoiler *n* 97
spoke *n* 101
sponge *n* 31, 34, 37
sponge cake *n* 63
spontaneous *adj* 10
spores *n* 170
sport fishing *n* 121
sports bra *n* 15
sports car *n* 97
sports center *n* 43
sports drink *n* 52
sports field *n* 80
sports game *n* 136
sports jacket *n* 15
sports shoes *n* 17
sports show *n* 137
sportsperson *n* 89
sportswear *n* 15
Spotted Lake *n* 145
sprain *n* 19
spray *n* 49
spray *v* 39
spray nozzle *n* 40
sprayer *n* 40
spring *n* 57, 172
spring a leak *v* 33
spring greens *n* 55
spring onion *n* 55
spring roll *n* 72
springboard *n* 118, 125
springbok *n* 158
sprinkle *v* 29
sprinkler *n* 40

# T

# U

unclog the toilet v 35
under prep 180
under par adj 115
undercoat n 37
undergraduate n 80
underpass n 96, 102
underscore n 175
undersea features n 145
undershirt n 14
understand v 11
underwater camera n
  118
underwater diving n
  118
underwear n 14
unemployment
  benefit n 81
unenthusiastic adj 06
uneven bars n 125
unfasten v 14
unfriendly adj 10
unfurnished adj 32
unhappy adj 06
unicorn n 139
unicycle n 101
uniform,
  uniforms 13, 50, 88
unimpressed adj 06
United Arab
  Emirates n 151, 153
United Kingdom n
  151, 153
United States
  of America n 150, 152
universe n 144
university
  departments n 80
university schools n
  80
unkind adj 10
unleaded n 97
unload the
  dishwasher v 34
unpack v 11, 32
unpasteurized adj 61
unpeeled prawn n 54
unpick v 142
unpleasant adj 177
unreasonable adj 10
unreliable adj 10
unsalted adj 61
unsaturated fat n 23
upload v 83
upper deck n 99
upper level n 47
uppercase n 175
upscale adj 47
upset adj 06
upstairs adv, n 25
uranium n 78
Uranus n 143
urinary n 04
urology n 21

Uruguay n 149, 152
Uruguayan adj 152
USB drive n 83
useful adj 177
useful
  expressions n 179-180
useless adj 177
usher n 126
uterus n 04, 08
utility knife n 36-37
utility power n 33
UV tubes n 18
Uzbek adj 153
Uzbekistan n 151, 153

# V

V-neck n 14
vacancies n 92, 131
vacation n 81, 104
vaccination n 08, 20
vacuole n 77
vacuum n 75
vacuum cleaner n 34
vacuum the carpet v 34
vagina n 04
Vaisakhi n 07
valance n 30
valley n 146
valve n 101
vampire n 139
vanadium n 78
vandalism n 85
vanilla milkshake n 61
vanity n 30
Vanuatu n 150, 153
Vanuatuan adj 153
varnish n 37
vase n 26
Vatican City n 151
vault n 125
veal n 53
vegan adj 23
vegan n 23
vegetable garden n 41, 86
vegetables n 48, 55-56
vegetarian adj 23
vegetarian n 23
veggie burger n 70
veil n 15
vein n 04
Venetian blinds n 26
Venezuela n 149, 152
Venezuelan adj 152
venison n 53

vent n 145
Venus n 143
Venus fly-trap n 168
verdict n 85
vermilion
  flycatcher n 160
vertebrate n 77
verticals n 120
vest n 14
vest n 15
vet n 89
veteran n 88
vial n 36
vibraphone n 128
Victoria Falls n 145
vicuña n 158
video chat n 83
video conference n 83
video games n 136
video on demand n 137
Vietnam n 150, 153
Vietnamese adj 153
view a house v 32
viewing platform n 44
viewpoint n 148
villa n 32, 131
village n 43
villain n 127
Vincentian adj 152
vinegar n 60, 64
vineyard n 86
vintage adj 13
vintage n 97
vinyl records n 129
viola n 128
violet n 38
violin n 128-29
violin sonata n 128
Virginia creeper n 168
Virgo n 144
virus n 19, 77
visa n 104
visible light n 75
vision n 22
visitor n 107
visor n 100
vitamins n 23, 49
vivarium n 164
vlog n 84
vlogger n 84
vocal cords n 04
vodka n 68
vodka and orange n 68
voice recorder n 83
volcano n 145
volley n 114
volleyball n 112
volleyball positions n
  112
volt n 75
voltage n 33
volume n 74, 136, 174
volunteer v 92

vomit v 20
vote n 85
vulture n 160

# W

waders n 121
wading pool n 25, 133
waffle, waffles n 65, 70-71
wages n 81
waist n 01, 129
waistband n 15, 142
wait in line v 104
wait on v 178
wait up v 178
waiter n 69, 89
waiting room n 20, 102
waitress n 69, 89
wake up v 09, 178
walk v 120
walk the dog v 09
walkie-talkie n 50
walking boots n 135
walking trail n 148
wall n 25, 44, 87
Wallace's flying frog n 163
wallet n 94
wallet n 16
wallflower n 169
wallpaper n 37
wallpaper v 37
wallpaper border n 37
wallpaper brush n 37
wallpaper hanger n 37
wallpaper paste n 37
wallpaper roll n 37
wallpaper stripper n 37
walnut n 58, 168
walnut oil n 60
walrus n 166
wand n 139
want v 46
war n 79, 88
war elephant n 79
ward n 21
wardrobe n 30
warehouse n 44, 106
warfare n 79
warhorse n 79
warm adj 154
warm front n 155
warning track n 113
warp thread n 142
warrant n 85
warrior n 79

warrior pose n 24
warthog n 159
wasabi n 60
wash the car v 34
wash your face v 09
wash your hair v 09, 12
washer n 36
washer fluid n 97
washer fluid
  reservoir n 98
washing machine n 34
wasp n 162
wasp nest n 162
waste n 33
waste disposal n 135
watch n 16
watch TV v 09
watching television n 137
water n 48, 91, 118
water v 39
water bottle,
  water bottles n 101, 135
water carrier n 135
water chestnut n 56
water cooler n 82
water features n 145
water garden n 41
water hazard n 115
water jet n 50
water lilies n 167
water phenomena n 145
water plants n 41
water polo n 119
water rail n 161
water shoes n 17
water skier n 119
water skiing n 119
water sports n 119
water the plants v 09, 34
water vapor n 51
watercolor n 130
watercolor paints
  n 141
watercress n 55
waterfall n 146
waterfront n 132
watering n 40
watering can n 40
watermark n 94
watermelon n 58
waterproof
  fishing gear n 121
wave n 75, 119, 134, 147
wave v 02
wavelength n 75
wavy hair n 12
wax adj 176
wax n 18, 176
waxcap n 170
weapons n 79, 88
wear v 14
weasel n 158
weather n 137, 154

# XY



# Z

# German word list

The numbers after each word or phrase refer to the units in which they can be found. The article precedes the word in cases where the suffix would change without it.

# A

# B

Berghütte 32
Bergsteigen 133
Bergziege 159
Bericht 82
Berkelium 78
Berliner 63
Bermudashort 14
Berufe 89, 90
berufliche Fähigkeiten 93
Berufsverkehr 42, 102
in Berufung gehen 85
Beruhigungsmittel 49
berühmte Gebäude 44
Beryllium 78
Besaitung 114
Besatzung 119
Besatzungsluke 143
beschleunigen 98
Beschriftung 40
der / die Beschuldigte 85
Beschwerde 50
Besen 34, 40, 139
Besetzung 126, 127
besitzen 32
besonders 177
besorgt 06
Besprechung 81, 82, 95
Besprechung beenden 95
Besprechungszimmer 82
der beste Freund / die
    beste Freundin 07
Bestechung 85
Besteck 26, 27
bestehen 73
bestellen 46, 69
Bestellung verfolgen 46
bestimmt 10, 93
bestreuen 29
Bestseller 138
Bestuhlung 126
Beton 35, 176
Betonmischer 87
Betrag 45
Betreff 83
Betrug 85
Bett 30
Bett beziehen 34
ins Bett gehen 09
Bett machen 09, 34
betteln 164
Beugung 75
Beutel 158
bewaffnete Drohne 88
Bewährung 85
bewegliche Wand 82
Beweise 85
Beweisstück 50
Bewerber / Bewerberin 81
Bewerbungen 92

Bewerbungsformular 92
Bewerbungsgespräch
    haben 92
bewölkt 154
bezahlen 46
Bezahlkanal 137
Beziehungen 05, 07
Bezirk 42
BH 14
Bhangra 129
Bhutan 150, 153
bhutanisch 153
Biathlon 122
Bibliothek 43, 80, 148
Bibliothekar /
    Bibliothekarin 80, 90
Bibliotheksausweis 80
Bidet 31
biegsam 176
Biene 165
Bienenstock 86, 162, 165
Bier 52, 68
Big Ben 44
Bikini 134
Bildhauer / Bildhauerin 89
Bildhauerei 141
Bildschirm 45, 83, 136, 137
Bildschirm teilen 95
Billard 125
Bimsstein 31, 156
Binde 49
Bindedraht 40
binden 14
Bindestrich 175
Bio- 23, 39, 53
Bioabteilung 23
Biochemie 76
Biogemüse 55
Biografie 138
Bioladen 23, 46, 47
Biologe / Biologin 77
Biologie 73, 77, 80
Biomassekraftwerk 51
der biometrische Pass 104
Biomüll 33, 155
Biotechnologie 91
Birdseye-Chili 59
Birke 168
Birkenspanner 162
Birne 58, 169
bis später 179
Bischofsmütze 56
Bismut 78
Biss 19
Bistro 69
bitter 52, 56
Bizeps 03
Bizepscurl 124
Blase 19

blasen 11
Blasloch 166
Blässhuhn 161
Blatt 55
Blätterteig 63
blau 01, 141
Blaubeere 57
der Blaue Doktorfisch 166
der blaue Fleck 19
Blaue Krabbe 166
Blaue Linie 110
Blaukäppchen 161
Blaulicht 50
Blaumohn 168
Blaustern 167
Blauwal 166
Blauzungenskink 163
Blechblasinstrumente 128
Blei 78
Bleiche 34
Bleichen 22
bleifrei 97
bleihaltig 97
Bleistift 73, 82, 141, 175
Blinddarm 04
Blinddarmentzündung 19
Blindenschrift 175
blinken 98
Blinker 97, 100
blinzeln 02
Blitz 154
Blitzer 96
Blizzard 154
blocken 112, 117
Blockflöte 129
Blockhütte 32
blockieren 84
Blog 84
Blogger / Bloggerin 84
das blonde Haar 12
Blues 129
Bluetooth-Headset 83
Bluetooth-Lautsprecher
    136
Blumen 38
Blumen gießen 09, 34
Blumenbeet 41
Blumenkohl 56
Blumenrabatte 41
Blumenstand 47
Blumenstrauß 15
Blumentopf 40
Bluse 14
Blutdruck 20
Blutdruckmessgerät 21
Blüte 169
bluten 20
Blütenaufbau 38
Blütenblatt 38

Blütenboden 38
Blütenpflanze 157
Blütenstrauch 41
Blütezeit des Islam 79
Bluthochdruck 19
Blutknoten 121
Blutkreislauf 04
Blutorange 57
Blutung 19
Blutuntersuchung 20, 21
Blutwurst 71
Bob 12, 122
Bobfahren 122
Boccia 125
Bock 165
Bockshornklee 59
Boden 25, 30, 39
Boden kehren 34
Boden schrubben 34
Boden wischen 34
Boden-Luft-Rakete 88
Bodenarten 39
bodenlang 15
Bodenmatte 125
Body 13
Bodyboarding 119, 134
Bogen 24, 41, 44, 79, 125
Bogenfenster 32
Bogenhanf 38
Bogenschießen 125
Bogenschütze /
    Bogenschützin 125
Bohlenweg 134
Bohne 56
Bohnensprosse 55
Bohreinsatz 35, 36
bohren 35
Bohrer 22
Bohrfutter 35
Bohrium 78
Boiler 33
Boje 106, 119, 134
bolivianisch 152
Bolivien 149, 152
Bolognesesauce 64
Bombay-Schildschwanz
    163
Bombaykatze 164
Bombenflugzeug 88
Bomberjacke 15
Bommelmütze 16
Bonbons 67
Bongo 128
Bonsai 38
Boogiebrett 119
Booster 143
Boote 105
Bootsschuhe 17
Bor 78

Border Collie 164
Bordkarte 104
Börse 94
böse Roboter 139
Bösewicht 127
Bosnien und Herzegowina
    151, 153
bosnisch und
    herzegowinisch 153
Botanik 77
Botaniker / Botanikerin 77
der botanische Garten 132
Botsuana 149, 152
botswanisch 152
Bougainville 168
Boundary 111
Bouquet 47
Boutique 46
Bowler / Bowlerin 111
Bowling 125
Bowling Crease 111
Bowlingball 125
Box 52
Boxen 117
Boxengasse 123
Boxenstopp 123
Boxer 117
Boxershorts 14
Boxgymnastik 124
Boxhandschuh 117
Boxkampf 117
Boxspring-Matratze 30
Brachiosaurus 157
Brachvogel 161
Branchen 91
Brandteig 63
Brandung 119
Brandungsangeln 121
Branntwein 68
brasilianisch 152
Brasilien 149, 152
braten 29
Bratengabel 28
Bratenthermometer 28
Bratenwender 28
Bratpfanne 28
Bratsche 128
braun 01, 141
Braunbär 159
das braune Haar 12
der Braune Weiderich 168
Braut 07
Brautente 161
Bräutigam 07
Brautjungfernkleid 15
Brechung 75
Brechungsteleskop 144
breit 176
Breite 74

# C

# D

# E

# F

# G

Gabel 27, 40, 101, 119
Gabelschlüssel 36
Gabelstapler 87, 106
Gabun 149, 152
gabunisch 152
Gadolinium 78
Gagat 156
gähnen 02
Galapagosschildkröte 163
Galerie 130
Galiamelone 58
Gallenblase 04
Gallium 78
Gallone 174
galoppieren 120, 165
Gambia 149, 152
gambisch 152
Gameshow 137
Gaming-Industrie 91
Gammastrahlung 75
Gang 25, 80, 126
Ganges 145
Gangesgavial 163
Gangway 104, 105
Gans 53, 165
Gänseblümchen 38
Gänseei 61
Garage 25
Garantie 47
Gardenie 38
Garderobe 130
garnieren 29
Garten gestalten 39
Gartenarbeit 39
Gartenbuch 138
Gartencenter 46
Gartenelemente 41
Gartengeräte 40
Gartenhandschuhe 40
Gartenkorb 40
Gartenpflanzen 38
Gartensalat 72
Gartenschere mit langem
  Griff 40
Gartenschlauch 40
Gartenschuppen 39
Gartentypen 41
Gärtner / Gärtnerin 89
Gärtnern 133
Gas 76, 99
Gasfackel 51
Gasheizung 33

Gaskocher 135
Gasriesen 143
Gasse 42
Gassi gehen 09
Gast 26
Gast / Gästin 65, 69
Gäste 131
Gastgeber / Gastgeberin
  26
Gastgewerbe 91
Gasthaus 131
Gastmannschaft 107
Gastornis 157
Gastredner / Gastrednerin
  95
Gastroenterologie 21
Gastronomiebereich 47
Gate 104
Gatenummer 104
Gaube 25
Gaumen 04
Gazelle 158
gebacken 72
Gebänderte Seekobra 166
Gebärmutter 04, 08
Gebärmutterhals 04
Gebäude 42, 43, 44, 148
Gebäudeplan 130, 132
Gebetswand (quibla) 44
Gebinde 142
Gebirge 146
Gebirgsausläufer 147
Gebirgskette 146
Gebirgspflanze 41
Gebiss 120
geboren werden 07
gebraten 72
die gebratenen Pilze 71
Gebrauchtwarenladen 46
gebrochene Knochen 19
Gebühr 85
das gebundene Buch 138
Geburt 08
Geburtshelfer 08
Geburtshilfe 21
Geburtstag 07
Geburtstagskarte 07
Geburtstagskerzen 63
Geburtstagskuchen 63
Geburtstermin 08
Geburtsurkunde 07
Gebüsch 41
gedankenlos 10
Gedankenstrich 175
Gedeck 27, 69
Gedrängehalb 108
geduldig 10, 93
gedünstet 72
gefährdete Art 155

Gefahrenstelle 96
Gefahrenzone 117
das gefangene Insekt 168
Gefängnis 85
Gefängniswärter /
  Gefängniswärterin 85
Geflügel 48, 53, 165
Gefrierfach 27
Gefrierfach abtauen 34
Gefriergut 48
Gefrierpunkt 154
Gefrierschutzmittel 97
gefroren 54, 56
Gefühle 06
gefüllt 72
gefüllte Olive 64
das gefüllte Weinblatt 64
gegen den Uhrzeigersinn
  148
Gegengewicht 87
Gegenspieler /
  Gegenspielerin 112
Gegensprechanlage 25
gegenüber 148
Gegner / Gegnerin 117
gegrillt 72
gegrillte Tomate 71
Gehalt 81
Gehaltserhöhung 81
Gehaltskürzung 81
geheimniskrämerisch 10
gehen 179
gehen lassen 62
Gehirn 04
Gehirnerschütterung 19
gehoben 47
Gehörn 158
Gehsteig 25, 43, 65
Geier 160
Geige 128, 129
Geißblatt 38
Geisteswissenschaften 80
gekocht 56, 72
das gekochte Ei 61, 71
das gekochte Fleisch 53,
  64
das gekochte Gemüse 72
das gekräuselte Haar 12
gekühlt 52
gekündigt werden 81
Gel 49
Geländemotorrad 100
Geländer 25, 65
gelangweilt 06
gelb 141
der Gelbbraune
  Kofferfisch 166
der Gelbe Doktorfisch 166

Gelbe Kanarische 58
gelbe Karte 109
der Gelbe
  Segelflossendoktor 166
Gelbsenf 59, 60
Geld 45, 94
Geld abheben 45
Geld überweisen 45
Geld und Finanzen 94
Geld wechseln 45
Geldautomat 45
Geldbeutel 16, 94
Geldbörse 94
Geldschein 45, 94
Geleebonbon 67
Gelenk 03
Gelenkbus 99
gemahlener Zimt 59
Gemälde 26, 130, 141
gemein 10, 177
der Gemeine
  Kartoffelbovist 170
Gemeine Kröte 163
Gemeine Platane 168
Gemüse 48, 55, 56
Gemüsegarten 41, 86
Gemüsehändler /
  Gemüsehändlerin 89
Gemüsehobel 28
Gemüsestick 72
Gen 77
genau 93
General / Generalin 88
Generator 33, 51
genervt 06
Genitalien 01
Genres 138
Geode 156
geöffnet 48, 132
Geografie 73, 146, 147
geografische Merkmale
  146
geologische Zeitalter
  157
der geometrische Garten
  41
Georgien 150, 153
georgisch 153
Gepäck 131
Gepäckablage 102
Gepäckausgabe 104
Gepäckfach 102, 103, 104
Gepäckraum 99
Gepäckträger 100
Gepäckwagen 102, 104,
  131
Gepard 158
gepökelt 72
das gepökelte Fleisch 53

gepunktet 13
Gerade 74
geradeaus fahren 96
geradeaus gehen / fahren
  148
die geraden
  Bauchmuskeln 03
der geraffte Rock 142
Geranie 38
Geräte 83
Gerätetauchen 118
geräuchert 54, 72
das geräucherte Fleisch 53,
  64
der geräucherte
  Schellfisch 64
der geräucherte Makrele
  64, 71
Gerbera 47
Gericht 85
Gerichte 72
Gerichtsgebäude 43
Gerichtsmitarbeiter /
  Gerichtsmitarbeiterin 85
Gerichtssaal 85
Gerichtsschreiber /
  Gerichtsschreiberin 85
Gerichtstermin 85
Gerichtsverhandlung 85
Gerichtsvollzieher /
  Gerichtsvollzieherin 85
der geriebene Käse 61
Germanium 78
Gerste 86
Gerte 120
Geruchsverschluss 33
gesalzen 54, 61, 64
die gesättigten Fettsäuren
  23
geschäftliche Einstellung
  93
Geschäftsabschluss 81
Geschäftsessen 81
Geschäftsfrau 81, 90
Geschäftsmann 81, 90
Geschäftsreise 81
geschälte Garnele 54
Geschenk 07
Geschenkeladen 46, 130
Geschichte 73, 79, 80
Geschichten 139
geschieden 05
das Geschirr 27, 122
Geschirr abtrocknen 34
Geschirr spülen 34
Geschirrspülmittel 34
Geschirrspültab 34
Geschirrtuch 28
geschlossen 48, 132

# H

# K

# L

# N

# O



# P

# Q



# R

# S

# T

# U

# V



# W

# XY

Xenon **78**
Xylofon **128**
Yacht **105, 119, 134**
Yak **159**
Yamswurzel **56, 86**
Yard-Linie **107**
Yards gewinnen **107**
Yoga **24**
Yogahose **24**
Yogalehrer / Yogalehrerin **90**
Yogamatte **24**
Yogastunde **24**
Ysop **59**
Ytterbium **78**
Yttrium **78**

# Z

zählen **11, 74**
Zahlen **173**
mit der Karte zahlen **94**
Zähler **74**
Zahn **03**
Zahn ziehen **22**
der Zahnarzt **22**
Zahnarzt / Zahnärztin **22, 89**
zahnärztliche Krankengeschichte **22**
Zahnarztstuhl **22**
Zahnbürste **31**
Zähne **01, 03**
Zähne putzen **22**
Zahnfleisch **03**
Zahnkranz **101**
Zahnmark **03**
Zahnpasta **31**
Zahnpflege **49**
Zahnpfleger / Zahnpflegerin **22**
Zahnröntgenaufnahme **22**
Zahnschmelz **03**

Zahnschmerz **22**
Zahnseide **22, 31**
Zahnseide benutzen **22**
Zahnspange **22**
Zahnstein **22**
Zahnzwischenraumbürste **22**
Zander **54**
Zange **28, 68, 76**
Zäpfchen **49**
Zapfhahn **68**
Zapfsäule **97**
Zartbitterschokolade **67**
Zauberbuch **139**
Zauberer **139**
Zauberlampe **139**
zaubern **139**
Zauberstab **139**
Zaubertrank **139**
Zaumzeug **120**
Zaun **41, 86**
Zaun reparieren **35**
Zaunkönig **160**
Zebra **158**
Zeh **02**
Zehenknochen **03**
Zehennagel **02**
Zehenraum **126**
zehn **173**
zehn nach eins **171**
zehn vor zwei **171**
zehntausend **173**
zehnter / zehnte **173**
Zeichenblock **141**
Zeichendreieck **73, 74**
Zeichenkohle **141**
zeichnen **73, 141**
Zeigefinger **02**
Zeit **107, 171**
Zeit ablesen **171**
Zeitalter **157**
Zeiten **109**
Zeitmanagement **93**
Zeitmesser **76**
Zeitplan **132**
Zeitschrift **48**
Zeitschriftenseite **84**
Zeitung **48, 138**
Zeitung lesen **09**
Zeitungskiosk **46**
Zelle **50, 77, 85**
Zellkern **77**
Zellwand **77**
Zelt aufstellen **135**
Zeltboden **135**
Zelthering **135**
Zeltstange **135**
Zement **87**
Zentaur **139**

Zentimeter **174**
zentralafrikanisch **152**
Zentralafrikanische Republik **149, 152**
Zentrifugalkraft **75**
Zentripetalkraft **75**
Zeppelin **103**
zerbrechlich **45**
zerhacken **29**
zerlegen **29**
zerstampfen **29**
Zerstäuber **40**
Zerstörer **88**
Zerstörung von Lebensräumen **155**
Zeuge / Zeugin **85**
Zicklein **165**
Zickzackschere **142**
Ziege **53, 165**
Ziegel **35, 87, 176**
Ziegenmilch **61**
Ziegenkäse **61**
ziehen **11, 140**
in den Süden / Norden ziehen **161**
Ziel **104**
Zielflagge **123**
Zielgerade **123**
Ziellinie **115, 116, 123**
Zielscheibe **125**
Zierleiste **26**
Zierpflanze **41**
Ziffer **175**
Zimmer frei **131**
Zimmer mit Ausblick **131**
Zimmerpflanzen **38**
Zimmerreinigung **131**
Zimmerservice **131**
Zimt **59**
Zimtschnecke **71**
Zimtstange **59**
Zink **78, 156**
Zinn **78, 156**
Zinne **44**
Zinssatz **45**
Zirkel **73, 74**
Zirkeltraining **124**
Zirkonium **78**
Zitrone **57**
Zitronengras **59**
Zitronenmelisse **59**
Zitronenmus **60**
Zitronenpresse **28**
Zitronenschale **57**
Zitrusfrüchte **57**
Zitrusmarmelade **60, 71**
zittern **02**
Zoll **104, 174**
das zollfreie Geschäft **104**

Zollhaus **106**
Zombie **139**
Zoologe / Zoologin **77**
Zoologie **77, 80**
zu Abend essen **09, 52**
zu früh **171**
zu Mittag essen **09**
zu spät **171**
zu spät kommen **09**
zu viel essen **23**
Zubehör **17**
Zubereitung **54, 72**
Zucchini **56**
züchten **120**
Zuchtpilze **170**
Zucker **23**
Zuckererbse **55**
Zuckerrohr **86, 167**
Zuckerstange **67**
Zuckerwatte **67**
Zufahrtsstraße **106**
Zufluss **147**
zufrieden **06**
Zug **102**
mit dem Zug fahren **09**
Zug nehmen **102**
Zug verpassen **102**
Zugabe **126**
Zugbrücke **44**
Züge **102**
Zügel **120**
Zugfahrer / Zugfahrerin **90**
Zugnetz **102**
Zugterminal **106**
Zugtypen **102**
Zuhause **25–41**
zuhören **11**
Zündkerze **98**
Zündung **99**
zunehmen **20**
der zunehmende Mond **143**
Zunge **04, 17, 53**
zur Kasse gehen **46**
zurückgeben **46, 80, 178**
zurückschneiden **39**
zurückspulen **137**
zusammenarbeiten **92**
zusammenbauen **178**
zusammenfassen **95**
zusammenlegen **14**
zusammenrechen **39**
Zusatzleistungen **81**
Zusatzstoffe **23**
Zuschauer / Zuschauerin **110, 115, 116**
zuschneiden **39**
Zuspieler / Zuspielerin **112**
zuverlässig **10, 93**

zwanzig **173**
zwanzig Minuten **171**
zwanzig nach eins **171**
zwanzig vor zwei **171**
zwanzigster / zwanzigste **173**
zwei **173**
zwei Spieler / zwei Spielerinnen **114**
zwei Uhr **171**
zwei Wochen **172**
Zweibettzimmer **131**
Zweig **169**
zweihundert **173**
zweijährige Pflanze **41**
zweimal in der Woche **172**
Zweipersonenzelt **135**
Zweispännerrennen **120**
zweitausend **172**
zweitausendeins **172**
zweite Abzweigung rechts abbiegen **148**
zweite Abzweigung rechts nehmen **96**
zweite Base **113**
der / die zweite Innendreiviertel **108**
Zweite-Reihe-Stürmer / Zweite-Reihe-Stürmerin **108**
zweiter / zweite **173**
zweiundzwanzig **173**
Zwerg **139**
Zwergflaschenputzer **168**
Zwergmispel **169**
Zwergplaneten **143**
Zwergspitz **164**
Zwiebel **41, 56**
Zwiebelkuppel **44**
Zwillinge **05, 144**
zwinkern **02**
Zwirn **40**
zwischen **148, 180**
zwischenmenschliche Kompetenz **93**
Zwischenrippenmuskel **03**
zwölf **173**
Zylinder **74**
Zylinderkopf **98**
Zypern **151, 153**
zyprisch **153**
Zytoplasma **77**

# Acknowledgments

**The publisher would like to thank:**
Dr. Steven Snape for his assistance with hieroglyphs. Elizabeth Blakemore for editorial assistance; Mark Lloyd, Charlotte Johnson, and Anna Scully for design assistance; Simon Mumford for national flags; Sunita Gahir and Ali Jayne Scrivens for additional illustration; Adam Brackenbury for art colour correction; Claire Ashby and Romaine Werblow for images; William Collins for fonts; Lori Hand, Kayla Dugger, and Jane Perlmutter for Americanization; Justine Willis for proofreading; Elizabeth Blakemore for indexing; Helen Peters for the wordlists; Christine Stroyan for audio recording management and ID Audio for audio recording and production.

**DK India**
**Senior Art Editors** Vikas Sachdeva, Ira Sharma; **Art Editor** Anukriti Arora;
**Assistant Art Editors** Ankita Das, Adhithi Priya; **Editors** Hina Jain, Saumya Agarwal;
**DTP Designer** Manish Upreti

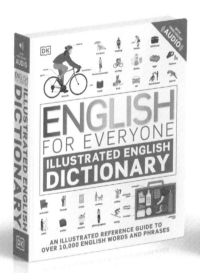

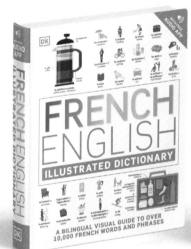

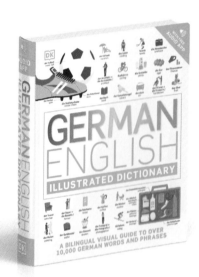

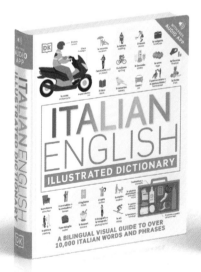

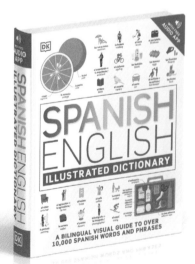